THE ECONOMY OF CERTAINTY

RESOURCES IN ARABIC
AND ISLAMIC STUDIES

series editors

Joseph E. Lowry
Devin J. Stewart
Shawkat M. Toorawa

Number 2
THE ECONOMY OF CERTAINTY

THE ECONOMY OF CERTAINTY
An Introduction to the Typology of Islamic Legal Theory

Aron Zysow

LOCKWOOD PRESS
Atlanta, Georgia
2013

THE ECONOMY OF CERTAINTY
An Introduction to the Typology of Islamic Legal Theory

ISBN: 978-1-937040-09-3

Library of Congress Control Number: 2013946525

Cover image: From an elegant copy of the compendium on Ḥanafī law, the *Kitāb Majmaʿ al-baḥrayn wa-multaqā al-nayyirayn* by Ibn al-Sāʿatī (d. 694/1294 or 1295). Source: Wikimedia Commons.

Printed in the United States of America on acid-free paper.

CONTENTS

Series Editors' Preface

We are extremely pleased to be able to publish for the first time Aron Zysow's *The Economy of Certainty: An Introduction to the Typology of Islamic Legal Theory*, a lightly revised version of his now classic 1984 Harvard University Ph.D. dissertation of the same title. For anyone working in the history of Islamic thought generally, and the history of Islamic legal thought and theology in particular, Zysow's work remains fundamental. It is still challenging and fresh, and most would agree that it has yet to be surpassed as an account of Islamic legal theory.

This edition includes a foreword by Robert Gleave of the University of Exeter, a new preface, and addenda by the author at the end of each chapter and to the bibliography. We also provide a table of page correspondences between this volume and the 1984 dissertation.

We would like to express our gratitude to Asiya Toorawa for time-consuming word-processing; to Elias Saba for careful editorial work and for preparing the indices; to Rob Gleave for writing an illuminating foreword; and to a generous anonymous donor for financial assistance. Above all, we are indebted to Aron Zysow for agreeing to let us publish this important work, and for taking the time to provide a new Preface, furnish very useful addenda, and attend to many details. Billie Jean Collins continues to provide us with encouragement and a venue for the publication of important work in the fields of Arabic and Islamic Studies—for this too we are most grateful.

Joseph E. Lowry
Devin J. Stewart
Shawkat M. Toorawa

Foreword

The continued importance of "The Economy of Certainty" to the study of Islamic legal theory is a tribute to the precision employed at its inception; the work's persistent relevance to the research into *uṣūl al-fiqh* makes its publication here more than welcome: it is, to use the language of *uṣūl*, imperative. Originally presented as a doctoral dissertation at Harvard University, "The Economy of Certainty" has retained its position as "essential reading" on many university curricula since its submission in 1984. In many disciplines, thirty-year old research borders on being antique; however, when read today, Zysow's presentation retains both its originality and its authority. Indeed, his characterization of the *uṣūl* discipline has been confirmed by research since he submitted "The Economy of Certainty"; Zysow's account might in fact be said to have *controlled* many subsequent lines of enquiry. Grand expositions of a discipline deserve to be written after, not before, the slog of discrete, detailed studies; in this case the order was reversed. It can be frustrating to spend much time reading up on an element of *uṣūl al-fiqh* and reach what one thought was an original observation, only to find Zysow has already expressed the idea, with typical prescience, deep in the 541 pages of "The Economy of Certainty." Certainly, I can recall no doctoral thesis so widely and continuously cited in the field of Islamic legal studies.

Ironically, the influence of "The Economy of Certainty" can be credited, in part, to its remaining in thesis form and its lack of formal publication. The conclusions of any thesis are understood to be provisional, exploratory and unofficial, even when the thesis has a wide scope (as indicated by a subtitle such as "An Introduction to the Typology of Islamic Legal Theory"); theses invite further research, either by the authors themselves, or by those who have had the tenacity to dig out a thesis and digest its findings. A thesis is not designed, in truth, to convince anyone beyond the examiners; and it is usually intended to be read by no more than a few dogged enthusiasts. These qualities have meant that subsequent researchers have felt free to use Zysow's ideas as a platform for their own research, or have been influenced by his approach without always given him due reference, or have explored the same questions, along the same lines as those found in "The Economy of Certainty," without fearing any accusation of duplication because it remained a thesis rather than a series of articles or a single volume.

Had "The Economy of Certainty" been available as a published monograph, scholarly interaction with Zysow's conclusions and analysis may well have taken on a different character. Even with the advent of the Portable Document Format (in which "The Economy of Certainty" has, for some time now, been available almost on demand), its status as a thesis has given it a certain cachet, enhanced rather than diminished by the protracted period it has remained unpublished. Its release here as a monograph, albeit in a lightly revised form and with additional thoughts from the author after each chapter and additional references, will undoubtedly alter that dynamic. People may now stumble across "The Economy of Certainty" serendipitously whilst browsing through a library (be it actual or virtual) and it will no longer be the preserve solely of those who seek it out. Publication will popularize it (as much as *uṣūl al-fiqh* can ever be popular), and it will lose some of its exclusivity thereby. This is not an argument against publication: the time is right—indeed, it has been for some time—for "The Economy of Certainty" to be more widely, and permanently, available. As a thesis and as an intellectual resource, "The Economy of Certainty" has influenced the field of *uṣūl* studies, perhaps to maximal effect, such has been its widespread distribution amongst devotees. Now, as a book, it will not only raise the assessment of *uṣūl* within the academic study of Islam, but also contribute to the understanding of the Muslim intellectual tradition more broadly as scholars in cognate fields are introduced to the sophistication both of *uṣūl*, and of Zysow's examination. Zysow himself, of course, has already exerted an influence in Islamic studies more generally. The penetrating critique and depth of understanding in "The Economy of Certainty" in relation to both *uṣūl* scholarship (and pre-1984 scholarship on *uṣūl*) has also been much in evidence in Zysow's engaging contributions to seminars and conferences and in his subsequent publications (see, for example, Zysow 2002, 2008).

The sustained standing of "The Economy of Certainty" within the field over three decades does not, however, indicate an intellectual catalepsy extinguishing any dynamism in the study of *uṣūl al-fiqh*. Whilst *uṣūl* remains an exclusive niche relative to the study of *fiqh* or actual legal practice, there has, in the intervening years, been a steady increase in the number of scholars engaged with Islamic legal theory both on its own terms, and in relation to various other disciplines of Islamic thought. Many of these, particularly in Anglophone scholarship, have been directly and obviously influenced by a reading of "The Economy of Certainty." For example, there has been an ongoing debate around the function or role of *uṣūl al-fiqh*. Wael Hallaq, who published widely on *uṣūl*-related topics in the 1980s, following the submission of "The Economy of Certainty," has argued eloquently and passionately for what might be termed the "practicality" of *uṣūl al-fiqh* (Hallaq 1984, 1992, 1997). For Hallaq, *uṣūl al-fiqh*'s function is best displayed when an *uṣūlī* writer devises or proposes a workable method of deriving practical law from the sources. Indeed the criterion for assessment of an *uṣūl* discussion, or even an *uṣūl* author, is the link with social reality and legal practice. This chimes with what many *uṣūl* writers themselves claim. The rhetoric of *uṣūl al-fiqh*—that is, its internal justification for its existence—is regularly linked by *uṣūl* writers themselves to the derivation of legal norms (*fiqh*). Works of *uṣūl al-fiqh* are written (supposedly self-consciously) to describe the method whereby *fiqh* can be known. Furthermore Hallaq has argued that *fiqh* and social reality are themselves intimately linked, creating a seamless coherence to Islamic legal literatures from *uṣūl* to the implementation of law.

Other scholars have modified, developed or rejected Hallaq's characterization or developed wholly independent descriptions (Ahmed 2006; Lowry 2007). According to some, *uṣūl al-fiqh* serves, *ex post facto*, to justify existing *fiqh*—it is retrospective, rather than creating new law, explaining how we know what we know of the law (Jackson 2002). For others, *uṣūl al-fiqh* serves to "theologize" the *fiqh*—that is, make it more than simply law but religious law, as it links the law to revelatory texts (Weiss 2010). For yet others, *uṣūl* writers were concerned with the beauty and intellectual coherence of their own system rather than its practicality (Calder 1996). For all these scholars (and the various amalgam and hybrid positions spawned as scholarship develops), Zysow's "The Economy of Certainty" proved an essential starting point and conduit to understanding legal theory, and the examination of *uṣūl*'s purpose or role was possible only subsequently. Only after understanding *uṣūl* can one speculate as to its purpose: "The Economy of Certainty" enabled that primary understanding, and so academics felt able to speculate on the meta-question of function. Indeed, one could argue that those working in *uṣūl* are able to ask such questions because reading Zysow gave them a firm grasp of the basic geography of the principal questions animating *uṣūl al-fiqh*. It is not that "The Economy of Certainty" described all *uṣūl al-fiqh*, and that there was no need for further research: rather the framework of "The Economy of Certainty" is sufficiently ambitious and firmly established in the texts of *uṣūl* that one can legitimately turn to grander issues, and then do so on a firmer footing.

Zysow's reading for "The Economy of Certainty" was broad and, considering the material available at the time, quite extraordinary; consequently, his understanding of what is typical (and what is not; see p. 2) enabled readers to move on to other questions with sufficient confidence that the groundwork had been done. "The most basic patterns" (p. 2) of *uṣūl al-fiqh* have, for now, been adequately, described and presented in this accomplished piece of *recherche fondamentale*. His method was to focus on ʿAlāʾ al-Dīn al-Samarqandī (d. 539/1144), a scholar whose *Mīzān* he had studied in manuscript form, and for whom, one suspects, Zysow has enormous respect. Al-Samarqandī was a Central Asian Ḥanafī who did not conform to all the doctrines of his contemporaries. He reflected a community of Samarqand-based scholars who ploughed their own furrow, devising clever, theologically informed answers, to established *uṣūl* questions. A critique of "The Economy of Certainty" could be that Zysow's reliance on Samarqand makes its utility as a general account limited: but al-Samarqandī's originality (and his often lucid expressions of the central issue at stake in a problem) is set against the range of views and arguments across the various theological trends and movements. Whenever al-Samarqandī is not the most informative source, Zysow presents the views of an alternative author who discusses the issue more appropriately.

Before "The Economy of Certainty," one really had to resort to Goldziher's *The Ẓāhirīs* for an account of *uṣūl al-fiqh*, an account that had its own problems as a general description of legal theory (Goldziher 2008 [1971], German original published in 1884). After "The Economy of Certainty," the field of Islamic legal theory (at least in the English-speaking research community) was opened up to informed speculation as to the nature of the discipline itself. Zysow himself touches on the issue of *uṣūl*'s nature and purpose in his introduction to "The Economy of Certainty" (though questions of the *uṣūl*'s purpose do not form the primary focus of his enquiry). In some brief comments, he states first that "the study of these systems of legal theory is an end in itself" (p. 4) for the intellectual historian of Islam. This validation alone might be enough: *uṣūl al-fiqh* can be treated, as it was in many institutions of medieval Muslim learning, as a self-justified area of study, without immediate reference to its function or purpose in the broader "hierarchy of the Islamic religious sciences," let alone in wider society. Zysow was clearly aware, however, that this would not be enough for some. *Uṣūl* can be studied as an independent discipline, but for many writers, both in a Western academic and in a Muslim educational context, mere intellectual curiosity was an insufficient basis to justify a whole science. *Uṣūl* should also be studied because it is a science connectied with other sciences: Zysow specifically mentions scholastic theology (*kalām*) and law (or jurisprudence, *fiqh*). The study of *uṣūl* can help the historian of Islamic theology, for *uṣūl al-fiqh* (even in its so-called "legal" expressions) was intensely theological. *Uṣūl* was, at times, "theology-in-use," and this led to theological compromise as it encountered the law. With regard to the debated *uṣūl-fiqh* relationship, Zysow sees "no reason to doubt" (p. 5) the fact that jurists saw *uṣūl* as informing their derivation of the law; having said that, Zysow also states that the legal theorists were "conscious enough of the limitations of their attempt to reconstruct their own practices." These are not categorical statements arguing for any of the various views which emerged subsequently in the field concerning the relationship between *uṣūl* and *furūʿ*, and between *uṣūl* and legal practice (*furūʿ* is not, of course, practice, despite the temptation to view it as such). However, with characteristic foresight, Zysow's comments recognize the issues which will inevitably emerge in the study of *uṣūl* once the basic ground is marked out, namely, what the point of this legal theory might be—surely more than an intellectual game. A pressing issue at this stage for Zysow is procedural: "Before we can begin to determine how far the practice of the Muslim jurist diverges from his theory, we must first have a far better grasp on what that theory is" (p. 5).

Any debate over the rationale for studying *uṣūl al-fiqh* (beyond the "value in itself" argument of the purist academic) is premature when we do not yet have a decent grasp of the theory itself. For Zysow, if one wants a pragmatic reason to study *uṣūl*, it can be found in *uṣūl*'s ability to reveal how Muslim jurists conceived of the law before they carried out any actual legal derivation: that is, *uṣūl* aims to present a unified theory of how the law of God operates ("system and method" as Zysow puts it, p. 5). The notion of a unified system of law, in which each piece and procedure fits with another perhaps reflects the theological commitment to a single, unified deity. Most importantly, becoming aware of such a notion enables us to understand how Muslim legal thinking is imbued with religious concerns. This is true of the Central Asian Ḥanafī *uṣūlīs* who form the primary focus of Zysow's analysis in "The Economy of Certainty," even though they are normally classed as "jurist-*uṣūlīs*" (*fuqahāʾ*). Jurist-*uṣūlīs* supposedly had an eye fixed squarely on the theory's ramifications for *fiqh* derivation, as opposed to the "theologian-*uṣūlīs*" (*mutakallimūn*) such as the Shāfiʿīs, who were more concerned with the theological implications of *uṣūl*.

What then are the patterns which run through *uṣūl* discussions, according to Zysow? The primary one is signalled in the title of the work itself: epistemology. For each question or issue (*masʾala*) of legal theory, there is an underlying epistemological question. So, the question of reports of the Prophet's words and acts (*akhbār*) and their ability to act as a source of law (*ḥujjiyya*) is, essentially, a question of knowledge. Theology might establish that the Prophet must be obeyed, but how knowledge of his exemplary action might be gained is the pressing issue of legal theory. Zysow examines the position of various Ḥanafī thinkers, often setting them against other theological and legal groupings, and positioning the issue within a broader set of concerns about religious doctrine generally. Theological truth is known with certainty, and the extent to which this mechanism of knowledge acquisition can be applied to *fiqh* is the focus of *uṣūl* discussions. The general position is that such gold-standard knowledge was not necessary, and legal derivation could proceed with less than certain knowledge of an individual report's authenticity: the resultant legal opinions and rulings were always colored by the fact that their origins (relative to *mutawātir* sources forming the bedrock of theological doctrine) were, relatively speaking, epistemologically compromised. The distinctive Ḥanafī position on these matters was to require varying the acceptable level of certainty for legal derivation depending on the content of the report: matters of "general [legal] concern" (p. 41) require a higher standard (*mashhūr*; though still less than *mutawātir*) than reports on the legal specifics. It was, Zysow argues, their theology, and the epistemology developed within that intellectual context, which explained the Ḥanafīs' distinctive legal views on the authenticity of prophetic reports.

Once a record of a speech act or an action (i.e., a text) is established as a potential source of law, understanding the legal significance of the words or action becomes crucial. Hence, Zysow next turns to "Interpretation." Here, once again, epistemology takes center stage. "How does one know what was said or done?" at some time past was a challenge to legal certainty; "how does one know what was meant?" is, in many ways, an even greater test of a coherent legal theory. Zysow establishes the *optimism* of the Ḥanafīs: words, when used by a Prophet, mean what they appear to mean, and it takes significant evidence to shift one's assessment of the apparently intended meaning to something else. One can know intended meaning from the natural workings of language, without the need for analogy. Analogy is not invalid, but it should not be used to replace the meaning to be found in the language system itself. This linguistic optimism (perhaps) contrasts with the greater incorporation of ambiguity (and perhaps a hint of pessimism as to the self-sufficiency of language) in the Shāfiʿī system. In many elements, Zysow notes how the Central Asian Ḥanafī views represent a departure from, or radical development of, those of the Iraqi Ḥanafī founders of the school, or how one group of Central Asian Ḥanafīs adopted the Iraqi position, but others developed something new and distinctive. Among the Central Asian Ḥanafīs, Zysow is particularly impressed by the school of Samarqand (using al-Samarqandī as the principal source), who are committed to a theological distinction between belief and action, and carry this through to their legal-linguistic philosophy. Since the law is focused on regulating action, language's outward, natural, obvious meaning is sufficient to establish duties of performance. For example, a verb in the imperative mood, ordering a person to perform an action, does not indicate that the action is an obligation under the law; it might, however, indicate that the person should treat the action as if it is obligatory. Thus, he or she must perform the action, but it does not mean he or she need be committed to believing that the action is (in the mind of God, as it were) obligatory. Zysow returns again and again to the sophisticated connection between theology and legal theory found in the Samarqandī school, hinting at how it takes the well-worn paths of *uṣūl* debate to a new level, beyond the Shāfiʿī-Ḥanafī polemics of the earlier period, which by the thirteenth century had arguably become arid and predictable.

Theological and epistemological themes are also present in the exposition of the doctrine of consensus (*ijmāʿ*) being a source of legal knowledge. Whilst some have promoted *ijmāʿ* as the basis for all legal enquiry, Zysow rightly corrects such a portrayal. The sources of law, and their interpretation are not established by some consensus in the post-Prophetic period. Rather, consensus is "declaratory," confirming one opinion amongst many as the law, or discovering a new opinion where the sources are silent. The sources of law are established as reliable records of legal and theological messages by *tawātur*—their recurrent transmission within the community over time; *ijmāʿ* plays no role here. *Ijmāʿ* is, in fact, most akin to prophecy, and as the Prophet's mission was limited to certain areas of human life, so was consensus to be limited.

Zysow's respect for theologically informed *uṣūl al-fiqh* is demonstrated by his detailed exposition of analogical reasoning and debates among the Central Asian Ḥanafīs about whether speculation over the "causes" of legal rulings (a crucial part of the process of transferring rules from known to novel cases) constituted an (inadmissible) assessment of the workings of the divine mind. To avoid this theological problem, the Ḥanafīs opined that it was the ability of a reason to act as an effective cause of a rule which one was assessing, and the ultimate reason for the causal chain operating as it does is not available for rational scrutiny. This Zysow calls "the doctrine of effectiveness" (*taʾthīr*, p. 188), and that this cause is effective in bringing about that rule is the result of explicit designation by the Lawgiver (who effectively declares this to be the case) or by consensus (which, as we have seen, can act in a similar manner to Prophecy in revealing the workings of the law). The alternative notion of "appropriateness" ("it seems appropriate for this to be the cause of that") is debunked by the Ḥanafīs as thoroughly unconvincing, personal and, most damningly, failing to be a revelation-based method of elaborating *uṣūl*. The most dangerous and radical expression of this trend is the theory of Najm al-Dīn al-Ṭūfī, in which the overall aim of the law is postulated as producing benefit for God's subject, and any individual law perceived to be at variance with that aim can be adjusted or discarded. Similarly, preference (*istiḥsān*) and the specialization of the cause (*takhṣīṣ al-ʿilla*), in which an analogy is rendered legally inoperative by other considerations (an "explicit" text, a consensus, a stronger analogy), seek to avoid any appeal to ultimate motives or benefits of law (see Opwis 2010). Once again, Zysow turns to al-Samarqandī for a sophisticated expression of the doctrine. His account has to be read to be fully appreciated, but it involves a nuanced accommodation of effectiveness to anti-specialization. When Zysow writes that "its very subtlety ensured that this accommodation would have no following" (p. 254), one detects a level of intellectual sympathy. Sometimes a discipline is not quite ready to encounter another level of sophistication and fully internalize its implications. This could be said both of al-Samarqandī's doctrine of effectiveness and also, perhaps, of Zysow's own presentation in "The Economy of Certainty."

In the final exposition, Zysow tackles *ijtihād*, aware of the sensitivity of the topic and the investment of Muslims in the modern period in its potential as a panacea for Islamic religion and law. There is, perhaps, nowhere else in his account of *uṣūl al-fiqh* that Zysow is better able to express his deep interest in and sensitivity to the epistemological dimensions of *uṣūl* than in this account of fallibilism (*takhṭiʾa*), infallibilism (*taṣwīb*), and probability. For the *uṣūlīs* the problem was acute, as the number of juristic opinions was multiplying with each generation, and a theoretical framework to encompass as many acceptable views as possible became essential. For Zysow, those arguing for some version of *taṣwīb*—saying that every qualified jurist is "correct" in his *ijtihād*—were pragmatic. That is, by arguing in this way, certainty is attained, but it is also emptied of singular content. Those arguing for *takhṭiʾa*—that one jurist is correct, and the others are justified but wrong in their *ijtihād*—had the advantage of supporting the institutional structure of the medieval law schools. One could accept their existence without accepting they they all were right and the that the truth was multiple. This gave the *takhṭiʾa* position the edge amongst the "solidly Ḥanafī" (p. 277) region of Central Asia, where Ḥanafī school tradition was dominant, whereas in other more mixed areas, *taṣwīb* survived. I do not think Zysow is necessarily entertaining a social cause for the persistence or demise of an *uṣūl* doctrine, but his comments on how infallibilism may have helped in the political unification of the Zaydīs, or on its rejection by various reformer movements (p. 275), reveal an interesting set of contexts in which certain doctrines might thrive, whilst others might perish.

Zysow's analysis in these chapters follows, approximately, the logical order of their exposition in works of *uṣūl*. From the outset, though, he postulates two broad categories of legal theory: those that incorporate probability (and hence uncertainty) into the theory, and those that reject this, and continually demand certainty. This is the major division proposed in his "typology" of *uṣūl* writers and it is, of course, an epistemological criterion of classification. For the first group, there is commitment to the "formal" framework in which norms are created (in particular, the skills of the jurist and his employment of *ijtihād*). Zysow contrasts these "formalists" with "materialists" who argue that "every rule of law must be certain in order to be valid" (p. 3)—that it is the material content of the law, which is of prime importance, rather than the formal mechanisms of its creation. The majority of legal theorists in the history of *uṣūl al-fiqh* writings have been formalist in this sense. Examples of materialists include Twelver Shiᶜism and Ẓāhirism and these are examined in some brief remarks in Zysow's Epilogue. In both cases, I would argue, materialism gave way to formalism in time. Ẓāhirism did not survive long enough as a vibrant intellectual tradition to fully formalize, but one can see the tendency already in Ibn Ḥazm (d. 456/1064) (Sabra 2007 and 2008). Twelver Shiᶜism, notwithstanding the re-emergence (though not, as is sometimes portrayed, total dominance) of the materialist Akhbārism in the sixteenth–nineteenth centuries, eventually became thoroughly formalist, with a highly technical valorization of probability and *ijtihād* (Gleave 2000). Zysow suggests that the Twelvers moved from materialism to formalism, but there may have been juristic dispute and a theoretical encounter with probability before the demand for certainty found in the early Imāmī *uṣūl* writers.

Whatever the detailed critiques of Zysow's typology of materialist/formalist systems of legal theory, it has not (yet) been fully utilized in subsequent studies of *uṣūl*. This may be because it revolves too much around epistemological principles when the debate within the field of Islamic legal studies (at least since the emergence of the journal *Islamic Law and Society* in 1994) has emphasized the link between theory and practice rather than the internal operation of *uṣūl*. It may be because it has had a restricted readership (rectified, somewhat, by the present publication). Two additional actors, though, might be more pertinent here. First, there is the inherent problem with a classification system in which the vast majority of items fall into one category: most *uṣūl* writings have been unswervingly formalist, hence their extensive coverage in Zysow's work (materialist systems receive an eloquent, but nonetheless much briefer epilogue). Second, there is the rise of formidable "materialist" tendencies in modern Islamic thought. Whether because of increased exchange with alternative systems of legal thought, or as a rejection of them, the notion that a legal rule is merely probable, or the result of an individual scholar's fallible legal reasoning, is proving less persuasive both intellectually and popularly. *Uṣūl* scholars were products of educational systems which lost their authority and status during colonial domination in the Muslim world, a trend that continued during the subsequent era of national states.

Along with the loss of educational institutions, there has been the attempt to dismantle the intellectual institution of the *madhhab* in the name of reform. Rather like al-Samarqandī, Zysow's subtlety in expressing the materialist/formalist distinction may have restricted the potential influence of his ideas in the current climate. What the typology has done, though, is to introduce to the field of Islamic legal theory, a potentially fruitful exchange of the ideational structures of Western legal theory (formal and material sources of the law; references to Kelsen, Hart and others, and so on). Employing these tools of analysis in the dissection *uṣūl al-fiqh* has proved popular, and developed into an interesting subfield within *uṣūl* studies. It perhaps could only have been due to someone with Zysow's interdisciplinary interests and training (jurisprudence, legal theory, Rabbinics, Jewish law) that the possibilities of alternative frameworks for understanding *uṣūl al-fiqh* could have emerged. It is because of this that "The Economy of Certainty" casts a long shadow over the years of subsequent research. It has been read and reread by those working on *uṣūl*, and now, hopefully, those working in linked fields of enquiry will be able to benefit from Zysow's masterly account of the epistemological and theological factors which make *uṣūl al-fiqh* such a distinctive and absorbing theory of law.

Robert Gleave

Works Cited

Ahmed, Ahmed Atif. 2006. *Structural Interrelations of Theory and Practice in Islamic Law: A Study of Six Works of Islamic Jurisprudence*. Leiden: Brill.

Calder, Norman. 1996. "Al-Nawawī's Typology of Muftīs and Its Significance for a General Theory of Islamic Law." *Islamic Law and Society* 3: 137–64.

Gleave, Robert. 2000. *Inevitable Doubt: Two Theories of Shīʿī Jurisprudence*. Leiden: Brill.

Goldziher, Ignaz. 2008 [1971]. *The Ẓāhirīs: Their Doctrine and Their History: A Contribution to the History of Islamic Theology*. Ed. and trans. Wolfgang Behn with an Introduction by Camilla Adang. Boston: Brill.

Hallaq, Wael B. 1984. "Considerations on the Function and Character of Sunnī Legal Theory." *Journal of the American Oriental Society* 104: 679–89.

——. 1992: "Uṣūl al-Fiqh: Beyond Tradition." *Journal of Islamic Studies* 3(2): 172–202.

——. 1997. *A History of Islamic Legal Theories: An Introduction to Sunnī uṣūl al-fiqh*. Cambridge: Cambridge University Press.

Jackson, Sherman. 2002. "Fiction and Formalism: Toward a Functional Analysis of Uṣūl al-Fiqh." In *Studies in Islamic Legal Theory*. Ed. Bernard Weiss. Leiden: Brill. Pp. 177–201

Lowry, Joseph E. 2007. *Early Islamic Legal Theory: The Risāla of Muḥammad ibn Idrīs al-Shāfiʿī*. Leiden: Brill.

Opwis, Felicitas. 2010. *Maṣlaḥa and the Purpose of the Law: Islamic Discourse on Legal Change from the 4th/10th to 8th/14th Century*. Leiden: Brill.

Sabra, Adam. 2007 and 2008. "Ibn Hazm's Literalism: A Critique of Islamic Legal Theory." *al-Qantara* 28: 7–40, and 28: 307–48.

Weiss, Bernard. 2010. *The Search for God's Law: Islamic Jurisprudence in the Writings of Sayf al-Dīn al-Āmidī*. Revised Edition. Salt Lake City: University of Utah Press.

Zysow, Aron. 2002. *Muʿtazilism and Māturīdism in Ḥanafī Legal Theory. In Studies in Islamic Legal Theory*. Ed. Bernard G. Weiss. Leiden: Brill. Pp. 235–65.

——. 2008. "Two Theories of the Obligation to Obey God's Commands." In *The Law Applied: Contextualizing the Islamic Sharīʿa*. Ed. Peri Bearman, Wolfhart Heinrichs, and Bernard Weiss. London: I. B. Tauris. Pp. 397–421.

Author's Preface

The publication of my 1984 Harvard doctoral dissertation "The Economy of Certainty" brings with it what can only be described, however blandly, as mixed feelings. While I am happy to present the work in this new more accessible version, I had long hoped to produce a totally expanded and revised book of the same name, a book that would have far surpassed its predecessor in scope, depth of analysis, and insight. That work, I have rather lately come to realize, while perfect in every respect, would most likely have been perfectly unreadable. There are limits to what can go into the making of a single book. Moreover, years of teaching have finally succeeded in making it clear to me that a balance between historical research and conceptual exposition is no easy achievement.

The *uṣūl al-fiqh* landscape has undergone enormous changes in the decades since this book was written. There is now a steadily growing academic literature on Islamic legal theory in Western languages, and interest on the part of graduate students in the discipline is probably at an all time high.[1] There are now, wonder of wonders, even courses on *uṣūl al-fiqh* at American universities (I have taught a few myself). The most dramatic change, however, has come from the Muslim World. A veritable flood of new text editions and re-editions as well as an enormous number of book-length studies and articles have put research in the field upon a far firmer footing. [2] The advent of the internet has now made it possible to amass without travel or cost an impressive *uṣūl al-fiqh* library, including publications of the utmost rarity, and even copies of manuscripts. The internet also provides a vital link among scholars worldwide, professional and amateur, who are interested in legal theory and its vast literature and who daily freely share their knowledge.

1. A landmark event was the September 1999 conference in Alta, Utah, papers from which were published in the volume, *Studies in Islamic Legal Theory*, ed. Bernard G. Weiss (Leiden: Brill, 2002). A second Alta conference was held in September 2008, and a further volume of papers, dedicated to Professor Weiss, is scheduled to appear.

2. The variety of work exceeds easy categorization. There is even a codification of the discipline, Muḥammad Zakī ʿAbd al-Barr's *Taqnīn uṣūl al-fiqh* (Cairo: Maktabat Dār al-Turāth, 1409/1989), an apparently unprecedented effort as the author notes (pp. 8–9).

These developments are only in very small measure reflected in this edition of *The Economy of Certainty*. Its present publication has provided me with a welcome opportunity to correct some obvious mistakes and to append short notes to each chapter. It has not been possible, however, to undertake the considerable work (the drudgery, to be blunt) that would have been involved in updating the references to manuscripts that have since been published in one or more editions.[3] The original bibliography has been slightly expanded and corrected but otherwise reflects the state of research several decades ago. In this preface and in the additional notes I make rather selective reference to recent scholarship, limited almost exclusively to that in Western languages, in the hope of meeting the needs of those who may happen to first approach Islamic legal theory through this book and reasonably expect such guidance.[4]

"The Economy of Certainty" was an effort to catalog and map a broad range of opinions in Islamic legal theory rather than to focus on any single theorist or tradition.[5] For this purpose I naturally enough turned in the first instance to the classical treatises on the subject that were available. These treatises typically report the opinions of what is after all a rather restricted number of jurists and theologians. Indispensable as these general treatises are for a more or less systematic orientation in the field, they are far from exhausting its riches. Issues of legal theory are touched upon in many areas of Islamic learning, including the exegesis of the Qurʾān and *ḥadīth*, theology, and philology, not to mention the substantive law itself. The study of legal theory along historical lines needs to be put into contact with the history of these other disciplines, and the opinions of those who appear marginally or not at all in the standard treatises of *uṣūl al-fiqh* must be reflected in the on-going work of cataloging and mapping.[6]

3. These include two editions of the work that plays so large a role in this book, al-Samarqandī's *Mīzan al-uṣūl* (ed. Muḥammad Zakī ʿAbd al-Barr [Doha: Maṭābiʿ al-Dawḥa al-Ḥadītha, 1404/1984]; ed. ʿAbd al-Malik ʿAbd al-Raḥmān al-Saʿdī [Mecca: Wizārat al-Awqāf, 1407/1987]). Other editions have appeared bearing the name of al-Samarqandī's *al-Mīzān* that are in fact the work of Muḥammad ibn ʿAbd al-Ḥamīd al-Usmandī, first published under the title *Badhl al-naẓar* by Muḥammad Zakī ʿAbd al-Barr (Cairo: Maktabat Dār al-Turāth, 1417/1997).

4. Editors' note: These references to recent scholarship appear in an addendum after the main bibliography.

5. Recent valuable studies of individual legal theorists include Sherman A. Jackson, *Islamic Law and the State: The Constitutional Jurisprudence of Shihāb al-Dīn al-Qarāfī* (Leiden: Brill, 1996) and Joseph E. Lowry, *Early Islamic Legal Theory: The* Risāla *of Muḥammad ibn Idrīs al-Shāfiʿī* (Leiden: Brill, 2007). Lowry's translation of the *Risāla* has now appeared in the Library of Arabic Literature series: *Al-Shāfiʿī, The Epistle on Legal Theory*, ed. and trans. Joseph E. Lowry (New York: New York University Press, 2013).

6. For classical law there is now Christopher Melchert, *The Formation of the Sunni Schools of Law, 9th-10th Centuries C.E.* (Leiden: Brill, 1997); for the formative period of theology, the monumental work of Josef van Ess, *Theologie und Gesellschaft im 2. und 3. Jahrhundert Hidschra*, 6 vols. (Berlin: de Gruyter, 1991–1997) has important discussions of developments in legal theory. For theology the writings of Richard Frank, Daniel Gimaret, Wilferd Madelung, and now Sabine Schmidtke and her colleagues in

Whatever the precise relation between Islamic legal theory and Islamic law, the fact is that the great treatises of classical law of all the schools make constant reference to the terms and concepts of *uṣūl al-fiqh*.[7] *Uṣūl al-fiqh* has long been an indispensable part of the training of every Muslim jurist. While the passing years have witnessed an enormous growth in academic work on Islamic law by Western scholars in many disciplines, it is my distinct impression that many of these scholars have not taken the trouble to learn even the rudiments of legal theory from its original sources. Instead they rely on the summaries of the experts. Without doubt such re-statements have their use (I certainly hope that "The Economy of Certainty" has been and will continue to be useful).[8] But it is my conviction that even the best second-hand accounts cannot substitute for the careful study of even a short classical work on *uṣūl al-fiqh*.[9]

Berlin, are particularly noteworthy. A survey of the Muʿtazilī contribution to *uṣūl al-fiqh* is prefaced by Sabine Schmidtke and Hasan Ansari to their facsimile edition of Ibn al-Malāḥimī's *al-Tajrīd fī uṣūl al-fiqh* (Tehran: Markaz-i Dā'irat al-Maʿārif-i Buzurg-i Islāmī, 2011). A study with a very significant theological component is A. Kevin Reinhart, *Before Revelation: The Boundaries of Muslim Moral Thought* (Albany: State University of New York Press, 1995). Joseph E. Lowry, "The Legal Hermeneutics of al-Shāfiʿī and Ibn Qutayba: A Reconsideration," *Islamic Law and Society* 11 (2004) 1–41, and Scott Lucas, "The Legal Principles of Muḥammad b. Ismāʿīl al-Bukhāri and their Relationship to Classical Salafī Islam" *Islamic Law and Society* 13 (2006) 289–324, address figures not prominent in the *uṣūl al-fiqh* treatises.

7. Ahmad Atif Ahmad, *Structural Interrelations of Theory and Practice in Islamic Law: A Study of Six Works of Medieval Islamic Jurisprudence* (Leiden: Brill, 2006) introduces the genre of *takhrīj al-furūʿ ʿalā al-uṣūl* works.

8. A superb short introduction, accurately described by its title, is Bernard G. Weiss, *The Spirit of Islamic Law* (Athens, GA: University of Georgia Press, 1998). An introduction along historical lines is Wael B. Hallaq's comprehensive *A History of Islamic Legal Theories: An Introduction to Sunnī uṣūl al-fiqh* (Cambridge: Cambridge University Press, 1997). Mohammad Hashim Kamali, *Principles of Islamic Jurisprudence*, 3rd ed. (Cambridge: Islamic Texts Society, 2003) is heavily based on modern Arabic textbooks. An academic study focused on the modern period is Birgit Krawietz, *Hierarchie der Rechtsquellen im tradierten sunnitischen Islam* (Berlin: Duncker & Humblot, 2002)

9. Translations into Western languages of works of classical legal theory are sadly lacking. There is a French translation of the very short and popular introductory text of al-Juwaynī, *al-Waraqāt* with the commentary of al-Ḥaṭṭāb by Léon Bercher, *Les fondements du fiqh: Kitab al-Warakat fi uçoul al-fiqh: le livre des feuilles sur les fondements du droit musulman* (Paris: Iqra, 1995). An English translation of *al-Waraqāt* by David R. Vishanoff is available on his University of Oklahoma website. An annotated French translation of a classical intermediate-length text, Abū Isḥāq al-Shīrāzī's *Kitāb al-Lumaʿ* is available in Éric Chaumont's *Traité de théorie légale musulmane* (Berkeley: Robbins Collection, 1999), which contains a valuable *uṣūl al-fiqh* bibliography (pp. 367–401) covering both primary and secondary literature. Chaumont's critical edition of the Arabic text of *Kitāb al-Lumaʿ* was published in *Mélanges de l'Université Saint-Joseph* 53 (1993–1994). The fullest exposition of classical Sunnī *uṣūl al-fiqh* in any Western language is probably Bernard G. Weiss's *The Search for God's Law: Islamic Jurisprudence in the Writings of Sayf al-Dīn al-Āmidi*, rev. ed. (Salt Lake City: University of Utah Press, 2010). The first of the three levels of the Twelver Shiʿi jurist Muḥammad Bāqir al-Ṣadr's *al-Durūs* has appeared in two English translations, *Lessons in Islamic Jurisprudence*, trans. Roy Parviz Mottahedeh (Oxford: Oneworld, 2003) and *Principles of Islamic Jurisprudence: Shiʿi Law*, trans. Arif Abdul Hussain (London: ICAS: 2003). The ultimate and quite

There are, of course, those who will need no special encouragement to pursue the study of *uṣūl al-fiqh* either because its practical significance is immediately obvious to them or because they quickly come to fall under its spell. I number myself among the latter, and it is precisely the bearing of the questions of *uṣūl al-fiqh* on so many fields of thought that has kept my interest alive. Those with a philosophical bent, for example, will find that *uṣūl al-fiqh* touches upon epistemology, the philosophy of language, moral theory, and the philosophy of science. For scholars to fail to attend to such obvious connections is not only for them to miss an opportunity to bring an apparently arcane corner of Islamic studies into the wider fold of human learning but equally to impoverish Islamic studies.[10]

difficult test of such translations is whether they are intelligible to a reader without knowledge of the original. With few exceptions, such as "analogy" for *qiyās* and "consensus" for *ijmā*ʿ, there is currently little uniformity in the renderings of even common technical terms, and such uniformity is unlikely to emerge. In any case, it is questionable whether agreement in the translation of technical terms in works of *uṣūl al-fiqh* should even be a goal, the point being to capture the sense of such terms, not to imprison them.

10. It is worth noting that Islamic legal theory left its mark on medieval Jewish law, both Rabbinite and Karaite, and the surviving Jewish texts documenting this influence are apt to shed important light on *uṣūl al-fiqh*. See David E. Sklare, *Samuel b. Ḥofnī Gaon and His Cultural World: Texts and Studies* (Leiden, Brill, 1996) and Gregor Schwarb, "*Uṣūl al-fiqh* im jüdischen *kalām* des 10. und 11. Jahrhunderts: Ein Überblick," in *Orient als Grenzbereich?: Rabbinisches und außerrabbinisches Judentum*, ed. Annelies Kuyt and Gerold Necker, Abhandlungen für die Kunde des Morgenlandes 60 (Wiesbaden: Harrassowitz, 2007), 77–104.

Acknowledgments

I would like to take this opportunity to thank my teachers, Professors Muhsin Mahdi, George Makdisi, and Isadore Twersky, who are sadly no longer with us, and Professor A. I. Sabra, in whose seminar on Muʿtazilī *kalām* I wrote my first paper on *uṣūl al-fiqh*. Thanks too to those many colleagues and students who generously responded to my requests for books and other research materials over the years. I owe a special debt of gratitude to Professors Frank Vogel and Bernard Haykel for making it possible for me to continue my research and teaching at two great universities. Professors Joseph Lowry, Devin Stewart, and Shawkat Toorawa have selflessly assisted in the preparation of the volume.

Professor Wolfhart Heinrichs made every effort to arrange for the publication of this book many years ago, and my unreasonable resistance in no way reflects on the respect in which I hold him.

For hope and inspiration I thank Sarah, Esther, and David, a threefold blessing.

I dedicate this book to my mother and to the memory of my father. I wish I could offer them far more.

Abbreviations

Āmidī: al-Āmidī. *al-Iḥkām fī uṣūl al-aḥkām.*
Asnawī: al-Asnawī. *Nihāyat al-sūl fī sharḥ minhāj al-wuṣūl.*
Badakhshī: al-Badakhshī. *Manāhij al-ʿuqūl fī sharḥ minhāj al-uṣūl.*
Baḥr: al-Zarkashī, *al-Baḥr al-muḥīṭ*
Bājī: al-Bājī. *al-Minhāǧ fī tartīb al-hiǧāǧ.*
Bazdawī: al-Bazdawī, Fakhr al-Islām. *Uṣūl al-fiqh.*
Bukhārī: al-Bukhārī. *Kashf al-asrār ʿan uṣūl Fakhr al-Islām al-Bazdawī.*
Burhān: al-Juwaynī. *al-Burhān fī uṣūl al-fiqh.*
Dabūsī: al-Dabūsī. *Taqwīm al-adilla fī uṣūl al-fiqh.*
Dharīʿa: al-Sharīf al-Murtaḍā. *al-Dharīʿa ilā uṣūl al-sharīʿa.*
Fawātiḥ: al-Anṣārī, ʿAbd al-ʿAlī. *Fawātiḥ al-raḥamūt sharḥ musallam al-thubūt fī uṣūl al-fiqh.*
Fuṣūl: al-Mufīd. *al-Fuṣūl al-mukhtāra min al-ʿuyūn wa'l-maḥāsin.*
Ḥujaj: al-Bazdawī, Abū'l-Yusr. *Kitāb Maʿrifat al-ḥujaj al-sharʿiyya.*
Ḥuṣūl: Ṣiddīq Ḥasan Khān. *Ḥuṣūl al-maʾmul min ʿilm al-uṣūl.*
Ibn ʿAqīl: Ibn ʿAqīl. *Le livre de la dialectique d'Ibn ʿAqīl.*
Iḥkām: Ibn Ḥazm. *al-Iḥkām fī uṣūl al-aḥkām.*
Intiṣār: al-Khayyāṭ. *Kitāb al-Intiṣār.*
Irshād: al-Shawkānī. *Irshād al-fuḥūl ilā taḥqīq al-haqq min ʿilm al-uṣūl.*
Jamʿ: al-Subkī, Tāj al-Dīn. *Jamʿ al-jawāmiʿ.*
Jaṣṣāṣ: al-Jaṣṣāṣ. *al-Fuṣūl fī al-uṣūl.*
Jawāmiʿ: al-Nāṭiq bi'l-Ḥaqq. *Kitāb Jawāmiʿ al-adilla fī uṣūl al-fiqh.*
Lumaʿ: al-Shīrāzī. *al-Lumaʿ fī uṣūl al-fiqh.*
Madkhal: Ibn Badrān. *al-Madkhal ilā madhhab al-Imām Aḥmad ibn Ḥanbal.*
Maḥṣūl: al-Rāzī. *al-Maḥṣūl fī uṣūl al-fiqh.*
Manār: al-Nasafī, Abū 'l-Barakāt. *Sharḥ al-Manār wa-ḥawāshīhi min ʿilm al-uṣūl.*
Mankhūl: al-Ghazālī. *al-Mankhūl min taʿlīqat al-uṣūl.*
Māwardī: al-Māwardī. *Adab al-qāḍī.*
Mīzān: al-Samarqandī. *Mīzān al-uṣūl fī natāʾij al-ʿuqūl.*
Mughnī: ʿAbd al-Jabbār. *al-Mughnī fī abwāb al-tawḥīd wa'l-ʿadl.*
Musawwada: Ibn Taymiyya. *al-Musawwada fī uṣūl al-fiqh.*

Mustaṣfā: al-Ghazālī. *al-Mustaṣfā min ʿilm al-uṣūl.*
Muʿtamad: al-Baṣrī. *Kitāb al-Muʿtamad fī uṣūl al-fiqh.*
Nasafī: al-Nasafī, Abū 'l-Barakāt. *Kashf al-asrār fī sharḥ al-Manār.*
Nuʿmān: al-Nuʿmān ibn Muḥammad. *Kitāb Ikhtilāf uṣūl al-madhāhib.*
Qarāfī: al-Qarāfī. *Sharḥ tanqīḥ al-fuṣūl fī ikhtiṣār al-maḥṣūl fī al-uṣūl.*
Qawāṭiʿ: al-Samʿānī. *Qawāṭiʿ al-adilla.*
Rawḍa: Ibn Qudāma. *Rawḍat al-nāẓir wa-junnat al-munāẓir.*
Sarakhsī: al-Sarakhsī. *Uṣūl al-Sarakhsī.*
Shifāʾ: al-Ghazālī. *Shifāʾ al-ghalīl fī bayān al-shabah wa'l-mukhīl wa-masāʾil al-taʿlīl.*
Tabṣira: al-Nasafī, Abū 'l-Muʿīn. *Kitāb Tabṣirat al-adilla.*
Talwīḥ: al-Taftāzānī. *al-Talwīḥ.*
Taqrīr: Ibn Amīr al-Ḥājj. *al-Taqrīr wa'l-taḥbīr.*
Taysīr: Amīr Bādshāh. *Taysīr al-taḥrīr.*
Ṭūsī: al-Ṭūsī. *Kitāb ʿUddat al-uṣūl.*
ʿUdda: Abū Yaʿlā. *al-ʿUdda.*

INTRODUCTION

At the heart of Islamic law, as of all legal orders, there lies the question of legitimacy. From where do the rules that purport to bind Muslims come? What is the source of their validity? Who is entitled to make authoritative pronouncements as to the content of the law? What are the standards for resolving disagreement as to the law? From a very early period, for reasons upon which we are free to speculate, Muslims came to treat the question of legitimacy along explicitly epistemological lines. Certainty and probability were the fundamental categories with which they approached every question of law. This concern with epistemology sets Islamic law apart from other legal systems that treat their problem of legitimacy in institutional terms: for example, Anglo-American law, where the fundamental division is between common law and statute, and Jewish law, which distinguishes between the law of the Torah and the law resting on Rabbinic authority. Its constant preoccupation with epistemology makes Islamic law much more self-conscious than either of these two systems, and for those of a philosophical bent, much more sophisticated.

Uṣūl al-fiqh, the subject of this study, is one genre of Islamic legal literature and corresponds roughly to the general part of jurisprudence as practiced by such Western writers as Austin and Kelsen. It is not directly concerned with the institutions of substantive law but with the more basic question of how one derives a legal system from the materials of the Islamic revelation. The voluminous literature on *uṣūl al-fiqh* contains a vast body of observations on language, legal reasoning and argument, and the assessment of historical evidence. When one takes into consideration the entire range of Islamic legal schools, it seems that activity in the field of *uṣūl al-fiqh* continued with undiminished vigor for over a thousand years, from about the beginning of the ninth century well through the nineteenth. A great expert, Badr al-Dīn al-Zarkashī (d. 794/1392), already estimated that the number of questions dealt with in *uṣūl al-fiqh* was closer to eight thousand than to the eight hundred suggested by another authority, and further reflection, he noted, only generated more.[1]

1. *Baḥr*, f. 370a.

It is clear that a study such as this cannot reasonably deal with more than a small fraction of these many topics. I have therefore chosen to limit my work to those subjects that reflect the role of *uṣūl al-fiqh* as the science of the sources of law, and my treatment of each subject has been dictated by a single consideration: the creation of a framework within which the history of this discipline can be undertaken. The richness of *uṣūl al-fiqh* and its obvious dependence on other disciplines such as theology and grammar make it only too easy to despair of finding those intelligible structures that intellectual history requires. There is a real question as to the autonomy of *uṣūl al-fiqh*. My own view is that there are patterns that emerge from the study of *uṣūl al-fiqh*, and it is with some of these patterns, the most basic, that this study is concerned.

It should be readily apparent that this is more a study of *uṣūl al-fiqh* than it is of any particular Muslim jurist or legal tradition. Without a knowledge of what is typical, one cannot grasp what is original in the work of the individual jurist. Whatever the institutional importance of the legal schools, when it comes to legal theory, the most illuminating groupings often cut across school lines. Nonetheless, in the interests of intelligibility, I have taken Ḥanafism as a focal point and within Ḥanafism the Central Asian tradition. Among the Central Asians I have devoted particular attention to ʿAlāʾ al-Dīn al-Samarqandī (d. 539/1144). My decision to concentrate on this school and this author is largely, but not entirely, arbitrary. I have had several collateral purposes in view. In the first place, I wished to show that Ḥanafī *uṣūl al-fiqh* is informed by the same theological concerns as the writings of the famous Shāfiʿī theologians such as al-Ghazālī and Fakhr al-Dīn al-Rāzī. Ḥanafī *uṣūl al-fiqh* is not, as is sometimes suggested, particularly legal in any but a superficial sense.[2] Secondly, the autonomy of Ḥanafī *uṣūl al-fiqh* should make it clear that the history of *uṣūl al-fiqh* is not a series of footnotes to al-Shāfiʿī's *Risāla*, generally regarded as the first work in the field. Excessive concern with origins has led to the unfortunate neglect of the classical theory, and this despite the wealth of information in the classical treatises that could illuminate the early period. I shall be concerned with origins only insofar as determining the origin of a doctrine enables us to fit it into its legal or theological setting. Finally, al-Samarqandī's treatise appears to be our chief source for the legal theory of the school of Samarqand, the most famous representative of which was Abū Manṣūr al-Māturīdī (d. 333/944). Al-Samarqandī's reports of al-Māturīdī's teaching offer a good illustration of how *uṣūl al-fiqh* can contribute in the most direct fashion to our knowledge of Islamic theology.

Ḥanafism has the further advantage of providing us with an example of an unusually consistent formalist system, and the great dividing line in Islamic theory is between

---

2. Cf. ʿAbd al-Rahmān Ibn Khaldūn, *Muqaddimat al-ʿallāma Ibn Khaldūn* (Cairo, n.d.; reprint ed., Beirut: Dār Iḥyāʾ al-Turāth al-ʿArabī, n.d.), p. 455.

formalists and materialists.[3] For the formalists, the practice (*ijtihād*) of the jurist is of paramount concern. Ordinarily the results of his practice are only probable, but their validity is ensured by the fact that the framework within which he practices is known with certainty. This framework is provided by the main legal institutions and by *uṣūl al-fiqh*. Where certainty is attainable there is no room for disagreement. But where there is only probability, disagreement is to be expected. Even here, however, disagreement is not inevitable. Should the jurists come to agree on a solution to a question of law, their consensus elevates this solution from probability to certainty. The conditions under which probability enters the law and the mechanism of its elevation to certainty differ from system to system. But in each case there is achieved a balance between certainty and probability. Where the balance is precarious, it tends over time to give way to another that provides greater satisfaction to those within and offers less of a target to those from without.

For the materialist jurists, probability has no place in the formulation of the rules of law. Every rule of law must be certain in order to be valid. There is no balancing of certainty and probability in materialist systems, and the line between legal theory and law is erased. Because no probability is allowed to enter into these systems, there is no need for its elevation to certainty in the shape of consensus. The sources of certainty, however, to which the materialists can look differ significantly. The Shiʿis recognize an infallible Imām; the Sunni Ẓāhirīs do not. Furthermore, the standards for certainty that are invoked can change over time. In the cases of both Shiʿism and Ẓāhirism, we shall see how the importation of Muʿtazilī standards of certainty led to a reduction in the body of information regarded as certain.

The line between formalists and materialists generally coincides with that between analogists and anti-analogists. One need only cite Ẓāhirism. This follows simply from the common recognition that analogy could provide only probable results. But anomalous systems do exist. A formalist system can reject analogy if it can find a reasoned basis for distinguishing between analogy and other sources of probability.[4] On the other hand, if

3. My distinction between formalists and materialists is inspired by, but by no means coincides with, Salmond's distinction between formal and material sources of law. "A formal source of law is defined by Salmond as that from which a rule of law derives its force and validity; the material source is that from which is derived the matter, not the validity, of the law" (George Whitecross Paton, *A Text-book of Jurisprudence*, ed. G. W. Paton and David P. Derham, 4th ed. [Oxford: Oxford University Press, 1972], p.188). This study throughout is concerned with formal sources in Salmond's sense. Needless to say, the Muslim formalists bear no relation to the formalists of Anglo-American jurisprudence. These jurists are contrasted with the instrumentalists. On this topic, see now Robert Samuel Summers, *Instrumentalism and American Legal Theory* (Ithaca: Cornell University Press, 1983).

4. For example, Ibn ʿArabī, discussed below.

the conditions for the practice of analogy are stringent enough, its results may be raised to the level of certainty and admitted into a materialist system.[5]

For the historian of Islamic intellectual history, the study of these systems of legal theory is an end in itself. Their identification and elucidation is as legitimate as the analogous activity undertaken in the study of Islamic philosophy, theology, or mysticism. This would be true even if legal theory were totally divorced from any other Islamic discipline. But such is not the case. The ties between legal theory and theology, on the one hand, and law, on the other, are too obvious to be missed. At least something should be said about its relation to each.

In the hierarchy of Islamic religious sciences, theology ranks above legal theory in the sense that it establishes such premises as the veracity of God that the work of the legal theorist presupposes. But the significance of theology for legal theory goes well beyond its role of providing essential premises. Legal theory and theology were both born out of the early fragmentation of the Muslim community that forced Muslims to identify and defend the essential elements of their belief and practice. The epistemological, rather than the institutional, basis of Islamic law testifies to this origin. Subsequently, developed theology, above all in the form of Muʿtazilism, managed to penetrate to the very heart of legal theory. The impress of Muʿtazilism can be found centuries after the highpoint of its influence had passed. Ashʿarism and Māturīdism, too, in their turn, exercised a notable, though lesser, influence on legal theory.

The literature of legal theory provides new information of direct relevance to each of these theological movements. But the chief significance of legal theory for theology lies elsewhere. Legal theory can guide the historian of theology in viewing the object of his study in Islamic terms. By becoming familiar with the interconnections between legal theory and theology, he will be able to see an added dimension to the theological arguments. No longer oblivious to their legal consequences, he will not be so likely to confine his attention to the Greek precursors but will also consider the role of these arguments in their own culture. *Uṣūl al-fiqh* will teach the historian of theology to read his texts with added powers of discrimination. In some instances, he will have to distinguish between the reconstructed theology of the theological treatises and the theology-in-use of the legal texts.[6] In being put to use in the law, theology is sometimes forced to bend, and the theologians and legal theorists, often the same individuals, were well aware of this.

All of these remarks apply with equal if not greater force to the passage from legal theory to law. I am far from thinking that the study of legal theory should be conducted apart from the study of the substantive law. The theorists were conscious enough of the

5. For example, al-Aṣamm.

6. The distinction in these terms is suggested by Abraham Kaplan's distinction between "logic-in-use" and "reconstructed logic" in *The Conduct of Inquiry: Methodology for Behavioral Science* (Scranton: Chandler, 1964), p. 8.

limitations of their attempts to reconstruct their own practice.[7] But while it would be foolish to detach the theory from the legal system it was meant to serve, it would be even more foolish to ignore the work done by the Muslim jurists in disengaging the principles that guided their activity. Those who counsel us to do so in the name of legal science, only elevate ignorance into a method.[8] Before we can begin to determine how far the practice of the Muslim jurist diverges from his theory, we must have a far better grasp on what that theory is.

It is not difficult to find statements of the most illustrious jurists testifying to the importance of *uṣūl al-fiqh* for the practicing jurist.[9] I see no reason to doubt the validity of their remarks. The primary role of legal theory for the historian of Islamic law is that it aids him in seeing law as a discipline in its own right, with evolving methods and styles. It brings the historian closer to the inner and, to my mind, more significant side of Islamic law for the outsider. It inculcates concern for system and method, not merely for the single rule of law or the single legal institution. Having immersed himself in legal theory, the student of Islamic law will come to see the law as the Muslim jurist does, and this, if not the final, is at least the first stage toward understanding.

Addenda to the Introduction

P. 2

The reports on the opinions of al-Māturīdī on questions of *uṣūl al-fiqh* have been collected and studied in an unpublished dissertation of Şükrü Özen, "Ebû Mansûr el-Mâtürîdî'nin fıkıh usûlünün yeniden inşası" (Marmara University, 2001).

7. For example, with reference to hermeneutics, Ibn Taymiyya, *Rafʿ al-malām ʿan al-aʾimma al-aʿlām* (Damascus: al-Maktab al-Islāmī, 1383/1964), p. 26.

8. This was the position of Chafik T. Chehata going back to his *Essai d'une théorie générale de l'obligation en droit musulman*, vol. 1 (Cairo: F. E. Noury, 1936) and has been maintained by his student Yaʿakov Meron ("The Development of Legal Thought in Ḥanafi Texts," *Studia Islamica* 30 [1969]: 94–101).

9. For example, Ṭūsī, p. 2; Sarakhsī, 1:10.

1
THE AUTHENTICATION OF PROPHETIC TRADITIONS

I. The Concurrent Tradition

1. The Conditions of Concurrency

The Muslim jurist has the task of interpreting the divinely revealed legal texts and of extending their application by analogy. It is clear, however, that before he can undertake these tasks the jurist must have access to the legal information furnished by revelation.[1] The veracity of the miracle-wielding prophet, at least in his function of laying down the law, is demonstrated by the theologian and is assumed by the legal theorist. Generally speaking, no distinction is made between the validity of the Qurʾān and prophetic utterances that are non-Qurʾānic.[2] The division between the two is drawn from the

1. This priority is impaired, however, by the introduction of interpretation and analogy into the process of authentication. *Mutawātir* traditions must go back to a sensory experience. Unit-reports are tested by the *balwā* standard (see below) and when they are inconsistent with analogy, by the requirement that the transmitter be a jurist.

2. With respect to interpretation, see al-Faṣīh al-Harawī, *Jawāhir al-uṣūl fī ʿilm ḥadīth al-rasūl*, ed. Abū 'l-Maʿālī Aṭhar al-Mubārakfūrī (Medina: al-Maktaba al-ʿIlmiyya, n.d.), p. 18. The major issue in this connection is that of abrogation. Famous is al-Shāfiʿī's doctrine that the Qurʾān could be abrogated only by the Qurʾān and the *sunna* only by the *sunna* (*Risāla*, paras. 322, 324). This doctrine, defended by al-Shāfiʿī in both versions of his *Risāla* (Ṭūsī, p. 203), was meant to protect the *sunna* from widespread rejection (*Risāla*, para. 332). This doctrine, theologically retrogressive, was rejected by the majority of Shāfiʿīs (*Irshād*, p. 191), and the opposing doctrine was even attributed to al-Shafiʿī by some of his followers (Ṭūṣi, p. 203 [sceptical]; *Mīzān*, f. 191a [*ahl al-taḥqīq min aṣḥābihi*]). This issue raises four points of general significance in the study of *uṣūl al-fiqh*: 1. the actual doctrine of an early master; 2. the understanding of his doctrine by his followers; 3. the understanding of his doctrine by his opponents; 4. the polemical dimension, illustrated here by Abū Bakr ibn Masʿūd al-Kāsānī, *Badāʾiʿ al-ṣanāʾiʿ*, 1:160.

point of view of authenticity, the Qurʾān being an identifiable whole of absolutely certain authenticity as opposed to the *sunna*, where the question of authenticity is of serious concern.

Common *uṣūl* doctrine recognizes two classes of transmitted information: one consists of concurrent reports (*al-khabar al-mutawātir*) and the other of unit-reports (*khabar al-wāḥid*, pl. *akhbār al-āḥād*), that is, those reports that fall short of the dissemination of the first category.[3] The distinction is an epistemological one, it being claimed that if enough people under certain circumstances tell us something, we can have certain knowledge of the veracity of their report, whereas unit-reports cannot give us this certainty. This distinction is fundamental to the *uṣūl* treatment of *ḥadīth*, which is often found under the heading of *akhbār* ("reports").[4] The *ḥadīth* takes the form of a report to the effect that various people one from another have transmitted a saying or action of the Prophet; the final transmitter is the reporter, the rest of the *isnād* ("chain of transmitters") and the *matn* ("text") are the report.[5] One should note that the Qurʾān itself was transmitted in precisely the same fashion; its transmission is equivalent to a report that the Prophet spoke the text of the Qurʾān in the name of God. That the authenticity of the Qurʾān is not treated in the *uṣūl* texts is, however, not surprising, for the controversies about the Qurʾān were, as Ibn Ḥazm notes, the province of the theologian:

> There is no disagreement among the sects belonging to Islam, the *Ahl al-Sunna*, the Muʿtazila, the Murjiʾa, and the Zaydiyya as to the obligation of accepting the Qurʾān nor as to the fact that the Qurʾān is that very same one which is recited among us. Only a group of extreme Rāfiḍīs have disputed this and are thereby unbelievers, heretics according to all the people of Islam. It is not with them that we are holding discourse in this work but only with the people of our

Some achieved the same result as al-Shāfiʿī without his rigid compartmentalization. For the Syrian al-Awzāʿī (d. 157/774), the *sunna* could abrogate the Qurʾān but not vice versa (al-Harawī, *Jawāhir al-uṣūl*, p. 8); so also for the *muḥaddith* al-Dārimī (d. 255/869) (Nuʿmān, editor's introduction, p. 82). Only Qāḍī Abū ʾl-Faraj (d. 331/942) attributed this, the "Kufan" view, to Mālik (Ibn ʿAbd al-Barr, *Jāmiʿ bayān al-ʿilm wa-faḍlihi*, 2:192).

3. We also find *khabar al-āḥād* (Bājī, p. 37) and *al-ḥadīth al-āḥādī* (al-Amīr al-Ṣanʿānī, *Tāwḍīḥ al-afkār li-maʿānī Tanqīḥ al-anẓār*, ed. Muḥammad Muḥyī al-Dīn ʿAbd al-Ḥamīd [Cairo: Maktabat al-Khānjī, 1366 H], 1:87). The distinction roughly corresponds to that found in al-Shāfiʿī between *khabar al-ʿāmma* and *khabar al-khāṣṣa* (e.g., *Risāla*, paras. 998, 1115). Al-Shāfiʿī uses the verb *tawātara* in a nontechnical sense (*Risāla*, para. 1190; see Zayn al-Dīn al-ʿIrāqī, *al-Taqyīd wa'l-īḍāḥ*, pp. 265–66). Significantly, al-Shāfiʿī uses *khabar al-wāḥid* where there is one transmitter (*Risāla*, para. 999).

4. On the distinction between *khabar* and *ḥadīth*, see Ibn Ḥajar al-ʿAsqalānī, *Nuzhat al-naẓar sharḥ Nukhbat al-fikar fī muṣṭalaḥ ahl al-athar* (Medina: al-Maktaba al-ʿIlmiyya, n.d.), pp. 18–19.

5. The *ḥadīth* scholars differed as to whether the *matn* was only what the Prophet said or included the quotation of the Companion, the latter view being dominant (al-Harawī, *Jawāhir al-uṣūl*, p. 9).

> religion (*milla*), for we have already established the falsity of the other religions in our book *al-Fiṣal*.[6]

But although the question of the authenticity of the Qurʾān is raised only cursorily in the *uṣūl* texts, one must keep in mind that the Qurʾān is, as it were, the *matn* of a *mutawātir* report and that any attack on the *mutawātir* report is at the same time an attack upon the Qurʾān.[7]

In general, one can say that the Ḥanafī treatment of *ḥadīth* has two aims: to admit enough sound material for analogy to function and to exclude materials that would obliterate the outlines of the legal system. The secure basis is comprised of those *ḥadīth* that are *mutawātir* and *mashhūr* ("widespread"), an intermediate category recognized by most Ḥanafī scholars. Traditions whose mode of transmission cannot entail certainty, the *akhbār al-āḥād*, are measured against these sources in addition to being subjected to other tests. Only after they meet these criteria can they form the basis for action (*ʿamal*), that is, constitute a legal norm. This distinction between sources that are of absolutely certain authenticity and those that are merely presumptive is a characteristic feature of the formalist legal systems of Islam.

The *mutawātir* report figures as a source of certain knowledge throughout Islamic thought, and a study of its various uses could well form the subject of a separate treatise.[8] Our discussion will center about two issues: What conditions must be met for a report to be *mutawātir* and which of the two sorts of certain knowledge does it yield, *ḍarūrī* ("immediate") or *muktasab* ("acquired")?[9] It will emerge that the Ḥanafīs were apparently unanimous in holding that the knowledge yielded by the *mutawātir* tradition was *ḍarūrī*, in spite of the spread of the *muktasab* position in other circles. We shall also see that a number of prominent Ḥanafī scholars stipulated conditions for the *mutawātir* tradition that were peculiar to themselves.

As the standard definition of a *mutawātir* report we may take that which states that it is "the report of something sensible by a group of people whom experience precludes from acting in concert."[10] The *mutawātir* report is one transmitted by enough people to

---

6. *Iḥkām*, 1:96. The Qurʾānic counterpart of the problem of authenticity is in the *qirāʾāt*: "*wa-ammā al-qirāʾāt fa-innahā bi-manzilat al-riwāya fī al-ḥadīth*" (Muḥammad ibn Aḥmad Ibn Juzayy, *Kitāb al-Tashīl li-ʿulūm al-tanzīl*, ed. Muḥammad Muḥammad ʿAbd al-Munʿim al-Yūnusī and Ibrāhīm ʿAṭwa ʿAwaḍ [Cairo: Dār al-Kutub al-Ḥadītha, n.d.] 1:11).

7. *Mankhūl*, p. 282 (*wa-manāṭ al-sharīʿa wa-ʿumdatuhā tawātur al-qurʾān*).

8. The leading development appears to be the extension of *tawātur* to the authentication of the inner experience of *ijtihād* for consensus.

9. On these terms, see Josef van Ess, *Die Erkenntislehre des ʿAḍudaddīn al-Īcī: Übersetzung und Kommentar des ersten Buches seiner Mawāqif*. Akademie der Wissenschaften und der Literatur, Veröffentlichungen der orientalischen Kommission, vol. 26 (Wiesbaden: Steiner, 1966), pp. 114–28.

10. Qarāfī, p. 349.

eliminate the possibility of their concurrence stemming from chance or collusion.[11] The source of knowledge must reside in the senses because sense knowledge is free from obscurity or confusion. It is not liable to the errors of reasoning.[12] Thus the unbelievers can report in all their numbers that God is "one of three" without this producing certain knowledge.[13] The basis for *tawātur* knowledge is experience (*ʿāda*), not reason, for reason does not exclude the possibility of any number of people lying. The impossibility is only one based on experience.[14]

The precise number of those who constituted a *tawātur* quorum was, however, a matter of uncertainty. Various numbers were suggested, usually those that figured prominently in Qurʾānic stories or in early Islamic history.[15] It was argued that since even when four men testify to fornication, the judge still must investigate their moral credentials, one could be sure that four fell short of the number.[16] Al-Ghazālī discusses the difficulties involved:

> If we assume the absence of concomitant circumstances, the minimum number by which *ḍarūrī* (in this case, best rendered "irresistible") knowledge takes place is known to God but not to us. We have no way to know, for we do not know when we first came to know of the existence of Mecca, of al-Shāfiʿī, or of the Prophets by means of concurrent reports reaching us. We do not know whether it was after the hundredth report or the two hundredth. And we cannot easily test this even if we try. The way to try is to observe ourselves when a man is killed in the market place, for example. A number of people leave the scene and come to us with the report of his murder. The first statement arouses a presumption of truth; the second and the third confirm it. It keeps growing in

11. *Muʿtamad*, 2:558.

12. *Muʿtamad*, 2:559.

13. *Mīzān*, f. 108b; *Mustaṣfā*, p. 163.

14. Qarāfī, p. 349.

15. *Irshād*, pp. 47–48; *Musawwada*, p. 236; *Muʿtamad*, 2:565–66; Jaṣṣāṣ, f. 162b (twenty reporters for Abū 'l-Hudhayl). Ibn Ḥazm identified a tradition (from Wābiṣa ibn Miʿbad) as concurrent in content on the basis of its transmission by twelve Companions (*Iḥkām*, 2:62; cf. *Manār*, pp. 627–28, below [analogy is superior to this tradition]). Al-Suyūṭī regarded the number ten as sufficient (*Kitāb al-Taḥadduth bi-niʿmat Allāh*, vol. 2 of E. M. Sartain, *Jalāl al-Dīn al-Suyūṭī, Biography and Background* [Cambridge: Cambridge University Press, 1975], p. 23). He was the author of a collection of *mutawātir* traditions, *al-Azhār al-mutanāthira fī al-akhbār al-mutawātira* (al-Suyūṭī, *Tadrīb al-rāwī fī sharḥ Taqrīb al-Nawāwī*, ed. ʿAbd al-Wahhāb ʿAbd al-Laṭīf [Medina: al-Maktaba al-ʿIlmiyya, 1379/1959], p. 374 and note 1).

16. *Musawwada*, p. 236. Ibn Barhān (d. 520/1126) claimed that there was a consensus that the number three was insufficient (*Musawwada*, p. 236). Ibn Tūmart regarded "two, four, ten or the like" as too small (*Le Livre de Mohammed Ibn Toumert, Mahdi des Almohades*, ed. J. D. Luciani [Algiers: Pierre Fontana, 1903], p. 46); Muḥammad Bāqir al-Bihbihānī, *al-Fawāʾid al-jadīda*, with Muḥammad Ḥusayn ibn ʿAbd al-Raḥīm al-Rāzī, *al-Fuṣūl al-gharawiyya fī al-uṣūl al-fiqhiyya* (N.p., 1261/1845), p. 8 (pagination supplied): "six or seven or ten."

> confirmation until it becomes *ḍarūrī;* we are unable to cause ourselves to doubt it. Now, if one could conceive of being aware of the instant in which this knowledge became *ḍarūrī* and of retaining the number of the informants, then knowledge of this matter would be possible. But grasping this instant is difficult, for the force of our conviction increases subtly in the same way as the intellect of a "discerning youth" (*ṣabī mumayyiz*) increases until he becomes legally responsible or in the same way that the light of dawn increases until it is full. For this reason this number remains obscure, and its grasp is beyond human powers. As to the fixing of the number at forty on the basis of the quorum of the Friday noon prayer or at seventy on the basis of the Qur'anic verse (7: 155), "And Moses chose seventy men of his people to meet Us," or at the number of the people of Badr (more than three hundred), these numbers are all arbitrary and inappropriate to the question under discussion. Their mutual contradiction is enough to show that they are groundless. Thus there is no way to fix the number. From the existence of *ḍarūrī* knowledge we infer that the full number, known only to God, has concurred in the report.[17]

More concisely, al-Jaṣṣāṣ (d. 370/981) observes that "in matters based on experience, there is no way to draw limits and to fix a minimum boundary."[18]

There was thus general agreement that the minimum number of reporters for a *mutawātir* tradition was unascertainable. The *uṣūlīs* are content to speak of a "large number." The basis for the certainty of this kind of tradition was, of course, the exclusion of chance agreement and, more importantly, of collusion. A large number would be necessary to exclude these possibilities under ordinary circumstances. But under controlled conditions, numbers would no longer be significant. Ibn Ḥazm insists upon this point:

> If you set a man to invent a long, false tale, he can do it. This is known absolutely from experience. But if you put two men in two houses so that they cannot meet and have each one produce a false narrative, there is no way for the tales to agree from beginning to end, no way at all. It does happen, but so infrequently that we hardly ever see it, that two talents coincide for a few words or so, and we have seen two poets produce the same hemistich; this we have seen only twice in our life.... As for what the literary critics call *al-muwārada*, in which the poetic talents agree on a number of verses, the cited cases are tall tales, absolutely unsound. They are nothing but instances of plagiarism and mutual borrowing among the poets.[19]

The usual stipulation of a "great number" was not sufficient for a number of Transoxanian Ḥanafī scholars. They posed stricter, so-called controverted conditions (*mukhtalaf*

17. *Mustaṣfā*, pp. 161–62.
18. Jaṣṣāṣ, f. 170a.
19. *Iḥkām*, 1:108.

fīhi).[20] In the *Uṣūl* of al-Sarakhsī (d. 483/1090), a *mutawātir* tradition is defined as one "transmitted by a group of people of whom one cannot imagine their collusion on account of the greatness of their number and the distances between their habitations."[21] In the *Uṣūl* of Fakhr al-Islām al-Bazdawī (d. 482/1089), the people are said to be such that "their number cannot be counted nor can one conceive of their collusion on account of their number, their probity, and the distances between their habitations."[22] Leaving aside the question of probity for the moment, one notes that the two conditions of being innumerable and of living in widely separated habitations are related and, in fact, they are treated by al-Ghazālī as a single condition, which he rejects.[23] Both al-Sarakhsī and al-Bazdawī were theological conservatives, and these conditions may well represent an old Ḥanafī tradition. The condition of separate habitations may be directed against local *ḥadīth* such as those of Medina.[24]

The stipulation of probity calls for separate consideration, since it raises the question of the use of *mutawātir* reports in a theological context. The "controverted conditions" do not appear explicitly in the *Mīzān* of al-Bazdawī's theologically minded student al-Samarqandī nor does ʿAbd al-ʿAzīz al-Bukhārī (d. 730/1329), the commentator of al-Bazdawī, take the three conditions seriously. They are, he says, "more effective in precluding the possibility of collusion and clearer in refuting the opponent but are not really conditions in the sense that knowledge by *tawātur* depends on them."[25] Now, probity includes adherence to Islam, and in order to show that this condition is not a real one, al-Bukhārī notes that al-Bazdawī rejects certain Zoroastrian and Jewish reports for which *tawātur* was claimed on the grounds that the numerical condition is not met at every stage of their transmission. If probity were really necessary, then these reports could have been dismissed out of hand.[26]

In fact, another explanation is possible. Al-Bazdawī bases his definition on the use of the *mutawātir* tradition in Islamic law. Under ordinary circumstances, the traditions of unbelievers, *mutawātir* or not, do not constitute a source of Islamic law. This point can be obscured because the texts speak of *akhbār* ("reports") whether the context is a religious one or not. In theological circles the *mutawātir* report had quite early become a weapon with which to meet the challenge of various forms of scepticism. In this theological context, Muslims were not averse to supporting their claims by referring to the experiences

20. Bukhārī, 3:361; Āmidī, 2:27.

21. Sarakhsī, 1:282.

22. Bazdawī, 2:361.

23. *Mustaṣfā*, p. 163.

24. Suggested by *Mustaṣfā*, p. 163.

25. Bukhārī, 2:361. Al-Samarqandī's definition of concurrence refers only to a source in sensory experience and a multitude excluding collusion (*Mīzān*, f. 108b), but his defense of the doctrine does assume the controverted conditions (e.g., *Mīzān*, f. 109b). It is unclear how seriously he takes them.

26. Bukhārī, 2:361.

of Jews and Christians that confirmed the historicity of prophetic miracles. Thus Ibn al-Rāwandī (d. ca. 250/864), replying to the Muʿtazilī criticism of the Shiʿis for not recognizing knowledge based on the *mutawātir* report, says that "not all of them hold this view, for we find Hishām ibn al-Ḥakam (d. 198/814) claiming that the occurrence (*majīʾ*) of a *mutawātir* report imposes knowledge even when the reporters are unbelievers."[27] Ibn al-Rāwandī wants to show that even among the Shiʿis there were those who accepted the *tawātur* doctrine in its most liberal version. The stipulation of probity thus harks back to the use of the *mutawātir* report within Islamic circles before the theological version became dominant by reason of its greater generality. Most works of *uṣūl* either present the theological formulation without reference to the older doctrine or dismiss the more stringent conditions as theologically unsophisticated. Yet the old conditions do sometimes appear. Apart from the Ḥanafī works, we find that the *ʿUdda* of the Ḥanbalī Abū Yaʿlā ibn al-Farrāʾ (d. 458/1066) states that the reporters of a *mutawātir* tradition must be such that it is not conceivable that they conspire to tell an untruth "either because of their great number or because of their religion and probity."[28]

2. The Classification of Concurrent Knowledge

A much-discussed problem among the *uṣūlis* is the precise degree of knowledge produced by a *mutawātir* report. Three positions are to be noted. One denied that the *mutawātir* report produced certainty. This view is attributed, on the one hand, to two non-Islamic sects, the Sumaniyya and the Barāhima, the archetypic deniers of prophecy,[29] and, on the other, to the Muʿtazilī al-Naẓẓām (d. 231/846) and was deemed one of his infamies (*faḍāʾiḥ*).[30] The other two positions recognize *tawātur* knowledge as certain but differ as to whether it is *ḍarūrī* or *muktasab*.[31] A common classification of knowledge among the Ḥanafīs recognizes two categories of knowledge proper, certainty (*yaqīn*), in its two varieties of *ḍarūrī* and *muktasab*, and confidence (*ṭumaʾnīna*), in which the balance is entirely in favor of truthfulness.[32] Opposed to these is the mere presumption (*ẓann*) of truthfulness. Basing themselves upon this classification, some of the sources distinguish between the views of the Sumaniyya and the Barāhima and of al-Naẓẓām. The non-

27. *Intiṣār*, p. 113.

28. *ʿUdda*, f. 127a; *Musawwada*, pp. 236–37.

29. On the Sumaniyya, see van Ess, *Die Erkenntnislehre des ʿAḍudaddīn al-Īcī*, pp. 257–65.

30. ʿAbd al-Qāhir al-Baghdādī, *al-Farq bayn al-firaq*, ed. Muḥammad Muḥyī al-Dīn ʿAbd al-Ḥamīd (Cairo: Muḥammad ʿAlī Ṣubayḥ, n.d.), p. 143.

31. *Muʿtamad*, 2:552 and *Qawāṭiʿ*, f. 104b (foliation supplied) agree that the dispute is a theological one, with little connection to *uṣūl al-fiqh*. For Ibn Qayyim al-Jawziyya, *Mukhtaṣar al-ṣawāʿiq al-mursala ʿalā al-jahmiyya waʾl-muʿaṭṭila*, abridged by Muḥammad ibn al-Mawṣilī, ed. Zakariyyāʾ ʿAlī Yūsuf (Cairo: Maṭbaʿat al-Imām, n.d.), p. 94, it is simply "profitless."

32. Sarakhsī, 1:284.

Muslims accorded *tawātur* information the status of a presumption;[33] al-Naẓẓām thought that it inspired confidence.[34] Yet the difference is not regarded as one of major significance, for to deny *tawātur* as a source of certainty is to deny that the Qurʾān is of certain authenticity. It would introduce doubt as to our knowledge of history, of geography, and even of our own place in the world: the identity of our parents, the foods we may safely enjoy and those that threaten our life.[35]

"The majority of jurists and theologians," writes al-Samarqandī, "hold that the *mutawātir* report imposes certainty by itself without external evidence (*qarīna*). The Muʿtazilī al-Naẓẓām held that it does not impose certainty by itself but only with external evidence. Equally the unit-report can impose certainty with external evidence. An example of this is the report that someone has died. When there is a crowd at his door, the sound of weeping is heard, and a bier appears, this report imposes certainty."[36] Al-Naẓẓām argued against the infallibility of the *mutawātir* report by noting that if each person was individually capable of lying (his view of human nature was pessimistic in this connection), this fact was not altered by their mere coming together (*ijtimāʿ*).[37] This is the same argument al-Naẓẓām used in attacking the doctrine of consensus.[38] Al-Naẓẓām illustrated his contention by *mutawātir* reports that were known to be false, such as that of the Jews concerning the crucifixion of Jesus and those of the Zoroastrians concerning the miracles of their prophet.[39] We know from the Qurʾān that Jesus was not really crucified, and we know that Zoroaster was no prophet because his dualist doctrine is false. What is obscure about al-Naẓẓām's teaching is how he dealt with the authenticity of the Qurʾān. Did he claim the existence of external evidence or did he bypass the *tawātur* issue entirely?[40] This question is all the more intriguing in that a Ḥanafī jurist of considerable repute, the Muʿtazilī Muḥammad ibn Shujāʿ al-Thaljī (d. 266/879), is reported to have followed al-Naẓẓām's teaching.[41]

Those who took the orthodox position that *tawātur* knowledge is certain were divided as to whether it was *ḍarūrī* or *muktasab*. *Ḍarūrī* knowledge is immediate in the sense

33. Bukhārī, 2:362.

34. *Manār*, p. 617, margin.

35. Abū 'l-Yusr al-Bazdawī, *Uṣūl al-Dīn*, ed. Hans Peter Linns (Cairo: ʿĪsā al-Bābī al-Ḥalabī, 1383/1966), p. 7; Bukhārī, 2:363; *Manār*, p. 617.

36. *Mīzān*, f. 108b. The certainty was *ḍarūrī* for al-Naẓẓām (*Mankhūl*, p. 339; *Musawwada*, p. 240; *Baḥr*, f. 224a).

37. Bukhārī, 2:363. The attribution to al-Naẓẓām is my own, but is suggested by such texts as Abū 'l-Yusr al-Bazdawī, *Uṣūl al-Dīn*, p. 10.

38. Sarakhsī, 1:295.

39. *Mīzān*, f. 108b.

40. Abū 'l-Ḥusayn al-Baṣrī already suggests that al-Naẓẓām may have been referring to the usual attendant circumstances of a concurrent tradition (*Muʿtamad*, 2:567).

41. *Manār*, p. 615, margin.

that it does not rest upon a chain of inference; it is knowledge that forces itself upon one (hence its etymology) and is thus immune to doubt. It has both an internal (*badīhī*) and external (*ḥissī*) aspect. It includes the perception of pain, the axioms of thought, and sensory knowledge.[42] Because the knowledge we obtain through our senses is *ḍarūrī*, it is evident why the traditional view considered *tawātur* knowledge to be *ḍarūrī*. To hear a *mutawātir* tradition is in effect to come into direct contact with the Prophet, to hear his words or "see" his actions.[43] The opposing doctrine, that this knowledge is *muktasab*, goes back to Bishr ibn al-Muʿtamir (d. 210/825), the founder of the Baghdadi school of the Muʿtazila.[44] It is often linked with the name of Abū ʾl-Qāsim al-Kaʿbī (d. 319/931), an adherent of this school.[45] Al-Kaʿbī was a Ḥanafī, and his teaching in Central Asia elicited a refutation on the part of al-Māturīdī.[46]

In time the *muktasab* position came to acquire important adherents of various persuasions: the Imamī al-Shaykh al-Mufīd (d. 413/1023),[47] the Shāfiʿīs Abū Bakr al-Daqqāq (d. 392/1002)[48] and Imām al-Ḥaramayn (d. 478/1088),[49] the Basran Muʿtazilī Abū ʾl-Ḥusayn al-Baṣrī (d. 436/1045).[50] Indeed we even find al-Sarakhsī identifying it as that of the Shāfiʿīs without qualification.[51] Abū ʾl-Ḥusayn al-Baṣrī presents the standard argument for this position in justifying his rejection of the view of his predecessors Abū ʿAlī al-Jubbāʾī, Abū Hāshim, and ʿAbd al-Jabbār:

> Inference (*istidlāl*) is the ordering of knowledge to arrive at further knowledge. Everything whose existence depends on the ordering of knowledge is inferred. The knowledge that follows upon a *mutawātir* report occurs in this way. For we know what has been reported to us only when we know that the reporter has not reported on the basis of his opinion but on the basis of what is not at all doubtful and that there is no motive for him to lie. Thus we know that he has not lied intentionally because we know that he has no motive for lying, and we know that the report cannot be unintentionally false because we know that it is

42. ʿAbd al-Qāhir al-Baghdādī, *Uṣūl al-Dīn* (Istanbul, 1346/1928. Reprint. n.p., n.d.), pp. 8–9.

43. Bukhārī, 2:361–62.

44. A. S. Tritton, "Some Muʿtazilī Ideas about Religion: in Particular about Knowledge Based on General Report," *Bulletin of the School of Oriental and African Studies* 14 (1952): pp. 617–18 (Arabic). On the identity of this text, see R. L. Martin, "The Identification of Two Muʿtazilite MSS," *Journal of the American Oriental Society* 98 (1978): 389–93.

45. *Muʿtamad*, 2:552 (opposed to the Jubbāʾīs, for whom it was *ḍarurī*).

46. See the list of al-Māturīdī's writings on p. 6 (Arabic) of Fathalla Kholeif's introduction to his edition of al-Māturīdī's *Kitāb al-Tawḥīd* (Beirut: Dar el-Mashreq, 1970).

47. Al-Shaykh al-Mufīd, *Awāʾil al-maqālāt fī al-madhāhib al-mukhtārāt*, ed. Faḍl Allāh al-Zānjānī (Tabriz: Maṭbaʿat Riḍāʾī, 1371 H), pp. 65–66.

48. *Lumaʿ*, p. 42.

49. *Burhān*, f. 161; Asnawī, 2:218.

50. *Muʿtamad*, 2:552.

51. Sarakhsī, 1:291. For other attributions, see *Musawwada*, p. 234.

> a matter of clarity with no doubt. Once its being false is excluded, it follows that it is true. When one of these conditions is not met, we do not know the soundness of the report.[52]

Al-Kaᶜbī is reported to have argued that if it were possible to know what is absent from the senses immediately, then it would be possible to have sensory knowledge by inference. Since the latter is impossible, so is the former.[53]

This account of *tawātur* knowledge was, however, faced with several glaring anomalies. It seemed to take place unconsciously without the usual chain of reasoning. Adolescents and the common people had knowledge of this sort, and they were not considered capable of inference. It appeared to have that immunity to arguments (*shubah*, "specious arguments") that was characteristic of *ḍarūrī* knowledge. How could it depend upon a knowledge of the attributes of the reporters when the latter was so obscure and subtle a topic that it was beyond many mature rational men, even theologians?[54]

The nature of *tawātur* knowledge was, then, of a peculiar sort, as al-Ghazālī illustrates.[55] While preferring the label *ḍarūrī*, he grasped the difficulties of the question and was prepared to call the dispute a purely verbal one. This position is already outlined in his treatise *al-Mankhūl* and developed in *al-Mustaṣfā*.[56] Later Ashᶜarīs, for example, Fakhr al-Dīn al-Rāzī, himself a supporter of the *ḍarūrī* view, saw al-Ghazālī as an adherent of *iktisāb*;[57] this in turn brought others to al-Ghazālī's defense.[58] Especially interesting is the fact that among those who supported *iktisāb* we find a rehabilitation of the former heretics. Abū 'l-Ḥusayn al-Baṣrī already suggests that al-Naẓẓām's stipulation of external circumstances may be identified with the usual conditions for *tawātur*, and in the *Burhān* of Imām al-Ḥaramayn the position of the Sumaniyya and Barāhima is boldly reinterpreted in a similar fashion.[59]

Among the Ḥanafīs, however, the *ḍarūrī* position was firmly maintained. The Ḥanafīs could and did claim that this knowledge, being *ḍarūrī*, needed no arguments; assertion was enough.[60] But they were quite ready to borrow and elaborate upon Muᶜtazilī arguments for the certainty of *tawātur* knowledge. Thus al-Samarqandī offers an especially elegant proof showing that the usual motives for lying are not applicable in a sufficient-

52. *Muᶜtamad*, 2:552.

53. *Dharīᶜa*, 2:695.

54. Tritton, "Some Muᶜtazili Ideas," pp. 615, 618 (Arabic).

55. This point is clearly made by *Jawāmiᶜ*, f. 40a. It is significant that al-Sharīf al-Murtaḍā abstained from taking a position on the classification of *tawātur* knowledge (*Dharīᶜa*, 2:485; Asnawī, 2:218).

56. *Mankhūl*, pp. 237–38; *Mustaṣfā*, pp. 156–57.

57. *Maḥṣūl* f. 117a.

58. Asnawī, 2:218.

59. *Muᶜtamad*, 2:567; *Burhān*, f. 161. See *Musawwada*, p. 236, on al-Juwaynī's *taʾwīl* of al-Naẓẓām's doctrine and *Musawwada*, p. 233, on the Sumaniyya.

60. Bukhārī, 2:368; *Mīzān*, ff. 109b–110a.

ly large group, including people of all classes. The pressure, for example, to which the weak and poor can be subjected may be safely ruled out in the case of the powerful and wealthy.[61]

This steadfastness of the Ḥanafīs in upholding the *ḍarūrī* doctrine calls for some explanation. A number of considerations suggest themselves. In the first place, we may be dealing here with a theological conservatism that appears to be characteristic of the Ḥanafīs. Furthermore, the Ḥanafīs may have been inclined to retain a doctrine that they felt divided them from the Shāfiʿīs, who were, as we have seen, identified by some with the *iktisāb* position. In the case of some Ḥanafīs, however, the explanation is closer to hand. They could not classify *tawātur* knowledge as *muktasab*, because that category already had an occupant, the *mashhūr* tradition.

II. The *Mashhūr* Tradition

The *mashhūr* (or *mustafīḍ*) tradition is defined by al-Samarqandī as one "which was in the *āḥād* category in the beginning but which in the second generation became widespread (*ishtahara*) among the scholars to the point that it was transmitted by a number whose conspiracy to lie is inconceivable."[62] We are obviously dealing here with an innovated category, one that depends on the traditional division into *mutawātir* and non-*mutawātir* (*āḥād*). It is therefore not surprising that al-Samarqandī continues, "Our masters have differed as to its epistemological status (*ḥukm*), for there is no transmitted teaching (*riwāya*) from our founders."[63]

The history of the *mashhūr* tradition within the Ḥanafī school takes us back to ʿĪsā ibn Abān (d. 221/836) and al-Jaṣṣāṣ (d. 370/981). In his *Refutation of Bishr al-Marīsī*, Ibn Abān had accepted the common classification of traditions into *mutawātir* and non-*mutawātir*, but within the second category he had made a distinction between various classes of traditions. The denial of the validity of a tradition from a given class entailed a corresponding degree of condemnation. He recognized three degrees of condemnation aside from unbelief, which, of course, followed upon rejection of a *mutawātir* tradition. The most severe was to be found erring (*taḍlīl*); such was the status of one who rejected the stoning of those who engaged in illicit sexual intercourse and met the appropriate legal conditions (*iḥṣān*). Following this was the condition of the "sinner" who rejected, for example, the wiping of the foot covering in place of the washing of the feet in the minor ablution (*al-masḥ ʿalā al-khuffayn*). Finally, error (*khaṭaʾ*) would characterize someone who

61. *Mīzān*, f. 109a (perhaps developing *Muʿtamad*, 2:559).

62. *Mīzān*, f. 110a. A tradition that is not *mashhūr* or *mutawātir* is *gharīb* (*Manār*, p. 724). Al-Māwardī uses *istifāḍa* in the sense of *tawātur*, and *mutawātir* in the sense of *mashhūr* (Māwardī, 1:371).

63. *Mīzān*, f. 110a.

rejected the traditions fixing the minimum period of menstruation.[64] Thus within the *āḥād* traditions, Ibn Abān recognized various degrees of validity based on the reception that had been accorded these traditions by the early Muslim community. He does not seem, however, to have employed an epistemological terminology to correspond to these categories; the terms of condemnation apparently served this purpose.

Al-Jaṣṣāṣ, on the other hand, claimed that alongside of the *ḍarūrī mutawātir* tradition there existed another grade of *mutawātir* tradition that was known to be authentic by inference. This is the *mashhūr* tradition. Its acceptance in the second generation can only be due to the fact that the Followers were certain of its authenticity. But since we gather this by inference, the knowledge produced by such a tradition is distinct from that produced by a tradition that is *mutawātir* at every stage in its transmission.[65] The widespread acceptance that these traditions found is likened to consensus. "The *mashhūr* tradition is that which the scholars (of the age) have favorably received, so that there exists a consensus of the people of the age to accept it. Its status is thus that of consensus, and since the latter imposes certain knowledge, so does the former."[66]

Al-Jaṣṣāṣ claimed to find support for his view in the teaching of Abū Yūsuf that the tradition of wiping the footgear abrogated the Qurʾān. Since the Qurʾān can be abrogated only by a *mutawātir* tradition, this "indicates that he held that among the *mutawātir* traditions there are those whose authenticity is known by inference, this being the case with the rubbing of the footgear. No one can claim to know its authenticity and soundness without inference."[67] The tradition in question, it should be noted, is one that ʿĪsā ibn Abān had associated with the second level of condemnation.

Al-Jaṣṣāṣ considers the rejection of this tradition as equivalent to the rejection of a *mutawātir* tradition, and presumably this would entail unbelief. This in any case came to be seen as al-Jaṣṣāṣ's position.[68] In opposition to this view, other Ḥanafīs upheld and elaborated upon the position of ʿĪsā ibn Abān. A tradition of this sort did not, in their opinion, yield certain knowledge; it was in this sense non-*mutawātir*. But it did stand apart from the ordinary unit-tradition and called for a category of its own. But whereas Ibn Abān had spoken of several degrees of validity within the category of non-*mutawātir*, the later scholars recognized a separate category, the *mashhūr* tradition, which inspired confidence (*ṭumaʾnīnat al-qalb*) but not certainty.[69]

One advantage of this new position was apparent in theology. Al-Naẓẓām had been able to attack the *mutawātir* category by pointing to traditions of the Jews and Zoroas-

---

64. Jaṣṣāṣ, f. 167 a,b.
65. Jaṣṣāṣ, f. 168a; Sarakhsī, 1:292.
66. *Mīzān*, f. 110a.
67. Jaṣṣāṣ, f. 168a.
68. Bukhārī, 2:368, noting that there is disagreement whether any scholar took this position.
69. This position being attributed to ʿĪsā ibn Abān (Bukhārī, 3:368).

trians that were *mutawātir* but false. These traditions, it was now argued, were not really *mutawātir* but only *mashhūr*. The reports of Zoroaster's miracles had originated in the narrow circles of the king and been spread abroad to enhance royal power. There was, in fact, a conspiracy at the root of these traditions. As *mashhūr* traditions they could inspire no more than confidence and were to be rejected in the face of the Qurʾān, whose authenticity was absolutely certain because its transmission was *mutawātir*.[70]

Thus there emerged two views on the *mashhūr* tradition. One, associated with ʿĪsā ibn Abān, refused to brand as an unbeliever one who rejected a *mashhūr* tradition. The other view regarded the *mashhūr* tradition as a subcategory of the *mutawātir*; to reject it was to become an unbeliever. For the first view the *mashhūr* was a category in its own right, parallel to the *mutawātir* and the *āḥād*. The disagreement was evidently regarded as a significant one, for article sixteen of the *Waṣiyya* of Abū Ḥanīfa reads as follows:

> We confess that the moistening of shoes is obligatory, for those who are at home during day and a night, for travellers during three days and nights. This is founded on a tradition in this sense. Whosoever should reject it would be in danger of unbelief (*yukhāf ʿalayhi al-kufr*), this tradition being nearly equivalent to an absolutely reliable report.[71]

Wensinck, in his classic *Muslim Creed*, regards this article as being directed against the Shiʿis and the Khārijīs, who rejected the wiping of sandals as a substitute for the washing of the feet.[72] He misses its reference to the internal Ḥanafī dispute. A late commentator, Mullā Ḥusayn ibn Iskandar (d. ca. 1084/1673), is more informative. For him the dispute is between Abū Ḥanīfa, the author of the work, and Abū Yūsuf, who held that rejection of this tradition amounted to unbelief, because it was *mutawātir*.[73] Apparently what has happened is this: al-Jaṣṣāṣ, as we have noted, based his position on a teaching of Abū Yūsuf. This identification with Abū Yūsuf became common, and those who took the opposing view, the followers of Ibn Abān, tried to identify their own view with Abū Ḥanīfa. The *Waṣiyya* is a document stemming from this group and thus, at least in part, should be dated considerably later than the ninth century, as suggested by Wensinck;[74] it can be no earlier than the end of the tenth century.

---

70. Sarakhsī, 1:285–88, 293.

71. A. J. Wensinck, *The Muslim Creed: Its Genesis and Historical Development* (1932. Repr. London: Frank Cass, 1965), p. 129.

72. Wensinck, *The Muslim Creed*, p. 158.

73. Mullā Ḥusayn ibn Iskandar, *Kitāb al-Jawhara al-munīfa fī sharḥ Wasiyyat al-Imām al-Aʿẓam Abī Ḥanīfa* (Hyderabad: Maṭbaʿat Dāʾirat al-Maʿārif al-Niẓāmiyya, 1321 H), pp. 29–30. In legal works, the "danger of unbelief" formula is ascribed both to Abū Ḥanīfa (ʿAbd Allāh ibn Maḥmūd al-Mawṣilī, *al-Ikhtiyār li-taʿlīl al-Mukhtār*, ed. Maḥmud Abū Daqīqa [Cairo, 1951. Repr. Beirut: Dār al-Maʿrifa li'l-Ṭibāʿa wa'l-Nashr, 1395/1975], 1:23) and to al-Karkhī (al-Kāsānī, *Badāʾiʿ al-ṣanāʾiʿ*, 1:95).

74. Wensinck, *The Muslim Creed*, p. 187.

The position linked with al-Jaṣṣāṣ was for a long time the dominant one and is reported as that of the majority by al-Samarqandī.[75] It even won approval outside of the Ḥanafī camp among a group of Ashʿarī Shāfiʿīs, Ibn Fūrak (d. 406/1015),[76] Abū Isḥāq al-Isfarāyīnī (d. 418/1027),[77] and his student ʿAbd al-Qāhir al-Baghdādī (d. 429/1037).[78] Al-Isfarāyīnī especially was favorably disposed to the Ḥanafīs, and his teaching shows their influence at many points. The Ibn Abān view, however, ultimately came to be dominant among the Ḥanafīs. It was supported by such figures as Abū Zayd al-Dabūsī (d. 430/1038–39) and al-Sarakhsī (d. 483/1090). By the time of al-Bukhārī (d. 730/1329) it has won the day.[79]

Even among the late supporters of al-Jaṣṣāṣ, the original position was eroded. This is manifested in their refusal to attach unbelief to a rejection of a *mashhūr* tradition. It was thus not accorded the same status as the *ḍarūrī mutawātir*, an anomaly that al-Samarqandī explains as follows:

> The difference between them is that to reject a *mutawātir* tradition is to give lie to the Prophet, for the reports of a *mutawātir* tradition are beyond number at the beginning and at the end, and consequently it is equivalent to what is heard from the Prophet himself. But the rejection of a *mashhūr* tradition is not giving the lie to the Prophet, because a number who could not have conspired to lie have not heard it from the Prophet. It is only a unit-tradition which the scholars of the second generation have accepted, so that to reject it is to accuse them of error in accepting it and suspect them of insufficient attention to its really coming from the Prophet. To accuse the scholars of error is not, however, unbelief but innovation and error.[80]

Thus even those like al-Samarqandī who claimed certainty for the *mashhūr* tradition denied that belief was at stake. According to al-Sarakhsī, there had never been any disagreement on this point at all.[81] The sharp line that had formerly divided the two groups was now obliterated, and the dispute, which no longer had any practical bearing (*lā yaẓhar athar al-khilāf fī al-ahkām*), lost importance.[82]

Behind some of the developments we have been looking at is the very significant question of whether there are any concurrent traditions at all. This question was raised by some distinguished scholars of *ḥadīth*.[83] In their case, one could claim that the ques-

75. *Mīzān*, f. 110a.
76. *Burhān*, f. 163.
77. *Burhān*, f. 163; *Musawwada*, p. 240; *Jamʿ*, 2:130.
78. Al-Baghdādī, *Uṣūl al-dīn*, pp. 12–13, giving *al-masḥ ʿalā al-khuffayn* as an example.
79. Bukhārī, 3:368.
80. *Mīzān*, f. 110b.
81. Sarakhsī, 1:296.
82. Bukhārī, 2:368.
83. The existence of any significant number of *mutawātir* traditions was doubted by such famous

tion was based on a misunderstanding of a concept foreign to their discipline. But the problem takes on a new importance when the same question is raised by those known primarily as jurists. Thus the Mālikī al-Qarāfī (d. 684/1285) regards the mutual specialization of two concurrent traditions as a purely theoretical matter:

> It is difficult to give an illustration (*taṣwīr*) of this topic with respect to two concurrent *sunnas* in our day, for concurrence in traditions is infrequent in our day or nonexistent because of the lack of attention to the transmission of traditions, and there are no traditions left except those that provide probability (*ẓann*) only. Thus one of the jurists has said that there is no concurrent tradition except "Actions are judged by intention," but upon examination we do not find this concurrent for us either. Where is the number that cannot possibly conspire to lie in all the generations between us and the Messenger of God?[84]

For al-Qarāfī, concurrent traditions had once existed but then become extinct.[85]

For the Ḥanafī Abū 'l-Yusr al-Bazdawī (d. 493/1099), the problem of concurrent traditions lay at the other end of the chain, at its origin. According to him, there are no concurrent traditions on legal topics (*aḥkām*), but only on such matters as the existence of Mecca. This meant that it was *mashhūr* traditions upon which the law was based.[86] It is thus not surprising to find Abū 'l-Yusr al-Bazdawī among the strongest supporters of the treatment of *mashhūr* traditions as virtually equivalent to concurrent ones, even to the

---

ḥadīth scholars as Abū Bakr al-Ḥāzimī (d. 584/1188) (*Shurūṭ al-āʾimma al-khamsa*, p. 37) and Ibn al-Ṣalāḥ (d. 643/1245) (al-ʿIrāqī, *al-Taqyīd*, p. 266). Ibn al-Ṣalāḥ's challenge to the traditionists to produce such traditions was taken up by al-Suyūṭī in particular (see n. 15, above, and al-ʿAsqalānī, *Nuzhat al-naẓar*, p. 23). However, the problem was, as Ibn al-Ṣalāḥ himself suggested, that the *mutawātir* tradition was foreign to the work of the traditionists (al-ʿIrāqī, *al-Taqyīd*, p. 265); the point of labeling a tradition as concurrent was precisely to preclude the need for an *isnād*. In the same sense, see William Marçais, "Le *Taqrīb* de en-Nawawi, traduit et annoté," *Journal asiatique*, n.s., 18 (1901):105, n. 1, and Carlo Nallino, "Classificazione del '*ḥadīth*' dal punto di vista dei tradizionisti," in *Raccolta di scritti editi e inediti*, ed. Maria Nallino, 6 vols. (Rome: Istituto per l'Oriente, 1939–48), 2:142–45. This point is repeatedly made by Ṭāhir al-Jazāʾirī, *Tawjīh al-naẓar ilā uṣūl al-athar* (Medina: al-Maktaba al-ʿIlmiyya, n.d.), pp. 48, 49, 64. The issue also arises in modern discussions of the old problem of whether the concurrent report of non-Muslims is acceptable, with al-Jazāʾirī (*Tawjīh*, p. 54) affirming this view and Muḥammad Jamāl al-Dīn al-Qāsimī attempting to identify a traditionist use of *tawātur*, which would require Islam, as opposed to the *uṣūlī* use, which would not (*Qawāʿid al-taḥdīth min funūn muṣṭalaḥ al-ḥadīth*, ed. Muḥammad Bahjat al-Bayṭār [Cairo: ʿĪsā al-Bābī al-Ḥalabī, 1380/1961], p. 147).

84. Qarāfī, p. 206; Abū Isḥāq al-Shāṭibī, *al-Muwāfaqāt fī uṣūl al-aḥkām*, ed. Muḥammad Muḥyī al-Dīn ʿAbd al-Ḥamīd (Cairo: Muḥammad ʿAlī Ṣubayḥ, n.d.), 4:8 (*tawātur* is now only hypothetical).

85. Qarāfī, p. 207.

86. *Ḥujaj*, f. 33a; al-Qasṭallānī, *Irshād al-sārī ilā sharḥ Ṣaḥīḥ al-Bukhārī* (Cairo: al-Maṭbaʿa al-Kubrā al-Amīriyya, 1304–5), 1:56 (denying that *innamā al-aʿmāl bi'l-niyyāt* is *mutawātir*: *naʿam al-mashhūr mulḥaq bi'l-mutawātir ʿinda ahl al-ḥadīth*).

point that he attaches unbelief to their denial. In this, he tells us, he was following his teacher Shams al-Aʾimma al-Ḥalwānī (d. 448/1056).[87]

Whereas al-Bazdawī looked to the *mashhūr* category to remedy the deficiency in concurrent traditions, others reinterpreted the *mutawātir* category itself. This is the upshot of the rehabilitation of al-Naẓẓām's position that has already been mentioned. Not mere numbers, but the precise circumstances of the transmission became critical. Out of this tendency grew the division of *mutawātir* traditions into general and special (*ʿāmm, khāṣṣ*) that was particularly dear to Ibn Taymiyya (d. 728/1328).[88] There were *mutawātir* traditions peculiar to each group of specialists. To this extent, the reception of *tawātur* knowledge was seen as an active rather than a passive experience in which all could equally share.

III. The Unit-Tradition

1. The Unit-Tradition in Ḥanafism

Despite the controversies with respect to the *mutawātir* and *mashhūr* traditions, the heart of the *uṣūl* treatment of traditions lies elsewhere. It is the unit-tradition that is the focus of concern. The positions taken in regard to this sort of tradition are truly fundamental and serve as an infallible touchstone of the character of the legal thought in question. The basic division is between the formalists, who recognize the unit-tradition as the source of a valid norm but deny it certain authenticity, and the materialists, who claim that there are unit-traditions whose authenticity is beyond question.

The formalist position may be stated briefly. The most that can be expected of a given chain of reporters is that each be of attested probity (*ʿadāla*) and exactness (*ḍabṭ*), that is to say, his scrupulous observance of the divine law indicates that he is not one to tell a lie, and his faculties are such as not to render him suspect of some significant alteration in what he transmits. Yet the possibility remains that men of this sort do tell lies and do commit errors. A unit-tradition, consisting as it does of one or several chains of this sort, can yield no more than a presumption (*ẓann*) of authenticity. Can it then serve as the source for a valid norm? The formalist answer is yes, provided that its presumptive authenticity is not rebutted. Such a rebuttal occurs under a number of circumstances,

87. *Ḥujaj*, f. 33b; Bukhārī, 2:368.

88. *Musawwada*, p. 249; also in the following works of Ibn Taymiyya: *Rafʿ al-malām*, pp. 41–42; *Bayān muwāfaqat ṣarīḥ al-maʿqul li-ṣaḥīḥ al-manqūl*, 1:113; *Naqḍ al-manṭiq*, ed. Muḥammad ibn ʿAbd al-Razzāq Ḥamza, Sulayman ibn ʿAbd al-Raḥmān al-Ṣāniʿ, and Muḥammad Ḥāmid al-Fiqī (Cairo: Maṭbaʿat al-Sunna al-Muḥammadiyya, 1370/1951), p. 28; *Kitāb al-Radd ʿalā al-manṭiqiyyīn*, ed. ʿAbduṣ-Ṣamad Sharafud-Din al-Kutubī (Bombay: Qayyimah Press, 1368/1949), p. 100; *al-Furqān bayn al-ḥaqq wa'l-bāṭil*, in his *Majmūʿat al-rasāʾil al-kubrā*, 1:5–172 (Cairo: Muḥammad ʿAlī Ṣubayḥ, 1385/1966), p. 89; Ibn Qayyim al-Jawziyya, *Mukhtaṣar al-ṣawāʿiq*, p. 484.

some of which will be treated below. These grounds for rebuttal may be said to be of a material nature in that they are connected with the norm contained in the *ḥadīth*, with the content of the tradition. Distinct from them are formal conditions that pertain to the chain of transmitters. These conditions concern the standards for probity and exactness that must be met by each of the transmitters and the state of the chain in question, its completeness. Generally speaking, the Ḥanafīs exhibit extreme tolerance with regard to these formal conditions, and this is so, because they are so exacting when it comes to the material conditions for validity.

The materialists, for their part, reject the distinction between authenticity and validity. A source of law is valid because and only because its authenticity is certain. To admit presumptive sources into the law is to fall into the formalist camp, to relinquish the basis for opposition to analogy, and ultimately to shape God's law out of recognition. To realize their aim of building the law out of absolutely sound materials, the materialists need criteria for judging traditions that enable them to have certain knowledge and not mere presumption. These criteria they claim to possess.

The Ḥanafīs do not consider the epistemological status of the unit-tradition problematical. "The claim of the traditionists that it yields certainty," writes Fakhr al-Islām al-Bazdawī, "is false without a doubt since common experience (*ʿiyān*) refutes it."[89] They

89. Bazdawī, 2:375–76. One must be careful not to confuse the claim of the *ḥadīth* scholar that a tradition is "sound" (*ṣaḥīḥ*) with the claim that it is of certain authenticity. On this point, see al-Bāqillanī quoted in *Burhān*, f. 63; Zayn al-Dīn al-ʿIrāqī, *Sharḥ alfiyyat al-ʿIrāqī al-musammā biʾl-Tadhkira waʾl-tabṣira*, ed. Muḥammad ibn al-Ḥusayn al-Irāqī al-Ḥusaynī. 3 vols. (Fez: al-Maṭbaʿa al-Jadīda, 1354 H), 1:14; Ibn Rajab quoted in al-Ḥāzimī, *Shurūṭ*, p. 52, note; al-Harawī, *Jawāhir al-uṣūl*, pp. 17, 18. Clear evidence that *ṣaḥīḥ* is not to be taken in the sense of authentic is its frequent use in the elative (e.g., Abū Dāwūd al-Sijistānī, *Risālat Abī Dāwūd ilā ahl Makka fī waṣf sunanihi*, ed. Muḥammad al-Ṣabbāgh [Beirut: al-Maktab al-Islāmī, 1401 H], p. 22).

Whether all or some sound traditions were of certain authenticity is another question, on which *ḥadīth* scholars differed. Al-Khaṭīb al-Baghdādī denied that the traditions in the collections could support a claim of knowledge (*Kitāb al-Faqīh waʾl-mutafaqqih*, ed. Ismāʿīl al-Anṣārī, 2 vols. [Beirut: Dār al-Kutub al-ʿIlmiyya, 1395/1975], 1:96), and this is identified as the view of the majority by al-Harawī, *Jawāhir al-uṣūl*, p. 21. With this, contrast Ibn al-Ṣalāḥ's view that what al-Bukhārī and Muslim had both accepted into their collections was a source of *naẓarī* knowledge (al-ʿIrāqī, *al-Taqyīd waʾl-īḍāḥ sharḥ Muqaddimat Ibn al-Ṣalāḥ*, ed. ʿAbd al-Raḥmān ʿUthmān [Medina: al-Maktaba al-Salafiyya, 1389/1969], p. 41 and note; see also Abū ʾl-Faḍl al-Maqdisī, *Shurūṭ al-āʾimma al-sitta*, ed. Muḥammad Zāhid al-Kawtharī [Cairo: Maktabat al-Qudsī, 1357 H.], p. 13 and note).

The *Ṣaḥīḥs* of al-Bukhārī and Muslim and the other standard collections have no particular significance in the history of the legal schools, although their traditions are, it is true, sometimes accorded predominance (*tarjīḥ*) (Ibn ʿAqīl, p. 180). The real importance of such *ḥadīth* works for the jurists was in their convenience as repositories of acceptable traditions so that *isnāds* could be dispensed with (ʿAbd al-Raḥmān ibn Ibrāhim al-Maqdisī, *al-ʿUdda sharḥ al-ʿUmda* [Cairo: al-Maktaba al-Salafiyya, n.d.], p. 21; Bājī, p. 78 [on the relation of this practice in debate to the acceptance of *marāsīl*]). The hermeneutic apparatus was fully adequate to handle any threat this might otherwise have posed to

see their task as being to show that reason does not exclude accepting sources of this character as norms for action and that this, in fact, is what the divine Lawgiver intended. We thus find arguments of two sorts, rational (*maʿqūl*) and traditional (*samʿī*); we shall take up the latter first.

Although there are some Qurʾānic verses commonly cited in support of this position,[90] the real foundation for the acceptance of the unit-tradition as a source of law is the practice of the Companions of the Prophet, what amounts to a consensus.[91] This practice is considered to be so unambiguous that it virtually makes superfluous recourse to other normative sources, such as the practice of the Prophet himself, where there is also supporting evidence.[92] But since the reports on which our knowledge of the practice of the Companions is based are themselves unit-traditions, the question naturally arises as to whether we are not dealing with a vicious circularity. This difficulty is resolved by the notion of a concurrence in content (*al-tawātur biʾl-maʿnā*). The stock examples of this are the valor of ʿAlī and the generosity of Ḥātim al-Ṭāʾī.[93] Although no specific incidents in which these qualities are demonstrated have been reported at the degree of *tawātur*, nonetheless all the unit-reports taken together reach the level of *tawātur* and give us certain knowledge of the qualities in question. The same is claimed of the practice of the Companions in regard to the acceptance of unit-traditions as standards of action.[94] One can also cite the consensus of the nation of Islam to accept "unit-reports" in their business dealings.[95] This latter practice, however, is only analogous to the acceptance of unit-traditions as sources for general norms. In any case, it is clear that the Ḥanafīs felt no great difficulty in justifying by arguments from tradition the place of the unit-tradition in their legal system.

As might be expected, it is in the rational arguments that theological differences make themselves felt. The conservative al-Bazdawī contents himself with pointing to

---

settled doctrine. Thus *Talwīh*, 3:63: "Investigating the circumstances of the transmitters in our time is virtually impossible because of the length of time and the many intermediaries, so that it is best to make do with the approbation of the reliable experts in the science of tradition like al-Bukhārī, Muslim, al-Baghawī, al-Ṣāghānī, and others." The relation between the jurists and the traditionists is summed up in the statement that al-Aʿmash is supposed to have made to Abū Yūsuf: "You are the physicians; we the druggists" (Ibn ʿAbd al-Barr, *Jāmiʿ bayān al-ʿilm wa-faḍlih*, 2:13; Majd al-Dīn Ibn al-Athīr, *Jāmiʿ al-uṣūl fī aḥādīth al-rasūl*, ed. ʿAbd al-Qādir al-Arnāʾūt. 11 vols. [Damascus: Maktabat al-Ḥalwānī, 1969–73], 1:38).

90. Bukhārī, 2:372; *Lumaʿ*, p. 43.

91. Bukhārī, 3:28.

92. Bukhārī, 2:372–73.

93. In place of ʿAlī one also finds ʿAmr ibn Maʿdīkarib (*Dharīʿa*, 2:530) and ʿAntara (Abū Bakr al-Bāqillanī, *Nukat al-Intiṣār li-naql al-Qurʾān*, ed. H. Z. Salam [Alexandria: Munshaʾat al-Maʿārif, 1971]), p. 294. The use of ʿAlī may have originally been polemical: the reports of ʿAlī's valor are *mutawātir* but not those of his designation as imām.

94. Bukhārī, 2:375.

95. Bukhārī, 2:375–76.

the reliance put on presumption in the use of analogy and the decisions of judges.[96] For al-Samarqandī, on the other hand, the practice of the courts is only another example of the consensus of the nation to use unit-reports in matters of legal consequence.[97] The rational argument that he uses to support the acceptance of the unit-tradition is not based on an analogy with any legal institution but rather on the purpose of law in general. It is unmistakably Muʿtazilī. Although only presumption is possible in the case of the unit-tradition, not to act on this presumption would be to fly in the face of wisdom (*ḥikma*). To reject all unit-traditions would undoubtedly mean rejecting some elements of truth. To accept them all indiscriminately would mean accepting falsehood. To refuse to do anything (*tawaqquf*) would also mean rejecting truth. In all cases, one would be liable to the charge of folly (*safah*). The answer is to make a distinction. "And so one must act according to what is most probable (*al-rājiḥ wa'l-ghālib*), for acting in accord with what is most probable is part of wisdom." This principle is common to all areas of life:

> It is obligatory to act according to a unit-report in rational matters for an intelligible reason (*maʿnā maʿqūl*) that is also found in legal matters. The explanation of this is the following. We know by reason the obligation to avoid harm and the propriety (*ḥusn*) of gaining benefit when this is certain. Cases in which this is most probable are assimilated to those in which it is certain, with respect to the obligation of avoiding harm and the propriety of gaining benefit. An example is the case of the man who has before him two roads and is informed by a person of probity that one road is secure while the other is infested with bandits. He is rationally obligated to act in accordance with this report, because warding off harm is the most probable result. Similarly, when a doctor tells his patient that his blood is in excess and he needs to be bled, he is obliged to undergo this treatment. Likewise if one is sitting under a sloping wall and a man who has some knowledge of these matters tells him to remove himself, he is obliged to do so. In all these cases he acts according to what is most probable where action would be obligatory with certainty. What is most probable is assimilated to what is certain. The same reason operates in the divine law, for the law was instituted for the benefit of man. Its prohibitions are meant to lead to abstention from what is bad and to which is attached blame in this world and punishment in the next. The assimilation of what is most probable to what is certain is all the more necessary, because the harm in the earlier cases is confined to this world, but in the law it includes the next.[98]

This argument clearly originated in Muʿtazilī circles and was meant to answer those Muʿtazilīs who, al-Samarqandī himself informs us, held that the unit-report was a norm

96. Bazdawī, 2:375.
97. *Mīzān*, f. 116b.
98. *Mīzān*, f. 116b.

only in matters of reason, not in the law.[99] From other sources we know that among these Muʿtazilīs were Abū Bakr al-Aṣamm (d. 200/815) and his pupil Ismāʿīl ibn Ibrāhīm, known as Ibn ʿUlayya (d. 218/833).[100] Although our knowledge of their doctrine is in the highest degree fragmentary, these Muʿtazilīs seem to have had an enormous impact on later *uṣūl* thought, both among Muʿtazilīs who opposed them and among a group of Ẓāhirīs who carried on their teachings. In turn, the lines of thought stimulated by this challenge penetrated into other circles, Ashʿarī and orthodox Ḥanafī.

Al-Aṣamm is reported to have said that if there were a collection of a hundred traditions, all authentic except for one, and that one was not specifically known, it would be necessary to refrain from acting upon any of them.[101] This is precisely the kind of "folly" against which al-Samarqandī's argument was directed.

A number of arguments appearing in the *uṣūl* texts can be traced with confidence to this group of Muʿtazilīs. Perhaps the most revealing is that which distinguishes between the reliance placed on presumption in ordinary business matters, on the one hand, and in the acceptance of the unit-tradition, on the other. The Ḥanafīs, as we have seen, regard the trust placed in presumption in all these instances as analogous. The opposing argument is a characteristically Muʿtazilī one. God is characterized by perfect ability (*mawṣūf bi-kamāl al-qudra*) to make known His will in such a way that no doubt remains. This is clearly not the case with the *khabar al-wāḥid*. Humans, on the other hand, are incapable of protecting their rights and doing their business in such a way as to do without the unit-report: messengers must be sent, agents must be employed, and thus reliance on the individual reporter is inevitable.[102]

---

99. *Mīzān*, f. 116a. One of these was al-Khayyāṭ, whose student Abū 'l-Qāsim al-Kaʿbī wrote a work in refutation of his master's doctrine (al-Baghdādī, *al-Farq*, p. 180). Lest his readers become too partial to unit-traditions, al-Kaʿbī wrote another work in which he collected the mutual reproaches of the traditionists, *Kitāb Qabūl al-akhbār wa-maʿrifat al-rijāl* (Cairo: Dār al-Kutub. Muṣṭalaḥ al-ḥadīth MS 14), f. 1b (foliation supplied). (I would like to thank Kevin Reinhart for the opportunity to consult this work.) Wāṣil ibn ʿAṭāʾ required concurrence for a report to be a source of law (ʿAbd al-Jabbār ibn Aḥmad al-Hamadhānī, *Faḍl al-iʿtizāl wa-ṭabaqāt al-muʿtazila*, ed. Fuʾād Sayyid [Tunis: al-Dār al-Tūnisiyya li'l-Nashr, 1393/1974], p. 234); ʿAmr ibn ʿUbayd, however, relied on the unit-reports of al-Ḥasan al-Baṣrī (*Iḥkām*, 1:114).

100. *Irshād*, p. 49. Ibn ʿUlayya's rejection of the *khabar al-wāḥid* is probably to be understood as the rejection of the unit-tradition in a literal sense, that is, as the rejection of those traditions that did not have at least two transmitters at each stage, what is termed *ʿazīz* in the literature of *uṣūl al-ḥadīth* (al-Ḥāzimī, *Shurūṭ*, p. 23, n. 1; al-Suyūṭī, *Tadrīb al-rāwī*, p. 28). Ibn Ḥibbān (d. 354/965) regarded the stipulation of this condition as tantamount to the rejection of the *sunna*; all traditions, he claimed, were unit ones (Ibn Ḥibbān, *Ṣaḥīḥ*, p. 118, loosely quoted al-Ḥāzimī, *Shurūṭ*, p.32). Traditions were collected to vindicate this strict condition (al-Suyūṭī, *Tadrīb al-rāwī*, pp. 28–29).

101. *Iḥkām*, 1:114.

102. Sarakhsī, 1:322; al-Baghdādī, *al-Kifāya* (Hyderabad: Dāʾirat al-Maʿārif al-ʿUthmāniyya, 1357 H), p. 18.

Other arguments pointed to the undesirable consequences of the position that accepted the *khabar al-wāḥid* as a norm. The ordinary man of probity was placed on a higher plane than the Prophet, for he was taken at his word, whereas the Prophet had to perform miracles to win assent.[103] If the unit-traditions were accepted as a basis for religious action, what grounds were there for maintaining the uncontested Muʿtazilī principle that they were not sufficient as a basis for religious belief, in matters such as the nature of God and His attributes?[104] Questions such as these forced the mainstream Muʿtazilīs to examine the rational basis for the acceptance of the unit-tradition more closely than others. We have already seen the general trend of their answer as it appears in al-Samarqandī's *Mīzān*. Just as we rely on the unit-report in ordinary matters that affect our welfare, so also we rely on it in matters of religion, where so much more is at stake. This reply was meant to show that the principle underlying secular and religious action was the same, that of wellbeing (*maṣlaḥa*) and that the distinction introduced by the opponent was unfounded.

But the Muʿtazilī defenders of the unit-tradition did not stop here. They introduced a device to maintain their position that we may term "the displacement of certainty." This device marks a significant concession to the demand for certainty put forth by the opposition. Its attractiveness was such that it was used by a number of Ashʿarīs, notably al-Ghazālī, and it is not without an echo in some later Ḥanafī texts, undoubtedly under Ashʿarī influence. But for al-Samarqandī, the ploy was unacceptable. We shall not undertake an extended treatment of this issue here but shall, like al-Samarqandī, refer the reader to the question of the infallibility of the *mujtahid*, an older and more famous version of the problem.

Two elements, say the Muʿtazilīs, must be present for us to act on a unit-tradition. First, the unit-tradition itself and, secondly, the master rule that informs us of the obligation to conform to the norm contained in the tradition. The unit consisting of the master rule along with the relevant tradition now bears the load of certainty. This master rule does not differ in any significant respect from an ordinary command of God. "There is no difference between God saying to us, 'When the veracity of the reporter seems probable to you, then act according to his report,' and His saying, 'Do so and so.' In all these cases we *know* the obligation of the act in question."[105]

The fact that the identification of the obligatory act rests on mere presumption is not a fatal flaw as the opponent claims. "The actions of the divine law are obligatory only because they constitute a benefit (*maṣlaḥa*), and it is not impossible that an act be of benefit when we do it in a particular state (*wa-naḥnu ʿalā ṣifa makhṣhūṣa*). Our presuming

103. Sarakhsī, 1:322; *Muʿtamad*, 2:575.
104. Sarakhsī, 1:322; *Muʿtamad*, 2:577.
105. *Muʿtamad*, 2:573.

the veracity of the reporter is precisely one of our "states."[106] Al-Ghazālī as an Ashʿarī voluntarist has no use for the Muʿtazilī argument from benefit, but he is nevertheless able to make use of the same displacement of certainty. "For," he argues, "what impossibility is there in God's saying to His subjects, 'If a bird flies past and you think that it is a raven, then I have made so-and-so an obligation for you and have made your presumption a sign (*ʿalāma*) of the obligation to act, just as I have made the declination of the sun from the meridian a sign of the obligation of prayer'?"[107] It is because our own state of being is a condition for the obligation of action that the uncertain authenticity of the tradition is of no importance. All that matters is our knowledge of the master rule, and that is certain.

In questions of religious belief, however, the situation is different, and it is for this reason that the unit-tradition has no place in determining dogma. For here what is required is knowledge, and knowledge must correspond to reality. "God's being beyond vision is a fact that exists in its own right and not in virtue of our presumption, so that it is not necessary that God be beyond vision because we presume the veracity of someone who reports this to us."[108] In the domain of belief there can be no master rule to convert presumption into certainty. We either know, or we do not know. In brief, the efficacy of action may well depend upon a subjective element; knowledge is concerned solely with what is objective.

In this respect, the Ḥanafīs take a very different position. For action, too, there exists an objective standard. The fact is that we do not know for certain that we are doing what God wants in conforming to a particular unit-tradition. There can be no master rule of the sort that the Muʿtazilīs posit. For God's will, like God's invisibility, exists apart from our states of being. We can only strive to know God's will; we cannot take part in the creation of valid law merely by entertaining some presumption or other. It is true, however, that we do not have unimpeachable sources for determining every legal question and are thus called upon to use sources that fall short of certainty. In such cases we are not immune to error. We obey God in employing our minds to find the truth through these sources, but we do not know whether our particular solution corresponds to God's will. We must be content with affirming generally (*ʿala al-ibhām*) that what God wills is the truth. [109]

Al-Samarqandī, belonging as he does to the school of Samarqand, makes the same sharp distinction between belief and action that we have seen to be characteristic of the Muʿtazila. Accordingly, he rejects the unit-tradition in questions of theology. In the case of belief, there is no room for anything less than certainty. Presumption can be a basis

---

106. *Muʿtamad*, 2:574.
107. *Mustaṣfā*, p. 71.
108. *Muʿtamad*, 2:578.
109. *Mīzān*. f. 117b.

for action in the absence of certainty, but presumption is of no use when it is precisely certainty that is called for.[110]

It is on this point, however, that some Ḥanafīs of a less rationalistic bent took a sharply contrasting position. They did accept the unit-tradition in questions of belief (*iʿtiqād*), and their reason for doing so is that knowledge and belief are not the same thing at all. One can be found without the other. There are those who have knowledge of the truth without belief, such as the *ahl al-kitāb*, who know that Muḥammad is a prophet but will not become Muslims. Again, there are those who have belief without knowledge. Such is the *muqallid*; he is incapable of understanding the proofs for what he believes. Belief (*iʿtiqād*), in fact, consists in an act, the setting of one's heart (*ʿaqd al-qalb*) on something. "And our being tested by having to set our heart on something is just like our being tested by having to do something, if not more important."[111] Although the only traditions specifically mentioned in this connection are those that deal with the afterlife, there is an unmistakable tendency displayed here to do away with the dichotomy of action and knowledge in favor of the former. This is perhaps not surprising in the case of those who were primarily jurists and for whom theology was frequently linked with an ascetic Sufism that aimed at checking the wayward impulses of the heart.

The Muʿtazilīs were apt to go in the opposite direction and view everything as a question of knowledge. ʿAlāʾ al-Dīn al-Samarqandī and the Samarqandī school were thus in the middle. As proper Ḥanafīs, they recognized the objectivity of God's will and gave action its due, but as rationalists they demanded room for theology to use its own methods in attaining the certainty that must underlie belief.

2. The Unit-Tradition in Ẓāhirism and Ḥanbalism

Among the legal schools that are associated with the *ahl al-ḥadīth*, the Ẓāhirīs and the Ḥanbalīs are of particular historical importance. The study of the Ẓāhirī school is, of course, greatly handicapped by the lack of sources. This was true when Goldziher wrote his classic study (1884) and remains true to this day, despite the publication of major works of Ibn Ḥazm. The danger, indeed, is great that Ẓāhirism will be identified with its greatest representative and that other aspects of the movement will be overlooked. In what follows we shall trace, on the basis of very scanty reports, a significant disagreement within early Ẓāhirism as to the standing of the unit-tradition and then show how Ibn Ḥazm, possibly with this disagreement in mind, elaborated an argument that raised the unit-tradition to its greatest eminence.

Among those who are commonly cited as having held that the unit-tradition affords certain knowledge is Dāwūd ibn ʿAlī ibn Khalaf, the founder of the Ẓāhirī school. Dāwūd

110. *Mīzān*, f. 111b.

111. Sarakhsī, 1:329; Bazdawī, 2:377; Abū 'l-Yusr al-Bazdawī quoted in Bukhārī, 2:377.

is said to have considered this knowledge inferential (*istidlālī*), and his reasoning is supposed to have been that the Qurʾān forbids us to follow what is only presumptive (17:36): "And follow not that of which thou hast no knowledge!" and condemns those who do follow it (53:28): "They follow naught but conjecture (*ẓann*) and conjecture avails not against truth." Yet we know that there is a consensus to accept the unit-tradition; we may then properly infer that the unit-tradition is a source of knowledge.[112] This, of course, is the same sort of argument we encountered in al-Jaṣṣāṣ's defense of the *mashhūr* tradition as a source of certainty.

Dāwūd's reasoning contrasts neatly with that of those Ẓāhirīs who rejected the unit-tradition on the basis of the same Qurʾānic verses. Action must depend on knowledge, but since the unit-tradition is not a source of knowledge, it cannot serve as a basis for action.[113] This view is most commonly attributed to al-Qāsānī.[114] It is also linked now and then to Abū Bakr ibn Dāwūd and to al-Nahrawānī.[115] Abū Bakr ibn Dāwūd is, of course, the son of Dāwūd al-Ẓāhirī. Ibn Dāwūd (d. 297/909) was a scholar of wide learning and the chief exponent of his father's system.[116] Al-Qāsānī is Abū Bakr Muḥammad ibn Isḥāq, a follower, but a very critical one of Dāwūd.[117] He was the object of a refutation by Abū 'l-Ḥasan ʿAbd Allāh ibn al-Mughallis (d. 324/935), the leading Ẓāhirī of his day.[118] Al-Nahrawānī is another Ẓāhirī, Abū Saʿīd al-Ḥasan ibn ʿUbayd.[119] A work of his against analogy is mentioned in the *Fihrist* of Ibn al-Nadīm.[120]

Thus at the very beginning of the history of Ẓāhirism, we find a rejection of the *khabar al-wāḥid* as a source of law, and this despite the teaching of Dāwūd. In holding this view, Ibn Dāwūd would be set squarely against his great rival, the Shāfiʿī Ibn Surayj (d. 306/918), who argued that acceptance of the *khabar al-wāḥid* was rationally obligatory. This and other positions that were regarded as Muʿtazilī were held by a significant body

112. Bukhārī. 3:371; *Qawāṭiʿ*, f. 106a; *Dharīʿa*, 2:517 (those for whom knowledge follows action).

113. *Iḥkām*, 1:114; Jaṣṣāṣ, f. 180b.

114. E.g., *Irshād*, p. 49.

115. E.g., *Musawwada* , p. 238.

116. On Ibn Dāwūd, see Louis Massignon, *La Passion de Husayn Ibn Mansour Hallaj*, 4 vols. (Paris: Gallimard, 1975), 1:386–416.

117. On him, see Abū Isḥāq al-Shīrāzī, *Ṭabaqāt al-fuqahāʾ*, ed. Iḥsān ʿAbbās (Beirut: Dār al-Rāʾid al-ʿArabī, 1970), p. 176.

118. Al-Shīrāzī, *Ṭabaqāt*, p. 176. For the Ẓāhirī division on the unit-tradition, see *Mīzān*, f. 136b. It follows that some Ẓāhirīs allowed for the abrogation of a concurrent tradition by a unit-one (al-Muḥaqqiq al-Ḥillī, *Maʿārij al-uṣūl*, ed. Ḥabīb Allāh al-Jīlānī al-Ashkfūrī [Tehran, 1310/1893], p. 113).

119. Also found as al-Nahrabīnī (Māwardī, 1:560). He is incorrectly identified as Abū 'l-Faraj al-Muʿāfā ibn Zakariyyāʾ, a follower of al-Ṭabarī, by the editors of Māwardī (p. 560, n. 2) and *Mankhūl* (p. 326, n. 2). The correct identification is suggested by the juxtaposition of al-Qāsānī and al-Nahrawānī in al-Shīrāzī, *Ṭabaqāt*, p. 176, and confirmed by *Baḥr*, f. 270a.

120. Ibn al-Nadīm, *Kitāb al-Fihrist*, ed. Gustav Flügel. 2 vols. (Leipzig: F. C. W. Vogel, 1871–72. Repr. Beirut: Maktabat Khayyāṭ, 1964), p. 218.

of Shāfiʿīs, among them al-Qaffāl al-Shāshī (d. 365/976). This embarrassing fact was explained by the later Ashʿarī theologians al-Bāqillānī and Abū Isḥāq al-Isfarāyīnī as due solely to the incompetence of these jurists in questions of theology; they picked up what they read in the Muʿtazilī treatises.[121] In fact, in the case of Ibn Surayj at least, these positions would have been just the ones that he would have been able to use against his Ẓāhirī opponents. Ibn Surayj was also the author of *A Reply to al-Qāsānī* (*Jawāb li'l-Qāsānī*). The contents of this work are completely unknown, but it is reported that al-Qāsānī came to embrace Shāfiʿism and to defend the use of analogy.[122]

Unfortunately, Ibn Ḥazm makes no reference to this group that we can identify. For him, those who rejected the unit-tradition are the Muʿtazilī theologians who in the eighth century were the first to deviate from the consensus on this matter.[123] He may well consider these Ẓāhirīs as tainted with the Muʿtazilī heresy. Although the Muʿtazilīs who rejected the unit-tradition are supposed to have done so on the basis of reason as opposed to the Ẓāhirīs, whose rejection was based on scripture (the distinction we have maintained), the arguments are combined in some sources.[124] Moreover, al-Ghazālī contrasts the majority position that accepts the *khabar al-wāḥid* with that of most of the Qadariyya and their Ẓāhirī *followers* such as al-Qāsānī, who held that to act in accordance with a *khabar al-wāḥid* is forbidden by revalation.[125]

The important question, and one that we are not now in a position to answer, is, how did this change in legal theory affect the legal practice of the Ẓāhirī school? The Ẓāhirīs as deniers of analogy needed all the material sources they could find. To have done away with all the norms contained in the corpus of unit-traditions would have meant a radical reduction of the scope of the system constructed by Dāwūd. What had been regulated under that system would thus revert to its original status of legal indifference (*barāʾa*); this position was, in fact, taken by some who rejected the *khabar al-wāḥid*.[126] Alternatively, they could have and most probably did claim that many traditions considered unit were in fact *mutawātir*, for, as Ibn Ḥazm notes, "Anyone can claim for any tradition he wishes that it is *mutawātir*; indeed, it is the collectors of *isnāds* (*aṣḥāb al-isnād*) who can put forth the most valid claim to this effect, since they have so many reporters and varied *isnāds* to vouch for this claim."[127]

121. Tāj al-Dīn al-Subkī, *Tabaqāt al-shāfiʿiyya al-kubrā*, ed. ʿAbd al-Faṭṭāḥ Muḥammad al-Ḥulw and Maḥmūd Muḥammad al-Ṭanāḥī (Cairo: ʿĪsā al-Bābī al-Ḥalabī, 1964–76) 3:201–3.; al-Muḥaqqiq al-Ḥillī, *Maʿārij al-uṣūl*, p. 82.

122. Ibn al-Nadīm, *al-Fihrist*, p. 213.

123. *Iḥkām*, 1:114.

124. Sarakhsī, 1:321–22.

125. *Mustaṣfā*, p. 172. *Mīzān*, f. 136b, speaks of "most of the Ẓāhirīs and al-Qāshānī from the Muʿtazila." See below, Chapter Four, n. 114.

126. *Mustaṣfā*, p. 172; *Rawḍa*, p. 53.

127. *Iḥkām*, 1:134. See also *Iḥkām*, 7:113.

Ibn Ḥazm himself (d. 456/1064) signals a return to the teaching of Dāwūd, which he identifies as that of al-Ḥārith al-Muḥāsibī (d. 243/857) and al-Ḥusayn ibn ʿAlī al-Karābīsī (d. 245/859).[128] It is also reported by Ibn Khuwayz Mindād (first half of fifth/tenth century) as that of Mālik (d. 179/795).[129] The unit-tradition is a source of certain knowledge and a basis for action. Ibn Ḥazm's argument for the *khabar al-wāḥid* takes up the challenge of the Muʿtazilīs that God is capable of giving us certainty in the sources of the law and would not leave us in puzzlement by commanding us to act on our presumptions of authenticity. In fact, claims Ibn Ḥazm, God is not only capable of giving us certainty but has taken it upon Himself to ensure the preservation and transmission of the divine law. Revelation includes the utterances of the Prophet, which are exactly on a level with the Qurʾān. The Prophet "does not speak out of his own desire; it is nothing but revelation (*waḥyun yūḥā*)" (Qurʾān 53:3). But we know that God has guaranteed the preservation of His revelation in the verse (15:9): "Verily we Ourselves have sent down the Exhortation and most surely We will be its guardian." This verse is generally taken to refer only to the preservation of the Qurʾān, but this, according to Ibn Ḥazm, is a mere assertion without foundation. This being so, it follows that all of Muḥammad's law survives; it is by God's gracious intervention immune to alteration and all the more so to obliteration. The unit-tradition, which God has commanded us to accept, is thus an infallible guide to God's will. The Qurʾān, the *mutawātir*, and the *āḥād* traditions form a body of revelation that is impervious to error and falsehood. To claim that a unit-tradition that meets all the legal requirements may nonetheless be unauthentic is to admit that the truth is indistinguishable from falsehood and that God has not kept His promise to preserve the revelation. This, briefly put, is Ibn Ḥazm's bold argument for the *khabar al-wāḥid*. The unit-tradition in the form of a chain of reliable authorities going back to the Prophet is a source of certain knowledge. It is, moreover, aside from the Qurʾān and the *mutawātir* tradition, the only source that Ibn Ḥazm will recognize. For him, too, as we shall note, all weight is put on the formal considerations for authenticity, on the impeccability of the *isnād*.[130]

Ibn Ḥazm set much store by this proof and appears to have considered it original. Others were not so impressed, among them his contemporary the Ḥanbalī Abū Yaʿlā ibn al-Farrāʾ (d. 458/1066). He reasserts the accepted view that the Qurʾānic guarantee of divine preservation refers only to the Qurʾān itself and settles the issue by noting that there is a *ḥadīth* that threatens with damnation those who fabricate lies in the Prophet's

128. *Iḥkām*, 1:108, 119; Abū ʿĀṣim Muḥammad ibn Aḥmad al-ʿAbbādī, *Kitāb Ṭabaqāt al-fuqahā aš-šāfiʿīya*, ed. Gösta Vistestam (Leiden: Brill, 1964), p. 24; Ibn ʿAbd al-Barr, *al-Tamhīd li-mā fī al-Muwaṭṭaʾ min al-maʿānī wa'l-asānīd*, 1:8.

129. *Iḥkām*, 1:108, 119; Ibn ʿAbd al-Barr, *al-Tamhīd*, 1:8. On him, see Ahmed Bekir, *Histoire de l'école malikite en orient jusqu'à la fin du moyen age* (Tunis, 1962), p. 86.

130. *Iḥkām*, 1:121–50. See the quotation from Abū Bakr al-Bayhaqī (d. 458/1066) in Bukhārī, 3:49. Cf. Ibn Taymiyya, *Rafʿ al-malām*, p. 13 (some of the *sunna* may never have reached us).

name. If this *ḥadīth* is genuine, then the possibility is recognized that lies may pass as sayings of the Prophet. If the *ḥadīth* is forged, then here is an example of one such lie often taken for the truth.[131]

Abū Yaʿlā's own views on the *khabar al-wāḥid* are of interest, for in him we find a prime exponent among the Ḥanbalīs of the formalist position. The Ḥanbalī movement was above all united by allegiance to one man, Aḥmad ibn Ḥanbal (d. 241/855), a figure of heroic proportions, and it was the views of Ibn Ḥanbal that formed the basis (*aṣl*) for the school both in law and theology.

It is not surprising then to find that the controversy concerning the *khabar al-wāḥid* in the Ḥanbalī school centers about the doctrine attributed to Aḥmad by Abū Yaʿlā. This teaching had been found by Abū Yaʿlā in the handwriting of Abū Ḥafṣ al-ʿUkbarī, who had heard it from Abū Ḥafṣ ʿUmar ibn Zayd. Ultimately it went back to Abū Bakr Aḥmad ibn Muḥammad ibn Hāniʾ al-Athram (d. 260/873), who in his book *Maʿānī al-ḥadīth* had quoted Aḥmad as saying, "When a sound tradition from the Prophet reaches me in which there is an ordinance or an obligation, I put the ordinance or obligation into practice and serve God in this way, but I do not testify that the Prophet said this." For Abū Yaʿlā, the upshot of this statement was clear. Ibn Ḥanbal had stated unequivocally (*ṣarraḥa*) that the tradition is not of certain authenticity, that is, that there is only presumption, not knowledge.[132]

Ibn Taymiyya (d. 728/1328), who held that the unit-tradition could be a source of certainty, was obviously embarrassed by so explicit an affirmation of the opposing doctrine coming from Aḥmad himself. He thus set out statements of Aḥmad that could be interpreted to indicate that the master was really on the other side of the issue, his own.[133] Ibn Qayyim al-Jawziyya (d. 751/1350), Ibn Taymiyya's foremost disciple, was more outspoken in rejecting Abū Yaʿlā's citation. It was, he argued, very likely not authentic at all. Al-Athram was the only source for it, and even he did not state explicitly that he had heard it from Aḥmad himself. Even if it is genuine, the proper explanation is that Aḥmad refrained from testifying to the authenticity of the tradition out of pious scruple (*waraʿ*). Ibn al-Qayyim then reproduces Ibn Ḥazm's proof of the certain authenticity of the *khabar al-wāḥid*.[134]

In these sharply contrasting viewpoints we are witness to a battle that concerned nothing less than the character of Ḥanbalism. The formalists, Abū Yaʿlā and his successors, had already gained the day. We know from Muwaffaq al-Dīn ibn Qudāma (d. 620/1223), the great Syrian Ḥanbalī, that a majority of the school and especially the later authorities favored the formalist position.[135] The doctrine of Ibn Taymiyya and his disciple thus

131. *ʿUdda*, f. 136.

132. *Musawwada*, p. 242; *ʿUdda*, f. 135a.

133. *Musawwada*, p. 242.

134. Ibn Qayyim al-Jawziyya, *Mukhtaṣar al-ṣawāʿiq*, pp. 480–81.

135. *Rawḍa*, p. 52.

represents a bold but unsuccessful attempt to recapture what had been lost generations earlier. The twentieth century Ḥanbalī author Ibn Badrān regards the formalist position as standard Ḥanbalī doctrine.[136]

IV. Discontinuity

1. *The* Mursal *Tradition*

There is nothing remarkable about the Ḥanafīs' acceptance of the unit-tradition as a legal source; this they share with the majority of legal schools. What is remarkable is the consistency with which they, the Samarqandī school included, refused to compromise their ancient position that the authenticity of these traditions, being only presumptive, was subject to rebuttal. The content of an ostensibly sound tradition must measure up to certain standards before it can constitute a legal norm. Because the authenticity of a *ḥadīth* is equivalent to its connectedness (*ittiṣāl*) to the Prophet, the Ḥanafīs speak of a *ḥadīth* whose contents fail to meet these standards as "discontinuous" (*munqaṭiᶜ*). Discontinuity of this sort is termed "inner" or "material" (*bāṭin, maᶜnan*) as distinct from "external" or "formal" discontinuity (*inqiṭāᶜ ẓāhir, ṣūratan*). Material discontinuity has reference to both the *matn* and the *isnād*; both the content of the tradition and its reporters must be acceptable. Formal discontinuity is found when there is a gap in the *isnād*. Material discontinuity is revealed when the reporters do not meet the relevant standards of character and attentiveness or when the *matn* is measured by canons (*uṣūl*) considered of greater certainty than the authenticity of the unit-tradition and is found to fall short. Only formal discontinuity is discontinuity in the literal sense.

The only case of formal discontinuity discussed by the *uṣūlīs* is that of the "detached" (*mursal*) tradition. This detachment consists in someone quoting the Prophet without his actually having heard the Prophet make the particular statement. It is the case of the reporter who omits the transmitter or transmitters who link him to the Prophet.[137] Even a Companion can report a *mursal* tradition, for example, one he has heard from another

136. *Madkhal*, p. 91.

137. *Irshād*, p. 64. The question, of course, is whether the requisite probability (*ẓann*) of authenticity now exists (al-Ṣanᶜānī, *Tawḍīḥ al-afkār*, 1:298). On the term "*mursal*," see Joseph Schacht, *The Origins of Muhammadan Jurisprudence*, pp. 38–39, and Marçais, "Le *Taqrīb*," 16:515, n. 1. According to Abū Dāwūd al-Sijistānī (d. 275/889), "the scholars of the past like Sufyān al-Thawrī, Mālik ibn Anas, and al-Awzāᶜī used to cite them (*yaḥtajj bihā*) until al-Shāfiᶜī came and spoke against them. Aḥmad ibn Ḥanbal and others followed him in this" (*Risāla ilā ahl Makka*, p. 24, quoted in al-Jazāʾirī, *Tawjīh al-naẓar*, p. 152). Al-Ṭabarī, it appears, also regarded al-Shāfiᶜī as the first to introduce this innovation (*bidᶜa*) (Ibn ᶜAbd al-Barr, *al-Tamhīd*, 1:4). Note also the recent study Muḥammad Ḥasan Hītū, *al-Ḥadīth al-mursal: ḥujjiyyatuhu wa-atharuhu fī al-fiqh al-islāmī* (Beirut: Dar al-Fikr, n.d.).

Companion. But here the detachment must be known from an external source, since a Companion is presumed to report from his own hearing.[138]

Among the Ḥanafīs there was no uniform position on the validity of the *mursal* tradition. The view that would accept them all without discrimination is associated with Abū 'l-Ḥasan al-Karkhī.[139] It is to be contrasted with the position of those who distinguished among the reporters of the *mursal* according either to their chronology or their outstanding moral qualities. Among these is ʿĪsā ibn Abān, who accepted the *marāsīl* of the first three generations of Islam, whose outstanding qualities had been testified to by the Prophet, and thereafter accepted only the *marāsīl* of outstanding religious scholars (*aʾimmat al-dīn*).[140] Al-Jaṣṣāṣ follows ʿĪsā in the main but reserves the right to reject the *marāsīl* of the second and third generations if the reporter is known to have been lax in his choice of informants.[141]

The issue underlying the entire discussion of the *mursal* is to what extent the immediate reporter, the one who detaches the *ḥadīth* (*al-mursil*), ensures the probity of the reporter he omits by the very fact of reporting from him. For the reporters of a tradition must possess certain qualities for the tradition to be valid, and these qualities are vouched for by those who know and themselves possess these qualities (*ahl al-taʿdīl*). The chain stops with the Companions, whose qualities are ensured by the Qurʾān and the *sunna*.

The position of al-Karkhī is thus the simplest. Any person of probity in reporting a *mursal* tradition thereby vouches for those he omits. It also seems to have been the most popular among the Ḥanafīs. The position attributed to al-Karkhī is taken as that of the Ḥanafīs in a number of Shāfiʿī works.[142] Moreover, it is for al-Samarqandī the teaching of "our scholars" (*ʿulamāʾunā*). Al-Karkhī is not mentioned. ʿĪsā ibn Abān's position, on the other hand, is mentioned only briefly and there is no indication given that it had any wide following.[143] Al-Samarqandī's exposition of the problem, which is quite extended, is meant to answer the arguments of those who supported al-Shāfiʿī. Al-Shāfiʿī's position, according to al-Samarqandī, was that apart from the *marāsīl* of the Companions other *marāsīl* were to be rejected unless their continuity could be shown externally. For this reason, al-Shāfiʿī accepted the *marāsīl* of Saʿīd ibn al-Musayyab. "I followed them up," al-Shāfiʿī is supposed to have said, "and found them to be continuous (*musnad*)."[144] In fact, al-Shāfiʿī's view on the *mursal* was much discussed among his followers. We shall have

138. *Manār*, p. 644.
139. *Musawwada*, p. 250; *Manār*, p. 646.
140. Jaṣṣāṣ, f. 193a.
141. Jaṣṣāṣ, f. 193a.
142. *Lumaʿ*, p. 44; Āmidī, 2:112.
143. *Mīzān*, f. 111b.
144. *Mīzān*, f. 111b.

more to say about this presently, but for now shall confine ourselves to summarizing al-Samarqandī's discussion, which brings out with admirable clarity some of the key issues at stake in the controversy over the *mursal*.

The main argument attributed to al-Shāfiʿī is that an explicit *isnād* is necessary in order that the recipient of the tradition (*al-sāmiʿ*) be in a position to conduct his own inquiry into the probity of the reporters. In a continuous tradition, where there has been no explicit approbation by the reporter, the recipient will not accept the tradition until he is himself convinced of the probity of the reporters. Rejection is all the more necessary where not only the character of the reporters but their very identity is unknown. This personal inquiry is called for because the grounds for disapprobation (*jarḥ*) may be concealed, and the tendency is only too great to rely on externals. We cannot assume an implied guarantee of probity in the act of reporting since there are many cases of reliable authorities (*thiqāt*) reporting both continuous and discontinuous traditions from informants who are not acceptable.

In reply, al-Samarqandī claims that *irsāl* was a common practice among the Companions and one that took place without opposition. This acceptance constitutes a kind of consensus as to the legitimacy of the practice. We are entitled to posit an implicit guarantee of probity in the act of reporting because it is inconceivable that the *mursil*, himself a reliable authority, would impose a new legal rule upon his hearers without being prepared to vouch for the quality of his informants. The enormity of the offense of attributing to the Prophet something he did not say would be deterrent enough.

Having made his case for an implicit approbation in the *mursal*, al-Samarqandī insists that this approbation is sufficient and no personal inquiry is called for. This principle, he claims, is also accepted by al-Shāfiʿī, for he, too, like the Ḥanafīs, accepts a general approbation without the mention of specific grounds (*asbāb*). Thus al-Shāfiʿī also reaches a point at which personal probity is all that is demanded for a valid approbation. Where al-Shāfiʿī does differ is in his demand that disapprobation be for a specific ground. The Ḥanafīs reject a specific disapprobation; apparently they regarded it as an invitation to character assassination. Indeed, such was often the case, with the Ḥanafīs themselves frequent victims. Thus, according to al-Samarqandī, it is enough to say that a reporter is *mastūr*, that is, of unknown moral standing, or in some other oblique way indicate that he is unacceptable.[145]

In al-Samarqandī's defense of the *mursal*, we find the antithesis of what after al-Shāfiʿī had come to be the position of the *ahl al-ḥadīth*. For al-Samarqandī says nothing

145. *Mīzān*, ff. 112b–113a. Whether this implicit guarantee also existed in traditions where the reporters were mentioned by name was the subject of controversy among the Ḥanafīs. Some were willing to rely upon the probity of the reporter in every case. Others considered the naming of the reporters without explicit approbation a way of putting their examination in the hands of the hearer; the reporter himself was not sure of his authorities (*Mīzān*, f. 112b–113a).

less than that the *isnād* is unnecessary.[146] Once he has ascertained the fact of approbation on the part of a man of probity, the hearer is relieved of making a personal inquiry into the subject of the approbation. He must accept the approbation at face value. This position is one of extreme subjectivity when contrasted with that of the *muḥaddith*, who saw the *isnād* as a whole to be tested in all places for weaknesses. His goal was by applying the most stringent standards to eliminate whatever was at all suspect and thus to come into possession of the corpus of the Prophet's utterances, for the traditions that survived such minute scrutiny were regarded as of certain authenticity.

Al-Samarqandī, as we have noted, presents his position as that of the Ḥanafīs at large, and there are Shāfiʿī sources that so consider it. In fact, the situation was not at all so simple. The doctrine of ʿĪsā ibn Abān, which he merely notes in passing, and the closely related doctrine of al-Jaṣṣāṣ, which he does not refer to at all, had found important adherents among the Central Asians.[147] The dispute centered about *marāsīl* after the third generation. Ibn Abān accepted only those that had won the approval of great scholars; al-Jaṣṣāṣ considered them to be under a presumption of unsoundness until proof to the contrary. Thus al-Jaṣṣāṣ's position was the most reserved with regard to the *mursal*. It differs from that of Ibn Abān in another point as well. Ibn Abān is said to have regarded the *mursal* as of greater validity than the *musnad*. The fact that the *mursil* took all responsibility for the authenticity of the *ḥadīth* upon himself was a clear indication of the special confidence he placed in it. This preference of the *mursal* is supported by reference to the early practice of *irsāl* when numerous reporters attested to the authenticity of the *ḥadīth*. The names of the reporters were omitted precisely because there were so many.[148] The preference of the *mursal* to the *musnad* also had the advantage of forestalling the objection of those *ḥadīth* scholars who justifiably asked what point was there in having an *isnād* if a *mursal* was as good as a *musnad*. Ibn Abān, a former follower of the traditionists, would have been sensitive to this objection. His answer, that the *mursal* was in fact more valid than the *musnad*, would be more persuasive than the answer sometimes found, that the occupation of the *ḥadīth* scholars with the *isnād* was an avocation of theirs and no more impugned the *mursal* than did the collection of varied *isnāds* impugn the tradition with a single *isnād*.[149] At the same time, however, ʿĪsā's claim for the superiority of the *mursal* could only apply to those traditions in which the personal authority of the *mursil*

146. Thus *Talwīḥ*, 2:257 defines *irsāl* as the absence of an *isnād*.

147. Al-Bazdawī favoring ʿĪsā ibn Abān's view and al-Sarakhsī that of al-Jaṣṣāṣ (Bukhārī, 3:7; Sarakhsī, 1:323). ʿĪsā's doctrine is presented as that of the Kufans in al-Ḥākim al-Nīsābūrī, *Kitāb Maʿrifat ʿulūm al-ḥadīth*, ed. Muʿaẓẓam Ḥusayn (Cairo: Matbaʿat Dār al-Kutub al-Miṣriyya, 1356/1937), p. 26,· but the *mursal* is not said to be superior to the *musnad*.

148. Bukhārī, 3:4, 7: Ibn ʿAbd al-Barr, *al-Tamhīd*, 1:3. Majd al-Dīn Ibn al-Athīr, *Jāmiʿ al-uṣūl*, 1:117. See Schacht, *Origins*, p. 39.

149. Sarakhsī, 1:363; Bukhārī, 3:7.

would be of significance, in the case of the first three generations and thereafter of great scholars.

Al-Jaṣṣāṣ's position rests not upon the technical probity of the *mursil*, as does that of al-Karkhī, but upon a more specific quality, that of abstaining from transmitting the *ḥadīth* of unreliable authorities. This quality is presumed in the early period; its opposite thereafter. It thus grants the point of the opposing camp that simple probity is not enough. Among the later Ḥanafīs, however, even those who reject al-Karkhī's position that the *mursal* is always acceptable base the implied approbation of the omitted informants on the probity of the reporter. Unlike al-Samarqandī, who follows al-Karkhī completely, they accept the rationale of probity but rather inconsistently restrict its application.[150]

Al-Samarqandī's contrast of the Ḥanafī and Shāfiʿī positions on the acceptability of a nonspecific disapprobation calls for some comment. The Ḥanafī teaching on this issue, as al-Samarqandī presents it, corresponds to his liberal doctrine on the *mursal*. The word of the single man of probity is enough to guarantee his *mursal* and to admit or disqualify another reporter. In those Ḥanafī sources, however, which take a more reserved view of the *mursal*, the only position reported is that which corresponds to al-Shāfiʿī's.[151] It would be rash to conclude that al-Samarqandī has erred or fabricated a new position for the Ḥanafīs. The Shāfiʿī Abū Isḥāq al-Shīrāzī (d. 476/1083) quotes Abū Ḥanīfa to the effect that the branding of a reporter as a wrongdoer (*fāsiq*) without explanation suffices for disapprobation.[152] We may thus take it that al-Karkhī's position on the *mursal* had its counterpart in respect to disapprobation and that these views were widely enough held for them to be seen by some Shāfiʿīs as the standard Ḥanafī doctrines.

The usual argument for making a distinction between approbation that is general and disapprobation is that the grounds for probity are innumerable, whereas improbity can be confirmed by the mention of only one specific shortcoming. Alternatively, it is argued that there is only one ground for probity, while there are many grounds for improbity, some of them controversial.[153] It is this latter consideration that stands out in the Ḥanafī justification for their position. The *ahl al-ḥadīth* had for a long time been accusing the Ḥanafīs both of undervaluing the role of traditions and of exhibiting incompetence in their criticism. These charges were leveled against the early masters of the school as well as against later scholars.[154] Such open attacks the Ḥanafīs felt themselves in a position to answer. In supporting the demand that disapprobation be based on a specific

150. *Taysīr*, 3:105.

151. Bazdawī, 3:68; Sarakhsī, 2:9.

152. *Lumaʿ*, p. 47.

153. *Mankhūl*, p. 262.

154. For a collection of this material, see ʿAbd al-Ḥayy al-Laknawī, *al-Rafʿ wa'l-takmīl fī al-jarḥ wa'l-taʿdīl*, ed. ʿAbd al-Fattāḥ Abū Ghudda (Aleppo: Maktab al-Maṭbūʿāt al-Islāmiyya, n.d.).

charge, they hoped to make it impossible for their opponents to prevail in the domain of *ḥadīth* transmission by applying tacitly their own, often debatable, standards. They demanded that the standards for approbation take into consideration their role in the community. The ways of the jurist are not those of the ascetic (*akhlāq al-fuqahāʾ tukhālif akhlāq al-zuhhād*). What was fitting for one who had to set a public example (*ahl al-qudwa*) might not be fitting for the solitary (*ahl al-ʿuzla*).[155] Clearly, the Ḥanafīs had to react when such grounds for disapprobation were advanced as lack of expert competence in *ḥadīth* transmission and excessive preoccupation with *fiqh*![156]

The position attributed to al-Karkhī was not confined to the Ḥanafīs but was the standard Malīkī doctrine and was popular among the Muʿtazilīs as well.[157] Among the latter it was held by Abū ʿAlī al-Jubbāʾī, who demanded two *mursil*s consistently with his stipulation of two reporters at every stage of a tradition, his son Abū Hāshim, ʿAbd al-Jabbār, and Abū 'l Ḥusayn al-Baṣrī.[158] Consequently, al-Karkhī, in rejecting the position of ʿĪsā ibn Abān, was completely in accord with mainstream Muʿtazilī thought.

The acceptance of the *mursal* tradition increased the range of possibilities for filling in details of the law. It did not in anyway bind those who accepted it, for the material conditions that the Ḥanafīs and Mālikīs set for the unit-tradition were such as to leave them ample room for rejecting both *mursal* and *musnad* traditions. Nor did the forgoing of the *isnād* mean that anyone could quote a statement in the Prophet's name and expect it to become a legal norm. If such a tradition were previously unknown, it would be rejected, Abū 'l-Ḥusayn al-Baṣrī states, "not because it is a *mursal*, but because the *ḥadīth* have been recorded and collected, and what is unknown to a *ḥadīth* scholar of our day is falsehood."[159]

Among those who rejected the *mursal*, the case of al-Shāfiʿī offers particular problems of its own. Al-Shāfiʿī was generally considered to have accepted the *marāsīl* of the *ṣaḥāba* without reservation. Outside of this, he accepted only the *marāsīl* of Saʿīd ibn al-Musayyab, because those he had checked and found to be continuous. Some Shāfiʿīs, however, rejected all *marāsīl* except those of Saʿīd; they could find no principle on which to make an exception of the Companions.[160] Others denied that the *marāsīl* of Saʿīd were special; al-Shāfiʿī had approved of them because he was familiar with them.[161] There was

155. Bazdawī, 3:73.
156. Bazdawī, 3:75.
157. Qarāfī, p. 379.
158. *Muʿtamad*, 2:628–29.
159. *Muʿtamad*, 2:637.
160. *Musawwada*, p. 259. Apparently this was the position of al-Qaffāl al-Shāshī (d. 365/976) (al-Suyūṭī, *Tadrīb al-rāwī*, p. 121).
161. *Lumaʿ*, p. 44. This was the position of Abū Isḥāq al-Isfarāyīnī (d. 418/1027) (al-ʿIrāqī, *al-Taqyīd*, p. 80, note) attributed to al-Shāfiʿī by Ibn Baṭṭāl (al-Ṣanʿānī, *Tawḍīh al-afkār*, 1:292). Al-Shāfiʿī is supposed

thus a current of Shāfiʿī thought that was ready to go beyond al-Shāfiʿī in the rejection of the *mursal*.

Closely associated with the problem of the *mursal* was that of the tradition in which the reporter was approbated but not named (*akhbaranī al-thiqa*). Indeed, it was on the basis of al-Shāfiʿī's use of these traditions in the *Mukhtaṣar* of al-Muzanī that al-Bāqillānī had argued that al-Shāfiʿī accepted the *mursal*. Obviously, al-Shāfiʿī had meant for these traditions to be accepted on his authority.[162] Although some who rejected the *mursal* accepted traditions of this sort, mainstream Shāfiʿī opinion refused to make a distinction. Al-Shāfiʿī's use of these traditions called for an explanation. Thus Abū 'l-Ṭayyib al-Ṭabarī (d. 450/1058) claimed that al-Shāfiʿī had meant to bind only himself.[163] A more convincing answer was given by those who claimed to know the identity of the reporters to which al-Shāfiʿī was referring. Al-Shāfiʿī's "an authority" was a known personage, and there was consequently no *irsāl*.[164] It thus came about that when Imām al-Ḥaramayn made his case for the acceptance of these traditions as they stood, he was breaking with what was regarded by the Shāfiʿīs as the view of al-Shāfiʿī himself. Noting that to oppose al-Shāfiʿī in *uṣūl al-fiqh* is a serious matter for "he knew the field inside out" (*ibn bajdatihā wa-mulāzim arūmatihā*), he tried to find support for his view in al-Shāfiʿī's writings.[165] The Ḥanafī position was to accept these traditions; the sufficiency of probity was once again the dominant consideration.[166]

The accepted view among the *ahl al-ḥadīth* was to reject the *mursal*. Indeed, some went so far as to reject a *musnad* tradition with a corresponding *mursal*.[167] Presumably the omitted reporter had some flaw and was therefore dropped from the *isnād*. There was thus an implied disapprobation, and disapprobation always outweighed approbation. Ibn Ḥazm, in keeping with his principle that a unit-tradition must have a sound *isnād*, rejects the *mursal* out of hand.[168] The omitted reporter is unknown, and we cannot judge the *isnād* without knowing his identity. The explicit warranty found in the form "a reliable authority reported to me" is equally unacceptable. One must conduct one's own inquiry into the probity of the reporters. He rejects vigorously, however, the view that a *musnad* is impaired by a corresponding *mursal*.[169] The silence of the reporter cannot be grounds for rejecting what he or someone else says elsewhere.

---

to have eventually treated the *marāsīl* of Saʿīd ibn al-Musayyab like the others (al-Suyūṭī, *Tadrīb al-rāwī*, p. 122).

162. *Mankhūl*, p. 276.
163. *Musawwada*, p. 257.
164. *Irshād*, pp. 67–68.
165. *Burhān*, f. 177.
166. Bukhārī, 3:72.
167. *Irshād*, p. 64; Sarakhsī, 1:364; *Musawwada*, p. 251. See also n. 137 above.
168. *Iḥkām*, 2:1.
169. *Iḥkām*, 2:88.

Ibn Ḥazm's bitterness is primarily directed against the Mālikīs and the Ḥanafīs. While claiming to accept the *mursal*, they are in fact the first to reject it when it runs counter to the teaching of their *imām*. The number of cases in which this occurs runs into the thousands. Because they used a *mursal* tradition to defend some legal positions, they said that they accepted the *mursal* on principle. Their aim was solely to defend the point in question with whatever was at hand, regardless of whether they simultaneously demolished a thousand other positions of theirs. Furthermore, having made this one point, they were unconcerned about invalidating it somewhere else.[170]

The Ḥanbalīs are divided along more or less the same lines as in the case of the unit-tradition. Once again two contradictory teachings are attributed to Aḥmad ibn Ḥanbal. Abū Yaʿlā ibn al-Farraʾ and Ibn ʿAqīl (d. 513/1120) are the main proponents of the view that accepts the *marāsīl* of all periods.[171] In the case of the rejection of the *mursal*, the Ḥanbalīs of the opposing camp are less rigid than we found them to be in their claims for the unit-tradition. Ibn Taymiyya considered Abū Yaʿlā to have had in mind a *mursal* in which a reporter was omitted rather than one without any *isnād* whatsoever. This he finds acceptable for "the omission of one or two is not like the omission of ten."[172] In the case of two versions of a tradition, one *musnad* and the other *mursal*, the *musnad* is not thereby impugned.[173] The tradition in which there is an explicit approbation of an unnamed reporter is also accepted.[174] The issue of the *mursal* tradition was one on which the conservative Ḥanbalīs were willing to make concessions that did not jeopardize their claim that law recognized only "unit-traditions" of certain authenticity. Those who were closer to the Muʿtazilīs, such as Abū Yaʿlā and Ibn ʿAqīl, had already rejected the pretensions of the unit-tradition to certainty and thus felt free to apply the principle of an implied approbation.

2. *Inner Discontinuity*

The Qurʾān and the *mutawātir* and *mashhūr* traditions form a body of certain or nearly certain materials against which the presumed validity of a unit-tradition, *musnad* or *mursal* can be tested. A unit-tradition that is inconsistent with these is rejected, what constitutes inconsistency being a question of hermeneutics. But apart from these certain material sources, the Ḥanafīs also measure the presumed validity of a tradition against rational canons. Thus a unit-tradition that regulates a matter of general concern or a matter that was in dispute among the Companions will also be rejected. In such cases,

170. *Iḥkām*, 2:5.
171. *Musawwada*, p. 251.
172. *Musawwada*, p. 252.
173. *Musawwada*, p. 251.
174. *Musawwada*, pp. 256–57.

only *mutawātir* and *mashhūr* traditions are acceptable. Reason and experience dictate that traditions in these areas be of wide circulation. It is in rejecting traditions that fail to meet this second series of standards that the Ḥanafīs diverge most markedly from the other legal schools.

The doctrine of the major legal schools, the Ḥanafīs, the Shāfiʿīs, and Mālikīs, recognizes the unit-tradition as of only prima facie validity and will thus reject a unit-tradition when it conflicts with sources of certain validity. What is recognized as a conflict may, of course, and in fact does differ among the schools. When it comes to the extension of these sources by analogy, significant differences emerge. The Shāfiʿīs prefer a unit-tradition to analogy and are thus diametrically opposed to the Mālikīs, who prefer analogy.[175] The Ḥanafī position that became standard makes a distinction between the traditions of Companions who were recognized jurists and those who were not. It is only the traditions of a jurist that are preferred to analogy.

The Ḥanafī position does not rest, as one might suppose, on a general preference for analogy as against the unit-tradition. For the Ḥanafīs, the unit-tradition is of greater validity than analogy. The word of the Prophet is known with certainty to be binding, and the doubt that attaches to a tradition arises from its mode of transmission. In analogy, on the other hand, the very construction of the analogy is fraught with uncertainty.[176] When the tradition of a nonjurist is rejected, it is because there is now the additional doubt occasioned by the possibility of an inadequate transmission of the sense of the Prophet's statement. Transmission according to sense (*al-naql bi'l-maʿnā*) was formerly a widespread practice.[177] One who lacks the proper legal aptitude might very well fail to transmit the Prophet's utterance in such a way as to convey its full sense. Yet even in the case of the nonjurist, his tradition is rejected only after it has proved to be incompatible with every possible analogy that is relevant (*insidād bāb al-raʾy*). It is rejected, that is, only as a last resort (*lā yutrak illā bi'l-ḍarūra*).[178] The Ḥanafīs find support for their preference of the unit-tradition to analogy and their rejection of the tradition of the nonjurist in the well-known practice of the early community.[179]

The standard example of a tradition rejected on the grounds of its incompatibility with analogy is the *ḥadīth* of the *muṣarrāh* reported by Abū Hurayra (d. 58/678). The *muṣarrāh* is a she-camel, ewe, or she-goat whose udders have been tied until they swell and give the appearance that the animal is rich in milk. It can thus fetch a higher price

175. Qarāfī, p. 387. *Iḥkām*, 7:54 (Qāḍī Abū 'l-Faraj and Abū Bakr al-Abharī were the first among those who accepted unit-traditions to hold this), 8:45; Ibn Qayyim al-Jawziyya, *Iʿlām al-muwaqqiʿīn ʿan rabb al-ʿālamīn*, ed. Ṭāhā ʿAbd al-Raʾūf. 4 vols. (Cairo: Maktabat al-Kulliyyāt al-Azhariyya, 1388/1968), 1:469. Abū 'l-Muẓaffar al-Samʿānī questioned its attribution to someone the stature of Mālik (Bukhārī, 2:347).

176. Sarakhsī, 1:339; Bazdawī, 2:378.

177. Bukhārī, 3:55; *Musawwada*, p. 281; *Iḥkām*, 2:86.

178. Bazdawī, 2:379.

179. Sarakhsī, 1:340.

on the market. The tradition that condemns this deceptive practice lays down that "the buyer has the option after he has milked the animal of keeping it, if he is pleased with it, or, if displeased, of returning it with a *ṣāᶜ* of dates." The stipulation of a *ṣāᶜ* of dates is incompatible with legal analogy, for compensation for fungibles is the equivalent in kind and for nonfungibles the monetary value. How then can a *ṣāᶜ* of dates compensate for the consumed milk? Abū Hurayra is not one of those who are known for legal skill, and the tradition is rejected. The point is clearly made that this implies no belittling of the reporter.[180]

The position we have just outlined is that of ᶜĪsā ibn Abān, who was followed by Abū Zayd al-Dabūsī (d. 432/1041) and most of the moderns, among whom Fakhr al-Islām al-Bazdawī was the most prominent example.[181] We know that ᶜĪsā was in fact charged with spreading a slanderous tradition on the authority of ᶜAlī that Abū Hurayra was one of the thirty Antichrists who were to come out of the Islamic community.[182] Thus ᶜĪsā's distinction between jurists and nonjurists among the Companions was for some an invidious one.[183]

There was another Ḥanafī position of importance that held that the unit-tradition was to be preferred to analogy in all cases. This is the position of Abū 'l-Ḥasan al-Karkhī. It, too, had its prominent followers. It was the teaching of Abū 'l-Yusr al-Bazdawī and of his student ᶜAlaʾ al-Dīn al-Samarqandī.[184] They claimed that the distinction based on the juridical competence of the reporter was a new one for which there was no support in the teachings of the early masters. Abū Yūsuf is even supposed to have accepted the tradition of the *muṣarrāh*.[185]

The argument of these scholars is that the probity and exactitude of the reporter were a sufficient guarantee of his faithful reproduction of the tradition. His familiarity with the Arabic language ruled out the possibility of misapprehension on his part, and his probity excluded the possibility of his having altered a tradition in such a way as to add to or subtract from its meaning. Thus here, as in the case of the *mursal*, the principle of the sufficiency of probity is one of ruthless simplification, impatient with the fine distinctions of ᶜĪsā ibn Abān. But those who held this simpler doctrine were not thereby bound to accept the *ḥadīth* of the *muṣarrāh* or other traditions that fell into the same category. These traditions, they claimed, had been generally rejected by the school not

---

180. Bukhārī, 2:380; Bājī, p. 89 (*al-muḥaffala*). Al-Jaṣṣāṣ regarded the tradition as inconsistent with the Qurʾānic prohibition of usury (Jaṣṣāṣ, f. 187a).

181. Bukhārī, 2:383.

182. Jaṣṣāṣ, f. 180b.

183. Bukhārī, 2:382.

184. Bukhārī, 2:383; *Mīzān*, f. 114a,b.

185. Bukhārī; 2:382. This may be another instance of a split between Abū Yūsuf and al-Shaybānī, who is supposed to have taken ᶜĪsā ibn Abān's position in disputation with al-Shāfiᶜī (Ibn Qayyim al-Jawziyya, *Mukhtaṣar al-ṣawāᶜiq*, p. 526) and Abū ᶜUbayda (Kaᶜbī, *Qabūl al-akhbār*, f. 29b).

because of a shortcoming in the reporter but because they conflicted with the text of the Qurʾān or authentic traditions.[186]

The second set of criteria against which a tradition must be tested is of a different sort. These criteria are based on reason and are Muʿtazilī in principle. That they were not accepted by the mainstream of the Muʿtazilīs is a further example of the line that divides even those Ḥanafīs who were most closely linked with the Muʿtazilī movement from the rest of their theological colleagues. Failure to satisfy these criteria is tantamount to discontinuity.

The first doctrine to be considered holds that when there is a general need for a legal rule (*mā yaʿumm bihi al-balwā*), that rule will be transmitted at least at the level of a *mashhūr* tradition. This means that a unit-tradition that purports to regulate matters of this sort is to be rejected either as abrogated (*mansūkh*) or as having been subject to a lapse (*sahw*) in transmission.[187] Thus the transmitters are not accused of outright fabrication, but merely of being insufficiently informed or attentive. The basis for this doctrine is the Prophet's obligation to spread his message, as attested to by the Qurʾān. From this, one reasons that the Prophet would not allow his nation to violate the law regularly through ignorance. The Prophet is thus bound to see to it that the rules for the main institutions of law reach an adequate audience, who in turn will transmit the Prophet's directives on a broad scale. Two steps, then, are involved in the working out of the doctrine. The first deduces from the Prophet's overall obligation to promulgate the revelation his obligation to set a multitude on the right path (*tawqīf*). Barring some calamity, this multitude will transmit the prophetic teaching to another multitude and so forth. This we know by common experience.[188] There was also a version of the argument that mitigated its Muʿtazilī character. The initiative is now that of the people. Instead of the Prophet being under an obligation of promulgation, the people will necessarily inquire as to the rules regulating such common actions.[189]

The other criterion in this category is related to that of the foregoing doctrine. It holds that when there was a controversy on a point of law among the Companions, the transmission of a tradition regulating the controverted question must be at least at the level of the *mashhūr*. In such a case, the Companions who knew of the pertinent tradition would necessarily cite it to terminate the speculations of their fellows; it is inconceivable that they would conceal it (*kitmān*). Put forth in this atmosphere of public controversy, the tradition would be assured an adequate transmission.[190]

186. Bukhārī, 2:383.

187. Sarakhsī, 1:368; Jaṣṣāṣ, f. 187a.

188. *ʿUdda*, ff. 131b–132a; *Manār*, p. 648 (criticizing the force of the second step).

189. Qarāfī, p. 372; Shihab al-Dīn Maḥmūd ibn Aḥmad al-Zanjānī, *Takhrīj al-furūʿ ʿalā al-uṣūl*, ed. Muḥammad Adīb Ṣāliḥ (Damascus: Maṭbaʿat Jāmiʿat Dimashq, 1382/1962), p. 16.

190. Sarakhsī, 1:369–70; Bukhārī, 3:18–20.

The *balwā* ("public need") doctrine was the dominant one among the Ḥanafīs and won the support of the Muʿtazilī Abū ʿAbd Allāh al-Baṣrī (d. 369/970), a close associate of al-Karkhī, but it was not universally held by them.[191] Those masters who rejected the *balwā* doctrine and the related doctrine of publicity following controversy were not forced to accept the traditions that their colleagues spurned. These traditions they, too, rejected on the ground that they were in conflict with traditions whose validity was better established.[192]

We have observed the sharp distinction the Muʿtazilīs made between knowledge (*ʿilm*) and action (*ʿamal*). Action could be based on presumption, but knowledge depended on certainty. Basing themselves on this distinction, the Muʿtazilīs accepted a criticism of traditions that was perhaps the origin of the Ḥanafī doctrines we have been examining. Their criticism recognized a category of unit-reports that the hearer could know to be false by their very content. These were traditions reported in a "private" (*khafī*) manner that ought to have been reported publicly (*ẓāhir*). Such traditions are by this very fact known to be false. This is the case only when the subject of the report is public and there are secular or religious motives or both leading to its transmission. Examples are the foundations (*uṣūl*) of religion, where the motives are purely religious, public events such as court cases, where the motives are secular, and miracles, where both sorts of motives are at work.[193] What we have here is the *balwā* doctrine before the Ḥanafīs extended it to law.

The Muʿtazilī argument holds that where we are held accountable to know something, the Prophet will have ensured the adequate promulgation of this information. Otherwise there would exist an obligation impossible to fulfill. "It is not possible that the Prophet impose upon us the obligation to know something without giving us a path to knowledge. But the unit-tradition is not a path to knowledge."[194] The Ḥanafīs had a different view of religious action from that of the Muʿtazilīs. For them it had an objective basis in the will of God. It was for this reason that they went beyond the Muʿtazilīs and demanded that traditions regulating the key elements of religious action be subject to the same rigorous standards as traditions that were the basis of knowledge. The matters to which the Ḥanafī version of the doctrine applied were precisely those that both "scholars and common people needed to know in order to act" (*yaḥtāj al-khāṣṣ wa'l-ʿāmm ilā maʿrifatihi li'l-ʿamal bihi*).[195]

191. *Irshād*, p. 56.

192. Bukhārī, 3:19.

193. *Muʿtamad*, 2:547–48. The principle at issue is significant in the polemic between Sunnism and Shiʿism (*ʿUdda*, f. 132b; Ṭūsī, p. 39).

194. *Muʿtamad*, 2:659.

195. Sarakhsī, 1:368. The doctrine in its full scope is found in al-Kaʿbī, *Kitāb Qabūl al-akhbār*, f. 2a: "And you also know that in the agreed-upon principles of theology only concurrent traditions are accepted in which there is no need for *isnāds* or N. from N. Similarly in common matters for which most have need

Summary

Rooted in an historical revelation, Islamic law requires criteria by which to judge the authenticity of its material sources, the Qurʾān and *sunna*. The authenticity of the Qurʾān and some part of the *sunna* is guaranteed by their widespread and unbroken transmission. These sources are *mutawātir*. As to the non-*mutawātir* traditions, there is disagreement whether they must be of absolutely certain authenticity in order to serve as binding legal norms. Those who required certainty were themselves divided as to whether it could be found outside of what was *mutawātir*. Generally, however, certainty was not required; a valid norm could be based on traditions of only probable authenticity, unit-traditions. For the Ḥanafīs there is an intermediate category, which is the standard for those traditions that purport to regulate matters of general concern. They must be *mashhūr*. This is a less rigorous version of the requirement that all binding traditions be of absolute certainty and like it, is founded on theological postulates. Because they imposed such rigid standards for the content of traditions, the Ḥanafīs were able to adopt relatively lenient requirements with respect to the chain of transmitters.

Addenda to Chapter One

Recent years have witnessed a dramatic increase in English-language philosophical writing on the epistemology of testimony, a subject that had fallen into great neglect. The turning point appears to have come with the study of the Australian philosopher C. A. J. Coady, *Testimony: A Philosophical Study* (Oxford: Clarendon, 1992). Not long thereafter appeared the volume *Knowing from Words: Western and Indian Philosophical Analysis of Understanding and Testimony*, ed. Bimal Krishna Matilal and Arindan Chakrabarti (Dordrecht: Kluwer Academic, 1994). Testimony as a source of knowledge is currently receiving enormous attention from philosophers. Their work represents a sharp shift away from the individualism that long dominated the theory of knowledge toward what has come to be called social epistemology. On the question of how we come to acquire knowledge from listening to what others tell us, there are two competing approaches: reductivism, following Hume, seeks to explain reliance on testimony as ultimately warranted by non-testimonial experiences; anti-reductivism follows in the footsteps of Thomas Reid and regards testimony as an independent source of knowledge. Both approaches can be discerned in the extensive Islamic writings on the topic, although study of these is still in its infancy. Those working on testimony as a source of knowledge in its Islamic context, *kalām*, *uṣūl al-fiqh*, *ḥadīth*, and the law of evidence, to name only the most salient areas, will want to avail themselves of this philosophical literature.

---

only the tradition of a multitude (*khabar al-jamāʿa*) and the practice of the nation is accepted, for the fame of what the Prophet says corresponds to the need (*ḥāja*) for it."

In *uṣūl al-fiqh* and even more obviously in *kalām* the great dividing line is between *mutāwatir* and *āḥād* reports. The notion of *tawātur* that we encounter in classical *uṣūl al-fiqh* represents the confluence of a number of disparate concerns, and it in turn served to generate further developments beyond legal theory proper in the study of both the Qur'ān and *ḥadīth*. Despite its appearance of inevitability *tawātur* has a long and complex history that has yet to be examined in detail. Moreover, the apparent simplicity of the classic version of *tawātur* is deceptive; its logic managed to elude some of the greatest *ḥadīth* scholars.

P. 8

Hüseyin Hansu, "Notes on the Term *Mutawātir* and Its Reception in *Ḥadīth* Criticism," *Islamic Law and Society* 16 (2009): 383–408, is a broader discussion than its title might suggest.

P. 9

More needs to be said about *tawātur* in relation to the Qur'ān. See now Shady Hekmat Nasser, *The Transmission of the Variant Readings of the Qur'ān: The Problem of Tawātur and the Emergence of Shawādhdh* (Leiden: Brill, forthcoming, based on his 2011 Harvard University doctoral dissertation).

P. 17

On ʿĪsā ibn Abān, see Murteza Bedir, "An Early Response to Shāfiʿī: ʿĪsā b. Abān on the Prophetic Report (*khabar*)," *Islamic Law and Society* 9 (2002): 285–311.

P. 23, n. 89

Jonathan A. C. Brown, "Did the Prophet Say It or Not? The Literal, Historical, and Effective Truth of *Ḥadīths* in Early Sunnism," *Journal of the American Oriental Society* 129 (2009): 259–85, has argued that early *ḥadīth* scholars worked with a notion of historical, not literal, truth and believed that they could attain such historical truth via *ṣaḥīḥ* traditions. In this their approach is at odds with that of the legal theorists, whose focus on literal truth is to be traced back to Greek thought. Brown's conclusions and premises sharply contrast with those of the Saudi *ḥadīth* scholar al-Sharīf Ḥātim ibn ʿĀrif al-ʿAwnī in his *al-Yaqīnī wa'l-ẓannī min al-akhbār: sijāl bayna al-imām Abī 'l-Ḥasan al-Ashʿarī wa'l-muḥaddithīn* (Beirut: al-Shabaka al-ʿArabiyya li'l-Abḥāth wa'l-Nashr, 1432/2011), 71–108. In connection with Ibn al-Ṣalāḥ's famous claim of certainty for the collections of al-Bukhārī and Muslim, see now Jonathan Brown, *The Canonization of al-Bukhārī and Muslim: The Formation and Function of the Sunnī Ḥadīth Canon* (Leiden: Brill, 2007), 178–204, 252–55.

Pp. 25–26

On the Muʿtazilīs and *ḥadīth*, see Hüseyin Hansu, *Mutazile ve hadis* (Kızılay, Ankara: Kitâbiyât, 2004) and Racha El-Omari, "Accommodation and Resistance: Classical

Muᶜtazilites on *Ḥadīth*," *Journal of Near Eastern Studies* 71 (2012): 231–56 (mainly on al-Kaᶜbī's *Qabūl al-akhbâr*).

P. 32

Among al-Qāsānī's arguments against unit-traditions was that they were too dispersed to provide a stable basis for analogy (Muḥammad ibn ᶜAlī al-Māzarī, *Īḍāḥ al-maḥṣūl min Burhān al-uṣūl*, ed. ᶜAmmār al-Ṭālibī [Beirut: Dār al-Gharb al-Islāmī, 2001], 448–49). The extent of his acceptance of analogy was variously reported (al-Zarkashī, *al-Baḥr al-muḥīṭ*, ed. ᶜAbd al-Qādir ᶜAbd Allāh al-ᶜĀnī [Kuwait: Wizārat al-Awqāf, 1413/1992], 5:17–21).

P. 34

I suggest "unsupported" as a better translation for *mursal* as it captures the opposition with *musnad* ("supported") "Unsupported" might also serve for *maṣlaḥa mursala.*

P. 41

A collection of examples of Ḥanafī inconsistency in the treatment of *mursal* traditions can be found in the surviving parts of Ibn Ḥazm, *al-Iᶜrāb ᶜan al-ḥayra wa'l-iltibās al-mawjūdayn fī madhāhib al-ra'y wa'l-qiyās*, ed. Muḥammad ibn Zayn al-ᶜĀbidīn Rustam (Riyadh: Aḍwāʾ al-Salaf, 1425/2005), 1:309–53.

2

INTERPRETATION

I. The Nature of Islamic Hermeneutics

Generally speaking, the *uṣūlīs* were interested in putting forth a system of interpretation acceptable to a rational man, one consonant with the workings of language as known from common experience. In some instances there is found a distinct interest to discover the interpretative principles that had guided the earlier jurists, and where explicit statements were lacking, as was often the case, these principles had to be induced from the legal cases. The fidelity with which these principles were adhered to depended upon the individual *uṣūlī* and the tradition within which he worked. What was not done, however, was to defend principles of interpretation on the basis of the legal authority of their proponent. Authority in the language of the Arabs was a different matter, and clearly one's master could be and perhaps had to be an authority in language as well as law. To the extent that the *uṣūl* works do deal with the methodology and technical terms of the early jurists, they can serve to direct further research. But one must not expect to find fully documented histories of these subjects.

The principles of hermeneutics expounded in the *uṣūl* texts are at one and the same time both wider and narrower than the sacred texts of Islam. On the one hand, *uṣūl* hermeneutics is not specifically scriptural but rather encompasses legal discourse in general. The mainstream *uṣūl* tradition approaches the Qurʾān and *ḥadīth* as specimens of Arabic prose; they do, it is true, represent that language at its most eloquent but do not break with its normal usages. To this extent, the work of the *uṣūlī* presupposes the results of the inquiries of the lexicographers and grammarians. Where necessary he can fill in the gaps they have left.[1] The Ḥanafīs in particular show a tendency to illustrate their principles of interpretation with the analysis of such nonsacred utterances as vows

1. Sarakhsī, 1:220. Abū 'l-Ḥusayn al-Baṣrī regarded mastery of the linguistic portions of *uṣūl al-fiqh* as sufficient for the requirements of *ijtihād* (al-Amīr al-Ṣanʿānī, *Irshād al-nuqqād ilā taysīr al-ijtihād*. In

and formulae of divorce and manumission. Such expressions, like the sacred texts, had been the object of the closest scrutiny and were thus especially suited to serve as models of interpretative practice. Although it is proper to regard the hermeneutics of the *uṣūl* as legal, this qualification must be taken in the broadest sense, in the sense in which the Qurʾān is, for the medieval Muslim scholar, primarily a legal document, one instituting a new legal order. It would be a grave error, however, to automatically associate the canons of interpretation with strictly legal questions. There is unmistakable evidence that a number of central issues were originally and most forcefully raised in connection with subjects of theological concern, with questions such as the fate of the believer after death. Hermeneutics like the other parts of *uṣūl* doctrine was sensitive to considerations that are not legal in the narrow sense at all.

It cannot be too much emphasized that the rules of interpretation are presented as standing on their own. They emerge from the natural, automatic understanding of language that we all have. The task of the *uṣūlī* is to uncover the presuppositions of this understanding and to exhibit more or less systematically its subtle workings. This does not mean that attempts were not made to show that some of these principles were in fact part of the legal system, that they themselves were legal rules. But such attempts could never yield an adequate set of interpretative principles. The logic of the circumstances is such that a point must be reached at which some norms of the legal system are faced with nothing more than ordinary linguistic competence. The norms that control interpretation themselves need to be understood. Attempts were also made to infer principles of interpretation from reports about the early Muslims. Their understanding of the law was sure to be correct in as much as their mastery of the language of the revelation was secure. But these reports unfortunately lent themselves to conflicting interpretations. It could, moreover, be argued that the early Muslims had in some instances based their interpretations on particular circumstances and not merely upon the words of the revelation. Those who came later could not properly be held responsible for the knowledge of such special circumstances. They had to interpret the words as they were transmitted.[2] It is thus that the major principles of interpretation ultimately rest on the rational consideration of the use of language. The results of this consideration can then be confirmed by the sacred texts or the practice of the early community. The Prophet, it was asserted, had been sent to teach the Law and not the Arabic language.[3]

On the other side, it must be recognized that the sacred texts of Islam represent particular difficulties. Because the Qurʾān is "a deep ocean whose wonders never fail and whose marvels never cease," the *uṣūlī* must admit that his hermeneutics is inadequate

---

Majmūʿat al-rasāʾil al-munīriyya, ed. Muḥammad Munīr [Cairo: Idārat al-Ṭibāʿa al-Munīriyya, 1343 H. Vol. 1, pp. 1–47. Repr. Beirut: Dār al-Jīl, 1970], p. 23).

2. Jaṣṣāṣ, f. 17a.

3. *Mīzān*, f. 74b; *Muʿtamad*, 1:248, 2:912–13; Ṭūsī, p. 116.

to the task of exhausting the content of God's Word. He does not claim to offer a tool for comprehending the force of the Qurʾānic stories, parables, aphorisms, and homilies (*qiṣaṣ, amthāl, ḥikam, mawāʿiẓ*).[4] In so far as the inimitability (*iʿjāz*) of the Qurʾān rests upon such elements, it is to the study of rhetoric that the *uṣūlī* must turn for guidance. In this sense, the hermeneutics of the *uṣūl* is not capable of the task of interpreting the Qurʾān.[5] The traditions, too, have a density far beyond that of ordinary discourse. The Prophet was gifted with "pregnant speech" (*jawāmiʿ al-kalim*).

But even apart from these considerations, there are further difficulties. The new legal order was instituted over a considerable period of time, and it is almost universally admitted that instances of abrogation (*naskh*) were not infrequent. Moreover, the traditions from the Prophet are not available in a single readily identifiable collection. No jurist can claim to know all the traditions that may be relevant to a given topic. In short, the sacred texts are far from constituting an ideal code. This apparent inadequacy the formalist jurists were quick to turn to their advantage. Had the revealed texts assumed the form of a set of abstract, neatly articulated norms, then the claims of the materialists that the revelation was complete in itself would have been more plausible. In point of fact, however, the texts were often strikingly specific. This limitation on the part of the texts was not accidental. God could have issued an elegantly drafted code for the guidance of His subjects. Instead, He gave them a law that called upon them to exercise all their powers of reasoning. In this way the jurists are able to merit their special reward in the world to come and to assume their role of authority in this world. The very nature of the revealed legislation requires the hierarchy that preserves society. "As long as people are distinct, they are well off; but if they are equal, they perish."[6]

Within the scope of this chapter we cannot hope to give even a general account of the doctrine of interpretation of the Ḥanafīs, let alone that of the other schools. Rather, we shall focus on a number of key issues in the history of the hermeneutics of the *uṣūl*. To treat these issues in isolation demands a radical oversimplification of *uṣūl* doctrine. This doctrine is characterized by a remarkable subtlety, one which increasingly impresses the careful reader. The issues we shall touch upon are already fully articulated in the first great Ḥanafī *uṣūl* treatise that we possess, that of al-Jaṣṣāṣ, and are debated there at great length. We shall not be especially concerned to reproduce the arguments deployed, but shall concentrate on eliciting the presuppositions upon which these arguments rest, especially on the varying views of language that underlie the *uṣūl* discussions. Once again the problem of epistemology will be at the center, the question of certainty and uncertainty. In this connection, some of the issues related to the imperative mood (*ṣīghat al-amr*) and

4. Bukhārī, 1:26; Nasafī, 1:15.

5. On the other hand, Ibn Juzayy (d. 741/1340) argues for a greater role for *uṣūl al-fiqh* in the science of *tafsīr* (*Kitāb al-Tashīl*, 1:14). See also Ibrāhīm ibn Mūsā al-Shāṭibī, *al-Muwāfaqāt fī uṣūl al-aḥkām*, 3:248.

6. Bukhārī, 1:57.

special and general terms (*al-khāṣṣ wa'l-ʿāmm*) shall be examined, and directly connected with the latter, the topic of the specialization (*takhṣīṣ*) of general texts. The anomalous position of the school of Samarqand on these matters will be of special interest. In addition, two typical forms of legal argument will be discussed, the *argumentum a fortiori*, which the Ḥanafīs accept, and the *argumentum a contrario*, which they reject.

II. The Hermeneutical Apparatus

Before entering upon these particular issues, it will not be amiss to present a sketch of a standard Ḥanafī systematization of the principle technical terms of interpretation, one found in the works of Abū 'l-ʿUsr al-Bazdawī and al-Sarakhsī and taken up in the later texts of al-Nasafī and Ṣadr al-Sharīʿa al-Maḥbūbī. It must be acknowledged, however, that the basis for the classification gave the commentators much room for discussion. In the main we shall follow the scrupulous treatment of al-Bukhārī, the authoritative commentator of al-Bazdawī's text.

A useful guiding thread through the labyrinthine way ahead is provided by a rather simplistic division of the legal texts into four categories. The significance of this division should be immediately apparent. At the highest level stand those texts that are of both certain authenticity and certain reference (*qaṭʿī al-thubūt wa'l-dalāla*). In the second place come those texts that are of certain authenticity but only of presumptive reference (*qaṭʿī al-thubūt wa-ẓannī al-dalāla*). These texts find their converse in those that are of presumptive authenticity and certain reference (*ẓannī al-thubūt wa-qaṭʿī al-dalāla*). Finally, we have texts that are presumptive with respect to both authenticity and reference (*ẓannī al-thubūt wa-ẓannī al-dalāla*).[7] This classification is that of the legal sources once they have passed through the process of interpretation. It is the goal of interpretation to reduce the legal provisions of the revelation to the foregoing scheme. Action ordained by texts of the highest level is absolutely obligatory (*farḍ*), by texts of the second and third levels binding (*wājib*), and by those of the fourth level merely recommended (*sunna, mustaḥabb*).[8]

An important point to be noted is the difference between interpretation, that is, construction, and abrogation.[9] As long as the provisions of a text are not abrogated, any interpretation attaches directly to it. When a text of the Qurʾān is interpreted in accordance with a unit-tradition, it is the Qurʾānic text that supports the *wājib* qualifica-

7. A text is of certain reference when its sphere of application is so delimited as to exclude any possible ambiguity (*inqiṭāʿ al-iḥtimāl*) (Bukhārī, 1:84; *Manār*, p. 74; Ibn Taymiyya, *Rafʿ al-malām*, p. 41).

8. The distinction between the qualifications *farḍ* and *wājib* is characteristically Ḥanafī. A major consequence of the Samarqandī position on interpretation is an unprecedented enlargement of the *wājib* category (see n. 83, below).

9. The same term *naskh* was, however, used for both in the early period (Ibn Taymiyya, *Rafʿ al-malām*, p. 30).

tion of the action (*iḍāfat al-ḥukm ilā al-dalīl al-aqwā awlā*).[10] This follows from the postulate of the consistency of the law. The extent to which there may remain after interpretation unresolvable obscurities or inconsistencies is an interesting question.[11] Al-Samarqandī for one is prepared to admit the possibility of an irreducible conflict of norms (*taʿāruḍ*). All this means is that the law is not effective on this point, and because God is not obliged to reveal any particular law in the first place, there is nothing offensive to reason in a conflict of this sort.[12]

In attempting to reduce the sacred law to a coherent set of norms, the Muslim jurists had elaborated an extensive hermeneutical terminology. The classical *uṣūlī* as heir to this tradition was faced with the task of presenting these terms in an orderly fashion. This was a most delicate undertaking involving as it did a consideration of the terminology that had been employed within the particular school as well as without. Among the attempts made at systematization that which we shall now consider stands out. It represents an ambitious ordering of the Ḥanafī exegetical tradition and has no obvious parallel elsewhere in *uṣūl* literature.

That this attempt was not altogether successful need occasion no surprise. The fluidity in terminology was so great that no rigid scheme could do justice to the practice of the jurists. That the scheme was not conceptually elegant did not unduly trouble the *uṣūlī*s. The commentator al-Bukhārī rejects any simple theoretical underpinning for the system; it is, he observes, based on an exhaustive examination (*istiqrāʾ*) of the Qurʾānic text and by the justice it does to that text must it be judged.[13] A radically simpler scheme involving only two categories was derived from the Qurʾān itself: "It was He who sent down to you the Book of which there are perspicuous verses (*āyāt muḥkamāt*)—they are the substance of the Book—and others intricate (*mutashābihāt*)" (3:7). But this was rejected as being totally inadequate.[14] In any case, the scheme we are interested in, involving twenty terms, was much more manageable than that of one scholar who is cited as having elaborated a scheme with 768 divisions![15]

The twenty terms fall into four groups, the second of which includes eight terms, the other three groups four each.[16] Although the scheme purports to be a classification of the words and meaning (*al-naẓm wa'l-maʿnā*) of the Qurʾānic text, there is no reason to take this restriction very seriously: "It appears," notes one commentator, "that these divisions are not peculiar to the Book but hold for all of Arabic speech (*yajrī fī jamīʿ kalimāt*

10. Bukhārī, 1:44–45 (note the reservation); *Manār*, pp. 347–48; Abū Bakr ibn Masʿūd al-Kāsānī, *Badāʾiʿ al-ṣanāʾiʿ*, 1:88.

11. See Imām al-Ḥaramayn, quoted in *Irshād*, p. 168.

12. *Mīzān*, f. 91a.

13. Bukhārī, 1:28.

14. Nasafī, 1:15, margin; Bukhārī, 1:42. Cf. *Baḥr*, f. 55b.

15. *Manār*, p. 60.

16. Bazdawī, 1:28–29; Nasafī, 1:18.

al-ʿarab)."[17] One should also note that the frequent mention of a speaker (*mutakallim*) and listener (*sāmiʿ*) makes it clear that the spoken language is being focused upon. Speech is the primary (*aṣl*) means of communication for which writing is a substitute (*khalaf*). [18]

The first group of terms (*khāṣṣ, ʿāmm, mushtarak, muʾawwal*) considers words according to the nature of their denotation. A word that is special (*khāṣṣ*) refers to one thing only.[19] Proper names, Zayd, Bakr, are the models for this category. From the legal point of view, it is significant to note that numbers are special.[20] Moreover, grammatical structures can be special. Thus the dual is special, as is the imperative.[21] It is thus that some central problems of *uṣūl* hermeneutics relating to the imperative and prohibitive find their place under the heading of the special term.

A term is general (*ʿāmm*) when its denotation is unrestricted (*ghayr maḥṣūr*); it thus refers to an indefinite number of individuals.[22] A plural form with the article is general: the Muslims (*al-muslimūna*), the polytheists (*al-mushrikūna*). These are examples of words that are general by virtue of their structure (*ṣīgha*).[23] Other words are general by virtue of their meaning: the people (*al-qawm*), whoever (*man*), whatever (*mā*).[24]

A term that has two or more separate denotations is called "equivocal" (*mushtarak*). An equivocal term bears (*yaḥtamil*) these different, even opposite significations from its very introduction (*waḍʿ*). Its use for one of these significations depends on the intention (*irāda*) of the speaker. When one of the meanings that the term bears has been identified as the intended one, the term is said to be "interpreted" (*muʾawwal*).[25]

The second group of terms regards, not the single word as does the first category, but words in combination (*tarkīb*), in discourse (*khiṭāb*, *kalām* as opposed to *kalim*). It is a classification of degrees of distinctness (*wujūh al-bayān*).[26]

---

17. Nasafī, 1:19; Bukhārī, 1:23.

18. *Manār*, p. 349.

19. Bazdawī, 1:30; *Muʿtamad*, 1:251.

20. *Mīzān*, f. 65b.

21. Sarakhsī, 1:152; *Talwīḥ*, 1:168, margin; Nasafī, 1:33.

22. *Talwīḥ*, 1:163, margin. Aḥmad ibn Ḥanbal claimed to have learned the terms *khāṣṣ* and *ʿāmm* from al-Shāfiʿī (*Baḥr*, f. 121b). For Wāṣil ibn ʿAṭāʾ's use of the terms, see ʿAbd al-Jabbār, *Faḍl al-iʿtizāl*, p. 234.

23. Bukhārī, 1:31. The terms *hayʾa*, *ṣūra*, and *bināʾ* are synonymous (*Manār*, p. 51; Sarakhsī, 1:152).

24. *Mīzān*, f. 65a.

25. Sarakhsī, 1:126; Bazdawī, 1:38.

26. See *Encyclopaedia of Islam*, 2nd ed., s.v. "*bayān*." To the references there, add Abū Bakr al-Bāqillānī, *Nukat al-intiṣār li-naql al-Qurʾān*, ed. M. Z. Salām (Alexandria: Munshaʾat al-Maʿārif, 1971), pp. 256–72; Ibn Ḥazm, *al-Taqrīb li-ḥadd al-manṭiq wa'l-madkhal ilayhi bi'l-alfāẓ al-ʿāmmiyya wa'l-amthila al-fiqhiyya*, ed. Iḥsān ʿAbbās (Beirut: Dār Maktabat al-Ḥayāt, n.d.), pp. 4–5; Nabil Shehaby, "The Influence of Stoic Logic on al-Jaṣṣāṣ's Legal Theory," *The Cultural Context of Medieval Learning: Proceedings of the First International Colloquium on Philosophy, Science, and Theology in the Middle Ages, September 1970*, ed. John E. Murdoch and Edith D. Sylla. Boston Studies in the Philosophy of Science, 26 (Boston: D. Reidel, 1975), pp. 61–71. *Bayān* is a rather elusive term, about which at least something must be said. For al-Bukhārī, "what is meant by

This second group of terms consists of words that indicate clarity or obscurity. Those terms that indicate clarity refer to legal provisions that do not require clarification (*bayān*), or to use the scholastic terminology, the *bayān* that removes obscurity (*khafāʾ*) (*bayān al-tafsīr*) because they are already clear (*bayyin*) in themselves (*clara non sunt interpretanda, interpretatio cessat in claris*).[27] In those cases where some uncertainty (*iḥtimāl*) but no obscurity exists, it may be removed by a *bayān*, in a wider sense.[28]

Discourse (*kalām*) is "obvious" (*ẓāhir*) when its meaning is grasped by a speaker of the language immediately (*min ghayr taʾammul*) upon the mere hearing of the words (*bi-ṣīghatihi, bi-nafs al-samāʿ*).[29] Thus the verse "O you people, fear your Lord" (4:1) is obvious. Discourse that is "explicit" (*naṣṣ*) stands above that which is obvious by virtue of the explicit context (*qarīna nuṭqiyya*), which either preceding or following the discourse in question (*sibāq* or *siyāq*) indicates a particular intention (*qaṣd*) on the part of the speaker.[30] The discourse is explicit with respect to this intention.

Discourse that is "explained" (*mufassar*) is of greater clarity than that which is explicit. The explanation (*tafsīr*) spoken of may result from the elimination of any obscurities in the discourse that call for clarification or from the desire of the speaker to exclude certain uncertainties that remain in discourse that is otherwise clear. In a case of the first sort, the clarification (*bayān*) of what is obscure must be certain (*qaṭʿī*), or we are dealing with an interpretation (*taʾwīl*) not an explanation (*tafsīr*). In the second case, there is *bayān* for the sake of confirmation (*bayān al-taʾkīd waʾl-taqrīr*), not *bayān* in the sense of removing a real obscurity.[31] In the Qurʾānic verse "So the angels prostrated themselves, all of them together" (*fa-sajada al-malāʾikatu kulluhum ajmaʿūn*) (15:30), the term "angels" being general (*ʿāmm*), the possibility (*iḥtimāl*) is not excluded that not every angel is meant.

---

bayān is 'making the meaning clear' (*iẓhār al-maʿnā*) or its being clear (*ẓuhūr*) to the listener'" (Bukhārī, 1:27). We note at once that the term may be taken in both an intransitive and a transitive sense. But between the making clear and the clarity, there is the means of clarification, and the term is thus used in the Qurʾān: "This is an exposition (*bayān*) for mankind and a guidance and admonition for such as are godfearing" (3:138). Al-Shāfiʿī already observed that "*bayān* is a term that encompasses things that have a common basis but are much ramified." He further held that although there were degrees of *bayān* (distinctness), this diversity was merely a matter of intensity (*taʾkīd*) for those in whose tongue the Qurʾān had been revealed. It was all immediately accessible to them (*Risāla*, paras. 53, 54). This vague understanding of *bayān* was defended by the Shāfiʿī Abū 'l-Muẓaffar al-Samʿānī (d. 489/1095) against the criticism of Abū Bakr ibn Dāwūd al-Ẓāhirī (d. 297/909), who had found it more obscure than the word *bayān* itself (*Qawāṭiʿ*, f. 79a). See also *Ṭūsī*, pp. 152–53; *Mustaṣfā*, pp. 275–76. On the scholastic terminology of *bayān*, see Nasafī, 1:20, margin; al-Shāshī, *Uṣūl al-Shāshī* (Hyderabad, 1306), pp. 55–60.

27. Bazdawī, 1:39; Sarakhsī, 1:128.

28. *Manār*, pp. 68–69.

29. Sarakhsī, 1:163–64.

30. *Talwīḥ*, 1:409.

31. Bukhārī, 1:50; Sarakhsī, 1:49 (to be emended by reading *gharīban* for *ʿarabiyyan* in line 7 and striking out *lā* in line 8). On the opposition of *muʾawwal* and *mufassar*, see Bukhārī, 1:42–45.

This possibility is, however, excluded by the word *kulluhum* ("all of them"). There still remains the possibility that they prostrated themselves separately, but this is excluded by the word *ajmaʿūn* ("together"). The only possibility not excluded in discourse that is explained is that of abrogation (*naskh*). When that, too, is excluded, the discourse is termed "fixed" (*muḥkam*).[32]

The terms of this category mark claims made by the interpreter. The weaker the claim he puts forth, the greater the room he leaves for seeing his interpretation challenged. The strongest claim, that the discourse is fixed, means that the jurist will not accept any reading of the legal provision but his own and that his reading makes law since abrogation is excluded. Of course, in order to support his claim, the interpreter is bound to show how the relevant uncertainties are excluded.

To each of the four terms of clarity, *ẓāhir, naṣṣ, mufassar, muḥkam*, there corresponds a term of obscurity: "obscure" (*khafī*), "difficult" (*mushkil*), "indeterminate" (*mujmal*), and "unintelligible" (*mutashābih*). The primary focus here is on what procedure the interpreter has to follow in order to remove the obscurity. The greater the obscurity, the more demanding the task of the interpreter.[33]

In the first group of terms, words were classified from the point of view of their being coined for their denotation, neither speaker nor listener entering into consideration. In the second group, discourse was regarded from the point of view of the listener. Thus the *mujmal* expression, al-Samarqandī points out, "requires clarification (*bayān*) with respect to the listener although its meaning is known to the speaker."[34] In the third group, with which we are now concerned, the point of view is that of the speaker. It is his usage of language that is considered. From this aspect all of language is seen as falling under one of the two terms that dominate the group. For every expression (*lafẓ*) is used either in its proper sense (*ḥaqīqa*) or in a figurative one (*majāz*). In addition, a term, whether proper or extended, is either "direct" (*ṣarīḥ*) or "oblique" (*kināya*).

An expression is proper when used for that meaning for which it was originally introduced. A figurative expression is one used for some meaning other than that for which it was introduced. The introduction of a word for a meaning is taken in a wide sense, and three levels of usage are recognized (*al-iṣṭilāḥ alladhī waqaʿa al-takhāṭub bihi*): the linguistic (*lugha*), legal (*sharʿ*), and customary (*ʿurf*). It thus may happen that an expression that is proper at the legal level is figurative in relation to the meaning for which it was introduced (here coined) before the law was revealed.[35]

An expression is direct when its frequency of use is such that its meaning is of unmistakable clarity. It is oblique when what is intended is concealed. The meaning of the

32. Bazdawī, 1:50.
33. Bukhārī, 1:51–55.
34. *Mīzān*, ff. 90a–90b.
35. Sarakhsī, 1:170; Bazdawī, 1:62.

expression in itself is not what is intended, rather it points beyond itself. For example, a generous man is spoken of as being "of many ashes" (*kathīr al-ramād*); the great number of guests he entertains results in an accumulation of ashes in the cooking area.[36]

In the last group of terms we find not a classification of the Qurʾānic text itself, but of the ways in which the revealed text serves as the foundation for legal rules (*istidlāl*). The interpreter familiar with the distinctions identified in the preceding categories is able to draw out from the texts the rules they contain. Each term here indicates a procedure that can be employed in this process. The validity of the rules arrived at rests on the validity of the procedures that have been employed. The procedures grouped in this fourth classification have this in common, that they proceed from the language of the text (*al-naṣṣ*) and do not penetrate to the level of the reason (*maʿnā*) of the text. Analogy (*qiyās*) is thus excluded.[37] Each procedure is based on a different feature of the text: its plain expression (*ʿibāra*), its allusiveness (*ishāra*), its sense (*dalāla*), and its requirement (*iqtiḍāʾ*).

A rule that rests upon the plain expression of the text is one based upon the literal meaning of the text as gathered according to the hermeneutics we have been considering. A rule, however, may also be drawn from an allusion in the text. That the revealed texts can convey such allusions is an element of their stylistic superiority (*iʿjāz, jawāmiʿ al-kalim*).[38]

The sense of the text (*dalālat al-naṣṣ*) is the basis for the *argumentum a fortiori*. The classic example refers to Qurʾān 17:23 where it is forbidden to utter the contemptuous expression *uff* to one's parents. Upon the basis of the sense of this prohibition, it was ruled that striking one's parents was also forbidden.[39]

The requirement of the text (*iqtiḍāʾ*) is the legal background necessary for the text to take effect (*mā lam yaʿmal illā bi-sharṭ taqaddumihi ʿalayhi*). The standard example is the sale required before someone can free his slave in your name for a thousand (*dirhams*) (*iʿtiq ʿabdaka ʿannī bi-alf*).[40]

---

36. Nasafī, 1:247. The significance of the opposition is in the area of legal formulas. One that is *ṣarīḥ* is operative regardless of the speaker's intention.

37. Sarkhsi, 1:236 (chapter heading).

38. Sarakhsī, 1:241; Bukhārī, 1:69.

39. Sarakhsī, 1:241.

40. Bukhārī, 1:75. We find among some Ḥanafīs a further category in this group, that of the "ellipsis of the text" (*al-iḍmār, al-ḥadhf*). This is the case with al-Samarqandī, who is following his teacher Abū 'l-Yusr al-Bazdawī. Others refuse to distinguish between the requirement and the ellipsis of the text. The distinction would lie in the fact that the ellipsis is a linguistic, not a legal, phenomenon. An elliptical expression is to be so completed as to produce discourse that is correct (*taṣḥīḥ al-kalām*). The importance of the distinction rests upon the scope of the supplied ellipsis. The ellipsis, as a linguistic phenomenon, would be subject to the same classifications as other linguistic phenomena; most significantly it could be general (*ʿāmm*). It was just this feature of the ellipsis that led others to deny it a category of its own. Once restored, it is part of the plain expression (*ʿibāra*) of the text. See *Mīzān*. ff. 19a, 102b; Bukhārī, 1:76; *Manār*, p. 536.

Even the short sketch that we have presented of the Ḥanafī hermeneutical apparatus should be sufficient to show that it rests upon an impressive body of observations of the semantic and pragmatic aspects of language. In what follows we shall consider some of the postulates about language that are the foundation of Ḥanafī hermeneutics and then examine the role that these postulates have played in determining the mainstream Ḥanafī positions on a number of controversial issues.

III. The Linguistic Postulates

The classical Ḥanafī *uṣūl* doctrine stands out from that of other legal schools in the consistency with which it defends a view of language that permits confident, secure interpretation. In this respect it stands close to the doctrine of Ẓāhirīs such as Ibn Ḥazm and that of certain Ḥanbalīs such as Ibn Taymiyya. What all these systems of interpretation have in common is that they seek to explain the workings of language, or at least the language of the sacred texts, in such a way as to exclude uncertainty from the process of interpretation. As far as the Ḥanafīs are concerned, their optimism with respect to language appears to rest upon four postulates: 1. language is an adequate means of communication about the world outside and within man; 2. language is made up of distinct elements that correspond to significant distinctions in reality; 3. language is a system; 4. language is a public instrument. The use of each of these postulates will be illustrated in the discussion that follows, but let us say something more about them here.

Language is seen by the Ḥanafīs as a means of communicating information. This is its *raison d'être*. The postulate of the adequacy of language is put in these terms by al-Sarakhsī: "Expressions are adequate for intentions, and this adequacy is realized only when for each intention there exists a special expression."[41] There are enough expressions available for all human intentions because the unused phonetic combinations exceed those that are used. The more important a notion is, the more deserving it is of having its own expression.[42] Precisely because it is adequate, language is not indefinitely flexible. Words can indeed be used in extended senses, but such departures from the proper sense must be signalled. The intention of the speaker must be made tangible or it is beyond our grasp. Language is based on external appearances. It is a public medium, and private intentions must adjust themselves to this medium if they are to be communicated. In this respect language is like the law, which is also based on externals.[43]

Moreover, language has its own particular way of corresponding to reality. It is characterized by an inner order, an order that it is the task of the grammarian to display.[44]

41. Sarakhsī, 1:12; Nasafī, 1:35.
42. Sarakhsī, 1:16.
43. Sarakhsī, 1:140.
44. Abū 'l-Qāsim al-Zajjājī, *al-Īḍāḥ fī ʿilal al-naḥw*, ed. Māzin Mubārak (Cairo: Dār al-ʿUrūba, 1378/1959),

For this reason, one test of whether a word is used in its proper rather than extended sense is that it exhibits the normal range of morphological patterns.[45] What is true of one part of the verbal system, for example, may be presumed to be true of the others.[46] The way in which language is adapted to its end and its inner harmony are, for the Ḥanafīs, evidence of the rationality of its inventor.[47] It was in a human language that the Lawgiver addressed mankind, and it is the ordinary canons of interpretation which must be applied to understanding the sacred texts (*ṣāḥib al-sharᶜ khāṭabanā bi-lisān al-ᶜarab fa-innamā yufham min khiṭāb al-sharᶜ mā yufham min mukhāṭabāt al-nās fīmā baynahum*).[48]

It follows from the postulates that we have just considered that the principal features of language correspond to significant human intentions and that the linguistic forms that signal these intentions are not to be taken in another sense without adequate justification. The mere possibility (*iḥtimāl*) that the speaker has intended a common linguistic form to be the sign for a private intention is of no consequence in the absence of some substantial indication of this intention. A valid interpretation of discourse cannot be expected to go beyond the evidence. In this respect, the Ḥanafī position on interpretation may be seen to represent a clinging to the *ẓāhir* of the text, its apparent meaning, and historically the Ḥanafīs were partisans of the natural reading of the texts against those who claimed to be pursuing a more sophisticated analysis of language.

We shall consider two areas of controversy, which in fact present similar problems, as the *uṣūlīs* were well aware.[49] The issues may be formulated in simple terms: in the Qurᵓān we find the imperative form used for a variety of functions; similarly we find general terms that are known from other sources to be intended for only a part of their denotation. What then is the force of an imperative when there are no specific indications of how it is to be taken? How sure can we be that a general term is meant to include everything to which the term can be applied? It should be readily appreciated that the two controversies, that of the imperative mood (*ṣīghat al-amr*) and the general term (*ᶜāmm*) are of central importance to the law. For with the imperative is connected the binding force of the law and with the general term its range of application.

Neither of these issues can be fully treated here for both are of considerable complexity. The imperative form is, as we have seen, classified as a special term (*khāṣṣ*). But

---

p. 41 (*al-naḥw ᶜilm qiyāsī*); Abū ᾿l-Barakāt ibn al-Anbārī, *Lumaᶜ al-adilla fī uṣūl al-naḥw*, ed. A. Amer (Stockholm: Almqvist & Wiksell, 1963), p. 44 (*al-naḥw kulluhu qiyās*).

45. Sarakhsī, 1:12.

46. Sarakhsī, 1:20.

47. On the intriguing debate as to the origin of language, see the recent discussion in C. H. M. Versteegh, *Greek Elements in Arabic Linguistic Thinking* (Leiden: Brill, 1977), pp. 162–77. The role of the issue in *uṣūl al-fiqh* is obscure (*Mustaṣfā*, p. 261; *Baḥr*, f. 61a; *Jamᶜ*, 1:269). The Ḥanafī texts allow for either divine or human invention (e.g., *Mīzān*, f. 97a).

48. Sarakhsī, 1:141.

49. *Musawwada*, p. 12; *Baḥr*, f. 128b.

because the imperative refers to action, it is necessary to determine what reference if any the imperative contains to the time in which the particular action is to be performed (*adāʾ*), how often it is to be performed, what action is called for in the case of a failure to discharge the primary obligation (*qaḍāʾ*), to what extent performance of the action represents a discharge of the original obligation. In addition, the Ḥanafīs discuss the question of the ethical qualities of the act that may be known to follow from its being commanded. Together with the general term is raised the delicate interplay of texts that falls under the head of the specialization of the general term (*takhṣīṣ al-ʿāmm*). Their safeguarding of the force of the general term is the main pillar of Ḥanafī hermeneutics.

IV. The Imperative

1. *The Deontological Value of the Imperative*

"It is most fitting," writes Imām al-Sarakhsī, "that we begin with the imperative and prohibition because the greatest part of our trial (*ibtilāʾ*) results from them, and through knowledge of them knowledge of the law is complete, and what is lawful is distinguished from what is prohibited."[50] For al-Sarakhsī, knowledge of *uṣūl al-fiqh* is meant to guide the student in his understanding of the works of *furūʿ* and the importance of the imperative was such that it deserved to be treated first.[51] The approach is that of the interpreter of the legal texts and may be contrasted with that of al-Ghazālī. For the Ashʿarī al-Ghazālī, the focus is on the qualification of the action (*ḥukm*), and because these qualifications are conveyed by numerous linguistic forms, a rational presentation of the *uṣūl* demands that the qualifications be treated in their own right and only subsequently the linguistic forms by which they are conveyed.[52]

The command (*amr*) for the Ḥanafīs is the imperative form (*ṣīghat al-amr*) accompanied by an attitude of superiority (*istiʿlāʾ*). The attitude of superiority distinguished the use of the same linguistic form in request (*iltimās*) where there is equality (*tasāwī*) between the speaker and the addressee, and petition (*suʾāl, duʿāʾ*) where the speaker assumes an attitude of inferiority (*khuḍūʿ, taḍarruʿ*).[53] The linguistic form in question is exemplified by *ifʿal*, etc. for the second person and *li-yafʿal*, etc. for the third.[54] The imperative for the majority of the Ḥanafīs creates an obligation (*wujūb*) to perform the act that is ordered. Obligation is the consequence (*ḥukm, mūjab, muqtaḍā*) of the imperative.[55] More than that, the imperative is the only linguistic form available for imposing an obligation.

50. Sarakhsī, 1:11.
51. Sarakhsī, 1:10.
52. *Mustaṣfā*, pp. 16–17.
53. *Manār*, p. 108; Ṭūsī, p. 65.
54. *Manār*, p. 109.
55. Nasafī, 1:37.

A statement such as "I have imposed such and such upon you" (*awjabtu ʿalayka*) requires the understanding of an imperative in order to have force.[56] This definition explains why an inferior should not assume the attitude of one in authority and give commands. In such a case he is liable to the charge of stupidity and bad manners. Having no authority, he is guilty of abusing the linguistic institution.[57]

In addition to these two elements of a particular linguistic form and a particular attitude on the part of the speaker, the Basran Muʿtazilī analysis of the imperative included one or more elements of intentionality. The most important intention required was that the speaker desire that the addressee perform the action.[58] This was rejected by the orthodox theologians because for them God's will (*irāda*) is always effective. Since not all of God's commandments are obeyed, we may gather that He sometimes does not will what He commands.[59] This issue is significant in that it illustrates how important theological controversies have a curious way of losing their edge in the actual practice of interpretation. The fact is that the linguistic form of the imperative for the Muʿtazila is itself the evidence of the intention which they posit.[60] The question then is one of the explanation of the command and not its recognition, for here Sunnis and Muʿtazilīs agree. As an issue in the hermeneutics of the sacred texts, the dispute is irrelevant.[61]

The relation between authority, command, and obligation is explained in these simple terms by *Uṣūl al-Shāshī*:

> Disobedience with respect to the Law is the cause of punishment. The explanation (*taḥqīq*) of this is that the obligation of obedience corresponds to the authority (*wilāya*) of the one giving the command over the one addressed. For this reason if you direct the imperative form towards one who does not owe you any obedience this will not impose an obligation. But if you direct it at some slave who owes you obedience, he will definitely be bound to obey you so that if he willingly neglects the obligation, he merits punishment according to both common opinion and the Law (*ʿurfan wa-shar ʿan*). Thus we know that the obligation of obedience is in accord with the one who gives the command. This much being established, we say that God has complete dominion (*milk kāmil*) over every

56. *Manār*, p. 127.

57. *Manār*, p. 109; *Muʿtamad*, 1:49.

58. *Muʿtamad*, 1:50–56; Ibn Taymiyya, *Bayān muwāfaqat ṣarīḥ al-maʿqūl li-ṣaḥīḥ al-manqūl*, 2:55 (from the *Taʿlīq fī uṣūl al-fiqh* of Abū Ḥāmid al-Isfarāyīnī).

59. *Mustaṣfā*, p. 292.

60. *Muʿtamad*, 1:80. For this reason, Ibn Mattawayh does not mention *irāda* in his definition of the command (*al-Tadhkira fī aḥkām al-jawāhir wa'l-aʿrāḍ*, ed. S. N. Lutf and F. B. ʿAwn [Cairo: Dār al-Thaqāfa, 1975], p. 384). See also the following Shiʿi texts: 180 *Dharīʿa*, 1:50–52; Ṭūsī, pp. 65–66; Muṣṭafā al-Iʿtimādi, *Sharḥ Maʿālim al-dīn*, pp. 16–17; al-ʿAllāma al-Ḥillī, *Mabādiʾ al-wuṣūl ilā ʿilm al-uṣūl*, ed. ʿAbd al-Ḥusayn Muḥammad ʿAlī ibn Yūsuf al-Baqqāl (Najaf: Maṭbaʿat al-Ādāb, 1390/1970), pp. 90–91.

61. Or almost so. See the discussion of Abū Hāshim al-Jubbāʾī, below.

> part of the world and can do with it as He pleases. Now if it is established that disobedience of one who has limited dominion (*milk qāṣir*) over a slave is the cause of punishment, what do you think about disobeying the command of the one who brought you into being from nothingness and rained showers of benefits upon you?[62]

The Ḥanafī jurists offer a variety of arguments for their view that the command imposes strict obligation. In the first place, they cite Qurʾānic verses that either illustrate the force of the command in God's acts of creation or threaten those who disobey His command:

> And our word unto a thing when we intend it is only that we say unto it—Be! and it is. (16:40) And of His signs is this: the heavens and the earth stand fast by His command. (30:25) So let those who go against His command beware lest a trial befall them or there befall them a painful chastisement. (24:36) It is not for any believer, man or woman, when God and His Messenger have decreed a matter, to have the choice in the affair. (33:36)[63]

From our point of view, however, more interesting are the arguments characterized as that from consensus (*dalālat al-ijmāʿ*) and from reason (*dalālat al-maʿqūl*). The consensus in this case does not refer to a fact of legal history but to a feature of the pragmatics of language.[64] A speaker wishing to demand some action has no other means available than to issue a command. The consensus of reasonable men (*al-ʿuqalāʾ*) on this matter does not explicitly endorse the Ḥanafī claim but does lend it support.[65]

The rational argument proceeds from the nature of language. In the first place, the imperative is one of the parts of the verbal conjugation (*taṣārīf al-afʿāl*). The postulate of the adequacy of language is fulfilled only if to the imperative there is attached a particular meaning. The notion of obligation (*ījāb*) is so important as to demand a particular linguistic expression. This is the imperative. The imperative thus takes its place beside the past and present tenses, each of which has only a single primary time reference. In this respect, the integral structure of the verbal system is maintained.[66]

Furthermore the verb "command" (*amara*) is transitive and demands an intransitive counterpart "being commanded" (*iʾtamara*), just as the verb "break" (*kasara*) has as its counterpart "to be broken" (*inkasara*). When one breaks something, that something is broken. True "being commanded" would consist of something taking place, but if God's commands were always followed by obedience, then there would be no room for human

62. *Uṣūl al-Shāshī*, p. 29.
63. Sarakhsī, 1:18.
64. Cf. Nasafī, 1:39, margin; *Manār*, p. 126.
65. Bazdawī, 1:116.
66. Bazdawī, 1:117; Nasafī, 1:41.

freedom and thus no legal responsibility. The consequence of the command is for this reason shifted from external reality to that of the consciousness of obligation, which can lead to the performance of what is commanded.[67] In the same way, the prohibition does not lead to the nonexistence of what is prohibited but to a negative obligation.[68] All this is not to deny that the imperative, like the other verbal forms, may be used in other senses as well. But when this happens, there must be an indication (*dalīl*) that this is the case. The imperative by itself (*muṭlaq al-amr*) imposes obligation.

Enough has been said here to indicate how the postulates about language function in the argument of the Ḥanafī *uṣūlīs*. Of all the various senses in which the imperative is used, one must be its primary signification. Pragmatic, semantic, and theological considerations show that this signification is that of obligation. The position here attributed to the Ḥanafīs was, as might be expected, shared by a considerable body of Muslim jurists of all affiliations. In what follows we shall examine some positions that question the identification of the imperative with obligation and that, seen together, are evidence of a significant trend towards linguistic scepticism.

At the basis of this scepticism lies the fact that the imperative is used in a wide variety of significations. There was in fact an inclination that proved difficult to resist to come up with longer and longer lists of such usages.[69] Thus we find the imperative form used for what is a recommended act (*nadb*): "Those your right hands own who seek emancipation, contract with them (*kātibūhum*) accordingly, if you know some good in them" (24:33); for guidance in this life (*īrshād*): "And take witnesses when you are trafficking one with another" (2:282); for permission: "Eat what they (animals trained to hunt) catch for you" (5:4); to express powerlessness (*taʿjīz*): "Bring a verse like it!" (2:23).[70]

67. Bukhārī, 1:117; Nasafī, 1:41.

68. Nasafī, 1:141.

69. Sarakhsī, 1:14, lists seven uses; Bukhārī, 1:107, has eighteen; *Jamʿ*, 1:372, has twenty-six. This tendency to find more and more uses is already criticized by al-Ghazālī as stemming from a craving for embellishment (*Mustaṣfā*, p. 294). One may also see here a desire to document the wonders of Qurʾānic style.

70. Sarakhsī, 1:14; Bukhārī, 1:107; *Mankhūl*, pp. 132–33. It should be noted that *ırshad* (*al-irshād ilā al-awthaq* for Sarakhsī, 1:14, and Bukhārī, 1:108) is found in al-Shāfiʿī and his disciple al-Muzanī. See Robert Brunschvig, "Le Livre de l'ordre et de la défense d'al-Muzanī," *Bulletin d'études orientales* 11 (1945): p. 165, n. 7. At the time of this article, Brunschvig seems to have been unaware of the meaning assigned to this term by the Shāfiʿī exegetical tradition of the *Risāla*, "an action by which worldly benefit is gained" (*Mustaṣfā*, p. 294; Bukhārī, 1:107). This tradition is tacitly acknowledged in Brunschvig's "Encore sur la doctrine du Mahdī Ibn Tūmart," *Folia orientalia* 12 (1970): p. 35. Al-Shāfiʿī also used the term *rushd*; al-Ṣayrafī used *khaṭṭ* (*Baḥr*, f. 108a). See also Ibn Ḥibbān, *Ṣaḥīḥ Ibn Ḥibbān bi-tartīb al-Amīr ʿAlāʾ al-Dīn al-Fārisī*. Vol. 1, ed. Aḥmad Muḥammad Shākir (Cairo: Dār al-Maʿārif, 1372/1952), pp. 56, 61–62.

It is significant that already in the *Risāla* we find *aḥkām* such as *irshād* and *adab* (*Risāla*, para. 128) which do not fit into the traditional scheme of five *aḥkām*: *wājib*, *sunna*, *mubāḥ*, *makrūh*, *ḥarām*. That the later jurists used more than these five qualifications is well documented (Ignazio Guidi, "Sunnah e nadb

The problem then was to distinguish which of these usages represented the primary meaning of the imperative. There were three major candidates: obligation (*wujūb*), recommendation (*nadb*) and permission (*ibāḥa*).[71] In the first instance, there were those who supported one of these alternatives. The Ḥanbalīs and many others, jurists as well as the theologians, defended obligation.[72] Al-Shāfiʿī in one opinion (*qawl*) held for recommendation.[73] Some Mālikīs preferred permission.[74] The answers that interest us, however, do not claim that one of these choices is the primary sense, but rather than the primary sense is some element common to two or more of these possibilities (*ishtirāk bi'l-maʿnā*) or that there is no primary sense and that the sense cannot be known without further evidence (*waqf*). Quite obviously, the latter solution is a sceptical one; but this is true also of the former when it is contrasted with the position of those who claim that one distinct deontological value is primary. This will become readily apparent when we consider the doctrine of the school of Samarqand.

The position of hesitation was apparently held by Ḥanafīs, Mālikīs, and Shāfiʿīs. These jurists, wrote Ibn Ḥazm, "testify against themselves that they do not do what they are commanded (by God) until Abū Ḥanīfa or Mālik or al-Shāfiʿī commands them."[75] Because the imperative is vague (*mujmal*) for the Hesitators, they need further evidence, but in

---

presso i giuristi malechiti," in *Festschrift Eduard Sachau zu siebzigsten Geburtstage gewidmet*, ed. Gotthold Weil (Berlin: Riemer, 1915), pp. 333–37; see also Erwin Gräf, "Zur Klassifizierung der menschlichen Handlungen nach Ṭūsī dem Šaiḫ Al-Ṭāʾifa (gest. 460) und seinen Lehrern," *Zeitschrift der Deutschen Morgenländischen Gesellschaft*, Supp. 3, pt. 1 (1977), pp. 388–422). Scholars have regarded the five *aḥkām* as representing the original scheme, to which the others were later accretions (Guidi, "*Sunnah e nadb*," p. 334; Fehmi Jadaane, *L'Influence du stoicisme sur la pensée musulmane* [Beirut: Dar El-Mashreq, 1968], p. 188). I believe this to be incorrect. The five *aḥkām* are a simplified schematization of the qualifications used by the jurists. This scheme is based on the presence and absence of otherworldly sanctions and was probably introduced for discussion in *kalām*, where the more complex scheme of the *fuqahāʾ* was not needed. The theologian was not concerned, as the jurist was, with the frequency or infrequency of the Prophet's actions (ʿAbd al-Ghanī al-Ghunaymī, *al-Lubāb fī sharḥ al-Kitāb*. 4 vols., ed. Muḥammad Muḥyī al-Dīn ʿAbd al-Ḥamīd [Cairo: Muḥammad ʿAlī Ṣubayḥ, 1381–83/1961–63], 1:16). The simpler scheme even excluded the epistemological considerations behind the Ḥanafī distinction between *farḍ* and *wājib*. I see nothing at all to be said for Simon Van den Bergh's assertion of borrowing from the Stoics (Averroes' *Tahafut al-Tahafut*, 2 vols. [London: Luzac, 1969], 1:117–18; see Jadaane, *L'Influence du stoicisme*, pp. 184–89), especially if the five-term classification is derived from a more complex one. See also Saul Horovitz, *Über den Einfluss der griechischen Philosophie auf die Entwicklung des Kalam* (Breslau: T. Schatszky, 1909), p. 44 (Stoic influence) and Martin Schreiner, *Studien über Jeshuʿa ben Jehuda, Achtzehnter Bericht über die Lehranstalt für die Wissenschaft des Judenthums in Berlin* (Berlin: H. Itzkowski, 1900), pp. 71–72 (three Muʿtazilī qualifications increased to five by the Ashʿarīs).

71. Bukhārī, 1:107, also gives *tahdīd* as one of the favorites.

72. *Musawwada*, p. 5.

73. *Mustaṣfā*, p. 297.

74. Sarakhsī, 1:16.

75. *Iḥkām*, 3:2.

weighing this evidence they rely on the founders of the law schools. In this doctrine, Ibn Ḥazm sees the working of *taqlīd*. The upshot of the position of hesitation is indeed a vast increase in that part of the law that is inoperative in itself; a greater body of textual information is called upon to resolve this crucial ambiguity.

It should be noted, however, that there were several routes to this scepticism. For some, among whom the Shāfiʿī Ibn Surayj is numbered, the imperative has not one but several primary senses. One needs further information in order to decide which of them is intended (*taʿyīn al-murād*).[76] For al-Ghazālī on the other hand, the hesitation arises from the fact that one is not in a position to know which of the significations of the imperative is primary. In the absence of an authoritative tradition about the original application of the imperative form, one can only examine its use. But examination does not permit any certain attribution. "We do not claim that hesitation is a doctrine," he writes, "but the Arabs do use this form sometimes for recommendation and sometimes for obligation, and they have not informed us that it was coined for one rather than the other. Our position then is not to attribute to them what they have not proclaimed explicitly and to refrain from fabrication against them."[77] This is hesitation as to the very significance of the imperative and is evidence of greater uncertainty than the position that holds that the intention of the speaker is unknown unless he specially indicates it. For al-Ghazālī, it is not merely a question of not knowing the intention of a particular speaker, but of having lost contact with the very foundations of the language.

Other positions do not proclaim themselves as sceptical in the same fashion, but nonetheless they also are rooted in uncertainty. The Muʿtazilī master Abū Hāshim al-Jubbāʾī is frequently reported to have held that the primary significance of the imperative is recommendation.[78] In fact, Abū Hāshim's position is considerably more complex than this simple formulation would indicate. The Basran Muʿtazila consider, as we have seen, the will (*irāda*) for the performance of the action to be one of the elements that constitute a command. For Abū Hāshim, this will is precisely what is communicated by the command (*idhā qāla al-qāʾil li-ghayrihi ifʿal afāda dhālika annahu murīd minhu al-fiʿl*). Now the deontological status of this act that is willed can within certain limits be gathered from the character of the speaker. If he is wise (*ḥakīm*), then the act is good (*ḥasan*) in the sense of being at least permitted. Where the speaker is God (*al-qadīm*), we know that the act is either recommended or obligatory since God does not order what is merely permitted. On the other hand, when an evil ruler gives orders, the acts are known to be willed but are not necessarily obligatory or even permitted. That an act that is commanded is recommended rather than obligatory cannot be gathered from the imperative alone but rather from the fact that the imperative is not accompanied by any indication that

76. *Talwīḥ*, 2:53; Sarakhsī, 1:15.

77. *Mustaṣfā*, p. 296.

78. Asnawī, 2:18.

disobedience is to be punished.[79] When the imperative is used in the sacred texts for an act which is merely permitted, this is not a true command (*amr*) because the burdens (*takālīf*) created by the law do not include what is merely permitted.[80] Thus we may say that Abū Hāshim's position is in fact one of hesitation; the imperative by itself yields no precise deontological qualification even in the speech of God. More information is needed to distinguish between acts that are obligatory and those that are recommended. The dispute that divided those Muᶜtazilīs who took the position of Abū Hāshim and those like Abū 'l-Ḥusayn al-Baṣrī, who held that obligation is the primary sense of the imperative, does not arise from disagreement as to the fact that the act that is commanded is also willed. Both sides agree on this. What the position of Abū Hāshim states is that nothing beyond the fact that the act is willed is communicated (*wa-laysa yadullu ᶜalā amr zāʾid*).[81]

The Ḥanafī school of Samarqand with al-Māturīdī at their head took a stance that ultimately comes close to that of Abū Hāshim al-Jubbāʾī. For them the primary sense of the imperative is that which obligation and recommendation have in common, the invitation (*ṭalab*) to act, a view that had other adherents.[82] Strictly speaking, both this doctrine and that of Abū Hāshim do not fall into the category of hesitation. Both assert that the primary sense of the imperative is determinate. Linguistically, there is no anomaly. It is only deontologically viewed, against the requirements of the legal system, that the information conveyed by the imperative turns out to be inadequate. In order for an imperative to be a source of obligation, one needs specific information that a sanction attends disobedience. The significant difference between the Muᶜtazilīs and the Samarqandīs, however, is that whereas the Muᶜtazilīs in the absence of a specific indication interpret the imperative in the sense of recommendation, the Samarqandīs take the side of obligation.

ᶜAlāʾ al-Dīn al-Samarqandī expounds the major positions on "the consequence of the unqualified imperative issuing from one who must be obeyed" (*fī bayān ḥukm al-amr al-muṭlaq al-ṣādir min muftaraḍ al-ṭāᶜa*):

> The Hesitators (*al-wāqifiyya*) say that it has no consequence without some contextual indication (*qarīna*) as we have explained. The majority of the jurists and most of the theologians other than the Hesitators say that its consequence is the certain (*qaṭᶜī*) obligation of action and belief. This is the view of the Iraqi masters from among our colleagues (the Ḥanafīs). The masters of Samarqand whose head is Abū Manṣūr al-Māturīdī hold that its consequence is the *prima facie* obligation of action but not of belief in a specific fashion: one does not

79. *Mughnī*, 17:116.

80. *Mughnī*, 17:115.

81. *Mughnī*, 17:107. Robert Brunschvig, "Encore sur la doctrine du Mahdī Ibn Tūmart," p. 38, regards the dispute as concerning the importance of *irāda*, thus missing the point.

82. *Mankhūl*, p. 107; Asnawī, 2:19.

> believe that the action is specifically recommended or obligatory but believes without specification that what God intends, be it obligation or recommendation, is the truth. But one does most certainly perform the action so that if obligation is intended by it (the imperative), he discharges his responsibility, and if recommendation is intended, he gains a reward. This is the meaning of (the category) of obligation (*wujūb*) for the jurists as when Abū Ḥanīfa said of the *witr* prayer that it is obligatory (*wājib*). The dispute among our colleagues concerns belief and not action.... As to the obligation of belief, it is a matter between the subject (*ʿabd*) and God. It is enough to believe simply that what God intends is true as in the case of a text (*naṣṣ*) which is indeterminate (*mujmal*) or unintelligible (*mutashābih*).[83]

For al-Samarqandī, the element of belief has been detached from that of action and is the same belief that attends an indeterminate or unintelligible text. Because there is a possibility that the act is obligatory, one avoids any risk by performing it. "Avoidance of harm is legally and rationally obligatory for caution's sake (*iḥtiyāṭan*)."[84] The same justification, it will be recalled, was given for acting in accordance with a unit-tradition, and it was there that the same formula of nonspecific belief was employed. In the realm of action, one is safe by going beyond what the evidence strictly warrants. In the realm of belief, the standards are more exacting, for unbelief (*kufr*) must be avoided. "Because of the possibility that the act is not intended to be obligatory, it is not permitted to believe that obligation is intended, for this amounts to believing obligatory what is not obligatory, and this is unbelief to say nothing of error" (*fa-maʿa iḥtimāl ghayr al-wujūb lā yajūzu iʿtiqād al-wujūb limā fīhi min iʿtiqād ghayr al-wājib wājib wa-hādhā kufr faḍlan ʿan al-khaṭaʾ*).[85]

---

83. *Mīzān*, ff. 23a–23b. The distinction between *farḍ* and *wājib* was perfectly suited to bring out the character of the Samarqandī doctrine. Yet the very distinction between the two was the object of considerable hostility outside of Ḥanafism. Abū Isḥāq al-Shīrāzī denied that there was any basis at any level of language, be it lexical, legal, or customary, for the distinction between an obligation based on a certain source and one based on a presumptive source (*Lumaʿ*, p.13). Similarly, he rejected the distinction between a *dalīl*, or source leading to certainty, and an *amāra*, or source leading to probability only (*Lumaʿ*, p. 3). The same position is taken by his student Abū 'l-Walīd al-Bājī (d. 474/1081) (*Kitāb al-Ḥudūd fī al-uṣūl*, ed. Nazīh Ḥammād [Beirut: Muʾassasat al-Zuʿbī, 1392/1973], p. 38 [*dalīl*], pp. 54–55 [*farḍ*: where the Ḥanafī distinction is misunderstood, on which see Guidi, "*Sunnah e nadb*," p. 336, n. 2]). See also the criticism in *Mankhūl*, p. 76; in *Mustaṣfā*, p. 81, the dispute is regarded as purely verbal (see Asnawī, 1:46). The discontinuity between knowledge and action was made too glaring for these jurists by the Ḥanafī terminology.

The Ḥanbalīs had two transmitted teachings from Aḥmad ibn Ḥanbal, one of which regarded *farḍ* and *wājib* as synonymous; the other corresponded to the Ḥanafī usage (*Musawwada*, p. 580; *Rawḍa*, p. 16; *ʿUdda*, f. 11b). For a Mālikī distinction, see al-Bājī, *Kitāb al-Ḥudūd*, p. 55. The Ḥanafīs sometimes used *wājib* for *farḍ* (Badakhshī, 1:43). On distinctions within the category of *farḍ*, see Bukhārī, 1:44–45.

84. *Mīzān*, f. 25b.

85. *Mīzān*, f. 25a.

For al-Samarqandī, the sophisticated theologian, the jurists' association of a particular linguistic form with the concept of a command is erroneous. He takes the theological doctrine of "inner speech" (*kalām nafsī*) quite seriously.[86] Linguistic forms merely convey the content of this inner speech. "The proper sense of 'command' is the demand for action which includes both recommendation and obligation."[87] This content of the inner speech is communicated in various ways, one of which is the imperative mood, but the imperative mood is a command only by extension. The view that a particular linguistic form is the proper sense of the word 'command' is not orthodox theological doctrine. It is the position of the Muʿtazila, who deny inner speech.[88]

The linguistic form of the imperative is not identical with the command because if it were, then it would always function as a command, and there would be no command without it, that is, it would have to meet the standards for a proper definition and be "consistent and convertible" (*muṭṭarid wa-munʿakis*).[89] But this standard is obviously not met, for the imperative does not always convey the sense of a command, and commands are communicated in a variety of linguistic forms:

> An exposition of the indications of God's command other than this linguistic form (the imperative): God's report (*khabar*) concerning His command is an indication of it such as God's saying, "He commands justice and charity." (16: 90) Similarly the report of God's Messenger that God commands so and so. Also the consensus of the nation on a command is a sign of it. Similarly the words "oblige," "set down," "compel," "write," etc. (*al-ījāb wa'l-farḍ wa'l-ilzām, wa'l-kitāba wa-naḥwahū*). Similarly the form of the prohibition is an indication that its opposite is commanded. Moreover God's command is known by reason with respect to those matters which are known by reason alone before the summons (of the prophet) arrives and before the sending of the Messenger in the period between prophets.[90]

86. In general, it may be said that the theological doctrine of *kalām nafsī*, was kept out of Ḥanafī *uṣūl al-fiqh*. "The jurists do not know (the usage of "command" for a notion subsisting in the mind of the speaker) but only know someone's saying *ifʿal* as a command in the literal sense" (Bukhārī, 1:101). For an attempt at a theologically acceptable interpretation of the traditional Ḥanafī formula, see *Uṣūl al-Shāshī*, pp. 27–28. The tendency of the doctrine of *kalām nafsī* was to reduce all language to the descriptive level, that is *istikhbār*, *amr*, and *nahy* to *khabar* (Fakhr al-Dīn al-Rāzī, *al-Masāʾil al-khamsūn fī uṣūl al-kalām*, in *Majmūʿat al-rasāʾil* [Cairo: Maṭbaʿat Kurdistān al-ʿIlmiyya, 1328], p. 371; *Tabṣira*, f. 6a; Abū 'l-Barakāt ʿAbd Allāh al-Nasafī, *ʿUmdat ʿaqīdat ahl al-sunna wa'l-jamāʿa*, ed. William Cureton [London: Society for the Publication of Oriental Texts, 1843], p. 7). For Ibn Ḥazm's views on the relation of *amr* and *khabar*, see his *Taqrīb*, pp. 38–39 and Robert Brunschvig, "Pour ou contre la logique grecque chez les théologiens-juristes de l'Islam: Ibn Ḥazm, al-Ghazālī, Ibn Taymiyya," *Atti dei convegni* 13 (1971): pp. 192–93.

87. *Mīzān*, f. 21b.

88. *Mīzān*, ff. 19b–20a.

89. *Mīzān*, f. 22b.

90. *Mīzān*, f. 23a.

The imperative is not a command itself, but functions as an indication of a command in the absence of contextual signs that exclude this sense.[91]

Linguistically, there is no problem with the imperative mood. By itself (*muṭlaq*) it stands for a command. Whether this command is to be taken in the sense of obligation or of mere recommendation is, however, another matter, and a serious one. The contrast between the position of a Hesitator such as al-Ghazālī and that of al-Samarqandī is clear. Whereas for al-Ghazālī it is a question of not slandering the Arabs by attributing to them a usage they did not intend, for al-Samarqandī it is God who must not be slandered. The position of the school of Samarqand raises the problem of the imperative form from the linguistic to the theological level, where it is resolved into the category of the obligatory (*wājib*). Al-Samarqandī, looking to the dispute among the Ḥanafīs themselves, sees his solution as one of compromise. Some Ḥanafīs claim that both belief and action are required; others hold that only action is demanded. There is thus no disagreement as to the obligatoriness of action (*lā taʿāruḍ fī ḥaqq wujūb al-ʿamal*).[92] The Samarqandī position upholds that which is certain, that one must act in accord with the imperative.

As for the arguments that purport to establish the connection between the imperative and obligation in the usual sense, these al-Samarqandī finds inconclusive. He agrees that conformity (*muwāfaqa*) to the command of the Prophet is required and disobedience (*mukhālafa*) prohibited, but the issue is in what do these consist (*lākinna al-kalām fī tafsīrihimā*). Perfect conformity consists in correlating our belief and action with that of the Prophet. We are to believe as he believed and act as he acted.[93]

The connection between the imperative and obligation "cannot be based on the conjugation of the verb because the indicative (*khabar*) is part of it, and falsehood is linguistically a proper indicative, although what is reported is not so. Similarly, the imperative in the sense of recommendation is an earnest demand (*ṭalab*) but not an absolute demand for the action."[94] Being commanded cannot be the consequence of the command as being broken is the consequence of breaking, for the consequences of all causes follow necessarily from their causes and do not depend on human freedom. "But being commanded is the act of a voluntary agent, so how can it be the consequence of the command?" Moreover, al-Samarqandī is at pains to point out, God's command is eternal *a parte ante* (*qadīm*) whereas causes come to be. Furthermore, the correct theological position is that being broken is not really the consequence of breaking, but a separate act on the part of God. In addition, "making the command the cause of being commanded without those who disobey being commanded is to hold the doctrine of the specialization of the cause (*takhṣīṣ*

91. *Mīzān*, f. 22a.
92. *Mīzān*, f. 25b.
93. *Mīzān*, f. 25b.
94. *Mīzān*, ff. 26a–26b.

al-ʿilla), the falsity of which will be made known, God willing."[95] No theological weapon is spared in al-Samarqandī's attack on the classical Ḥanafī position.

We have seen that for the Samarqandīs, the imperative can signal an act that is obligatory or recommended. When the act has a sanction applied to its nonperformance, it is obligatory. The question remains, however, why an act to which no sanction has apparently been applied cannot count as recommended only. This is, for example, the position of Qāḍī ʿAbd al-Jabbār; an act that is commanded is recommended unless its nonperformance is known to be subject to punishment.[96] With this question we approach the central issue of the Samarqandī doctrine of hermeneutics. Al-Samarqandī does not, however, put the matter as we have done. Rather, he addresses the question of why the possibility of the imperative being used for recommendation cannot be ignored, that is why the formula of belief is vague and does not identify the particular act as obligatory. It must be realized that the opposing position, the position that links the command and certain obligation is the dominant one among the Ḥanafīs.[97] Of course, these Ḥanafīs had recognized that the imperative could be used in other significations, prominently in that of recommendation. But for them the imperative used for recommendation is used in an extended sense (*majāz*). For one to recognize that a word is being used in an extended sense, there must be an indication (*qarīna*). It is this issue that al-Samarqandī addresses. The doctrine that he espouses is a direct attack on the postulate of language as a public means of communication. The principle that the law attends only to externals is not inviolable:

> If you say that the possibility of the imperative signifying recommendation and the intention of an extended usage is something hidden (*bāṭin*) so that it is given no consideration legally, we answer that in the principles of the Sacred Law one does not give consideration to the true state of affairs (*ḥaqīqa*) only when there is need not to do so, and there is no need here not to give it consideration because belief is a matter between the one commanded and God.[98]

The state of uncertainty that is occasioned by the inadequate evidence available to the believer is adequately reflected in the general formula of belief. And once the separation of action from belief is made, the characteristic suspension of belief that the Samarqandīs uphold does not touch upon the proper fulfillment of God's will in the sphere of action. The uncertainty that has entered the interpretation of the legal texts once the postulate of linguistic publicity has been rejected is absorbed into the sphere of belief. Action goes on apparently undisturbed.

---

95. *Mīzān*, f. 26b.
96. *Mughnī*, 17:116.
97. Cf. Bukhārī, 1:119.
98. *Mīzān*, f. 25a.

Al-Samarqandī is adamant in rejecting the claim that the apparent absence of any indication that obligation is not intended is enough evidence for upholding obligation as certain on the level of belief:

> If you say that the imperative form's being encountered without any indication from God that excludes obligation is a certain sign of obligation, for the imperative cannot be unqualified without obligation being intended, we answer: This is passing judgment on God and restricting Him, which is inadmissible. Moreover, the imperative form itself is not a sign, for it can be found without being the sign of obligation. Rather you hold that the imperative form without a contrary indication is the sign of obligation. But how do you know that there is no contrary indication? If you say that there is no indication attached to the form because none can be perceived, this is inadmissible, for the indication is sometimes a clarification (*bayān*) on the part of the Prophet. So why do you say that there is no clarification of the Prophet that God intends the form in the sense of recommendation? So, too, sometimes, the indication is rational not verbal. So why do you say that there is no rational indication associated with the imperative which specifies recommendation? There is no doubt that this is within the range of possibility. Thus the claim that the imperative form is without any indication excluding obligation is unfounded. We, however, uphold *prima facie* obligation together with uncertainty with respect to belief.[99]

This, then, is the foundation of the Samarqandī position. Various linguistic usages, in this case the imperative, can appear in more than one signification. This, for the Samarqandīs, creates uncertainty that only specific information can remove. In the absence of this information, a faithful interpretation of the law must take account of this ambiguity. "The sound position is that of the Samarqandī masters. They hold that linguistically the imperative is properly used for demanding action. It thus bears the sense of recommendation and obligation. Sometimes it is also used for other meanings by extension. The extended sense is used in discourse just like the proper one and is even predominant."[100] For the Iraqi Ḥanafīs and those Central Asians who follow them, the uncertainty upon which the Samarqandīs base their position was no foundation at all. It was a mere possibility arising without evidence and was consequently negligible.[101]

In the case of the imperative, the divergence of the Samarqandī position from that of the mainstream of the Ḥanafīs is of no practical consequence. It is this which explains why we can find al-Sarakhsī endorsing the possibility that the imperative is properly used for recommendation and obligation.[102] Since obligation includes recommendation,

---

99. *Mīzān*, f. 25a.
100. *Mīzān*, f. 24b.
101. Nasafī, 1:41; *Manār*, p. 68.
102. Sarakhsī, 1:17.

we cannot go wrong in acting upon the sense of obligation. Giving the imperative the force of obligation would thus be a precautionary measure (*iḥtiyāṭ*). For al-Sarakhsī, it is the action that counts. No attention at all is given to the question of belief, and it is clear that al-Sarakhsī, although using the arguments of his Iraqi predecessors, has in fact lost touch with their theology.

When we turn to the Shāfiʿī school, we find the issue equally complicated. For the doctrine of hesitation had, it appears, penetrated rather early into the mainstream Shāfiʿī tradition and was even identified as the position of al-Shāfiʿī himself. The Ḥanafīs were, of course, eager to find outside support for their view that the imperative determined obligation and were interested in the Shāfiʿī discussion of the problem. Thus we find al-Sarakhsī carefully reporting the dispute:

> The doctrine of most of the jurists is that the consequence of the imperative is obligation except where there is contrary evidence. Ibn Surayj the Shāfiʿī (d. 306/918) held (*zaʿama*) that its consequence was hesitation until what was intended was clarified by some evidence and claimed that this was the doctrine of al-Shafiʿī. For in the *Aḥkām al-Qur*ʾān, al-Shāfiʿī said regarding the verse: "Marry of the women who seem good to you" (4:3) that it bore two senses (obligation and recommendation). Most Shāfiʿīs, however, deny this and say that what al-Shāfiʿī meant was that the verse could be taken in a way other than complete unrestrictedness (*murāduhu annahu yaḥtamil an yakūn bi-khilāf al-iṭlāq*). Similarly he said of the general term that it was liable to specialization when there was some evidence which specialized it although its apparent sense for him was generality. And these Shāfiʿīs claim that in his other books he stated distinctly that the imperative is for obligation.[103]

Al-Sarakhsī's account covers the main points but fails to convey the passion with which the debate among the Shāfiʿīs was often conducted. Those who defended the doctrine linking the imperative with obligation zealously maintained that this was the only authentic doctrine of their school and indeed of the Muslim jurists. Thus Abū Isḥāq al-Isfarāyīnī (d. 418/1027) wrote that:

> It is reported of some Shāfiʿīs that the imperative indicates recommendation and permission, but the well-known doctrine from the time of the Companions to our day is that the imperative indicates obligation. As for this (other) doctrine, it is that of people who are not jurists but who intruded in what concerns the jurists, just as some attribute to al-Shāfiʿī the

103. Sarakhsī, 1:15–16.

> doctrine of hesitation for the general term, which is not his doctrine. Any other doctrine, we say, means rejection of the law.[104]

In a similar vein, Abū 'l-Muẓaffar al-Samʿānī (d. 489/1095) goes so far as to deny that a jurist of Ibn Surayj's rank could have held the doctrine of hesitation. As far as he is concerned, no scholar before al-Ashʿarī held the doctrine.[105]

Among the famous Ashʿarīs, al-Bāqillānī, al-Juwaynī, and al-Ghazālī, the question of al-Shāfiʿī's position and the doctrine of hesitation receive discrepant treatments. Al-Bāqillānī inferred from al-Shāfiʿī's writing that he had held the doctrine of hesitation.[106] According to al-Juwaynī, al-Shāfiʿī supported the doctrine of obligation but had been followed in this only by Abū Isḥāq al-Isfarāyīnī. Most Shāfiʿīs, according to him, took the position of hesitation.[107] Al-Ghazālī, on the other hand, in his *Mankhūl*, seeks to defend al-Shāfiʿī's upholding of the doctrine of obligation. The force of the imperative in the legal texts is that of obligation, not because this is the force of the linguistic form but because we know that to disobey the Prophet subjects one to punishment. Consequently, al-Shāfiʿī was right (*aṣāba*) in so understanding the form.[108]

What is striking about this dispute is the clear demarcation made between theology and law. Even so distinguished a theologian as al-Isfarāyīnī argues that the doctrine of hesitation is an unwanted theological importation into legal hermeneutics. For al-Samʿānī, it is the theologian al-Ashʿarī who initiated this pernicious trend. And even al-Ghazālī defends al-Shāfiʿī's view as the correct one for the interpretation of the sacred texts, although not as the proper understanding of the linguistic form. This line of defense is one that appears to be absent from the Ḥanafī writings, where the doctrine put forth is one of the imperative simply and not of the legal imperative. This is a further example of the fact that must be very plain by this point, that the standard representation of the *uṣūl* of the Ḥanafīs as peculiarly legal in contrast to the theological *uṣūl* of the other schools is without foundation.

---

104. *Burhān*, f. 114.

105. *Qawāṭiʿ*, f. 10b. The attribution of *waqf* to al-Ashʿarī was in itself controversial. *Mankhūl*, p. 105, simply asserts it. But according to Abū Isḥāq al-Shīrāzī, al-Ashʿarī taught the doctrine of obligation to the students of Abū Isḥāq al-Marwazī (d. 340/951) in Baghdad (*Baḥr*, f. 109a: the citation is from al-Shīrāzī's commentary to his own *Lumaʿ*. In *Lumaʿ*, p. 8, al-Shīrāzī is careful to attribute *waqf* to some of the Ashʿarīs). Asnawī, 2:19, has Abū Isḥāq al-Isfarāyīnī instead of al-Marwazī, but al-Isfarāyīnī died in 418/1027, al-Ashʿarī in 324/935. Al-Marwazī was al-Ashʿarī's teacher in Shāfiʿī law, and in turn learned *kalām* from al-Ashʿarī (Tāj al-Dīn al-Subkī, *Ṭabaqāt*, 3:367).

106. *Baḥr*, f. 109a.

107. *Burhān*, f. 114. This appears to be typical of al-Juwaynī, who is careful to determine al-Shāfiʿī's doctrine without regard to his own position (Tāj al-Dīn al-Subkī, *Ṭabaqāt*, 5:192). Cf. *Lumaʿ*, p. 8, on the majority of the Shāfiʿīs.

108. *Mankhūl*, p. 108. In *Mustaṣfā*, p. 299, al-Shāfiʿī is reported to have been a Hesitator.

2. Performance of the Commanded Act

The *uṣūl* treatment of the imperative is by no means exhausted in the determination of its deontological value. Of the other issues that are raised, we shall examine only two: How often is the act commanded to be performed? Only once (*al-marra*) or repeatedly (*ʿalā takrār*)? And is the act to be performed immediately (*ʿalā al-fawr, ʿalā bidār*) or may performance be postponed (*ʿalā tarākhin, muhla*)?[109] On both of these questions, three main positions may be distinguished: 1. The minimalist position holds that the act commanded by a simple imperative is to be performed only once and that its performance need not be immediate. 2. The maximalist position understands the imperative to demand repeated performance of the act commanded. This answer in itself determines that performance must begin at once, for as Abū Isḥāq al-Shīrāzī puts it: "if we say that the imperative requires repetition of the act as long as one is able, the act is immediately obligatory because the first instance is one of ability and one must not let it pass without performance."[110] Finally, there are the Hesitators who deny that the imperative by itself determines either of these issues; more information is required.

In the classical *uṣūl* treatises of al-Bazdawī and al-Sarakhsī, we find a strict version of the minimalist position. Not only does the imperative not require the repetition of the act commanded, it does not even bear this sense (*ṣīghat al-amr lā tūjib al-takrār wa-lā taḥtamiluhu*), that is, it will not have this sense even if the speaker intends it. This is because the sense of the imperative in this respect is already clear in itself. The key argument in favor of this view is that the imperative is equivalent to a demand for the realization of the content of the verbal noun (*maṣdar, lafẓ al-fiʿl*), which is an individual name like Zayd. In this respect, it is like the noun of agency (*ism al-fāʿil*), the participle, which is also applied on the basis of a single performance of the act in question. The dominant doctrine, moreover, refuses to modify this view even when the imperative is subject to a condition (*al-muʿallaq biʾl-sharṭ*) or the object of the imperative is identified by a special character (*al-muqayyad biʾl-waṣf*). There were Ḥanafīs who would distinguish these cases, but the view of al-Sarakhsī is that "this is not the doctrine in our school for if someone says to his wife, 'If you enter this house, you are divorced' she is liable on account of this declaration to one divorce only, even if she enters the house repeatedly." The other doctrine is for him that of al-Shāfiʿī.[111]

The classical Ḥanafī position with regard to the immediacy of the performance of the act that is commanded is that it need not take place at once. For, it is argued, if the

109. *Mustaṣfā*, p. 303, correctly observes that these issues are not peculiar to the imperative. On immediacy of performance, see Robert Brunschvig, "Le Culte et le temps dans l'Islam classique," *Revue de l'histoire des religions* 177 (1970): pp. 185–93.

110. *Lumaʿ*, p. 9.

111. Sarakhsī, 1:21–22.

imperative alone "do this" were equivalent to the imperative with a specific indication of immediacy "do this at once" this would obliterate the obvious distinction between the two forms. The imperative alone would then be taken in a qualified sense without any evidence (*al-taqyīd min ghayr dalīl*).[112]

The minimalist view that we find in the classical Ḥanafī authors was apparently contested in an earlier period. Thus we find that al-Karkhī held the doctrine of immediate performance and regarded it as the teaching of the Ḥanafī masters. This was also the view of al-Jaṣṣāṣ.[113] Similarly, while al-Jaṣṣāṣ reports that the view that the imperative does not even bear the sense of repetition was held by many later Ḥanafīs, he himself held the opposing doctrine.[114] External sources commonly attribute the position in favor of immediate performance to the Ḥanafīs, and there are even sources that attribute the doctrine of repetition to them as well.[115]

The issue of the possibility of a delayed performance of the commanded action was one over which the Ḥanafīs of the fourth/tenth century were clearly divided. This controversy was not confined to them, for the Mālikīs were also split. In their case, the Eastern branch of the school held for immediate performance; the Mālikīs of the West allowed delay. The dominant view even in the East seems to have been that one performance alone was called for.[116] Clearly, then, this period saw an attempt to come to a consistent position on the scope of the imperative. Both Ḥanafīs and Mālikīs reached much the same results: the imperative demanded only one performance. Whether this performance had to take place at once or might be postponed was, however, a matter of disagreement.

The Samarqandī position, or perhaps more accurately that of al-Māturīdī, goes back to this very period of controversy. Al-Māturīdī's solution was a simple application of the same principle we have already met with, the dissociation of action and belief. "The doctrine of our master the Imām Abū Manṣūr (al-Māturīdī)," al-Samarqandī informs us, "is that we do not believe apodictically (*ʿalā ṭarīq al-yaqīn*) with regard to the imperative that it determines one performance (*al-marra*) or continuous performance (*al-dawām*) but believe nonspecifically that what God wills is the truth and perform the act successively (*ʿalā al-tarāduf*) by way of precaution as long as there is no indication that only one performance is intended."[117]

In precisely the same fashion, al-Māturīdī resolved the issue of immediate as against postponed performance: "The doctrine of our master Abū Manṣūr al-Māturīdī is that one does not believe with respect to the imperative either in immediate or postponed

112. Sarakhsī, 1:27; Nasafī, 1:81.
113. Jaṣṣāṣ, f. 96b.
114. Jaṣṣāṣ, f. 58b.
115. *Burhān*, f. 48; *Mankhūl*, p. 111.
116. Qarāfī, pp. 128–29.
117. *Mīzān*, f. 27b.

performance unless there is an indication beyond the mere linguistic form (*warāʾ al-ṣīgha*), but there is a *prima facie*, not-certain, obligation to perform the act in the first possible instant together with nonspecific belief unless there is a further indication."[118] In both these cases, the teaching is presented as that of al-Māturīdī, not that of the scholars of Samarqand at large, and al-Samarqandī himself adheres to the standard minimalist position of the Central Asian Ḥanafīs.[119]

Al-Māturīdī was certainly not the only one, however, to think that safety lay in the repetition of the commanded act and in its immediate performance. This possibility is raised by Abū 'l-Ḥusayn al-Baṣrī in his *al-Muʿtamad*. In both cases, al-Baṣrī rejects the precautionary step as ineffective:

> If the subject knows that the imperative does not require repetition he is safe from harm because there is no repetition called for. But if he fails to examine the matter, he is not safe from harm in believing that repetition is obligatory and in repeatedly performing the action with the intent of (fulfilling) an obligation (*bi-niyyat al-wujūb*).[120]

Similarly, he notes that the way of precaution does not lie in believing immediate performance to be obligatory when "we have no guarantee against it being nonobligatory, so that we end up believing what may be false."[121]

Al-Māturīdī's dissociation of action and belief avoided the risk of incorrect belief, which for al-Baṣrī negated any apparent gain in security. Repeating the action commanded and performing it at once are the safe things to do, but only when one's belief has been neutralized or perhaps more accurately, only when one's commitment at the cognitive level is as free of risk as the action one undertakes.

V. The General and Special Terms

1. *Introduction*

The dissociation of action and belief characteristic of Samarqandī hermeneutics is not limited to the consequences of the imperative. The special term (*khāṣṣ*), apparent (*ẓāhir*) and definite (*naṣṣ*) discourse are all sources of certainty for the mainstream Ḥanafī tradition in Iraq and Central Asia. For the Samarqandīs, however, these provide a basis for action only, not for certain belief.[122] In each case, there is the possibility (*iḥtimāl*) that the

118. *Mīzān*, f. 59a.
119. *Mīzān*, f. 28b.
120. *Muʿtamad*, 1:111 (reading *al-mukallaf* for *al-mutakallim* in line 22).
121. *Muʿtamad*, 1:127.
122. *Mīzān*, ff. 75b–76a.

words in question may be intended in an extended sense. Only at the level of discourse that is explained (*mufassar*) is this possibility excluded. Thus, obvious (*ẓāhir*) and explicit (*naṣṣ*) discourse fall short of providing a basis for certainty as much as equivocal (*mushtarak*) discourse, which has been clarified by a weak source and is merely interpreted (*muʾawwal*) not explained (*mufassar*).

The displacement of the special term from the level of certainty to that of presumption must be regarded as of special significance within the context of the classical Ḥanafī legal system. Holding the special term to be of certain reference (*qaṭʿī al-dalāla*), thus clear in itself, the Ḥanafī jurists would not admit the restriction (*taqyīd*) of an unqualified (*muṭlaq*) special term under the heading of clarification (*bayān*), but rather considered it to amount to abrogation (*naskh*). Abrogation being the most radical modification of an existing legal provision, it could not be founded on a source weaker than the one whose abrogation was claimed. This meant that a Qurʾānic verse with a special term could not be abrogated by a unit-tradition or by analogy. An example will make the point clear. The Qurʾān commands: "O ye who believe, when ye rise up for prayer, wash your faces and your hands up to the elbows, etc." (5:6). The ritual washing (*wuḍūʾ*) consists of a series of acts, each of which is determined by a special term. The word "wash," explains Imām al-Sarakhsī, "is introduced at the linguistic level (*mawḍūʿ lughatan*) for the washing of these limbs. Thus the strict obligation (*farḍiyya*) of washing for the limbs that are washed and of wiping for the limb that is wiped rests on this text. Stipulating intention (*al-niyya*), continuity (*al-muwālāh*), order (*al-tartīb*), and the invocation of God's name (*al-tasmiya*) as equally obligatory so that impurity does not vanish without them although washing and wiping take place does not constitute giving effect (*al-ʿamal*) to this special term, but rather its abrogation."[123] Recalling the scheme presented earlier in which the text that is of certain authority and reference stands at the top and that which is presumptive in both authenticity and reference stands at the bottom, one can grasp the force of the criticism that the Ḥanafīs direct against their opponents, who on the basis of unit-traditions place intention and other additional elements on the same footing as washing and wiping one's limbs. Either they set the Qurʾānic text too low or they raise the unit-tradition too high. Only the Ḥanafīs give each source its proper value. The Qurʾānic text establishes obligation of the strictest sort (*farḍ*). The unit-tradition serves as the basis for action that is binding (*wājib*) or recommended (*sunna*).[124]

---

123. Sarakhsī, 1:128–29 (reading *al-mamsūḥ* in p. 129, line 1, as in note 1).

124. Sarakhsī, 1:129; Bazdawī, 1:84. The Ḥanafīs had several options with regard to a tradition that added to a legal provision of certain authenticity and reference. They could reject it completely when it concerned a matter of general interest and would have been *mashhūr* if authentic (*Manār*, 724). They could, on the other hand, base a legal rule on this tradition but one that did not have the deontological status of the original text. Whether a tradition of this sort was the basis for obligation (*wujūb*) or merely recommendation was, however, a delicate matter (*Manār*, pp. 74–76). Finally, they could accept the tradition but rob it of legal force by a suitable interpretation (*Manār*, p. 647). Traditions that the Ḥanafīs

"For the masters of Samarqand," notes al-Samarqandī, "these further stipulations do represent an addition to the text apparently (*ẓāhiran*), but an addition to the text is for them a clarification and can be based on a unit-tradition."[125] Those who refused to regard an additional legal provision as a case of abrogation justified their position on the ground that the restriction of an unqualified term (*taqyīd al-muṭlaq*) was analogous, not to say identical, to the specialization of a general term (*takṣīṣ al-ʿāmm*).[126] The specialization of the general term is, in fact, paradigmatic in the literature of *uṣūl al-fiqh* for the entire range of problems that arise in the mutual relations between legal provisions.

The importance of the general term lies, of course, in the fact that the range of application of the law is determined by general terms. But the very fact that a term is general means that it can stand in relation to other terms themselves general or specific whose denotation is less extensive. It is universally the task of the legal interpreter to resolve the incompatibilities that arise when general provisions suffer derogation at the hands of those of lesser generality, but in the case of Islamic law this task imposes itself with particular urgency. This follows from the nature of the Islamic revelation. For not only was the Qurʾān sent down piecemeal, but the traditions of the Prophet that have the same revealed status as the Qurʾān were never officially collected and the determination of their authenticity presented, as we have seen, a major problem for the Muslim jurist. It is not surprising, then, that the issues connected with the specialization of the general term generated a vast amount of discussion among the writers on *uṣūl*. What is surprising perhaps is that for a time that includes the fourth/tenth century, so crucial to the history of *uṣūl*, the problem of the general term was directly associated in the minds of the Muslim scholars with the theological question of the fate of the Muslim after death. The theological dimension of the issue, familiar to the earlier Iraqi masters, was revived among the Central Asian Ḥanafīs. One can see in the polemics surrounding this issue the depth of the division between the Central Asians, which no later effort could completely bridge.

The problem of the general term stands, as we have indicated, at the heart of the Ḥanafī exegetical tradition, for the mainstream Ḥanafīs were almost alone in regarding the general term as a source of absolute certainty. For them, the special and general terms were alike in this respect. Yet in the case of the general term, far more than in that of the special, the Ḥanafī view of language is submitted to severe testing. The criterion for a term's being general is that it admits of exception (*jawāz al-istithnāʾ ʿalāmat al-ʿāmm*).[127] It is, moreover, an undeniable fact that many, if not most, terms that are general

---

accepted in apparent contradiction to their own principles were often defended as *mashhūr* (*Manār*, p. 78).

125. *Mīzān*, f. 76a.

126. *Mīzān*, f. 193b; Nasafī, 2:90; Bukhārī, 2:192–93.

127. *Manār*, p. 125.

are not in fact intended to be taken in their fullest denotation, but have, that is, been subject to specialization (*takhṣīṣ*). This is reflected in the proverbial expression "there is not a general term which has not been specialized" (*mā min ʿāmm illā wa-qad khuṣṣa minhu al-baʿḍ*).[128]

The majority of Ḥanafīs may be said to have considered this fact of no consequence whatsoever. For them, each general term was to be taken in its fullest extension unless there was an accompanying indication that less than the full extension was intended.[129] For others, the possibility that the full extension of the general term was not intended had to be reckoned with. Thus we find here the same issues that we have already met in connection with the imperative and the solutions, too, are familiar. In the first place, we have those who take the general term as applying to its fullest denotation in the absence of contrary evidence (*aṣḥāb al-ʿumūm*). Their position is analogous to that of taking the imperative for strict obligation. There are those, on the other hand, who take the general term in its most restricted application unless there is evidence to the contrary (*aṣḥāb al-khuṣūṣ*). To this position corresponds that of those who associate the imperative with what is regarded as its minimal certain quality, recommendation, or more strictly permission.[130] Finally, we have the Hesitators (*aṣḥāb al-waqf*). They recognize the notion of generality but deny that any particular linguistic form is in itself evidence that

128. *Talwīḥ*, 1:201; *Manār*, p. 291, rejects the attribution of this maxim to Ibn ʿAbbās and cites Qurʾānic verses that have not been specialized. It is important to stress here the distinction between *khāṣṣ* in the absolute sense, a special term, and *khāṣṣ* for a legal provision that stands in relation to one of wider extension (see al-Shaykh al-Mufīd, *Awāʾil al-maqālāt*, p. 59; *Muʿtamad*, 1:251; Bukhārī, 1:31; *Talwīḥ*, 1:178). The distinction between *khāṣṣ* and *ʿāmm* does not correspond to that between particular (*juzʾī*) and universal (*kullī*) of the logicians (*Mustaṣfā*, pp. 319–20; *Rawḍa*, pp. 115–16), although the identification of the two schemes was made by some (Ibn Sīnā, *al-Shifāʾ*, *al-Manṭiq*: 4, *al-Qiyās*, ed. Saʿīd Zāyid [Cairo: Wizārat al-Thaqāfa, 1383/1964], pp. 555–56; see also Brunschvig, "Pour ou contre la logique grecque," p. 192). Al-Shāfiʿī was even accused of having come under the influence of logic in treating an unrestricted term as general (*Manār*, p. 326). The proper classification of indefinite nouns, both singular (*muṭlaq* = *nakira* [*Manār*, p. 324]) and plural (*jamʿ* = *munakkar*) was problematic (see Bukhārī, 1:30; *Manār*, p. 510; *Talwīḥ*, 1:241–42; and contrast *Lumaʿ*, p. 25, which treats the *muṭlaq* as general, with *Mīzān*, f. 75a, which treats it as special. Once the special term is uncertain, its classification is not very significant).

The terminology of specialization can be confusing. For *khāṣṣ* and *ʿāmm*, one often finds *khuṣūṣ* and *ʿumūm* (plurals *khuṣūṣāt* and *ʿumūmāt*) (Bukhārī, 3:9). The extension of the original term that turns out to be excluded is called *makhṣūṣ*; the original term once specialized is also called *makhṣūṣ* (more properly, *makhṣūṣ minhu*) (*Mīzān*, ff. 75a–75b). Al-Shāfiʿī used *khāṣṣ* for both (*Baḥr*, f. 154b). Specialization (*takhṣīṣ*), as seen from the point of view of the specializing provision, is sometimes referred to as *khuṣūṣ* (*Manār*, p. 296), the specializing text as *dalīl al-khuṣūṣ* (Bazdawī, 1:309). The specialized text, too, is infrequently called *khuṣūṣ* (*Muʿtamad*, 1:251). Al-Bājī preferred *takhṣīṣ* to *khuṣūṣ* for specialization as more explicit and in more frequent use in debate (*Kitāb al-Ḥudūd*, pp. 44–45). Finally, it may be noted that *takhṣīṣ* is sometimes used in a broad sense to include abrogation (*Talwīḥ*, 1:209; *Muʿtamad*, 1:251).

129. Jaṣṣāṣ, f. 11b; Bukhārī, 1:291.

130. Bukhārī, 1:129. *Mustaṣfā*, p. 297, identifies permission as the minimum for the imperative.

generality is what is intended. Those forms that are used to express generality only do so when accompanied by further evidence.[131]

The Samarqandī position need not surprise us either. For their solution to this issue exactly parallels that encountered in the case of the imperative. The general term is taken in its full extension only with regard to action. Belief is deliberately imprecise. Whatever God intends, generality or specificity, is true.[132] Clearly, however, the precautionary device involved in taking the imperative for obligation cannot be called upon in this instance; it is not safer to take the general term in its widest denotation. The issue must be seen in a theoretical rather than a practical light. Action is what the law is meant to direct, and for action one is guided by the externals of language. The Samarqandī position ultimately comes close to that dominant in the other legal schools. The chief difference lies in the fact that the element of belief is detached and couched in the characteristic Samarqandī formula.

The partisans of the general term thus fall into two camps: those for whom the generality of the term is certain, and those for whom it is merely presumptive. The practical importance of this disagreement lies in the relation of the text that is general to other apparently relevant sources, more specifically in the question, is a general text of certain authenticity to be specialized by a unit-tradition or analogy?

2. Theological Background

At this point, however, we wish to explore the theological background of this hermeneutical issue and as a starting point refer to the following passage from the *Uṣūl* of al-Jaṣṣāṣ:

> Abū 'l-Ṭayyib Ibn Shihāb related to me of Abū 'l-Ḥasan (al-Karkhī) that Abū 'l-Ḥasan said to him, "I hesitate with respect to the generality of the indicative but not with respect to the generality of the imperative and prohibitive (*innī aqifu fī ʿumūm al-akhbār wa-aqūlu bi'l-ʿumūm fī al-amr wa'l-nahy*)." So I said to Abū 'l-Ṭayyib, "This indicates that his doctrine was one of hesitation with respect to the punishment of the grave sinner of our faith (*al-waʿīd fī fāsiq al-milla*)," and he replied, "Yes, that was his doctrine." He also told me that he heard Abū Saʿīd al-Bardaʿī take the position of hesitation with respect to the generality of the imperative and prohibitive as well as of the indicative. Now, I do not doubt Abū 'l-Ṭayyib in anything he relates, for he did attend the classes of Abū Saʿīd al-Bardaʿī and our early masters. But I myself never heard Abū 'l-Ḥasan make a distinction between the indicative and the imperative and prohibitive in this matter, but rather he held for generality without restriction. There are people

131. *Musawwada*, p. 89; *Mankhūl*, p. 139; *Rawḍa*, p. 111 (identifying *waqf* as the minimum).
132. *Mīzān*, f. 70a.

> who think that the doctrine of Abū Ḥanīfa was hesitation with respect to the generality of the indicative and that he did not affirm with certainty generality or specificity in this without further evidence. This is because it is part of his well-known doctrine that he does not affirm with certainty the punishment of grave sinners of the faith.[133]

In fact, al-Jaṣṣāṣ goes on to say that Abū Ḥanīfa did hold this doctrine with respect to the grave sinner, but on the basis of specific texts that indicated that all sins except idolatry are subject to forgiveness: "God forgives not that a partner should be ascribed to Him, He forgives all but that to whom He will" (Qurʾān 4:48). One was not entitled to infer any sceptical doctrine with respect to the general term from this theological position of Abū Ḥanīfa's. Al-Jaṣṣāṣ, on the contrary, insists that all the Ḥanafīs held the doctrine that general terms were to be taken at face value. This was the doctrine that al-Karkhī had handed down from his teachers, and it was confirmed by al-Jaṣṣāṣ' personal contacts. Moreover, no one who had any knowledge of Ḥanafī legal teaching could fail to see that their legal views rested on this exegetical position.[134] This doctrine was not in fact peculiar to the Ḥanafīs, but was common to all the early Muslim scholars (*madhhab al-salaf*).[135] It continued to be the universally held view until "a sect of the Murjiʾa sprang up for whom the doctrine of support for *irjāʾ* was too constricting, and they had recourse to rejecting entirely the view in favor of generality so as not to have to concede to their opponents the doctrine of the punishment of the grave sinner on the basis of the apparent sense of Qurʾānic verses which require it."[136]

Al-Jaṣṣāṣ's ascription of the position of hesitation to Murjiʾa circles is confirmed by other sources, and in fact the theological background of the issue can be fairly well reconstructed. The Murjiʾa are sufficiently characterized for our purposes by the fact that they hold that the true believer will certainly see the fulfillment of God's promise of reward after death; they are the "people of the promise" (*aṣḥab al-waʿd*), and their position on this issue is the contrary of that of the Muʿtazila (and the Khārijīs) that all grave sinners will be punished after death regardless of their belief (*ahl al-waʿīd*). The problem is that there are Qurʾānic verses that can be used in support of both positions. Thus the rather extreme measure of denying that the general term is necessarily to be taken in its fullest extension in the absence of contrary evidence would only be of advantage to the Murjiʾa could they put forth reasons for taking the verses of promise, that is reward, at their face value while denying that the verses of threat, that is punishment, escaped the scepticism now attaching to the general term. This necessary distinction the Murjiʾa thought they could maintain. God's promise, they argued, had to be kept in full; reason

133. Jaṣṣāṣ, ff. 10a–10b, quoted in part, *Talwīḥ*, 1:189, margin.
134. Jaṣṣāṣ, f. 10a.
135. Jaṣṣāṣ, f. 12b.
136. Jaṣṣāṣ, f. 12b, quoted *Talwīḥ*, 1:189, margin.

demanded that this be so. But for God not to carry out in full His threat was no shortcoming on His part, but rather a mark of His generosity that did Him credit.[137] The distinction between the generality of the imperative, which these Murjiʾa by and large accepted, and that of the indicative rested on the fact that the point of God's threat was to induce fear as a motive for obedience. Mere possibility was strong enough to ground such fear. The proper observance of the law, however, required that the subject have no excuse (*muzāḥ al-ʿilla*) rooted in ambiguous language.[138]

It is clear from al-Jaṣṣāṣ' account that the exegetical doctrine of the general term was commonly considered to entail and to be entailed by the theological doctrine of the fate of the believer after death. Al-Jaṣṣāṣ accepts the first entailment. From what is supposed to be al-Karkhī's view on hermeneutics, he infers a theological position. He does not, however, recognize entailment in the other direction; from Abū Ḥanīfa's theology, one cannot legitimately infer his view on this issue of interpretation. One must note, moreover, that al-Jaṣṣāṣ himself clearly did not share the "well-known doctrine" of Abū Ḥanīfa, nor could it have been common in the Ḥanafī circles with which he was acquainted. This is why it makes sense for him to ask about al-Karkhī's theological position. Had Abū Ḥanīfa's theological doctrine been the prevalent one, the fact that al-Karkhī shared it would not have served to confirm the exegetical doctrine attributed to him.

Not much more than a century after al-Jaṣṣāṣ, we find the theological dimension of the dispute over the general term the topic of acrimonious debate among the Central Asian Ḥanafīs. The key text in this connection is found in Abū 'l-Muʿīn al-Nasafī's (d. 508/1114) theological treatise *Tabṣirat al-adilla*, in the section devoted to punishment and reward in the world to come. For al-Nasafī, the dispute is one between the Ḥanafīs and the Muʿtazila. The argument of the Muʿtazila in favor of the thesis that every grave sinner would suffer punishment in the afterlife was that the revealed texts that spoke of this punishment were unqualified and general (*muṭlaqa ʿāmma*). Any exception to these general statements would amount to lying on God's part, which was unthinkable. In the absence of any indication of specialization, the verses were to be taken at face value. The Ḥanafīs, al-Nasafī continues, saw things in a different light:

> Our early companions used to most vigorously dispute this principle and would not concede to them that the adherence to the general was obligatory at the level of belief. This is because it is a linguistic commonplace to use a general expression while intending specialization, to the point where this predominates over the intention of the proper sense, which is generality. Similarly a term without restriction may, according to our masters, be used for a restricted one. But they (the Muʿtazila) deny this most emphatically and treat any indication of specialization or restriction that is subsequent to the gen-

137. *Mughnī*, 17:56.188.
138. *Muʿtamad*, 2:239.

> eral or unrestricted text as abrogation, not as a clarification that the speaker intended by it from the very start only that which did not fall under the specialization or restriction. Our colleagues, however, used to treat this as a case of clarification. Both groups treat this principle as an upshot of the question of punishment (*min natāʾij masʾalat al-waʿīd*), and every early master of ours and theirs who discussed the question of the general and the unrestricted term said that a position on this entailed one with respect to the fulfillment of the threat of punishment and the possibility of pardon.[139]

Al-Nasafī then cites the relevant passage from al-Jaṣṣāṣ to substantiate the link between the two issues. In what follows, al-Nasafī traces the problem to his own time:

> The Shaykh Abū Manṣūr al-Māturīdī and other masters of ours used to hold that a general term could be used when specification was intended and that a subsequent indication of specialization or restriction was a clarification of what was intended, not abrogation. The general form without an indication of specialization or restriction was not evidence that generality was intended. This they considered the doctrine of the Muʿtazila, and the masters in our region used to attack people for holding this doctrine and accuse them of being Muʿtazilīs, until one appeared among them who inclined in *uṣūl al-fiqh* to the Iraqis of our school and followed them on the issue of generality. He cited what he imagined was a sound argument for his view on this issue and ascribed the position of our masters to al-Shāfiʿī, all this without paying any heed to the question of punishment. God knows best his belief in this matter, but in his book he stated flatly that the wrongdoer without qualification is one who commits a major infraction (*al-fāsiq al-muṭlaq huwa ṣāḥib al-kabīra*). I do not know whether he said this wittingly or whether it just came to him and he spoke without knowledge of what it entails. In any cases the innermost thoughts are entrusted to God. He knows best the beliefs of men and the recesses of their souls. All those who considered themselves experts followed him and took him as a model. Not one of them bothered himself with where he stood on the question of punishment. They called Shaykh Abū Manṣūr a Hesitator on this issue out of ignorance of his doctrine. For his true doctrine is that action according to the general term and the unrestricted form is an obligation (*wujūb*), since the obligatory is what rests on evidence that is not certain, evidence furnished by the apparent sense. What, on the other hand, rests on certain evidence is strictly incumbent (*farḍ*), and it has not been related of our companions that they said that the unqualified imperative indicates what is incumbent or that adherence to the general term is incumbent but rather that the unqualified imperative indicates obligation and that adherence to the general is obligatory. And this is what Shaykh Abū Manṣūr held. The true Hesitator is one who hesitates with respect to action

139. *Tabṣira*, f. 284a.

> and belief. Now, one who sides with the partisans of generality and yet admits the possibility of pardon for the grave sinner cannot very well make use of the claim of specialization as Shaykh Abū Manṣūr held and all those master theologians who side with us such as Abū 'l-Ḥasan al-Ashᶜarī and his followers, Ibn al-Rāwandī, al-Ḥusayn (Ibn Muḥammad al-Najjār) and others. So he claims that the generality of the threat includes every individual as if they were specified by name but that God may fail to fulfill His threat and that this is magnanimous whereas failure to fulfill His promise is blameworthy.[140]

"Many of our jurists," continues al-Nasafī, "used to take this position." It was, moreover, he tells us, attributed to Abū 'l-ᶜAbbās al-Qalānisī by ᶜAbd al-Qāhir al-Baghdādī, but al-Nasafī found al-Qalānisī arguing from specialization in his *Kitāb al-Jāmiᶜ*.[141]

Al-Nasafī is arguing that there is a direct connection between a particular exegetical position and a theological one. This connection had been lost sight of by a substantial body of Central Asian jurists who had thoughtlessly followed the lead of one among them who inclined toward the *uṣūl* of the Iraqis. This unnamed scholar would appear to be Abū Zayd al-Dabūsī.[142] The relation between the hermeneutical and the theological doctrines was well known to al-Jaṣṣāṣ, and al-Nasafī wished to restore it to the consciousness of his contemporaries. But al-Nasafī differs from al-Jaṣṣāṣ in a fundamental respect. For al-Jaṣṣāṣ did not argue from the correctness of a theological dogma to a particular exegetical position. Rather, he tried to show that even those Ḥanafīs who had taken a theological stance different from his own had not done so on the basis of a deviant view of the general term. Al-Jaṣṣāṣ, in short, is ready to sacrifice theology to hermeneutics. What al-Nasafī wants to do is something quite different. He is writing for a reader who accepts a particular theological doctrine as the correct one, as that of orthodox Islam. Al-Nasafī wishes to show that those who took the wrong position in interpretation either did not realize the theological consequences or incorrectly thought that they could reconcile it with sound dogma.

In order to make his point, al-Nasafī sets out to "raise" the historical consciousness of his contemporary Central Asians. Before the incorrect teaching had become prevalent, Abū Manṣūr al-Māturīdī, a great scholar from amongst them, had treated the issue exhaustively. Al-Māturīdī's position was identical with that of the early Ḥanafī masters. Al-Nasafī is thus determined to go over the head of the majority of Central Asian and Iraqi Ḥanafīs to identify the authentic doctrine of the school:

---

140. *Tabṣira*, f. 284b, quoted in part *Talwīḥ*, 1:190, margin.

141. *Tabṣira*, f. 284b. On al-Qalānisī, see Michel Allard, *Le Problème des attributs divins dans la doctrine d'al-Ašᶜarī de ses premiers grands disciples* (Beirut: Imprimerie Catholique, 1965), pp. 133–39.

142. Dabūsī, f. 1b, mentions two theological works of his, *al-Amad al-aqṣā* and *Khizānat al-hudā*.

> If it were not for fear of being too prolix, I would furnish some proofs with respect to the question of generality which would expose the way in which they (the Muʿtazila) fool the weak ones by citing legal doctrines of our companions and induce them to think that it is the teaching of our colleagues that one must believe that the scope of the general term includes everything it applies to verbally and that one is to testify that God intends this all and deny that He may intend some specialization or restriction. But the condition we set ourselves at the beginning of the book of avoiding longwindedness prohibits our undertaking this. Yet how can one make this claim against our fellows when in their books are to be found innumerable legal solutions which rest on the view that if one says something and claims "I did not intend its apparent sense," that is, the linguistically proper one, he is believed as long as he is not suspect, in that he makes things harder for himself by saying this and incurs some loss. The judge does not take him at his word only when he stands to gain were he to be believed in his claim of intending what was not the apparent sense. This amounts to their taking the view that if someone says something and intends by it a sense that the words will bear he is believed even if this constitutes a departure from the apparent sense of his words as long as there is no reason to suspect him. This proves that they did not regard the apparent sense of a statement unaccompanied by evidence that the non-apparent sense was intended as indicating that the apparent sense was intended. For if this were so then one's saying "I had the non-apparent sense in mind" would not be accepted even if there were no grounds for suspecting him. Just as one who claims to have intended a sense that the words will not bear is not credited even if not suspected. Now God is not suspect in the indications of specification which He furnishes, and this ought to show that He intended specification from the very time of the original revelation.[143]

The battle over the general term was fought with every available weapon, exegetical, theological, and legal. In the paragraph quoted, al-Nasafī seeks to dispose of the issue once and for all by pointing to a legal principle that is not in dispute. The position al-Nasafī was defending was, as he himself admits, the view of the minority of the Central Asian jurists. In the generation of al-Nasafī, the effort on the part of the Samarqandīs to gain a hearing for their position seems to have reached its peak. The length to which al-Nasafī is prepared to go to undermine the opposing view is clearly illustrated in the passages we have quoted from his *Tabṣirat al-adilla*. Not only does al-Nasafī hint at unorthodoxy on the part of al-Dabūsī, he does not hesitate to appeal to the authority of theologians from outside the Ḥanafī camp.

In the *uṣūl* treatise of al-Sarakhsī, the majority view is presented without any reference to a Ḥanafī opposition; the Samarqandī view is presented as that of al-Shāfiʿī, as

143. *Tabṣira*, f. 286a.

al-Nasafī indicates.[144] In the treatise of al-Fakhr al-Bazdawī, the majority view is characterized as the popular one (*al-mashhūr*) and some attention is given to establishing its claim to be the correct Ḥanafī doctrine.[145] It is from the short work *Maʿrifat al-ḥujaj al-sharʿiyya* of Abū 'l-Yusr al-Bazdawī (d. 493/1100), however, that one gets a sense of the reaction of the majority to the vehement attack of the Samarqandīs. That al-Bazdawī touches upon the issue at all is all the more remarkable in view of the fact that the work in question is only a brief sketch of the *uṣūl* and that al-Bazdawī, as we may gather from his *Uṣūl al-dīn*, pursued a policy of reconciliation between the different factions of the *Ahl al-Sunna wa'l-Jamāʿa*. To the accusation that the refusal to specialize a general text of the Qurʾān on the basis of a unit-tradition is a Muʿtazilī doctrine, al-Bazdawī replies that even if this were the case, it would make no difference. The fact of the matter, however, is that the majority of the Muʿtazila do in fact allow the specialization of a general verse on the basis of a unit-tradition.[146] The accusation of flirting with Muʿtazilism is thus neatly thrown back in the opponent's face.

3. *Specialization of the General Term*

The relation of the general term to the unit-tradition and to analogy lies at the heart of the legal side of the dispute. The split between the Samarqandīs and the other Central Asian Ḥanafīs over this issue is, however, only a late milestone in the history of the controversy. The dispute over whether one is to see a case of abrogation in the addition of a legal provision to a text already revealed or in the specification of a general term is already found in the earliest *uṣūl* literature. It may be recalled that al-Shāfiʿī's position that the Qurʾān and *sunna* could not abrogate one another was meant to save the Prophetic traditions from a blanket rejection. There was thus a longstanding trend in some circles, those of the firmest supporters of analogy, to cling to the main provisions of the Qurʾān and *sunna* in the face of traditions that would serve to surround each general principle with exceptions and thus severely limit the applicability of analogy. The problem of interpretation at this point converges with that considered in connection with prophetic traditions. We have here two sides of the same coin. The epistemological force of the unit-tradition is of significance in relation to the force of certain linguistic phenomena, paramount among them terms that are unrestricted or general. Al-Shāfiʿī's championing of the view in favor of the unit-tradition was continued by Aḥmad ibn Ḥanbal, who wrote "a well-known *Treatise in Refutation of those who Follow the Obvious Sense Even If It Runs Counter to the Way of the Prophet and his Companions*," this being, we are told, the practice of

144. Sarakhsī, 1:132.
145. Bazdawī, 1:308.
146. *Ḥujaj*, f. 19a.

many theologians and analogists (*ahl al-kalām wa'l-ra'y*).[147] The doctrine that we have presented as that of the majority of Ḥanafīs is not one that was limited to them but was espoused in a number of circles. In the dominant legal schools, however, it was only among the Ḥanafīs that it became the standard teaching.[148]

Both al-Nasafī, writing in favor of the Samarqandī position, and al-Bazdawī, writing in opposition to it, regard the issue as one of practical exegetical importance. The Samarqandīs specialize Qur'ānic provisions and those of *mutawātir* and *mashhūr* traditions on the basis of analogy and unit-traditions.[149] The other Ḥanafīs refuse to do so. This practical side of the issue, however, does not seem to have extended beyond the generation of al-Nasafī and al-Bazdawī. Al-Samarqandī, a student of both these masters, is much more cautious. As regards specialization by analogy, he writes:

> It has not been transmitted from the Samarqandī masters expressly whether they allow this or not. If it is said that this is permitted according to their principle, this is not unlikely (*la yabʿud*). But the sounder view held among them is that it is not permitted, although there is uncertainty in a general text. This is because the uncertainty in analogy is greater, for uncertainty is of varying degrees, lesser and greater. Is not the unit-tradition uncertain and yet preferred to analogy?[150]

Similarly, in connection with specialization on the basis of a unit-tradition, he writes, "As for the view of the Samarqandī masters, if it is said that this is allowed, this is unobjectionable (*lā ba's bihi*). But the sounder view is that it is not allowed because the uncertainty in a unit-tradition is greater than that in a general term."[151]

Al-Bukhārī, the commentator of al-Bazdawī, records the same view in his discussion of the unit-tradition. The opinion that specialization is not allowed on the basis of a unit-tradition is the better founded one.[152] The uncertainty in a unit-tradition concerns not only its meaning but its authenticity. Thus it appears that the generation preceding al-Samarqandī saw an intense effort on the part of the Samarqandīs to gain a hearing for

147. *Musawwada*, p. 12; Ibn Taymiyya, *Rafʿ al-malām*, p. 30. On specialization by analogy for the Shāfiʿīs, see Abū ʿĀṣim Muḥammad Ibn Aḥmad al-ʿAbbādī, *Kitab Ṭabaqat al-fuqahā' aš-šāfiʿīya*, p. 69.

148. One of those who took a similar position was the famous Andalusian Sufi Ibn Masarra (d. 319/931). According to Ibn Ḥazm, Ibn Masarra divided traditions into three categories: those that were consonant with the Qur'ān were to be accepted, as were those that supplemented the Qur'ān, but those traditions that were in apparent conflict with the Qur'ān were to be rejected (*muṭṭaraḥ*) (*Iḥkām* 2:81). This information confirms the connection between the doctrine of Ibn Masarra and Muʿtazilī teaching reported by Ibn Ḥazm and other sources. See A. E. Affifi, *The Mystical Philosophy of Muhyid Din-Ibnul Arabi* (1939; reprint ed., Lahore: Sh. Muhammad Ashraf, 1964), p. 179.

149. *Tabṣira*, f. 284a; *Ḥujaj*, ff. 16a, 18a.

150. *Mīzān*, f. 81b.

151. *Mīzān*, f. 82b.

152. Bukhārī, 3:9, quoted *Talwīḥ*, 3:75.

their view and that when this attempt proved abortive, the Samarqandīs set about blunting the edge of their doctrine on the issue of specialization. It is important to note that al-Samarqandī does not reject the lenient view on specialization as untenable. Rather, he claims that it is not supported by any authentic Samarqandī tradition, that is, presumably, it is not stated explicitly in the writings of al-Māturīdī. Although it can be defended as consistent with Samarqandī principles, it is not consistent with the highest standards of exegetical circumspection.

The standard Ḥanafī view rejecting the interpretation of a general term in the light of a unit-tradition amounts to an assertion that the general term is not indeterminate (*mujmal*). "For it is a condition of the unit-tradition attaching itself as a clarification of the Qurʾān that there be some indeterminacy in that to which it attaches itself. Otherwise this entails the abrogation of the Qurʾān by a unit-tradition."[153] The Ḥanafīs hold, then, that the general term is not indeterminate. An older usage that made "general" (*ʿāmm*) and "indeterminate" (*mujmal*) synonymous is rejected.[154] The situation is well formulated by Abū Isḥāq al-Shīrāzī: "All these (the definite, apparent, and general terms) fall under the category of what is clear (*mubayyan*), that is, they do not require any further information to know what is intended but only to know what is not intended.[155]

The view dominant among the Central Asian Ḥanafīs is that a general term, once it has been legitimately specialized, still remains a valid basis for action. It does not become indeterminate (*mujmal*). We shall not enter into the various types of specialization that the jurists recognize, but shall restrict our discussion to the question of the status of a specialized term. The classical Ḥanafī doctrine appears as one of great simplicity when contrasted with that propounded by earlier Ḥanafīs such as ʿĪsā ibn Abān and al-Karkhī.[156] It holds that a general term remains a basis for action whether or not the extent of specialization is definitely known. The general term, however, is now weakened to the extent that it is liable to further specialization by a unit-tradition or analogy. The practical consequence of this view is that general terms that are, according to other doctrines, indeterminate and thus unusable are retained by the Ḥanafīs.[157] The defense of this doctrine rests upon what is claimed to have been the practice of the Companions, that is, consensus.[158] In addition, there is a rational argument that seeks to show that the Ḥanafī position puts specialization in its proper place and does justice to its affinity with abrogation, on the one hand, and exception (*istithnāʾ*) on the other. For specialization

153. Bukhārī, 1:81–82.

154. Ibn Taymiyya, *al-Īmān*, ed. Muḥammad Khālid Harrās (Cairo: Dār al-Ṭibāʿa al-Muḥammadiyya, 1972), p. 343; *Baḥr*, f. 184b (al-Qaffāl al-Shāshī); *Mīzān*, f. 90a.

155. *Lumaʿ*, p. 28; Ibn Taymiyya, *al-Īmān*, pp. 340–41.

156. Jaṣṣāṣ, ff. 24b, 41a; *Mīzān*, f. 73a; *Muʿtamad*, 1:285, 289; *Iḥkām*, 3:141.

157. Bazdawī, 1:300–308.

158. Bukhārī, 1:301, 310.

resembles exception in so far as its effect (*ḥukm*) is to show that some range of the original provision was never intended. It resembles abrogation formally (*ṣīghatan*) since the specializing provision, like the abrogating one, is independent (*qāʾim bi-nafsihi*).[159] This, then, is the practical side of the question of the general term after specialization (*al-ʿāmm al-makhṣūṣ*). But as the commentator al-Bukhārī notes, there is another theoretical side to this topic. The other question is, How is one to classify the general term after specialization? Is it being used in its proper sense (*ḥaqīqa*) or is it now figurative (*majāz*)? Much has been said about this question, al-Bukhārī notes, in directing his reader to look elsewhere for a fuller exposition.[160]

This problem constitutes a curious chapter in the story of the concepts of *ḥaqīqa* and *majāz* and one that is apt to be overlooked. The question is related to the practical one already mentioned in that one argument advanced for rejecting the specialized general term as a source of law was that it was now figurative. Within the former indefinite range of the general term, one could isolate any number of subgroupings. Because each of these could equally claim to represent the figurative sense of the specialized term, its application to any one of them rather than another would be purely arbitrary. Nor could all these subgroupings be intended, for this would mean that several figurative senses were simultaneously intended.[161] The general term now that it was being used figuratively was indeterminate.

According to al-Jaṣṣāṣ, the majority of the scholars of his day regarded the usage of a specialized general term for its reduced range as figurative.[162] Jaṣṣāṣ's own view is that it is proper not figurative, but the important thing for him is to establish that a general term, once specialized, still has legal force.[163] This doctrine he identifies as that of the founding fathers of the school.[164] Even al-Karkhī, who held a very different doctrine, was careful to label it as his own and not to ascribe it to the early masters.[165] Al-Karkhī and before him Muḥammad ibn Shujāʿ al-Thaljī (d. 266/879) had treated a specialized general term as indeterminate because inasmuch as the word now had to be taken in a figurative sense, its present scope could only be determined by some further evidence.[166] But according to al-Jaṣṣāṣ, it was possible to hold that the general term was figurative and yet

159. Bazdawī, 1:310.

160. Bukhārī, 1:310. A parallel problem was presented by an imperative once it could no longer be taken in the sense of obligation (*ʿUdda*, f. 45a).

161. Bukhārī, 1:309. This was itself a controversial doctrine.

162. Jaṣṣāṣ, f. 33a.

163. Jaṣṣāṣ, f. 42a.

164. Jaṣṣāṣ, f. 41a.

165. Jaṣṣāṣ, f. 41a; Sarakhsī, 1:145.

166. Jaṣṣāṣ, f. 41a; Sarakhsī, 1:145.

continue to apply it to its unspecialized range. Although figurative, the term was being used in a sense that was no more indeterminate than its original one.[167]

There is no denying, however, the close connection between the practical issue of refusing to apply the specialized text and the figurative status of the specialized term. The problem for the jurists was how to justify their continued practice in the face of the arguments in favor of taking the specialized term as figurative. Ibn Taymiyya, a noted opponent of the *ḥaqīqa/majāz* distinction, observes that almost all the legal schools, the Ḥanbalīs, the Shāfiʿīs, and the Mālikīs, are split over whether the specialized general term is figurative or proper. Similarly, they are divided over the question of whether an imperative used for recommendation is being used figuratively. This, he claims, shows that there are no convincing criteria for distinguishing between a proper and figurative usage.[168]

The application of the theory of *majāz* to the general term after specialization was such as to test the foundation of the entire doctrine. If one claimed that the usage of the term remained proper because the combination of the general term and its context constituted a unity (*al-ḥaqīqa majmūʿ al-lafẓ wa'l-qarīna*), then this opened the way to arguing that there was never any figurative usage in language at all.[169] Al-Karkhī, for example, had held that when the specializing instrument was a condition, an excepting clause, or an attribute, then the usage of the general term was not figurative.[170] On the other hand, from insisting that specialization altered the application of the general term so as to make it figurative, it was only a short step to making all language figurative. For all discourse consisted of combining elements in such a way that in combination they acquired a sense they did not have in isolation.[171]

Let us glance briefly at two very different reactions to the challenge presented by the imposition of the *ḥaqīqa/majāz* theory upon the hermeneutical problem of the general term that has been specialized. The Shāfiʿī Abū 'l Muẓaffar al-Samʿānī follows the traditional Shāfiʿī teaching that the specialized term retains its legal force and can serve to ground a legal norm (*ḥujja*).[172] It is not being used figuratively. But in a remarkable passage, he advises his reader that "the dispute on this question is with the theologians and in discussions with them one ought to say that it becomes figurative."[173]

The stratagem that won popularity among the majority of Central Asian Ḥanafīs went beyond the merely verbal concession offered by al-Samʿānī. The definition of

167. Jaṣṣāṣ, f. 42b; Bukhārī, 1:310.
168. Ibn Taymiyya, *al-Īmān*, p. 88.
169. *Muʿtamad*, 1:283.
170. *Muʿtamad*, 1:285.
171. *Dharīʿa*, 1:283–84.
172. *Qawāṭiʿ*, f. 516; *Lumaʿ*, p. 18; *Rawḍa*, p. 124.
173. *Qawāṭiʿ*, f. 45b.

the general term was so framed that it did not have to cover every applicable instance (*istighrāq, istīʿāb*).[174] It was enough for a term to be general that it apply to three or more objects. This meant that a general term, although specialized, might nonetheless be used in a proper sense. Of course, this adjusted definition marked a tacit recognition of the claims of the opposition, the Samarqandīs and others, who argued that the grounds for taking a general term in a restricted sense were at least as strong as those for taking it in its fullest range.[175] In fact, some readers of al-Bazdawī understood his definition to exclude the application of a general term to its full range.[176] It was, however, recognized that even among those whose definition of the general term was more demanding, there were those who considered it to remain proper after specialization. One was therefore led to regard this issue as independent of that of the definition of the general term.[177]

4. Hermeneutical Procedure

Having examined in detail some of the problems associated with the general term, let us now review the topic by looking at the procedures to be followed by the interpreter. In the first instance, we divide the interpreters into two classes. Those who regard the general term as indeterminate will not proceed at all. Their position must be one of hesitation. This practice was necessarily anathema to those who found it inconceivable that God address mankind in such a way that no information be transmitted. They were thus led, as al-Jaṣṣāṣ puts it, to "empty all of God's discourse and that of the Messenger of their content, a view that brings its adherents to shed religion altogether."[178] Ibn Ḥazm offers a pointed analogy. Those who deny any force to a general term because such terms have on occasion been found to be specialized are like those who say, "Since I have seen many lie in speaking, I will assume all speech to consist of lies." They might as well assume every law to be abrogated until the contrary is proved.[179]

For those who do not take the position of hesitation, the question that must be decided is whether one may proceed to act in accord with the general legal provision and to commit oneself at the level of belief without taking any steps to search for specializing texts. Dominant opinion regards such a search (*baḥth*) as obligatory.[180] Al-Jaṣṣāṣ explains why: "When one knows that in the Qurʾān and *sunna* there are general and special provisions, those that abrogate and those abrogated, and yet believes that to be general that

174. *Mīzān*, f. 73a; *Muʿtamad*, 1:286.
175. *Mīzān*, f. 72a.
176. Bukhārī, 1:33.
177. Bukhārī, 1:307; *Mīzān*, f. 72b.
178. Jaṣṣāṣ, f. 12b.
179. *Iḥkām*, 3:125.
180. *ʿUdda*, f. 71b.

he does not know to be general or special, he has proceeded to believe what he does not know to be sound. But God cannot then charge him to recognize a specializing text, for this would mean that God had charged him with believing what was contrary to His intention, and this is a vicious contradiction."[181]

Given the case of a general provision and a special one of acceptable validity, two possibilities arise. The chronology (*taʾrīkh*) of the texts is sufficiently known for the interpreter to determine whether he is dealing with specialization or abrogation or it is not known what is the order of revelation nor the time intervening. Knowledge of the relative chronology is important because it underlies the distinction between specialization and abrogation. A specializing provision must be contemporaneous (*muqārin*) with the text that it specializes, that is, it must be promulgated before the time for action has arrived (*waqt al-ḥāja*).[182] If a text capable of specialization falls within this time span, we have specialization. If it falls outside of this time, we have abrogation. According to the Iraqi doctrine, which is dominant, a subsequent general provision always abrogates a special one unless the latter is precisely contemporaneous.[183] Others, however, allow for a period of time within which a subsequent general text could be specialized by an earlier provision.[184] Where the chronology is unknown, one must look beyond the two texts to make a determination (*tarjīḥ*). For it is not possible to decide whether the special provision is contemporaneous or subsequent and thus specializes or abrogates the general text or whether the general text is subsequent and there is abrogation.[185] The practical difference between the two cases is that a general provision remains certain (*qaṭʿī*) after abrogation but is only presumptive (*ẓannī*) after specialization.[186]

The Ḥanafīs contrast their procedure with that of al-Shāfiʿī, for whom the general text is always construed (*yubnā ʿalā*) to fit the special one. It makes no difference for him whether or not the chronology is known.[187] The Ḥanafīs, on the other hand, recognize cases where the general text predominates (*yaqḍī ʿalā*) over the special one.

The Samarqandī position differs in several points. Where the general text is subsequent, they follow the doctrine of the majority of their school, but only with respect to action. The Samarqandīs, it will be recalled, do not consider the general text as certain; it could very well be specialized. Consistently applied, this view would lead to the doctrine of al-Shāfiʿī. On the other hand, the Ḥanafīs may be correct in seeing abrogation here. The hesitation that would seem to be the proper response to these two possibili-

181. Jaṣṣāṣ, f. 17a.

182. Sarakshī, 1:47, 2:73–74; *Muʿtamad*, 1:251.

183. *Talwīḥ*, 1:205–6. *Mīzān*, f. 189b, characterizes the preference for abrogation as Muʿtazilī.

184. *Muʿtamad*, 1:278–79; *Taysīr*, 1:273.

185. *Taysīr*, 1:272; *Mīzān*, f. 83a.

186. *Talwīḥ*, 1:205, 207, margin.

187. *Lumaʿ*, p. 20. The verb *rattaba* was also used (Jaṣṣāṣ, f. 72a [quoting ʿĪsā ibn Abān]).

ties is confined to belief.[188] The general term remains a basis for action. Once again, the Samarqandī view is brought into line with that of the majority. The same solution is offered for the case where the chronology of the texts is unknown.[189] In these instances we see the flexibility of Samarqandī doctrine. Having refused to make a cognitive commitment with respect to the general text when there is no indication of specialization, the element of doubt introduced by ignorance of the chronology of the texts does not deflect their procedure as it does that of the majority. For them, action on the basis of a general text and the claim that such a text is certain were never associated. It is on this ground that al-Samarqandī criticizes those Ḥanafīs who postulated the contemporaneity of the two texts. This, he notes, is not compatible with the doctrine that holds that the reference of a general term to every member of its denotation is absolutely certain. Faced with the claims of certainty for the general provision, on the one hand, and for the special term, on the other, the proper solution is hesitation.[190]

VI. Ẓāhirī Hermeneutics

Interpretation does not take place in a vacuum. Every act of interpretation rests upon assumptions regarding the language in which the legislation is couched, the nature of the lawgiver, and the relevance of the social background of the law. In so far as interpretation is rationalized, these assumptions are made explicit in the form of rules that guide the interpreter. The overall aim of these rules is to resolve as much as possible uncertainty regarding the intention of the lawgiver. Guided by these rules, the interpreter is able to restrict the scope of ambiguity within the provisions of the law. There are, of course, cases in which the application of the rules of interpretation leads to results that are incompatible with other provisions of the law that are well established. In such instances, further rules come into effect. Thus the body of exegetical principles presents itself as an articulated network of rules. Within the context of Islam, the most powerful assumptions that underlie the rules of interpretation are those concerning the lawgiver, God. The point, however, must be insisted upon that very different conceptions of the nature of God can lead to interpretative principles that are very much alike. We have seen an example of this in connection with the Muᶜtazilī doctrine that will (*irāda*) is a constituent of the command. This point is of fundamental theological importance but is almost negligible insofar as interpretation is concerned.

A further example of this phenomenon is to be found in the writings of Ibn Ḥazm. A classic study of Goldziher gives the impression that Ibn Ḥazm stands apart from the

188. *Mīzān*, f. 82b.
189. *Mīzān*, f. 83b.
190. *Mīzān*, f. 83b.

mainstream hermeneutics.[191] This is not the case. Despite his uncompromising consistency in theological questions, Ibn Ḥazm's hermeneutics corresponds in important areas with that of the Iraqi Ḥanafīs, who were so very far from him in their theological outlook. What underlies this resemblance is Ibn Ḥazm's adherence to one fundamental assumption in his exegetical doctrine. This is that God does not impose what is impossible (*taklīf mā lā yuṭāq*). This principle is one that God Himself has communicated; it is part of revelation itself.

The operation of this principle may be briefly illustrated. Ibn Ḥazm, despite his extreme voluntarism, does not allow for the possibility of a legal prescription remaining indeterminate (*mujmal*) after the time for its performance has come. "We do not hold this view," he writes, "because reason excludes this happening but because there is a revealed text to this effect, that is, 'God charges no soul except with what it can bear' (Qurʾān 2:233)."[192] On the question of whether an imperative demands the earliest possible performance or whether performance may be delayed, Ibn Ḥazm holds the former view, and in so doing continues the controversy on this issue between Muḥammad ibn Dāwūd and the Shāfiʿī jurist Abū 'l-Ḥasan ibn al-Qaṭṭān (d. 359/970).[193] Responding to the argument that one only sins in postponing the pilgrimage if one dies before accomplishing it, Ibn Ḥazm observes that God has not obliged us to know when we will die. We are thus responsible for so arranging our affairs as to avoid sin. The conclusion is that postponement is not permitted.[194] Similarly, Ibn Ḥazm determines that an imperative is fulfilled by a single performance without repetition because it is impossible to perform a given act at all times. To demand any particular number of performances would be arbitrary.[195]

It is instructive to contrast Ibn Ḥazm's unexceptional approach to hermeneutics with that of earlier Ẓāhirīs. Although the doctrines we shall consider are anomalous, the logic behind them is not difficult to grasp. What characterizes these opinions are the constraints that they put on revelation. Possible modes of divine communication that others had recognized are rigidly excluded.

---

191. His introduction to Ibn Tūmart, *Le Livre de Mohammed Ibn Toumert*, pp. 52–55. Goldziher erroneously regarded the understanding of the imperative as imposing obligation as characteristic of Ẓāhirism (*The Ẓāhirīs: Their History and Their Doctrine*, ed. and trans. Wolfgang Behn [Leiden: Brill, 1971], pp. 67–76). See the correction to his view in Robert Brunschvig, "Encore sur la doctrine du Mahdī Ibn Tūmart," pp. 34–37. Goldziher correctly noted that Ẓāhirism retained more imperatives in the sense of obligation (*Ẓāhirīs*, p. 69), but the reason for this is to be found in the Ẓāhirī handling of sources in relation to one another, not in a simple hermeneutical principle (e.g., *Iḥkām*, 3:140).

192. *Iḥkām*, 1:83.

193. *Iḥkām*, 3:49. Ibn al-Qaṭṭān was Ibn Surayj's last surviving student (Jamāl al-Dīn ʿAbd al-Raḥīm al-Asnawī, *Ṭabaqāt al-shāfiʿiyya*, ed. ʿAbd Allāh al-Jubūrī. 2 vols. [Baghdad: Riʾāsat Dīwān al-Awqāf, 1390–91/1970–71], 2:298).

194. *Iḥkām*, 3:49.

195. *Iḥkām*, 3:73; *Irshād*, p. 97.

Prominent among those who denied that there is figurative language in the Qurʾān we find Ẓāhirīs such as Dāwūd, his son Muḥammad, and Mundhir ibn Saʿīd al-Ballūṭī (d. 355/965). This doctrine, which had adherents in a number of schools, especially the Ḥanbalīs, was most closely linked with Ẓāhirism.[196] Ibn Dāwūd is supposed to have said that the proper sense of *mustaʿīr*, one who uses language figuratively, is "one who takes what is not his, so that if anyone calls a word in the Qurʾān *mustaʿār*, this amounts to an assertion that it is put where it does not belong."[197] We also find the arguments cited that figurative language is equivalent to lying, that it is only resorted to when ordinary usage is found to be constraining. The answer to these arguments was to insist upon the fact that the meanings of figurative expressions can be known with as much certainty as non-figurative discourse and that figurative language, far from being a sign of inadequacy, was one of verbal mastery and eloquence.[198]

It is important to distinguish this doctrine, which denies the existence of figurative language in the Qurʾān, from that which refuses to recognize figurative language at all, a position attributed to Abū Isḥāq al-Isfarāyīnī and espoused by Ibn Taymiyya.[199] This doctrine is not open to a reply such as that of Ibn Fūrak, who held that to deny figurative language in the Qurʾān is to deny that it was revealed in Arabic.[200] The force of Ibn Fūrak's objection rests upon the recognition of figurative language in ordinary Arabic. This the Ẓāhirīs are prepared to admit. What they claim is that the interpreter of the Qurʾān has no need to take note of this linguistic possibility, which has been excluded by the nature of the Lawgiver. This doctrine reduces the need to consult outside sources in the task of interpretation. The blanket denial of *majāz* works in the opposite direction, and we find Ibn Taymiyya joining his attack on *majāz* with a call for the reading of the Qurʾān in the light of the prophetic traditions.

For Dāwūd, there could be no ambiguity in the *sunna* of the Prophet. The Prophet had been directed to clarify the Qurʾān, and this purpose would be defeated if the clarification he had given was itself in need of further elucidation.[201] In keeping with this assumption regarding the *sunna*, where there were two traditions in apparent conflict, such as one general and the other special, there was a trend in Ẓāhirī exegesis to reject them both rather than to attempt to harmonize them. This was not done in the case of Qurʾānic verses.[202] Not only was the means of divine communication restricted, so also

196. Ibn Taymiyya, *al-Īmān*, pp. 76–77. Ibn Dāwūd is supposed to have held the same of the *sunna* (*Baḥr*, f. 84a).

197. *Baḥr*, f. 84a.

198. Aḥmad ibn Muṣṭafā Tashköprüzāde, *Miftāḥ al-saʿāda wa-miṣbāḥ al-siyāda fī mawḍūʿāt al-ʿulūm*, ed. Kāmil Kāmil Bakrī and ʿAbd al-Wahhāb Abū ʾl-Nūr (Cairo: Dār al-Kutub al-Ḥadītha, 1968), 2:450.

199. Ibn Taymiyya, *al-Īmān*, p. 77.

200. *Baḥr*, f. 84a.

201. *Qawāṭiʿ*, f. 52b; *Lumaʿ*, p. 19.

202. *Lumaʿ*, pp. 19–20. According to Ibn Ḥazm, Ibn Dāwūd in his *Kitāb al-Wuṣūl* was moving toward a

was the divine will, for Dāwūd took the position, usually identified with the Muʿtazila, that the explanation of a law could not be deferred until the time for performance.[203]

The classical Ḥanafī system of hermeneutics stands between the severity of some Ẓāhirīs and Muʿtazilīs and the leniency of a consistent Hesitator like al-Bāqillānī. Starting from a view of language that insists upon its intersubjectivity, the Ḥanafīs are ready to take discourse at its face value. They presume that the apparent meaning is what is intended until proof to the contrary is brought. At the same time, they are most circumspect when it comes to restricting the tenor of general provisions, to the point of positing abrogation where others see specialization. What is gained in simplicity is lost in efficiency.[204] The Samarqandī school stands apart from this exegetical tradition in its dissociation of action and knowledge. The element of certainty having been removed, one is left with apparent meanings only. That this very different system did not disturb the entire structure of Ḥanafī law is due to the fact that action is now an autonomous realm. "What is intended from the Law," al-Samarqandī asserts, "is the obligation to act."[205] This may be contrasted with the opinion of al-Bazdawī, who defends the standard tradition of assimilating knowledge to action: "Since it is agreed that the intention of the speaker is not to be considered with respect to action, it should all the more be disregarded with respect to knowledge because knowledge is the action of the heart. The heart is primary (*al-aṣl*), whereas action takes place in the limbs, which are subordinate to the heart. Since true intention is disregarded with respect to what is subordinate, it is all the more to be disregarded with respect to what is primary."[206]

VII. The *Argumentum a Fortiori*

With the *argumenta a fortiori* and *a contrario* we arrive at a new level in the work of the *mujtahid*. For the rules that rest on these patterns of inference are said to fall under the "tenor of the text" (*mafhūm*) and together with the results of analogy, constitute "what is understood from the text" (*maʿqūl al-aṣl*).[207] Together they function to fill apparent lacunae in the law. The Ḥanafīs, however, do not accord these arguments equal acceptability. While wholeheartedly welcoming the *argumentum a fortiori*, they are almost unanimous in rejecting every form of the *argumentum a contrario*. Once the nature of the two procedures is grasped, the basic Ḥanafī tendency is immediately intelligible.

position like his own, but died before implementing this reform in Ẓāhirī doctrine (*Iḥkām*, 2:39).

203. *Irshād*, p. 174; *Rawḍa*, p. 96.

204. Bukhārī, 3:111; *Manār*, p. 724.

205. *Mīzān*, f. 70a.

206. Quoted Bukhārī, 1:306.

207. *Lumaʿ*, p. 60.

The *argumentum a fortiori* appears in two forms, the *a minori ad maius* and the *a maiori ad minus*. In the first type, an express prohibition is the basis for inferring a further prohibition. This is the type of the classic Islamic example. From the Qurʾānic prohibition (17:23) of saying *uff* to one's parents, it is inferred that it is all the more prohibited to strike them.[208] This, then, is the inference from the lesser to the greater. In the type *a maiori ad minus* ("from the greater to the lesser"), an express permission or command is the basis for inferring that some other action is permitted or obligatory. Thus if it were permitted to offer a blind animal as a sacrifice, one might infer that an animal with sight in one eye was all the more permitted.[209] What is common to these inferences is that they are axiological. They rest upon the jurist's grasping a particular value in the expressly formulated law and upon his ability to evaluate other actions with reference to this standard. Thus in the classic example, the value involved in the prohibition of saying *uff* is that of protecting the parents from harm (*adhā*), and the prohibition of striking

---

208. *Lumaʿ*, p. 26.

209. *Musawwada*, p. 222. The *argumentum a fortiori* in both its forms was almost universally accepted by Islamic jurists, although the nomenclature employed varied considerably. For early Ẓāhirism, *istidlāl* encompassed both the *argumentum a fortiori* and the *argumentum a contrario* (Ibn ʿAbd al-Barr, *Jāmiʿ bayān al-ʿilm wa-faḍlihi*, 2:74; *dalīl al-khiṭāb* was used for both arguments, and not by Ẓāhirīs only [*Iḥkām*, 7:3; *Muʿtamad*, 1:171]). Eventually a specialization of terminology took place. The Ḥanafīs did not in general accept the *argumentum a contrario*; for them, *dalālat al-naṣṣ* is used for the *argumentum a fortiori*, and *dalīl al-naṣṣ* for the inferred rule (Bukhārī, 1:74; *Manār*, p. 528). The Shāfiʿīs accepted both arguments, for which they had the general term "tenor of the text" (*mafhūm al-naṣṣ*) (*Lumaʿ*, p. 26), which was opposed to what was expressed (*manṭūq*) (Bukhārī, 2:235). In accordance with this terminology, one finds the tenor of agreement (*mafhūm al-muwāfaqa*) for the *argumentum a fortiori*, and the tenor of contrariety (*mafhūm al-mukhālafa*) for the *argumentum a contrario* (*Manār*, pp. 547–48). A popular and slightly more concrete terminology is that of Ibn Fūrak (d. 406/1015), the Shāfiʿī Ashʿarī. *Dalīl al-khiṭāb* is now used for the *argumentum a contrario*, and *faḥwa al-khiṭāb* for the *argumentum a fortiori* (Abū Bakr Muḥammad ibn al-Ḥusayn ibn Fūrak, *Muqaddima fī nukat min uṣūl al-fiqh*, p. 10). On its origination, see *Burhān*, f. 121. See also *Iḥkām*, 7:4. One also finds *faḥwā al-naṣṣ* (*Mīzān*, f. 77a, margin), *faḥwā al-qawl* (*Mīzān*, f. 77a, margin: a Muʿtazilī term), and *faḥwā al-lafẓ* (*Rawḍa*, p. 138). *Laḥn al-khiṭāb*, which for Ibn Fūrak had the sense of an ellipsis (Ibn Fūrak, *Uṣūl al-fiqh*, p. 10) came to acquire the sense of the *argumentum a simili* (Aboubekr Abdesselam Ben Choaib, "L'Argumentation juridique en droit musulman," *Revue du monde musulman* 7 (1909): pp. 73–74).

For the *argumentum a fortiori*, other terms are also used: *tanbīh*, *naṣṣ* (Māwardī, 1:588: used by the anti-analogists), and *awlā* (*Musawwada*, p. 341). Since *faḥwā al-khiṭāb* was classified as *qiyās* in some circles (*Iḥkām*, 7:4), it is clear why these other terms might be used. *Tanbīh* is an old term antedating *faḥwā al-khiṭāb* (*Lumaʿ*, p. 35: *faḥwā al-khiṭāb wa-huwa al-tanbīh*). It is used in distinguishing the *argumentum a maiori ad minus* (*al-tanbīh bi'l-aʿlā ʿalā al-adnā*) from the *a minori ad maius* (*bi'l-adnā ʿalā al-aʿlā*) (Abū 'l-Walīd Ibn Rushd, *Bidāyat al-mujtahid wa-nihāyat al-muqtaṣid*. [Cairo: al-Maktaba al-Tijāriyya al-Kubrā, n.d], 1:3; Ibn Ḥazm, *Mulakhkhaṣ ibṭāl al-qiyās wa'l-raʾy wa'l-istiḥsān wa'l-taqlīd wa'l-taʿlīl*, ed. Saʿīd al-Afghānī [Damascus: Maṭbaʿat Jāmiʿat Dimashq, 1379/1960], p. 29: al-Dhahabī's comments). Finally, on the question of origins, see Hassan Abdel-Rahman, "L'Argument a maiori et l'argument par analogie dans la logique juridique musulmane," *Rivista internazionale di filosofia del diritto* 48 (1971): pp. 140–48.

them depends upon the evaluation of physical injury as more inimical to this value than merely verbal insults. Both of these requirements are the subject of controversy among contemporary legal theorists.[210] In the Islamic discussion, only the first problem, the detection of the general value enshrined in the particular norm, attracted much attention. Very likely, the attack on the first step was regarded as decisive. If it could not be justified, the argument failed.

The critical dispute with respect to the *argumentum a fortiori* is already completely articulated in the *Risāla* of al-Shāfiʿī. In a remarkably lucid formulation, al-Shāfiʿī writes that "the strongest form of analogy is where God in the Qurʾān or His Messenger forbid a small degree of anything and it is known that if a small degree is forbidden, much of it is equally forbidden or more so in virtue of the excess of the large amount over the small.... Similarly if He permits a great deal of something, less of it is all the more permitted."[211] Al-Shāfiʿī then goes on to observe that "some scholars refrain from calling this analogy but say that it is the import (*maʿnā*) of what God has permitted or forbidden, praised or condemned because it is part of this; it thus stands on its own and is not an analogy to something else.... Other scholars, however, say that whatever is outside of the explicit scope of the Qurʾān or *sunna* and has the same import is analogy, and God knows best."[212]

The problem, then, was the classification of this argument. Was it a natural linguistic inference or was it a form of analogy? For those who reject analogy, the question, of course, was of immediate concern. But those who were not in principle opposed to the employment of analogy had to decide whether the constraints with which the use of analogy was hedged about also applied to the *argumentum a fortiori*. The Shāfiʿīs generally understood al-Shāfiʿī to have endorsed the view that the argument was a form of analogy, though one of particular obviousness (*al-qiyās al-jalī*).[213] The Ḥanafīs, on the other hand, claimed that the inference is based on a natural understanding of language and is one made by the jurist and nonjurist alike. This view is confirmed by the acceptance of the argument *a fortiori* even among those who reject analogy (*nufāt al-qiyās*).[214] Thus although the word *uff* refers to a particular expression of disdain, its prohibition conveys the prohibition of what the utterance of *uff* aims at, namely, injury, in this case, mental injury. In the same way, "beating" refers to the particular act of striking with an implement but conveys the notion of causing pain. Thus one who vows not to beat his wife does not break his vow in beating her corpse but does break it in pulling her hair.[215]

210. See Joseph Horovitz, *Law and Logic: A Critical Account of Legal Argument* (Vienna: Springer, 1972), pp. 96, 112.

211. *Risāla*, paras. 1483, 1485.

212. *Risāla*, paras. 1492, 1495.

213. *Lumaʿ*, p. 27.

214. Bukhārī, 1:73–74; Nasafī, 1:253, below and margin.

215. *Manār*, p. 526.

Those who deny that the simple prohibition of saying *uff* itself indicates that beating is prohibited suggest the case of a ruler who orders the execution of a person, but at the same time forbids that he be verbally abused.[216] More than the simple comprehension of the original prohibition was required to justify the inference in question. The attendant circumstances had to indicate that a general value was being safeguarded. To call this argument analogy was to identify the recognition of this general value with the discovery of the cause (*ʿilla*) in the process of analogy.[217] One might, however, be ready to concede that the *argumentum a fortiori* was more than the mere allusion (*tanbīh*) by one case to another and yet refuse to classify it with analogy in the usual sense.[218]

Although the view that the argument *a fortiori* is a form of analogy is particularly associated with al-Shāfiʿī and his school, it has supporters elsewhere as well.[219] The practical consequences of this distinction are not as obvious as might be hoped. Al-Sarakhsī points to the use of the argument in areas where analogy is excluded such as penal law.[220] But according to al-Bukhārī, even those Ḥanafīs who classified the inference as analogy regarded its use in these areas as legitimate.[221] It is thus common to find the dispute labeled a purely verbal one.[222] One consequence of the dispute would appear to be of significance. Some Shāfiʿīs excluded the *argumentum a fortiori* together with analogy from exercising abrogation.[223] This, in fact, is a severe restriction on the application of the inference, which cannot now be automatic.

There was also, it would appear, a polemical dimension to the insistence of the Shāfiʿīs on classifying the *argumentum a fortiori* with analogy. This was aimed at the Ẓāhirīs. The reports of Dāwūd's teaching on the matter conflict, and Ẓāhirī doctrine after him was divided.[224] His son Abū Bakr was among those who rejected the inference, and this appears to have been the mainstream Ẓāhirī doctrine.[225] But some Ẓahirīs did accept the argument and against them it could be urged that this amounted to a recognition of analogy.[226]

Ibn Ḥazm's attack on the *argumentum a fortiori* is part of his rejection of the process of "inference" (*istidlāl*) that was identified with Dāwūd and subsequent Ẓāhiris. Its mainstay was the *argumentum a contrario* (*dalīl al-khiṭāb*). The proposition that he defends is quite

---

216. *Burhān.*, f. 121; *Mustaṣfā*, p. 273; Āmidī, 3:65.
217. Āmidī, 3:64.
218. *Mustaṣfā*, p. 273.
219. *Musawwada*, p. 346; Bukhārī, 1:73; *Madkhal*, p. 126.
220. Sarakhsī, 1:242.
221. Bukhārī, 1:74.
222. Bukhārī, 1:74; *Baḥr*, f. 192b (Imām al-Ḥaramayn); *Rawḍa*, p.139; Ibn Taymiyya, *al-Īmān*, p. 348.
223. *Lumaʿ*, p. 35.
224. *Musawwada*, p. 346; *Manār*: p. 528, margin.
225. *Iḥkām*, 7:2, 61.
226. *Iḥkām*, 7:57.

simple: "Every communication and every decision gives you what is in it. It does not give you a rule for anything else, neither that it has the same rule nor the opposite rule. Everything else depends on its own ruling."[227]

Ibn Ḥazm's rejection of the *argumentum a fortiori* aims at showing that the inference is not linguistically valid.[228] The prohibition of saying *uff* is that and nothing more. The general obligation of refraining from injury to one's parents rests on other texts. Indeed, the very verse containing the prohibition of saying *uff* enjoins the showing of kindness (*iḥsān*) to one's parents (17:23) and forbids repulsing them. The following verse commands that "the wing of submission" be lowered unto them. If the prohibition of saying *uff* did, in fact, represent a general prohibition of injury, what sense would there be in these additional provisions? The "irresistible proof" of Ibn Ḥazm's contention that the prohibition of uttering *uff* tells us nothing about striking or murdering is that, were a witness to a murder to testify that the killer had merely said *uff* to the victim, all agree that this would be an instance of perjury. Yet the proponents of the *argumentum a fortiori* sanction this very lie.[229]

VIII. The *Argumentum a Contrario*

A similar impasse was reached in the dispute between the Ḥanafīs and the Shāfiʿīs over the validity of the *argumentum a contrario*. In the inference *a contrario*, the terms of a

227. *Iḥkām*, 7:58.

228. *Iḥkām*, 7:58.

229. *Iḥkām*, 7:58. Resting as it did upon claims about the natural understanding of the native speaker, the usual defense of the argument could only meet this line of attack with opposing assertions. The tone of the voices coming from the other side, however, was subject to some variation. Thus Ibn Rushd writes that "the Ẓāhirīs ought not to oppose the *argumentum a fortiori* because it is part of received usage (*al-samʿ*). Whoever rejects it, rejects a branch of the discourse of the Arabs" (*Bidāyat al-mujtahid*, 1:5, quoted *Irshād*, p. 179). Ibn Taymiyya, on the other hand, characterizes Ibn Ḥazm's opposition to the inference as nothing but contentiousness (*mukābara*) (*Irshād*, p. 179). Another dispute illustrates the same phenomenon. With regard to the fast of Ramaḍān, the Qurʾān fixes for one "who is sick or on a journey a number of other days" (2:184). The majority of jurists see an ellipsis (*laḥn al-khiṭāb*) here. One must understand: "for him who is sick or on a journey *and breaks his fast*." Hence if someone fasts on his journey, his fast is valid. The Ẓāhirīs, however, held that if someone fasts while journeying, his fast must be repeated. In his discussion of the dispute, Ibn Rushd is careful to point out that the Ẓāhirī reading without an ellipsis is the *ḥaqīqa* as opposed to the *majāz* of the majority (*Bidāyat al-mujtahid*, 1:250). This rather favorable view of the Ẓāhirī position may be contrasted with that of a later Mālikī, Ibn Juzayy, for whom the Ẓāhirī rule reflects their "ignorance of the tongue of the Arabs" (*Kitāb al-Tashīl*, 1:225). An even more pointed statement comes from the famous Mālikī Qāḍī Abū Bakr Ibn al-ʿArabī (d. 543/1148). Possibly referring to the Persian origin of Dāwūd al-Ẓāhirī, he writes, "Only weak-minded non-Arabs hold this. Correctness of expression and the force of elegance demand that 'and breaks his fast' be understood" (*Aḥkām al-Qurʾān*, ed. ʿAlī Muḥammad al-Bijāwī [Cairo: ʿĪsā al-Bābī al-Ḥalabī, 1376–78/1957–59], 1:78).

legal ruling are understood to be exclusive so that what does not correspond to them is by that very fact excluded from the application of the rule and given the contrary legal qualification. The gist of the argument lies in the claim that the exclusivity is equivalent to a verbal one. The statement of the Prophet that "*zakāt* is owed on sheep and goats that are put out to pasture" (*fī sāʾimat al-ghanam al-zakāt*) indicates that no *zakāt* is owed on other kinds of sheep and goats, such as those that are maintained on fodder (*maʿlūfa*).[230] This rule concerning sheep and goats that are not pastured is treated as a verbal one. It is thus capable of exercising abrogation and because it is general it is liable to specialization.[231] In this sense, the nonliability of sheep and goats that live on fodder is a strong permission and must be distinguished from the view that no *zakāt* is owed on these animals because there is no special rule regulating the matter. This is weak permission. The difference between the two points of view is evident when further texts come into the picture. For the proponents of the *argumentum a contrario*, these new texts deal with areas which are already regulated. For the advocates of weak permission, the texts represent original legislation. In the case in question, the Shāfiʿīs and the Ḥanafīs agree that no *zakāt* is due on nonpasturing sheep and goats, but the Ḥanafīs base their view on prophetic traditions, not on the *argumentum a contrario*.[232]

The *argument a contrario* allows one to infer that the deontic qualification of what is not expressly regulated is the contrary of that laid down, and it is for this reason that it is known as the "tenor of opposition" (*mafhūm al-mukhālafa*). The Ḥanafīs, however, generally refer to it as "the specific mention of something" (*takhṣīṣ al-shayʾ bi-dhikr*).[233] Numerous varieties of the *argumentum a contrario* are distinguished in the legal literature, each of which is referred to by the relevant element of specification. In the example we have considered, the attribute "put to pasture" (*sāʾima*) is what is specifically mentioned, and the rule excluding nonpasturing animals from *zakāt* is based on the "tenor of the attribute" (*mafhūm al-ṣifa*). The argument can thus rest on such elements as a specific number (*mafhūm al-ʿadad*), time (*mafhūm al-zamān*), or place (*mafhūm al-makān*).[234] Not all of these varieties enjoy equal acceptance. Ḥanafī doctrine stands out for its complete rejection of every form of the argument, and its treatment in Ḥanafī works of *uṣūl* aims at equipping the Ḥanafī jurist to repulse the arguments of the adversary.[235]

230. *Lumaʿ*, p. 27; Nasafī, 1:273.

231. *Lumaʿ*, p. 35.

232. Sarakhsī, 1:259; *Manār*, p. 548.

233. *Muʿtamad*, 1:161; *Mīzān*, f. 78b.

234. *Mankhūl*, p. 209; *Irshād*, p. 175; *Manār*, p. 546. For a full account, see Ben Choaib. "L' Argumentation juridique," pp. 74–86.

235. *Manār*, p. 546. Our discussion deals with the legitimacy of the *argumentum a contrario* with respect to the language of the Qurʾān and *ḥadīth*. The metalanguage of the jurists is another matter entirely. Here the Shāfiʿīs exclude its application. Similarly, it is excluded in the interpretation of the instrument constituting a *waqf*. The reason is that there is a presumption of carelessness in these cases that does

The least popular form of the *argumentum a contrario* is the *mafhūm al-laqab*.[236] Here the very mention of a thing by its name supports an inference that the rule does not apply to what does not bear the name. Thus if the Prophet had said that "*zakāt* is owed on sheep and goats," this would indicate that no other animals are liable. Among those who supported this view are the Shāfiʿīs Abū Bakr al-Daqqāq, Abū Bakr al-Ṣayrafī, Ibn Fūrak, and the Mālikīs Ibn Khuwayz Mindād, Abū 'l-Walīd al-Bājī, and Ibn al-Qaṣṣār.[237] The rejection of this form of the argument rests on the simple fact that there is no other way to refer to something than by its name. Two standard examples are cited to show the absurdity of upholding this inference. According to this form of the argument *a contrario*, to say that Muḥammad is the Messenger of God is equivalent to denying that there are any other messengers and to say that Zayd exists is to deny that God exists. Both of these inferences, of course, amount to unbelief. It is reported that these examples were actually used against Abū Bakr al-Daqqāq in a public debate in Baghdad.[238]

At the other end of the scale lies the "tenor of the limit" (*mafhūm al-ghāya*). Most of those who denied the argument *a contrario* accepted the view that the mention of a limit indicates that what is beyond the limit is differently regulated. This follows from the very notion of something being set as a limit. This doctrine is attributed to Abū Ḥanīfa and to the majority of his followers.[239] The classical Ḥanafī texts, however, do not make this exception, and this brought upon them the charge of a perverse consistency.[240]

The consistent rejection of the *argumentum a contrario* that we find in the Central Asian texts is inherited from Abū Bakr al-Jaṣṣāṣ. Among the important scholars who had preceded al-Jaṣṣāṣ, Abū ʿAbd Allāh al-Thaljī had recognized the argument *a contrario* based on the mention of a specific number (*mafhūm al-ʿadad*),[241] and al-Jaṣṣāṣ' teacher al-Karkhī, that based on the mention of a condition (*mafhūm al-sharṭ*).[242] Another student of

---

not apply to the Lawgiver (*Jamʿ*, 1:255; *Irshād*, p. 183). The Ḥanafīs, on the other hand, favor the view that the argument is applicable everywhere but in the case of the Lawgiver. The words of the Lawgiver are a "mine of eloquence," and there is no reason for restricting His intention as the Shāfiʿīs do (*Taysīr*, 1:101, and especially Muḥammad Amīn ibn ʿĀbidīn [d. 1252/1836], *Sharḥ al-manẓūma al-musammā bi-ʿUqūd rasm al-muftī*. In his *Majmūʿat rasāʾil* [Damascus: Maṭbaʿat Maʿārif Sūriya, 1301/1883], pp. 43–47). See also ʿAbd al-Jabbār ibn Aḥmad al-Hamadhānī, *Sharḥ al-uṣūl al-khamsa*, ed. ʿAbd al-Karīm ʿUthmān (Cairo: Maktabat Wahba, 1384/1965), p. 356 (exclusion in *furūʿ al-fiqh a fortiori* means exclusion in *uṣūl al-dīn*).

236. As the example shows, the name need not be proper (*Manār*, pp. 546–57). It is thus called *mafhūm al-ism* (*Musawwada*, p. 351).

237. *Irshād*, p. 182. For Mālikī attributions, see Bājī, p. 30, n. 5 (from his *Iḥkām al-fuṣūl*).

238. Asnawī, 2:318–19; *Talwīḥ*, 2:210.

239. *Lumaʿ*, p. 27.

240. *Mīzān*, f. 77a, margin; *Irshād*, p. 182. Abū 'l-Ḥusayn al-Baṣrī regarded its acceptance as universal (*Muʿtamad*, 1:161 and note 2).

241. Sarakhsī, 1:256; *Manār*, p. 550.

242. Bukhārī, 1:271; *Muʿtamad*, 1:153.

al-Karkhī, Abū ʿAbd Allāh al-Baṣrī, was even prepared to use the argument from a specific attribute under certain circumstances.[243]

The explanation for this clear trend toward a total rejection of the *argumentum a contrario* is not far to seek. It is in their unrelenting attachment to analogy that the roots of the Ḥanafī doctrine lie. The relationship between analogy and the *argumentum a contrario* is explained in this way by the modern German jurist Paul Oertmann: "Legal science has at all times provided two opposite tendencies for establishing new rules: analogy and the argument *a contrario* ... it is always possible to reason both ways, that is to say, either since *a* and *b* are expressly regulated by the law, but *c* is not, the law does not wish *c* to be treated in the same manner as *a* and *b*; or to say, since the law has regulated *a* and *b* in a definite manner, one may conclude that it intended the similar case *c* to be handled in the same manner."[244]

The difference between the problem as it appears in secular legal systems and in Islamic law is that the intention of the lawgiver is a theological problem in Islam. In a secular system it is, or at least should be, merely a historical one. The argument for the recognition of the *argumentum a contrario* rests upon the view that when God or the Prophet makes specific mention of something there must be a good reason for this, and the obvious reason is that a legally relevant distinction is being indicated.[245] The Ḥanafī argument against the inference runs in two lines that ultimately converge. In the first place, the undesirable consequences of the application of the argument are pointed out. In the second place, reasons are suggested for the specific wording upon which the argument rests. In both instances, it is analogy that is at the center of things.

The argument is fundamentally too coarse an instrument for the Ḥanafī jurists. This coarseness disqualifies it from serving as a basis for legal inference. "The proof that what we have said is correct," writes al-Jaṣṣāṣ,

> is that something cannot serve God as an indication of His law and yet be found without what it is supposed to indicate, not in any way entailing the rule it is supposed to point to. But this is exactly the case with the *argumentum a contrario* (*al-makhṣūṣ bi-dhikr*, "what is specifically mentioned"). For we have found God to specify certain things, mentioning some of their attributes and attaching legal consequences to them without this specification entailing the opposite rule in what is not mentioned. For example God says "Do not kill your children for fear of poverty" (17:31). The prohibition against killing one's children is specifi-

243. *Muʿtamad*, 1:161–62; *Mīzān*, f. 104a. For Imām al-Ḥaramayn, its rejection was due to an excessive consistency (*Burhān*, f. 122).

244. Paul Oertmann, "Interests and Concepts in Legal Science," in *The Jurisprudence of Interests*, ed. and trans. M. Magdalena Schoch (Cambridge, MA: Harvard University Press, 1948), p. 69.

245. Nasafī, 1:268; *Mīzān*, f. 104a.

> cally linked with the case in which poverty is feared. But the prohibition is the same in both cases.[246]

The automatic application of the *argumentum a contrario* would generate general propositions of law in conflict with those already established.[247] Moreover, its consistent application would mean that analogy can never be employed.[248] The very terms of a rule would fix its scope unalterably.

The question remains, however, why God should have conveyed His will through such specific legislation. In the words of a contemporary legal philosopher, "It can hardly be seen why the legislator should conceal his 'true intention' from those charged with the generalization of the law, thus imposing upon them the easily dispensable task of generalizing."[249] But the Qurʾān and the words of the Prophet are not ordinary speech in the density of what they communicate. The Qurʾān is a stylistic miracle and the Prophet was granted "pregnant speech," and perhaps they had in mind some point that we have not grasped.[250] This is the justification for shifting the burden of proof to the one who insists that the only possible point can be the indication that what does not fall under the specific text is differently regulated. But to prove this is to eliminate an indefinite number of possibilities, and "this can never happen 'until a camel pass through the eye of a needle.'"[251] Having made this negative point, the opponents of the argument *a contrario* proceed to suggest other reasons for the special language of the law.[252] There is one argument that stands out. "For us the point of specification," says al-Sarakhsī, "is that the investigators (*al-mustanbiṭūn*) reflect on the cause (*ʿilla*) of the text and on the basis of that establish the same rule in other instances so as to attain the rank of investigators and their reward. This would not be possible if the express regulation were general."[253] It would be wrong to take this as an *ad hoc* rationalization. Rather, it is a faithful expression of the ideology of the formalist jurists. The competition between analogy and the *argumentum a contrario* is readily apparent in the Ḥanafī texts, but appears also among those who were more favorably inclined to the inference. Al-Bayḍāwī (d. 680/1286), for example, argues against the argument from the specification of the name (*mafhūm al-laqab*) by pointing out that its application would exclude the use of analogy.[254]

246. Jaṣṣāṣ, f. 50a.
247. Jaṣṣāṣ, f. 52a.
248. Jaṣṣāṣ, f. 51b.
249. Horovitz, *Law and Logic*, pp. 96–97.
250. *Manār*, p. 551.
251. *Mīzān*, f. 104b; Nasafī, 1:269.
252. *Rawḍa*, pp. 141–42; Nasafī, 1:269; Bukhārī, 2:257–58.
253. Sarakhsī, 1:256; Nasafī, 1:269; Bukhārī, 2:257; Jaṣṣāṣ, f. 57a.
254. Asnawī, 1:314, 318.

What the arguments *a fortiori* and *a contrario* have in common is that both were defended as valid linguistic inferences. The Ḥanafīs claimed this for the argument *a fortiori*, and the same claim is made by the proponents of the *a contrario*. There is no longer any argument but only an appeal to authority. Against the mastery in Arabic of al-Shāfiʿī, the Ḥanafīs pit that of al-Shaybānī.[255] Among the prominent philologians on the side of the *argumentum a contrario* we find Abū ʿAmr ibn al-ʿAlāʾ (d. 154/770), Abū ʿUbayd al-Qāsim Ibn Sallām (d. 223/838), and Thaʿlab (d. 291/904), and against it al-Akhfash (d. 177/793), Ibn Jinnī (d. 392/1002), and Ibn Fāris (d. 395/1005).[256] Some way had to be found to tilt the balance to one side. It is claimed that al-Akhfash cannot compare with Abū ʿUbayd, al-Akhfash was a specialist in grammar and not in lexicography.[257] The Ḥanafīs recognize the merits of al-Shāfiʿī as an expert in language, but note that he and Abū ʿUbayd were both students of al-Shaybānī. Both praised him for his wonderful mastery of Arabic. Moreover, al-Shaybānī was closer to the first generations of Islam for whom native mastery of the language made the formal study of grammar superfluous.[258] One could, of course, refuse to pursue this line of discussion either because the weight of authority on each side was balanced, or because the opinions of individual scholars had no real bearing on the issue.[259]

The *argumentum a contrario* was a critical point of contact for the materialist and formalist views of the law, and the Muslim jurists were well aware of this. The following defense of the inference that al-Ghazālī puts into the mouth of al-Shāfiʿī is faithful to the doctrine of the master:

> If it is said: perhaps the law is specific so that those who do analogy (*al-qiyāsiyyūn*) can elicit the reason for what is expressly regulated and apply it to other matters so that the rules of the law are extended in this way, our reply is that this is nonsense (*hadhayān*). The Messenger of God would not have intentionally refrained from explaining it so as to delegate legal judgment to the dark confusions of the *mujtahid*s and their stumbling entanglements. Had God kept him alive longer, he would not have failed to clarify every obscurity in the law. It is only when there is no resort that we do analogy.[260]

The first and fundamental stage in the history of the *argumentum a contrario* is defined by the view of analogy just presented. At this stage, an attitude of reserve, if not downright

---

255. Jaṣṣāṣ, f. 53a.

256. *Musawwada*, p. 360; *Irshād*, p. 180; *Muʿtamad*, 1:173; *Iḥkām*, 7:7; *Mankhūl*, p. 210.

257. *Musawwada*, pp. 354–55; *ʿUdda*, f. 60b.

258. On al-Shāfiʿī: al-Suyūṭī, *Kitāb al-Iqtirāḥ fī ʿilm uṣūl al-naḥw*, ed. Aḥmad Muḥammad Qāsim (Cairo: Maṭbaʿat al-Saʿādah, 1396/1976), p. 57; *Iḥkām*, 7:10; *Mankhūl*, p. 209; denied by Jaṣṣāṣ, f. 53a; *Talwīḥ*, pp. 217–18, margin. On al-Shaybānī: al-Kāsānī, *Badāʾiʿ al-ṣanāʾiʿ*, 2:879; Ibn Taymiyya, *al-Īmān*, p. 76.

259. *Muʿtamad*, 1:172; *Mankhūl*, p. 210.

260. *Mankhūl*, p. 214.

rejection, towards analogy manifests itself in an acceptance of the *argumentum a contrario*. This is not only the position of al-Shāfiʿī but also that of Dāwūd al-Ẓāhirī.[261] This view is also attributed to Mālik, and of Aḥmad ibn Ḥanbal it is reported that "he was among its most vocal supporters" (*ashadd al-nās qawlan bihi*).[262] On the other hand, outside of the Ḥanafī school, there were those who took a similar position on the importance of analogy. Thus it is significant to observe that Ibn Surayj (d. 306/918), a famous commentator of al-Shāfiʿī's *Risāla*, attributed the rejection of the inference to al-Shāfiʿī and interpreted away anything that indicated a contrary view.[263] This basic opposition does not, however, go the whole way in explaining the controversy over the *argumentum a contrario*.

There were other grounds for rejecting the inference apart from the partisanship of analogy, for among those who opposed its use we find Ashʿarīs and Ẓāhirīs. In order to understand the Ashʿarī opposition, we must recall that the argument *a contrario* is regarded by its supporters as a linguistic inference. From the fact that *a* is regulated in a particular fashion, one immediately understands that *non-a* is regulated in a contrary fashion. What this means is that the express enactment is made the basis for a new regulation that is general in that it applies to every *non-a*. Now the Ashʿarīs were among those who took the position of hesitation with respect to linguistic forms that are general (*ṣīghat al-ʿāmm*). In rejecting the *argumentum a contrario*, the Ashʿarīs would be merely maintaining their position of hesitation. Imām al-Ḥaramayn explains the standpoint of the Hesitators and in passing clarifies the doctrine of Abū 'l-Ḥasan al-Ashʿarī:

> Those who deny the general forms because they are subject to equally balanced probabilities (*li-taqābul al-ẓunūn*) reject the argument *a contrario* for here the balance of probabilities is all the clearer and the inference all the more subject to hesitation. They have cited our master Abū 'l-Ḥasan al-Ashʿarī, as the head of the Hesitators, as rejecting the general form and the argument *a contrario*. But on the question of the vision of God, he bases himself on the words of God: "Nay, but surely on that day they will be veiled from their Lord." (83:15). The mention of the veil with reference to the abasement of the damned (*al-ashqiyāʾ*) suggests that the opposite is true of the saved (*suʿadāʾ*). I have determined after lengthy study of the writings of Abū 'l-Ḥasan that he is not among those who deny the general form as most writers believe. It was in disputation with the partisans of punishment (*aṣḥāb al-waʿīd*) that he rejected the general forms. The clue to his doctrine is that he rejects an argument from the general form where certainty is demanded. But we do not find him arguing against action in accordance with the apparent sense in the realm of opinion (*fī sulṭān al-ẓunūn*).[264]

---

261. *Musawwada*, p. 351; *ʿUdda*, f. 59a; *Qawāṭiʿ*, f. 72a.
262. *Musawwada*, p. 351.
263. *Dharīʿa*, 1:393. Al-Qaffāl al-Shāshī was more direct in rejecting al-Shāfiʿī's position (*Baḥr*, f. 192b).
264. *Burhān*, f. 121.

If Imām al-Ḥaramayn is correct, then al-Ashʿarī's doctrine on the general term is identical with that of the Samarqandīs, and it was not al-Ashʿarī but only his followers like al-Bāqillānī who rejected the general form in matters of action as well as belief and who rejected the *argumentum a contrario.* [265]

In response to this Ashʿarī challenge to the argument, we find an attempt made to justify the inference by establishing rules for its application. This is the approach of Imām al-Ḥaramayn followed by al-Ghazālī in *al-Mankhūl*. The application of the argument *a contrario* could not be mechanical. The specific quality had to be such as would fit the rule (*ṣifa mukhīla, munāsiba*).[266] To revert to the classical example: "The non-liability of foddered animals for *zakāt*," writes al-Ghazālī, "is comprehended not by the mere specification (of grazing) but from the connection (*rābiṭa*) established in the mind of the jurist between grazing, which is a benefit decreasing expenditures and producing wealth, and the obligation of *zākat*, which is due from the excess of the wealthy to benefit the poor."[267] In this fashion, the argument *a contrario* is reduced to a form of analogy. It is recognized that there are many cases in which the inference is not applicable, but this does not impair the validity of the argument, as al-Jaṣṣāṣ had claimed. As long as there is a suitable connection (*ikhāla*), the consistency of the argument is of no account since "the lawgiver has established what is not consistent (*muṭṭarid*) as a legal cause (*ʿilla*)"[268]

The assimilation of the argument *a contrario* to analogy meant that the inference was not a linguistic one (*laysa al-mafhūm jinsan min al-kalām*). This new view of the argument had the advantage of answering the claim of the opposition that any restriction of the rule established *a contrario* entailed the abrogation of part of the range of regulation based on the original express enactment. This followed from the understanding of the argument as creating a single linguistic form "*a* is *b*, and *not-a* is *not-b*." The modified doctrine held that there was no abrogation but merely specialization. The range of regulation established *a contrario* was analogous to a general term and just as much subject to specialization.[269] Although the *argumentum a contrario* was preserved, much of its force was lost, and al-Juwaynī is careful to note that it rarely leads to the level of certainty of the argument *a fortiori*.[270] Thus undermined, it was only a short step to the rejection of the inference in the *Mustaṣfā* of al-Ghazālī. The very assimilation of the argument *a contrario* to analogy was its undoing. For analogy cannot establish that what does not fall under a given cause is not subject to the same rule. Another cause could very well

265. *Mustaṣfā*, p. 374; *Musawwada*, p. 351.

266. *Burhān*, ff. 126–27; *Musawwada*, p. 360. Cf. *Baḥr*, f. 195b, quoting al-Juwaynī's *Asālīb*, a work on *khilāf* (Tāj al-Dīn al-Subkī, *Ṭabaqāt*, 5:172, n. 4).

267. *Mankhūl*, p. 216.

268. *Mankhūl*, p. 216.

269. *Mankhūl*, pp. 216–17; Bukhārī, 2:252.

270. *Burhān*, f. 129.

result in the same regulation.[271] Dāwūd al-Ẓāhirī was, as has been noted, among the famous jurists who accepted the argument *a contrario*. It was indeed the cornerstone of his doctrine of "inference" (*istidlāl*).[272] If the Ẓahirīs were to modify his doctrine, it could not be because of the claims of analogy, which they rejected, or because of the uncertainty of general terms, for they did not find them uncertain. It was rather a refinement of their own teaching that led some leading Ẓāhirīs to deny the validity of the *argumentum a contrario*, and ultimately that of the *argumentum a fortiori* as well. The attack on "inference" was parallel to the attack on analogy. In both cases it was denied that language had anything but an exterior (*ẓāhir*) level. In the divine legislation, there was neither "a ground" (*maʿnā*) that could serve as the basis for analogy nor "a tenor" (*mafhūm, dalīl*) that could be immediately grasped. Everything not in the words of the Lawgiver must be regulated by its own text, Ibn Ḥazm had insisted. Moreover, the two arguments *a fortiori* and *a contrario* are incompatible, for the application of the one immediately excludes the other. Their use is therefore totally arbitrary. Rather than saying that anything more injurious than exclaiming *uffa* to a parent is prohibited, one could just as well say that anything more injurious was allowed *a contrario*.[273] Ibn Ḥazm is thus able to pit one inference against the other and to pit analogy against the *argumentum a contrario*, which is its opposite (*ḍidd*).[274]

The partisans of "inference" claimed that a specific text could have a general range, its "tenor" (*mafhūm*). But there is no such linguistic phenomenon (*laysa hādhā mawjūdan fī al-lugha*).[275] "Whoever wants to find all the laws in a single verse," writes Ibn Ḥazm, "is bereft of reason, looking for a pretext to destroy the Sacred Law."[276] The point (*fāʾida*) of the specific language of a divine enactment cannot be identified with the argument *a contrario*. This is a heretical doctrine. There is indeed a point, but that point is obedience to the precise sense of the law. There can be no greater point than this, which leads to paradise and saves one from hell.[277]

The Ẓāhirī rejection of analogy did not rest upon the exclusion of analogy in each instance by a particular text. It was a principled opposition, based on the uncertainty of the results of analogy.[278] In no sense, then, were they bound to the argument *a contrario*. In the second generation of Ẓāhirism, we find Dāwūd's son Muḥammad among those

---

271. *Mustaṣfā*, p. 380; Bazdawī. 2:259.

272. See n. 209, above. Jaṣṣāṣ, ff. 261b, 262b, has a fuller form: *al-dalīl alladhī la yaḥtamil fī al-lugha illā maʿnā waḥid*.

273. *Iḥkām*, 7:57.

274. *Iḥkām*, 7:46; see also *Iḥkām*. 1:44.

275. *Iḥkām*, 1:131.

276. *Iḥkām*, 7:5.

277. *Iḥkām*, 7:12.

278. Sarakhsī, 1:255; Bukhārī, 2:255.

who reject the argument.[279] A similar position is attributed to al-Qāsānī.[280] One can surmise that as with the unit-tradition, this deviation from Dāwūd's doctrine grew out of contact with Muʿtazilī circles. On this Ibn Dāwūd and his rival Ibn Surayj were for once in agreement. The tradition of Dāwūd was, however, maintained by others, among them Abū'l-Ḥasan ʿAbd Allāh Ibn al-Mughallis.[281] This split in the Ẓāhirī ranks had practical consequences. Ibn Ḥazm, for example, applies the obligation of *zakāt* to animals that were fed on fodder, not merely those that grazed.[282]

Summary

In the theory of interpretation, we find the same convergence of theology and epistemology as elsewhere in *uṣūl al-fiqh*. The jurist had not only to assess the authenticity of the sources he was working with, he had also to determine how certain was their apparent signification. From their Muʿtazilī predecessors in Iraq, the Central Asian Ḥanafīs inherited a tradition of optimism as to the workings of language. The texts meant what they appeared to mean, and only the strongest evidence warranted departing from their obvious sense. Only the Samarqandīs succumbed to the growing scepticism toward language found in other circles, and even they apparently managed to resolve their doubts so as to leave the edifice of Ḥanafī *fiqh* intact. Of the arguments *a fortiori* and *a contrario*, the Ḥanafīs rejected the latter entirely in the interests of analogy. The former they accepted as a linguistic inference, yielding greater certainty than the results of analogy.

Addenda to Chapter Two

A student of *uṣūl al-fiqh* would do well to familiarize himself with the modern fields of semantics and pragmatics, on which there is no shortage of introductory works. The interest of the *uṣūlīs* is primarily in actual utterances that occur in a particular setting, including a specific time and place, rather than in the abstract sentences that underlie these utterances. The meaning that they seek to grasp is specific speaker meaning, not general linguistic meaning. The speakers of primary interest to them are God and the Prophet. Whatever its ultimate metaphysical status, the Qurʾān for the purposes of *uṣūl al-fiqh* is best regarded as a collection of utterances tied to particular settings in the life of the early Muslim community, although often enough precise information about these settings is lacking. Similarly the *ḥadīth* report specific prophetic utterances. The

279. *Iḥkām*, 7:21; *Musawwada*. p. 351; *ʿUdda*, f. 59a.

280. *Musawwada*, p. 360.

281. *Iḥkām*, 7:15.

282. *Iḥkām*, 2:24; Abū 'l-Walīd Ibn Rushd, *Bidāyat al-mujtahid*, 2:214. For other legal examples, *Iḥkām*, 7:19–33; Ibn Juzayy, *Kitāb al-Tashīl*, 1:246 (on Ibn al-Qāsim [d. 191/806]).

uṣūlīs are not concerned as such with how words and grammatical structures originally got assigned to specific meanings by acts of imposition (cf. the scholastic *impositio),* in Arabic *waḍʿ*, but in how the words and grammatical structures made available by imposition were actually used (*istiʿmāl*) by God and the Prophet. It turns out, however, that the shortest path to determining actual usage, the concern of pragmatics, may run through semantics, i.e., imposition, if one adopts the reasonable assumption that the original linguistic meaning is the intended utterance meaning in the absence of evidence to the contrary. Like modern students of pragmatics, the *uṣūlīs* work with speech-acts such as commands, well known from the writings of the Oxford philosopher J. L. Austin and his American student John Searle, and conversational implicatures, such as the *argumenta a fortiori* and *a contrario,* given currency by another Oxford philosopher H. P. Grice. And like contemporary philosophers and linguists, they sometimes have to grapple with where to draw the line between semantics and pragmatics. Studies in *uṣūl al-fiqh* are already beginning to make use of the analytical tools provided by modern theorists. These include Mohamed M. Yunis Ali, *Medieval Islamic Pragmatics: Sunni Legal Theorists' Models of Textual Communication* (Richmond, Surrey: Curzon Press, 2000), Šukrija (Husejn) Ramić, *Language and the Interpretation of Islamic Law* (Cambridge: Islamic Texts Society, 2003), David R. Vishanoff, *The Formation of Islamic Hermeneutics: How Sunni Legal Theorists Imagined a Revealed Law* (New Haven: American Oriental Society, 2011), and Robert Gleave, *Islam and Literalism: Literal Meaning and Interpretation in Islamic Legal Theory* (Edinburgh: Edinburgh University Press, 2012).

Pp. 52–58

This section is hardly a model of lucidity, and in retrospect it would have been better to present the complex Central Asian Ḥanafī scheme as an elaboration of more widely held distinctions.

Pp. 60–91

The classical *uṣūl* discussions of the imperative and the general term illustrate the formative role of theology in certain areas of *uṣūl al-fiqh*. The protracted debate on the otherworldly fate of the grave sinner (*fāsiq*) generated an enormous body of arguments, best preserved today, it would appear, among the Zaydīs, one of the surviving pockets of the *waʿīdiyya*, those who upheld the eternal punishment in the hereafter of such sinners. The debate was focused on the general language of the Qurʾān, but skeptical Murjiʾī strategies designed to undermine recourse to certain general Qurʾānic statements were carried over in the name of consistency to the imperative. For a long time *uṣūl al-fiqh* bore the burden of these theologically motivated positions. Eventually the cost to straightforward legal interpretation came to be regarded as too high. Murjiʾī theology was made to rest upon other bases than linguistic skepticism, and this link between theology and *uṣūl al-fiqh* slipped into general oblivion. Two recent German studies that focus on *ʿāmm* and *khāṣṣ* are Cornelia Schöck, *Koranexegese, Grammatik und Logik: Zum Verhältnis von arabisch-*

er und aristotelischer Urteils-, Konsequenz- und Schlusslehre (Leiden: Brill, 2006) and Hans-Thomas Tillschneider, *Die Entstehung der juristischen Hermeneutik (uṣūl al-fiqh) im frühen Islam* (Würzberg: Ergon Verlag, 2006). Both appeal to debates originating in Greek logic to explain the Islamic theological and *uṣūl* disputes, quite unconvincingly for reasons well stated by Vishanoff (*Formation*, 29–30).

P. 52 n. 8

See A. Kevin Reinhart, " 'Like the Difference between Heaven and Earth:' Ḥanafī and Shāfiʿi Discussions of *Wājib* and *Farḍ*," in Bernard G. Weiss, ed., *Studies in Islamic Legal Theory*, 205–34.

Pp. 54–55, n. 26

On the role of *bayān* in al-Shāfiʿī's *uṣūl al-fiqh* see Lowry, *Early Islamic Legal Theory*, 23–59.

P. 58

A far-ranging article on principles of interpretation in *uṣūl al-fiqh* is Gregor Schwarb's "Capturing the Meaning of God's Speech: The Relevance of *Uṣūl al-Fiqh* to an Understanding of *Uṣūl al-Tafsīr* in Jewish and Muslim *Kalām*," in Meir M. Bar-Asher, Simon Hopkins, Sarah Stroumsa, and Bruno Chiesa, eds., *A Word Fitly Spoken: Studies in Medieval Exegesis of the Hebrew Bible and the Qurʾān Presented to Haggai Ben-Shammai* (Jerusalem: Ben-Zvi Intitute, 2007), 111–56.

P. 60

Amend the first sentence of bottom paragraph to read "The command for the Ḥanafīs is the *utterance* of the imperative form etc.

P. 73, n. 105

On al-Ashʿarī's position on the force of the imperative form, see Ibn Fūrak, *Mujarrad maqālāt al-shaykh Abī 'l-Ḥasan al-Ashʿarī*, ed. Daniel Gimaret (Beirut: Dar al-Machreq, 1987), 197. According to Ibn Fūrak (p. 193), on most questions of *uṣūl al-fiqh* al-Ashʿarī followed the opinions of al-Shāfiʿī in his *al-Risāla fī aḥkām al-Qurʾān* as did Ibn Surayj.

P. 95, n. 202

On Ibn Dāwūd as a legal theorist, see Devin Stewart, "Muḥammad b. Dāwūd al-Ẓāhirī's Manual of Jurisprudence: *Al-Wuṣūl ilā maʿrifat al-uṣūl*," in Bernard G. Weiss, ed., *Studies in Islamic Legal Theory*, 99–158.

P. 101, n. 235

Here and throughout the attribution of *Sharḥ al-uṣūl al-khamsa* should be to the Caspian Zaydī Mānkdīm (d. 425/1034).

3
CONSENSUS

I. Introduction

With consensus, we come to that doctrine of *uṣūl al-fiqh* that has unquestionably attracted the most attention from modern scholarship. Snouck Hurgronje was perhaps the first to insist upon the centrality of this doctrine. "The *ijmāʿ* has in practice," he wrote, "become an adequate basis for the whole law which makes all other bases superfluous."[1] The primacy of *ijmāʿ* is now a commonplace of writing about Islam.[2] Two citations show how pervasive this view is, even in the work of the most eminent authorities. Hamilton Gibb writes:

> Indeed on a strict logical analysis, it is obvious that *ijmāʿ* underlies the whole imposing structure and alone gives it final validity. For it is *ijmāʿ* in the first place which guarantees the authenticity of the text of the Koran and of the Traditions. It is *ijmāʿ* which determines how the words of these texts are to be pronounced and what they mean and in what direction they are to be applied. But *ijmāʿ* goes much father; it is erected into a theory of infallibility, a third channel of revelation.[3]

Anderson and Coulson, leading scholars of Islamic law, see *ijmāʿ* in much the same light:

> It is the paramount criterion of legal authority inasmuch as it is the *ijmāʿ* alone which, in the ultimate analysis, guarantees the authenticity of the Qurʾān and the *ḥadīth*s as records of the divine revelation, the validity of the method

1. C. Snouck Hurgronje, *Selected Works*, ed. G.-H. Bousquet and J. Schacht (Leiden: Brill, 1957), p. 56.
2. G. F. Hourani, "The Basis of Authority of Consensus in Sunnite Islam," *Studia Islamica* 21 (1964): 13–60, is a well justified criticism, but his own conclusion, that the doctrine of consensus has no valid base, is uncalled for.
3. H. A. R. Gibb, *Mohammedanism*, 2nd ed. (New York: Oxford University Press, 1962), p. 96.

> of *qiyās* and, in short, the whole structure of the legal theory. As such *ijmāʿ* is the self-asserted hypothesis of Muslim jurisprudence. For while the doctrine formally rests upon a *ḥadīth* in which the Prophet states: "My community will never agree upon an error," it is the *ijmāʿ* itself which guarantees the authenticity of the *ḥadīth*.[4]

An examination of the classical texts, however, does not support these great claims made for *ijmāʿ*. It would indeed be a pathetic example of incompetence if the Islamic jurists had failed to observe so obvious a circularity as is suggested. To assert that the authenticity of the Qurʾān rests on *ijmāʿ* is unaccountably to ignore concurrence (*tawātur*). In a similar fashion, it can be shown that the doctrine of consensus has been wrenched out of the legal theory of which it is a part. But these critical observations are more properly placed not before but after a discussion of the main features of the doctrine.

In works on *uṣūl al-fiqh*, the treatment devoted to *ijmāʿ* usually falls short of that given to *ḥadīth* criticism, not to mention interpretation or analogy. This is especially true of the Ḥanafī literature, in which there is presented an *ijmāʿ* doctrine of striking simplicity and consistency. This doctrine holds that the Islamic community always contains those who espouse the truth on any point of law that should arise. Any general agreement of the competent authorities must of necessity include those in possession of the truth, which is now known to all. This truth immediately binds all those who entered into the original agreement as well as all later generations. Moreover, when a point of law is in dispute and a number of opposing positions emerge, the truth must be found among these views, and no one is allowed to introduce a new solution. A later generation can, however, come to agree that only one of these views is correct. The classical Ḥanafī theory is entirely in favor of *ijmāʿ* and consistently adopts those positions that were felt to facilitate the application of the doctrine.

This partiality toward *ijmāʿ* is not hard to explain. The acceptance of the doctrine bound the Ḥanafīs to nothing that they did not gladly accept. Given the age of the school and its roots in the ancient Kufan tradition, there was no likelihood that an opponent could claim *ijmāʿ* against the Ḥanafīs and receive a favorable hearing. Unless they agreed, there was no consensus. Similarly, the prohibition of new legal solutions in case of dispute only reinforced the strong school tradition that is so characteristic of the Ḥanafīs. Above all, however, one must stress the relation of consensus to the presumptive legal sources, the unit-tradition and analogy. It is the primary function of *ijmāʿ* to elevate these presumptive sources, or at any rate the norms they embody, to the certainty with which

4. N. D. Anderson and N. J. Coulson, "Islamic Law in Contemporary Cultural Change," *Saeculum* 18 (1967): 26. These views are by no means confined to English writers. One can find similar claims made by David Santillana, *Istituzioni di diritto musulmano malichita con riguardo anche al sistema sciafiita*, 2 vols. (Rome: Istituto per l'Oriente, 1938), 1:41, and José López Ortiz, *Derecho musulmán* (Barcelona: Labor, 1932), p. 26.

the Qurʾān and the *mutawātir* traditions were invested. This last consideration is of capital importance for it brings us back to the distinction between materialist and formalist legal thought. The formalist Ḥanafīs are only too ready to have the legal sources they accepted accorded a new status of certainty. The materialists, on the other hand, had nothing to gain from *ijmāʿ*; the sources they worked with were already considered to be of absolute authenticity, the unit-traditions that they accepted rested on more than mere presumption, and analogy they rejected outright. This opposition to *ijmāʿ* is amply documented in the works of Ibn Ḥazm and Qāḍī al-Nuʿmān.

Between the Ḥanafī position and that of clear-cut rejection, there lies a body of writing on *ijmāʿ* that is more difficult to classify. If the Ḥanafī *ijmāʿ* doctrine goes back to an early Iraqi receptivity to the doctrine, which is also found among some Muʿtazilīs, this middle-ground doctrine had its roots in the reserved acceptance of *ijmāʿ* which was common elsewhere. The picture one gets from the classical Shāfiʿī and Ḥanbalī texts is one of extreme diversity, and any generalizations made about these schools are apt to be open to challenge. Among the Shāfiʿīs, we find that the influence of al-Ashʿarī kept alive a highly critical attitude toward *ijmāʿ* that comes out in such thinkers as al-Juwaynī and al-Ghazālī. Those Shāfiʿīs who are theological conservatives, such as Abū Isḥāq al-Shīrāzī (d. 476/1083) and the former Ḥanafī Abū 'l-Muẓaffar al-Samʿānī (d. 489/1095), are much closer to the Ḥanafī position. This is also true of Abū Isḥāq al-Isfarāyīnī (d. 418/1027), whose affinity to the Ḥanafīs has already been mentioned. Among the Ḥanbalīs, the split runs along the same lines we have observed in the case of the unit-tradition, and once again the dispute shows itself in divergent reports of Aḥmad ibn Ḥanbal's teaching. Our consideration of the Mālikīs will be limited to their identification of *ijmāʿ* with the agreement of the Medinese.

II. The Basis of the Doctrine of Consensus

The answer given to the question of what is the proof (*dalīl*), that is, the basis of the doctrine of *ijmāʿ*, is of fundamental importance. The Ḥanafīs, who considered the doctrine to be solidly based on revelation (*samʿ*) and reason (*ʿaql*), felt free to interpret it in such a way that it could actually be applied. This accounts for the consistency and simplicity of their version of *ijmāʿ*. For others, the foundation of *ijmāʿ* was more problematic, and this initial uneasiness shows itself throughout their doctrine.

The Ḥanafīs based their teaching upon a number of Qurʾānic verses, of which the following may be cited:

> (2:143) Thus we have appointed you a middle nation (*ummatan wasaṭan*) that ye may be witnesses against mankind.
>
> (3:110) You are the best nation raised for mankind, enjoining what is good and forbidding evil.
>
> (4:115) And who so opposes the Messenger after the guidance has been manifested unto him and follows other than the way of the believers (*ghayra sabīl*

> *al-mu'minīn*), We appoint for him that unto which he himself has turned and expose him to hell—a hapless journey's end.[5]

There were also numerous traditions that had the advantage of setting forth the doctrine in more forthright terms: "God will not unite my people in error (*ḍalāla*)"; "What the Muslims consider good is good according to God, and what the Muslims consider bad is bad according to God." Although these were unit-traditions, they confirmed one another and amounted to what was concurrent in content. Moreover, they had been transmitted in the presence of large groups without the objection that would inevitably have followed were they groundless.[6]

In addition, the Ḥanafīs elaborated an interesting rational justification for the doctrine, which we quote in the version of al-Sarakhsī:

> There is also a rational argument (*shay' min al-maʿqūl*) in favor of *ijmāʿ*. God has made the Messenger the Seal of Prophets and has ruled that this law (*sharīʿa*) will continue until the Day of Resurrection, there being no prophet after him. To this the Messenger referred when he said, "A party (*ṭā'ifa*) of my people will never cease to triumph in the truth (*ʿalā al-ḥaqq ẓāhirīn*), unharmed by those who oppose them." His law must be manifest (*ẓāhira*) among mankind until the Last Hour. But revelation (*al-waḥy*) has come to an end with his passing. We know then of necessity that the way for his law to continue is for God to protect his people from uniting in error. For them to unite in error amounts to the abolition of the law, which is contrary to the survival which has been promised. Once it is established that the whole people are preserved from uniting in error, what they agree upon is like what was heard directly from the Messenger. That imposes certain knowledge, so does this.[7]

In this argument, the connection between *ijmāʿ* and *ijtihād* is apparent. The law, originally a limited body of revealed texts, must be maintained by extending it to cover the new cases that arise. One of the solutions put forth must be correct, or the law would have broken down. The criticism directed at this argument takes us to the very heart of the Ḥanafī conception of law. The objection is raised that the law that is to be preserved is the law as it appears in the original body of revelation, and this does not need the support of *ijmāʿ*. Furthermore, even if new solutions are to be understood as falling under the scope of the divine guarantee of the preservation of the law, the law as a whole cannot be said

5. Bukhārī, 3:253–57; Sarakhsī, 1:296–99; *Mīzān*, f. 140b. It may be noted that the use of the Qur'ānic verse 9:119: "O you who believe, fear God and be with those who speak the truth," is specifically identified with al-Māturīdī (Bukhārī, 3:257; *Mīzān*, f. 141b).

6. Bukhārī, 3:258–59; Sarakhsī, 1:299; *Mīzān*, f. 142a.

7. Sarakhsī, 1:300.

to have broken down (*inqiṭāʿ*) so long as its main institutions remain. The answer is given by the commentator al-Bukhārī:

> All the legal rules are actually instituted (*mashrūʿa*) and in force (*thābita*) before *ijtihād*, some of them in virtue of the apparent sense of the texts (*ẓawāhir al-nuṣūṣ*) and some in virtue of their latent reasons (*maʿānīhā al-khafiyya*). The part that was latent is manifested by *ijtihād*, not put in force by *ijtihād*, for analogy makes the rule manifest but does not put it in force. This being so, all fall under the texts that require the continuation of the law, and a break in the latent part would conflict with these texts. To say that the failure (*intifāʾ*) of a part does not mean a failure of the law as a whole is false. "Law" (*sharīʿa*) is a name which applies to all that the Prophet brought, and the whole fails with a failure of the part. Do you not observe that there is agreement (*ittifāq*) that the past laws (*al-sharāʾiʿ al-māḍiya*) were abrogated by this law, but this abrogation applies to only a part of their legal rules?[8]

The conception of the law here is of a functioning whole. The law can be said to continue only if it emerges from the texts, for the law is a system. Islam did not perpetuate the legal systems that preceded it merely because it took over some of the same rules. The role of *ijmāʿ* is to identify the correct solution that has been attained through *ijtihād* and is present in the community. Neither *ijtihād* nor *ijmāʿ* are creative; they are both declaratory. And of the two, it is clearly *ijtihād* that is the more significant. *Ijtihād* manifests the truth and maintains the continuity of the legal system; *ijmāʿ* merely broadcasts this truth to a wider public and fixes it beyond the reach of dispute.

This argument rests on a premise derived from revelation, the continuity of Islamic law until the Day of Judgment. More strictly rational arguments were not favored; this is true of every school. The working of *ijmāʿ* was not felt to be demonstrable by reason. This much was conceded to those who denied *ijmāʿ*. Al-Sarakhsī, for example, introduces his discussion of the doctrine by observing that "the consensus of this people imposes certain knowledge as a divine favor (*karāma*) to them for their religion, not because it is inconceivable on some rational ground (*maʿnā maʿqūl*) that they agree upon an error. The Jews, Christians, and Zoroastrians are greater in number than us and yet have been found to agree upon error.[9]

In the *Mīzān* of ʿAlāʾ al-Dīn al-Samarqandī, we find a bold rejection of this almost universally held view and a direct assault on the predominant conception of *ijmāʿ* as a

8. Bukhārī, 3:260–61. This argument is accepted by *ʿUdda*, f.161b, and *Qawāṭiʿ*, f. 155b. It is rejected by *Mughnī*, 17:200, and *Muʿtamad*, 2:477–78, for it means that *ijmāʿ* applies to other revealed religions as well. But the notion of law as a system and not merely a collection of rules is defended in *Muʿtamad*, 2:902.

9. Sarakhsī, 1:295. *Muʿtamad*, 2:482, speaks of *luṭf*. See also *Lumaʿ*, p. 51; *Mankhūl*, p. 366; Santillana, *Istituzioni di diritto*, 1:41.

divine grace of the Islamic community. This conception was worked out in response to those who claimed that the unanimity of a large group was inconceivable. This is the view often attributed to al-Naẓẓām.[10] Al-Samarqandī takes up positions that had been long abandoned and defends them with a new vigor and consistency. Here we shall confine ourselves to a brief summary of al-Samarqandī's argument. The full implications of his doctrine will be examined below.

Al-Samarqandī, in the first instance, claims that men of mature reason (*al-ʿuqalāʾ*) when confronted by controversy, naturally incline to resort to what they agree upon; the resemblance between what is in dispute and what is agreed upon enables them to resolve the former by appealing to the latter. This universal fact indicates that God sanctions the results of their agreement, for it was He who created them in this way. Similarly, when men are uncertain about what is good, they appeal to reason, which is the competent faculty. When they are uncertain about what the color of something is, they resort to the sense of sight. In the second place, when we find men in agreement, this indicates that something significant has served to bring them together. Men are of the most varied temperaments and intentions, and it is inconceivable that they agree by chance. We cannot, for example, imagine any large group agreeing in what they eat and drink on a particular day. Employing the device of enumeration and elimination (*al-sabr wa'l-taqsīm*) that he especially favors, al-Samarqandī reduces the number of possible motives for agreement to four: imitation (*taqlīd*); a misleading argument (*shubha*); a probable argument (*al-dalīl al-rājiḥ*); or a conclusive argument (*al-dalīl al-mūjib li'l-ʿilm*). Al-Samarqandī's frame of ref-

10. The doxographical tradition is split over whether al-Naẓẓām claimed that *ijmāʿ* was inconceivable, whether he rejected it as a legal source (*ḥujja*), or whether he accepted it in some fashion (*Baḥr*, f. 235a; Bukhārī, 3:252; *Musawwada*, p. 315). The second appears to be the case. For al-Naẓẓām, consensus had no independent force of its own. He defined *ijmāʿ* as any statement for which there is authority, even if it be the word of a single person (*Mustaṣfā*, p. 199; Josef van Ess, *Das Kitāb an-Nakt des Naẓẓām und seine Rezeption im Kitāb al-Futyā des Ǧāḥiẓ: Eine Sammlung der Fragmente mit Übersetzung und Kommentar.* Abhandlunden der Akademie der Wissenschaften in Göttingen, Philologisch-historische Klasse. Ser. 3, no. 79 [Göttingen: Vandenhoeck & Ruprecht, 1972], p. 118). But so did Ibn Surayj (*Irshād*, p. 90). Since analogy was no authority for him, there could be no consensus based on analogy, but there could be a consensus based on a tradition (*Mughnī*, 17:298). This doctrine is not eccentric, but resembles that of Ibn Ḥazm discussed below. As for the prophetic tradition that "My people will never agree upon an error (*khaṭaʾ*)," al-Naẓẓām did not regard himself as bound by what was a unit-tradition (van Ess, *Das Kitāb an-Nakt*, p. 116). But he did admit that all Muslims could not agree upon a particular error, although they might all be in error (*ḍalāla*) (*Fuṣūl*, 2:40; van Ess, *Das Kitāb an-Nakt*, p. 115). It was with respect to agreement on a particular error that al-Naẓẓām reservedly endorsed the argument of the jurists that unanimity was inconceivable in people of such varied views and temperaments (van Ess, *Das Kitāb an-Nakt*, p. 116). Furthermore, the general error of the whole community could only stem from the use of analogy, not from what depended on a report from sense perception (*Intiṣār*, p. 44; van Ess, *Das Kitāb an-Nakt*, p. 115). It should be noted that I do not think van Ess correct in attempting to draw a technical distinction between *khaṭaʾ* and *ḍalāla* (*Das Kitāb an-Nakt*, p. 115).

erence is that of a divine law, and he proceeds to show that only the last motive can be relevant.[11] The following passage, which deals with the misleading argument (*al-shubha*) may be considered the core of his argument:

> It is inconceivable that the misleading argument encompass all those who are subject to the law (*al-mukallafūn*), because God has imposed upon them the search for what is true and correct. There must then be a way for them to reach the truth. The misleading argument exists as a source of trial (*ibtilāʾ*), so that it may be rejected in favor of a conclusive argument by reasoning along the way leading to what is true and correct. Without this way we would have a case of an impossible imposition (*taklīf mā laysa fī al-wusʿ*), and this we know to be impossible by reason and revelation. Given that both these paths exist, the one leading to the truth and the other to error (*shubha*), the way of truth is more evident (*awḍaḥ*). So it is inconceivable that all fall into error when there is *ijtihād* and the seeking of truth for the sake of God.[12]

Large groups can indeed fall into error, but error can never encompass all as the truth can (*al-shubha lā taʿumm al-kull wa'l-ḥaqq yaʿumm*).[13]

The Ḥanafīs are confident that the bases for *ijmāʿ* are unshakable. Revelation, in the form of the Qurʾān and the *ḥadīth*, and rational argument all supported this central doctrine. With this confidence, one may contrast the embarrassment of some leading Shāfiʿī theorists. The uncertainty goes back to al-Shāfiʿī himself. In the *Risāla*, al-Shāfiʿī is asked what is the basis for following a consensus that is not founded on a Qurʾānic text or a tradition: "Do you agree with others that their consensus is always founded on a sound *sunna* even if they do not transmit it?"[14] Although unwilling to go so far, al-Shāfiʿī does insist that no tradition can ever be lost. A *sunna* of the Messenger may escape some of the people, but it cannot escape them all. Nonetheless, he claims that "we know that all will not agree upon what is contrary to the *sunna* of the Messenger nor upon an error, God willing."[15] As support for this wider claim, he cites a pair of traditions. It is clear that al-Shāfiʿī was not unsympathetic to the view that traced every consensus back to a prophetic tradition. But evidently he found this doctrine inadequate, for it would limit

---

11. *Mīzān*, f. 142a,b.

12. *Mīzān*, f. 142b. The text of this argument is a bit jumbled. The third possibility, the probable proof, seems to have dropped out, only to return on f. 143b. Furthermore, the conclusion of the argument identifies the conclusive argument that unites them as a *mutawātir* tradition. This conclusion would fit the argument from common experience (*ʿāda*), which is discussed below. Dabūsī, f. 5b, had held that agreement in conformity to one's forebears was a natural instinct. But this did not make it a legal authority, as one could gather from the history of the unbelievers. God's favor was necessary for this.

13. *Mīzān*, f. 143b.

14. *Risāla*, para. 1309.

15. *Risāla*, para. 1312.

the application of *ijmāᶜ* to the past. One inferred from the consensus of the Muslims that there was a directive from the Prophet that regulated the behavior in question. The *ijmāᶜ* doctrine which al-Shāfiᶜī did assert was that "it is not possible for the community (*al-jamāᶜa*) to all lose sight of the sense of the Qurʾān, *sunna*, or analogy, God willing."[16] In the face of the growing disunity of the law, the doctrine of *ijmāᶜ* must have been a source of considerable consolation.

To secure the basis for this critical doctrine was of continuing concern to al-Shāfiᶜī. It is related that, asked to find a proof text for *ijmāᶜ* from the Qurʾān, he read the Holy Book three hundred times until he found the verse (4:115) that promises hell to those who follow "other than the path of the Believers."[17] Al-Shāfiᶜī is regarded as the first person to found *ijmāᶜ* on a Qurʾānic verse.[18] It is undeniable that the verse in question more than any other became an object of contention. A host of objections and counter-objections accumulated about it and are registered in the *uṣūl* works.[19] But this spate of dialectics must not distract us from the main point, that a respectable circle of Shāfiᶜīs rejected this verse as a proof for *ijmāᶜ*. "Many objections," observes Imām al-Ḥaramayn, "have been raised, but my opinion is that in most cases the authors went to the trouble of concocting these groundless objections only in order to refute them. I have no use for such objections, instead I raise one of my own which effectively disposes of the verse as a proof-text."[20] Similarly, al-Ghazālī did not consider the verse an appropriate proof (*laysa naṣṣan fī al-gharaḍ*).[21] The traditions commonly cited in support of *ijmāᶜ* are also rejected by Imām al-Ḥaramayn and by al-Ghazālī in his *Mankhūl*.[22] These, too, are subject to alternative interpretations. In place of scriptural proofs, al-Juwaynī elaborated an argument from common experience (*al-ᶜāda*), in which he was followed by al-Ghazālī.[23] Subsequently in his later work *al-Mustaṣfā*, al-Ghazālī came to regard the *ḥadīth* as the strongest support for *ijmāᶜ*;[24] this shift is indicative of the uncertainty that still marks the treatment of this topic for these Shāfiᶜīs.

The argument for *ijmāᶜ* from common experience is presented in several versions (*ṣuwar*), all of which resort to a single phenomenon, the manifestation of an attitude of

---

16. *Risāla*, para. 1320. See Joseph Schacht, *The Origins of Muhammadan Jurisprudence*, pp. 88–94.

17. Fakhr al-Dīn al-Rāzī, *al-Tafsīr al-kabīr* (Cairo: al-Maṭbaᶜa al-Bahiyya al-Miṣriyya, n.d.), 11:43, on Qurʾān 4:115.

18. *Musawwada*, p. 315; *Mankhūl*, p. 305.

19. For example, *Muᶜtamad*, 2:462–69; *Irshād*, pp. 74–75.

20. *Burhān*, f. 191. Al-Samᶜānī, on the other hand, writes that "This verse is a proof text of the utmost reliability. Al-Shāfiᶜī used it to establish *ijmāᶜ*" (*Qawāṭiᶜ*, f. 155b).

21. *Mustaṣfā*, p. 201. On the interpretation of the verse, see Bukhārī, 3:254–55.

22. *Burhān*, f. 192; *Mankhūl*, p. 306.

23. *Burhān*, f. 192; *Mankhūl*, p. 306. *Baḥr*, f. 253b, wrongly attributes the origination of this argument to al-Ghazālī.

24. *Mustaṣfā*, p. 201.

certainty where certainty is not expected (*qaṭᶜ lā fī maḥall al-qaṭᶜ*). For example, if the Muslims agree upon a legal solution where there is no revealed text and manifest certainty in their view, one is entitled to infer that this consensus is based upon a revealed text of certain authenticity. We know of their determination to learn God's will, and we know that their large numbers remove the possibility of their conspiring to lie about their real view. Their certainty can have only one explanation. Al-Ghazālī notes that this argument is close to that used to establish the authenticity of a *mutawātir* tradition.[25] The text that underlay their agreement was not transmitted because there was no longer any need to do so. It will be observed that this amounts to the same claim made in the time of al-Shāfiᶜī that authentic prophetic traditions underlay the consensus of the Muslims. This is not the establishment of a doctrine of *ijmāᶜ* but its reduction to another source, the *sunna*.

There is a more ambitious and subtle form of the argument. The Companions have come to an agreement upon a question unregulated by a revealed text, but they do not claim certainty for their solution. Their Followers attack any violation of this earlier consensus. They treat as certain a solution that is not intrinsically so. The explanation is that they know on the basis of a certain text that consensus is a source of law. Once again this controlling text is not transmitted, at least not at the level of *tawātur*; it may, however, be identical with one of the unit-traditions commonly cited in support of *ijmāᶜ*.[26] In the *Mustaṣfā*, al-Ghazālī terms this argument "weak" inasmuch as it supposes that a large enough group cannot mistakenly consider something certain that is not certain at all. But that it is possible we know from the example of the Jews, who claim to be certain that Jesus and Muḥammad are not prophets. *Tawātur* excludes the possibility of falsehood, but not that of an erroneous conviction.[27]

III. The Operation of Consensus

The importance of the answer to the question of the basis of *ijmāᶜ* is apparent in the working out of the specific conditions for its operation. The Ḥanafīs begin with the broadly formulated principles they derive from the Qurʾān and *ḥadīth*. They reject any but the most necessary restrictions (*quyūd*) upon these principles. Those who establish the force of consensus from the past behavior of the community hold no such key to the application of the doctrine. They were led by the logic of their position to look for the conditions for the operation of *ijmāᶜ* in the past practice of the Muslims. Those Shāfiᶜīs, on the other hand, who entertained no doubts about the scriptural foundation of consensus, took the same positions in nearly every instance as the Ḥanafīs. In the one case, we have *ijmāᶜ* worked out from a textual base, in the other from inference. Despite the

25. *Mankhūl*, p. 307.
26. *Mankhūl*, pp. 306–9.
27. *Mustaṣfā*, p. 207.

fact that the Ḥanafīs had rational arguments with which to support the doctrine, in determining the conditions for its application, they stress its quality as a specific grace conferred upon the Islamic community. Having grounded *ijmāʿ* in reason, they found that the ambiguities urged against its scriptural foundations were illusory.

The discussion of *ijmāʿ* in the works of *uṣūl* centers about who enters into the consensus of the community and under what circumstances a consensus may be said to have been reached. There is agreement among the Ḥanafīs that on issues that require legal reasoning (*raʾy*), only legal scholars enter into the consensus. In fact, the discussion of *ijmāʿ* in the *uṣūl* treatises of all schools deals with the consensus of the scholars. This is readily understood if we recall that the chief function of *ijmāʿ*, its *raison d'être*, is to confirm the results of legal procedures, analogy, interpretation, and the acceptance of unit-traditions that are not in themselves certain. The masses lack the intellectual equipment (*al-āla*) to deal with these issues. The texts that speak of the agreement of the Muslims cannot properly apply to them, for one cannot speak of their agreement upon issues they cannot understand.[28] On questions where there is no need for legal reasoning, the Ḥanafī tradition was to recognize the layman (*al-ʿāmma*) as entering into the consensus. This would encompass those cases for the knowledge of which there was a general need (*balwā ʿāmma*);[29] such cases, as we have seen, would have to be regulated by *mutawātir* or *mashhūr* traditions. Al-Samarqandī appears to form an exception. For him, the chief role of *ijmāʿ* in the filling in of those areas where there is no text of certain authenticity is never lost sight of. Decisions based on analogy or the examination of unit-traditions can, of course, be made only by scholars. Apparently al-Samarqandī would deny that there was any need to consider the opinion of the laity, even in matters where explicit texts exist. The consensus of the scholars alone would already be sufficient.[30]

Some *uṣūlīs* are supposed to have denied the status of consensus to any decision, even one requiring legal reasoning, in which the whole community, scholars and laymen, had not participated. This view is attributed to al-Bāqillānī, but erroneously it seems.[31] On the other hand, there can be found those like Abū 'l-Ḥusayn al-Baṣrī who argued for

28. Bukhārī, 3:239. This is rather a polite way of putting the matter. For Abū Isḥāq al-Shīrāzī, they are like children in this regard (*Lumaʿ*, p. 54). Nasafī, 2:106, compares them to lunatics as far as *ijmāʿ* is concerned. It is also said that the laity "are like cattle and are under the obligation of following the *mujtahids*" (*Manār*, p. 739; Nasafī, 2:106, below).

29. Sarakhsī, 1:303; Jaṣṣāṣ, f. 221a.

30. *Mīzān*, f. 127b. See *Manār*, p. 739, margin, for the meaning of the inclusion of the *ʿawāmm* and *Manār*, p. 737, margin, on the definition of *ijmāʿ* so as to exclude the *ʿawāmm*; so also, al-Khwārizmī, *Mafātīḥ al-ʿulūm* (Cairo: Maṭbaʿat al-Sharq, 1342 H. Repr. Cairo: Maṭbaʿat al-Sharq, n.d.), p. 7.

31. On the propriety of this attribution to al-Bāqillānī, see *Baḥr*, f. 256a. What seems to be a conclusive argument against it is the fact that al-Bāqillānī argued in favor of the conceivability of *ijmāʿ* by suggesting that some powerful ruler might well gather all the scholars of his day in a single place and get their opinions without difficulty (*Burhān*, f. 189). The inclusion of the laity is defended by Āmidī, 1:204–6.

the total exclusion of the laity. Legal issues, even the most well known, require reasoning (*istidlāl*), and the laity are incapable of reasoning.[32]

The relation between the scholars and the laity does not receive much attention in the Ḥanafī texts; they make no attempt to bridge the gap between the two. In other circles we do find suggested solutions. The masses delegate the decision on issues beyond their competence to the scholars and may be said to participate in a general way (*bi'l-jumla*) in the consensus they reach.[33] One of the proof texts for *ijmāʿ*, it may be observed, is the Qurʾānic verse (4:59): "Obey God and obey the Messenger and those in authority from amongst yourselves."[34]

Stipulations are made as to the belief, piety and intellectual qualifications of the scholars whose opinions count for *ijmāʿ*. Because the infallibility of the community was a divine grace (*karāma*), it could apply only to those who merited grace. This would exclude those whose opinions deviated to the extent of unbelief (*kufr*). There is disagreement as to those who were merely "errant" (*ḍāll*). Some Ḥanafīs admit their opinion in cases unrelated to their error. Al-Sarakhsī approves of this policy upon condition that there is no public manifestation of their heresy.[35] Al-Samarqandī refers to this opinion but rejects it. "The soundest view," he writes, "is to reject them completely, for the standard (*aṣl*) in consensus is the consensus of the Companions, and God guarded (*ṣāna*) them from any dissent that would necessitate their being branded as errant, in order that their consensus might be an absolute proof (*ḥujja muṭlaqa*)."[36]

The treatment of specific groups is not without historic interest. The Khārijīs could have been treated as errant. They were rejected, however, on the grounds of their ignorance. Regarding so many of the Companions as unbelievers, they neglected the traditions transmitted by these Companions.[37]

The standing of the Ẓāhirīs in the constitution of consensus is a well known topic of dispute.[38] The Ḥanafī position is not easy to document, but it can be safely surmised that

32. *Muʿtamad*, 2:480–83.

33. *Mustaṣfā*, pp. 208–9; *Mughnī*, 17:212.

34. *Muʿtamad*, 2:470; *Mīzān*, f. 140b.

35. Sarakhsī, 1:311. The Shīʿīs are an example of this group (Sarakhsī, 1:311; *Mīzān*, f. 128a). The Shaykhs of Bukhara and Balkh ruled that the Shiʿis were unbelievers because they rejected the imamate of Abū Bakr, which rests on consensus (Nasafī, 2:108, margin). It should be noted that this was a consensus based on analogy with Abū Bakr's imamate in prayer.

36. *Mīẓān*, f. 128b.

37. Sarakhsī, 1:311. ʿĪsā ibn Abān left out the Khārijīs in recognizing a consensus on the lapidation of adulterers (Jaṣṣāṣ, f. 168b).

38. See Goldziher, *Ẓāhirīs*, pp. 103–4, and *Encyclopaedia of Islam*, 2nd ed., s.v. "Dāwūd ibn ʿAlī." For a summary, see *Baḥr*, f. 257a. Note also the defense of Dāwūd al-Ẓāhirī in Ibrāhīm al-Bājūrī, *Tuhfat al-murīd*, p. 151. Al-Bājūrī (d. 1263/1860) states that Imām al-Ḥaramayn's ruling that no attention is to be paid to the views of the Ẓāhirīs, is to be taken to apply to a specific group of Ẓāhirīs like Ibn Ḥazm, not to Dāwūd, who was "a mountain in learning."

it was one of total rejection. The disdain in which Dāwūd al-Ẓāhirī was held by al-Jaṣṣāṣ probably reflects a prevalent attitude on the part of the Iraqi Ḥanafīs. Al-Jaṣṣāṣ excoriates Dāwūd, not because he rejected analogy, but because he denied the possibility of a rational proof of the existence of God:

> He used to say that neither in the heavens and earth nor in ourselves are there any evidences of the existence of God and His unity. He claimed to know God only on the basis of prophetic report (*khabar*). The fool (*jāhil*) did not understand that the way to know the truth of the Prophet's report, to distinguish between his report and that of Musaylima and the other false prophets, to know their falsehood, is reason alone and the investigation of the miracles, wonders, and signs of which only God is capable.... This being the extent of his intellect and the range of his knowledge, how can he be counted among the scholars and those whose disagreement is reckoned with? He admits that he does not know God, because his saying, "I do not know God by rational proof," is an admission that he does not know Him at all. He is more ignorant than the layman and more abject than the dumb beast (*ajhal min al-ʿāmmī wa-asqaṭ min al-bahīma*).[39]

Dāwūd had not stopped at rejecting legal analogy, but had gone so far in denying the role of reason as to undermine the very foundations of the law. In this passage from al-Jaṣṣāṣ, we can glimpse the theological tendencies of early Ẓāhirism, which put it squarely at odds with Iraqi Ḥanafism, which was predominantly Muʿtazilī.[40]

From the words of the Qurʾān (2:143), "Thus He has appointed you a middle nation, that ye might be witnesses against mankind," it was inferred that those who enter into consensus must have the legal capacity to give testimony (*ahliyyat adāʾ al-shahāda*). The Iraqi Ḥanafīs were strict on this point. Any grave sinner (*fāsiq*) was excluded. This was also al-Samarqandī's opinion.[41] Al-Sarakhsī, however, distinguished between a sinner who is careful to shield his transgression from the public eye and one who takes no such steps. The latter's opinion is not reckoned with because it may be presumed that just as he commits in public an action he knows to be wrong, he may enunciate a legal opinion that he inwardly rejects. The more circumspect sinner is not suspected of such lying, and although he is disqualified from legal testimony, he merits grace in the afterlife and thus also shares in the grace of constituting consensus.[42]

The Shāfiʿīs took a different course. Only the unbeliever was excluded. The dissent of a heretic or a sinner was enough to prevent the formation of consensus. For al-Ghazālī, this stipulation was a necessary consequence of the manner in which the doctrine of *ijmāʿ* was founded. *Ijmāʿ* was based on an inference from the past practice of the Islamic

39. Jaṣṣāṣ, f. 224a; also f. 247b, where Dāwūd is not named.
40. See Goldziher, *Ẓāhirīs*, pp. 126–27.
41. Jaṣṣāṣ, f. 223a; Sarakhsī, 1:312; *Mīzān*, f. 127b.
42. Sarakhsī, 1:312.

community; there was no precedent for excluding any scholar from consensus. To do so would threaten the very foundation of the doctrine.[43] The problem posed by the sincerity of the sinner was variously dealt with. Al-Ghazālī insisted that his sincerity would become evident in the debate that would precede any consensus.[44] Other Shāfiᶜīs stipulated that a sinner's opinion was to be reckoned with if supported by an adequate argument. An expert of attested good character need not offer an argument to support his view.[45]

As for the intellectual equipment of the scholars, the Ḥanafīs demanded competence in the law, its theory and rules.[46] In other circles, the status of the pure theorist and the pure lawyer were debated. Al-Ghazālī in the *Mankhūl* excluded the latter, but in the *Mustaṣfā* argues for his inclusion.[47] The case for inclusion is especially strong in the case of the theorist (*uṣūlī*), who may not know the answer to a given legal question now but is able to derive it from the sources if need be. This is confirmed by the practice of the early Muslim community, which took note of the disagreement of men not known for their mastery of the legal rules. As a matter of fact, the legal system was not elaborated in their time. Even now the best lawyers may not have a ready grasp of all the details of the law in such intricate areas as testaments and menstruation.[48] This tendency to promote the status of the *uṣūlī* (and the theologian) had already been noted and rejected by Abū Isḥāq al-Shīrāzī. Like the Ḥanafīs, he demanded a competence in both *uṣūl* and *furūᶜ*.[49] Two very different views of the law are in opposition here. Al-Ghazālī perceives the law as a whole in virtue of its revealed sources and methodology. The opposing view goes further. It demands an active, not merely a potential, grasp of the law as a whole. The interplay of the various legal institutions is only apparent at an advanced stage in the working out of the sources. One cannot join the game anywhere in the middle. The relation between this view of the law and *taqlīd*, the adherence to a particular school, is obvious.

IV. Tacit Consensus

Among those who attacked the doctrine of *ijmāᶜ* several strategies were employed. The first was to deny that a large group could agree on anything that was not already of certain validity. But if such a source existed, consensus would serve no purpose. The Ḥanafīs did not accept the force of this argument. The revealed texts that indicated that the Muslims would never agree upon an error would be meaningless, unless agreement

43. *Mankhūl*, pp. 310, 312.
44. *Mustaṣfā*, p. 210.
45. *Musawwada*, p. 331; Bukhārī, 3:238.
46. Sarakhsī, 1:312.
47. *Mankhūl* p. 231; *Mustaṣfā*, p. 209.
48. *Mustaṣfā*, p. 200. See Bukhārī, 3:240.
49. *Lumaᶜ*, pp. 53–54; similarly *ᶜUdda*, f. 171a.

could be a reality and a significant one at that. As a second strategy, the opponents pointed to the great distances that separated the Muslim scholars from one another. Under such circumstances, it would be impossible for anyone to ascertain the existence of a consensus. In the face of this challenge, there was formulated the doctrine of a tacit consensus (*ijmāʿ sukūtī*), which the Ḥanafīs regarded as a relaxation (*rukhṣa*) of the strict law (*ʿazīma*), which demanded that each scholar explicitly express his opinion. This doctrine is of great moment in the development of the theory of consensus. It was severely condemned by those who rejected *ijmāʿ* altogether, as well as by those who feared its abuse. The importance of the tacit *ijmāʿ* to the Ḥanafīs may be gathered from the fact that in a number of *uṣūl* treatises it is the first topic to be discussed of those that concern *ijmāʿ* and is presented even without the basis for *ijmāʿ* having been established.[50]

The doctrine of a tacit consensus holds that there is a large body of questions upon which scholars are bound to seek the truth. When he is faced with an opinion (*qawl*) on such a question, the silence of a scholar may properly be taken as indicating his agreement. Because he must reach some conclusion in the matter, for him to refrain from denouncing a view he holds to be incorrect would amount to a violation of the Qurʾānic description of the Muslims as a people "enjoining what is right and forbidding what is wrong" (3:110).[51] According to the accepted Ḥanafī view, this doctrine is widely applicable. Only such trivial questions are excluded as the merits of Abū Hurayra as against those of Anas ibn Mālik.[52] The doctrine operates in the field of dogma (*ʿaqliyyāt*), where there was almost universal agreement that there could be only one correct view, as well as the law (*sharʿiyyāt*), for here, too, the Central Asian Ḥanafīs held that only one opinion could be correct (*al-mujtahid yukhṭiʾ wa-yuṣīb*). There was, however, a considerable body of scholars who held that every legal opinion was correct (*kull mujtahid muṣīb*), and they could argue that a scholar was under no obligation to oppose a view that he regarded as correct although different from his own. Those who defended a tacit *ijmāʿ* had to show that it could be reconciled with this opposing doctrine.

For al-Samarqandī, at least, this was easily accomplished. It is true, he admits, that according to this doctrine, every *mujtahid* is correct and entitled to his opinion. This does not mean, however, that every *mujtahid* will want to adopt the view of his colleague as his own. Although believing his fellow jurist to be entitled to his opinion, he will nonetheless seek to publicize his own view by offering arguments in its behalf. When such an opposing view fails to appear, we may safely infer that there is a consensus.[53]

---

50. This is true of Bazdawī, Nasafī, and *Mīzān*.

51. Nasafī, 2:104; *Mīzān*, f. 134b.

52. *Mīzān*, f. 134b. In *Muʿtamad*, 2:532, the example is ʿAmmār vs. Ḥudhayfa.

53. *Mīzān*, f. 136a, quoted Bukhārī, 3:231. Bazdawī, 3:231, distinguishes between *ʿarḍ* and *ishtihār*, assimilating the latter to the former, but this is only a minor refinement. *Qawāṭiʿ*, f. 165b, speaks of *intishār*.

The classical Ḥanafī doctrine of the tacit *ijmāᶜ* is substantially that which we find in al-Jaṣṣāṣ. In al-Jaṣṣāṣ's day, however, the doctrine was still a controversial one within the school, and he was called upon to answer the arguments of ᶜĪsā ibn Abān and Abū 'l-Ḥasan al-Karkhī. ᶜĪsā is said to have based his opposition to the doctrine on the well known incident of Dhū 'l-Yadayn (*qiṣṣat Dhī 'l-Yadayn*). The Companion Khirbāq Ibn ᶜAmr, known as Dhū 'l-Yadayn, one day noticed that the Prophet abbreviated his prayers. Dhū 'l-Yadayn brought this to his attention. Evidently, the Prophet did not consider the congregation's failure to contradict Dhū 'l-Yadayn enough. He asked Abū Bakr and ᶜUmar whether Dhū ᶜl-Yadayn had spoken the truth, and only after they confirmed his story did the Prophet complete his prayers.[54] Al-Jaṣṣāṣ suggests that ᶜĪsā may have objected to the sort of tacit agreement involved in this particular case. Here there was not time for people to show their reaction. The Prophet could, it is true, have waited to see if any objection would be raised, but instead he chose (*ikhtāra*) to make inquiries, speech during prayer having not yet been forbidden.[55]

Al-Karkhī based his opposition to a tacit *ijmāᶜ* on the fact that "it is not permissible (*jāʾiz*) for anyone to manifest disapproval (*iẓhār al-nakīr*) toward someone who holds a view different from his own." Silence therefore does not necessarily indicate agreement. Al-Karkhī's position is based on the right of the *mujtahid* to follow the truth as he sees it, that is, on the view that every *mujtahid* is correct. Against him, al-Jaṣṣāṣ argues that what is taken as a sign of approval is not failure to manifest disapproval but the failure to offer an opposing view (*tark iẓhār al-khilāf*). If there is an opposing view, it cannot fail to make itself known, above all in matters of religion where interest runs so high. The early Muslims felt a special responsibility to speak out, since they believed that their consensus would bind those who came after them.[56]

According to later Ḥanafī sources, the difference between ᶜĪsā ibn Abān and al-Karkhī is that the former rejected the tacit *ijmāᶜ* entirely, whereas the latter accepted it as a *ḥujja*, a basis for action but not a source of certain knowledge.[57] Abū Abd Allāh al-Baṣrī, al-Karkhī's favorite student, went further and rejected the tacit *ijmāᶜ* even as *ḥujja*.[58] The debate was one common to Iraqi Muᶜtazilism. Abū ᶜAlī al-Jubbāʾī accepted the tacit *ijmāᶜ* as a full one. But unlike the Ḥanafīs, he stipulated the extinction of the relevant generation of scholars (*inqirāḍ al-ᶜaṣr*) as the time span that had to be allowed for an opposing view

54. Jaṣṣāṣ, f. 221b; Sarakhsī, 1:304. The incident is also used by those who deny that the report of one person is an adequate basis for action (*Muᶜtamad*, 2:623; al-Suyūṭī, *Tadrīb al-rāwī*, p. 28). See also *Dharīᶜa*, 1:554; al-Bājūrī, *Tuḥfat al-murīd*, p. 122. On Dhū 'l-Yadayn, see al-Nawawī, *Tahdhīb al-asmāʾ wa-'l-lughāt* (Cairo, n.p. Repr. Tehran: Maktabat al-Asadī, n.d.), 1 (pt. 2): 185–86.

55. Jaṣṣāṣ, f. 222a; Sarakhsī, 1:307.

56. Jaṣṣāṣ, f. 222a; Sarakhsī, 1:308.

57. Bukhārī, 3:229. Al-Jaṣṣāṣ makes no such distinction.

58. Bukhārī, 3:229.

to be manifested.[59] His son, Abū Hāshim, refused to accord the tacit *ijmāᶜ* full recognition but did consider it a legal norm (*ḥujja*) inasmuch as there was a consensus to treat it as such, just as there was a consensus that recognized the unit-tradition as a legal norm.[60] Abū ᶜAbd Allāh al-Baṣrī rejected this view. Those who had treated the tacit *ijmāᶜ* as a legal norm had done so, according to him, only because they had considered it a completely valid consensus.[61] The later Muᶜtazilī masters such as ᶜAbd al-Jabbār and Abū 'l-Ḥusayn al-Baṣrī accepted the tacit *ijmāᶜ*.[62] The same considerations that won over al-Jaṣṣāṣ were dominant in the Muᶜtazilī school at large.

By the time of al-Jaṣṣāṣ, the tacit *ijmāᶜ* was widely considered to be the issue upon which hinged the entire doctrine of consensus. The opponents of *ijmāᶜ* had claimed that it was not possible for anyone to know the views of all the Muslim scholars. The only exception some of these opponents were prepared to recognize was with respect to the generation of the Companions, who had not yet spread over the face of the earth. Such was the view of the early Ẓāhirīs. Even among those who accepted a more liberal *ijmāᶜ* doctrine, there were those who recognized the weight of the opposing arguments. Al-Juwaynī was among those whose reservations on the possibility of the operation of *ijmāᶜ* in his own time nearly amounted to a denial of the doctrine:

> Whoever thinks that the occurrence of consensus on some presumptive question of law is easily conceivable in our time despite the absence of unifying motives does not know what he is talking about (*laysa ᶜalā baṣīratin min amrihi*). The fact is that most of the questions on which there is a consensus go back to the Companions, when they were together.[63]

Al-Jaṣṣāṣ, too, sees the weight of these arguments. One simply cannot know the individual view of every scholar. But this means only that the conditions for *ijmāᶜ* have been set too high by some. "The validity of consensus cannot rest upon each scholar expressing his agreement with the others, for if this were a condition for consensus, there would never be a valid consensus."[64] Al-Jaṣṣāṣ further argues that this holds good for every generation, that of the Companions not excepted. To demand explicit agreement is to destroy the doctrine of consensus, a doctrine that is established by divinely revealed texts. The same point is made very clearly by ᶜAbd al-Jabbār: "God meant by 'consensus'

59. *Muᶜtamad*, 2:533.
60. *Mīzān*, f. 135b; *Mughnī*, 17:237.
61. *Muᶜtamad*, 2:534.
62. *Muᶜtamad*, 2:533–34; *Mughnī*, 17:237–38.
63. *Burhān*, f. 191
64. Jaṣṣāṣ, f. 221a.

a view without opposition, since God cannot impose upon us what is unattainable. Since this is the only possibility, we know that it is what God intended."[65]

Various arguments were advanced to show that the principle upon which the tacit *ijmāʿ* rested was a familiar one. The miraculous nature of the Qurʾān was demonstrated by the fact that no one of the contemporary Arabs had been able to emulate it. Had they been able to do so, they would have done so, and we would know their feat.[66] It was argued that one's knowledge that the Byzantines were all Christians had an analogous basis. No one had actually counted all the inhabitants of that land.[67] We find a curious and rather more sophisticated way of making the same point in the *Mīzān* of al-Samarqandī. Al-Samarqandī claims that we know the names of things—genera, species, and individuals—in the same way that we know that there is a consensus on a question of law. We do not know that everyone who speaks the language calls bread "bread," but because no objection is raised to the common usage, we infer that there is a consensus: "Whoever would stipulate a statement (*nuṭq*) from everyone and deny consensus by diffusion (*intishār*) coupled with the silence of the others denies that he is "man" and an "animal" and must refrain from calling meat, bread, and water by name because he has not expressly heard these names from everyone. But all rational people reject this, and this amounts to a consensus on their part that an explicit consensus on legal matters is not stipulated."[68] We see here a leading feature of the thought of al-Samarqandī, an attempt to break down the barriers between law and life. Consensus, we have seen, is a rationally valid principle for regulating human affairs. A closer examination of language reveals that this most vital of human institutions rests upon consensus, a tacit consensus. To continue to use language despite this fact is to participate oneself in a consensus which validates not only language itself but the recognition of a tacit consensus in the law.

It is not implausible that ʿĪsā ibn Abān in rejecting the tacit consensus was following in the footsteps of his master Muḥammad al-Shaybānī. The circle of Abū Yūsuf, on the other hand, may have been more favorably disposed toward the tacit consensus.[69] At any rate, Bishr al-Marīsī, a student of Abū Yūsuf, was among those associated with a liberal *ijmāʿ* doctrine. Aḥmad ibn Ḥanbal is reported by his son ʿAbd Allāh to have proclaimed, "Whoever claims consensus is a liar. Perhaps the people are not in agreement. This is the

65. *Muʿtamad*, 2:536.

66. *Mughnī*, 17:236; Sarakhsī, 1:309.

67. *Muʿtamad*, 2:536–37. Cf. *Iḥkām*, 4:179, 182–83.

68. *Mīzān*, f. 135b.

69. One argument against a tacit consensus was that a young but otherwise fully accomplished scholar might refrain from expressing his opinion out of deference to his seniors. This, we are told, would be permissible according to Abū Ḥanīfa and Abū Yūsuf, but not according to Muḥammad al-Shaybānī. According to him, the young scholar is obliged to form his own opinion, which, if different, would prevent the formation of a consensus. Thus for al-Shaybānī, silence that stems from a failure to exercise legal reasoning is not an acceptable basis for consensus (*Mīzān*, f. 135b).

claim of Bishr al-Marīsī and al-Aṣamm. Let him rather say, 'I do not know that the people have disagreed,' if no disagreement has reached him."[70] This statement was one that any opponent of *ijmāʿ* would have been only too happy to use, and it is quoted with approval by Ibn Ḥazm.[71] The doctrine of the tacit *ijmāʿ* is linked with two disreputable theologians.

Within the Ḥanbalī school, we find Ibn Taymiyya taking Ahmad's statement at face value. He sees in it a condemnation of the claim of *ijmāʿ* after the generation of the Companions or perhaps their Followers. In Aḥmad's own teaching, there is hardly to be found any claim of consensus except from the first generations. Aḥmad's statement is to be interpreted as a prohibition of making such a claim. It applies to the claim of a general express consensus (*ijmāʿ ʿāmm nuṭqī*) for this is in fact equivalent to a tacit *ijmāʿ*. The theologian-jurists (*fuqahāʾ al-mutakallimīn*) like al-Marīsī and al-Aṣamm were given to making such claims because they were familiar only with the teachings of people like Abū Ḥanīfa and Mālik. Of the views of the Companions and Followers they were ignorant.[72] Ibn Taymiyya thus comes close to the old Ẓāhirī position that would restrict the working of *ijmāʿ* to the first generation of the Muslims. To claim the consensus of a later period is inadmissible because this amounts to claiming a tacit *ijmāʿ*. With this, one may contrast the interpretation of Aḥmad's dictum that Qaḍī Abū Yaʿlā puts forth. He admits that its apparent sense (*ẓāhir*) is a rejection of the validity of consensus. "But this is not to be taken in its literal sense. He only said this by way of pious scruple because of the possibility that there was dissent that had not reached him." This must be the meaning of Aḥmad's statement because only in this way is it to be reconciled with his own use of consensus in legal discussion.[73] It will be recalled that in the dispute over the unit-tradition, Ibn al-Qayyim, one of those who claimed that it was a source of certain knowledge, similarly interpreted a discordant dictum of Aḥmad's as a token of piety.[74] The reputation for saintliness that Aḥmad had earned at so great a cost stood his followers in good stead.

It is in accordance with this basic disagreement that one must understand the doctrine of the tacit consensus in the Ḥanbalī texts. Ibn Taymiyya and Abū Yaʿlā both accept a tacit consensus of the Companions with the stipulation of the extinction of the age (*inqirāḍ al-ʿaṣr*) and claim that this was Aḥmad's teaching. But the formulation of the issue must not mislead us. For Ibn Taymiyya, the doctrine is limited to the first two generations; the lifespan of *ijmāʿ* was a brief one. This was the way in which he understood

70. *Musawwada*, p. 315; *ʿUdda*, f. 159b; Ibn Qayyim al-Jawziyya, *Mukhtaṣar al-ṣawāʿiq*, p. 510 (Ibn ʿUlayya instead of Bishr al-Marīsī), p. 528 (several versions); Ibn Qayyim al-Jawziyya, *Iʿlām al-muwaqqiʿīn*, 1:30; *Talwīḥ*, 3:309; *Ḥuṣūl*, p. 67. It should also be noted that Ibn ʿUlayya excluded Followers from the consensus of the Companions (*Musawwada*, p. 333; *Ḥuṣūl*, p. 73).

71. *Iḥkām*, 4:188–89. Josef van Ess, *Die Erkenntnislehre des ʿAḍudaddīn al-Īcī*, p. 379, correctly questions the state of this passage.

72. *Musawwada*, p. 316.

73. *ʿUdda*, f. 159b, quoted *Musawwada*, p. 316.

74. See above, ch. 1, n. 134.

Aḥmad's pronouncements on consensus: "When Aḥmad speaks of the consensus of every age, he refers to the Followers (*wa-kalāmuhu fī ijmāᶜ kull ᶜaṣr innamā huwa fī al-tābiᶜīn*)."[75] Abū Yaᶜlā, on the other hand, must be understood to espouse a tacit consensus that encompasses all generations. The doctrine is formulated in terms of the Companions only because they serve as the model. That this is so is confirmed by the modern Ḥanbalī Ibn Badrān, who carefully notes that the tacit *ijmāᶜ* applies equally to the Companions and to those who come after them.[76]

V. Consensus of the Majority

The Ḥanafīs championed the tacit *ijmāᶜ* because they came to identify it with *ijmāᶜ* in general. There could be no consensus if it were necessary to canvas the opinion of every scholar individually. The same consideration prompted al-Jaṣṣāṣ to adopt a position that was chiefly associated with Muḥammad ibn Jarīr al-Ṭabarī (d. 310/923), the famous historian. Al-Jaṣṣāṣ held that a few dissenting opinions would not prevent the formation of a valid consensus. This view he maintained in opposition to his teacher al-Karkhī, there being, as al-Jaṣṣāṣ was quick to claim, no accepted Ḥanafī doctrine on the question.[77] In favor of his position, he argued that to accept a tacit consensus already meant ignoring the possibility of the question at issue not having come to the notice of a scholar or two. If this were so, then it was only a short step to discounting the opposition of these few should it be expressed. Unless one was prepared to do so, no consensus would be possible. Those cases in which one Companion had been able to prevent the formation of a consensus were explained by postulating a special license (*taswīgh*) of *ijtihād*, which the majority had been willing to grant.[78]

When the community was divided into two camps, one consisting of the vast majority of the scholars and the other of a few dissenters, the possibility of the great majority being in error was excluded. The vast majority would form a body whose report was of certain reliability; the dissenters, on the other hand, might not be telling the truth as to their views. They could have been subject to pressures that could not possibly have been brought to bear on the main body of scholars.[79] This point is of special importance. It presents us with new evidence of the operation of the *tawātur* concept. The *tawātur* number guarantees the authenticity not only of the corpus of revelation but also of the elaboration of that revelation by the Muslim scholars. If the error of the vast majority were possible, then it would be possible for the majority to apostatize while one person

75. *Musawwada*, p. 316.
76. *Madkhal*, p. 131.
77. Jaṣṣāṣ, f. 224b.
78. Jaṣṣāṣ, f. 224b; Sarakhsī, 1:317.
79. Jaṣṣāṣ, f. 224b.

remain a believer. If this were possible, then the law would come to an end for want of those whose transmission of the law would be authoritative. The other possibility is that the one believer would have to be considered worthy of absolute confidence, and one would then have to affirm that he is God's proof against mankind through consensus.[80]

There are two questions at issue here. First, can the number of those who constitute *ijmāʿ* drop below *tawātur*? And secondly, can the Muslims drop below this number? Al-Jaṣṣāṣ's negative reply to the first question, of course, contains the answer to the second. The law must continue to function normally until the end of time. His conception of the functioning of the law is one which lays special emphasis on the role of *ijtihād* as a preparation for certainty in the form of consensus.

Al-Ghazālī's answer to these questions is worth considering. In the *Mankhūl*, he takes the position that the body of scholars must be at *tawātur* level for *ijmāʿ* to have any force.[81] This, as he notes in the *Mustaṣfā*, is entailed by the view that bases *ijmāʿ* on the argument from common experience. The group whose behavior allows us to infer the validity of consensus must be too large to be susceptible to error or collusion.[82] In the *Mustaṣfā*, al-Ghazālī came to base *ijmāʿ* on revelation and now considered himself to be in a position to reject the claim that the number constituting consensus must be *mutawātir*. The sincerity of the scholars is to be founded in God's promise that some Muslims would always uphold the truth. It is enough that there be an external manifestation of belief; when they agree, we can infer that they are telling the truth. Al-Ghazālī was more inclined to favor the view that the Muslim community as a whole had always to be *mutawātir*. This would ensure the transmission of the foundations of the law. But even on this point, he suggests that God could attain an equivalent result either by having unbelievers share in the transmission or by bypassing the *tawātur* principle altogether and simply creating certain knowledge where it was suitable.[83]

The difference between these two positions is quite clear. Al-Jaṣṣāṣ takes the point of view that presupposes God's constant and uniform supervision of the development of the law. A crucial element in the consistent development of the law is consensus, and the conditions required for consensus to operate must be realized. The Muʿtazilī faith in the justice of God is linked with the Ḥanafī understanding of law as a gradually emerging body of truths. Al-Ghazālī has no such conception of the law. For him it is enough if the main institutions of the law (*aʿlām al-sharʿ*) are transmitted by the community.

In the later development of Ḥanafī *uṣūl*, al-Jaṣṣāṣ's doctrine of a majority consensus was not widely maintained. Outside of al-Jaṣṣāṣ's immediate circle, the most important

80. Jaṣṣāṣ, f. 225a.

81. *Mankhūl*, pp. 313–14.

82. *Mustaṣfā*, p. 215.

83. *Mustaṣfā*, pp. 215–16.

proponent of this view was al-Sarakhsī,[84] but al-Sarakhsī rejected the notion that the constituents of consensus had to reach *tawātur* level.[85] The majority of Ḥanafīs saw no basis in the revealed texts that instituted consensus for the exclusion of the opinion of any qualified *mujtahid*. "These texts," says al-Samarqandī, "refer to all the people of consensus, the majority of the people are only part of the believers."[86] The prophetic traditions that were cited in support of the majoritarian doctrine, such as "Cling to the great mass" (*ʿalaykum bi'l-sawād al-aʿẓam*) were rejected as unit-traditions in an area that regulated belief, or they were subjected to reconciling interpretation.[87] Equally rejected was the curious argument that in order for a consensus to have immediate legal force, there had to be some opposition.[88] The point of this argument is that the doctrine of consensus is not primarily concerned with the fact of agreement, but rather with its normative character. How could this normative character manifest itself among those who constituted the original consensus? The consensus did not appear to impose upon them anything they did not already accept. The answer is that once their consensus was ascertained, they no longer had the option of taking a different view. It could also be said that there was now a new obligation to believe that the result of their consensus was identical with what God willed.[89] The later Ḥanafīs were thus united in rejecting al-Jaṣṣāṣ's assimilation of *ijmāʿ* to the *tawātur* principle. They insisted that the doctrine of consensus be worked out from the texts that instituted it, and these texts did not make the operation of consensus contingent on the number of those in agreement.[90]

The most famous scholar to have held that the dissent of one or two jurists was of no account was al-Ṭabarī. Al-Ṭabarī, it seems, did not hesitate to put his theory into practice. He is reported to have enumerated four hundred legal questions on which al-Shāfiʿī had violated consensus![91] The Shāfiʿī Abū Isḥāq al-Isfarāyīnī astutely observed that al-Ṭabarī's idiosyncratic view on *ijmāʿ* would exclude itself.[92] Two prominent Muʿtazilīs, al-Khayyāṭ and Ibn al-Ikhshīd, are also cited in connection with the majoritarian *ijmāʿ*. Al-Khayyāṭ held that a minority falling short of *tawātur* was to be discounted.[93] This position

84. Sarakhsī, 1:316–17. Abū ʿAbd Allāh al-Jurjānī, like al-Jaṣṣāṣ a student of al-Karkhī, also held this doctrine (Bukhārī, 3:245; *Musawwada*, p. 330).

85. Sarakhsī, 1:312; Dabūsī, f. 7b.

86. *Mīzān*, f. 128b.

87. *Mīzān*, f. 129a, quoted Bukhārī, 3:246–47.

88. Bukhārī, 3:247.

89. Bukhārī, 3:247.

90. Bukhārī, 3:247; *Manār*, p. 742.

91. *Iḥkām*, 4:189. Recall al-Ṭabarī's position on the *mursal* tradition (see above, ch. 1, n. 137). On al-Ṭabarī's place in the Shāfiʿī school, see Tāj al-Dīn al-Subkī, *Ṭabaqāt*, 3:126–27, and al-Nawawī, *Tahdhīb al-asmāʾ*, 1 (pt. 1): 79. *Risāla*, para. 388, suggests that al-Shāfiʿī himself gave weight to a consensus of the majority, but I have not found a discussion of this in the *uṣūl* literature.

92. *Baḥr*, f. 258a.

93. *Intiṣār*, p. 94; *Muʿtamad*, 2:486–87; Bukhārī, 3:245; Qarāfī, p. 336.

was held by other Muʿtalizīs and some Mālikīs.[94] Ibn al-Ikhshīd discounted the dissent of one or two on questions of theology.[95]

Al-Jaṣṣāṣ is careful to distinguish his position from that which identified consensus with the simple majority (*akthar*); this is the view of the Ḥashwiyya.[96] Similarly, Qaḍī al-Nuʿmān considers this doctrine as that of "most of the Ḥashwiyya and Nawāṣib."[97] The Ḥanbalis come to mind immediately, and there is evidence, though only scanty evidence, that this view did find support among them. Our classical Ḥanbalī sources are for once united in rejecting this doctrine.[98] We are told, however, that Aḥmad ibn Ḥanbal could be understood as supporting it (*wa-qad awmaʾa ilayhi*).[99] Ibn Badrān is more explicit. He identifies the opposing position as that of the majority, but states that from Aḥmad's own views it could be inferred that the majority constituted consensus except in the time of the Companions, for a complete canvassing was thereafter impossible.[100] Because al-Nuʿmān refers to the Nawāṣib, those hostile to ʿAlī, the possibility suggests itself that the doctrine was intended to exclude the Shiʿis from consensus. Al-Jaṣṣāṣ, in fact, argues against the consensus of a simple majority by noting that most of the people in the time of the Umayyads accepted the imamate of Muʿāwiya and Yazīd and their like from among the Marwānids. The minority were against this, and we know that they were right.[101]

The tacit consensus and the consensus of the majority were not the only doctrines that served to put consensus more within reach. Some made the "irregular" (*shādhdh*) stipulation that only the opinion of well known *muftīs* be considered.[102] Some held that only the scholars of Mecca, Medina, and the two "encampments" (*miṣrayn*), Basra and Kufa, entered into consensus.[103] Clearly, this latter doctrine was formulated in reaction to the Mālikī claim that the consensus of the scholars of Medina was all that mattered.

This claim aroused considerable controversy. It was furthermore subject to varying interpretations among the Mālikīs themselves. Here only some of the relevant issues can be outlined. The strongest version of the claim would identify the consensus of the Muslims with that of Medina. This version was upheld by Abū Bakr Ibn Bukayr (d. 305/917).[104] The most important alternative version of the claim is linked with the name

94. Qarāfī, p. 336. One of the Mālikīs was Ibn Khuwayz Mindād (*Mankhūl*, p. 312, n. 3).

95. Qarāfī, p. 336. See the quotation from Ibn al-Ikhshīd in Nuʿmān, pp. 59–60.

96. Jaṣṣāṣ, f. 227b.

97. Nuʿmān, p. 84.

98. *Rawḍa*, p. 71; *Musawwada*, p. 329.

99. *Rawḍa*, p. 71; Bukhārī, 3:245.

100. *Madkhal*, p. 130.

101. Jaṣṣāṣ, f. 228a. On Muʿāwiya and Yazīd, see Henri Laoust, *Les schismes dans l'Islam* (Paris: Payot, 1965), pp. 425–27.

102. *Baḥr*, f. 254a.

103. Nuʿmān, p. 100.

104. *Iḥkām*, 4:145.

of Abū Bakr al-Abharī (d. 375/985). He held that the consensus of Medina was binding where it was based on a tradition of the Prophet (*naql*). Medina was the Prophet's home, and its scholars were the most familiar with what he had said and done.[105] Ibn Bukayr had held that the *ijmāʿ* of Medina was valid whether based on a text or on legal reasoning (*raʾy wa-qiyās wa-naql*). Qāḍī al-Nuʿmān refers to a third version, according to which every consensus of Medina was in fact based on revelation, on what they had "heard and seen," even if they made no explicit attribution (*wa-in lam yusnidūhu*).[106] This is precisely what some supporters of *ijmāʿ* had been claiming in al-Shāfiʿī's day, and is probably the original justification for the Medinan consensus. Ibn Bukayr's version is a bolder claim, for it makes the consensus of Medina a principle in its own right. Al-Abharī's version was a concession to the opposition; it appears to have become the dominant view in the school.[107]

It was the strong version of the Mālikī claim that attracted the notice of the rival *uṣūlis* and drew their consistent abuse. For al-Jaṣṣāṣ, it is a modern doctrine (*qawl muḥdath*) that has no basis in the teaching of any early Muslim.[108] Imām al-Ḥaramayn, too, considers the doctrine to have been foisted into Mālik's teachings.[109] Ibn Ḥazm went even further. He showed that what Mālik in the *Muwaṭṭaʾ* claimed to be the consensus of Medina was not always his own doctrine. Give up your claim that the consensus of Medina is binding, he challenged the Mālikīs, or condemn Mālik as a conscious violator of consensus.[110] As for the traditions in praise of Medina, to interpret the general texts dealing with *ijmāʿ* in their light was illegitimate; one might just as well say that all the

105. *Iḥkām*, 4:145. The fourth/tenth century, especially its first half, seems to have been a crucial period in the elaboration of this doctrine. Qāḍī Abū 'l-Ḥusayn ʿUmar ibn Muḥammad wrote a *Refutation of Those Who Reject the Consensus of the People of Medina* (Ibn Farḥūn, *Kitāb al-Dībāj al-mudhhab fī maʿrifat aʿyān ʿulamāʾ al-madhhab* [Cairo, 1351 H.], p. 184; al-Shīrāzī, *Ṭabaqāt*, p. 166; Ahmed Bekir, *Histoire de l'école Mālikite*, p. 107), in which he defended the consensus of Medina as a source in its own right (Ibn Qayyim al-Jawziyya, *Iʿlām al-muwaqqiʿīn*, 2:392, and *Irshād*, p. 82, both quoting ʿAbd al-Wahhāb ibn Naṣr al-Baghdādī (d. 422/1031) against the Shāfiʿī al-Ṣayrafī (d. 330/941), who would not go beyond recognizing concurrent traditions peculiar to Medina (ʿIyāḍ ibn Mūsā, *Tartīb al-madārik wa-taqrīb al-masālik li-maʿrifat aʿlām madhhab Mālik*, ed. Aḥmad Bakīr Maḥmūd. 5 vols. [Beirut: Dār Maktabat al-Ḥayāt, 1387 H], 1:68, reproduced in Robert Brunschvig, "Polémiques médiévales autour du rite de Mālik," *al-Andalus* 15 [1950]: p. 421). ʿAlī ibn Maysūma, a contemporary of al-Abharī, was the author of *Ijmāʿ ahl al-Madīna* (Bekir, *Histoire de l'école malikite*, p. 113). For the early history of the dispute, see Brunschvig, "Polémiques."

106. Nuʿmān, p. 95.

107. *Musawwada*, p. 332 (Ibn Taymiyya calls it a flight from the issue). It was the position of al-Bājī (Bājī, p. 142; *Baḥr*, f. 258b) and al-Qarāfī (Qarāfī, p. 334; for his vacillation between this claim and the wider one [*taʿmīm*] see *Baḥr*, f. 259a). For a list of its supporters, who, according to ʿAbd al-Wahhāb al-Baghdādī, included most of the Western Mālikīs, see Ibn Qayyim al-Jawziyya, *Iʿlām al-muwaqqiʿīn*, 2:392.

108. Jaṣṣāṣ, f. 228b. For later Ḥanafī responses, Bukhārī, 3:241–42; Sarakhsī, 1:314; *Mīzān*, f. 144a.

109. *Burhān*, f. 204.

110. *Iḥkām*, 4:217. Abū Marwān ʿAbd al-Mālik ibn al-ʿĀṣ al-Qurṭubī (d. 330/941) already responded to such attacks in his *Kitāb al-Radd ʿalā man ankara ʿalā Mālik al-ʿamal bimā rawāhu* (Muḥammad Makhlūf,

obligations of the law applied only to the people of Medina.[111] Even if one granted special virtues to Medina, Medina could not simply be identified with the Mālikīs.[112] The learning of Medina was common property.[113] Personal experience made it painfully clear that there were no special qualities that Medina conferred on its population. "It is known," writes al-Jaṣṣāṣ, "that in this time the Medinese are the most ignorant people, the least learned, the furthest from any good."[114] Similarly, Imām al-Ḥaramayn, whose residence in the Holy Cities was a prolonged one, claims that "should anyone come to know what takes place in the dwellings of Medina, he would be struck with amazement."[115]

The doctrine of Medinese superiority in the transmission of prophetic teaching did, however, find support among rival schools. Al-Shāfiʿī, who had studied with Mālik, was supposed to have given preference (*tarjīḥ*) to the traditions of Medina, and other Shāfiʿīs could claim to follow his example in doing so.[116] One version of the Mālikī assertion of superiority claimed nothing more than this: that the Medinese traditions were to be preferred in case of conflict.[117] Abū Yūsuf is also known to have followed Medinese usage in some areas of the law.[118] The Ḥanbalī Ibn ʿAqīl (d. 513/1120) went so far as to accept the dominant version of the Mālikī claim:

> I hold that their consensus is binding (*ḥujja*) in what concerns transmission but not in what concerns legal reasoning (*ijtihād*). For we have what they have in the way of legal reasoning (*raʾy*) but not in the way of transmission (*riwāya*), especially in those areas they had need of (*mā taʿumm bihi balwāhum*). They are

Shajarat al-nūr al-zakiyya fī ṭabaqāt al-mālikiyya. [Cairo: al-Maṭbaʿa al-salafiyya, 1349–50 H. Repr. Beirut: Dār al-Kitāb al-ʿArabī, n.d.], 1:87–88).

111. Jaṣṣāṣ, f. 228b.

112. Jaṣṣāṣ, f. 228b.

113. Jaṣṣāṣ, f. 229b; Bukhārī, 3:242.

114. Jaṣṣāṣ, f. 228b.

115. *Burhān*, f. 204. According to *Ihkām*, 4:204, Medina was populated by Shiʿis.

116. *Lumaʿ*, p. 50; *Qawāṭiʿ*, f. 172b; Muḥammad ibn Mūsā al-Ḥāzimī, *Kitāb al-Iʿtibār fī bayān al-nāsikh wa'l-mansūkh min al-āthār* (Ḥimṣ: Maṭbaʿat al-Andalus, 1386/1966), pp. 15, 85 (the superior knowledge of *ahl al-Madīna* of what is abrogated).

117. *Lumaʿ*, p. 53. On the dispute as to the authority of the various local *isnāds*, see Ibn Taymiyya, *Rafʿ al-malām*, pp. 16–17.

118. *Manār*, p. 740. On the time of the call for the morning prayer, al-Ghunaymī, *al-Lubāb fī sharḥ al-Kitāb*, 1:64, note. On Abū Yūsuf's conversion to the Medinese *ṣāʿ*, Aḥmad ibn Muḥammad al-Fayyūmī, *Kitāb al-Miṣbāḥ al-munīr fī gharīb al-sharḥ al-kābir li'l-Rāfiʿī* (Cairo: al-Maṭbaʿa al-Amīriyya, 1922), p. 480; for a reconciliation of the figures, al-Ghunaymī, *al-Lubāb fī sharḥ al-Kitāb*, 1:10 (from *al-Zaylaʿī*). Ibn Ḥazm disputes the claim of unanimity as to the *ṣāʿ* of Medina (*Iḥkām*, 6:169 [an example of *aqallu mā qīla*]). The *ṣāʿ*, among other topics, was the subject of debates between Abū Yūsuf and Mālik before the Caliph Hārūn al-Rashīd (Bājī, pp. 23, 76; ʿIyāḍ, *Madārik*, 1:224–25; al-Kāsānī, *Badāʾiʿ al-ṣanāʾiʿ*, 1:462).

> cultivators of date trees and fruit, and their transmission is put above every other, especially in this area.[119]

The common element in the varying versions of the Mālikī claim for the consensus of Medina is that the traditions upon which the scholars of Medina agree have the force of *ijmāʿ*. It will be recalled that the dominant Mālikī doctrine on the unit-tradition differs from that of the other major schools in giving preference to analogy over the unit-tradition. That this should be so appears less surprising when it is realized that the unit-traditions the Mālikīs would be called upon to consider would have to be those that were not current in the Mālikī school, for the Mālikī traditions would be part of the legacy of Medina and thus fall under consensus.[120]

With regard to the limitation of the participants in consensus (*al-mujmiʿūn*), there is a widely reported doctrine that merits our attention, especially since it was espoused by a prominent Ḥanafī, Qaḍī Abū Khāzim ʿAbd al-Ḥamīd ibn ʿAbd al-ʿAzīz (d. 292/905). The fullest report of his doctrine is that of al-Jaṣṣāṣ, who had it from a student of Abū Khāzim. Abū Khāzim held that whenever the first four Caliphs were in accord, their decision was binding. He based himself upon the prophetic tradition: "Keep to my *sunna* and the *sunna* of the orthodox Caliphs after me, seize it with your teeth." Putting this doctrine into practice, Abū Khāzim ruled that the government had acted improperly in appropriating property that belonged to the uterine heirs (*dhawū al-arḥām*) of deceased Muslims and that the property was to be restored to its rightful owners. The opinion of the Companion Zayd ibn Thābit, a great authority on succession, which had been the basis of the government's action, was of no consequence alongside the consensus of the four Caliphs. The Caliph al-Muʿtaḍid bi'llāh (reigned 279/892–289/902) gave Abū Khāzim's ruling the force of law. From within the Ḥanafī school, Abū Khāzim drew the rebuke of his former student Abū Saʿīd al-Bardaʿī (d. 317/929), but the Qāḍī refused to yield.[121] The *uṣūl* literature

---

119. *Musawwada*, pp. 332–33 (from *Kitāb al-Naẓariyyāt al-kibār*).

120. "Those who come afterwards transmit from those who come before, sons from fathers, and the report departs from the realm of presumption and speculation and enters the realm of certainty" (Qarāfī, p. 334, reading *ḥayyiz* in place of *khabar* twice). Where there was consensus, the Medinese traditions were concurrent (*Irshād*, p. 82; ʿIyāḍ, *Madārik*, 1:88). Note also, Ibn ʿAbd al-Barr, *al-Tamhīd*, 1:79, glossing a statement of ʿAbd al-Raḥmān Ibn Mahdī (d. 198/813): "'The longstanding *sunna* of the Medinese is better than a tradition'—that is, an Iraqi tradition." Presumably those who regarded the consensus of the Kufans as a source of law would reject traditions opposed to it (Taqī al-Dīn al-Subkī, *Maʿnā qawl al-imām al-muṭṭalibī idhā saḥḥa al-ḥadīth fa-huwa madhhabī*, in *Majmūʿat al-rasāʾil al-munīriyya*, ed. Muḥammad Munīr [Cairo: Idārat al-Ṭibāʿa al-Munīriyya, 1346 H. Vol. 3, pp. 98-114. Reprint. Beirut: Dār al-Jīl, 1970], p. 114).

121. Jaṣṣāṣ, f. 225b; Sarakhsī, 1:317 (al-Muʿtaṣim is incorrectly given as the Caliph). O. Spies and E. Pritsch refer to al-Muʿtaḍid's introduction of *dhawū al-arḥām* among the heirs in 896, but do not mention Abū Khazim or give a source ("Klassiches Islamisches Recht," in *Orientalisches Recht*, Handbuch der Orientalistik, pt. 1, supp. 3 [Leiden: Brill, 1964], p. 233). Jalāl al-Dīn al-Suyūṭī, *Taʾrīkh al-khulafāʾ* (Beirut:

considers this doctrine a curiosity.[122] Badr al-Dīn al-Zarkashī (d. 794/1392), however, argues that Abū Khāzim's doctrine is not eccentric at all, but represents a view shared by others such as Aḥmad ibn Ḥanbal that the agreement of the four Caliphs was the basis of a legal norm (*ḥujja*), to be preferred over the views of others. "There is no reason for our colleagues (the Shāfiʿīs) to attribute it specifically to Abū Khāzim." According to this interpretation, Abū Khāzim was not talking about *ijmāʿ* at all.[123]

VI. *Inqirāḍ al-ʿaṣr*

The Ḥanafī theory of consensus facilitates the operation of *ijmāʿ* not only by narrowing the range of those who must actively participate in its formation, but also by putting the consensus into immediate effect once agreement has been reached or dissent has failed to appear. This is to be contrasted with the view that held that consensus did not take effect until the original body of scholars who had considered the question of law had died off. This doctrine, that of "*inqirāḍ al-ʿaṣr*" ("the extinction of the generation"), found support among *uṣūlīs* of various allegiances—Ḥanbalīs, Shāfiʿīs, Muʿtazilīs, Ashʿarīs. This support it lost only gradually. Thus we find the doctrine espoused in a number of versions. For example, the Shāfiʿī Abū Isḥāq al-Isfarāyīnī, while abandoning the doctrine generally, retains it for the tacit consensus.[124]

The stipulation of *inqirāḍ al-ʿaṣr* apparently originated in an attempt to explain how it happened that the agreement of the Companions upon a question did not prevent subsequent dissent. Thus Aḥmad Ibn Ḥanbal is reported to have said: "The evidence (*al-ḥujja*) is against one who claims that if something was agreed upon but followed by disagreement, we stand by what was agreed upon as consensus. The *umm al-walad* was classified as a slave by consensus; then ʿUmar set them free. After ʿUmar's death ʿAlī was of the opinion that they were slaves."[125] The *umm al-walad*, the slave who has given birth to her master's child, was originally given no special protection by the law. But this original consensus did not prevent ʿUmar from deciding that she was not to be sold but rather was to be set free at her master's death. Nor did the consensus that formed around ʿUmar's decision prevent ʿAlī from later reverting to the original view. The doctrine of

Dār al-Thaqāfa, n.d.), p. 400, gives the same date for al-Muʿtaḍid's decree and speaks of the abolition of *dīwān al-mawārīth*; the change was a popular one. Abū Khāzim is not mentioned, but his defiance of the Caliph in another matter is reported on the following page.

122. *Mustaṣfā*, p. 215; *Iḥkām*, 4:191; Qarāfī, p. 335.

123. *Baḥr*, f. 260b; *Rawḍa*, p. 73. According to al-Jaṣṣāṣ, however, Abū Khāzim is supposed to have said, "I do not regard the question as a controverted one because of Zayd's view" (Jaṣṣāṣ, f. 226a). Sarakhsī, 1:317, understands Abū Khāzim's doctrine to be that the agreement of the caliphs is a consensus that imposes certain knowledge (*ijmāʿ mūjib li'l-ʿilm*).

124. *Burhān*, f. 196.

125. *Musawwada*, pp. 323–24. See *Encyclopaedia of Islam*, 2nd ed., s.v. "ʿabd," sec. 3.

inqirāḍ al-ʿaṣr posits that there was no valid consensus in the first place and that what appears to be a breach of consensus was in fact the entirely legitimate exercise of *ijtihād*.

The justification for the stipulation of the extinction of the generation rests on the right of those jurists who had originally come to agreement to continue to pursue the solution of the question at issue, even if it meant that they abandoned (*al-rujūʿ*) what had earlier appeared correct. This right Abū Yaʿlā ibn al-Farrāʾ derives from the Qurʾānic verse (2:143) establishing consensus. The Muslim doctors are witnesses against mankind. God has made their agreement a "testimony against others; He did not make it a testimony against themselves."[126] The *mujtahid* is responsible for locating a relevant prophetic tradition or constructing a proper analogy. His responsibility comes to an end only with his death; and only when all the scholars have died without changing their opinion is it proper to speak of a firm consensus.

In opposition to this doctrine, the Ḥanafīs held that when all the scholars are in agreement even for an instant, a valid consensus is formed.[127] This agreement can take place verbally (*qawlan*) or by the opinion of some *mujtahids* going unopposed. In the latter case, that of the tacit consensus, a period of consideration (*muddat al-taʾammul*) is provided for.[128] There is no need to stipulate the lifetime of the generation. The *mujtahid* does not require an entire lifetime to attain certainty;[129] neither is the stipulation of *inqirāḍ al-ʿaṣr* called for by the revealed texts on which the doctrine of consensus is based.[130] The historical cases that had been adduced to support the doctrine were rejected by the Ḥanafīs. They could furnish another account of the events, one in which there was either no dissent or no consensus in the first place.[131] The proponents of *inqirāḍ al-ʿaṣr*, in turn, were called upon to reconcile their doctrine with reports such as that which had al-Ḥasan al-Baṣrī claiming the consensus of the Companions as a valid norm (*ḥujja*) in the lifetime of Anas ibn Mālik.[132]

The chief drawback of the doctrine of *inqirāḍ al-ʿaṣr* was that it provided for a period between the original agreement of the scholars and their death in which the consensus-

---

126. *ʿUdda*. f. 163b.

127. Bukhārī, 3:243–45; Nasafī, 2:106. In *Mīzān*, f. 130b, the argument assumes the *mujtahid*'s liability to error, which gives it greater weight, for if every *mujtahid* were correct, the additional time called for by the doctrine of *inqirāḍ al-ʿaṣr* would serve no useful purpose. The *muftī* could be certain that his original opinion was correct.

128. *Taysīr*, 3:246; Nasafī, 2:104; *Manār*, p. 738; *Muʿtamad*, 2:1023 (*zamān al-muhla*). *Mīzān*, f. 131b, speaks of "three days or a month or so." The shortest period is that of the session of the arrival of the report (*Taysīr*, 3:246, which ascribes it to *Mīzān* [not in my ms.]). Nasafī, 2:104, margin, states that for the majority of Ḥanafīs the period is not precisely fixed but is left to common practice. In *Taysīr*, 3:246, this is reported in the name of al-Jaṣṣāṣ.

129. *Mīzān*, f.131a (clearly expanding upon *Muʿtamad*, 2:505).

130. Bukhārī, 3:243-44; Nasafī, 2:106; *Mīzān*, f. 130b.

131. Bukhārī. 3:244; *Mīzān*, f. 131a.

132. *ʿUdda*, f. 164b, quoted *Musawwada*, p. 321, and criticized, p. 322.

to-be was incubating. But this period of incubation brought with it a new host of problems. It was quite simply an anomaly in the Islamic legal system. This point of vulnerability did not escape al-Jaṣṣāṣ, who observed that the effect of God's norm (*ḥujja*) is not bound up with time but takes place at once.[133] The unhappy consequences that proceeded from this anomalous intermediate period were seized upon by its opponents, and its proponents were compelled to make the necessary accommodations. The growing dissatisfaction with these *ad hoc* solutions ultimately led to the abandonment of the stipulation of *inqirāḍ al-ʿaṣr.*

It was incumbent upon those who upheld *inqirāḍ al-ʿaṣr* to define the status of the *mujtahids* who appeared during the lifetime of those who were part of the original agreement. If they were to be excluded from the matter entirely, this would appear to be inconsistent with their right as qualified jurists to express an opinion on a matter that was not yet decided. On the other hand, if they were admitted as equals into the original body of scholars, there could never be a consensus; before these new jurists died others would join them. The matter would always be in suspense. This is the problem of the "overtaker" (*al-lāḥiq, al-mudrik*) who figures prominently in the *uṣūl* texts.[134] The Ḥanbalīs, who clung tenaciously to the *inqirāḍ* doctrine, offered two solutions to the problem, both of which were attributed to Aḥmad ibn Ḥanbal. The first held that only the original body of jurists had any role in the consensus. According to the second, the new *mujtahids* could prevent the formation of consensus by expressing a dissenting opinion, but this privilege extended only to the scholars of the generation immediately following the original one (*innamā yasūgh al-khilāf li-man ʿāṣarahum fa-ammā man ʿāṣara man ʿāṣarahum fa-lā*). In neither formulation, Abū Yaʿlā insists, can the opponent charge that consensus is made impossible.[135] But the weaknesses of the two solutions are nonetheless apparent. The first solution isolates the original body of jurists and creates a complex pattern of legal privilege that runs counter to the accepted notion of *ijtihād*. The second solution involves a subtle and, it seems, arbitrary distinction that Ibn Taymiyya neatly formulates: "The secret of the question is that no regard is paid to the agreement of the overtaker, but only to his lack of dissent" (*sirr al-masʾala anna al-mudrik la yuʿtabar wifāquhu bal yuʿtabar ʿadam khilāfihī*).[136] The new *mujtahid* never fully acquires the status of the old. He can only influence the *ijmāʿ*-to-be by a dissenting opinion that is expressed before the original group dies. Once they are gone, the matter is out of his hands. To give him equal standing with the original *mujtahids* would in fact have been to set in operation a process in which

133. Jaṣṣāṣ, f. 227a.

134. E.g., *Musawwada*, p. 323.

135. *ʿUdda*, f. 165a.

136. *Musawwada*, p. 323. To use another terminology, their consensus is formed (*inʿaqada*) but is not yet an argument (*ḥujja*) (*Muʿtamad*, 2:502; *Manār*, p. 740, margin).

consensus could never be fixed, for the new scholars would in a sense be survivors of the original group, as would those who came after them.

The doctrine of *inqirāḍ al-ʿaṣr* was also open to the charge of undermining the validity of consensus. The original participants retained the right to change their opinion as long as they lived. It was possible that all might come to hold another opinion than their original one. But this, said the critics of the doctrine, would mean that all the Muslims had agreed upon an error.[137] The force of this argument is not lost upon Ibn Taymiyya. In response, he suggests that what is possible is their temporary agreement upon an error. They are, however, safeguarded against a lasting agreement upon an error (*innamā hum maʿṣūmūn ʿan dawām al-khaṭaʾ*), for should they persist in error, the error could become so rooted among the Muslim masses as never to be eradicated.[138]

The drawbacks of the doctrine have been sufficiently dealt with for it to be clear why the stipulation of *inqirāḍ al-ʿaṣr* steadily lost ground. This was true even among the Ḥanbalīs. Defended by such figures as Abū Yaʿlā ibn al-Farrāʾ, Ibn Qudāma, al-Ḥalwānī, and Ibn ʿAqīl,[139] it was subjected to searching criticism by Ibn Taymiyya, who ultimately maintained the doctrine.[140] There were nonetheless those such as Abū 'l-Khaṭṭāb al-Kalwadhānī[141] (d. 510/1116) and Najm al-Dīn al-Ṭūfī (d. 715/1316) who defended the opposing doctrine and claimed that it could be supported from Aḥmad's *fiqh* (*awmaʾa ilayhi*).[142] Ibn Badrān is aware of the overwhelming Ḥanbalī acceptance of the *inqirāḍ* stipulation, but regards the view that omits it as the sound one in the school.[143]

The Ḥanafīs commonly associate the *inqirāḍ* doctrine with al-Shāfiʿī,[144] but within the Shāfiʿī school its popularity was limited. The doctrine was upheld by Abū 'l-Ḥasan al-Ashʿarī, and without his support the doctrine might have succumbed sooner.[145] Among those Shāfiʿī Ashʿarīs who did accept it are Ibn Fūrak and Sulaym al-Rāzī.[146] Al-Ashʿarī may have been following his teacher Abū ʿAlī al-Jubbāʾī in making the stipulation, for Abū 'l-ʿAbbās al-Qalānisī, al-Ashʿarī's contemporary and a prominent leader of orthodoxy, rejected it, according to ʿAbd al-Qāhir al-Baghdādī.[147] We have already observed that al-Baghdādī's teacher al-Isfarāyīnī retained *inqirāḍ* only for the tacit consensus. The

137. Bukhārī, 3:244.

138. *Musawwada*, p. 322.

139. *Musawwada*, p. 320.

140. *Musawwada*, p. 322.

141. *Musawwada*, p. 320.

142. *Madkhal*, p. 131.

143. *Madkhal*, p. 131.

144. Bazdawī, 3:243; *Mīzān*, f. 130a.

145. *Baḥr*, f. 262b. For Abū Yaʿlā, the Ashʿarīs were among those who rejected it (*ʿUdda*, f. 163b, quoted *Musawwada*, p. 320).

146. *Baḥr*, f. 262b; *Taysīr*, 3:230.

147. *Baḥr*, f. 262b.

solution of al-Juwaynī, who was followed by al-Ghazālī, was to require in place of the extinction of the generation a period that common experience (*ʿāda*) showed to be sufficient for a view to become stable. The *inqirāḍ* doctrine was felt to be unnecessarily dogmatic and was unable to maintain itself in the face of the increasing theological sophistication of the Ashʿarīs.[148] Among the Shafiʿīs who were not Ashʿarīs, its hold was even less secure. Al-Samʿānī, for example, labels the opposing doctrine the soundest Shāfiʿī teaching.[149] He, like the Ḥanafīs, approaches the question from the revealed texts, which furnish no basis for the stipulation of *inqirāḍ*.

VII. Consensus after Disagreement

The Ḥanafīs not only consistently take positions that facilitate the operation of consensus, they also resist any limitation to its applicability. They are almost alone in arguing that consensus can be formed even after disagreement has become established (*al-khilāf al-mutaqarrir*). Because their position would seem to be the obvious one, we must seek to grasp the motive that led so many to reject it. The problem is the counterpart of that which has preceded. Those who upheld *inqirāḍ al-ʿaṣr* had to determine the rights of the newly qualified *mujtahids*. In the point at issue here, the rights of the old *mujtahid*s are under discussion. A considerable body of opinion looked upon the early Muslims, above all the Companions, as specially favored to know the truth. (For the Ẓāhirīs, among others, consensus was in fact confined to the Companions.) A consensus in conflict with the view of a substantial body of the Companions would amount to these Companions being charged with error by their inferiors. That the question was seen in this light is indicated by the fact that most of those who held this view considered fully valid a consensus that followed upon disagreement within the space of the first generation, even when they rejected the stipulation of *inqirāḍ al-ʿaṣr*.[150]

Those, like al-Juwaynī and the early al-Ghazālī, who did not base consensus on revelation but on common experience, would accept the position against a subsequent consensus as a matter of course. The fact that the Companions had agreed upon a number of

148. *Mankhūl*, p. 318, which indicates that this is the way to understand al-Juwaynī's stipulation of a "long time" (*Burhān*, f. 196; *Musawwada*, p. 320), to be distinguished from *muddat al-taʾammul* (n. 128 above). Here *ʿurf* is to determine *istiqrār* (stabilization of views). Al-Bāqillānī had already rejected *inqirāḍ al-ʿaṣr* (*Burhān*, f. 196). It is important to note that this period applies only to a consensus based on probability (*Musawwada*, p. 320). Was the same true of *inqirāḍ al-ʿaṣr*?

149. *Qawāṭiʿ*, f. 169a; *Lumaʿ*, p. 52.

150. *Musawwada*, p. 324; *Rawḍa*, p. 73. For those who supported *inqirāḍ al-ʿaṣr*, there was no difficulty involved in taking this view. *Mustaṣfā*, p. 226, calls it a mainstay for those who stipulate *inqirāḍ al-ʿaṣr* and offers five ways out. The preceding disagreement might even have served the cause of truth, so that the subsequent consensus would be a superior one (Māwardī, 1:479).

conflicting solutions could only mean that there was no obviously correct answer. There could thus be no sound basis for a subsequent consensus.[151]

The justification for the majority position took two forms. The dominant, and it seems the earlier, argument held that the original disagreement amounted to a consensus to allow both views to be maintained.[152] A subsequent agreement upon one of the conflicting views could not invalidate this original consensus. Some who accepted this analysis claimed that a subsequent agreement was inconceivable inasmuch as it would entail two conflicting *ijmāʿ*s.[153] More commonly, however, the later agreement was merely denied the status of consensus. The new generation could not abrogate the old consensus.[154] The weak spot in this line of argument, a case of agreement that did not constitute consensus, is the same as that found in the *inqirāḍ al-ʿaṣr* doctrine."If all the Followers could agree and the truth nonetheless eludes them this could happen to all other generations."[155] This difficulty was avoided by the alternative analysis, which claimed that the new generation could not form a consensus because on the issue in question they did not constitute the whole nation. The earlier scholars were dead, but their arguments lived on and had to be considered. This notion, it was argued, was consistent with common usage, for there was nothing bizarre in claiming to agree or disagree with al-Shāfiʿī although he was long dead.[156] This second argument marks a significant shift. If what matters is the legal argument, then one dissenting view can prevent the formation of consensus from ever taking place in the future. In the earlier version, what had prevented the formation of consensus was a disagreement so widespread and fixed as to constitute a consensus in itself.

The Ḥanafīs could once again claim that the distinction their opponents made was not based on the revealed texts constituting consensus as a legal source.[157] The argument that the earlier disagreement was an implicit consensus that one view was not to exclude the others was answered in two ways. What may be termed the authentic Central Asian Ḥanafī response was based on the principle that there is only one correct solution to a legal question. A consensus that two or more views might be maintained with equal propriety would mean that it was proper to hold an erroneous view. Such a consensus would itself be an error, and the institution of consensus would be undermined.[158] Al-Samarqandī insists that there is an obligation to seek the truth from among the accepted

151. *Mankhūl*, p. 321.

152. *ʿUdda*, f. 166a. Abū Yaʿlā refers to the second argument as *ṭarīqa ukhrā*. In *Rawḍa*, p. 75, the order is reversed and more emphasis put on this "other way."

153. *Lumaʿ*, p. 54.

154. *Rawḍa*, p. 75; *Musawwada*, p. 325.

155. *Mīzān*, f. 132b.

156. *Mustaṣfā*, p. 225; *Rawḍa*, p. 75 (with Aḥmad for al-Shāfiʿī).

157. Bukhārī, 3:249; *Mīzān*, f. 132b; *Muʿtamad*, 2:501, 517–19.

158. Bukhārī, 3:250.

solutions and that this obligation itself falls under consensus. To deny the validity of a consensus upon one of the solutions is in effect to violate the consensus binding the Muslim to seek the truth and not be content with *taqlīd*, through adherence to the views of others. *Ijtihād* is not an end in itself but is for the sake of finding the truth; once there is consensus, it is known that the truth has been found. To deny the possibility of finding the truth, as the opponents do, is to charge God with having commanded the Muslim what is beyond his powers. But this is contrary to reason and revelation.[159] This argument depends on the assumption that there is only one correct view. But this assumption was not shared by all. Another, more commonly cited argument did not reject an implicit consensus on the acceptability of the divergent views but claimed that it was qualified by the condition (*sharṭ*) that no subsequent consensus favor one view to the exclusion of the others.[160] The use of this argument by the Ḥanafīs is another instance of their desire to elaborate a defense of their positions that would be compatible with either of the prevalent views of *ijtihād*.

As to the claim that later generations have always to reckon with the legal arguments of past scholars, al-Samarqandī denies that these legal arguments are sound. Because of the later consensus, we are in a position to know that what appeared to be a sound argument (*dalīl*) was only a misleading one (*shubha*). A sound argument is confirmed with the passage of time (*yataqarrar li-muḍiyy al-zamān*), whereas a misleading argument is liable to exposure.[161]

The subsequent consensus is not to be seen as a denigration of earlier scholars. It is true that one group is now known to have been correct and the other wrong. But those who were wrong can only be charged with error (*takhṭiʾa*) not with deviation (*taḍlīl*). The distinction rests upon a principle that we have already encountered and that al-Samarqandī repeatedly enunciates. The legal scholar is obliged to act in accordance with his notion of what is most probable, but he is not to affirm this as true, as identical with God's will:

> If, then, he does not believe in the absolute truth of his view, how can this be deviation (*ḍalāl*) so that the charge of error be equivalent to a charge of deviation? The fact is that deviation occurs only in rational judgments (*al-aḥkām al-ʿaqliyya*) because what is believed (*al-muʿtaqad*) is either necessary (*wājib al-wujūd*) or impossible (*mustaḥīl al-thubūt*). When one errs in these matters he believes what is necessary to be impossible. The disagreement of the Companions was confined to legal questions (*al-sharʿiyyāt*), God having shielded them from disagreement in rational questions so that no deviation or error be imputed to them. Legal questions, on the other hand, are among the things which are

159. *Mīzān*, f. 133a.
160. Bukhārī, 3:350; *Muʿtamad*, 2:501.
161. *Mīzān*, f. 133a.

> possible with respect to reason (*al-mumkināt al-ʿaqliyya*), so that it would not have been impossible for the law to be other than it is. Disagreement in legal questions is not a ground for the charge of deviation, since error (*al-jahl*) in the law is not harmful unless it amounts to giving lie to the Prophet by denying what rests on *tawātur*. This is to be guilty of unbelief (*kufr*). But to deny what is certain by way of consensus or a *mashhūr* tradition is not grounds for unbelief according to the sound teaching of the school.[162]

The question we have just considered, that of the elimination (*irtifāʿ*) of disagreement by the subsequent consensus of another body of scholars, is an unmistakable indication of how far the Ḥanafīs wished to press the claims of consensus. It was a question on which they were conscious of holding a minority opinion. As against the Ḥanafīs, al-Samarqandī ranges the majority of the jurists and theologians of the *ahl al-ḥadīth*.[163] Yet some of our sources do speak of a Ḥanafī division on the point, although no individuals are named. We can be reasonably sure, however, that whatever Ḥanafī opposition there was based itself on a legal teaching of Abū Ḥanīfa. Abū Ḥanīfa ruled that if a judge decreed that an *umm al-walad* was to be sold, the judicial decision was to stand.[164] Muḥammad al-Shaybanī held that it was to be reversed. The status of the *umm al-walad* was, we have seen, a matter of dispute among the early Muslims. According to the Ḥanafīs, it was only in the second generation, that of the Followers, that a consensus was reached prohibiting her alienation. On the basis of his ruling, Abū Ḥanīfa could be understood to have held that a consensus reached after a previous dispute was invalid. Apparently Abū 'l-Ḥasan al-Karkhī was the central figure in establishing the validity of consensus in such cases as sound doctrine. The report of Abū Ḥanīfa's opinion goes back to al-Karkhī, who reconciled it with the doctrine he favored.[165] Al-Karkhī's pupil al-Jaṣṣāṣ confesses to having forgotten how this reconciliation was effected, but later Ḥanafīs made good this lapse of memory.[166] Although no less a figure than Shams al-Dīn al-Ḥalwānī (d. 448/1056), al-Sarakhsī's teacher, held that both Abū Ḥanīfa and Abū Yūsuf did not recognize a consensus formed under such circumstances, this did not keep al-Sarakhsī from accepting its validity, a further indication of its general acceptance among the Ḥanafīs by this period.[167]

---

162. *Mīzān*, f. 133a. On *ijmāʿ* and *kufr*, see Ignaz Goldziher, "Über iğmāʿ." *Nachrichten von der Königlichen Gesellschaft der Wissenschaften zu Göttingen* (Philologisch-historische Klasse, 1916).

163. *Mīzān*, f. 131b. For a list of those on both sides, *Musawwada*, p. 325. There is some question as to the view of al-Ḥārith al-Muḥāsibi (contrast Māwardī, 1:483–84, with Abū ʿĀṣim Muḥammad ibn Aḥmad al-ʿAbbādī, *Kitāb Ṭabaqāt al-fuqahāʾ aš-šāfiʿīya*, p. 27 [no consensus]).

164. *Mīzān*, f. 132a; Bukhārī, 3:248; Jaṣṣāṣ, f. 231b.

165. Jaṣṣāṣ, f. 231b.

166. Jaṣṣāṣ, f. 231b. The dispute that matters is not the substantive one, but that concerning the validity of such a consensus, and the judgment stands because the matter is controverted (Bukhārī, 3:248; Sarakhsī, 1:320).

167. Sarakhsī, 1:319–20.

The close links between consensus and *taqlīd* are apparent in another issue to be considered. Once the Muslim scholars have come to hold a number of views on a question of law, is it permissible to introduce a new view (*iḥdāth qawl thālith*)? From the Ḥanafīs' principle that only one view can be correct, it would follow that the truth must be identical with one of the views already accepted. Otherwise, the community would be in error. Thus a new view cannot possibly be correct. In fact, the great majority of *uṣūlīs* denied that such a new view was admissible. The only dissent that is reported comes from the Ẓāhirīs, some Shiʿis, and surprisingly some Ḥanafīs.[168]

The mainstream Ḥanafī doctrine already appears fully developed in al-Jaṣṣāṣ, who attributes it to al-Shaybānī. According to Hishām ibn ʿUbayd Allāh, al-Shaybānī had said that "legal knowledge falls under four heads: 1. what is in the Qurʾān and what resembles it, 2. what is part of the *sunna* of the Messenger of God and what resembles it, 3. what the Companions have agreed and disagreed upon and what resembles it, and 4. what the Believers consider to be good and what resembles it."[169]

For those who held that every *mujtahid* is correct, the exclusion of a new view is based on the claim that the earlier disagreement was an implicit consensus that only the views already considered could be held. Because of its flexibility, this analysis was adopted by the Ḥanafīs as well, and we find al-Bazdawī, for example, justifying this consensus as analogous to a tacit one. The silence of the jurists is a sign of their rejection of any but the views in dispute.[170]

Unfortunately, none of the Ḥanafīs who held the opposing doctrine are named. We do know, however, that they made a distinction between a disagreement of the Companions and that of the other generations. Only a disagreement of the Companions was seen as limiting the range of possible solutions. This prerogative of the Companions is attributed to their special excellence and historical primacy (*al-faḍl wa'l-sābiqiyya*).[171]

---

168. *Musawwada*, p. 326.

169. Jaṣṣāṣ, f. 218a; Ṭūsī, p. 139; Ibn ʿAbd al-Barr, *Jāmiʿ bayān al-ʿilm wa-faḍlihi*, 2:26. The version in Sarakhsī, 1:318, does not mention *ikhtilāf*.

170. Bukhārī, 3:234; Nasafī, 2:112. Mullā Jīwan sees in this principle "the origin of the limitation of the legal schools to four" (Nasafī, 2:113, below and margin). Qāḍī al-Nuʿmān already regarded the doctrine of *ijmāʿ* as a feature of *taqlīd* (Nuʿmān, p. 56). In connection with this issue, *Muʿtamad*, 2:505–14, raises the subject of *talfīq*. See *Iḥkām*, 4:231–32, on the error of Dāwūd in this matter.

171. Bukhārī, 3:236; Nasafī, 2:112. These Ḥanafīs undoubtedly based themselves on a statement of Abū Ḥanīfa in which he claimed the right to practice *ijtihād* on the same level as the Followers, but limited himself to choosing from among the views of the Companions (several versions in Abū Shāma, *Mukhtaṣar Kitāb al-muʾammal li'l-radd ilā al-amr al-awwal*. In *Majmūʿat al-rasāʾil* [Cairo: Maṭbaʿat Kurdistān al-ʿIlmiyya, 1328 H], pp. 29–30). The mainstream solution is that Abū Ḥanīfa was himself a Follower (Jaṣṣāṣ, f. 219b).

VIII. Ẓāhirism and the Support of Consensus

In order to understand the Ẓāhirī opposition on this issue, as indeed their attack on the entire doctrine of consensus, it is necessary to grasp the relation of consensus to the other sources: Qurʾān, *sunna*, and analogy. This is the problem of the support of consensus (*al-mustanad, al-maʾkhadh, al-sabab al-dāʿī*). The classical doctrine of consensus allows for a consensus formed on a Qurʾānic text, a tradition, even a unit-tradition, and a solution reached by analogy.[172] Those who rejected analogy, such as the Ẓāhirīs, could not, of course, accept the last possibility. In this they were joined by al-Ṭabarī. Al-Ṭabarī himself accepted analogy, but he did not believe that all the Muslim scholars could ever come to agreement on an analogical solution. There was the inherent variability of human nature to be reckoned with. This in itself was what made the application of analogy less than entirely predictable. In addition, there already existed a body of determined opponents of analogy.[173] According to al-Samarqandī, the majority of Ẓāhirīs also rejected the unit-tradition as a basis for consensus.[174] This would indicate that the Ẓāhirī trend that rejected the unit-tradition had become dominant by this time. On the other hand, there were those who claimed that consensus could be based on divine inspiration (*ilhām, tawqīf*). God could bring the scholars to agree on a solution by directly suggesting it to their minds without the intermediary of a revealed text or analogy. Inspiration, they admitted, was suspect but only as long as it was confined to individuals. When all the Muslims were agreed, this suspicion was removed. Moreover, there were instances of consensus for which no basis was known.[175]

These two extremes, the Ẓāhirīs and the Inspirationalists, point to the crux of the problem of consensus. Consensus has the effect of investing its content with certainty. A unit-tradition is in itself of no more than probable authenticity. When there is a consensus on the content of the tradition, the legal norm that is the content of the tradition is now known to be of certain validity. It was in dispute whether the tradition itself was now known to be of certain authenticity.[176] Similarly, the content of an analogical solution can become of certain validity when it is confirmed by *ijmāʿ*. A materialist system by its very nature cannot make the same use of *ijmāʿ* as a formalist system, for which consensus validates the ever increasing body of analogical solutions. Because the materialist system is constructed of elements that are already certain, *ijmāʿ* is redundant. Wherever we find the rejection of analogy, we find a curtailment of the doctrine of consensus, if not its outright

---

172. Sarakhsī, 1:301; *Lumaʿ*, p. 51.

173. Bukhārī, 3:264.

174. *Mīzān*, f. 136b. Bukhārī, 3:264, questions the accuracy of this but probably without justification, since al-Samarqandī is careful to note that some Ẓāhirīs did admit the unit-tradition as a basis for consensus.

175. See n. 218, below.

176. Bukhārī, 3:265; *Muʿtamad*, 2:522–24.

repudiation: with the Ẓāhirīs, the Shiʿis,[177] al-Naẓẓām,[178] Jaʿfar Ibn Ḥarb and Jaʿfar ibn Mubashshir,[179] and al-Qāsānī.[180] Whatever role consensus may have had in the teaching of Dāwūd was immediately reduced among the early Ẓāhirīs, and in Ibn Ḥazm we find an attempt to undermine the doctrine of consensus entirely. Because this seems to have escaped the recent students of Ibn Ḥazm (only Goldziher, on the basis of very limited evidence, sensed Ibn Ḥazm's sleight of hand), we shall briefly consider Ibn Ḥazm's views.

Ibn Ḥazm focuses his attack upon the connection between *ijmāʿ* and analogy. Consensus cannot fill the lacunae of the law (*ḥukm lā naṣṣ fīhi*), because there is always a relevant text (*naṣṣ*). Whatever is not forbidden is permitted.[181] Consensus can thus only rest upon what is revealed. Every claim of consensus must be supported by the relevant text. Ibn Ḥazm does accept the authenticity of the tradition that states that some Muslims will always know the truth:

> All this is true. No Muslim will deny it. We do not oppose them as to the validity of consensus. We only oppose them on two points: their allowing for a consensus not based upon a text and their claim of consensus where it is groundless (*bāṭil*) and will not stand without proof. This is the case where we do find disagreement or where we do not know of any disagreement, but the existence of disagreement is possible.[182]

Although some Muslims always adhere to the truth, this fact is of no consequence. We can never hope to learn the truth by waiting for the Muslims to agree, for they cannot come to agreement. Ibn Ḥazm makes ample use of the two classic anti-*ijmāʿ* arguments. The Muslims are too many and too scattered ever to come to agreement. Men are of too varied dispositions for them to agree, except on the sense perceptions and immediate truths they have in common. Only revelation (*tawqīf*) can bring them together. This is an absolutely certain proof (*burhān qāṭiʿ ḍarūrī*).[183] The tacit consensus is entirely rejected. Disagreement is to be presumed (*al-aṣl min al-nās al-ikhtilāf fī ārāʾihim*). This is even guaranteed by God in the Qurʾān (11:118, 119): "They will not cease to disagree except those upon whom your Lord has mercy. For this He created them."[184] Agreement exists just as disagreement exists, but God has not charged us with knowing any of this. He has only charged us to follow the Qurʾān and the elucidation (*bayān*) of the Messenger that "those in authority from among you" (*ulū al-amr minkum*) have transmitted. Consensus

---

177. See below, Epilogue, sec. II.
178. See n. 10, above.
179. Ṭūṣī, p. 232; *Intiṣār*, pp. 63, 73.
180. Bukhārī, 3:252; *Mīzān*, f. 139b.
181. *Iḥkām*, 4:140; Ibn Ḥazm, *Mulakhkhaṣ*, pp. 36–37.
182. *Iḥkām*, 4:131.
183. *Iḥkām*, 4:138–39.
184. *Iḥkām*, 4:183.

cannot fail to agree with revelation, and obedience to revelation is obligatory whether the people agree or disagree. Revelation is no more obligatory because the people have agreed upon it nor any less obligatory because they dissent.[185]

The view that one finds attributed to the Ẓāhirīs and that Ibn Ḥazm identifies as the view of Dāwūd and many of his colleagues is that only the consensus of the Companions is valid.[186] The texts that institute consensus could only apply to this generation because they alone constituted the whole community. This could never again be the case. With their death, the Muslims were always only part of a community.[187] This argument was, of course, open to the same response as the Mālikī restriction of consensus to Medina: they alone in that case should be subject to the law.[188] The limitation of consensus to the Companions was also justified by the privileged position of the Companions as the eyewitnesses to revelation (*tawqīf*), the necessary basis for consensus, and their restricted numbers, which made it possible to know their opinions.[189]

Ibn Ḥazm is commonly credited with the traditional Ẓāhirī position.[190] But this is not accurate. In fact, Ibn Ḥazm argues that even the consensus of the Companions would have to be a tacit one. After extended research, Ibn Ḥazm could find the names of only 153 *muftīs* from among the tens of thousands who were the Prophet's Companions. To claim that no others responded to legal questions is a downright lie. Furthermore, some of the best Companions were *jinn*. Even if someone claimed to know the views of the human Companions, could anyone claim to know the thoughts of the *jinn*?[191]

Goldhizer, to whom the greater part of Ibn Ḥazm's writings was unavailable, knew from Ibn Ḥajar al-ʿAsqalānī's *Iṣāba* that Ibn Ḥazm had included *jinn* among the Companions. But he also knew that Ibn Ḥazm did make use of the claim of *ijmāʿ* and was thus forced to conclude that "he must have had his own opinion about it which can no longer be determined from our sources."[192] The problem remains, what are we to make of Ibn Ḥazm's arguments from consensus?

In the first place, the authentic consensus of the Companions (*ijmāʿ al-ṣahāba al-ṣaḥīḥ*) prohibits following the opinion of any Companion that is not found in the Qurʾān

185. *Iḥkām*, 4:141.

186. *Iḥkām*, 4:147; Bukhārī, 3:240.

187. *Iḥkām*, 4:147; *Mustaṣfā*, pp. 216–19.

188. Jaṣṣāṣ, f. 218b.

189. *Iḥkām*, 4:147.

190. For example, Y. Linant de Bellefonds, "Ibn Ḥazm et le zahirisme juridique," *Revue algérienne, tunisienne et marocaine de législation et de jurisprudence* 76 (1960): 13; Roger Arnaldez, *Grammaire et théologie chez Ibn Ḥazm de Cordoue* (Paris: J. Vrin, 1956), pp. 247–48. Ibn Ḥazm is open about his position in his *Fiṣal fī al-milal wa'l-niḥal*, 5:118: "Our opponents claim that what the opinions of our people are agreed upon is infallible (*maʿṣūm*) unlike other nations, but there is no proof for this."

191. *Iḥkām*, 4:177–78; Ibn Ḥazm, *Mulakhkhaṣ*, p. 19.

192. Goldziher, *Ẓāhirīs*, p. 32, n. 1.

and *sunna*.[193] From the point of view of content, one can distinguish two sorts of consensus. All those institutions that constitute the essential elements of Islam are part of *ijmāʿ*, for to reject them is automatically to be excluded from the Muslim community. Secondly, those actions that the Prophet performed in such a fashion that they had to be known to all the Companions also fall under *ijmāʿ*. These are the two parts that make up that *ijmāʿ* which is certain (*mutayaqqan*), "and there is no other *ijmāʿ*."[194] It follows that whenever something is claimed to be part of consensus and yet is not in accord with the Qurʾān and *sunna*, we know for certain that there is disagreement on the issue. To this extent, Ibn Ḥazm respects the tradition that guarantees that some Muslims will always know the truth.[195]

This, however, is only part of the story. For Ibn Ḥazm, the doctrine of consensus is indissolubly linked with the tragic history of the schools of law. Unscrupulous political leaders won the ready collaboration of ambitious scholars, who through their control of judicial offices gained a large following.[196] The claim of consensus was unknown among the Companions and the Followers, and has no inherent place in the law.[197] But once consensus became an issue, scholars (*ahl al-ʿilm*) took note of consensus and disagreement in order to exercise some restraint over those who were loose in their claims of consensus by bringing to their attention dissent they had overlooked. They took note of consensus to check those who had embarked on a course of dissent.[198] Ibn Ḥazm considers the claim of *ijmāʿ* an eristic device, and he makes no attempt to conceal this. "We often base our argument with our opponents on what they have agreed upon in common with us. Then we rebuke them for shifting to another rule." This device, "very much used by us" was regarded by an unlearned critic as inconsistent with Ibn Ḥazm's rejection of consensus as a slander against the community. There is, in fact, no inconsistency whatsoever:

> When we base our argument upon the opponent's agreement with us on some rule and censure him for departing from what he has agreed upon with us, we do this because he himself has departed from what he himself has judged to be valid to another position without any proof at all from the Qurʾān or *sunna*. We blame them for making statements about religion without proof, for this is forbidden and blamed in the Qurʾān and *sunna*. We do not claim a consensus, which we do not consider valid. We only claim against our opponent a consen-

193. *Iḥkām*, 4:15.
194. *Iḥkām*, 4:149–50.
195. *Iḥkām*, 4:184.
196. *Iḥkām*, 4:229–30.
197. *Iḥkām*, 4:184.
198. *Iḥkām*, 4:144.

> sus (*ijmāʿ*) with us, which he does not deny, in the sense that he is in agreement (*muwāfaqa*) with us.[199]

It is within this context that one should understand Ibn Ḥazm's collection in his *Marātib al-ijmāʿ* of the cases of consensus.[200] Consensus is used in two very similar ways, the *aqallu mā qīla* and *istiṣḥāb ḥāl al-ijmāʿ*. The first is adherence to the lowest common denominator, where a particular number or measure that figures in the law is in dispute. The second is a refusal to budge from the rule that is agreed upon in favor of one that is in dispute. These two forms of the "certain consensus which is transmitted from all the scholars of the community" are for Ibn Ḥazm a major way of finding the explanation of revealed texts that are indeterminate (*mujmal*).[201]

In making use of the *istiṣḥāb ḥāl al-ijmāʿ*, the assumption of the continuity of consensus, Ibn Hazm was following an old Ẓāhirī tradition.[202] The argument consisted in denying that a new case presented enough difference to prevent its being subsumed under a previous agreed-upon rule. The agreed-upon rule was certain and had to be adhered to unless there was a clearly relevant text for the new case.[203] The following interchange between Dāwūd's son Abū Bakr and his great rival, Ibn Surayj, is a pertinent example of its use:

> Ibn Dāwūd argued that the *umm al-walad* might be sold. There is agreement (*ittafaqū*), he said, that if she is a slave, she can be sold. Whoever claims that this rule no longer applies once she has given birth must bring proof. But Ibn Surayj turned the tables on him (*qalabahu ʿalayhī*) saying we agree that if she is pregnant she cannot be sold. Whoever claims that she can be sold once she has given birth must bring proof. Abū Bakr had no reply (*buhita*).[204]

The primary function of consensus being to ratify what is uncertain, consensus has no role in a system where only certainty is admitted in the first instance. Ibn Ḥazm's

---

199. *Iḥkām*, 4:233–34. Significantly, Bājī, p. 31, identifies *aqallu ma qīla* as a term of *jadal* (disputation).

200. Referred to in *Iḥkām* 2:79. See Ibn Ḥazm, *Marātib al-ijmāʿ fī al-ʿibādāt wa'l-muʿāmalāt wa'l-iʿtiqādat* (Cairo: Maktabat al-Qudsī, 1357 H), p. 7, n. 6. See also Robert Brunschvig, "Pour ou contre la logique grecque," p. 195.

201. *Iḥkām*, 3:154–55; 5:2–63; *Lumaʿ*, pp. 71–72; *Mustaṣfā*, pp.229–30. Ibn Ḥazm makes use of *ijmāʿ* in other ways as well. When there is a *mursal* tradition and a corresponding consensus, the *mursal* is irrelevant, and one has what amounts to a concurrent tradition (*Iḥkām*, 2:70). He accepts the commenda (*qirāḍ*) on the basis of consensus but avows himself ready to reject it if notice of one scholar who did so were brought to him (*Iḥkām*, 2:95). On the other hand, Ibn Ḥazm, unlike some Ẓāhirīs, denies the possibility of a sound tradition being abrogated by consensus (*Iḥkām*, 2:70).

202. The device was used by others as well: the Shāfiʿīs al-Muzanī (d. 264/878), Abū Thawr (d. 240/864), and al-Ṣayrafī (d. 330/941), and the Ḥanbalī Abū Isḥāq ibn Shāqlā (d. 369/979) (*Musawwada*, p. 343).

203. For criticism, see Jaṣṣāṣ, ff. 234b–235a.

204. *Baḥr*, f. 254a.

rejection of consensus is in this sense a more consistent position than that of the early Ẓāhirīs. The Ẓāhirī Ibn Ḥazm found that he had no more need of consensus than did the Ismāʿīlī al-Nuʿmān.[205]

We have noted that the standard doctrine of consensus does not discriminate between a basis for consensus that is certain in itself and one that only becomes certain through consensus. A consensus based on an explicit text of the Qurʾān or a *mutawātir* tradition would appear to be redundant. It seems that only a group of Ḥanafīs, probably Central Asian, were sufficiently troubled by this redundancy to limit the basis of consensus to the unit-tradition and analogy. This position, which for the very widely read al-Zarkashī represented a unique case of dissent from the standard doctrine, is known to us only from al-Samarqandī's *Mīzān*.[206] In answering their argument, al-Samarqandī took positions that are highly individual but perfectly consistent with his defense of the traditional doctrine.

The Ḥanafī opposition argued according to widely accepted principles of the school:

> We agree, they said, that consensus is certain legal proof (*ḥujja qaṭʿan*), but if it were only found where a conclusive source of law (*dalīl*) already existed and where the legal rules were known, there would be no benefit (*fāʾida*) in the formation of consensus as a legal proof. But the law does not include what is without advantage for men since the law was only instituted for the welfare (*maṣlaḥa*) of men and their benefit (*fāʾida*).[207]

The revealed texts that institute consensus as a source of law must be so understood as to apply to consensus as based on the sources that are uncertain in themselves, the unit-tradition and analogy. *Ijmāʿ* was instituted as a substitute for the Prophet; it was intended to fill the coming need for the renewal of the Prophetic Mission (*tajdīd al-risāla*). As the Muslims extend the law by *ijtihād*, it is only God's promise that ensures that they do not all fall into error. The religious communities of the past had no need of consensus because the law was certain as long as their prophets were alive, and when these died, new ones took their place. Similarly, as long as the Prophet Muḥammad was alive, consensus was not a source of law.[208]

In order to answer these arguments, al-Samarqandī was not content with asserting that agreement was consensus whatever its basis and that the revealed texts made no

205. The origin of Ẓāhirism in Sunni Islam probably accounts for the early Ẓāhirī interest in consensus, which still has its traces in Ibn Ḥazm.

206. *Mīzān*, f. 136b; *Baḥr*, f. 214b; *wa-huwa gharīb qādiḥ fī iṭlāq al-jamāʿa al-ijmāʿ ʿalā jawāzihi* (sc. *inʿiqād al-ijmāʿ ʿan dalāla*; *Irshād*, p. 80). The agreement *Baḥr* speaks of is mentioned in *Muʿtamad*, 2:524. Al-Bukhārī denies that al-Bazdawī belongs to this group of Ḥanafīs (Bukhārī, 3:264–65). Their point of view is defended by the nineteenth century commentator al-Marjānī (*Talwīḥ*, 3:208, margin).

207. *Mīzān*, f. 137a.

208. *Mīzān*, f. 137a.

such distinction. He attempted to meet the challenge on its own terms. There was, he argued, a real benefit in what appeared to be a redundancy of legal sources; a plurality of sources (*kathrat al-dalāʾil*) facilitated knowledge of the law. People could seek the truth from whatever source was most convenient. Thus some rules of law were found both in the Qurʾān and in a concurrent tradition. For the same reason, to make lighter the burden of men, God had given them the choice of three ways in which to expiate a broken vow. The most that could be said was that there was, strictly speaking, no need for this duplication of sources; but that there was advantage in it was beyond dispute.[209]

Because a consensus based upon a revealed text of certain authenticity is not redundant for al-Samarqandī, it follows that whenever there is a revealed text and agreement based on that text, there is consensus. He thus rejects the commonly held view that consensus as a legal source is confined to the period following the Prophet's death. A consensus could be formed in the religious communities of the past as well as in the lifetime of the Prophet of Islam.[210]

Others before al-Samarqandī, such as the Shāfiʿī Abū Isḥāq al-Isfarāyīnī and the Ḥanafī Abū Zayd al-Dabūsī, had held that consensus was not limited to the Muslims,[211] and Imām al-Ḥaramayn had explicitly limited the validity of the consensus of non-Muslims to cases where it rested on a certain source.[212] This extension of consensus to other religious laws was inherent in the position that founded consensus on common experience. The Jews and Christians had as much right as the Muslims to infer that the agreement of their scholars where it was not expected had some sound basis.[213] This was equally the case for those who founded consensus on reason, as al-Samarqandī did. It was impossible for all men to fall into error because the signs of the truth always existed. God had ensured this. Consequently, al-Samarqandī denies that the period before the coming of Islam in which no prophet was active (*al-fatra*) was one of total unbelief (*kufr*). There had always to be some people who knew the truth, but because power was in the hands of the unbelievers, the believers were compelled to summon others to the truth in secret.[214] Consensus for al-Samarqandī is not an anomalous feature of the Islamic legal system, but

209. *Mīzān*, f. 137b, 138a–138b.

210. *Mīzān*, f. 138b. How would al-Samarqandī explain the absence of consensus in the famous tradition of Muʿādh ibn Jabal? He could not argue that consensus was not valid in the lifetime of the Prophet as do *Ḥujaj*, f. 12b, *ʿUdda*, f. 162a, and Āmidī, 3:185, 191. Perhaps he would have argued that the content of any possible consensus in the Prophet's lifetime would have to be identical to that of the Qurʾān and *sunna*. He does say that consensus is required only where there is no text (*Mīzān*, f. 126b).

211. *Lumaʿ*, p. 53; *Baḥr*, f. 254a. See al-Bājūrī, *Tuḥfat al-murīd*, p. 2 (the consensus of the scholars of every religious group that all revealed books begin with the *basmala*). Cf. Ibn Taymiyya, *Rafʿ al-malām*, p. 3 (the scholars of other nations are their worst members).

212. *Baḥr*, f. 254a.

213. *Mankhūl*, p. 309.

214. *Mīzān*, f. 143b.

a principle rooted in the nature of God and man that ensures that the truth will never be extinguished.

Within the mainstream legal schools, two opposed tendencies can be discerned. With the growth of scepticism as to the working of language, there was increased uncertainty in the interpretation of legal texts, and there are indications that some regarded consensus as the only way out of a paralyzing "hesitation." We already find al-Jaṣṣāṣ rejecting the notion that hermeneutics can rest on consensus.[215] Ibn Taymiyya similarly insists that our understanding of the revealed texts must precede rather than follow consensus.[216] Both writers denounce the vicious circularity involved in giving primacy to consensus.[217]

The majority was equally hostile to those who claimed that consensus could rest on inspiration. Insistent as they were that the basis for consensus might be of either certain or presumptive validity, the Ḥanafīs were equally insistent that without some base there could be no consensus. Inspiration was not enough. To base consensus on inspiration would be to put the community on a higher level than the Prophet, who proclaimed the law only through revelation (*waḥy*) or legal reasoning (*istinbāṭ*). Furthermore, those who entered into consensus were scholars, and it was inconceivable that they would yield to their whims or the inspiration of the moment. That was the way of the heretics (*ahl al-bidʿa wa'l-ilḥād*). In those few cases where the base for consensus was unknown, the Ḥanafīs postulated a tradition that had not been transmitted because consensus was sufficient. [218]

Although it is doubtful whether those modern writers who have assigned so large a role to consensus have had these developments in mind, it is noteworthy that the enlarged claims made for consensus were categorically rejected by the majority of jurists.[219]

---

215. Jaṣṣāṣ, f. 12b.

216. Ibn Taymiyya, *Rafʿ al-malām*, p. 59. Cf. Sulaymān ibn ʿAbd al-Qawī al-Ṭūfī, *Risāla fī riʿāyat al-maṣāliḥ*, in ʿAbd al-Wahhāb Khallaf, *Maṣādir al-tashrīʿ al-islāmī fī mā lā naṣṣ fīhi* (Kuwait: Dār al-Qalam, 1390/1970), p. 125 (*al-ẓawāhir al-samʿiyya innamā wajaba al-iḥtijāj bihā bi'l-ijmāʿ fa-law uthbita al-ijmāʿ bihā lazima al-dawr*).

217. Jaṣṣāṣ, f. 12b; Ibn Taymiyya, *Rafʿ al-malām*, p. 59. Cf. al-Ṭūfī, *Risāla*, p. 125 (cited in n. 216) for the "modern view."

218. *Mīzān*, f. 138a; Bukhārī, 3:263. On the rejection of *ilhām* as a source of knowledge, see Saʿd al-Dīn al-Taftāzānī, *Sharḥ al-ʿAqāʾid al-nasafiyya* (Istanbul, 1326 H. Repr. Baghdad: Maktabat al-Muthannā, n.d.), p. 45, and Abū 'l-Yusr al-Bazdawī, *Uṣūl al-dīn*, p. 108 (subjectivism would lead to social chaos). Examples of rules which rest on *ijmāʿ* without a known support are the wordless sale by the conduct of the parties, i.e., implied-in-fact (*bayʿ al-taʿāṭī or al-murāḍāt*) and the hire of a bathhouse (*ujrat al-ḥammām*) (Bukhārī, 3:263; *Muʿtamad*, 2:521; al-Kāsānī, *Badāʾiʿ al-ṣanāʾiʿ*, 5:134; Majalla, art. 175).

219. Thus Ibn Taymiyya, *Maʿārij al-wuṣūl*, in his *Majmūʿat al-rasāʾil al-kubrā*, 1:175–211 (Cairo: Muḥammad ʿAlī Ṣubayḥ, 1385/1966), p. 201: "Those moderns who say that consensus is the foundation (*mustanad*) of the greater part of the Law only disclose their own status, for it is inadequate knowledge of the Book and *sunna* that makes them resort to this." Henri Laoust in a note to his translation of this

Opposed to this trend toward the expansion of consensus, there are indications suggesting a reduction of the role of consensus in the wake of infallibilism, the doctrine that every opinion of a qualified jurist was correct. This tendency is more difficult to document since the theorists committed to infallibilism still retained consensus as part of their systems. But it is clear that for an infallibilist system, consensus is redundant. This is the point made by the question that al-Ghazālī strives to answer: If infallibilism is correct, why is the *mujtahid* obliged to follow consensus? After all, his own view is equally correct. Al-Ghazālī's answer is that "the nation has agreed upon the obligation of following consensus."[220] This is probably not a circular response, as it first appears to be, but it does suggest the oddity of the question from the usual point of view.[221]

Infallibilism did not simply do away with consensus, but over time it worked to rob it of its force. Particularly among the Ashʿarī Shāfiʿīs, we begin to find consensus treated as a presumptive, no longer a conclusive, source of law.[222] This view, associated with Fakhr al-Dīn al-Rāzī,[223] was also held by al-Āmidī,[224] and can be found even earlier.[225]

IX. Conclusion

Enough has been said to suggest why the usual presentation of *ijmāʿ* as the cornerstone of Islamic legal theory is misleading. How can consensus possibly be the basis for the law when there is a significant body of jurists who reject *ijmāʿ* altogether? It is *tawātur* that provides Islamic law with its historical basis, the existence and actions of the Prophet, the authenticity of the Qurʾān in its various readings. These are prior to the possibility of a doctrine of consensus. Furthermore, the consensus of the Muslims is itself a fact that must be transmitted. So here too *tawātur* is paramount.[226] The interpretation of the revealed texts rests on an understanding of language that is prior to consensus. Without

---

work identifies these "moderns" as al-Juwaynī, al-Ghazālī, and Ibn Qudāma (*Contribution à une étude de la méthodologie canonique de Taki-d-din Aḥmad Ibn Taimiya* [Cairo: L'Institut Français d'Archéologie Orientale, 1939]), p. 110, n. 2, but I see no basis for this.

220. *Mustaṣfā*, p. 207; *Baḥr*, f. 254a.

221. Presumably the primary consensus here is of a higher order. It is part of *uṣūl al-fiqh*, where infallibilism is excluded.

222. Bukhārī, 3:254.

223. Ibn Qayyim al-Jawziyya, *Mukhtaṣar al-ṣawāʿiq*, p. 172. Al-Rāzī observed that "In fairness there is no way for us to know of the existence of a consensus except in the time of the Companions, when the believers were few and could all be known specifically" (*Maḥṣūl*, f. 135b). Citing the already limited *ijmāʿ* doctrine of Aḥmad ibn Ḥanbal, al-Rāzī's commentator Shams al-Dīn al-Isfahānī (d. 688/1289) denied the possibility of a concurrent transmission of a consensus, except for the Companions (*Irshād*, p. 73).

224. *Irshād*, p. 79.

225. Māwardī, 1:456. On al-Ghazālī's uncertainty, see Goldziher, "Über *iǵmaʿ*," p. 84.

226. Some Ḥanafīs even denied all force to a consensus that was not transmitted concurrently (*Musawwada*, p. 344; *Irshād*, pp. 73, 79, 89–90).

this understanding, one could not even comprehend the texts on which the doctrine of consensus is based. It would also be rash to regard the entire body of Islamic law as invested with the infallibility of consensus. Even among those who accept its authority, consensus is the exception rather than the rule.[227]

Whereas the *uṣūl* treatment of traditions is dominated by an analogy with reports (*akhbār*) within the legal system, the role of consensus is most often compared with that of prophecy. This analogy not only serves to support the claims for consensus, it also and perhaps more importantly limits the scope of consensus. Consensus is a substitute for the infallible guidance of the Prophet. It is as close as one can come to the renewal of the prophetic mission that has come to an end with Muḥammad, the Seal of Prophets. At the same time, however, the uniqueness of the Prophet must be preserved. Through consensus, ordinary Muslims must not gain prerogatives that surpass those of the Prophet. We have already seen that consensus could not be founded on inspiration because the Prophet never legislated by inspiration. This is but one of many examples.[228]

There were those who claimed that consensus should apply to secular matters such as methods of agriculture, building, and the planning of war. The sacred texts did not, after all, limit the scope of consensus. But against this, it could be argued that the Prophet had never exercised absolute authority in these areas. His judgment in such matters had been challenged on more than one occasion.[229] It thus came about that consensus was restricted, on the one hand, by logic, which excluded consensus on those basic questions of theology such as the existence of God and prophecy that underlay consensus itself, and, on the other hand, by the perception of the prophetic mission of Muḥammad as limited to theology and law.[230]

Some of the misunderstanding of consensus is perhaps due to its being confused with the fact of agreement. Consensus cannot be identified with the simple fact of agreement. For one thing, consensus in the standard doctrine requires a basis. Secondly, the agreement of the Muslims is not binding in every area. According to the usual view, even if all the Muslims agreed to practice a particular strategy of warfare, this practice would not bind them or the generations to follow, for the matter is not one that falls under the

227. *Mankhūl*, p. 310; *Mustaṣfā*, p. 218; Ibn Taymiyya, *Rafʿ al-malām*, p. 56.

228. Bukhārī, 3:263; *Mīzān*, f. 138a; *ʿUdda*, f. 164b (on *inqirāḍ al-ʿaṣr*). See also *Intiṣār*, p. 71 (the collectivity of the Jews superior to the Prophet). The text that comes closest to admitting that the Muslims *en masse* can surpass the rank of the Prophet is Jaṣṣāṣ, f. 220b. The argument has been made that the Prophet was rebuked for his *ijtihād*; how then can consensus be based on *ijtihād*? Al-Jaṣṣāṣ answers that the Prophet's *ijtihād* is better than that of any one person but not better than their collective *ijtihād*, just as his prayer is not better than the prayer of the community.

229. Bukhārī, 3:252; *Lumaʿ*, p. 52; *Mīzān*, f. 139a.

230. Bukhārī, 3:251; *Muʿtamad*, 2:493–94.

sacred law instituted by the Prophet. Consensus, in short, is not a behavioristic notion, but a normative one.[231]

One reason for the interest in consensus that exceeds that in the other sources appears to rest on the hopes many entertain for a new era in the history of Islamic law. Consensus has seemed to provide an ideal means of validating what are regarded as needed changes in the law. Some have even looked to the establishment of colleges of *mujtahids* to facilitate the formation of consensus.[232] To see consensus in this light, however, as a procedure aiming at some sort of codification of the law, marks a very significant departure from the doctrine of consensus even as it is found among the Ḥanafīs, its strongest supporters. This point is very well made by an heir of the Central Asian Ḥanafī tradition, the little known but remarkable scholar Shihāb al-Dīn al-Marjānī (d. 1306/1889):[233]

> The occurrence of consensus is not sought in itself in order to lay down the rule, for this is legislation, which is unacceptable (*tashrīʿ mardūd ʿalā ṣāḥibihi*). But it is a necessary consequence (*min ḍarūrāt*) of the application of a presumptive legal source, a unit-tradition or analogy, which provides a ready rule (*ḥukm nājiz*) on a case that arises (*ḥāditha mutajaddida*). There is no text (*naṣṣ*) from the Lawgiver, and one must act in one way or another, either to proceed or refrain.[234]

Summary

Contrary to what is often claimed, consensus is not the arbitrary basis of all of Islamic law. Far from being arbitrary, the doctrine of consensus ensures that the integrity of the revealed law will remain unimpaired throughout the ages despite the increasing reliance on probability. It is the expression of a profound theological insight. Those systems like Ẓāhirism that reject probability have at most a very limited doctrine of consensus. Not only is consensus not the basis of Islamic law, its function is not creative but declaratory, although there are instances in which consensus is evidence of laws for which there is no known source.

231. Note in this connection *Muʿtamad*, 2:466.

232. See Kemal A. Faruki, *Ijma and the Gate of Ijtihad* (Karachi: Gateway, 1373/1954).

233. See, on him, ʿUmar Riḍā Kaḥḥāla, *Muʿjam al-muʾallifīn: tarājim muṣannifī al-kutub al-ʿarabiyya* (Damascus: Matbaʿat al-Taraqqī, 1957–61), 4:308, 13:128. Al-Marjānī is a remarkably original student of the Islamic tradition, a combination of ardent Ḥanafī and Sufi (e.g., *madhhab ahl al-ḥaqq* = Ḥanafīs and Sufis [*Talwīḥ*, 3:336, margin]). It is perhaps noteworthy that he was acquainted with the *Muqaddima* of Ibn Khaldūn (Jalāl al-Dīn al-Dawwānī, *Sharḥ al-ʿAqāʾid al-ʿaḍudiyya* [Istanbul: Dār al-Saʿādat, 1316], p. 162, margin; *Talwīḥ*, 1:82–83, margin [quotation without attribution]).

234. *Talwīḥ*, 3:202, margin.

Addenda to Chapter Three

P. 132

On the possibility of the breakdown (*futūr*) of the Sharīʿa, see Ahmad Atif Ahmad, *The Fatigue of the Sharīʿa* (New York: Palgrave Macmillan, 2012).

Pp. 134–37

Important texts for the Mālikī understanding of the consensus of the Medinese have been collected and published by Muḥammad al-Sulaymānī together with his edition of Ibn al-Qaṣṣār's *al-Muqaddima fī al-uṣūl* (Beirut: Dār al-Gharb al-Islāmī, 1996). These include pertinent material from Ibn al-Fakhkhār's *al-Intiṣār li-ahl al-Madīna*, a work that has now been published in full (ed. Muḥammad al-Idrīsī, Rabat: Markaz al-Dirāsāt, 2009). The consensus of the Prophetic family (*ahl al-bayt, ʿitra*), not treated here, is a critical element of Zaydī legal theory. A classic presentation can be found in al-Ḥusayn b. al-Qāsim's *Kitāb Hidāyat al-ʿuqūl ilā ghāyat al-sūl fī al-uṣūl*, (Ṣanʿāʾ: al-Maktaba al-Islāmiyya, 1401/1981), 1:509–53. Twelver Shiʿi concern with consensus is traced by Devin Stewart, *Islamic Legal Orthodoxy: Twelver Shiite Responses to the Sunni Legal System* (Salt Lake City: University of Utah Press, 1998).

P. 157, n. 233

On al-Marjānī, see Michael Kemper, *Sufis und Gelehrte in Tatarien und Baschkirien, 1789–1889; der islamische Diskurs unter russischer Herrschaft* (Berlin: Klaus Schwarz, 1998), 429–65. A new edition of his important work *Nāẓūrat al-ḥaqq fī farḍiyyat al-ʿishāʾ wa-in lam yaghib al-shafaq*, has recently been published, ed. Ūrkhān ibn Idrīs Anjaqār and ʿAbd al-Qādir ibn Saljūq Yılmaz (Istanbul: Dār al-Ḥikma, 1433/2012).

4
ANALOGY

I. Introduction

If *fiqh* is, as so commonly claimed, the predominant "science" of medieval Islam, then *uṣūl al-fiqh* is the Islamic counterpart of the philosophy of science, and the problem of juristic analogy, *qiyās*, is the equivalent of the problem of induction. The identification of *qiyās* with induction is not novel. Ibn Ḥazm already observed that "what the ancients call induction (*istiqrāʾ*) the people of our faith call *qiyās*."[1] He and other astute students of Islamic intellectual life were able to penetrate to the crux of the issue. They saw that in the dominant kind of analogy practiced by the jurists, the crucial step was that of identifying the cause (*ʿilla*) of the original rule (*aṣl*) and that the common identification of legal analogy with the case-to-case inference known to the Islamic logicians as *al-tamthīl* was misleading. "That in virtue of which analogy exists is the cause," insisted the Ḥanafī Ṣadr al-Sharīʿa al-Maḥbūbī (d. 747/1346), himself a logician of repute.[2]

The classical example of legal analogy will elucidate the point at issue. The canonical form for the presentation of an analogy in the works of *fiqh* is as follows: Whisky inebriates so that it is prohibited like wine. The accepted analysis identifies four elements in such an analogy: the derived case (*farʿ*), whisky; the original case (*aṣl*), wine; the character they have in common (*jāmiʿ*), their power to inebriate; and their common legal qualification (*ḥukm*), prohibition. The crucial step that underlies this analogy is the identification of "the cause" (*ʿilla*), the factor in the original case that lies behind its prohibition. Here it is the quality of inebriating that is so identified rather than the color, taste, or smell of the wine. The dominant view among the practitioners of analogy is that in such a case, the identification is only probable, and it is this fact that lies at the heart of the issue of *qiyās*. Once the cause is isolated, it is no great feat to throw the analogy into the

1. Ibn Ḥazm, *al-Taqrīb*, p. 163.
2. *Talwīḥ*, 2:353. On his standing as a logician, see Tashköprüzāde, *Miftāḥ al-saʿāda*, 1:303.

form of an Aristotelian syllogism to please the logician.[3] All substances that inebriate are prohibited; whisky inebriates, therefore whisky is prohibited.

The problem of *qiyās* does not lie in its formulation, but in its epistemology. Linant de Bellefonds has drawn attention to a striking feature of Islamic jurisprudence: "In that enormous output which constitutes Muslim legal writing one finds only very rarely an attempt to systematize, to deduce a general rule from the specific rule for each legal act. It has been said that because of the religious character of the law, the Muslim jurist feels a certain reticence to lay down principles which would be generally applicable and thereby might seem to rival the revealed precepts."[4] The proper explanation, however, lies in the fact that it is only the original rule that is certain. The middle term and the conclusion are only probable. This is a point of significance and will be taken up later in connection with the topic of the "intransitive cause" (*al-ʿilla al-qāṣira*).

Like the familiar problem of induction, the theory of *qiyās* falls into two parts. The first, which we may term the foundation of *qiyās*, treats of the justification of analogy and is thus the counterpart of the Western literature written under the influence of Hume. The second part deals with the methodology of *qiyās*. It would be difficult to exaggerate the importance of both of these topics for the study of Islamic law and indeed for the study of Islamic intellectual history as a whole. Nowhere else in Islamic literature is there so fully developed a discussion of the problem of induction, and there is evidence that the legal discussion was not without influence on the methodology of the physical sciences.[5] The *uṣūlīs* themselves were aware of the scope of the issue that confronted them, and it is not uncommon for them to remark upon the role of *qiyās* in the various sciences

---

3. Ibn Sīnā, *al-Shifāʾ*, *al-Manṭiq*: 4, *al-Qiyās*, pp. 575–76; Ibn Sīnā, *al-Ishārāt wa'l-tanbīhāt*, ed. Sulaymān Dunyā (Cairo: Dār al-Maʿārif, 1968–71), 1:368–69; Naṣīr al-Dīn al-Ṭūsī's comment on Fakhr al-Dīn al-Rāzī, *al-Muḥaṣṣal*, p. 33; Ibn Taymiyya, *al-Radd*, p. 118; *Musawwada*, p. 395. Cf. *Musawwada*, p. 402 (*maḥḍ tamthīl*). This is unrelated to the rather trivial issue that was raised as to whether the prestigious term *qiyās* was more properly applied to the procedure of the jurists or to the Aristotelian syllogism (Ibn Taymiyya, *al-Radd*, pp. 6, 119). "Our analogist brethren have used a weak, sophistical trick and given the name of *qiyās* to arbitrary judgment and sophistry, calling their arbitrary judgment on the basis of reprehensible induction *qiyās*" (Ibn Ḥazm, *al-Taqrīb*, p. 173). See also the interpretation of al-Shaykh al-Mufīd's use of the term *qiyās* as *burhān* in al-Muḥaqqiq al-Ḥillī, *Maʿārij al-uṣūl*, p. 128. Related to this theme is the explanation offered in Jalāl al-Dīn al-Khwārizmī, *al-Hidāya maʿa sharḥihā al-Kifāya fī al-masāʾil al-fiqhiyya wa'l-dalāʾil al-naqliyya wa'l-ʿaqliyya*, ed. Hukeem Mouluvee Abdool Mujeed (Calcutta: al-Maṭba al-Ṭibbī, 1831–34), 1:31, that the early jurists used the term *maʿnā* to avoid the philosophical term *ʿilla*. The standard explanation traces *maʿnā* to a prophetic tradition (Bukhārī, 1:12; *Mīzān*, f. 154a). For Ibn Ḥazm's criticism of this use of *maʿnā*, see *Iḥkām*, 8:101.

4. Y. Linant de Bellefonds, *Traité de droit musulman comparé*, 1:54–55, translated in Herbert J. Liebesny, *Law of the Near and Middle East: Readings, Cases & Materials* (Albany: State University of New York Press, 1975), p. 30.

5. See most recently, Jalāl Muḥammad Mūsā, *Manhaj al-baḥth al-ʿilmī ʿinda al-ʿarab* (Beirut: Dār al-Kitāb al-Lubnānī, 1972), pp. 110–12, 275.

and in everyday life. They were interested in working out a definition of *qiyās* that would hold for all its varieties,[6] mindful at the same time of the differences between legal and rational causes.[7]

We shall restrict our attention to legal analogy. But even with this restriction, the importance of the debate over analogy is unmistakable. According to its partisans, the great bulk of the law rests on analogy. Imām al-Ḥaramayn defended his exclusion of the Ẓāhirīs from consensus on the ground that "the revealed texts do not cover one hundredth of the cases."[8] For him, analogy is the legal source (*aṣl*) most worthy of the student's attention.[9] It is the prime element in the work of the jurist, his *ijtihād*.

For a preliminary orientation it will be useful to specify further the procedure at issue in the debate over analogy. In doing so, we shall follow a classical scheme set forth by al-Ghazālī, who distinguishes three procedures (*taṣarruf*) concerned with the "cause" (*ʿilla*) of the rule of law or, as it is termed in the present context, the "nexus of the qualification" (*manāṭ al-ḥukm*). Two of the three procedures are relatively uncontroversial. These are the "verification of the nexus" (*taḥqīq al-manāṭ*) and the "reduction of the nexus" (*tanqīḥ al-manāṭ*). In verifying the nexus, we do not generalize the original rule as we did in the example of the prohibition of wine cited earlier. Rather, we go from the rule to a particular case that is regulated by the rule. The problem here is the proper application of the law where the standards set by the lawgiver are not precise enough to obviate any further legal effort (*ijtihād*). A judge, for example, is obligated to accept the testimony of a competent witness or to fix the proper amount of support in the case before him. "This is inevitable (*ḍarūra*) in every revealed law (*sharīʿa*)," writes al-Ghazālī, "for it is impossible to specify the probity of each individual or the amount of support each individual requires."[10] Under this procedure falls the determination of the proper direction for prayer (*qibla*) when the Kaʿba is not in sight. Such uncertainty and the accompanying recourse to probable opinion are unavoidable. Consequently, this has nothing to do with the analogy that is in controversy.[11]

In the reduction of the nexus, the rule of law is generalized, but only to the extent that we ignore what is known to be of no legal relevance. No attempt is made to locate

6. Ibn Taymiyya was familiar with over twenty definitions, all of them subject to some objection, evidence for his attack on the role of definition in knowledge (*al-Radd*, p. 8). Of one famous definition, that of al-Bāqillānī, which al-Juwaynī regarded as the best available (*Burhān*, f. 206), Ibn Ḥazm said that "it is more like the talk of the insane than anything else" (*Iḥkām*, 7:53). See also *Musawwada*, p. 369.

7. The *uṣūlī*s were especially interested in distinguishing between rational, that is, natural, causes and those of the law (*Dharīʿa*, 2:670; Ṭūsī, p. 254; *Talwīḥ*, 2:372–73; *Mughnī*, 17:335).

8. Quoted *Ḥuṣūl*, p. 73, and without attribution Bukhārī, 2:279.

9. *Burhān*, f. 206.

10. *Mustaṣfā*, p. 396; *Rawḍa*, p. 146.

11. *Mustaṣfā*, p. 396. In holding this, al-Ghazālī is implicitly abandoning al-Shāfiʿī's argument for analogy, which starts from this accepted practice (see n. 131, below).

the precise cause of the law.[12] We are satisfied with knowing that a case not covered in terms by the law nonetheless falls under it by virtue of the fact that there is no relevant difference.[13] This procedure is known to the Ḥanafīs as *istidlāl* and is regarded by them as of greater epistemic force than analogy.[14] Al-Ghazālī claims that most of those who reject analogy accept this procedure, and that those opponents of *qiyās* and Ẓāhirīs who do reject it are oblivious to the absurdity of what they say.[15] There was, in fact, disagreement among Ẓāhirīs as to this procedure. Al-Qāsānī and al-Nahrawānī, whom we have already encountered as among those who reject the unit-tradition as a source of law, are supposed to have recognized this procedure.[16] But other Ẓāhirīs did not. There is a prophetic tradition from Abū Hurayra that says: "Let no one of you urinate into stagnant water that does not flow and then perform his ablution from it." With respect to this, Ibn Daqīq al-ʿĪd (d. 706/1302), the great Shāfiʿī, writes:

> We know without question the falsity of the doctrine of the inflexible Ẓāhirīs that the rule is restricted to urination into water so that should some one urinate into a vessel and then pour it into the water, this would be unobjectionable according to the law, or should he urinate outside the water and urine run into the water. Now there is certain knowledge that what they hold is wrong. In both cases the urine does enter the water and what is meant is that we avoid water into which an impurity has entered. This is not a matter of opinion but is absolutely certain.[17]

Ibn Ḥazm was among those who took the position attacked by Ibn Daqīq al-ʿĪd, and so we are told in another source was Dāwūd.[18] The epithet applied to the Ẓāhirīs here, "inflexible" (*jāmid*) is revealing. It is one that is found elsewhere in the literature and seems to be used not where *qiyās* is in dispute but where the object of contention, as here, is claimed to be certain. The obduracy of the Ẓāhirīs lay not so much in their principled rejection of *qiyās*, but in their refusal to distinguish between *qiyās* and other procedures that should be legitimate according to their own criteria.[19]

---

12. *Mustaṣfā*, p. 396.

13. Qarāfī, p. 399.

14. *Lumaʿ*, p. 59; *Mustaṣfā*, p. 397; Sarakhsī, 1:141–47; 2:163.

15. *Mustaṣfā*, p. 397.

16. *Musawwada*, p. 388.

17. Ibn Daqīq al-ʿĪd, *Iḥkām al-aḥkām*, ed. Alī ibn Muḥammad al-Hindī (Cairo: al-Maktaba al-Salafiyya, 1379 H), 1:131, and al-Amīr al-Ṣanʿānī's long note.

18. Ibn Daqīq al-ʿĪd, *Iḥkām al-aḥkām*, 1:131; al-Amīr al-Ṣanʿānī, *Subul al-salām* (Cairo: Muṣṭafā al-Bābī al-Ḥalabī, 1379/1965), 1:21; *Burhān*, f. 250.

19. For example, al-Dhahabī on Ibn Ḥazm, *Mulakhkhaṣ*, p. 29; Zakariyyāʾ al-Anṣārī on Zayn al-Dīn al-ʿIrāqī, *Sharḥ alfiyyat al-ʿIrāqī*, 1:78–79; Muḥammad ibn ʿAbd al-Raḥmān al-Sakhāwī, *Fatḥ al-mughīth sharḥ Alfiyyat al-ḥadīth li'l-ʿIrāqī*, ed. ʿAbd al-Raḥmān Muḥammad ʿUthmān (Medina: al-Maktaba al-Salafiyya, 1388/1968), 1:56; Aḥmad Zarrūq, *Qawāʿid al-taṣawwuf*, fd. Muḥammad Zahrī al-Najjār (Cairo: Maktabat

The procedure about which the greatest dispute raged, *qiyās* in the proper sense, is the "extraction of the nexus" (*takhrīj al-manāṭ*), the isolation of that specific factor in the original case that is the cause of the rule. Implied in this account of the controversy over analogy is the recognition of causal analogy (*qiyās al-ʿilla*) as the predominant type of analogy as opposed to other forms such as *qiyās al-shabah* and *qiyās al-dalāla*. It is this version of *qiyās*, that characterized by the identification of a specific cause, with which we shall be most concerned.

II. The Foundations of Analogy

1. *Arguments for Analogy*

Although a Humean attack on causality is part of the Ashʿarī theological tradition, it nonetheless appears that this line of argument never amounted to the full-blown scepticism that we find in the Scottish philosopher. The justification of induction in daily life and in the physical sciences was not regarded as a problem by the Muslim theologians, who could rest their confidence in God's customary regulation of the universe.[20] Hume, on the other hand, was compelled to fall back upon a merely psychological explanation of inductive behavior. It is only in the legal sphere that we find a fully developed Islamic counterpart of the problem of induction. Indeed, the issue is one of the great topics of medieval intellectual life. "The question of whether analogy is a source of law (*ḥujja*) is difficult. On both sides there are great questions and to every legal and rational argument objections and replies."[21] We can examine only some of the salient lines of argument. The main arguments were put forth early in the history of the dispute and remained a part of the subsequent debate. What we find in the later writers is not a new series of arguments, but rather varying assessments and deployments of the classical positions. Since the early texts are not now accessible, the attribution of the arguments can hardly be certain, but wherever possible, an attempt will be made to situate them in their appropriate historical setting. We shall begin by reviewing the arguments for analogy and then take up the arguments of the other side in the form of a sketch of the early history of the anti-analogist movement. Finally, we return to the problem of induction in the special form presented by the "explicit cause" (*al-ʿilla al-manṣūṣa*).

According to a common doctrine, the valid sources of Islamic law are hierarchically arranged. "The Book," writes al-Ghazālī, "indicates the validity of the *sunna*, the *sunna*

al-Kulliyyāt al-Azhariyya, 1388/1968), p. 47 (the text has *juhūd*); *Ḥuṣūl*, p. 73. See also Robert Brunschvig, "Averroès juriste," In *Études d'orientalisme dediées à la mémoire de Lévi-Provençal*. 2 vols. (Paris: G.-P. Maisonneuve et Larose, 1962), 1:54.

20. *Irshād*, p. 199.

21. *Mīzān*, f. 145a.

that of consensus, and consensus that of analogy." In point of fact, this is merely a convenient scheme. It does not reflect the logical interrelation of the sources nor does it even summarize adequately the standard *uṣūl* positions. We have already seen that it is analogy that calls for consensus, so that to rest the validity of analogy on consensus is to miss the point of the doctrine of *ijmāʿ*.[22] The classical defense of analogy does perhaps favor consensus as the most common argument for analogy, but it hardly rests its case on this one claim. The kind of arguments used are by now familiar from our treatment of the unit-tradition; and the *uṣūlī*s were, of course, completely conscious of how closely related the two issues were.[23]

As in the case of the unit-tradition, we find the arguments divided into those labeled rational and those religious. As already indicated, the task confronting modern scholarship is that of disentangling these arguments and situating them in their historical setting not in the hope of identifying the "real" basis of analogy, but in the interests of illuminating the history of Islamic legal theory and theology. The quest for a true account of the origins of analogy, on the other hand, pertains to the history of Islamic law before *uṣūl al-fiqh*, although it cannot be undertaken in disregard of the information supplied by legal theory.

We may start with what is commonly identified as the strongest argument for analogy, that from consensus. It is in the nature of an appeal to consensus that it represents a claim introduced to put a swift end to controversy. In this sense, like the other religious textual arguments, it has no "depth," that is to say, it does not take us into the ideologies in conflict but is merely a short expression of that conflict. "The analogists," Ibn Ḥazm dryly observes, "claim a violation of consensus against us while our colleagues claim a violation of consensus against them."[24] In a similar fashion, the Imāmī Abū Jaʿfar al-Ṭūsī notes that the strongest positive argument against analogy is the consensus of the "righteous sect" (*al-ṭāʾifa al-muḥiqqa*), that is, the Imāmīs.[25] All this does not mean that the claims of consensus were not put forth with complete sincerity. Ibn Rushd (d. 520/1126), the grandfather of the philosopher, claimed that "I do not know a question upon which consensus is claimed in which this consensus is more firmly established than that of analogy."[26] Moreover, he did not hesitate to give practical effect to his view, but went so far as to exclude the Ẓāhirīs from giving testimony on the ground that their re-

22. *Mustaṣfā*, p. 515.

23. E.g., Jaṣṣāṣ, f. 265a; *Rawḍa*, p. 148.

24. Ibn Ḥazm, *al-Fiṣal fī al-milal wa'l-ahwāʾ wa'l-niḥal* (Cairo, 1317–21 H. Repr. Baghdad: Maktabat al-Muthannā, n.d.), 3:250. In this connection, note the revealing exchange between Abū Hāshim al-Jubbāʾī and Abū 'l-Ḥasan al-Karkhī in Ibn al-Murtaḍā, *Ṭabaqāt al-muʿtazila*, pp. 94–95.

25. Ṭūsī, p. 262.

26. Muḥammad ibn Aḥmad Ibn Rushd, *al-Muqaddamāt al-mumahhadāt li-bayān mā iqtaḍāhu rusūm al-Mudawwana min al-aḥkām al-sharʿiyya* (Cairo: Maṭbaʿat al-Saʿāda, 1325 H), 1 :21.

jection of analogy constituted an unacceptable innovation (*bidʿa*).[27] For the Sunnis, the nexus between consensus and analogy is crucial to the history of the attack on analogy, an attack that for them does not go back before al-Naẓẓām. According to ʿAbd al-Jabbār, al-Naẓẓam's attack on analogy stemmed from his error in rejecting consensus as a source of law. In this instance, moreover, al-Naẓẓam was guilty of a particularly egregious error, for according to his own principle (*ʿalā ṭarīqatihī*), a consensus resting on a prophetic report was binding, and this was obviously the case here.[28]

One nicety of the argument from consensus is worth noting. Precisely what kind of consensus is being claimed here? Since the issue is one pertaining to the *uṣūl*, certainty is required. Did every Companion of the Prophet expressly sanction the use of analogy? Or is there only a tacit consensus? And is such a consensus sufficient to decide the issue in dispute? The question is of special concern to al-Juwaynī, who was among those who did not recognize the force of a tacit consensus. His answer is that precisely because an issue of legal theory is involved, one that will determine the bulk of the law, silence is not tolerated. That is, this is a special case, and the absence of an objection to the practice of analogy does count as a consensus.[29] Others made the stronger claim that every Companion who was a qualified jurist did practice analogy. The consensus was one of action (*ijmāʿ fiʿlī*).[30] It must also be noted that the consensus here represents an endorsement of analogy in principle rather than of a particular method of analogy. This will concern us later. Furthermore, it does not in itself exclude the anti-analogists from entering into the consideration of a particular case in which some would apply analogy and preventing the formation of a consensus.[31]

Closely related to the claim of consensus for analogy is the citation of prophetic traditions in its favor. (The various statements of the Companions in favor of analogy, on the other hand, are pieces of direct evidence for the claim of consensus.) The most famous of these traditions is that containing the instructions of the Prophet to Muʿādh ibn Jabal, whom he was sending to serve as judge in Yemen. In the absence of a text of the Qurʾān or *sunna*, Muʿādh is to apply his powers of reasoning to find the correct legal judgment. The authenticity of this and similar traditions came under severe questioning, and they were subject to varying interpretations.[32] The partisans of analogy had several

27. From his *Majmūʿa fī al-fatāwā* quoted in Abdel Magid Turki, "Argument d'autorité, preuve rationelle et absence de preuves dans la méthodologie juridique musulmane," *Studia Islamica* 42 (1975): p. 89. See also ʿIyāḍ ibn Mūsā, *Tartīb al-madārik*, 1:96.

28. *Mughnī*, 17:298.

29. *Burhān*, f. 213.

30. Bukhārī, 3:271.

31. *Lumaʿ*, pp. 60–61.

32. On al-Shāfiʿī's use of the tradition of Muʿādh, see Joseph Schacht, *The Origins of Muhammadan Jurisprudence*, p. 106. According to *Burhān*, f. 241, al-Shāfiʿī originally made greater use of the tradition. We know that it was taken seriously enough by Dāwūd al-Ẓāhirī (n. 106 below). For an anti-analogist

options. They could claim that a given tradition, say that of Muʿādh, was totally accepted by the Muslims (*tuluqqiya bi'l-qabūl*). This elevated its content to the rank of a consensus. Alternatively, the sum of these various traditions constituted a concurrent report that the Prophet had sanctioned the use of analogy.[33] A third possibility is suggested by Abū 'l-Ḥusayn al-Baṣrī. He admits that the tradition of Muʿādh does not provide certainty but denies that certainty is required. Analogy is, after all, an action (*istiʿmāl al-qiyās min al-ʿamal*) and actions can be regulated by probable opinion.[34]

The Qurʾān, too, was held by some to command the use of analogy. The verse most often cited is 59:2, "Reflect you who have understanding" (*iʿtabirū yā ulī al-abṣār*). We are told that Ismāʿīl Ibn ʿUlayya (d. 218/832), one of the great partisans of analogy in Islam, used this verse as a proof text.[35] Whether this use was original with him is not clear. In any case, its citation became popular, and we find Ibn Surayj depending on it in his polemic with al-Qāsānī.[36] Like the tradition of Muʿādh, this verse was the subject of much contention.[37] In identifying it as "the strongest rational argument which we rely on in this question," al-Sarakhsī tacitly admits the force of the objection raised by those who noted that the verse does not refer to analogy but to reflecting. The general command of reflecting implies the reflection that constitutes analogy.[38] At the same time, al-Sarakhsī shows his disregard for the more suspect rational arguments for analogy that we shall now consider.

Those who based the legitimacy of analogy on rational grounds were a distinct minority.[39] It may be recalled that Ibn Surayj and al-Qaffāl al-Shāshī, leading Shāfiʿīs, fell under a cloud of suspicion precisely because they claimed that the status of the unit-tradition and analogy as sources of law could be rationally justified.[40] Apart from these two, others who argued for this position were Bishr al-Marīsī, al-Aṣamm, Abū Bakr al-Daqqāq, and the Ḥanbalī Abū 'l-Khaṭṭāb al-Kalwadhānī.[41] Abū 'l-Ḥusayn al-Baṣrī is reported to have been forced to rely on a rational argument when he rejected the traditional arguments as insufficient.[42] In fact, we have seen that al-Baṣrī suggests that the foundation of

---

version, see *Dharīʿa*, 2:723. Ibn Kathīr (d. 774/1373) compiled a *juzʾ* on the subject (Muḥammad ibn ʿAlī al-Shawkānī, *Irshād al-sāʾil ilā dalāʾil al-masāʾil*. In *Majmūʿat al-rasāʾil al-munīriyya*, ed. Muḥammad Munīr [Cairo: Idārat al-Ṭibāʿa al-Munīriyya, 1346 H. Repr. Beirut: Dār al-Jīl, 1970], 3:85).

33. *Muʿtamad*, 2:736; Māwardī, 1:566 (as *mutawātir*, not *ijmāʿ*).

34. *Muʿtamad*, 2:737.

35. Jaṣṣāṣ, f. 249b.

36. Jaṣṣāṣ, f. 249b. Ibn ʿUlayya is also reported to have made use of Qurʾān 4:83 (*Irshād*, p. 201).

37. *Irshād*, pp. 200–201.

38. Sarakhsī, 2:138.

39. Ṭūsī, p. 255.

40. Tāj al-Dīn al-Subkī, *Ṭabaqāt*, 3:201–2. (See above, ch. 1, n. 121.)

41. For the first three, see Turki, "Argument d'autorité," pp. 75–76; for al-Kalwadhānī, *Musawwada*, p. 369.

42. Bukhārī, 3:270; *Irshād*, p. 195.

analogy, regarded as a mere action, does not have to be certain. In any case, the rational argument he does put forth may be identified as the standard one. We have already encountered it in connection with the unit-tradition:

> When we say that reason indicates the use of analogy what we mean is that when we have probable opinion on the basis of legal evidence (*amāra*) as to the cause of the rule of the original case and also know by reason or the senses that this cause is present in something else, reason requires that we analogize that thing to the original case on the basis of that cause.... We only say that reason obliges analogizing fermented date juice (*nabīdh*) to wine (*khamr*) because reason establishes the evil of that which we think shows evidence of harm, and the evidence of prohibition is the evidence of harm.[43]

The basis for the argument is the rule of reason that bids us act so as to maximize our welfare and avoid harm wherever we can. Probable opinion based on the law is a valid basis for the application of this maxim.[44] Here it is probable that wine is prohibited because it inebriates, and this is enough to make us treat fermented date juice, which also inebriates, as prohibited. Analogy and the unit-tradition are both merely instances in which this rule of reason is relevant. Apart from this standard argument of Muʿtazilī stamp, there are a number of others. Abū 'l-Muẓaffar al-Samʿānī, having cited al-Baṣrī's argument, states explicitly that "it is better that we mention a rational argument that does not entail any doctrine of theirs (the Muʿtazila)." For him it is a rule of reason (*qaḍiyyat al-ʿaql*) that "two things similar have one rule (*ḥukm*) with respect to this similarity."[45] Other rational arguments will be examined below in our treatment of anti-analogism.

2. Anti-Analogism

The mainstream Sunni tradition appears to be unanimous in regarding Ibrāhīm al-Naẓẓām (d. 220/835—230/845) as the first person to question the validity of analogy; the attack on analogy was originally the heresy of a single individual. In fact the history of Islamic law shows that the rejection of analogy found support among many groups. It would be simplistic to seek to trace the roots of this widespread phenomenon to a single adventitious source. The disagreement over analogy stems from the clash of fundamentally opposed views as to the character of the Islamic revelation. Those who constitute the "rejecters of analogy" (*nufāt al-qiyās*) are in fact a larger segment of the Islamic community than the term might first suggest. For here are lumped together not only the Ẓāhirīs but many of the Sunni *ḥadīth* scholars, a sizeable proportion of the Muʿtazila,

43. *Muʿtamad*, 2: 725.
44. *Muʿtamad*, 2:717.
45. *Qawāṭiʿ*, f. 183a.

most Khārijīs, and most Shiʿis. What links these very disparate groups in their rejection of analogy is not their suspicion of a particular technical procedure, but the epistemological standards they demanded of any law that lay claim to being truly Islamic. As important a feature of each of these systems as the rejection of analogy may be, in itself it is too imprecise a feature to characterize them adequately. The history of each system needs to be studied in its own inner development, although there is evidence of considerable cross influences at work. In what follows we shall drawn upon the chief Sunni accounts. These focus upon al-Naẓẓām, the Muʿtazilīs who succeeded him, and the Ẓāhirīs.

A particularly valuable summary of these matters is furnished by Ibn ʿAbd al-Barr (d. 463/1071) in his *Jāmiʿ bayān al-ʿilm*:

> The scholars did not cease to allow analogy until there appeared Ibrāhīm Ibn Sayyār al-Naẓẓām and a group of the Muʿtazila who followed his path in the rejection of analogy and *ijtihād* in the rules of law thereby departing from the practice of the Predecessors (*al-salaf*). Among those who followed al-Naẓẓām in this were Jaʿfar ibn Ḥarb, Jaʿfar ibn Mubashshir, and Muḥammad ibn ʿAbd Allāh al-Iskāfī. These men were Muʿtazilīs, leaders of Muʿtazilīs among its adherents. Among the *Ahl al-Sunna* Dāwūd ibn Khalaf al-Isbāhānī followed them in rejecting analogy in the law, but he propounded the *dalīl*, a kind of analogy which we shall discuss, God willing. Dāwūd was not opposed to the *Jamāʿa* and *Ahl al-Sunna* in his belief and in the acceptance of unit-reports. Abū 'l-Qāsim ʿUbayd Allāh ibn ʿUmar in the *Book of Analogy* among his books on *uṣūl* says that, "I do not know any Basran or anyone else with any intelligence who preceded Ibrāhīm ibn al-Naẓẓām in the rejection of analogy and *ijtihād*. And the majority paid him no heed. Abū 'l-Hudhayl opposed him in this and checked and refuted him, Abū 'l-Hudhayl and his followers. Bishr ibn al-Muʿtamir, the head of the Baghdādīs, was among the most ardent supporters of analogy and *ijtihād* in the law, he and his followers. And it was as if he and Abū 'l-Hudhayl spoke on this with one voice.[46]

Although we shall attempt to fill in some of the details left out in this account, it nonetheless brings out clearly the inner-Muʿtazilī split over analogy. Ibn ʿAbd al-Barr also asserts the relation of Dāwūd's Ẓāhirism to these Muʿtazilī anti-analogists. This affiliation is confirmed by other sources and will have to be more precisely defined.

The mainstream *uṣūl* tradition distinguishes between those who based their opposition to analogy on rational grounds such as al-Naẓẓām and the Baghdādī Muʿtazilīs and

46. Ibn ʿAbd al-Barr, *Jāmiʿ bayān al-ʿilm wa-faḍlihi*, 2:62–63 (reading *tarīqahu* on p. 62, line 19). Abū 'l-Qāsim ʿUbayd Allāh ibn ʿUmar (d. 365/975) was a Shāfiʿī scholar who emigrated to Spain (ʿAbd Allāh ibn Muḥammad ibn al-Faraḍī, *Taʾrīkh ʿulamaʾ al-Andalus* [Cairo: al-Dār al-Miṣriyya li'l-Taʾlīf wa'l-Tarjama, 1966], pp. 253–55).

those who did so on the basis of the revealed texts such as Dāwūd and his son.[47] In fact, even the scanty evidence we have indicates that that is an oversimplification. Nonetheless, it is reasonable to make such a distinction provided that it is regarded as a matter of emphasis rather than an exclusive dichotomy. If we do so, we shall find a clear movement in Ẓāhirism away from the anti-rationalism of Dāwūd to the theologically sophisticated Ẓāhirism of the second generation, that of Dāwūd's son Muḥammad, al-Qāsānī, and al-Nahrawānī. This shift is confirmed by the development of Ẓāhirī doctrine on the unit-tradition. It is also important to keep in mind that many of the strongest supporters of analogy denied that it could be established rationally.[48] Al-Ghazālī even goes so far as to include among those who undermine analogy those who base its validity on reason.[49]

The argument against analogy most closely linked with al-Naẓẓām is one that rests its case on the nature of the Islamic revelation. Islamic law is characterized by such inconsistencies when measured by human standards that there is simply no place for analogy. Al-Naẓẓām supported this claim by giving examples of cases where if analogy had been applied, the result would have been the exact opposite of the established law. The law, for example, allows a man to look at the hair of a beautiful slave girl despite the lustful thoughts this may arouse, but forbids him to look at the hair of a freewoman however ugly she may be.[50] Apparently, for al-Naẓẓām, Islamic law was unique in possessing this arbitrary quality. Previous revelations had shown agreater consistency and were thus amenable to analogous development.[51] One could, of course, argue that al-Naẓẓām's examples were not to the point, since a proper analogy had to go below the surface and seek the true cause of the original ruling.[52] The reply of al-Māwardī (d. 450/1058), however, takes the opposite tack. All the examples relied upon by al-Naẓẓām are merely exceptions that prove the rule. They constitute that part of the law that is apparently arbitrary, and for this reason they were expressly regulated.[53] The other part of the law is not so constituted and is a proper sphere for the application of analogy. For al-Naẓẓām, then, adherence to the law was based on blind obedience rather than understanding. Its goals were not accessible to human reason.[54] Where the lawgiver did explicitly indicate the cause of the law, the rule was to be applied to all instances of the cause. But this was a linguistic operation and did not constitute analogy.[55]

---

47. For example, *Musawwada*, pp. 367–68 (quoting Ibn ʿAqīl).
48. *Lumaʿ*, p. 56; *Mughnī*, 17:286–87.
49. *Mustaṣfā*, p. 398.
50. *Muʿtamad*, 2:746.
51. *Irshād*, p. 199.
52. *Muʿtamad*, 2:747.
53. Māwardī, 1:576.
54. Bukhārī, 3:272.
55. *Muʿtamad*, 2:753, 759.

That feature of al-Naẓẓām's rejection of analogy that most impressed later writers was his attack on the Companions. For the Sunnis, this attack put al-Naẓẓām in the same camp as the Shiʿis.[56] In fact, al-Naẓẓām did not spare ʿAlī from his attacks. He, too, was among those who used analogy. The Imāmī leader al-Shaykh al-Mufīd (d. 413/1022), in seeking to vindicate ʿAlī from this slander, furnishes us with the fullest account we have of al-Naẓẓām's position.[57] His quotations from al-Naẓẓām go back to the *Kitāb al-Futyā* of al-Jāḥiẓ (d. 255/869), al-Naẓẓām's most famous disciple, a work that Josef van Ess has sought to reconstruct.[58] From these citations and from others, we can get a reasonably clear account of al-Naẓẓām's place in the dispute over analogy.

According to al-Naẓẓām, only a minority of the Companions exercised reasoning in the law, but those who did were the Companions who wielded the greatest influence, the first four Caliphs, Ibn Masʿūd, Zayd Ibn Thābit, Muʿādh Ibn Jabal, Abū 'l-Dardāʾ, and Abū Mūsā al-Ashʿārī, as well as a group of the younger Companions. The others were in no position to object to the behavior of their leaders and practiced "caution" (*taqiyya*).[59] Statements of these very Companions in condemnation of analogy, which were often cited by anti-analogist authors, al-Naẓẓām took as indications of their insincerity. They knew that what they were doing was wrong, and only did it to arrogate power to themselves.[60] Behind this attack on the Companions there lies a conception of the nature of Islamic law with which we are already familiar and which is put in unmistakable terms by al-Naẓẓām himself. Commenting upon a report that ʿAbd Allāh ibn ʿUmar, when asked a legal question, replied, "I don't know, but if you like, I'll give you an answer based on my opinion (*akhbartuka bi-ẓannī*)," al-Naẓẓām writes:

> They come and admit against themselves that on the basis of opinion they shed blood, on the basis of opinion allow sexual relations, on the basis of opinion award property, on the basis of opinion make obligatory acts of worship. God has forbidden them to pass judgment or testify on the basis of opinion: "Saving him who bears witness unto the truth knowingly" (43:86) and has commanded knowledge and certainty. But these people disobeyed and acted on the basis of opinion knowing that the people would obey them and that whatever they said would be binding and compulsory.[61]

Here we find the same issue of opinion versus certainty that we have come to recognize. At the core of al-Naẓẓām's view of the Companions is his conception of Islamic law as

56. Jaṣṣāṣ, f. 247a; Sarakhsī, 2:118; *Burhān*, f. 211; *Mustaṣfā*, p. 465.

57. *Fuṣūl*, 2:13–41.

58. van Ess, *Das Kitāb an-Nakṯ*.

59. *Fuṣūl*, 2:39; *Intiṣār*, p. 74; Bukhārī, 3:281–82; *Mustaṣfā*, pp. 405–6 (Ibn Masʿūd, Ibn ʿAbbās, Ibn al-Zubayr mentioned as young Companions).

60. *Fuṣūl*, 2:39.

61. *Fuṣūl*, 2:18.

requiring certainty in each of its elements. The Companions who exercised legal reasoning found such a system too constraining. The power they took to themselves was that of legislating. In so doing, they opened the way to disagreement, and this ultimately led to the bloody wars that marked the early history of Islam.[62] The doctrine of free reasoning once taken up, the Companions were led to elaborate a doctrine of consensus with which to prop it up.[63] Behind the various idiosyncrasies of al-Naẓẓām's teaching there lies a commonly held view of the nature of the law.

According to the *uṣūl* sources, those like the Muʿtazilī Jaʿfar ibn Mubashshir (d. 234/848–9) of Baghdad, who followed al-Naẓẓām in rejecting analogy, were careful to dissociate themselves from his attack on the Companions. They did not dispute the facts that al-Naẓẓām had pointed to, but they chose to interpret them differently: "The opinion of the Companions on the various cases that came up was by way of mediation and compromise (*al-tawassuṭ wa'l-ṣulḥ*) or by way of the theoretical study of legal questions (*bawr al-masāʾil*) not by way of a definitive ruling (*qaṭʿ al-ḥukm wa-ibrām al-qawl*)." But this interpretation flew so far in the face of the facts as to be absurd.[64] In fact, this way of construing the Companions' activity was already familiar to al-Naẓẓām and was one that he rejected,[65] although al-Khayyāṭ in his defense of al-Naẓẓām against the attack of Ibn al-Rāwandī sought to interpret al-Naẓẓām's views along this line.[66]

Apparently, also, Ibn Mubashshir did not entirely renounce the style of al-Naẓẓām for, according to Ibn al-Rāwandī, he accused the Companions of having introduced a fixed penalty (*ḥadd*) on the basis of their reasoning.[67] The case meant is that of the imbibing of wine. According to Ibn al-Rāwandī, Ibn Mubashshir regarded the consensus of the Companions and Followers to punish the imbibing of wine with lashes as an error since it was based on their own reasoning.[68] In any case, the interpretation of the Companions' legal activity as a form of conciliation did not die with the Baghdādī Muʿtazila but was taken up by Ibn Ḥazm, as we shall see.

The legal theory of those Baghdādī Muʿtazilīs classified among the opponents of analogy did not receive the attention accorded to that of al-Naẓẓām. Aside from the two Jaʿfars, Jaʿfar ibn Ḥarb and Jaʿfar ibn Mubashshir, other Baghdādīs mentioned as opponents of analogy are Muḥammad ibn ʿAbd Allāh al-Iskāfī, ʿĪsā al-Murdār, and Aḥmad ibn

62. Bukhārī, 3:282.

63. *Burhān*, f. 211.

64. Jaṣṣāṣ, f. 247a; Sarakhsī, 2:118; *Mughnī*, 17:298.

65. *Fuṣūl*, 2:14.

66. *Intiṣār*, p. 74. Another defense of al-Naẓẓām held that he presented his unflattering reconstruction of early Islamic history merely as an inevitable consequence of the low standards in admitting reports entertained by his opponents (*Fuṣūl*, 2:37).

67. *Intiṣār*, p. 104.

68. *Intiṣār*, p. 63.

ʿAlī al-Shaṭawī.[69] There is also mentioned a student of al-Naẓẓām, Abū ʿAffān al-Naẓẓāmī.[70] Al-Iskāfī was a student of Jaʿfar ibn Ḥarb, himself a student of ʿĪsā al-Murdār.[71] One should also probably associate with this group another student of al-Naẓẓām, the Shiʿi theologian Ṣāliḥ Qubba, who was known for his rational argumentation against the unit-tradition.[72] Presumably he took a similar course in rejecting analogy. There is also mentioned among this group a certain al-Maghribī or al-Maʿarrī, whose identity is elusive.[73]

It appears from the limited information at our disposal that the legal theory of this group was very close to that of al-Naẓẓām. Al-Khayyāṭ, a student of Jaʿfar ibn Mubashshir,[74] reports that "Jaʿfar's doctrine of law is well known," and characterizes it as the "adherence to the plain sense (*ẓāhir*) of the Qurʾān, the *sunna*, and consensus, and the rejection of the doctrine of opinion and analogy."[75] Jaʿfar's teaching on consensus may not have been as straightforward as al-Khayyāṭ suggests. We have already noted that according to Ibn al-Rāwandī, Jaʿfar regarded the punishment of the drinker of wine with lashes as an erroneous consensus founded on legal reasoning.[76] If this is the case, then his doctrine of consensus would appear to be like that of al-Naẓẓām, who is reported by ʿAbd al-Jabbār as having recognized only a consensus based on report.[77] Furthermore, Ibn al-Rāwandī also attacked the Baghdādī Muʿtazilī for holding that "unbelief is possible with regard to the whole nation and that the saying of the Prophet, 'God will never join my people in error' was not sound."[78] We may also note that Jaʿfar was very active in expounding his doctrine. He was the author of a book against the proponents of opinion and analogy[79] and engaged in debate on legal questions with Bishr al-Marīsī, one of the great supporters of analogy and consensus.[80]

Although no specific argument against analogy is attributed to this group, one argument appearing in the literature would seem to be associated with them. This is the argument that "because the apparent (*jalī*) rule of law is known by explicit texts so also the

69. *Iḥkām*, 7:203 (ʿĪsā al-Murādī); *Mīzān*, f. 145a. On al-Shaṭawī, see Muḥammad ibn ʿAbd al-Karīm al-Shahrastānī, *Kitāb al-Milal wa'l-niḥal*, ed. ʿAbd al-ʿAzīz Muḥammad al-Wakīl (Cairo: Muʾassasat al-Ḥalabī, 1387/1967), 1:30; Ibn al-Murtaḍā, *Ṭabaqāt al-muʿtazila*, ed. Suzanna Diwald-Wilzer. Bibliotheca Islamica, vol. 21 (Wiesbaden: Steiner, 1961), p. 93.

70. *Iḥkām*, 7:203 (Abū ʿAfār). See Ibn al-Murtaḍā, *Ṭabaqāt al-muʿtazila*, p. 78.

71. Ibn al-Murtaḍā, *Ṭabaqāt al-muʿtazila*, pp. 75, 78.

72. See the epilogue, n. 25.

73. Māwardī, 1:566 (the identification of the editor in n. 1 is not convincing); Ibn ʿAqīl, p. 192; *Musawwada*, p. 367 (al-Maʿarrī).

74. Ibn al-Murtāḍā, *Ṭabaqāt al-muʿtazila*, p. 85.

75. *Intiṣār*, p. 68.

76. *Intiṣār*, p. 63.

77. *Mughnī*, 17:298.

78. *Intiṣār*, p. 75.

79. *Intiṣār*, p. 63.

80. *Intiṣār*, p. 68 (the debate is legal, not theological, as Nyberg seems to think, pp. 134–35, note 82).

obscure (*khafī*) rule must be known in the same way, just as apparent and obscure objects of perception are known only by the senses."[81] This argument from the modality of sense perception is one that was used by Abū 'l-Qāsim al-Balkhī to establish the inferential nature of knowledge based on concurrent reports, the accepted Baghdādī view.[82] Al-Balkhī, in fact, was regarded as the classic case of one who confused the modality of knowledge.[83] This may, then, represent a popular style of argument among the Baghdādī Muʿtazila.

Among those prominent Muʿtazilīs who supported the use of analogy we find Abū 'l-Hudhayl, al-Aṣamm, Jahm ibn Ṣafwān, Bishr ibn al-Muʿtamīr, Muʿammar, Bishr al-Marīsī, and Aḥmad ibn Khābiṭ;[84] that is, the use of analogy was firmly established in the Basran school and had some support in the Baghdādī school, which was thus split on the issue.[85] Apart from the fact that each of these figures may be safely presumed to have defended the use of analogy on rational grounds, we can say little more about them as a group. The possible constitution of systems recognizing analogy is much more varied than that of those that reject it. It would thus be rash to assume that we are necessarily dealing with a view of analogy like that of the majority of jurists. Abū 'l-Hudhayl, for example, refrained from referring to the results of analogy as God's religion (*dīn Allāh*). "Religion" applied to that which was fixed and constant (*thābit wa-mustamirr*).[86] Whatever Abū 'l-Hudayl may have meant by this, it is clear that he would not have accepted the commonly held view of analogy as merely declarative, the view enshrined in al-Māturīdī's definition of analogy as a means of making evident (*ibāna*).[87]

In turning now to Ẓāhirism, we arrive at what is the most familiar of the movements opposed to analogy. In fact, the evidence for the reconstruction of the history of Ẓāhirism is not nearly so extensive as that available for the history of Imāmī Shiʿism. The close relation, however, that existed between Ẓāhirism and the mainstream Sunni legal tradition makes the study of Ẓāhirism more significant in the present context. In what follows we shall attempt not only to set forth the main features of the Ẓāhirī rejection of analogy, but also to touch upon the most obvious consequences following upon that rejection.

In order to appreciate the radical transformation of Ẓāhirism from Dāwūd al-Isfahānī to Ibn Ḥazm, we must look beyond the issue of analogy in the narrow sense to that of reason in general. A convenient point of departure is the classification in our sources of

---

81. Āmidī, 4:10; *Dharīʿa*, 2:695; Māwardī, 1:582–83.

82. See above, ch. 1, n. 53.

83. *Mustaṣfā*, p. 71.

84. *Iḥkām*, 7:203–4.

85. Al-Ghazālī's identification in *Shifāʾ al-ghalīl fī bayān al-shabah wa'l-mukhīl wa-masāʾil al-taʿlīl*, ed. Ḥamad al-Kubaysī (Baghdad: Riʾāsat Dīwān al-Awqāf, 1390/1971), pp. 399–401, of Abū Hāshim al-Jubbāʾī as an opponent of analogy is erroneous. Abū Hāshim did, however, hold unusually rigorous standards for its application (as the editor correctly points out, *Shifāʾ*, p. 400, n. 1).

86. *Muʿtamad*, 2:766; *Musawwada*, p. 370. This usage probably reflects Abū 'l-Hudhayl's infallibilism.

87. *Mīzān*, f. 144b.

the various schools according to their acceptance or rejection of both rational and legal analogy. By rational analogy is meant the theological method of analogy, the analogy upon which is founded the assertion of the attributes of God.[88] Within the context of the Islamic discussion, the rejection of rational analogy is tantamount to the rejection of rational theology, indeed, of reason (*ʿaql*).[89] Four possibilities exist. The dominant view is that both sorts of analogy are legitimate.[90] This is the view of the mainstream legal schools, which accepted a theological doctrine, be it Muʿtazilism, Ashʿarism, Māturīdism, or something more conservative. Al-Naẓẓām, on the other hand, is an example of one who rejected legal analogy but insisted upon analogy in theology. Al-Naẓẓām had not stopped at attacking the Companions for their use of legal analogy. He had also pointed to the inconsistent statements they made. One such statement he cites is the saying of ʿUmar, "If religion were based on analogy, the underside of the boot would require wiping rather than the top."[91] Al-Naẓẓām comments, "This saying of ʿUmar's (excluding analogy) does not hold except in legal rules and obligations. But as for reward and punishment, theodicy and its denial, and anthropomorphism and its denial, what is contrary to analogy does not hold."[92] The converse of al-Naẓẓām's position, the rejection of theology and the acceptance of legal analogy, we find attributed to Aḥmad ibn Ḥanbal and the more moderate of his followers.[93] Finally, there were those who rejected both varieties of analogy. These are the "extremists of the *ḥashwiyya* (anthropomorphists) and the Ẓāhirīs."[94] As imprecise as such a classification may be, it nonetheless affords us a useful framework within which to set the changes that Ẓāhirism underwent in its as yet largely unknown development.

Dāwūd (d. 270/834), the founder of Ẓāhirism, was by all accounts a staunch anti-rationalist. It is, in fact, this aspect of his teaching that drew the particular ire of al-Jaṣṣāṣ, as we have already noted.[95] It is from al-Jaṣṣāṣ that we learn of Dāwūd's well-known (*mashhūr*) saying, "Piss on reason!" (*bul ʿalā al-ʿaql*).[96] Dāwūd's place in the history of Islamic law must be considered in the light of this anti-rationalism. Only the briefest

88. Naṣīr al-Dīn al-Ṭūsī on al-Rāzī, *al-Muḥaṣṣal*, p. 29; Ibn Sīnā, *al-Ishārāt*, 1:368–69.

89. Sarakhsī, 2:119.

90. Cf. Ibn ʿAbd al-Barr, *Jāmiʿ*, 2:74, where the *fuqahāʾ* are said to be agreed against the use of *qiyās* in *tawḥīd*.

91. *Fuṣūl*, 2:13. This tradition is cited in the Sunni sources in the name of ʿAlī (e.g., al-Mawṣilī, *al-Ikhtiyār li-taʿlīl al-Mukhtār*, 1:24). The Shiʿi sources cite it, however, in the name of ʿUmar as here. The Shiʿis, it should be noted, reject the wiping of the boots. See on this, Ignaz Goldziher, *Introduction to Islamic Theology and Law*, trans. Andras and Ruth Hamori (Princeton: Princeton University Press, 1981), p. 207, n. 110, and generally, A. J. Wensinck, *The Muslim Creed*, pp. 158–60.

92. *Burhān*, 2:14.

93. *Burhān*, f. 208; *Mīzān*, f. 145a; *Musawwada*, p. 366.

94. *Burhān*, f. 208. I take it that *ghulāt* refers to both groups.

95. See above, ch. 3, nn. 39, 40.

96. Jaṣṣāṣ, ff. 224a, 237b, 261a. See also ʿUthmān ibn ʿAbd al-Raḥmān ibn al-Ṣalāḥ, *Fatāwā Ibn al-Ṣalāḥ*,

sketch of the issue can be attempted here. A full study would amount to nothing less than an account of the early history of Islamic law and theology.

The partisans of tradition (*aṣḥāb al-ḥadīth*) represent a perennial trend within Islamic intellectual life. Their view of the use of *qiyās* is captured in the saying attributed to the Caliph ʿUmar: "Beware of the partisans of opinion for they are the enemies of the *sunna*. The traditions were too much for them to preserve so they spoke according to their opinion and went astray, taking others with them."[97] This is the understandable view of the *ḥadīth* expert who has spent his life collecting and sifting the hundreds of thousands of traditions from the Prophet. For him, the key to the law is the preservation of the revealed texts. Some of the most prominent of traditionists found a spokesman if not a colleague in al-Shāfiʿī, most notably Aḥmad ibn Ḥanbal, whose doctrine in relation to that of al-Shāfiʿī is likened to that of Abū Yusūf and al-Shaybānī in relation to that of Abū Ḥanīfa.[98] In no sense, however, did the work of al-Shāfiʿī represent a definitive answer to the fragmentation of Islamic thought and of Islamic law in particular. This is very clear if we consider the hostility that marked the relations between three men who all considered themselves in some sense followers of al-Shāfiʿī: Aḥmad ibn Ḥanbal, al-Karābīsī, and Dāwūd al-Ẓāhirī.[99] The legacy of al-Shāfiʿī was rich enough and at the same time ambiguous enough to support very different interpretations and emphases. Aḥmad was apparently pleased with al-Shāfiʿī's assertion of analogy as a matter of constraint (*ḍarūra*).[100] Dāwūd denied that there was any such constraint.[101] The same view of the revealed texts as all sufficient was also the source of Dāwūd's rejection of rational theology. "There is no place for reason in establishing or controverting anything. The truth and falsity of doctrines are known by way of report."[102] This is the substance of Dāwūd's teaching and, it should be stressed, it was one he shared with many of the traditionists.

In view of this established anti-rationalism, we must distinguish in Dāwūd's rejection of analogy that line of attack that represents his authentic viewpoint. This is

---

Fatāwā Ibn al-Ṣalāḥ (Cairo, 1348 H.; Repr. Diyarbakr: al-Maktaba al-Islāmiyya, n.d.), p. 33, who notes al-Jaṣṣāṣ' particular bias.

97. Quoted *Rawḍa*, p. 149.

98. Walī Allāh al-Dihlawī, *al-Inṣāf fī bayān sabab al-ikhtilāf fī al-aḥkām al-fiqhiyya*, ed. Muḥibb al-Dīn al-Khaṭīb (Cairo: al-Maktaba al-Salafiyya, 1385), p. 37.

99. Al-Karābīsī's attack on Aḥmad was famous (al-Ḥāzimī, *Shurūṭ*, p. 50). For Aḥmad's attacks on al-Karābīsī and Dāwūd, see Walter M. Patton, *Aḥmed Ibn Ḥanbal and the Miḥna* (Leiden: Brill, 1897), pp. 32–33, 46. Dāwūd wrote a work against al-Karābīsī (Abū 'l-Qāsim al-Kaʿbī, *Dhikr al-muʿtazila*, with *ʿAbd al-Jabbār, Faḍl al-iʿtizāl*, pp. 78–79).

100. Abū ʿĀṣim Muḥammad ibn Aḥmad al-ʿAbbādī, *Kitāb Ṭabaqāt al-fuqahāʾ aš-šāfiʿīya*, ed. Gösta Vitestam (Leiden: Brill, 1964), p. 15; *Musawwada*, p. 367 (several versions).

101. Sarakhsī, 2:119. The mention of *istiṣḥāb al-ḥāl* indicates a Ẓāhirī source, but of the second generation.

102. Jaṣṣāṣ, f. 237b.

clearly the demand founded on Qurʾānic citations that Islamic law be based on certain knowledge and not on opinion (*ẓann*). In this sense, Abū Isḥāq al-Shīrāzī correctly puts Dāwūd among those whose rejection of analogy was based on revelation rather than reason.[103] This does not mean that Dāwūd was not ready to use any argument that came to hand to make his point. According to al-Jaṣṣāṣ, Dāwūd did not scruple to "steal" the rational arguments of his predecessors without apparent regard for their inconsistency with his rejection of reason and without grasping their purport.[104] Even allowing for al-Jaṣṣāṣ's obvious animus, we are safe in distinguishing between the essential thrust of Dāwūd's attack and that of later Ẓāhirism.

At the same time we must recognize that Dāwūd's attack was quite fully developed, one waged on many fronts. We can be sure that he cited the Qurʾānic demands for certainty. He was obviously also concerned with the large amount of traditional material dealing with analogy both in praise and in condemnation. Thus we find Dāwūd appearing in the chain of transmitters of the tradition containing the instructions of the Caliph ʿUmar to his judge Shurayh, but not in the familiar version that explicitly endorses analogy.[105] Dāwūd is also reported to have attacked the chain of transmitters of the tradition of Muʿādh, the tradition most widely cited in behalf of analogy.[106] Apart from this, Dāwūd used a variety of rational arguments, as we have indicated, which he borrowed from his Muʿtazilī predecessors. A further argument, or rather question, posed by Dāwūd is cited by al-Jaṣṣāṣ as indicating the man's ignorance of the nature of analogy, "Tell me," he said, "is analogy a root or a branch? If it is a root then there ought not be any dispute concerning it. And if it is a branch, then a branch of what root?"[107] Dāwūd's question was meant to point out the peculiar nature of analogy as a legal method rather than a legal source in the material sense. As a root, a foundation of the law, the institution of analogy should not be subject to dispute any more than the Qurʾān or *sunna*. As a branch, analogy would have to be traceable to some legal principle already established. The question quite clearly is directed at those who grounded analogy in revelation. One possible reply was, as we have noted, to reduce the status of analogy to that of a legal act (*ʿamal*). As such, it could be represented as coordinate with the actions demanded by the law. The issue raised is that of the standing of analogy as one of the four foundations of the law. But the question, as al-Jaṣṣāṣ observes, applied equally to Dāwūd's own method of inference, *istidlāl*.[108]

103. *Lumaʿ*, p. 56; *Jawāmiʿ*, f. 62b.

104. Jaṣṣāṣ, f. 265a; Sarakhsī, 2:119.

105. Ibn ʿAbd al-Barr, *Jāmiʿ*, 2:56.

106. Ibn ʿAbd al-Barr, *Jāmiʿ*, 1:65.

107. Jaṣṣāṣ, f. 267a. Dāwūd put this question to al-Muzanī (*Baḥr*, f. 271a).

108. Note Muḥyī al-Dīn Ibn ʿArabī's distinction between the Qurʾān and *sunna* as active (*fāʿil*) sources and *ijmāʿ* and *qiyās* as passive (*munfaʿil*) (*Risāla fī uṣūl al-fiqh*, in *Majmūʿ rasāʾil fī uṣūl al-fiqh*, ed. Jamāl al-Dīn al-Qāsimī [Beirut: al-Maṭbaʿa al-Ahliyya, 1324 H], p. 19).

With the second generation of Ẓāhirīs, we encounter a marked attempt to construct a legal system of greater coherence than that propounded by Dāwūd. In part, this meant the dropping of legal sources that Dāwūd had accepted, such as the unit-tradition and the *argumentum a contrario*. It also meant a more rigorous approach to the rejection of analogy, one that went beyond the scriptural foundations upon which Dāwūd had most heavily based his case. These Ẓāhirīs took the path of al-Naẓẓām, who "made action subordinate to knowledge" rather than that of Dāwūd, who "made knowledge subordinate to action."[109] There is no reason, however, to think that Dāwūd did not have followers who clung more or less strictly to his original definition of Ẓāhirism. We find that al-Māwardī still regards the acceptance of the *argumentum a contrario* as well as the *argumentum a fortiori* as characteristic of Ẓāhirism.[110] And Ibn Ḥazm specifically mentions Ibn al-Mughallis among the leading Ẓāhirīs who maintained the *argumentum a contrario*.[111]

Among that group of Ẓāhirīs we are most interested in, we must distinguish between Ibn Dāwūd and someone like al-Qāsānī. The position of al-Qāsānī and al-Nahrawānī, who is almost always mentioned alongside of him, could be seen as a compromise with analogy on some specific issues. This meant that their standing among Ẓāhirīs was not so clear. Al-Qāsānī, for example, is sometimes regarded as a Shāfiʿī.[112] In a rare, if not unique, reference to this group, Ibn Ḥazm speaks of "a group who are held of no account amongst us like al-Qāsānī and his ilk."[113] In the second place, the influence of Muʿtazilism that is evident in the thought of these figures was apparently not of the same degree. In the case of al-Qāsānī, it was such that he is often identified as a Muʿtazilī, and al-Sharīf al-Murtaḍā even speaks of "a group of the masters of the Muʿtazilī theologians like al-Qāsānī."[114] In this instance, then, we must go beyond speaking of a Muʿtazilī influence and speak rather of a Muʿtazilī affiliation. In any case, the interaction between Ẓāhirism and Muʿtazilism is unquestionable. The highpoint of this contact appears to have been precisely in the second generation of Ẓāhirism, the generation contemporary with the Shāfiʿī master Ibn Surayj (d. 306/918), a disputant of both Ibn Dāwūd and al-Qāsānī. In theology, Ibn Surayj was a student of Abū 'l-Ḥusayn al-Khayyāṭ, and we are told of how he, the Mālikī *faqīh* Ibn al-Mintāb, and a certain Ẓāhirī al-Iyādī were embarrassed to encounter each other in al-Khayyāṭ's home.[115] We also learn of a certain ʿAbd Allāh ibn Aḥmad ibn Rasūl (d. 319/931) who followed Dāwūd in *fiqh* and inclined to *iʿtizāl*.[116]

---

109. *Dharīʿa*, 2:517.
110. Māwardī, 1:642.
111. *Iḥkām*, 7:19, 21.
112. Ibn al-Nadīm, *al-Fihrist*, p. 213.
113. *Iḥkām*, 8:72.
114. *Dharīʿa*, 2:530.
115. ʿAbd al-Jabbār, *Faḍl al-iʿtizāl*, p. 301.
116. Ibn Ḥajar al-ʿAsqalānī, *Lisān al-mīzān* (Hyderabad: Maṭbaʿat Majlis Dāʾirat al-Maʿārif al-Niẓāmiyya, 1329–31 H), 2:252.

In what follows, the paucity of sources prevents our consistently distinguishing between the doctrine of Ibn Dāwūd, on the one hand, and that of al-Qāsānī (and al-Nahrawānī), on the other. We can surmise, however, that there were considerable similarities between their systems. Both, for example, rejected the unit-tradition and in so doing spared themselves a host of arguments for analogy. The literary activity centering about analogy reached monumental proportions in this period; Ibn Surayj and al-Qāsānī between them produced at least a thousand folios on both sides of the issue.[117] Although we cannot even guess at the details of these great battles, the main lines of strategy are tolerably clear, and indeed, familiar, for we have already encountered them in the debate over the unit-tradition.

One argument specifically attributed to "some followers of Dāwūd" proceeds from God's omnipotence (*qudra*).[118] God has the will and the power to do what is best (*aṣlaḥ*). If God had intended the law to encompass the details that the analogists claim, He would not have chosen to communicate this by the very imperfect means of analogy. He could have simply prescribed the general rules required and not have left their formulation to the jurists. This is the same argument we have met with earlier in connection with the unit-tradition. There it was used to reject the claims made for the unit-tradition as a basis for action. Had He so chosen, God could have ensured the transmission of these unit-traditions at the level of concurrence (*tawātur*). This argument was there attributed to the Muᶜtazilīs al-Aṣamm and Ibn ᶜUlayya. Al-Aṣamm and Ibn ᶜUlayya were, however, among the strongest supporters of analogy. Whatever the differences between their doctrine of analogy and that of the mainstream, it is clear that their position has to encompass a denial that God could have forgone the institution of analogy. The issue that divided al-Aṣamm from these Ẓāhirīs was one of fact. Al-Aṣamm denied that all cases to come could be regulated once and for all.[119] The Ẓāhirīs argued that this was possible, and that God had failed to do so indicated that His law was meant to retain its unique form. It was not to be generalized by the process of analogy.

It was, however, not necessary for all upholders of analogy to take the position of al-Aṣamm. It was quite compatible with the use of analogy to admit the possibility of a definitive revelation. On this view, one would look to other explanations of the institution of analogy. The justifications we find may be treated under two heads: psychological and sociological. The structure of a legal system that provides for analogy can attain psychological and sociological goals that are not within the reach of a system that excludes it. Under the heading of psychology we may cite in the first instance the view widespread among both proponents and opponents of analogy that it represents a natu-

---

117. Jaṣṣāṣ, f. 249b (from Abū ᶜAbd Allāh ibn Yazīd al-Wāsiṭī).

118. *Dharīᶜa*, 2:674.

119. Nasafī, 2:10; Bukhārī, 2:370–71. The acceptance of analogy and the rejection of the unit-tradition defended in this argument lead me to identify it with al-Aṣamm.

ral tendency of the human mind. "The fancy (*wahm*) of man is inclined to look for the cause and ground of every rule," writes al-Ghazālī.[120] To have found the reasons for the law even if certainty cannot be claimed is a great joy and relief. [121] For man to have been denied the satisfaction of looking behind the surface of the law would have constituted a great hardship (*ḥaraj*).[122] This notion of analogy as a natural tendency of the human mind is also reflected in those anti-analogist traditions that report how the lust after analogy destroyed the Israelites.[123] Closely associated with the relief achieved by penetrating to the basis of the law are the pedagogical advantages to be gained by structuring the law around its chief principles.[124]

The institution of analogy also serves the significant goal of creating a social pyramid headed by the jurists. It provides for the display of human excellence in various degrees.[125] This argument is already found in the writing of Qāḍī al-Nuʿmān, whose interlocutor looks in vain for the element of "understanding" (*dirāya*) in the Ismāʿīlī legal system. Without this element, the hierarchy necessary for a stable social order is undermined.[126] This view of analogy as the basis for the leadership of the jurist coexists in the literature with a more modest one. The jurist is portrayed as a specialist whose specialization allows the other elements of society to pursue their equally valuable work.[127]

One line of argument, combining psychological and sociological elements, is more specifically linked with the anti-analogist argument from God's omnipotence and merits special attention. It was clearly elaborated against the kind of Ẓāhirism represented by Ibn Dāwūd and al-Qāsānī and may very well have been used by Ibn Surayj himself. As it appears in the *ʿUdda* of Abū Jaʿfar al-Ṭūsī, the argument is couched in unmistakably Muʿtazilī terms. It is admitted that analogy may represent a lesser grade (*rutba*) of communication than textual regulation. But to regard it as such is to acknowledge that it is indeed a means of communicating God's will and one that very possibly represents a "grace." The Arabic term here is *luṭf*. The grace in the Muʿtazilī scheme of ethics is that which leads man to choose to do what is obligatory or to refrain from what is bad.[128] It thus represents an instrumental good. In the case of analogy, it is suggested that "God knew that the welfare of the subject lies in it and that if he arrives at the rule of law by means of it and experiences hardship (*mashaqqa*) in this process, he will be more ready to

120. *Mustaṣfā*, p. 478; *Mīzān*. f. 195b.
121. Sarakhsī, 2:128.
122. Dabūsī, f. 118a.
123. For example, Māwardī, 1:579.
124. Māwardī, 1:515; *Mīzān*, f. 195b.
125. Māwardī, 1:515.
126. Nuʿmān, p. 132.
127. *Lumaʿ*, p. 127.
128. Ṭūsī, p. 264.

observe the law.[129] Here again the possibility of a definitive legislation is acknowledged. The advantage of analogy is that it gives men a share in the elaboration of the law so that it is dearer to them and gains their loyalty.[130] In this way, they come to observe the law, and in observing it gain the eternal rewards it offers. These rewards are the benefit that analogy ultimately serves.[131]

The anti-analogist argument from God's omnipotence was apparently also cited by those Ẓāhirīs who did not reject the unit-tradition but maintained Dāwūd's position that the unit-tradition was a source of certainty.[132] This is further evidence of the complex pattern of rational and traditional argumentation that characterized early Ẓāhirism. The disunity of early Ẓāhirism emerges quite clearly, for the Ẓāhirīs were divided not only with respect to the unit-tradition, but also with respect to analogy itself. Like Jaʿfar ibn Ḥarb and Jaʿfar ibn Mubashshir, al-Qāsānī along with other Ẓāhirīs recognized the validity of analogy where the cause was textually identified (*al-ʿilla al-manṣūṣa*); Ibn Dāwūd did not. Ibn Dāwūd, in fact, represents a particularly consistent form of the new retrenched Ẓāhirism after Dāwūd, and in this sense he is Ibn Ḥazm's leading predecessor. The unit-tradition, analogy, and the arguments *a contrario* and *a fortiori* were all rejected by Ibn Dāwūd.[133] It is to his doctrine of analogy that we now turn.

Our sources indicate two important elements of Ibn Dāwūd's rejection of analogy, one logical, the other ethical. The question of logic relevant here is a procedural one. Is

129. Ṭūsī, p. 261; *Dharīʿa*, 2:693; *Rawḍa*, p. 193.

130. *Mustaṣfā*, p. 398.

131. That this argument was used against Ẓāhirism and by a Shāfiʿī is suggested by the fact that it takes up al-Shāfiʿī's argument from the use of legal reasoning (*ijtihād*) in such matters as determining the direction of prayer and the allotment of maintenance, where the Ẓāhirīs, too, recognized the inevitability of opinion. This argument was generally regarded as missing the point even by later Shāfiʿīs. The new version argues that these areas, too, could have been explicitly regulated "leading to knowledge." That this was not the case and that, despite this, divine wisdom (*ḥikma*) is upheld here suggest that the rest of the law (*sāʾir al-aḥkām*) could also be based on *ẓann*. It will be recalled that Ibn Surayj was one of the leading commentators of al-Shāfiʿī's *Risāla*, and this may represent his improved version of al-Shāfiʿī's argument. For Ibn Surayj's use of al-Shāfiʿī's argument, see *Baḥr*, f. 27lb (from his *Kitāb Ithbāt al-qiyās*). It is important to note that, at least in this context, the possibility of a definitive regulation is presupposed by the argument. The admission of this possibility also for all future cases would strengthen Ibn Surayj's position against those like al-Aṣamm who argued that *qiyās* was necessary because a definitive legislation was impossible. This amounts to claiming that analogy is at the highest level of communication (*bayān*). At this level, on Muʿtazilī principles, analogy would have to provide certain results, and this, in fact, was al-Aṣamm's view. The argument quoted here seeks to avoid this result. Analogy is established but not analogy that is certain. It thus represents a weaker claim for analogy. The combination of a rational basis for analogy and the possibility of a definitive revelation is found in the case of the Ḥanbalī Abū 'l-Khaṭṭāb al-Kalwadhānī (d. 510/1116–7) (*Musawwada*, pp. 369, 374).

132. Sarakhsī, 2:121 (if we assume a Ẓāhirī provenance).

133. See above, ch. 1, n. 115, and vch. 2, nn. 225, 279.

it incumbent on someone denying a thesis to prove his claim or is proof incumbent only on someone making a positive assertion? The traditional Ẓāhirī answer is that no proof of the negative assertion is required. A version of this doctrine and one that we want to identify with Ibn Dāwūd holds that proof of the negative is required only in matters of reason but not in matters of law. Al-Jaṣṣāṣ gives the rationale for this view:

> He who says that proof has to be adduced for denying matters of reason but not matters of revelation argues as follows. There is rational proof for both the denial and the assertion of propositions of reason so that the cases of denial and assertion do not differ. But in matters of revelation the source of knowledge is revelation, and there is no place for reason to establish anything. So if someone has not learned something by way of revelation he can say it is not evident to him that this is valid. If anyone claims its validity he must establish its validity. Otherwise, the presumption (*aṣl*) is that it is not established.[134]

The distinction between reason and revelation is, as we shall see, a crucial one for Ibn Dāwūd. The argument adduced here is itself a rational one. The presumption follows the nature of the subject matter. The traditional Ẓāhirī doctrine, however, based itself on the prophetic tradition: "Proof is incumbent on the claimant and the oath on the denier."[135] According to Ibn Ḥazm, it was their rejection of analogy that led the Ẓāhirīs to raise this issue in the first place. As far as he is concerned, this is not a suitable device. There are real arguments that can be brought against analogy.[136] What we have here is, of course, a debater's ploy. The position against analogy requires no defense. The burden of proof rests entirely on those who claim its legitimacy.

This logical argument is, however, only an extrinsic feature of Ibn Dāwūd's rejection of analogy. The core of his doctrine is ethical. In order to grasp the difference between Ibn Dāwūd and the Ẓāhirism that preceded him, or for that matter the Ẓāhirism of Ibn Ḥazm, we must introduce the distinction between "weak" and "strong" permission, now a standard notion in deontic theory, specifically as it relates to the problem of normative closure.[137]

Classical Ẓāhirism is characterized by ethical noncognitivism, that is, it denies that reason can independently of revelation perceive ethical value. In the case of Dāwūd, this doctrine is only part of a general antirationalist posture. Knowledge is dependent on information transmitted from a Prophet. This is Dāwūd's anti-rationalism of the report (*khabar*). Ibn Ḥazm's break with this anti-rationalism was complete. "Reason," he wrote,

---

134. Jaṣṣāṣ, f. 241b.
135. *Iḥkām*, 1:66.
136. *Iḥkām*, 1:77.
137. Carlos E. Alchourron and Eugenio Bulgin, *Normative Systems* (Vienna: Springer, 1971), pp. 125–30.

"whose proofs are never in contradiction."[138] Nonetheless, he too denied that reason could independently of revelation perceive value. For him, the good is identified with God's command, evil with God's prohibition, and these are conveyed by revelation.[139] What this means is that for Dāwūd and Ibn Ḥazm, there are two sets of actions: those regulated by the law and those not regulated. In the case of Dāwūd, the first set includes not only actions expressly regulated but also those whose qualification can be arrived at by inference (*istidlāl*), that is, the arguments *a contrario* and *a fortiori*. These inferences, Ibn Ḥazm rejects. But in both systems, what is not regulated is permitted by virtue of the fact that it is not prohibited. This is permission in the weak sense.

The doctrine of Ibn Dāwūd is quite different. For him, reason can perceive value. "Abū Bakr ibn Dāwūd said in his book that what God has not commanded so as to be obligatory (*lāzim*) and whatever He has not forbidden so as to be prohibited (*ḥarām*) is permitted (*mubāḥ*). One who does it does not sin in so doing nor does one suffer in omitting it." So wrote ʿAbd al-Qāhir al-Baghdādī distinguishing the teaching of Ibn Dāwūd from that of Dāwūd and the Ẓāhirīs, which is identified with that of orthodox noncognitivism.[140] It is upon this rational perception of value that Ibn Dāwūd based his rejection of analogy. The gist of this position is couched in these terms by Abū 'l-Ḥusayn al-Baṣrī:

> Reason functions like a text in indicating the qualification of a particular case. And just as God cannot enjoin us to an analogy which contradicts a specific text, similarly He cannot enjoin us to an analogy which contradicts the qualification of reason. Now all cases have a rational qualification. Consequently God cannot enjoin us to analogize with reference to them.[141]

The rational value of permission is as certain as any revealed text. When it is set aside, it is only by a text of equal certainty. In this sense, the law abrogates the values perceived by reason. Wherever there is no text to accomplish this abrogation, the "law of reason" remains valid. The results of analogy being merely probable cannot claim to be legitimate extensions of the texts that are certain. They are not of the same epistemological strength as the strong permission established by reason. The result is that human conduct is regulated by norms of disparate origin: some rational, others revealed. It is obvious that this argument against analogy presupposes ethical cognitivism and would be most of all directed at those circles that adhered to this theological doctrine. It is to

---

138. *Iḥkām*, 1:17. See also Ibn Ḥazm, *Fiṣal*, 1:82: *wa-man abṭala al-ʿaql fa-qad abṭala al-tawḥīd.*

139. See George Hourani, "Reason and Revelation in Ibn Ḥazm's Ethical Thought," in *Islamic Philosophical Theology*, ed. Parwiz Morewedge (Albany: State University of New York Press, 1979), pp. 142–64.

140. ʿAbd al-Qāhir al-Baghdādī, *Uṣūl al-dīn*, p. 25. For a direct confrontation between the methods of Dāwūd and Ibn Dāwūd, see *Baḥr*, 19b. Note also, *Musawwada*, p. 474, which attributes Ibn Dāwūd's doctrine to the Ẓāhirīs.

141. *Muʿtamad*, 2:175; *Burhān*, f. 209.

those who share this view and yet practice analogy that we must look for the other side of the story.[142]

The bifurcation of the normative into the rational and the revealed as it appears in Ibn Dāwūd evoked a rather paradoxical response. The traditional Ẓāhirī rejection of analogy based itself on Quʾrānic texts that spoke of the completeness of the law: "We have sent down the book unto you as an exposition of *all things*" (16:89); "We have left out *nothing* in the Book" (6:38); "*Nothing* wet or dry but in a clear book" (6:59). "Is it not enough for them that We have sent down unto them the Scripture which is read unto them?" (29:59) was cited by al-Qāsānī.[143] The claim of the completeness of the revealed law was, in fact, identified with the opponents of analogy and specifically with the Ẓāhirīs.[144] It was, however, this very claim that was now made in opposition to Ibn Dāwūd's doctrine and in favor of analogy. Thus Ibn Surayj argued that every law is in the Book of God.[145] Analogy is merely a process of discovery. The revealed law and its analogical extension are complete. There is no rational system that stands side by side with it. Rather, the law confirms some rational judgments while modifying others.

According to Qāḍī ʿIyāḍ, "Dāwūd called whatever he did not find within the scope of the plain sense of a text (*naṣṣ ẓāhir*) 'exempt' (*ʿafw*) from regulation and some instances he referred to as 'permitted' (*ibāḥa*)."[146] The "exemption" from regulation of which Dāwūd spoke is one form of weak permission. Another, slightly different version of weak permission is the presumption of continued nonprohibition (*istiṣḥāb li-ʿadam al-taḥrīm*). What is not known to be prohibited is presumed not to be prohibited.[147] This presumption is, in fact, not foreign to mainstream Islamic jurisprudence and is regarded by Abū 'l-Barakāt al-Nasafī as the "closest of their doctrines to the truth."[148] Ibn Dāwūd's position also amounted to a presumption of continuity, in this case, the continuity of the rational qualification of permission. We already find Dāwūd referring to followers of his who argued for the weaker form of continuity on the basis of noncognitivism.[149] They claimed the continuity of nonprohibition; Ibn Dāwūd that of permission. In both instances, the

---

142. Sarakhsī, 2:120.

143. Jaṣṣāṣ, f. 249b.

144. *Muʿtamad*, 2:744. For the Ḥanbalis, *Mīzān*, f. 145a.

145. *Baḥr*, f. 20a. For a possible reference to the confrontation of Ibn Dāwūd and Ibn Surayj, *Mughnī*, 17:304–5, 317.

146. ʿIyāḍ ibn Mūsā, *Tartīb al-madārik*, 1:96. For a quotation from Dāwūd illustrating his use of *ʿafw*, see Tāj al-Dīn al-Subkī, *Ṭabaqāt*, 2:290; *Baḥr*, f. 270a. Note also *ʿafw* as one basis for permission in *Musawwada*, p. 479. *Ibāḥa* presumably referred to strong permission based on an application of the *argumentum a contrario*. Cf. Ibn Taymiyya, *Kitāb Iqāmat al-dalīl ʿalā ibṭāl al-taḥlīl*. In *Majmūʿat fatāwā Shaykh al-Islām Ibn Taymiyya* (Cairo: Maṭbaʿat Kurdistan al-ʿIlmiyyah, 1329 H), 3:166–67.

147. *Musawwada*, p. 479.

148. Nasafī, 2:120; Sarakhsī, 2:119.

149. *Musawwada*, p. 476.

arguments rested on ignorance of a modifying text. Against these presumptions of continuity, it could be argued that the results of analogy stand at a higher epistemological level.[150] This reply was particuarly apt when directed at Ẓāhirīs who accepted unit-traditions. For in such cases they were abandoning their presumption of continuity on the basis of merely probable information, probable at least according to the majority.[151] Both strategies of Ibn Dāwūd, the logical and the ethical, met with a similar response. Ignorance was not comparable to knowledge. The analogists knew that analogy was a valid method for extending the law, and in each particular instance their solutions, though only probable, were based on evidence that clearly outweighed the presumption of their opponents, which was necessarily based on ignorance.

For Ibn Ḥazm, the strict voluntarist, there could be no place for the kind of legal system that Ibn Dāwūd had propounded. Ibn Ḥazm could not oppose the operation of analogy with an independent source of legal norms founded in reason. He had to attack analogy directly. For this attack, Ibu Ḥazm drew upon the vast body of anti-analogist arguments devised by his predecessors. We will review here only the most salient points of his massive campaign against analogy. What concerns us is what makes Ibn Ḥazm special, not what he shares with his forerunners. And this lies not in the specific arguments Ibn Ḥazm employs, but in the consistency of the system he puts forth.

In contrast to earlier opponents of analogy, Ibn Ḥazm has a precise target in view, the formal analogy practiced by his contemporaries. In this connection, he distinguishes between *qiyās* and *raʾy*, "free judgment" as legitimately practiced by the Companions. "Free judgment" is a ruling on a religious question without a text but according to what the respondent (*muftī*) regards as more circumspect or more just to prohibit or to allow.[152] The key element here is "circumspection" (*iḥtiyāṭ*). The Companions did not intend their free judgments to serve as legislation (*sharʿ*), but merely as a guide to what was the most circumspect behavior. It is in the second century that *qiyās* first appeared in the sense of an analogical ruling based on an existing text. But even in this period, the analogical solutions were not meant to form binding rules (*lā ʿalā wajh ījāb al-ḥukm*), and the respondents did not allow their answers to be written down.[153] It was only in the fourth century that the analogy predominant in Ibn Ḥazm's day, the causal analogy, appeared. Ibn Ḥazm's attack is aimed at this sort of analogy and the legal structure based upon it. For with this new form of analogy came the view that the law (*dīn*) could be legitimately extended, and the solutions now propounded were meant to be binding. The doctrine of "adherence" (*taqlīd*) was born.[154] For Ibn Ḥazm, free judgment alone has some basis

150. Nasafī, 2:122.
151. Nasafī, 2:123; *Muʿtamad*, 2:175.
152. Ibn Ḥazm, *Mulakhkhaṣ*, p. 4.
153. *Iḥkām*, 8:38.
154. *Iḥkām*, 8:38. Josef van Ess, "Ein unbekanntes Fragment des Naẓẓām," In *Der Orient in der Forschung:*

in the Islamic past.[155] This doctrine serves to explain the behavior of the Companions and is a development of the view that the Companions used analogy in cases admitting of compromise. It is to be distinguished from the much stronger claim that the use of analogy was a privilege (*khuṣūṣiyya*) of the Companions alone as a token of honor (*ikrām*). This doctrine, reported by al-Sarakhsī, may also come from a Ẓāhirī source since it corresponds to the traditional Ẓāhirī restriction of consensus to the Companions.[156]

The central point of Ibn Ḥazm's rejection of analogy is methodological. In reply to the question whether God could have imposed analogy, Ibn Ḥazm denies that this is possible once the verses were revealed: "God hath not laid upon you in religion any hardship (*ḥaraj*)" (22:78) and "God tasketh not a soul beyond its scope" (2:286). To demand the use of analogy without laying down precise directions would be to demand what is impossible.[157] Ibn Ḥazm puts his finger on the great problem of the Muslim analogists: the proper method of analogy. In a world in which everything bears some resemblance to everything else, how does one even begin to lay down the steps that lead to a rule of God?[158] Only inspiration (*waḥy*) can serve as a basis for religious law.[159]

The negative side of Ibn Ḥazm's view of legal methodology is his rejection of analogy and other fallible inferences like the argument *a contrario*. Its positive side is his championing of the cause of deductive inference in the form of Aristotelian logic. In this respect, he insists upon the importance of his book on logic:

> We have explained the method of sound proof without which nothing is sound and the proof which is always sound, and we have explained what is thought to be a proof but is not in our book entitled *Taqrīb li-ḥudūd al-manṭiq, An Introduction to the Rules of Logic*—a book of great benefit, indispensable for one seeking reality.[160]

The significance of Ibn Ḥazm's commitment to Aristotelian logic has often gone unnoticed. One cannot, of course, claim that Ibn Ḥazm's writing on logic had the influence later exercised by the works of al-Ghazālī. It is submitted, however, that what al-Ghazālī did was to put law into logic rather than to put logic into the law. Al-Ghazālī states explicitly, and indeed apologetically, that he larded his work *Miʿyar al-ʿilm* with legal examples to attract the interest of the jurists who formed the majority of his contemporary

---

Feschrift für Otto Spies zur 5. April 1966, ed. Wilhelm Hoernerbach (Wiesbaden: Harrassowitz, 1967), pp. 193–94, apparently accepts Ibn Ḥazm's dating of *taʿlīl*. But the technical use of *ʿilla* goes back to al-Aṣamm (d. 200 or 201/816 or 817) (*Jawāmiʿ*, f. 70a,b).

155. *Iḥkām*, 8:25.

156. Sarakhsī, 2:134–36.

157. *Iḥkām*, 8:47; Ibn Ḥazm, *Mulakhkhaṣ*, p. 73.

158. *Iḥkām*, 1:48; Nuʿmān, p. 138.

159. *Iḥkām*, 8:35.

160. *Iḥkām*, 5:82. On the perfection of his *al-Taqrīb*, see *Iḥkām*, 1:14.

intellectuals.[161] Ibn Ḥazm, on the other hand, set out to expound a doctrine of reality that did not bypass the law.[162] No inference that was not strictly deductive had any place in the law. The nature of Ibn Ḥazm's program was not lost upon his contemporaries. One of the charges brought against him by a group of Mālikī jurists to which he felt called upon to respond was just this, "that he rebuts what is legal with what is logical" (*yaruddu bi'l-manṭiqī ʿalā al-sharʿī*).[163] In a similar vein, his critic denied that law was like language.[164] And it was Ibn Ḥazm's book on logic that was singled out for censure.[165]

In effect, what Ibn Ḥazm was doing was imposing alien standards on the work of the jurists. As far as they were concerned, he was removing from the law precisely those features that gave it its name, *fiqh* ("understanding"). The law for the jurist only becomes the object of *fiqh* when its structure is grasped. Ibn Ḥazm was well aware of this fact. In offering his own definition of *fiqh* in terms of understanding and recall, he notes, "The analogists make an addition to what has been said here, namely, a man's knowledge of the similarities (*naẓāʾir*) in legal rules and cases and his discernment thereof."[166] For Ibn Ḥazm, however, there is no structure to be grasped beyond the language of the revealed texts. One rule never serves as the basis (*aṣl*) for another. All rules are equally basic. "There is nothing in religion except obligatory, prohibited, or permitted; there is no way to a fourth division. So which of this is basic and which derivative? What they say is groundless, and the truth is that the religious rules are all bases with no derivatives at all, and all of them are textual."[167] For the Ẓāhirī, the law is atomistic. To speak of bases at all means that there are derivatives. But Ẓāhirism denies that the law has bases at any but a verbal level. It denies that there is any validity to the level at which *fiqh* operates, the level of causes or reasons. *Fiqh* is precisely the inner rationale, and what determines the rule is the inner rationale. To seek it is to seek *fiqh*.[168] It is clear how apt a name Ẓāhirism, literally "externalism," is.

In summary, the opponents of analogy command a wide variety of arguments for their position. These fall into two categories. In the first place are the various strategies

---

161. Al-Ghazālī, *Miʿyār al-ʿilm fī fann al-manṭiq*, ed. Muḥammad Muṣṭafā Abū 'l-ʿIlāʾ (Cairo: Maktabat al-Jundī, n.d.), pp. 14–15.

162. On the role of his *al-Fiṣal*, see *Iḥkām*, 5:82. Ibn Ḥazm preceded al-Ghazālī in using nontechnical language and legal examples as the full title of his work indicates: *al-Taqrīb li-ḥadd al-manṭiq wa-ʾl-madkhal ilayhi biʾ l-alfāẓ al-ʿāmiyya waʾl-amthāl al-fiqhiyya.*

163. Ibn Ḥazm, *Risālatān lahu ajāba fīhimā ʿan risālatayn suʾila fīhimā suʾāl al-taʿnīf.* In his *al-Radd ʿalā Ibn al-Naghrīla al-yahūdī wa-rasāʾil ukhrā*, ed. Iḥsān ʿAbbās (Cairo: Maktabat Dār al-ʿUrūba, 1380/1960), p. 86.

164. Ibn Ḥazm, *Risālatān*, p. 101. Cf. al-Ghazālī, *Kitāb Miḥakk al-naẓar fī al-manṭiq* (Cairo: al-Maṭbaʿa al-Adabiyya, n.d.), p. 30 (*faḥwā al-khiṭāb* is not properly linguistic but has its place).

165. Ibn Ḥazm, *Risālatān*, p. 101.

166. *Iḥkām*, 5:131.

167. *Iḥkām*, 8:3.

168. Sarakhsī, 2:234.

directed at undermining the claim of a consensus of the Companions in favor of analogy. Apart from the validity of consensus altogether and this particular consensus, a tacit one, the practice of the Companions lent itself to other explanations. What the analogists regarded as instances of analogy were only cases of legal speculation, or nonbinding arbitration, of a least common view (*aqallu mā qīla*), or the application of a rule of reason or a revealed text.[169] In the second place, there are the arguments against analogy founded on reason. Analogy is not legitimate because it is fallible, because its results are contradictory, because there is no way to bridge the gap from case to reason, because the nature of the revealed law is such as to exclude analogy, because its imposition is repugnant to obligations that bind God.[170]

One feature of the analogist response we have yet to consider. This is the claim that the opponents of analogy covertly introduce it into their own systems. This notion of a false consciousness is one that appears at several points in the literature of Islamic law and theology as al-Jaṣṣās reminds us. The anti-analogists, he writes, "do not escape from using analogy and legal reasoning on new cases but unwittingly. Or they do know but brazenly call it by another name for the sake of being controversial.... Similarly we find those who reject rational arguments using them of necessity but without knowing or knowing but denying it. Similarly he who rejects the unit-tradition only rejects it verbally. So if you examine their doctrines you will find him using unit-traditions and adopting them without knowing."[171]

From this assertion it was only a short step to claiming the possibility of a consensus based on analogy.[172] This is a stronger claim and is forcefully rebutted by the Imāmī al-Sharīf al-Murtaḍā, on the grounds that while conceivable in the case of one or two, a methodological error of this magnitude was not compatible with the hairsplitting exactitude of the anti-analogists.[173] To embrace the anti-analogists in a consensus in this fashion was theologically questionable. Since the anti-analogists still regarded the use of analogy, even their own, as illegitimate, this meant that the consensus from their point of view was erroneous.[174] The dominant position simply refused to regard the anti-analogists in the constitution of consensus. Their systematic error in methodology was of no legal consequence. It was merely further evidence of their incompetence.[175]

169. *Dharīʿa*, 2:707; *Mustaṣfā*, p. 405.
170. *Dharīʿa*, 2:673–74.
171. Jaṣṣāṣ, 7:138–39.
172. *Iḥkām*, 7:138–39.
173. *Dharīʿa*, 2:647; *Muʿtamad*, 2:527; *Lumaʿ*, p. 60.
174. *Dharīʿa* 2:647.
175. See above, ch. 3, n. 38.

3. *The Explicit Cause*

The legal theorists are fond of a prototype with reference to which they elaborate their various doctrines. In the case of *ḥadīth* transmission (*riwāya*), the fudamental analogy is with testimony (*shahāda*).[176] Consensus, on the other hand, is worked out with an eye to the legislative prerogatives of the Prophet. These set the boundaries for any defensible doctrine of consensus.[177] In their discussion of analogy, the test case is one closer to home. The touchstone for any theory of analogy is provided by those reasons for the law that are explicitly identified by the Lawgiver (*al-ʿilla al-manṣūṣa*). The controversial doctrines are always examined in the light of how well they fare when applied to the "explicit cause." Consequently, our treatment of some of these controversies will expand on the preliminary discussion of the explicit cause offered here. Apart from this function of setting boundaries, a formal one, the "explicit cause" appears at the core of the Ḥanafī doctrine of effectiveness (*taʾthīr*). For effectiveness, what is of concern are the particular causes that are in fact explicit rather than the possibility of an explicit cause.

The question of how an explicit cause is recognized is a hermeneutical one, and was elaborately treated as such, particularly in *Shifāʾ al-ghalīl* of al-Ghazālī.[178] Assuming that an explicit cause is identified, the problem that arises is whether the communication of the cause is enough to license the application of the rule of the case to every instance of the cause, or is a separate rule establishing the legitimacy of analogy required? This question is examined with reference to both revelation and everyday discourse. The anti-analogists, of course, recognized no such rule. For them, the question was whether an explicit cause was to operate on its own or not at all. Most of them did regard the explicit cause as generalizing the original rule. Paradoxically, the pro-analogists were much more divided. Many required a special rule for analogy. Without this master rule, an explicit cause would not license any extended application of the original rule. It is this paradox that we now want to examine. To grasp the issues raised by this problem is to possess a valuable key to the entire theory of analogy.

The controversy surrounding the explicit cause is of the same type as that surrounding the *argumentum a fortiori*. There, it will be recalled, three positions can be distinguished: the total rejection of the argument, its acceptance as a linguistic inference, and its acceptance as a form of analogy.[179] The same choices are found here. Among the opponents of analogy, the majority appear to have regarded an explicit cause as sufficient for generalizing the original rule of law. For some of them, the rule of law together with

176. E.g., *Muʿtamad*, 2:624.

177. See above, ch. 3, n. 228. But this is not true of the Shiʿi doctrine of consensus since it rests on the principle of the imamate, which is logically prior to revelation (*Dharīʿa*, 2:626–27).

178. *Shifāʾ*, pp. 23–109.

179. See above, ch. 2, sec. VII.

its explicit cause was linguistically equivalent to a general norm. This was the position of al-Naẓẓām.[180] Others abandoned their general rejection of analogy where the cause was explicit. This is reported to have been the doctrine of al-Qāsānī, al-Nahrawānī, and al-Maghribī.[181] To them, one may add the *ḥadīth* scholar Ibn Ḥibbān.[182] Other anti-analogists consistently maintained their position even in the face of the explicit cause. For them, only a master rule for analogy could justify generalizing the rule of law, and no such master rule existed. This was the position of the two Jaʿfars, Jaʿfar ibn Mubashshir and Jaʿfar ibn Ḥarb.[183] Among the Imāmīs, al-Sharīf al-Murtaḍā held this view against the majority of his colleagues.[184] As might be expected, Ibn Ḥazm also rejects generalizing on the basis of an explicit cause. According to him, this is the uniform doctrine of the Ẓāhirīs from Dāwūd on.[185] The doctrine in favor of generalization is "the view of some people of no account among us like al-Qāsānī and his ilk."[186] But it appears from a passage of Dāwūd's *Uṣūl* quoted by al-Subkī that Dāwūd, contrary to what Ibn Ḥazm claims, held the same view as al-Naẓẓām: generalizing is a legitimate linguistic procedure where the cause is explicit.[187]

The analogists are also divided on the topic of the explicit cause. The majority of Muslim jurists regarded generalization as legitimate without a master rule for analogy. But for them, generalization was analogical not linguistic.[188] Abū Hāshim al-Jubbāʾī stood apart in regarding it as lingusitic.[189] A significant number of jurists, however, refused to recognize the legitimacy of generalization without a rule for analogy. Among these are Qāḍī ʿAbd al-Jabbār,[190] Abū 'l-Ḥusayn al-Baṣrī,[191] Abū Ḥāmid al-Isfarāyīnī,[192] al-Ṣayrafī,[193] al-Ghazālī,[194] and Ibn Qudāma.[195] For Abū ʿAbd Allāh al-Baṣrī, such a rule was not required where the original norm was a prohibition.[196]

---

180. *Jawāmiʿ*, f. 69a; *Mustaṣfā*, p. 422; *Muʿtamad*, 2:713.
181. *Jawāmiʿ*, f. 69a; *Mustaṣfā*, p. 419.
182. Ibn Ḥibbān, *Ṣaḥīḥ*, p. 72.
183. *Jawāmiʿ*, f. 69a; *Muʿtamad*, 2:753.
184. *Dharīʿa*, 2:684; al-Muḥaqqiq al-Ḥillī, *Maʿārij al-uṣūl*, p. 123; al-ʿAllāma al-Ḥillī, *Mabādiʾ al-wuṣūl ilā ʿilm al-uṣūl*, p. 218.
185. *Iḥkām*, 8:76–77.
186. *Iḥkām*, 8:77.
187. Tāj al-Dīn al-Subkī, *Ṭabaqāt*, 2:290.
188. *Muʿtamad*, 2:753; Ibn ʿAqīl, p. 191.
189. *Mughnī*, 17:310.
190. *Mughnī*, 17:310.
191. Ibn ʿAqīl, p. 191.
192. *Musawwada*, p. 390.
193. *Mustaṣfā*, p. 419.
194. *Mustaṣfā*, p. 422.
195. *Rawḍa*, p. 154.
196. *Musawwada*, p. 391.

This complex state of affairs cannot be reduced to a single pattern. Epistemological, ethical, and polemical considerations exercised varying degrees of influence. The position of Abū ʿAbd Allāh al-Baṣrī is particularly significant for our purposes, and the issues it raises will be examined below. At this point, however, the doctrine of the anti-analogists is what concerns us.

On the one side stand those anti-analogists who reject entirely the notion of causation in the law.[197] "Abū Sulaymān (Dāwūd al-Ẓāhirī) and all his fellows," observes Ibn Ḥazm, "say that God produces absolutely nothing, whether a law or anything else, for a cause." [198] On this account, the nature of God's activity in general and His legal activity in particular excludes the possibility of distinguishing between a rule and its cause. The only possibility outside of ignoring the explicit cause is to argue that a general norm can be conveyed in a linguistic form that appears to be making a causal statement. This, as noted, is al-Naẓẓām's doctrine and that of Dāwūd. There were analogists who also regarded the application of the explicit cause as a linguistic procedure. One of them was Abū Hāshim al-Jubbāʾī,[199] another the Shāfiʿī Ibn Fūrak.[200] To recognize it as such was at the same time to claim special virtues for this general norm, significantly the power to abrogate.[201] Here, as with the arguments *a fortiori* and *a contrario*, the analogists and anti-analogists meet. But the question for the anti-analogist is whether or not the inference is legitimate at all, the choice being outright rejection or acceptance as a linguistic phenomenon. The analogists are divided over the classification of the procedure. For them to term it linguistic is to refuse to countenance its rejection by the anti-analogists. By recognizing the generalization as linguistic, al-Naẓẓām escapes the attack of Ibn Fūrak but he falls into the hands of al-Ghazālī. For in denying that the extension of an explicit cause without a master rule for analogy is legitimate, al-Ghazālī is in a position to attack al-Naẓẓām from his other flank. "If al-Naẓẓām thinks that he rejects analogy, he has actually gone beyond us (*zāda ʿalaynā*) since he practices analogy where we do not."[202]

While some of the anti-analogists are theologically set against the notion of legal causality, others take the position that the law is founded on causal principles, on the well-being of mankind. But it does not follow that the cause of a particular law can be known. It is possible that the cause that appears to be explicit is not the complete cause. Even apart from this possibility, for some the operation of legal causes is not such as to permit the extension of a cause that is known, an explicit cause. The anti-analogist al-

197. For Abū Isḥāq al-Shīrāzī, these are the majority of the anti-analogists (*Lumaʿ*, p. 60).

198. *Iḥkām*, 8:77; Ibn Ḥazm, *Mulakhkhaṣ*, p. 5.

198. *Iḥkām*, 8:77; Ibn Ḥazm, *Mulakhkhaṣ*, p. 5.

199. *Mughnī*, 17:310.

200. *Irshād*, p. 211; Ibn Fūrak, *Muqaddima fī nukat min uṣūl al-fiqh*, in *Majmūʿ rasāʾil fī uṣūl al-fiqh*, ed. Jamāl al-Dīn al-Qāsimī (Beirut: al-Maṭbaʿa al-Ahliyya, 1324 H), p. 10.

201. *Musawwada*, p. 390.

202. *Mustaṣfā*, p. 422.

Sharīf al-Murtaḍā is at one with the analogist ʿAbd al-Jabbār in looking at the matter in this way. Both demand a master rule for analogy. But for al-Murtaḍā, no such rule can be found. On this view of the matter, everything depends on the existence of a master rule. We will come back to the question of what it means for the practice of analogy to be linked in this way with a rule, albeit one of a higher order.

Finally, we find those anti-analogists for whom the issue of analogy is one of epistemology alone. This is true of al-Qāsānī and al-Nahrawānī. For them, the law has causes and, provided that these causes are known, they can be applied to new cases. One way to know the cause is for it to be explicitly named. This doctrine represents a considerable weakening of the anti-analogist position maintained by Ibn Ḥazm. In fact, it is very close to the view of so radical an analogist as al-Aṣamm. The difference is that the sphere of what is certain and with it the scope of analogy is greater for al-Aṣamm. What distinguishes the two positions are their divergent views as to what is certain and what is practicable. Their epistemological demands and the theology behind these demands are the same.

In what follows, we shall be concerned with the counterpart of the explicit cause, the "educed cause" (*al-ʿilla al-mustanbaṭa*), which is equivalent to the "cause found by legal reasoning" (*al-ʿilla al-mujtahad fīhā*).[203] The analogy that revolves about educed causes is only one type of analogy. But because the causal analogy is the most highly regarded analogy and the one to which the Ḥanafīs are most attached, it will receive most of our attention. Two aspects of the cause will be of particular concern, its epistemology and its ontology. We will want to know what criteria the jurist considered in striving to identify that cause that was most probable. We will also want to know how the jurist conceived of the nature of the causes he was seeking. These two matters, the epistemology and the ontology of the cause, are closely linked. Tests that for some jurists disqualified a putative cause are entirely immaterial on another view of the cause. It should be noted that the technical details of analogical doctrine will be almost completely absent from our treatment. This in no way represents a denigration of these technicalities. Indeed, the opposite is the case. The technical apparatus of analogy and the sister discipline of legal controversy (*jadal*) deserve the most careful study. The literature of legal theory abounds in references to different styles of legal reasoning. Obviously, the clarification and documentation from contemporary legal texts of these methods is indispensable if progress is to be made in the study of Islamic legal history.

203. *Musawwada*, p. 386.

III. Noncausal Analogy

The leading species of analogy in classical Islam is that known as causal analogy (*qiyās al-ʿilla, qiyās al-maʿnā*). For the Ḥanafī theorists, there is really no other kind. Among others, particularly the Shāfiʿīs, more attention is given to competing varieties of analogy, and we sometimes find elaborate classifications reminiscent of the highly developed hermeneutical apparatus. Here we can only touch lightly upon some points of interest. A broad classification distinguishes positive from negative analogy, *qiyās al-ṭard* from *qiyās al-ʿaks*.[204] *Qiyās al-ṭard* moves forward from the point of resemblance to the assertion of the common qualification (*modus ponendo ponens*).[205] *Qiyas al-ʿaks* establishes that a proposed analogy does not hold. If the two cases were linked by a relevant resemblance, then a particular state of affairs would have to be the case. But it is not (*modus tollendo tollens*).[206]

More important, from our point of view, is the classification that recognizes types of analogy coordinate with the causal kind. A simple classification of this sort is that used by Abū Isḥāq al-Shīrāzī. For him, there are three kinds of analogy, *qiyās al-ʿilla*, *qiyās al-dalāla*, and *qiyās al-shabah*.[207] *Qiyās al-dalāla* ("evidential analogy") as used by Abū Isḥāq and his followers denotes a particularly legal kind of analogy.[208] It typically moves from one legal qualification of the case in question (*al-farʿ*) to another. For example, it is argued that a minor (*al-ṣabī*) owes *zakāt* because "the tithe (*al-ʿushr*) is owed on his agricultural produce so that *zakāt* is owed on his property as in the case of one of legal age (*al-bāligh*)."[209] This analogy does not look to the actual cause but merely indicates its existence (*yadullu ʿalā ʿillat al-sharʿ*). It presupposes the existence of functioning causes but makes no direct reference to them.

Qiyās al-shabah, or the "analogy of resemblance," is a particularly controversial topic especially among the Shāfiʿīs. The accounts of this procedure are far from uniform. And there is clearly something in ʿAbd al-Jabbār's observation that the controversy is partly terminological "in that what others call a resemblance we call a cause."[210] But at the core of the issue there are issues of substance. The problem for us is to identify those issues,

---

204. *Muʿtamad*, 2:103.

205. *Ṭard* as a type of analogy is not to be confused with *ṭard* as a test of causes treated below.

206. Also, *istidlāl min ṭarīq al-ʿaks* (Ibn ʿAqīl, p. 186). Émile Tyan mistakenly identifies *qiyās al-ʿaks* with the *argumentum a contrario* ("Méthodologie et sources de droit en Islam," *Studia Islamica* 10 [1959]: 82).

207. *Lumaʿ*, p. 58.

208. Bājī, p. 158. For the justification of this kind of analogy in terms of the sign model of the cause, see *Musawwada*, p. 411 (al-Kalwadhānī).

209. *Lumaʿ*, p. 59.

210. *Mughnī*, 17:330. See Josef van Ess, *Die Erkenntnislehre des ʿAḍudaddīn al-Īcī*, p. 387.

keeping in mind the statement of Ibn al-Anbārī that, "I know of no question of legal theory more obscure than this."[211]

The most detailed treatment of *qiyās al-shabah* appears to be that of al-Māwardī. He distinguishes two subspecies, *qiyās al-taḥqīq*, in which the relevant resemblance (*shabah*) is of a legal nature, and *qiyās al-taqrīb*, which regards nonlegal qualities. Within each of these he further distinguishes three types.[212] The example given to illustrate the first of these six varieties of the analogy of resemblance is one that appears throughout the literature and may safely serve as the basis of our discussion. The question is, Does a slave have property rights? If we regard his resemblance to a freeman, then he would have such rights. But if his resemblance to a beast is dominant, then he does not possess such rights. The problem is how to assess the force of these resemblances. On the one hand, the slave resembles the freeman in being subject to the religious law as well as to the fixed penalties (*ḥudūd*) and in possessing the right to marry and the power to divorce. But he resembles the beast in that he himself is the object of ownership and when converted is indemnifiable at market value (*al-qīma*).[213] For al-Māwardī, this example is an illustration of a situation in which the case to be decided cannot consistently be treated like one of the primary cases (*aṣlān*). In this instance, since we know that a slave cannot take by inheritance, we are justified in upholding the analogy that likens him to a beast.[214]

Al-Māwardī presents two accounts of the difference between causal analogy and that based on resemblance. According to some, the difference lay precisely in the distinction between the cause or reason (*maʿnā*) that was the basis of the causal analogy and the mere resemblance that grounded the other kind of analogy. For others, an analogy based on resemblance was distinguished by the fact that there were competing primary cases. In causal analogy, there was only one primary case.[215] This is true of the example we have considered, and it is true of the examples presented by al-Shīrāzī. In fact, the analogy based on resemblance is sometimes called *qiyās ghalabat al-ashbāh* ("analogy based on the dominant resemblance").[216] Which of the competing cases was dominant was variously determined: by the simple enumeration of the positive analogy, by the consideration of the negative analogy as in the example above, or by the introduction of specific criteria of relevance.[217]

To get a more precise notion of the relation between causal analogy and the analogy of resemblance, we should consider the different attitudes toward the two. On the

211. *Irshād*, p. 219.
212. Māwardī, 1:601.
213. Ibn ʿAqīl, p. 193 (reading *al-abḍāʿ wa-ṣiḥḥat ṭalāqihi* and *bi'l-qīma bi'l-ghaṣb*).
214. Māwardī, 1:601–2.
215. Māwardī, 1:586.
216. *Muʿtamad*, 2:632.
217. Māwardī, 1:600–601, 608.

one hand, we find the exclusive recognition of one or the other form. Al-Samarqandī is among those who recognize only a causal analogy. Without the requirement of a properly identified cause, analogy would become a mere plaything. And he echoes Ibn Ḥazm in noting "that there are no two things which do not bear some resemblance to each other."[218] In the case of competing analogies, the enumeration of the positive analogy as practiced by some Ḥanafīs is valid only if each positive analogy meets the criteria for a cause. [219] This appears to have been the position of the Shāfiʿīs Ibn Surayj, Abū Isḥāq al-Marwazī, and Abū 'l-Ṭayyib al-Ṭabarī.[220] On the other side, Ibn Fūrak writes of those "who limited themselves to the resemblance and denied the doctrine of the cause."[221] It is here that ʿAbd al-Jabbār's observation, noted above, is most relevant and the issue comes closest to being a purely verbal one.

Between these two extremes there exist a variety of intermediate positions. One of these is that of Abū Isḥāq al-Shīrāzī. As we have seen, al-Shīrāzī operates with a threefold classification of analogy, but for him all three kinds are not equally valid. In addition to the causal analogy, he recognizes the legitimacy of the analogy of indication (*qiyās al-dalāla*). The analogy based on a mere resemblance he rejects. Once again it is the cause that is of central concern. "The most likely view in my estimation is that the analogy of resemblance is not valid (*lā yaṣiḥḥ*) because it is not the cause of the rule for God nor an indication (*dalāla*) of the cause."[222] The analogy of indication is legitimate only because we have reason to regard the legal institutions it relies upon as resting upon a common cause. This analysis, however, was contested, and it was argued that the analogy of indication did not merit independent status. Such, for example, is the view of Fakhr al-Dīn al-Rāzī.[223] It could always be classified either as a causal analogy or as one based on resemblance.[224] A similar disagreement as to its status existed among the Ḥanbalīs.[225]

For the Shāfiʿīs, there was the further consideration that al-Shāfiʿī had spoken of resemblance in his famous *Risāla*. For those who rejected any but the causal analogy, al-Shāfiʿī's position required explanation. According to them, the resemblances were called upon to favor one or another of the competing causal analogies.[226] For other Shāfiʿīs, the recognition of the analogy based on resemblance involved a defense of al-Shāfiʿī's argument for analogy. Al-Shāfiʿī had argued that analogy entered the legal system with such rules as that which called for the pilgrim who had killed an animal while in the

---

218. *Mīzān*, f. 159a.
219. *Mīzān*, f. 159b. This is *ṭariqāt al-shabahayn* (*Musawwada*, p. 376).
220. *Baḥr*, f. 273b; *Musawwada*, p. 375; *Mankhūl*, p. 378.
221. *Irshād*, p. 206; *Baḥr*, f. 284b.
222. *Lumaʿ*, p. 59.
223. *Baḥr*, f. 274b.
224. See *Baḥr*, f. 273b, for such a classification.
225. *Musawwada*, p. 411.
226. *Lumaʿ*, p. 59.

state of sacralization (*iḥrām*) to replace it with its likeness (*mithl*) from among the beasts (Qur'ān 5:95).[227] Some theorists sought to identify this procedure with *qiyās al-shabah* in its totality or in part.[228] In so doing, they were defending al-Shāfiʿī's line of argument for analogy. According to others, this inevitable element of discretion was not analogy at all, and even those who rejected analogy recognized this procedure.[229] For still another group of Shāfiʿīs, the way to save the doctrine of *qiyās al-shabah* lay in narrowly regulating its application. Only where the resemblance was of a legal nature was there a valid analogy.[230] Insisting on the legal character of the resemblance took them toward the analogy of indication and apparently mitigated the danger of arbitrariness in the unregulated procedure.

In this way, there was an unmistakable erosion of the doctrine of the analogy of resemblance. There were, however, those who did not shrink from the unenviable task of defending an autonomous and fully developed analogy of resemblance, among them al-Juwaynī and al-Ghazālī.[231] For al-Ghazālī in particular, the defense of the analogy of resemblance comes close to representing a defense of analogy in general, for, he writes, "most of the analogies of the jurists go back to it."[232] In the face of the great claims made for the causal analogy, claims that he recognizes, al-Ghazālī could not argue for the analogy of resemblance as a simple alternative possibility. His position was rather that the applicability of the causal analogy was severely limited. The function of the analogy of resemblance was to complement the causal analogy. It addresses those cases where there was a need (*ḍarūra*) to determine the scope of a rule of law by laying down some criterion for its application where none had been given by the Lawgiver.[233]

For al-Ghazālī and the considerable body of later literature written under his influence, the chief problem posed by the analogy of resemblance was the elucidation of its autonomy. More particularly, how was this form of analogy related, on the one hand, to that in which the policy of the law served to identify the causal factor and, on the other, to that in which the cause had merely to satisfy certain formal criteria (*ṭard*)?[234] The analogy of resemblance is indeed sometimes rather fancifully stated to derive its name from its dubious status between these two forms of analogy.[235] The theorists were particularly

227. *Risāla*, paras. 1394–1398
228. *Mustaṣfā*, p. 451; Māwardī, 1:605.
229. See above, nn. 10, 11.
230. *Lumaʿ*, p. 59.
231. *Burhān*, f. 244; *Mankhūl*, pp. 378–84.
232. *Mustaṣfā*, p. 444.
233. *Mustaṣfā*, p. 450.
234. *Mankhūl*, p. 379; *Mustaṣfā*, p. 444; Fakhr al-Dīn al-Rāzī, *Munāẓarāt Fakhr al-Dīn al-Rāzī fī bilād mā warā' al-nahr*, ed. and trans. Fathalla Kholeif in *A Study on Fakhr al-Dīn al-Rāzī and His Controversies in Central Asia* (Beirut: Dar El-Machreq, 1966), pp. 43–45 (Arabic), pp. 68–69 (English).
235. Asnawī, p.73.

concerned to distinguish between *qiyās al-shabah* and the merely formally valid cause identified by *ṭard*. If this were not possible, then resemblance was liable to the charge of arbitrariness commonly leveled against *ṭard*. It must be admitted that their attempts to do so were not entirely successful.[236] But a suggestive principle is offered by al-Juwaynī: "In my view the resemblances that support probability, though they do not accord with the qualification in question, nonetheless accord with the requirement that the original and derivative cases fall under the same rule, and this is the great secret in the matter."[237] The analogy of resemblance is thus a classificatory rather than an explanatory procedure, one of the second order in distinction to causal analogy. It is for this reason that it is applicable in those instances where no intelligible ground for the law exists (*mā lā yuʿqal maʿnāhu*), above all, that is, in the area of religious ritual (*al-ʿibādāt*).[238]

IV. The Epistemology of the Cause

1. Appropriateness

In seeking to characterize the various schools of Islamic law, modern scholarship has consistently regarded its attachment to analogy as a peculiarity of the Ḥanafī tradition, a proposition defended in these pages.[239] But without a more precise formulation, this characterization is apt to be misleading. In the first instance, it is probably impossible to point to any set of features of the classical Ḥanafī system that did not have its adherents in other schools. The study of Islamic law along school lines often has nothing to recommend it but convenience. Secondly and more importantly for our purposes, a close study of the doctrine of analogy presents difficulties for the common view that identifies Ḥanafism with analogism. Prominent among these apparent paradoxes is the severely restricted scope granted analogy by the Ḥanafīs in comparison with other schools. In several significant substantive and formal areas of the law, extension by analogy is precluded according to classical Ḥanafī doctrine.

In what follows we shall consider two aspects of the Central Asian doctrine of analogy, its epistemology and its ontology. By the epistemology of analogy, we refer to those methods by which a putative cause is validated. Here the central development is the doctrine of effectiveness (*taʾthīr*), which represents a major development in the history of Islamic law. Once the cause is identified, the question remains, What is its function both in the original case and in its derivative? The answer to this question constitutes the

236. *Irshād*, p. 219.

237. *Burhān*, f. 249.

238. *Mankhūl*, pp. 380, 383; *Mustaṣfā*, p. 452.

239. For example, Asaf A. A. Fyzee, *Outlines of Muhammadan Law* (Delhi: Oxford University Press, 1974), pp. 33–34.

ontological aspect of the doctrine of analogy. Whereas the doctrine of effectiveness was common to Central Asian Ḥanafism, the ontological side of analogy was less conclusively settled. Indeed, not only were the problems of ontology controverted throughout the history of Islamic law in general, but the implications to be drawn from the different answers were not always agreed upon. Nonetheless, several difficult problems in the theory of analogy and some of the paradoxes of Ḥanafī doctrine alluded to become clearer in the light of the ontology of the cause.

The methods of identifying the cause of a particular law with a view to its extension can be variously classified. We have already considered a cause that is textually explicit. There are also those causes that have been identified by consensus. These together form a class of particular significance for the Ḥanafī jurist. A third set consists of those causes that have been educed. It is the process of eduction (*istinbāṭ*) that concerns us.

The methods we are about to consider are methods of validation, not discovery. They do not give directions for educing a cause, but rather for testing a cause already educed. Of the actual eduction, Abū 'l-Yusr al-Bazdawī says merely that "it entails enormous effort which only the master jurists know."[240] The methods (*masālik*) for validating an educed cause are applicable by the solitary jurist as well as by the disputant in public debate. They are of two sorts, material and formal. The most widely accepted methods are material, that is, they require some relation of substance between the cause and the rule of law from which it is drawn (*aṣl*). The leading formal methods require only that the cause (*ʿilla*) and the deontic qualification (*ḥukm*) appear together without exception. It is important to point out that it was the exclusive reliance on formal methods that was by and large rejected. The use of material methods coupled with formal tests was, on the other hand, generally accepted.

A mainstay of the rejection of analogy was the claim that there was no authentic method for its practice. "What is absolutely known to be false is that analogy be permitted in religion without the Messenger of God having taught to what we apply analogy and upon what we base it nor where we analogize or how."[241] There was no way to identify the causes that analogy required.[242] In the face of this challenge, we may note two very different responses. On the one hand, there were those like al-Juwaynī and al-Ghazālī who admitted the point of this objection. There were no authoritative methods laid down for analogy. There was, however, a master rule validating analogy. Working within the scope of this rule, the jurist had at his disposal a variety of methods. What mattered was that he honestly analogize on the basis of his own probable opinion. Thus al-Ghazālī writes, "In the consensus of the Companions to practice legal reasoning (*ijtihād*) we note only their consideration of the most probable opinion. Otherwise, they did not fix the types

240. *Ḥujaj*, f. 59b.

241. *Iḥkām*, 8:118.

242. *Dharīʿa*, 2:674.

of probable opinion or distinguish one kind from another."[243] On this view, the practice of the Companions, while it did not fix the method or methods for analogy, did at least indicate that the field was open. This is the claim put forth by al-Juwaynī against the severely restricted analogy practiced by those like al-Qāsānī.[244] Opposed to this methodological autonomy is the view that definite methods were already fixed at the beginning of Islamic history. This, for example, is the position of al-Bāqillānī, for whom several valid methods are available. The Central Asian Ḥanafīs go even further, for they tend toward a methodological monism. Only the method of effectiveness (*taʾthīr*) is fully legitimate. Yet despite the very different premises underlying these opposed points of view, the most widely accepted method, that of *munāsaba* ("appropriateness") forms the core also of the Ḥanafī method of effectiveness.

The method of appropriateness is described in this way by Ibn Qudāma: "When there is a benefit in establishing a rule as a consequence of a character (*waṣf*), the character is 'appropriate,' such as need and the institution of sale, or gratitude and kindness conferred, and this indicates that it is to be taken as the cause (*al-taʿlīl bihi*), since we know that the Lawgiver does not establish a rule except for some benefit. So when we see a rule leading to a benefit in a case in which we are of the opinion that He intended to confer that benefit in establishing the rule, the character which encompasses the benefit is to be taken as the cause."[245] What this amounts to is clear enough. Given a rule of law, one determines the benefit that the rule serves. Then in the light of this, one isolates that aspect of the original situation the regulation of which is appropriate to the benefit. Thus, for example, there is a rule punishing the drinking of wine. The benefit of this rule is that rational behavior is protected. It is then apparent that of all the factors that can be identified in the factual situation of drinking wine, the relevant property is the power of wine to intoxicate. This factor is isolated as the appropriate one and serves as the cause. Other factual situations in which the cause is present merit similar regulation, that is, they are also punishable.[246] Although in keeping with their interest in the cause, the Muslim jurists refer to the appropriateness of the cause to the qualification, more properly what is appropriate is the regulation of the cause in the light of a particular purpose.[247]

Munāsaba, which we have translated "appropriateness," is literally the "ratio" between the cause and its regulation, and indeed this forms the basis for the rationality of analogy. Causal analogy depends on recognizing in the law "an intelligible reason" (*maʿnā maʿqūl*). In fact, the term "an intelligible reason" is very nearly a redundancy, for it is virtually equivalent to a "reason." An unintelligible reason is no reason at all. The

243. *Shifāʾ*, p. 144; *Mustaṣfā*, p. 438.
244. *Burhān*, f. 217.
245. *Rawḍa*, p. 158.
246. *Irshād*, p. 216.
247. *Shifāʾ*, p. 47; Asnawī, 3:53; Badakhshī, 3:50.

doctrine of "intelligible reasons" as held by the proponents of appropriateness is crucial to understanding Islamic law. For it serves to demarcate areas of the law that are the domain of reason (*taᶜaqqul*) from those of pure obedience (*taᶜabbud*). "We practice analogy," al-Ghazālī emphasizes, "only in contracts and torts and what we know by many indications to be built on intelligible grounds and worldly benefits."[248] This principle is negatively put by Ibn Qudāma: "In that the reason of which is not intelligible, like the times of prayer or the number of ritual movements (*rakaᶜāt*), we are not acquainted with the necessitating reason nor is its extension known."[249] A study of the law will in fact reveal that the textual base of the *ᶜibādāt*, the ritual law, is far more extensive than that of the "civil law," those areas regulated in modern legal systems. The exclusion of analogy from the ritual law is, however, hardly complete. We have already observed that the analogy based on resemblance (*qiyās al-shabah*) is so constituted to lend itself to use in this area. Nonetheless, the study of Islamic law requires a constant sensitivity to this fundamental line of demarcation.

The development of the doctrine of appropriateness is obscure. That is not to say that it does not faithfully reflect the practice of analogy throughout much of Islamic legal history, that it is not "the pillar of analogy, the locus of its obscurity and clarity."[250] What is meant is that the theoretical treatment of analogy along these lines does not become at all widespread until a fairly late period in the history of *uṣūl al-fiqh*, and was apparently only widely adopted under the influence of al-Ghazālī.

The identification of the cause by the method of appropriateness depends upon grasping the relation between the rule of law and the end it serves. However problematic the relation between rule and policy is for modern legal systems, it is much more so within the context of medieval Islam. For a significant part of Ashᶜarī theology, ultimately the dominant theological tradition, was its ethical doctrine, and that doctrine appears to deny the very ethical cognition necessary for this method of analogy. For the Ashᶜarī theologian, it is only revelation that creates objective values. What is good is what God commands, and it is good simply by virtue of being commanded by God. Outside of revelation, there is no good in this superindividual sense. Each man regards as good that which conforms to his self-interest. The question thus arises, How is it possible upon this version of ethical facts to recognize the purpose of a given rule of law so as to identify, in the light of this purpose, the legal cause, that element that is appropriately regulated to serve this purpose? There exists an apparent incompatibility between Ashᶜarī ethics and that method of analogy that embodies legal rationality. It is our contention that not only were the Ashᶜarī *uṣūlīs* conscious of this problem, but that significant developments in their theory of appropriateness were meant to resolve it.

248. *Mustaṣfā*, p. 418.
249. *Rawḍa*, p. 168 (reading *yūqaf* in line 7).
250. *Irshād*, p. 214.

Even had they wished to remain oblivious to the difficulty posed to their theology by the practice of analogy, the medieval Ashʿarīs would not have been able to do so. Their opponents were only too ready to bring the inconsistency to their notice. The Ashʿarī ethical doctrine was false, and their own practice of analogy pointed to its falsity. "Our opponents," writes al-Shahrastānī, "say that should we remove good and bad from human actions and attribute them to the teachings of revelation, the rational reasons that we extract from those revealed laws would be without foundation. And it would not be possible to compare by analogy one act to another or one utterance to another. Nor would it be possible to say 'why' or 'because,' since there would be no causation for things or ethical attributes for actions to which to attach a disputed qualification or to which to compare by analogy a matter in contention. This amounts to the complete abolition of the revealed law instead of its establishment and the rejection of the religious law instead of its acceptance."[251] The identification of rational reasons depends upon some source of ethical knowledge independent of revelation, and this is precisely what the Ashʿarīs deny.

Here and there in the literature, we find further traces of the same criticism: the Ashʿarīs may defend their outrageous theological principles, but their practice of analogy shows that their ethical experience is the same as ours.[252] It is the theological point that has to be made. And even those who reject analogy like the Imāmī Muḥammad Bāqir al-Bihbihānī (d. 1205/1790) feel called upon to point out the inconsistency of the Ashʿarīs.[253] In the case of Ibn Taymiyya,[254] and even more in that of his disciple Ibn Qayyim al-Jawziyya,[255] what matters is the Ashʿarī error, the extent to which their theology is detached from their legal theory. For the Zaydī Ibn al-Wazīr, on the other hand, the universal Ashʿarī practice of analogy indicates that their theology has not been understood. Unlike the Muʿtazila, they deny that God was obliged to send Messengers, but they do not deny that God's actions have purposes. One need only consider, he notes, the immense popularity of a work on *uṣūl* like that of Ibn al-Ḥājib with its some seventy commentar-

---

251. Muḥammad ibn ʿAbd al-Karīm al-Shahrastānī, *Kitāb Nihāyat al-iqdām fī ʿilm al-kalām*, ed. Alfred Guillaume (Oxford: Oxford University Press, 1934), p. 374 (Arabic), p. 120 (English). Whereas al-Shahrastānī speaks of the "abolition of the law," another source, reworking this passage, speaks more specifically of the "abolition of analogy, which you do not hold" (Yūsuf ibn Muḥammad al-Miklātī, *Kitāb Lubāb al-ʿuqūl fī al-radd ʿalā al-falāsifa fī ʿilm al-uṣūl*, ed. Fawqiyya Ḥusayn Maḥmūd [Cairo: Dār al-Anṣār, 1977], p. 309).

252. ʿAbd Allāh ibn Majd al-Dīn al-Ḥusaynī, *Munyat al-labīb*, ed. Farmān ʿAlī Jaʿfar (Lucknow, 1315 H), p. 313.

253. Muḥammad Bāqir al-Bihbihānī, *al-Fawāʾid al-jadīda*, p. 11 (pagination supplied).

254. Ibn Taymiyya, *Qāʿida fī al-muʿjizāt waʾl-karāmāt*, in *al-Rasāʾil waʾl-masāʾil*, ed. Muḥammad Rashīd Riḍā, 5:2–36 (Cairo, 1349 H. Reprint. Lajnat al-Turāth al-ʿArabī, n.d.), 5:30.

255. Ibn Qayyim al-Jawziyya, *Miftāḥ dār al-saʿāda wa-manshūr wilāyat al-ʿilm waʾl-irāda*. 2 vols. in 1 (Beirut: Dār al-Kutub al-ʿIlmiyya, n.d.), 2:42.

ies, most of them the work of Ashʿarīs. Throughout the writings of al-Rāzī and al-Ghazālī, there is all the evidence one needs to establish that the Ashʿarīs make constant reference to God's purposes.[256]

How did the Ashʿarī theologians respond to this criticism? What they will have to argue, let it be remembered, is that the recognition of the purposes of the law, which the method of appropriateness requires, is not incompatible with their theology. They will have to show that Ibn Taymiyya is wrong when he says that "whoever denies that an action has inherent qualifications (and maintains) that it is good only because a command attaches to it and that (ethical) qualifications exist only in virtue of a command adhering to the act denies the benefit and evils the Law deals with, denies good and bad and appropriateness in the law between rules and causes. He specifically denies understanding (*fiqh*) in religion, which is the knowledge of the wisdom of the law and its excellences."[257]

A brief but most significant reply is that given by the North African Ashʿarī al-Miklātī (d. 626/1237). For al-Miklātī, we recognize the cause of a rule of law in two ways: by its being textually identified or by its appropriateness. If it is textually identified, there is no problem. "And if the cause is established by way of appropriateness there also does not follow from our abolishing (objective) good and evil its abolition, because we mean by appropriateness what is consonant with our welfare so that if the qualification is referred to this it fits. And by benefit we mean the protection of a policy of the law, the policies of the law for men being five: to guard their religion, their physical existence, their reason, their lineage, and their property."[258]

Al-Miklātī's reply is based upon the doctrine of the five (and in a later version, six) universal values (*kulliyyāt*), that all revealed religions safeguard.[259] The origin of this influential doctrine is obscure, as is indeed the development of an articulated doctrine of appropriateness. Both appear to stem from the Khurasanian branch of the Shāfiʿī school. One may speculatively link both with Abū Bakr al-Qaffāl al-Shāshī (d. 365/976).[260] In any case, by the time of al-Ghazālī both doctrines were well known.

The doctrine of the five universal values is meant to answer the question, How do we know what are the purposes of the law? It is a simple answer: The law itself informs us that its purposes are these five. This knowledge is the key to the legitimacy of analogy.

---

256. Muḥammad ibn Ibrāhīm ibn al-Wazīr, *Īthār al-ḥaqq ʿalā al-khalq fī radd al-khilāfāt ilā al-madhhab al-ḥaqq fī uṣūl al-tawḥīd* (Cairo: Sharikat Ṭabʿ al-Kutub al-ʿArabiyya, 1318/1900), p. 200.

257. Ibn Taymiyya, *Qāʿida fī al-muʿjizāt*, 5:30.

258. Al-Miklātī, *Lubāb al-ʿuqūl*, p. 310 (reading *rafʿuhā* in line 9).

259. Ibrāhīm al-Bājūrī, *Tuḥfat al-murīd*, p. 198. The sixth value is good repute (*ʿirḍ*).

260. Al-Shāshī adhered to Muʿtazilī ethics and based his book, *On the Excellences of the Sharīʿa*, on this view, that is, in terms of the purposes of the Law (Ibn Qayyim al-Jawziyya, *Miftāh*, 2:46). He is further supposed to have defended the universality of the prohibition against wine (*Baḥr*, f. 286b). In tracing the doctrine to him, we are able to follow how later Shāfiʿīs were compelled to make theological adjustments; the attack on the universality of these principles was at least in part an attack on Muʿtazilī principles.

For merely to know that a particular law protects life would not warrant the conclusion that the protection of life is its purpose. But once the purposes of the law are exhaustively determined, it is possible to recognize the function of a rule and thus to discover its cause. Once the end is given, the discovery of the means is within human competence. This constitutes the strictest version of the appropriateness doctrine.

What we commonly find, however, is a much less restricted procedure. In this version the key word is *ʿāda*, "practice or custom."[261] "All the cases of appropriateness," writes al-Ghazālī, "upon examination do not resort to grounds which necessitate in themselves, but there is only a kind of appropriateness that calls for the legal qualiflcation according to consistent practice."[262]

More fully, al-Ghazālī addresses the distinction between an acceptable doctrine of appropriateness and one that is heterodox:

> Although we say that God may do to His subjects as He will and that the observance of their good is not incumbent upon Him, we do not deny that reason indicates what is advantageous and disadvantageous and warns against ruin and urges the attractions of what is of benefit. Nor do we deny that the Messengers were sent for the good of creation in religion and worldly matters as a mere bounty of God, not as a duty obligatory upon Him and we have only made this point lest we be associated with the teaching of the Muʿtazila and lest the nature of the student recoil from what we say for fear of being soiled with a rejected dogma, contempt for which is rooted in the souls of the *Ahl al-Sunna*.[263]

Rather than restrict the purposes of the law to a small set that can then serve to identify relevant causes, this doctrine identifies the purposes of the law with those generally pursued by men. The scope of the purposes of the law could thus be considerably expanded, and in place of the five universals there is already in al-Ghazālī a more elaborate scheme, in which the five universals represent merely the purposes most in need of consideration (*al-ḍarūriyyāt*).[264] Once it is determined by "induction" (*istiqrāʾ*) that the law has regard for human well-being, "we can be sure," writes Abū Isḥāq al-Shāṭibī (d. 790/1388), "that this holds true for all details of the law."[265]

Another doctrine, one which fell by the wayside, was that put forth by Imām al-Ḥaramayn and earlier by al-Bāqillānī.[266] According to them, the principle of appropriateness was validated by the practice of the Companions. The Companions' use of causes

---

261. Incorporated into the definition of *munāsib* by Fakhr al-Dīn al-Rāzī (Asnawī, 3:53).

262. *Shifāʾ*, pp. 205, 640.

263. *Shifāʾ*, pp. 162–63; Ibrāhīm ibn Mūsā al-Shāṭibī, *al-Iʿtiṣām*, ed. Muḥammad Rashīd Riḍā (Cairo: al-Maktaba al-Tijāriyya al-Kubrā, n.d.), 2:113.

264. *Shifāʾ*, p. 162.

265. Ibrāhīm ibn Mūsā al-Shāṭibī, *al-Muwāfaqāt fī uṣūl al-aḥkām*, 2:4.

266. *Burhān*, f. 221; *Mankhūl*, p. 341; *Baḥr*, f. 300a.

identified by the method of appropriateness obviated any need for a direct consideration of the nature of the law. The disadvantage of this position, however, was that it did not address the issue of restricting the number of purposes to manageable proportions, although it was quite compatible with the tabulation of purposes already available.

George Hourani has correctly observed that "in Islamic ethics there is an unacknowledged tension between two standards, the command of God and the interest of man. The latter is equivalent to the standard of 'social eudaemonism' and survives throughout Islamic history as a natural standard which could not be entirely suppressed by any weight of theology."[267] But he and others have been wrong in locating this tension at the margins of Islamic legal teaching in such doctrines of the law as *istiḥsān* and *istiṣlāḥ*. In fact, as we have seen, the fundamental issues at stake are already raised in connection with analogy. In the case of the Ashʿarīs, the demands of legal practice produced a considerable mitigation of their anti-objectivism. For they were led to acknowledge not merely that God's actions are purposeful, a proposition that the Qurʾān itself supports, but, much the more significant, to claim that these purposes could be recognized by the human mind. In identifying God's purposes with those of man, the Ashʿarīs admitted that there were common standards for rational human action. But they could do so only by retreating from their ethical relativism. Alongside of purely personal ends, larger common purposes were recognized. This view is already established by the time of al-Ghazālī. But whereas al-Ghazālī is still inclined to reduce acts of courage to cowardice and to explain apparently unselfish acts as intellectual errors,[268] the Mālikī al-Qarāfī (d. 684/1285) simply accepts the conformity of such acts to reason.[269]

Whatever difficulties the Ashʿarīs may have had in reconciling their theology and legal practice, the bulk of jurists seem to have proceeded without regard to the question. Al-Fakhr al-Rāzī attributes the view of the Muʿtazila that God's actions aim at safeguarding human interests (*riʿāyat maṣāliḥ al-ʿibād*) to "most of the modern jurists."[270] Moreover, in every legal school there had been prominent jurists who subscribed to an objective

267. George Hourani, *Ethical Value* (London: George Allen and Unwin, 1956), p. 205. For Hourani independent judgments of value enter the law through *istiḥsan* in particular ("Two Theories of Value in Medieval Islam," *Muslim World* 50 [1960]: 269–78).

268. *Mustaṣfā*, p. 75; al-Ghazālī, *al-Iqtiṣād fī al-iʿtiqād*, ed. Muḥammad Muṣṭafā Abū 'l-ʿIlāʾ (Cairo: Maktabat al-Jundī, 1972), pp. 147–48.

269. Qarāfī, pp. 88–89. The change in Ashʿarī ethics is already perceived by Ibn Taymiyya in the case of Fakhr al-Dīn al-Rāzī (*Minhāj al-sunna al-nabawiyya fī naqḍ kalām al-shīʿa wa'l-qadariyya* [Cairo: al-Maṭbaʿa al-Amīriyya, 1322 H. Repr. N.p., n.d.], 1:125).

270. Fakhr al-Dīn al-Rāzī, *Kitāb al-Arbaʿīn fī uṣūl al-dīn* (Hyderabad: Maṭbaʿat Majlis Dāʾirat al-Maʿārif al-ʿUthmāniyya, 1353 H), p. 299; Naṣīr al-Dīn al-Ṭūsī on al-Rāzī, *al-Muḥaṣṣal*, p. 149. In this connection, note the attribution of causality to the majority of the jurists in Muḥammad ibn Yūsuf al-Sanūsī, *ʿUmdat ahl al-tawfīq wa'l-tasdīd sharḥ ʿAqīdat ahl al-tawḥīd al-kubrā* (Cairo: Muṣṭafā al-Bābī al-Ḥalabī, 1353/1936), p. 184.

ethics along Muʿtalizī lines.[271] The legal work of these masters remained part of the legacy of their schools. Shāfiʿī jurists, in particular, as we have noted, often had occasion to denounce Ashʿarī doctrines as innovations. Here, too, we find the Shāfiʿī Saʿd ibn ʿAlī al-Zanjānī (d. 471/1078) launching a bitter attack on al-Ashʿarī's relativist ethics, for which, al-Zanjānī claimed, he had no predecessor.[272]

2. *Effectiveness*

Developing parallel to and in competition with the method of appropriateness is that based on "effectiveness" (*taʾthīr*). The method of effectiveness constitutes an implied critique of appropriateness precisely on the grounds that the latter is merely rational. "Because we are talking about legal causes," wrote ʿAlāʾ al-Dīn al-Samarqandī, "their validity must be sought in the revealed law and not in reason alone, and the revealed law consists of texts and inferences therefrom (*al-naṣṣ wa'l-istidlāl*)."[273] More than the mere appropriateness of regulating a particular case to serve human purposes is called for. The additional element required is that the putative cause be related to causes known to be valid. But we can only know a cause to be valid when it has been explicitly identified as such by the Lawgiver or by consensus. The effectiveness of a cause lies in its relation to these causes, the validity of which is certain.

Before this method of analogy is more closely examined, it is important that its thrust be clearly grasped. A sense of what its proponents were aiming at may be gathered from the response of al-Ghazālī, their great critic. For him, the goals of the method of effectiveness were misconceived, the result of a grave error in epistemology. It is perhaps not surprising, then, that al-Ghazālī should see fit to raise the issue not only in his works of legal theory but in his logical writings as well. The following passage is, in fact, from his major work on logic, *Miʿyār al-ʿilm*:

> There plunged into *fiqh* one of the proponents of *raʾy* who had gathered loose bits of the rational sciences but had not mastered them, and he set about impugning most kinds of analogy, limiting himself to the "effective." He makes claims appropriate to reason against all that is used in *fiqh*. But when he comes to defend his own school in detail he cannot sustain it according to the standard he adopts in principle.... The point of what we say is that the exactitude we spoke of in connection with the rational sciences ought to be abandoned in *fiqh* entirely. To confuse the path leading to the attainment of certainty with that

271. See the list in Ibn Taymiyya, *Minhāj al-sunna*, 1:125.

272. Ibn Qayyim al-Jawziyya, *Miftāḥ*, 2:42; Ibn Qayyim al-Jawziyya, *Madārij al-sālikīn*, ed. Muḥammad Rashīd Riḍā (Cairo: Maṭbaʿat al-Manār, 1331–34 H), 1:127.

273. *Mīzān*, f. 159a.

> leading to the attainment of opinion is the work of one who has picked up a bit of both (disciplines) but not mastered either.[274]

The method of effectiveness is a mistaken demand for certainty in the law.[275] Its proponents, and al-Ghazālī is referring specifically to Abū Zayd al-Dabūsī (d. 430/1039), set their aim too high. In any event, they were unable to satisfy their own standards, for to have met those standards would have meant a radical contraction of the law. We shall now turn to the doctrine of effectiveness as presented by its classical aherents, Abū Zayd al-Dabūsī and the Central Asian Ḥanafīs. We will then take up al-Ghazālī's critique in more detail, and finally we shall examine briefly the later development of the doctrine.

The doctrine of effectiveness seeks to establish the necessary relation between what is claimed to be a cause and the causes that are known, and the development of the doctrine is in large measure an attempt to make increasingly explicit the possible varieties of this relation. According to al-Ghazālī, Abū Zayd al-Dabūsī and his followers laid down the strictest possible requirement for this relation: they claimed, in fact, to be using only causes identical to those identified textually or by consensus. This restriction would mean that all causes are certain, and accordingly al-Ghazālī considers Abū Zayd's aim to have been to raise the status of analogy to that of the rational sciences.[276] From the examples adduced by Abū Zayd, al-Ghazālī seeks to show that this requirement is not met and that al-Dabūsī's actual standards for analogy are those accepted by most jurists. Much hinges on al-Ghazālī's assumption that "effectiveness" (*taʾthīr*) is being used by al-Dabūsī with reference to explicitly identified causes. The term "effectiveness," however, appears in a variety of usages in the literature of *uṣūl al-fiqh*, and al-Ghazālī himself admits that al-Dabūsī may have meant something else by the term.[277]

It is reasonably clear that al-Dabūsī did not set his aim quite as high as al-Ghazālī claims. On the other hand, there are features of al-Dabūsī's doctrine that do indicate his inclination to the strongest form of effectiveness.[278] Unfortunately, he nowhere gives a precise definition of effectiveness. The important thing to note, however, is that once only certain causes are acceptable, there is no need to determine that the particular rule of law has a cause, at least according to the dominant Ḥanafī teaching.[279] All that is left is the application of a known cause to new cases. And it is controversial whether this is properly to be termed analogy.[280] ʿAlāʾ al-Dīn al-Samarqandī's definition of effectiveness is consciously framed to avoid any such misapprehension:

---

274. Al-Ghazālī, *Miʿyār al-ʿilm*, p. 146.
275. Al-Ghazālī, *Miʿyār al-ʿilm*, p. 147.
276. *Shifāʾ*, p. 300.
277. *Shifāʾ*, p. 178; *Mustaṣfā*, p. 436.
278. For example, the omission of any reference to the *aṣl*, discussed below.
279. Nasafī, 2:124, margin.
280. Ibn Taymiyya, *Iqtiḍāʾ al-ṣirāṭ al-mustaqīm mukhālafat ahl al-jaḥīm*, ed. Muḥammad Ḥamīd al-Fiqī

> We mean by it that the genus of the original character is effective upon the genus of the original qualification even if there is some difference with respect to quantity or quality (*al-qadr wa'l-waṣf*), for were it the same in every way with respect to the establishment of a similar qualification, this character would be the cause textually, not by inference.[281]

An almost identical definition is cited from the works of al-Samarqandī's teacher, Abū 'l-Yusr al-Bazdawī.[282] It is reasonable to assume that these definitions represent a common Central Asian doctrine and that they make explicit what is implicit in the writings of Abū Zayd al-Dabūsī and al-Sarakhsī, who closely follows al-Dabūsī. Effectiveness did not mean that only causes the certainty of which was established were legitimate. This doctrine, held by some such as the Ḥanbalī Ibn Ḥāmid, was tantamount to a rejection of analogy.[283] What was required was that a candidate for recognition as a valid cause be of the same *type* as one already known to be a cause. In the generations following al-Samarqandī, the notion of a legal genus merely alluded to in the definition quoted above became the basis for a sophisticated doctrine of legal kinds.

If not the attainment of absolute certainty in analogy, what, then, was the purpose of the doctrine of effectiveness? The answer to this question is clear from the Ḥanafī sources. Effectiveness is contrasted with other modes of doing analogy, particularly appropriateness. It is only effectiveness that provides a publicly accepted standard by which to judge the validity of an analogy. Just as their opponents seized upon the Ḥanafī use of the word *istiḥsān*, so the Ḥanafīs were quick to focus their attack on the Shāfiʿī use of the term *ikhāla*. For al-Ghazālī and some of the later literature, *ikhāla* is synonymous with *munāsaba*, appropriateness.[284] This unusual term and indeed the procedure of appropriateness both appear to be of Khurasanian Shāfiʿī origin.[285] A particular character in the original case suggests to the jurist that it is the cause; the character, and by extension the cause, are spoken of as suggestive (*mukhīl*). The note of subjectivity carried by the term made it a ready target for the Ḥanafīs.[286]

(Cairo: Maṭbaʿat al-Sunna al-Muḥammadiyya, 1369/1950), p. 284. This doctrine had many Ḥanbalī adherents.

281. *Mīzān*, f. 155a.

282. Bukhārī, 3:353.

283. *Musawwada*, p. 408; Ibn Taymiyya, *Iqtiḍā'*, p. 284.

284. *Shifā'*, p. 144, also mentions the terms *mushʿir* and *mu'dhin*. *Irshād*, p. 214, further gives *maṣlaḥa*, *istidlāl*, *riʿāyat al-maqāṣid*.

285. *Musawwada*, pp. 408, 438.

286. It is thus explained as *mūqiʿan fī al-qalb khayāl al-ṣiḥḥa li'l-ʿilla* (Sarakhsī, 2:177); similarly, *Ḥujaj*, f. 58b; *Mīzān*, f. 159a. The fifth form of the verb is used actively for the perception of the suggestiveness (*Shifā'*, p. 148), the sixth impersonally: *takhāyala fī qalbihi* (Sarakhsī, 2:185). Probably under the pressure of the Ḥanafī attack, some Shāfiʿīs offered explanations of the term that tended to mitigate its subjectivity (*Mīzān*, f. 159a; Bukhārī, 3:354). Others preferred to avoid its use altogether (Dabūsī, f. 133a).

The Ḥanafī texts refer to several methods of analogy that were popular among the Shāfiʿīs and that they contrast with their own method of effectiveness. What characterizes all of these methods, according to the Ḥanafīs, is the absence of any public test such as that provided by the requirement of effectiveness. The Ḥanafīs divide their own practice into two stages. In the first stage, the putative cause must be found to conform to the causes transmitted from the Prophet and the early Muslims.[287] This test is that of "conformity" (*mulāʾama*). The demand voiced here is that the cause not be repugnant to the legal qualification. Al-Samarqandī writes of "the agreement between the cause and the qualification, such that it is not rationally impossible to attribute that qualification to it, but rather it is fitting."[288] What we have here is a looser, negatively formulated version of the doctrine of appropriateness without the apparatus of the purposes of the law. For most purposes we can identify the two, although the Ḥanafīs generally do not do so. Neither do they mean by suggestiveness what we have treated as appropriateness. Rather, they regard suggestiveness either as a personal response to the appropriateness of a possible cause or as a kind of inspiration without foundation.[289] According to them, suggestiveness marks the first and, for some Shāfiʿīs, final stage in establishing a legal cause. Action in accord with a suggestive cause is obligatory for these Shāfiʿīs.[290] Other Shāfiʿīs demand a further test, that the cause be referred to the established legal rules and only accepted if it does not lead to any conflict (*al-ʿarḍ ʿalā al-uṣūl*).[291] The latter Shāfiʿī practice corresponds to that of Abū Isḥāq al-Isfarāyīnī who, stressing this second stage, referred to his doctrine by the misleading names of "consistency and currency" (*al-iṭṭirād wa'l-jarayān*)—misleading because they suggest the merely formal criteria for validity that he himself vigorously rejected.[292]

The Ḥanafīs acknowledge the personal persuasiveness of a suggestive cause and recognize the validity of action in accord with it. What they deny is that suggestiveness is acceptable as a public criterion for action. Suggestiveness, being an internal matter (*amr bāṭin*), is not a binding source of law against other parties and thus not a legal source at all.[293] Similarly, even their own standard of conformity only warrants action but does not impose it. Only when the effectiveness of a cause is ascertained is it appropriate to speak of an obligation to act.[294]

287. Bukhārī, 3:352.

288. *Mīzān*, f. 152b.

289. Sarakhsī, 2:183, 185. But al-Dabūsī does report of Shāfiʿīs who define *mulāʾama* as the Ḥanafīs do and reject *ikhāla* (Dabūsī, f. 133a).

290. Bukhārī, 3:353.

291. Bazdawī, 3:354.

292. *Burhān*, f. 224.

293. Bazdawī, 3:357–58; Sarakhsī, 2:185–86.

294. Bazdawī, 3:352.

Furthermore, no check of the sources can establish the validity of a cause, since no one can claim to know all the laws that are possibly relevant, and only a negative assertion is justified.[295] "For this reason," writes Abū Zayd al-Dabūsī, "the probity (*ʿadāla*), that is, validity, of the character is established only by its effect in requiring the like of this qualification in another place by consensus so that the known effect is evidence of its like. There is thus an inference based on a known existent, not on a negative or only on something that is inaccessible and cannot be disputed."[296]

The success of the doctrine of effectiveness lay in two directions. In public disputation, its appeal was such that it came to dominate even in Shāfiʿī circles, as al-Ghazālī testifies: "As for those who hold that only an effective cause is acceptable and they are the people of Marv and the people of Samarqand in our day, they do not cut off debate except when effectiveness is established. And when someone mentions suggestiveness amongst them, they recoil in disgust because they saw in the book of Abū Zayd that suggestiveness is worthless in disputation."[297] In Iraq, too, effectiveness later established itself as the highest standard.[298] In addition to and, of course, in conjunction with this external success, effectiveness opened up new possibilities for analogy both in precision and in scope.

These triumphs were only possible because there existed a fairly stable agreement as to the categories, the "legal kinds" that the doctrine of effectiveness required. The species and genera of legal causes and qualifications were part of the conceptual patrimony of the Islamic jurist. The historical study of these legal kinds does not appear to have been undertaken or even conceived. Such a study would perhaps bring to light important changes over time. It is nonetheless clear that a significant part of the amazingly rapid development of Islamic law that Goldziher and others have stressed was the systematization already apparent in Mālik's *Muwaṭṭaʾ*.[299] The doctrine of effectiveness rests on the view that these legal kinds are parallel to natural kinds, that the relatedness of one cause or one qualification to another is of relevance in doing analogy. Because a character is established as a cause in one case, we regard a related character as a more likely cause than one that is unrelated. This reasoning constitutes the analogy to which Ibn Taymiyya refers when he speaks of the doctrine of effectiveness as the identification

295. Bukhārī, 3:356.

296. Dabūsī, f. 137a.

297. *Shifāʾ*, p. 379. See also *Shifāʾ*, pp. 322–23.

298. Ibn Taymiyya, *Iqāmat al-dalīl*, 3:161.

299. See Ignaz Goldziher, "The Principles of Law in Islam," in *The Historians' History of the World*, ed. H. S. Williams, 25 vols. (New York, 1908), 8:294–304. See also W. Heffening, "Zum Aufbau der islamischen Rechtswerke," in *Studien zur Geschichte und Kultur des nahen und fernen Ostens*, ed. W. Heffening and W. Kirfel (Leiden: Brill, 1935), pp. 101–18.

of a cause by analogy.[300] There are thus two analogies: one establishing the cause and the other extending it.[301]

Effectiveness was already recognized as the soundest method of analogy by al-Karkhī. Furthermore, in the case of competing analogies, he gave preponderance (*tarjīḥ*) to the cause that was taken from the more closely related case. Indeed, the tendency to give weight to such familial resemblances must have been gaining ground, for in reporting al-Karkhī's doctrine, his student al-Jaṣṣāṣ saw fit to insist upon the legitimacy of analogies where this relatedness was only a distant one.[302]

While al-Bazdawī and al-Samarqandī were content to speak of the effectiveness of the genus of the cause upon the genus of the qualification, later scholars undertook a more exhaustive examination of the possible combinations of cause and qualification. A simple scheme of this sort is cited by the commentator al-Bukhārī (d. 730/1329) in the name of "one of the *uṣūlīs*," and is also found in Abū 'l-Barakāt al-Nasafī's (d. 710/1310) commentary to his own *Manār*.[303] Here the four obvious possibilities are considered: the effectiveness may be that of the individual cause upon the individual qualification, of the individual cause upon the genus of the qualification, of the genus of the cause upon the individual qualification, or finally, of the genus of the cause upon the genus of the qualification.

In the first possibility, there is no identification of a new cause but merely the application in new cases of an identified cause. We have here the explicit cause recognized even by many anti-analogists. An example of the effectiveness of the individual cause upon the genus of the qualification is the identification of minority (*ṣighar*) as the cause of the father's marital guardianship (*wilāyat al-nikāḥ*) over his virgin minor daughter. The effectiveness of this cause is already established by consensus in the case of his guardianship over her property (*wilāyat al-māl*). The two qualifications here fall under the genus of guardianship but the cause is the same. The four possibilities are presented hierarchically with the middle two regarded as cases of equal effectiveness.[304]

Interest in the notion of legal kinds did not stop at this point. If anything, constant attention to legal relatedness subtly worked to confuse what had been seen as distinct

---

300. Ibn Taymiyya, *Iqtiḍāʾ*, p. 284.

301. *Musawwada*, p. 408.

302. Jaṣṣāṣ, f. 281a (*taʾthīr fī al-uṣūl*); f. 276a (*tarjīḥ*).

303. Bukhārī, 3:353; Nasafī, 2:145.

304. *Taqrīr*, 3:147; *Fawātiḥ*, 2:265. The examples in these two texts are more carefully presented than elsewhere. *Irshād*, p. 217, gives priority to the second case (*adnā* probably to be read for *awlā* in the second line from the bottom), but Qarāfī, p. 394, regards this view as erroneous.

The individual is sometimes referred to as such (*al-ʿayn*), sometimes as the species (*al-nawʿ*). This latter usage was meant to exclude the erroneous notion that the particular cause or quality of the original case in its full individuality was meant (*Taysīr*, 3:310; *Taqrīr*, 3:147). The usage is clearly a later one, for the jurists ordinarily used the single term *jins* for species and genus.

aspects of analogy. Apart from the context that particularly concerns us, the identification of the cause of a revealed law, the examples cited in the texts to illustrate effectiveness often seem to refer to very different sides of analogy: restrictions on the application of a cause to a new case[305] or the assessment of the relatedness of a cause to its derivative cases.[306] In one Ḥanafī text, the example relating to the guardianship over minor girls is presented to illustrate the possibility of a cause producing a second qualification upon application, a process that calls for the "genericization of the cause" (*tajnīs al-ʿilla*).[307] The confusion caused by this promiscuous jumbling of contexts gave the more scrupulous commentators much grief.[308]

For the Ḥanafīs, the culmination of the development of the doctrine of legal kinds comes in *al-Tawḍīḥ* of Ṣadr al-Sharīʿa al-Maḥbūbī (d. 747/1346). The innovation in al-Maḥbūbī's method is that it takes into consideration a wider body of information. The four possible permutations of species and genus are now surveyed with regard to a single cause. The family relations are taken in combination (*tarkīb*) rather than merely individually (*ifrādan*). Thus the highest ranking cause will be one for which all four possibilities are realized. This is the fourfold combination. The cause is known to be effective in each way: species to species, species to genus, genus to species, and genus to genus. Should one possibility not be realized, there is a three-fold combination, and this can appear in four different structures. The two-fold combination can appear in six forms. Altogether, there are eleven possible structures. In this fashion, it is possible to work out a genealogy of causes in relation to qualifications that exhibits the force of a given character. "The force of a character," Saʿd al-Dīn al-Taftāzānī (d. 792/1390) explains, "is in proportion to its effectiveness, and its effectiveness is in proportion to the consideration (*iʿtibār*) accorded it by the Lawgiver, the greater the consideration, the more powerful the effectiveness. Thus the composite is of greater force than the simple and the composite of more parts of greater force than the composite of fewer parts."[309] The ideal of an inductive logic that inspired Rudolph Carnap and his followers already exercised its fascination on the Ḥanafī jurists of the fourteenth century.

At this point we may take note of al-Ghazālī's reaction to the spread of the doctrine of effectiveness in his day, particularly among the Shāfiʿīs of Marw. Al-Ghazālī's critique and his own positive teachings are of considerable value in helping a modern student grasp what was at stake. As already noted, al-Ghazālī claims that the doctrine of Abū Zayd al-Dabūsī was to reject all causes but those expressly identified by a revealed text or by

305. Bukhārī, 3:353–54.

306. *Taqrīr*, 2:138.

307. *Uṣūl al-Shāshī*, p. 73. It should be noted that for this work appropriateness, not effectiveness, is the fundamental method of establishing causes.

308. For example, *Taqrīr*, 3:147.

309. *Talwīḥ*, 2:397.

consensus. Accordingly, he sees the goal of the method of effectiveness as the attainment of certainty, a certainty that is misplaced in the law. Al-Ghazālī attempts to show that in his practice Abū Zayd was unable to comply with this severe standard. In fact, he was often unable to cite causes that were only appropriate.[310] The fact of the matter is that there was no substantial difference in method at stake between the partisans of effectiveness and the average Shāfiʿī jurist: for all, appropriateness was the standard method. At times, however, al-Ghazālī concedes that al-Dabūsī may have meant by an effective cause merely an appropriate one.[311] Upon this view, the entire issue would rest upon a verbal confusion. Indeed, at one point, al-Ghazālī counsels his reader on the proper terminology to employ when debating in the various regions: effectiveness (*taʾthīr*) in Samarqand, indication (*dalāla*) in Iraq, resemblance (*shabah*) in Nīsābūr.[312]

Al-Ghazālī's uncertainty about the aims of Abū Zayd and his followers is not without explanation. Abū Zayd does not offer an explicit definition of effectiveness in terms of species and genus, although he does speak of one form of guardianship as being of the genus of another. This failure was, as we have seen, corrected by al-Bazdawī and al-Samarqandī, who define effectiveness in terms of genus operating on genus. It is clear from al-Samarqandī's definition that he at least intended thereby to draw a sharp line between an explicit cause and an effective one. This was a reasonable course, but the later Ḥanafīs persist in regarding an explicit cause as an effective one and in rejecting a restrictive interpretation of al-Bazdawī's definition.[313] The explicit cause is thus the prototype of effectiveness. Al-Ghazālī may also, we have seen, have been misled by taking "effectiveness" in the narrow sense of "explicitness."

But there is more than merely verbal confusion at work here. Al-Ghazālī evidently regarded Abū Zayd's method of effectiveness as an attempt to elaborate upon and justify the practice of Abū Ḥanīfa who, according to al-Ghazālī, always sought explicit causes in his analogies.[314] Not only was this interpretation of effectiveness consistent with al-Ghazālī's understanding of legal history, it was confirmed by the practice of his contemporaries. In debate with the Shāfiʿīs of Marw, al-Ghazālī was struck by their refusal to allow any reference to original cases (*uṣūl*). Their style of analogy cited causes only. And they called anyone who cited an original case in his argument an *aḥkāmī* with no knowledge of *fiqh*.[315] This contempt for the rules, *aḥkām*, and exclusive interest in causes, could only mean that they were claiming for their causes the certainty of the original rules of

310. *Shifāʾ*, p. 321.
311. *Shifāʾ*, p. 178.
312. *Shifāʾ*, p. 381.
313. *Fawātiḥ*, 2:269.
314. *Shifāʾ*, p. 333. See also *Shifāʾ*, p. 82, and for Abū Ḥanīfa's failure to attain this goal in every case, *Shifāʾ*, p. 344.
315. *Shifāʾ*, p. 322.

law, and this could be so only if the causes were explicit. The cause, being general, was cherished; the original rule, the *ḥukm*, being specific, was discarded as a useless husk. Legal understanding, *fiqh*, is knowledge of the general, that is, of the causes.

The practice of not referring to an original case in formulating an analogy was, in fact, defended by Abū Zayd and his successors. According to him, this practice was that of the early masters, men like al-Shāfiʿī and al-Shaybānī.[316] The very fact that a cause alone was cited was to be explained in terms of effectiveness. Unless the cause was effective, there would be no point in citing it.[317] Apart from the validity of this practice, there was the question of whether it was properly denominated analogy. Abū Zayd is willing to distinguish between analogy, in which the original case is mentioned, and an inference based on a cause established by reasoning (*ʿilla thābita bi'l-raʾy*).[318]

We can see, then, that al-Ghazālī had some basis for regarding certainty as the aim of the method of effectiveness. The Ḥanafī texts, however, do not go nearly so far. There is no indication that Abū Zayd or any of his followers were claiming more than probability for their analogies. It is certainly true that they regarded effectiveness as the only sound method of doing analogy. But the claim of methodological exclusivity is not equivalent to the claim that certain results are always possible. What can safely be said is that effectiveness was regarded as a means to the attainment of greater probability than its competitors. Furthermore, within the method of effectiveness itself there was an attempt to establish a grading of analogies.

Can we accept al-Ghazālī's ultimate judgment of the failure of effectiveness, that it coincided with the standard practice of his day? This is a more difficult question, which only much research will answer. But even conceding a substantial agreement between effectiveness and appropriateness combined with conformity, there are real differences that remain. The issue is fundamentally one of rationality. The achievement of effectiveness lay not only vertically, so to speak, in the increased probability of its results; it lay also horizontally, in its extension of the scope of analogy.

The Ḥanafī doctrine of effectiveness and al-Ghazālī's appropriateness both revolve about considerations of means-to-end fittingness and of species-genus relatedness. This was the point al-Ghazālī was most concerned to make, and it was one that later Ḥanafī authors concede.[319] But the fact remains that the rationality of means to end is the cor-

316. Dabūsī, ff. 139a,b.

317. Dabūsī, f. 139b.

318. Dabūsī, f. 140b; *al-ʿilla al-mustanbaṭa bi'l-raʾy* (Sarakhsī, 1:191); *ʿilla sharʿiyya* (Bazdawī, 3:364); *ʿilla sharʿiyya thābita bi'l-raʾy* (Nasafī, 2:149). *Fawātiḥ*, 2:269, links the epithet *ahl al-raʾy* to this usage, which he criticizes. The term *raʾy* is puzzling here. It would seem to indicate some uncertainty in the cause. This could stem from the detachment of the cause from its original case. In any event, even an explicit cause would not operate with certainty upon another species of qualification than its original one, since the new case might be distinguishable (*Uṣūl al-Shāshī*, p. 73; *Fawātiḥ*, 2:269–70).

319. *Taqrīr*, 3:146–49.

nerstone of the method of appropriateness, whereas effectiveness focuses upon relatedness. Although these standards could be and were combined, they represent two fundamentally different ideals of rationality, with distinct tendencies.

Appropriateness as practiced by Abū Isḥāq al-Isfarāyīnī apparently corresponded to the suggestiveness spurned by the Ḥanafīs. It did without the genetic relatedness of al-Ghazālī's version.[320] Furthermore, even for al-Ghazālī, appropriateness extends beyond genetic relatedness. Causes that are appropriate but for which no prior specific or generic consideration on the part of the Lawgiver can be shown are termed "alien" (*gharīb*). In his writings on legal theory, al-Ghazālī consistently defended the acceptability of such "alien" causes.[321] Appropriateness thus encompasses a class of causes that are unacceptable to the Ḥanafīs since they do not meet the standard of effectiveness.[322] The extent to which their unyielding demand for effectiveness set them apart may be gathered from al-Ījī's (d. 756/1355) statement that Abū Zayd alone took the anomalous position of rejecting *appropriate* causes.[323]

It might be tempting to regard the difference between appropriateness and effectiveness as one between rationality and validity. The Ḥanafīs go beyond their opponents in calling for evidence of validity. But this formulation would fall far short of capturing the claims made for their doctrine by the Ḥanafīs. For just as appropriateness overlaps with but extends beyond effectiveness, so also effectiveness extends beyond the rationality of appropriateness and does not merely confirm it. Out of effectiveness there arises a second level of rationality. This point is made very clearly by the extended notion of an "intelligible reason" found in the Ḥanafī texts. Already Abū Zayd distinguishes between the kind of rational ground that reason itself can establish and that which depends on a consideration of revelation.[324] And the commentator al-Bukhārī speaks of "an intelligible ground based on effectiveness *or* suggestiveness (*an yuʿqal fīhā maʿnā min taʾthīr aw ikhāla*)."[325]

320. *Burhān*, f. 224.

321. *Shifāʾ*, pp. 194–95; *Mustaṣfā*, pp. 448–49. Admittedly, he held the view that "if the appropriateness of a ground is apparent, the law generally does not fail to regard its genus" (*Shifāʾ*, p. 153). Al-Suhrawardī al-Maqtūl was of the opinion that the appropriate cause can be alien (*Baḥr*, f. 301b). Al-Suhrawardī's legal writings have been ignored by his modern students. His *uṣūl al-fiqh* work *al-Tanqīḥāt* is quoted in the literature, particularly in Shams al-Dīn al-Isfahānī's long commentary to Fakhr al-Dīn al-Rāzī's *Maḥṣūl*. Al-Rāzī and al-Suhrawardī were both students of Majd al-Dīn al-Jīlī (Henri Laoust, *Les schismes dans l'Islam* [Paris: Payot, 1965], p. 230).

322. *Mīzān*, f. 159a.

323. ʿAḍud al-Dīn al-Ījī, *Sharḥ Mukhtaṣar al-Muntahā al-uṣūlī*, ed. Shaʿbān Muḥammad Ismāʿīl (Cairo: Maktabat al-Kulliyyāt al-Azhariyya, 1394/1974), 2:244. *Muʾaththir* as used here is equivalent to *munāsib* (Ṣafī al-Dīn al-Baghdādī, *Qawāʿid al-uṣūl wa-maʿāqid al-fuṣūl*. In *Majmūʿ mutūn uṣūliyya*, ed. Jamāl al-Dīn al-Qāsimī [Damascus: al-Maktaba al-Hāshimiyya, n.d.], p. 122).

324. Dabūsī, f. 123b; *Manār*, p. 845.

325. Bukhārī, 3:351; *Manār*, p. 845.

The rationality of appropriateness is a distinctively human one, depending upon the identification of the purposes of the law with those of mankind. In this sense, it offers an anthropomorphic jurisprudence. Effectiveness moves upon a more refined plane. In part, it is free to do so because the conformity of the Ḥanafīs is a considerably looser standard than the appropriateness of the Shāfiʿīs. It demands only that the putative cause not offend the Muslim jurist's sense of what is fitting. It does not prematurely exclude possible causes that only the more sensitive test of effectiveness can properly evaluate. Al-Dabūsī would not have found it surprising that his analogies appeared to outsiders like al-Ghazālī to be merely dressed up as appropriate.[326]

The independence of effectiveness as a source of rationality was facilitated by the inclusion of explicit causes under the heading of effective. For it was generally conceded that an explicit cause did not have to be appropriate, or at least not evidently so.[327] From this point of agreement, the dispensability of appropriateness could be extended to other forms of effectiveness.[328]

Effectiveness provided the foundation for a wider rationality than that of appropriateness. This was so because most of the time effectiveness validated causes that were already appropriate. This would certainly be the case if "alien" causes were of the utmost rarity, as al-Ghazālī and others claimed. To these causes, effectiveness would bring those that only it could detect. Because it incorporated appropriateness, effectiveness could assume such functions as distinguishing between conditions and causes that otherwise were the task of appropriateness.[329] Effectiveness, then, was not conceived of as narrowing that part of the law amenable to analogy, but rather was regarded as a technique for broadening it. It was the dominant Ḥanafī view that there was a presumption of causality in the law. Nonetheless, for any specific application of analogy, the Ḥanafīs required evidence that the case in question had a cause before considering specific candidates.[330] This position was more stringent than that which they attributed to al-Shāfiʿī, who required only evidence for a particular cause, not for causation.[331] This restrictive Ḥanafī doctrine was rejected by al-Samarqandī, who regarded the identification of an effective cause as sufficient.[332] Similarly, Ṣadr al-Sharīʿa al-Maḥbūbī regarded the Ḥanafī requirement as of "the utmost difficulty" and suggested that it could be dispensed with, given the demand for effectiveness.[333]

326. *Shifāʾ*, p. 321.

327. *Mustaṣfā*, p. 435; *Taqrīr*, 3:195.

328. This was the position of Abū Yaʿlā ibn al-Farrāʾ and the Iraqis (*Musawwada*, p. 408).

329. *Shifāʾ*, p. 553; Nasafī, 2:149.

330. *Mīzān*, f. 165a; Bazdawī, 2:293; Sarakhsī, 2:144.

331. Cf. *Talwīḥ*, 2:376, who reports this but observes *wa-qad ishtahara bayna aṣḥābihi anna al-aṣl huwa al-taʿabbud dūn al-taʿlīl*.

332. *Mīzān*, f. 165a.

333. *Talwīḥ*. 2:375. Perhaps Abū 'l-Yusr al-Bazdawī went furthest in this regard. For him, the common

The doctrine of effectiveness represents an impressive attempt to answer one of the cardinal arguments of the anti-analogists. In debate with the Ashʿarī theologian al-Bāqillānī, the Imāmī al-Shaykh al-Mufīd had argued that there could be no probable opinion in legal matters such as to warrant analogy. The opinions acted on in daily life depended on experience, but the revealed law gave one no foothold for attaining such experience. With respect to the law, we were like someone unfamiliar with the weather. He would have no reason to expect rain upon seeing clouds. Similarly, the law presented us with a realm that did not correspond to our expectations. "There is no custom or sign in the law based on experience (*durba*) or observation (*mushāhada*), for the texts of the law distinguish between what is associated in form and appearance and associate what is distinct in character."[334] Effectiveness answered this challenge by building upon the commonly held view of the jurists that the law had a custom (*ʿāda*) of its own with which it was possible to make acquaintance (*ʿahd*).[335] Perhaps no one makes this point more forcefully than Abū Zayd al-Dabūsī:

> And if it is said, "How is this (analogy) possible when the law is ever contrary to what our minds commonly understand of things?" we answer, "Yes, it is contrary to the common content of reason under the inspiration of our passions, but in conformity with a higher reason that we would not know without the declared law. It is contrary to the ordinary before revelation but in conformity after proof, so that upon study the legal becomes natural."[336]

3. *Formal Methods*

The successful assimilation of the law to nature was only possible by virtue of the discipline of effectiveness. Others took a less demanding course. "Our contemporaries," al-Dabūsī noted, "on account of their sloth in matters of religion have taken to the method of *ṭard*. Its use has become a standard habit and a fifth nature."[337] *Ṭard* was only one among a number of formal methods for identifying the cause of a law. Space does not permit more than a cursory treatment of these formal methods, and it will be necessary to eschew those disputes that constitute the principle interest of this branch of the theory of analogy. Some of the material has already been dealt with by Professor ʿAlī

---

distinction between caused and uncaused laws was erroneous. One should properly speak of laws that are caused insofar as we are concerned (*ʿindanā*) and laws caused in fact (*fī al-ḥaqīqa*). All laws, according to him, are of the latter sort (*Ḥujaj*, f. 6b).

334. *Fuṣūl*. 1:51; identified as al-Mufīd's argument in Ṭūsī, p. 254.

335. See *Muʿtamad*, 2:718–19, where the genetic relationship is presented as a possible source of *ʿāda*; *Rawḍa*, p. 161; al-Ghazālī, *Miʿyār al-ʿilm*, p. 139.

336. Dabūsī, f. 118b. Cf. the weaker statement of al-Sarakhsī, 2:129.

337. Dabūsī, f. 154b.

Sāmī al-Nashshār in his well-known book, *Manāhij al-baḥth ʿinda mufakkirī al-Islām*.[338] Al-Nashshār quite properly pointed to the *uṣūlīs*' anticipation of Mill's Canons of Induction. In some respects, however, al-Nashshār relied on an erroneous analysis of Mill's methods and consequently went wrong in describing their Islamic analogs. Today, thanks to the labors of C. D. Broad and G. H. von Wright, there exists a logic of conditions in connection with which a full technical study of these Islamic doctrines could be carried out.[339]

The doctrine of effectiveness was put forth by the Central Asian Ḥanafīs as the exclusive method for identifying legal causes. But the formal methods, particularly *ṭard*, the least demanding, persisted in use and were always a temptation to be guarded against in disputation. Not only were these formal methods without value in the face of effectiveness, they also represented an illegitimate importation into the law of methods proper to the rational sciences, that is, theology. The paradox is that these methods were not looked to in the mistaken belief that epistemologically the law could meet the standards of theology. Instead, they were introduced because their proponents despaired of finding a genuine legal rationality. The formal methods had the advantages of being readily applicable and publicly verifiable. Their introduction kept the legal process in motion. That the practice of these methods had a devastating effect on the science of law did not trouble their proponents. It is significant that al-Ghazālī's consternation with Abū Zayd al-Dabūsī stemmed from his impression that the goal of Abū Zayd was certainty, the standard appropriate for the rational sciences. He did not attack Abū Zayd for using the methods of the rational sciences for, in fact, it was al-Ghazālī himself who inclined to accept them in the law. From al-Ghazālī's point of view, the claims made for appropriateness, suggestiveness, and effectiveness equally represented a deviation from the practice of the ancients.[340] The proponents of these methods confused the law with the rational sciences. In fact, however, there was widespread agreement among jurists that the causes of theology set a standard of certainty generally unattainable in the law.[341] Where some jurists disagreed was in their assessment of the level of probability attainable outside of the rational sciences. For Abū Zayd and his followers, the role of probability in the daily life of rational beings was clear evidence that probability was in some sense knowledge.[342] Convinced that probability was a part of rationality, they set about making explicit the rationality of the law. They did not doubt that this task demanded a method of its own. They were fully in agreement with al-Jaṣṣāṣ when he condemned the terrible errors of

338. 1st edition, Cairo, 1947.

339. See Georg Henrik von Wright, *A Treatise on Induction and Probability* (London: Routledge and Kegan Paul, 1951).

340. Al-Ghazālī, *Miʿyār al-ʿilm*, p. 145.

341. *Qawāṭiʿ*, ff. 218b–219a.

342. Dabūsī, f. 118b; *Ḥujaj*, ff. 6b, 43a.

those who thought they could deal with legal matters on the basis of their familiarity with rational analysis.[343]

Among the formal methods is that known as *al-sabr wa'l-taqsīm*, literally "testing and division."[344] It consisted in marshalling the possible candidates for causation and in identifying one as the cause by eliminating the others. Its status as an independent method was subject to dispute. The process of identifying the cause was always one of choosing the best among the set of available alternatives, whether the alternatives were all effective, as for the Ḥanafīs, or of different types, as for the methodological pluralists.[345] Hence it could be argued that the method of determining the cause was not *al-sabr wa'l-taqsīm* but rather that *al-sabr wa'l-taqsīm* was presupposed for the application of the other methods.[346] The independence of *al-sabr wa'l-taqsīm* was defended by al-Ghazālī, who obviously had in mind the explicit presentation of the method with an exhaustive set of alternatives. In such a case, one could ignore the question of the type of cause that was left when the others were eliminated. There was no need to establish its appropriateness.[347]

With the notable exception of al-Jaṣṣāṣ and al-Marghīnānī (d. 593/1197), the author of *al-Hidāya*, the Ḥanafīs were set against this method.[348] Defenders of the method urged that it was valid where there was a consensus that the law in question had a cause and where all the possible causes except one were eliminated.[349] This more restricted claim did win some Ḥanafī approval.[350] The opposing arguments all boiled down to the inevitability of establishing effectiveness or at least appropriateness. Every cause had to stand on its own merits.[351] The propriety of the method of *al-sabr wa'l-taqsīm* for dealing with rational causes was not questioned. In nature, as opposed to law, causality was a universal principle. The true cause could thus be distinguished by elimination.[352]

The other two formal methods we shall consider can be dealt with together. The first is *ṭard*, "consistency," the second *al-ṭard wa'l-ʿaks*, "consistency and convertibility." A cause is said to be consistent (*muṭṭarid*) when it is uniformly found with the qualification

---

343. Jaṣṣāṣ, f. 303a.

344. It would appear that *al-taqsīm wa'l-sabr* is the more natural order (Qarāfī, p. 398). But Ibn al-Anbārī, quoted *Irshād*, p. 214, takes *sabr* in the sense of searching out and gathering the alternatives and *taqsīm* as the process of elimination. This understanding is caught by a further name, *al-ḥasr wa'l-taqsīm* (Ibn Taymiyya, *al-Radd*, p. 348). The process is also called *al-taqsīm wa'l-tardīd* (Ibn Taymiyya, *al-Radd*, p. 205), *al-taqsīm wa'l-muqābala* (Bājī, p. 171), and by the logicians *al-sharṭī al-munfaṣil* (al-Ghazālī, *Miʿyār al-ʿilm*, p. 126). More briefly, *al-taqsīm* (*Musawwada*, p. 426) and *al-sabr* (*Rawḍa*, p. 160).

345. Māwardī, 1:549.

346. *Baḥr*, ff. 302b–303a; *Shifāʾ*, pp. 454–55; *Mustaṣfā*, p. 471.

347. *Mustaṣfā*, p. 435; *Baḥr*, f. 303b.

348. *Fawātiḥ*, 2:300; *Musawwada*, p. 427, where its rejection is attributed to the Bukharans.

349. *Rawḍa*, p. 160.

350. *Mīzān*, f. 157b; Sarakhsī, 2:231.

351. Sarakhsī, 2:232; *Fawātiḥ*, 2:300.

352. Sarakshi, 2:232.

it is claimed to cause. To speak in terms of conditions, it is consistent when it is a sufficient condition of the qualification. A cause is said to be convertible (*munʿakis*) when the qualification is never found without the putative cause. The cause is thus a necessary condition of the qualification.[353] Convertibility is the "opposite" (*ḍidd*) of consistency.[354] In our discussion, we shall be concerned with consistency or with consistency combined with convertibility as sufficient to establish causality. This is quite another matter from the requirement that a cause otherwise identified also be consistent. This problem will be encountered in connection with the "specialization of the cause."

The doctrine that simple consistency without the further requirement of appropriateness or effectiveness is sufficient to establish causality was vigorously attacked by the Ḥanafīs. It was for them the fountainhead of the formalist heresy, which dispensed with the "intelligible grounds" necessary for analogy.[355] The Ḥanafīs contrasted it with their method of effectiveness,[356] but even more commonly with legal understanding (*fiqh*) in general.[357] Abū Zayd al-Dabūsī was a particularly vehement opponent of this dangerous innovation, and his characterization of the propnents of consistency as the *ḥashwiyya* ("anthropomorphists") of the analogists was well known.[358] Al-Dabūsī went so far as to develop a typology of consistency, and he elaborated techniques of argument to force the proponents of *ṭard* to accept effectiveness.[359] Consistency, according to al-Dabūsī's own testimony, was a widespread practice in his day, and its proponents are still spoken of as contemporaries by Abū l-Barakāt al-Nasafī (d. 710/1310).[360] Not only the Ḥanafīs, but the

---

353. Bukhārī, 3:365.

354. Sarakhsī, 2:241. When a definition is substituted for a cause, we have the common test of consistency and convertibility for definitions. A definition that is not consistent is too broad (not exclusive, *māniʿ*); one that is not convertible is too narrow (not inclusive, *jāmiʿ*) (Bukhārī, 1:21). See Robert Brunschvig, "Ǧāmiʿ māniʿ," *Arabica* 9 (1962): 74–76, and van Ess, *Die Erkenntislehre des ʿAḍudaddīn al-Īcī*, pp. 370–71. But a definition was subject to fewer attacks than an analogy (Ibn Taymiyya, *al-Radd*, p. 37).

Ṭard and *ʿaks* in the above usage, it should be repeated, apply to the cause and are to be distinguished from the same terms when applied to an analogy (e.g., *Muʿtamad*, 2:698–99).

It should furthermore be noted that our discussion will largely ignore the important disputational context of these methods and limit itself to the theoretical issues. The opposition between the two contexts is variously expressed: *uṣūl/jadal* (*Mustaṣfā*, p. 477); *uṣūl/munāẓara* (*Muʿtamad*, 2:1031), and, for our purposes, is synonymous with *fatwā/munāẓara* (*Mankhūl*, p. 397); *dīn/jadal* (*Irshād*, p. 228); *mufāqaha/mujādala* (Sarakhsī, 2:234); *nāẓir/munāẓir* (*Mustaṣfā*, p. 453), and so forth.

355. Sarakhsī, 2:231, attributes the method of *al-sabr wa'l-taqsīm* to some of *ahl al-ṭard*.

356. Bukhārī, 3:373; Sarakhsī, 2:276.

357. The opposition of *ahl al-ṭard* and *ahl al-fiqh* is frequent (Bukhārī: 3:351–52; Bazdawī, 3:365; Sarakhsī, 2:279).

358. Dabūsī, f. 132b; *Irshād*, p. 221; *Shifāʾ*, p. 305.

359. Dabūsī, ff. 160a–161b.

360. Nasafī, 2:122. Ibn Qayyim al-Jawziyya attributes *ṭard* along with the other methods of analogy to the Central Asian jurists (*Iʿlām al-muwaqqiʿīn*, 1:268). The statement of *Taqrīr*, 3:201, that the Ḥanafīs

mainstream of Muslim jurists of all allegiances, were united in their contempt for the practice of consistency, and the very term became synonymous with mere unfounded assertions.[361]

The method of consistency is a test for sufficient conditions and is so expounded by the legal theorists. If the cause exists, so does the qualification (c → q). It thus corresponds to Mill's *Method of Difference.*[362] By the Method of Difference, a factor is identified as a sufficient condition when its presence alone is enough to distinguish a case in which the conditioned phenomenon is present from one in which it is not. For the method of consistency, the causality of a character is established when no case can be found in which the claimed cause is not accompanied by the qualification it is supposed to cause. Such a counterexample, one in which the cause is present but not the qualification, eliminates the cause being defended just as it does in the *Method of Difference.* Upon the absence (*takhalluf*) of the qualification in the presence of the cause, the cause is "broken" (*naqḍ, intiqāḍ*).[363] Convertibility (*ʿaks*) tests for necessary conditions. In the absence of the cause, the qualification, too, should be absent (-c → -q). It corresponds to Mill's *Method of Agreement.*[364] The presence of the cause wherever the qualification is present is known as "effectiveness" (*taʾthīr*).[365] The requirement that a cause be both consistent and convertible corresponds to Mill's Joint *Method of Agreement and Difference.*[366] The technical term for this is *dawarān*, "concomitance," literally, "revolution."[367]

---

branded all those who did not require effectiveness as *ahl al-ṭard* is controverted by the explicit usage of the earlier authors (e.g., Bukhārī, 3:351).

361. *Aqallu rutbatan min ṭard al-fuqahāʾ* (al-Shahrastānī, *Kitāb Nihāyat al-iqdām*, p. 60); *daʿāwā mujarrada ... tushbihu al-aqyisa al-ṭardiyya al-khāliyya ʿan al-taʾthīr* (Ibn Taymiyya, *Bughyat al-murtād al-manʿūt bi'l-sabʿīniyya fī al-radd ʿalā al-mutafalsifa wa'l-qarāmiṭa wa'l-bāṭiniyya*, in Supplement to vol. 4 of *Majmūʿat fatāwā Shaykh al-Islām Ibn Taymiyya* [Cairo: Maṭbaʿat Kurdistān al-ʿIlmiyya, 1329 H], p. 22).

362. Not *Agreement* as in ʿAlī Sāmī al-Nashshār, *Manāhij al-baḥth ʿinda mufakkirī al-Islām* (Cairo: Dār al-Maʿārif, 1967), p. 111. The same erroneous analysis is standard and appears, for example, in J. M. Bochenski, *The Methods of Contemporary Thought*, trans. Peter Caws (New York: Harper & Row, 1968, p. 109). Cf. G. H. von Wright, *The Logical Problem of Induction*, 2nd ed. (New York: Macmillan, 1957), p. 69.

363. Bukhārī, 4:34; *Mustaṣfā*, p. 435. For consistency, one also finds the terms *ittisāq* (Jaṣṣāṣ, f. 283b) and *jarayān* (Ibn ʿAqīl, p. 188). *Irtifāʿ* is used for *takhalluf* in Mawardı, 1:542.

364. Not *Difference* as in al-Nashshar, *Manāhij*, p. 102. See Bochenski, *Methods*, p. 109, and cf. von Wright, *Logical Problem*, p. 69.

365. *Musawwada*, p. 406; *Mustaṣfā*, p. 435. In another usage, *taʾthīr* is the absence of the qualification upon the absence of the cause in a particular case and is opposed to *ʿaks*, which is the absence of the qualification upon the absence of the cause in all cases (Bājī, p. 198; Qarāfī, p. 401). Within the context of disputation, the failure to meet these standards (*ʿadam al-taʾthīr*, *ʿadam al-ʿaks*) is referred to by the simple terms *al-taʾthīr* and *al-ʿaks*; thus "*al-taʾthīr* is the presence of the qualification without the cause" (Ibn ʿAqīl, p. 149), "*al-ʿaks*, which is the presence of the qualification without the cause" (*Rawḍa*, p. 178).

366. Al-Nashshār, *Manāhij*, p. 124.

367. More fully *al-dawarān wujūdan wa-ʿadaman* (Bazdawī, 3:365). The qualification "revolves" (*dāʾir*) with the cause (*mudār*) (Bukhārī, 3:366; Qarāfī, p. 397). *Dawarān* is also used in a stricter sense with

The origins of these doctrines are obscure. According to Abū 'l-Ṭayyib al-Ṭabarī (d. 450/1058), consistency began among some later Shāfiʿīs and was then adopted by Iraqi Ḥanafīs.[368] Ibn Barhān (d. 520/1126) sets the origin of the doctrine among the earlier Shāfiʿīs and Ḥanafīs.[369] The tenth century would seem to be a good guess, and indeed Abū Bakr al-Ṣayrafī (d. 330/941)[370] is reported to have held the doctrine, as also Ibn Surayj (d. 306/918).[371] The association of consistency with the Shāfiʿīs is also made by ʿAbd al-Jabbār. According to him, some Shāfiʿīs regarded consistency as a warrant for analogy that dispensed with the need for a master rule. Others adopted it merely as a method of analogy.[372] The provenance of the doctrine of concomitance was similar. It, too, flourished among the Iraqi Shāfiʿīs.[373] Among its greatest supporters was Abū 'l-Ṭayyib al-Ṭabarī, for whom it produced results as secure as any probabilistic method could.[374] Some Muʿtazilīs are reported to have gone so far as to claim that it did lead to certainty.[375] This would appear to have been the view of the Shāfiʿī Ibn Abī Hurayra (d. 345/956), a student of Ibn Surayj.[376]

These formalist methods rest on the assumption that the methods of the rational sciences are suitable for law. The causes of the natural world are consistent and convertible, and this standard is applicable to the causes of the law. The justification for this applicability, however, was differently conceived. This is clear from the bits of argumentation preserved in the *uṣūl* literature and is also apparent from the attributions given above. That figures so different in outlook as al-Ṣayrafī and Ibn Surayj should agree upon the doctrine of consistency is significant. It appears that consistency was adopted upon quite opposed grounds. In the first place, there were those who took seriously the parallel between rational and legal causes. Among these were Ibn Surayj, and in the following generation, Ibn Abī Hurayra. The latter went a step beyond his master and demanded convertibility as well as consistency, that is, concomitance. The claim of certainty sometimes made for concomitance stems from these circles. This assimilation of legal to rational causes was repudiated by the Muʿtazilī master Abū ʿAbd Allāh al-Baṣrī, who explained

reference to a single case (*Irshād*, p. 221). The Ḥanafīs use the term *dawarān* for mere *ṭard* (*Musawwada*, p. 406; *Irshād*, p. 221), and conversely they use *ṭard* for *dawarān* (*Musawwada*, p. 406; *Talwīḥ*, 2:389; Sarakhsī, 2:186 [*iṭṭirād*]).

368. *Baḥr*, f. 306b; *Irshād*, p. 221.

369. *Baḥr*, f. 305b.

370. *Lumaʿ*, p. 66; *Baḥr*, f. 306b, questions this attribution.

371. *Shifāʾ*, p. 341.

372. *Mughnī*, 17:313.

373. *Baḥr*, f. 305b; *Fawātiḥ*, 2:302.

374. *Burhān*, f. 235; *Baḥr*, f. 305b; *Irshād*, p. 221.

375. Bukhārī, 3:365; Asnawī, 3:68.

376. He is reported to have been a partisan of concomitance (*Baḥr*, f. 305b) and also to have regarded the results of analogy as certain, at least at the end of his life (*Baḥr*, f. 157a).

that the two fields differed in subject matter and that the one cause could not be treated like the other "because the former really necessitates while the latter is like a sign and a motive."[377]

For al-Baṣrī, the status of legal causes as signs precluded their treatment by rational methods. For others it was precisely their quality as signs that legitimated the method of consistency.[378] (As we shall see in connection with the issue of the "specialization of the cause," the assertion that the causes of the law are signs did not have the same consequences for all those who made it.) It is probable that a view of this sort was held by al-Ṣayrafī. For him, the master rule for analogy demanded some action, and this demand could be fulfilled, albeit mechanically, by the method of consistency. Understood in this spirit, consistency marks the undermining of analogy from within. This view of consistency as the minimal fulfillment of the obligation of analogy is preserved by al-Qarāfī (d. 684/1285), for whom consistency is legitimate as a last resort "to exclude arbitrariness (in the law) insofar as possible" (*nafyan li-taʿabbud bi-ḥasab al-imkān*).[379]

Consistency pursued along these lines was parasitical upon the doctrine of a legal cause. The proponents of consistency spoke of legal causes but they were not in search of "intelligible grounds."[380] This search they regarded as a hardship (*ḥajr*) foreign to the law.[381] For the mainstream jurist, the difficult search for intelligible grounds was what constituted the "testing" of the jurist that distinguished him from the layman.[382] Contrasting the standard of the ancients (*salaf*) with the innovation of consistency, al-Sarakhsī observes that "for this reason one of them used to reflect for a period of time without coming up with more than an analogy or two for a case, while one of the moderns sometimes can cite fifty or more causes of this type (i.e., consistent) in one session (*majlis*)."[383]

The method of consistency, which at first sight would seem to bespeak a warm acceptance of analogy, was in fact regarded by the mainstream of jurists with contempt. They saw it as an affront to the dignity of the law (*istihzāʾ bi-qawāʿid al-dīn*).[384] Whatever its attractiveness, this aberration could not deflect the majority of jurists from the serious task of penetrating to the depths of the law, of understanding (*fiqh*) its workings. Abū 'l-Muẓẓafar al-Samʿānī (d. 489/1095) could confidently conclude his attack on the method of consistency with the observation that "in our day the grounds of *fiqh* have prevailed, and the jurists pursue one method in seeking pure *fiqh* and unadulterated truth. The

377. *Mughnī*, 17:325; *Muʿtamad*, 2:784.
378. *Fawātiḥ*, 2:261; Ibn Taymiyya, *al-Radd*, p. 162.
379. Qarāfī, p. 398.
380. Sarakhsī, 2:179.
381. Sarakhsī, 2:178.
382. Sarakhsī, 2:179.
383. Sarakhsī, 2:228.
384. Abū 'l-Muẓaffar al-Samʿānī quoted Bukhārī, 3:367; Bukhārī, 3:385: *hazl laʿb bi'l-dīn*.

grounds of the law have attained a point at which they approach in clarity the rational proofs adduced by the theologians in connection with the foundations of religion."[385]

V. The Ontology of the Cause

With the doctrine of effectiveness, the Ḥanafīs were able to set the epistemology of analogy on a firm basis. Their substantial agreement upon this matter, however, only underscores the unsettled state of what I have chosen to term the ontology of the cause. Under this heading I shall take up a series of controverted issues in the theory of analogy and show how they can be understood in the light of a basic disagreement over the nature of the legal cause. The most hotly disputed of these issues is probably that of the "specialization of the cause" (*takhṣīṣ al-ʿilla*), but a number of less prominent problems are more obviously related to the fundamental disagreement. Somewhat more speculatively, I shall attempt to draw into this picture the question of the scope of analogy. The issues taken up have this in common, that upon first sight they appear to be a merely technical accretion to the theory of analogy. The tendency to see purely verbal disputes here is not foreign to the later *uṣūl* literature.[386] But this tendency must be resisted if for no other reason that it suggests a grave incompetence on the part of the early masters.[387] The source of this embarrassing situation is not entirely obscure. For not only did the theorists differ with respect to their fundamental conceptions of the cause, they also differed as to the consequences to be drawn from these opposed conceptions. Some examples of this uncertainty will be touched upon, but in the interests of clarity our exposition will center about a few case studies, as it were, drawn from different periods of Ḥanafism. Within these smaller units there is substantial consistency in working out the possible solutions to the problem of the ontology of the cause.

For our purposes, it will be sufficient to recognize two competing models of the nature of the legal cause. Although more detailed divisions were elaborated, the one presented here is standard.[388] Thus Ibn Taymiyya refers to the question of whether "the

385. *Qawāṭiʿ*, ff. 218b–219a, quoted Bukhārī, 3:385–86. It is important to recognize that consistency and convertibility were evaluated very differently by the jurists. Although for most jurists, consistency was a necessary condition (*sharṭ*) for the validity of a cause, it was not a sufficient one (*dalāla*). The converse is true of convertibility. Because a plurality of causes was regarded as possible, failure of convertibility did not invalidate a cause. Convertibility was not a necessary condition of validity. On the other hand, convertibility was often held to be sufficient to establish causality (Ibn ʿAqīl, p. 153; Bājī, p. 195). Even Abū Zayd al-Dabūsī accepted convertibility as a factor in weighing one cause against another, although most later Ḥanafīs did not agree (Dabūsī, f. 152b; *Mīzān*, f. 197a; Sarakhsī, 2:241). And whatever the value of each of these tests individually, a further strength attached to their combination (*Rawḍa*, p. 162).

386. *Fawātiḥ*, 2:277 (*al-ʿilla al-qāṣira*); *Irshād*, p. 225 (*takhṣīṣ al-ʿilla*).

387. *Fawātiḥ*, 2:277. See also *Fawātiḥ*, 2:293.

388. *Baḥr*, f. 284b.

causes of the law are equivalent to a motive and incentive" (*al-dāʿī wa'l-bāʿith*) or to "an indication and sign" (*al-amāra wa'l-ʿalāma*).[389] The significance of these labels will become clear in due course. At this point a cautionary note is in order. The model of the cause as a mere "sign" cannot be simply identified with the use of the term "*amāra*" or "ʿ*alāma*." The use of these terms is very much context dependent. Because abrogation meant new qualifications for old causes, the causes of the law were not natural causes. With reference to abrogation, all theorists admit that legal causes are mere signs, in distinction to "necessitating causes" (ʿ*ilal mūjiba*), which could not exist without their consequences.[390]

Thus the acceptance of the sign model cannot be determined by vocabulary alone. A sounder course is to turn to the particular issues in dispute. For this purpose, we can distinguish core questions that touch directly upon the ontology of the cause and those that are more problematic consequences of the former. One could even go so far as simply to identify the models with these core issues. Among the disputed points that we can point to are the relation of the cause to the original case (*al-aṣl*), the possibility of an intransitive cause (*al-ʿilla al-qāṣira*), and the operation of an explicit cause (*al-ʿilla al-manṣūṣa*).

At the heart of the contest between the two models lies the question of the function of the cause. For one model, the cause serves to explain the law, for it is the "motive" (*bāʿith*) of the qualification. Opposed to this motive model is that in which the cause functions as a means of generalizing the original rule. Of course, a cause that explains the law can also be used to generalize it, but its function as explanation can remain even where generalization is not possible. For the sign model, to speak of causes is to speak of generalization. This difference is embodied in those disputed points of analogist theory that constitute the core of the disagreement. Four such issues may now be considered.

A very clear formulation of the two models is contained in the dispute as to whether the original qualification (*ḥukm al-aṣl*) is to be ascribed (*muḍāf*) to the revealed text or to the relevant cause. For the Iraqi Ḥanafīs, such as al-Jaṣṣāṣ, and for Abū Zayd al-Dabūsī and his followers in Central Asia, the text alone matters. The cause is a sign by means of which the original qualification may be applied to new cases and does not in any way explain the original case, which stands on its own.[391] The opposing view, which ascribed both the original and further instances of the qualification to the same cause, was held by the school of Samarqand.[392] In this issue as in others to be considered, ʿAlāʾ al-Dīn al-Samarqandī presents a consistent version of the motive model of the cause, and

389. Ibn Taymiyya, *al-Irāda wa'l-amr*, in *Majmūʿat al-rasāʾil al-kubrā* (Cairo: Muḥammad ʿAlī Ṣubayḥ, 1385/1966), 1:225. See *Muʿtamad*, 2:753, where *wajh al-maṣlaḥa* is contrasted with *amāra*.

390. *Lumaʿ*, p. 61. See *Musawwada*, p. 385, where the distinction is between mere *amārāt* and *amārāt* that are endowed with obligating force. Abrogation was, of course, an important argument for the adoption of the sign model.

391. Bukhārī, 3:344–45.

392. Bukhārī, 3:344.

his doctrine may profitably be contrasted with that of al-Jaṣṣāṣ, who defended the sign model. For al-Samarqandī, the original case is merely an instance of the operation of the cause. The function of the texts (*nuṣūṣ*) is to make known the dependence of the qualification upon the cause.[393] "God's law," he writes, "attaches not to words but to purposes and grounds."[394] The transparency of the text, its downgrading in favor of the cause, are possibly further manifestations of the scepticism toward language that characterized the school of Samarqand within the Ḥanafī tradition.

For the sign model, just as the original case stands on its own without the interposition of the cause, so also there is no place for an analogical extension to a case already regulated by a text. Nothing is to be gained (*lā fāʾida*) by making reference to the outside cause.[395] On this point, too, the Samarqandīs, according to ʿAlāʾ al-Dīn, upheld the motive model of the cause. They spoke of the mutual reinforcement of legal sources (*taʿāḍud al-adilla*).[396]

A more developed dispute concerns the legitimacy of an intransitive cause (*al-ʿilla al-qāṣira*). An intransitive cause is one that finds no application beyond the original case.[397] The classic example is the Shāfiʿī identification of the cause of usury (*ribā*) with respect to silver and gold. According to the Shāfiʿīs, it is their quality as media of exchange, a quality that no other substances share.[398] For the proponents of the sign model, the function of the cause is precisely that of extending the original qualification. An intransitive cause is thus a contradiction in terms. Indeed, some Ḥanafīs in their insistence upon the ready transitivity of the cause would not recognize a cause made up of more than four characters.[399] Most of those who rejected the intransitive cause appear to have made an exception of an explicit cause that happened to be intransitive.[400] But some would not go even this far.[401] Their intransigent doctrine marks the highwater mark of the sign model.

Although ʿAlāʾ al-Dīn al-Samarqandī upheld the motive model, and with it the possibility of an intransitive cause, he is careful to point out that an intransitive cause may not, like a transitive cause, be termed "analogy" (*qiyās*).[402] This is because no analogy is conceivable with it. In saying this, al-Samarqandī is dissociating himself from the pop-

393. *Mīzān*, f. 171a.

394. *Mīzān*, f. 176a.

395. Bukhārī, 3:329–30.

396. *Mīzān*, f. 167b.

397. *Baḥr*, f. 292a. Also called *wāqifa* (*Lumaʿ*, p. 63) and *lāzima* (Muḥammad ibn ʿAbd al-Raḥmān al-Dimashqī, *Raḥmat al-umma fī ikhtilāf al-aʾimma* [Cairo: Muṣṭafā al-Bābī al-Ḥalabī, 1359/1940], 1:166). Its opposite is *mutaʿaddiya* (*Lumaʿ*, p. 63).

398. *Baḥr*, f. 292a.

399. Māwardī, 1:553.

400. *Irshād*, pp. 208–9.

401. *Irshād*, p. 209.

402. *Mīzān*, f. 150b.

ular Shāfiʿī use of the intransitive cause, according to which "the intransitivity of the cause required the absence of the original qualification in other cases just as its transitivity required the presence of the qualification in other cases."[403] This negative analogy, however, is only valid if convertibility (*ʿaks*) is a necessary requirement of legal causes, so there cannot be a plurality of causes. At this point the motive model touches upon the assimilation of legal to rational causes.[404] It is not coincidental that Abū Isḥāq al-Isfarāyīnī was among the most vehement defenders of the intransitive cause (*min al-ghulāt fī taṣḥīḥ al-ʿilla al-qāṣira*), and even preferred it to transitive ones.[405] Al-Isfarāyīnī's doctrine of the cause was, we are told, influenced by his long study of theology.[406] It will be observed that the use of the intransitive cause in a negative analogy is nothing other than an *argumentum a contrario*. And it will be recalled that the *argumentum a contrario* was, in fact, analyzed by some Shāfiʿīs as a negative analogy requiring a suggestive cause for its validity.[407] Al-Samarqandī warns against careless analogizing on the basis of intransitive causes, and in its place proposes the correct doctrine of transitive causes with negative qualifications.[408]

As the fourth and final core issue, we revert to the problem of the explicit cause. Does an explicit cause in itself license analogy without a master rule? For the sign model of the cause, the answer is clearly yes. If this were not the case, writes al-Jaṣṣāṣ, there would be no point (*fāʾida*) to stating the cause. But God and His Messenger do not speak aimlessly (*ʿabathan*) nor are they capable of not meaning what they say (*waḍʿ al-kalām fī ghayr mawḍiʿihi*).[409] This is al-Jaṣṣāṣ's answer to those who argued against analogy by noting that should one person say to another, "Free my slave so-and-so because he is black," this would not warrant freeing all his black slaves.[410] The difference is in the nature of the speaker.[411] We require explicitness from a human being. For the sign model as held by al-Jaṣṣāṣ, the cause never properly acts as an explanation, the intransitive explicit cause being the exception that proves the rule.

The proponents of the motive model of the cause tended to hold that an explicit cause did not warrant generalization. This was the position of ʿAbd al-Jabbār[412] and

---

403. Māwardī, 1:547.

404. See Sarakhsī, 2:192, who says this explicitly.

405. *Irshād*, p. 209.

406. *Shifāʾ*, p. 482.

407. See above, ch. 2, n. 266.

408. *Mīzān*, f. 173a.

409. Jaṣṣāṣ, f. 267a.

410. Jaṣṣāṣ f. 266b. On the legal issue, see *Muʿtamad*, 2:756–57; *Rawḍa*, p. 151; Ibn Taymiyya, *Iqtiḍāʾ*, p. 284.

411. Jaṣṣāṣ, f. 266b; Sarakhsī, 2:145. See also *Mustaṣfā*, p.420; Bukhārī, 3:280.

412. *Mughnī*, 17:310.

al-Ghazālī,[413] for example. For them, the cause functioned primarily as an explanation, and there was no need to look beyond this to other cases. Some defenders of the motive model, however, did regard the explicit cause as sufficient warrant for analogizing. But to understand their doctrine, we have to examine the ethical background of the causal models and also to take up the vexed problem of the specialization of the cause.

A particularly apt introduction to these problems is provided by the teaching of Abū ʿAbd Allāh al-Baṣrī (d. 369/980). Al-Baṣrī's views are widely reported but most fully by his student, the Zaydī Imām Abū Ṭālib Yaḥyā ibn al-Ḥusayn al-Nāṭiq bi'l-Ḥaqq (d. 424/1033) in his *Jawāmiʿ al-adilla*. In the following passage, we learn that Abū ʿAbd Allāh originally held that an explicit cause was enough for analogy:

> Our master Abū ʿAbd Allāh used to hold this, then he gave it up, saying: "One may not make anything else agree with it (i.e., extend it) without the institution of analogy. Our reason for this is that benefit may attach to the rule with an explicit cause when it is performed by itself. But when there is joined to it what agrees with it in its cause, it may cease to be of benefit, and harm may attach to their combination. We know this from ordinary life (*al-shāhid*). A father may hold such an opinion of his son's conduct that should he give him an article of clothing or a dinar this would summon him to obey him and follow the path of righteousness and learn what the father wishes. But should the father double this and add other things to it this would become a source of harm, and the increase would summon the son to busy himself with vain pursuits and to depart from steadfastness in this path.... But our master Abū ʿAbd Allāh used to distinguish between whether the explicit cause was the cause of a positive action or of an omission. And he used to say that if the cause is one of a positive action, then the matter is as we have explained. But if it is the cause of an omission, one ought not to refrain from that action on account of some character peculiar to it without being bound to refrain from what agrees with it. This was because it is established that whoever refrains from some action on account of a character peculiar to it, necessarily refrains from all that agrees with it in that character. The opposite of this is impossible, and there can be no obligation with respect to what is impossible. As an example he cited what we know of reasonable men. If one of them refrains from taking a path only because wild beasts are there and for no other reason, he will not choose to follow another path with wild beasts. Motives cannot change in this matter. On this principle he based his view that legal causes are only specialized if they are the cause of a positive action and not an omission.[414]

413. *Mustaṣfā*, pp. 422–23.

414. *Jawāmiʿ*, ff. 69a,b. On al-Nāṭiq bi'l-Ḥaqq and this work, see Wilferd Madelung, *Der Imam al-Qāsim Ibn Ibrāhīm und die Glaubenslehre der Zaiditen*. Studien zur Sprache, Geschichte und Kultur des islamischen Orients, ed. Berthold Spuler, n.s., vol. 1 (Berlin: de Gruyter, 1965), pp. 178–80. On Abū ʿAbd Allāh al-Baṣrī,

The special significance of this and other accounts of Abū ʿAbd Allāh's doctrine is that they show us the causal models in action. The epistemology and ethics of the dispute are made especially clear, and the relations between the various technical issues are laid bare. The introduction of the problem of the specialization of the cause leads us to a very vexed area of legal theory, and one that goes beyond analogical doctrine in the narrow sense. Briefly put, the question is whether consistency, the presence of the qualification upon the presence of the cause, is a necessary condition of the validity of the cause. ʿAbd al-Jabbār explains Abū ʿAbd Allāh's views on this topic in a passage that complements that quoted above:

> Abū ʿAbd Allāh used to allow the specialization of the cause in all respects and used to say that it (the cause) is a sign of the qualification, and that it is not impossible for God (*al-ḥakīm*) to make it a sign in one case but not in another, as we have reported in *al-ʿUmad*. Then he changed his mind and came to regard legal causes as declarative of motives (*kāshifa ʿan al-dawāʿī*). He observed that the motive for an omission differs from the motive for an action. For it is not impossible that one of us do something for a cause but not do what shares in that cause. But it is not possible that one omit something, not doing it for a cause, without it following that he omit also whatever shares in that cause, as we have explained in the *Book on Repentance*. He thought that if the qualification of a cause is action, then specialization is allowed in every case. But if its qualification is prohibition and abstention, then specialization in it is not allowed, all things being the same. But if things are different, then it is not impossible. He took this course with regard to an explicit cause and said that without the obligation of analogy, it might be possible for the cause to be intransitive if its qualification were action, but if its qualification were abstinence, then that is not possible. He took the same course in topics parallel to this. And this is necessary if the cause is declarative of the motive but not if it is declarative of that in virtue of which the act is a benefit, in the case of a grace (*luṭf*).[415]

Couched as it was in such ethical terms, the dispute over the models of the cause raises issues that transcend the institution of analogy. The ethical issues raised are of such significance that even analogy itself can be drawn into their web. Thus for ʿAbd al-Jabbār, analogy is a contingent legal institution rather than a universal imperative of reason, and the ethical analysis at the heart of the dispute over the models is broad enough to subsume analogy as merely one more human action.[416] Even before the question is raised as

---

see *Encyclopaedia of Islam*, 2nd ed., Supplement, s.v. "Abū ʿAbd Allāh al-Baṣrī." See also *Muʿtamad*, 2:753; *Musawwada*, p. 391.

415. *Mughnī*, 17:337–38 (reading *al-tark* for *al-qawl* on p. 337, line 15). The reference is to *Mughnī*, 14:381–82.

416. *Mughnī*, 17:292.

to whether there is a rational or revealed rule of analogy, the problem of the cause from the ethical point of view has already taken shape, for it is one that goes to the heart of the workings of the law. The master rule for analogy acts merely as a signal to set in motion a structure already in place.

Abū ʿAbd Allāh al-Baṣrī and al-Jaṣṣāṣ, who represent for us the motive and sign models respectively, were both Iraqi Ḥanafīs of Muʿtazilī persuasion. The ethical doctrine to which they subscribed, however, was held by many beyond their circle, Shiʿis as well as Sunnis, adherents of other faiths as well as Muslims. In rejecting the notion of legal causes as signs, Abū ʿAbd Allāh was not turning his back on this ethical doctrine. Indeed, he might well have gone so far as to reject analogy altogether and still adhere to it. For this ethical doctrine did not in itself determine a particular legal theory, although it certainly did set limits on what could count as an acceptable one. For our purposes, the merest sketch of the pertinent background will have to suffice. Central to our concern is the concept of a "grace" (*luṭf*), synonymous with a "benefit" (*maṣlaḥa*).

As the prototype of a grace, we may take ritual prayer (*al-ṣalāt*). Prayer is not among that limited class of actions that are known to be obligatory by reason alone. Indeed, if not for revelation, reason might well have determined that the actions constituting prayer were demeaning and therefore wrong.[417] The actions known to be obligatory by reason alone are such in virtue of a particular inherent or relative quality. This quality is the ground (*wajh*) of their obligatoriness, and when an action is recognized as possessing this quality, when for example it constitutes thanks to a benefactor, it is thereby known to be obligatory.[418] All such actions are known to be obligatory by reason.[419] Actions, like prayer, on the other hand, are obligatory by virtue of their connection to other actions. They are "graces," that is, actions upon which one chooses what is obligatory or abstains from what is wrong. The vast majority of such actions are known to be obligatory only by revelation and constitute the greater part of the revealed law.[420] Their communication justifies the sending of prophets.[421] The relation that constitutes the ground of the obligatoriness of graces is our particular concern here.

The chain linking a grace to what is inherently good is fundamentally a psychological one, depending as it does on human choice (*ikhtiyār*).[422] The choice leading from the grace-bearing act to its object is only one aspect of the process, however. It constitutes "that by reason of which the act is a grace" (*mā li-ajlihi ṣāra al-fiʿl luṭfan*).[423] In addition,

---

417. Abd al-Jabbār, *Sharḥ al-uṣūl al-khamsa*, p. 779.
418. Ṭūsī, p. 305.
419. Ṭūsī, p. 264.
420. Ṭūsī, p. 264.
421. ʿAbd al-Jabbār, *Sharḥ*, pp. 564–65.
422. *Mughnī*, 17:289; ʿAbd al-Jabbār, *Sharḥ*, pp. 519–20; *Dharīʿa*, 2:702.
423. *Mughnī*, 17:290.

there is an act of will to perform the grace that goes back to "motives" in the mind of the agent.[424] The grace attracts the agent by arousing the requisite motive and at the same time brings him closer to the further act that the grace serves. According to ʿAbd al-Jabbār, all legal causes can be classified under one or another of these two aspects.[425] In the case of prayer, the Qurʾān identifies it as keeping one from what is abominable (29:45). The motives leading to its performance would be such things as the reward for its performance.[426]

The error of Abū ʿAbd Allāh al-Baṣrī, according to ʿAbd al-Jabbār and others, was to take all causes as motives. If this were the case, his analysis would be correct. But should the cause in question be the connection between the grace and the inherent good it serves, there is no basis for Abū ʿAbd Allāh's distinction between acts and omissions.[427]

To the sign model as put forth by al-Jaṣṣāṣ, this ethical system is of no direct relevance. But the choice of the sign model is itself justified with reference to the same ethical doctrines. Al-Jaṣṣāṣ distinguishes between the causes of the qualification (*ʿilal al-aḥkām*) and the causes of benefit (*ʿilal al-maṣāliḥ*). Analogy functions only with the former, which are mere signs (*amārāt, simāt, ʿalāmāt*), like names. He acknowledges the reality of causes of benefit but denies that they can be known by reason in an individual case. We know in a general fashion (*fī al-jumla*) that each law represents a benefit, and this knowledge is all we need.[428] The causes of benefit are not to be found in the regulations of the law but in those who are bound by the law (*al-mutaʿabbadīn*).[429] Al-Jaṣṣāṣ does not appear to regard even an explicit cause as necessarily equivalent to a cause of benefit. His is a very consistent version of the sign model. Only the intransitive explicit cause touches upon the real causes of the law.

As internal, psychological factors, the real causes of the law are inherently inaccessible. Largely unknown, they justify the law but do not form the object of juridical effort (*ijtihād*). Analogy works upon what are only figuratively causes. The jurist looks for a sign by means of which he may proceed to generalize the law. Such a sign is one which arouses probable opinion. For al-Jaṣṣāṣ, analogy is not an anomalous institution. On the contrary, the license it provides for juridical effort in religious matters is consistent with the policy of the law in leaving vast areas of human endeavor to private evaluation. In both cases,

---

424. *Mughnī*, 17:290.

425. *Mughnī*, 17:290.

426. *Mughnī*, 17:291.

427. *Mughnī*, 17:338; *Muʿtamad*, 2:757–58; *Dharīʿa*, 2:685: Ṭūsī, p. 258. For ʿAbd al-Jabbār's doctrine of analogy, see Robert Brunschvig, "Rationalité et tradition dans l'analogie juridique et religieuse chez le muʿtazilite ʿAbd al-Ǧabbār." *Arabica* 19 (1972): 213–22.

428. Jaṣṣāṣ, f. 23b.

429. Jaṣṣāṣ, f. 277b.

God clearly saw that the best interests of men were served by giving them this considerable measure of discretion.[430]

In place of this simple sign model, Abū ʿAbd Allāh al-Baṣrī puts forth a model of the legal cause that does not leave the ethical underpinning of the law so entirely in the background. Al-Baṣrī is above all concerned to do justice to the epistemology of the cause. For him, the explicit cause is a real cause, the cause of the benefit. The distinction he makes between action and omission is of secondary importance. It means that only the causes of omissions share in the consistency characteristic of rational causes: they do not require a rule of analogy and they are not subject to exception, that is, to specialization. In speaking of al-Baṣrī's change from a sign model to a motive model, ʿAbd al-Jabbār goes too far. In point of fact, al-Baṣrī distinguished sharply between explicit and elicited causes. Elicited causes cannot function like explicit ones because they are not known to be real causes. It is for this reason that al-Baṣrī did not admit of elicited causes that are intransitive. Only causes identified textually, by consensus, or by reason may be intransitive, precisely because they are known to be causes. Al-Baṣrī holds that every cause must be either known or must at least serve analogy.[431]

To speak of intransitive causes that are only probable is not merely an error in legal doctrine. It represents a grave threat to the integrity of the law. "For if this were possible, then it would be possible to explain by their purpose (*ḥikam*) such institutions as the obligation of fixed prayer, fasting in Ramḍān, and others like *zakāt* and the pilgrimage, even if nothing else could be made to agree. But this is the way of the Qarmaṭīs and the Bāṭiniyya, in that they give causes for the rules of the law in the way they do without requiring that further cases be regulated."[432] Divorced from action in the form of analogizing, the search for the reasons of the law is more than merely purposeless, it is inimical to the respect due to the institutions of the law. The Qarmaṭīs, indeed, are the archetype of those who propose to explain what is beyond explanation or at least is beyond human reasoning.[433]

Abū ʿAbd Allāh al-Baṣrī's doctrine of the cause is a combination of sign and motive models.[434] He was careful to stay clear of the search for the reasons of the law involved in a consistent motive model. Al-Baṣrī's doctrine follows the epistemology of the cause. When a cause is known with certainty, it is an explanation. A cause that is only probable is a sign. Al-Baṣrī went further and identified the explanatory causes as motives (*dawāʿī*). Upon this identification, he based his distinction between positive and negative motives. It was this identification rather than his distinction that drew later criticism. Al-Baṣrī,

430. Jaṣṣāṣ, f. 269b.

431. *Jawāmiʿ*, f. 74a; Bukhārī, 3:315.

432. *Jawāmiʿ*, f. 74a.

433. *Mughnī*, 17:333: *tajāhul al-qarāmiṭa idhā ʿallalū al-ḥurūf aw al-khalq.*

434. See *Mughnī*, 17:335, where Abū ʿAbd Allāh speaks of legal causes as *bi-manzilat al-amāra wa'l-dāʿī.*

however, was at one with the mainstream Ḥanafī tradition in regarding a nonexplicit intransitive cause as without purpose.[435] As uncertain, it could not explain the law. As intransitive, it could not serve to extend it.

Those who adhered to the motive model had several ways of justifying their acceptance of an intransitive cause that was educed. Consistency, of course, was on their side. An explicit cause could be intransitive; so could one that was only probable. In developing their justifications for an explanation that was only probable, these jurists were led to rehearse on a small scale the battle over analogy. Once again we hear of the natural propensity of man to follow probability and the spur toward obedience called forth by understanding.[436] There is a paradox here that must not be overlooked. Tailor-made, as it were, to fit the requirements of analogy, the sign model of the cause appears unable to sustain the claims made for analogy as a process of going beneath the surface of the revealed texts. Analogy is now seen to be a mere manipulation of signs without significance, a syntactic system without semantics, so to speak. It is al-Samarqandī and those who uphold the ethical understanding of the cause who alone remain faithful to the original claims for analogy. "The function of the cause," he writes, "is the existence of the qualification, that of the text the knowledge of the qualification. Thus the cause is of greater force than the text with respect to the qualification, since knowledge rests upon existence."[437]

Alongside this paradox, another must be set. The dominant Ḥanafī doctrine, that of the followers of Abū Zayd al-Dabūsī, severely restricted the applicability of analogy in comparison with other legal traditions. Their doctrine of the cause as a sign would seem to favor the widest possible scope for the practice of analogy. But it is instead with al-Samarqandī, the upholder of the motive theory of the cause, that we find an extended field for analogy like that common elsewhere. We shall seek to supply a solution to this second paradox. Having done so, we shall essay a broader view of the place of the ontology of the cause in the theory of analogy.

At first sight, those areas from which the Ḥanafīs exclude analogy appear to constitute very much of a hodge-podge: punishments[438] and expiations,[439] conditions (*shurūṭ*),[440] occasions (*asbāb*),[441] concessions (*rukhaṣ*),[442] and legally operative names (*asmāʾ*).[443] There is, of course, no *a priori* reason why the exclusion of analogy in all these areas must be

435. *Jawāmiʿ*, f. 74a.
436. *Mustaṣfā*, p. 474; *Rawḍa*, p. 171; Bukhārī, 3:318.
437. *Mīzān*, f. 168a.
438. *Irshād*, p. 223.
439. *Irshād*, p. 223.
440. Bukhārī, 3:390.
441. Bukhārī, 3:390.
442. Qarāfī, p. 415.
443. *Musawwada*, p. 394.

attributed to one principle. Indeed, the absence of a unified treatment of this topic in the Ḥanafī texts would suggest otherwise. Nonetheless, it is our contention that such a principle does exist and was more or less clearly articulated by several Ḥanafī authors, particularly Abū Zayd al-Dabūsī.

A Western jurist would probably experience no hesitation in identifying the exclusion of analogy from criminal law with a similar rule in Western legal systems. He would very likely see the exclusion of analogy from expiations in a similar light. These rules would rest on the principle of *nulla poena sine lege.*[444] To punish crimes on the basis of analogy would be to punish retrospectively. A similar account could be given of the Islamic rule: the controlling tradition being "Avert fixed punishments in case of doubt" (*idraʾū al-ḥudūd biʾl-shubuhāt*).[445] But what is missing in such an account is the formalism of the Islamic treatment of the problem. The Western account is not entirely on the wrong track. The problem is that it is not abstract enough and consequently does not go far enough. The Muslim jurists do not simply decide not to practice analogy in these areas of the law, nor are they kept from doing so by a rule. Rather, their doctrine of analogy is such that in these areas there is no place for analogy. The barrier is a conceptual one.

An examination of the structure of the relevant legal rules points the way to an understanding of the Ḥanafī doctrine.[446] The peculiarity of those areas of the law excluded from analogy is that they consist of rules that already contain the equivalent of a cause. In the case of conditions, this is obvious. The condition is the equivalent of a cause. Similarly, in each of these areas the law can naturally be formulated as a condition. The condition functions as an explicit cause. That such an analysis was present in the minds of the Muslim jurists is clear from their treatment of the "occasion" (*al-sabab*). The standard example of an occasion is found in the Qurʾānic injunction: "Perform the prayer at the inclination of the sun (*li-dulūk al-shams*)." (17: 78) The inclination of the sun is the "occasion" for the obligation of prayer. Any further treatment of the obscure doctrine of the occasion is beyond the scope of this study.[447] What

444. George Whitecross Paton, *A Text-book of Jurisprudence*, ed. G. W. Paton and David P. Derham, 4th ed. (Oxford: Oxford University Press, 1972), pp. 387–89.

445. *Muʿtamad*, 2:794–95. The question would remain, however, whether this tradition could operate as a meta-norm as well as a norm for individual cases.

446. On the analysis of the structure of criminal norms, see Tibor Király, *Criminal Procedure, Truth, and Probability*, trans. Kornél Balázs, rev. Árpád Erdei and Imre Gombos (Budapest: Akadémiai Kiadó, 1979), pp. 116–17.

447. The *sabab* is minimally a necessary and sufficient condition (Muḥammad ibn ʿAbd Allāh al-Qafṣī, *Kitāb Lubāb al-lubāb* [Tunis: al-Maṭbaʿa al-Tūnisiyya, 1346 H.], p. 4). The origin of the doctrine and its function are obscure. The core of the *sabab* doctrine appears to consist in those circumstances of time and place that are the "occasions" for a religious obligation. The repetition of the occasion or its continuity calls for the repetition of the obligation. By extension, the *Kaʿba* is the occasion for

is significant is that there is a clear tendency in the texts to regard the occasion as a cause.[448]

The foregoing analysis is meant to provide a basis for what follows. At issue is not the analysis itself, but once again its ontological significance. For the sign model of the cause, the fact that an occasion, for example, functions as a cause means that there is no place for further inquiry. As a sign, the cause has no ontological depth. It is like a mere name bestowed by an act of will. The motive model of the cause sees the cause as more than a mere pointer. The fact that a particular quality is a legal cause is itself a legal statement, the content of which is that the quality in question now requires the relevant qualification.[449] It is in this fashion that al-Ghazālī analyzes a rule depending on an occasion. In setting fornication as the occasion of a fixed legal punishment, God has communicated two rules: one, the imposition of a fixed punishment; and the other, the identification of fornication as the occasion of the punishment.[450] It is perfectly proper to inquire what is the cause of this second rule. Thus in order to extend an occasion by analogy, we must know the cause of the occasion. And inasmuch as the occasion itself functions as a cause, the search for its cause amounts to a search for "the cause of the cause" (*ᶜillat al-ᶜilla*). This is none other than the reason (*ḥikma*) or benefit (*maṣlaḥa*) of the original rule.[451]

Very simply put, the model of the legal cause as a sign does not justify the direct consideration of the policy of the rule of law. The Ḥanafīs' rejection of the validity of an

---

the pilgrimage, which is incumbent only once in a lifetime. This sense is precisely that caught by the definition of Ṣadr al-Sharīᶜa al-Maḥbūbī: "The occasion is that upon which depends the qualification without its effectiveness being understood and which is not the act of a person" (*Taqrīr*, 2:213–14). The unintelligibility of the *sabab* is also mentioned by Abū 'l-Yusr al-Bazdawī (Bukhārī, 2:347). See also *Jamᶜ*, 1:95, on the *sabab waqtī*. The application of the term to such transactions as a sale is by extension (*Taqrīr*, 2:347). The majority of the Ashᶜarīs, however, came to regard only occasions of the latter sort, human actions, as proper from a theological point of view (Bukhārī, 2:339–40).

The mainstream Ḥanafī view attributed the repetition of an obligation to its occasion, and this appears to have been its main function (see *Mustaṣfā*, p. 431). Abū 'l-Yusr al-Bazdawī rejected this analysis or at least its consistent application as a needless detour (*Ḥujaj*, f. 22a). "It is an inconsistency," he noted, "when it comes from those who say that it is not right to attribute an explicit rule to an intransitive cause, in that they say that an intransitive cause is no cause at all" (*Ḥujaj*, f. 21a). Just as they referred the rule to its text, not to its cause, they should similarly refer repetition of the obligation to the text and not the occasion. Al-Bazdawī did, however, retain the doctrine in some sense (Bukhārī, 3:348–50). The *sabab*, it should be noted, transcends the division between analogists and anti-analogists and forms part of Shiᶜi legal analysis (Ṭūsī, pp. 305–6). Compare the Talmudic concept of place and time as *gōrēm*, or *gerām*.

448. *Ḥujaj*, f. 6a; Sarakhsī, 2:194; Bazdawī, 3:375; and particularly *Jamᶜ*, 1:95. The identification of the *sabab* as a cause would be clearly facilitated by the adoption of the sign model of causes. The opposite tendency is represented by al-Bāqillānī (*Mustaṣfā*, p. 431).

449. *Mīzān*, f. 154a.

450. *Mustaṣfā*, p. 112; Qarāfī, p. 414.

451. Qarāfī, p. 415.

intransitive cause is one consequence of this basic doctrine. The principle is put very succinctly by Ṣadr al-Sharīʿa al-Maḥbūbī: "It does not pertain to man to explain the wherefor of God's laws" (*laysa li'l-ʿabd bayān limmiyyat aḥkām Allāh*).[452] We are now in a position to sharpen our understanding of the Ḥanafī position. The intransitive cause is not unacceptable simply because it is of no legal consequence (*fāʾida fiqhiyya*).[453] Certainly there is a great legal consequence in allowing analogy in all those areas from which the Ḥanafīs exclude it. If the question were simply one of action, there would be no need to exclude analogy from these parts of the law. That there is no practical application for an intransitive cause means that the cause is being offered as the reason for the law. But the reasons of the law, if known at all, must be known with certainty. The intransitive cause is rejected because it is neither of practical use nor known with certainty. Analogy is excluded just where it requires direct consideration of the reasons of the law. Only revelation or consensus can vouchsafe the knowledge of reasons. "The benefits and reasons of the law," writes al-Bukhārī, "are not causes in themselves because they are not accessible to probable opinion, and analogy is dependent on probable opinion."[454]

The consequence of mistaking the reason of the law for its cause was a grave one. In presumptuously basing their analogies on the policy of the rule, the opponents of the Ḥanafīs were legislating. One could not, in fact, properly speak of analogy in such cases. The original case was treated as transparent.[455] It was merely an instance of the implementation of the policy. "In establishing occasions, one establishes legal rules and in establishing conditions precedent (*shurūṭ māniʿa*) one does away with legal rules," is

452. *Talwīḥ*, 2:383.

453. *Talwīḥ*, 2:382. Probability is no substitute for knowledge except with respect to action.

454. Bukhārī, 4:7. See Bājī, p. 153, precisely in connection with the scope of analogy. Cf. Fakhr al-Dīn al-Rāzī, who reports finding the Bukhārans basing their analogies on policy alone (*Munāẓarāt*, pp. 24–26 [Arabic], pp. 47–49 [English]).

455. *Baḥr*, f. 287a. This is the point of the analysis of *Irshād*, p. 223, in which the *sabab* is said to become one with the *ḥukm*, that is, the *aṣl* has disappeared. His analysis is based on that of Ibn al-Ḥājib (*Kitāb Muntahā al-wuṣūl wa'l-amal fī ʿilmay al-uṣūl wa'l-jadal*, ed. Muḥammad Badr al-Dīn al-Naʿsānī al-Ḥalabī [Cairo: Maṭbaʿat al-Saʿāda, 1326 H.], p. 141), who excludes analogy from *asbāb* but allows for its application in *ḥudūd* and *kaffārāt*. The transparency of the *aṣl* is already a possible consequence of the attribution of the *ḥukm* to the *ʿilla* and not to the *naṣṣ*. In fact, the opposed points of view can be found reported in the name of the early masters, Abū Ḥanīfa and Abū Yūsuf. Abū Ḥanīfa saw the cause of the prohibition of wine as its power to intoxicate. In extending the rule on the basis of this cause, he prohibited only such amounts of other beverages as would intoxicate. Any amount of wine, however, was prohibited in accord with the original text (*Baḥr*, f. 283b). Abū Yūsuf is reported to have held that the original six species subject to the law of usury could be exempt from this law should the relevant cause cease to exist (ʿAbd al-Ghanī al-Ghunaymī, *al-Lubāb fī sharḥ al-Kitāb*, 2:39). Abū Yūsuf is supposed to have allowed analogy in those areas from which it was excluded by the mainstream (*Musawwada*, p. 398). But some authors present this as an inference from his acceptance of unit-traditions in these areas (*Muʿtamad*, 2:794; *Baḥr*, f. 275b [from Abū ʿAbd Allāh al-Ṣaymarī]).

the way al-Dabūsī puts the matter.[456] When the policy of the law is mistakenly used as a cause, the original rule is not generalized but new causes are created and thus new rules. When a condition is extended to previously apodictic rules, these rules are now suspended from operation. A similar objection could be brought against the application of analogy to legal names.[457] In fact, the same examples can represent the application of analogy to legal names as to occasions: e.g., the application of the *ḥadd* penalty to one who has intercourse with a beast. Is this case one of analogizing the original occasion of fornication (*zinā*) to a new case, or can the name "fornicator" (*zānī*) be applied by analogy to one who engages in this form of intercourse, as Ibn Surayj held?[458] In all such instances, Abū Zayd al-Dabūsī and his follwers saw an abuse of analogy. The task of analogy was to extend an original rule of law (*taʿdiya*), not to establish new rules (*ithbāt*). "The qualification," says al-Dabūsī, "follows the occasion, not the reason of the occasion. The reason is an end (*thamara*), not a cause."[459]

Up to this point we have made a sharp distinction between the methods of analogy and the causal models. What can be said about the relation between the two? Unfortunately, no simple formula will do justice to the problem. The most that can be said is that inferences are found moving in both directions, from the methodology to the cause and vice versa. We have already seen that the method of simple consistency (*ṭard*) was sometimes regarded as a consequence of the nature of the cause as a mere sign. Of more particular interest is the way in which the doctrine of effectiveness could be used to justify doctrines pertaining to the ontology of the cause. Insofar as this was of increasing concern to the Ḥanafīs, we may speak of aspirations toward an integrated theory of analogy. A telling example of this tendency is Ṣadr al-Sharīʿa al-Maḥbūbī's exposition of the Ḥanafī rejection of intransitive causes. According to him, the requirement of effectiveness is behind the Ḥanafī doctrine. The Shāfiʿīs, who demand only suggestiveness (*ikhāla*), could come to believe that a character, though not found elsewhere, is the cause of the rule. Effectiveness, which demands that every cause have a specific or generic parallel, rules out this possibility.[460]

Although this view of the matter is debatable, it is certainly true that the doctrine of effectiveness is highly compatible with the sign model, and thus with the position against intransitive causes. According to the doctrine of effectiveness, the validity of a cause depends on its family relation to proven causes rather than on its explanatory quality.

---

456. Dabūsī, f. 129a.

457. *Uṣūl al-Shāshī*, p. 70.

458. *Muʿtamad*, 2:795, 807; *Lumaʿ*, p. 7.

459. Quoted *Mustaṣfā*, p. 460; *Shifāʾ*, p. 604. See also *Mīzān*, f. 171a.

460. *Talwīḥ*, 2:383; *Fawātiḥ*, 2:277; *Baḥr*, f. 292b.

In a similar fashion, Abū Zayd al-Dabūsī argued that causes that met the standard of effectiveness were not invalidated by specialization. Because it was related to causes known with certainty, the causality of the effective cause was not subject to question, as it would be were the cause merely appropriate.[461]

Whatever the validity of these particular arguments, it is undeniable that the doctrine of effectiveness was particularly suited to serve the sign model of the cause. Without the doctrine of effectiveness, the sign model easily lent itself to the abuse of mere consistency. In this sense, effectiveness served to anchor the system of signs in the firm ground of the texts and consensus.

Ibn Taymiyya assumes the passage from sign model to effectiveness in expounding the view of the Ḥanbalī Abū Yaʿlā ibn al-Farrāʾ. Abū Yaʿlā's doctrine of the ontology of the cause was very close to that of al-Jaṣṣāṣ. Like al-Jaṣṣāṣ, he distinguished between the cause of the qualification and the cause of the benefit. Abū Yaʿlā, too, rejected an intransitive cause. It is on the question of the specialization of the cause that he diverged from the Ḥanafī jurist. In reporting Abū Yaʿlā's views on the intransitive cause and the model of the cause that underlay it, Ibn Taymiyya observes that "this means that he does not maintain an appropriate cause that is alien and probably does not establish analogy in occasions on the basis of reasons" (*la yaqūlu bi'l-munāsib al-gharīb wa-qad lā yuthbitu 'l-qiyās fī al-asbāb bi'l-ḥikam*).[462] The rejection of the appropriate but alien cause is here tantamount to the espousal of effectiveness.[463] Causes are signs that have to be at least generically confirmed by explicit texts in order to be valid. A cause that rests only upon its relationship to an assumed policy of the law is unacceptable. The policy of the law is unknown and can only be properly served by strict adherence to the means set down by the Lawgiver.

Appropriateness was correspondingly linked with the motive model. It looks to causes in the light of the policy of the law, and it is not surprising to find the appropriate cause identified with the motive (*bāʿith*) for the law.[464] Convinced that causes could be discerned by their function as means to the goals of the law, the proponents of appropriateness were not bound by the restraint of effectiveness. Once this freedom was assumed, how far could it be taken? This question was raised most pointedly among the partisans of appropriateness in connection with the problem of "unregulated benefits" (*al-maṣāliḥ al-mursala*).

---

461. *Irshād*, p. 225; *Baḥr*, f. 308b; Dabūsī, f. 153a.

462. *Musawwada*, p. 412; Ibn Taymiyya, *al-Radd*, p. 236.

463. See al-Ījī, *Sharḥ*, 2:244.

464. Āmidī, 3:186; Ibn al-Ḥājib, *Muntahā*, pp. 124, 135; *Talwīḥ*, 2:374, margin. The use of the term *bāʿith* was theologically odious to later Ashʿarīs, *Jamʿ*, 2:232–33. See also *Taqrīr*, 3:135.

VI. *Al-maṣāliḥ al-mursala*

The doctrine of unregulated benefits may be regarded as an extension of appropriateness. It goes one step beyond the discovery of an appropriate but generically uncorroborated cause in an existing rule of law. This is the alien cause. The problem of the alien cause is not the original rule but its extension by means of a cause invalid according to the Ḥanafī doctrine of effectiveness. The proponents of the unregulated benefit go further. They put forth new rules of law. The validity of these rules rests not on any cause, for there is no cause and thus no analogy at issue.[465] The validity of the new rule rests on its claim to safeguard a policy of the law, on sheer appropriateness.[466] In establishing these new rules, the jurist implements new means to serve the ends of the law, means that the Lawgiver left unimplemented (*mursal*).

Clearly, the Ḥanafīs, who regarded the extension of occasions by analogy as legislation, will have nothing to do with these unregulated benefits.[467] For those who do in principle accept the validity of such new regulations, a number of questions remain to be answered. For one thing, how far do the means adopted by the Lawgiver restrict the implementation of new measures? It was agreed that the new measures could not conflict with established law. The classic example of invalidity on this ground (*al-ilghāʾ*) is represented by a *fatwā* of Yaḥyā ibn Yaḥyā, the student of Mālik, ordering a king to expiate his breaking of the fast by fasting two consecutive months. Expiation by fasting is meant to apply only to one who is not in a position to set free a slave. But the wealthy king, reasoned Yaḥyā, would think nothing of freeing a slave and would be bound to repeat his offence.[468] The Ḥanafīs like to contrast this outrageous *fatwā* with that of their own ʿĪsā ibn Abān. ʿĪsā similarly ordered a king to make atonement by fasting, but only after it was clear that the burden of numerous dependents made it impossible for him to free a slave.[469] But apart from such obvious cases of repugnancy, did the new rule have to correspond to the established law? Or was its inherent appropriateness sufficient? Both positions were defended. In al-*Mankhūl*, al-Ghazālī supports the more lenient view on the grounds that "the established law (*uṣūl al-sharīʿa*) must necessarily testify for or against every unregulated benefit."[470] This amounts to the application of the principle of weak permission at the level of rules, not cases. Every new rule that protects a legal interest is

465. *Mustaṣfā*, p. 258.

466. *Irshād*, p. 242.

467. Cf. *Taqrīr*, 3:151.

468. To the list in *Shifāʾ*, p. 219, n. 2, add al-Shāṭibī, *al-Iʿtiṣām*, 2:113–14.

469. *Fawātiḥ*, 2:266; ʿĪsā ibn Māhān in *Taqrīr*, 3:150. Ibn ʿArafa explained Yaḥyā ibn Yaḥyā's ruling in a similar fashion (*Taqrīr*, 3:150).

470. *Mankhūl*, p. 363.

valid unless proven otherwise. The more demanding doctrine is a retrospective demand for effectiveness and did manage to win some Ḥanafī support.[471]

The doctrine of unregulated benefits was most commonly attributed to Mālik and his school, and their excessive use of it was a topic of some controversy.[472] But the attribution did not go unchallenged among the Mālikīs.[473] Ibn Daqīq al-ʿĪd regarded Mālik and Aḥmad ibn Ḥanbal as most attached to its use.[474] Al-Shāfiʿī, too, is supposed to have practiced it.[475] The strongest statement in behalf of its universal acceptance was made by the Mālikī al-Qarāfī (d. 684/1285) who wrote, "If you examine the schools you will find that when they do anything or analogize or distinguish two cases, they do not look for any evidence of the Lawgiver's consideration (*iʿtibār*) of this ground by which they analogize or distinguish. Rather, they are satisfied with mere appropriateness, and this is 'the unregulated benefit.' It is therefore in all the schools."[476]

The same claim is made by Najm al-Dīn al-Ṭūfī (d. 716/1316).[477] But al-Ṭūfī's own doctrine goes far beyond this point. For him, there can be no repugnancy between new regulations and the old law; in such cases, the old law gives way. The new rules abrogate the old. The ends are the same, but the means to attain these ends have changed. For al-Ṭūfī, the only restraint on change is inherent in appropriateness. Those areas of legislation in which the rationality of means and ends is not apparent, ritual law (*al-ʿibādāt*) and fixed measures (*al-muqaddarāt*) must be left unchanged. These he regards as the domain of consensus (*ijmāʿ*), that is, unalterability.[478]

Al-Ṭūfī's radical thesis is the highwater mark of the doctrine of appropriateness. Within analogy, appropriateness functions as a method of discovering the cause that permits the generalization of the revealed law. As the basis for the practice of unregulated benefits, appropriateness is the source of legislation complementary to the revealed law. For al-Ṭūfī, the claims of appropriateness supersede those of the revealed law. Analogy seeks to work with the means chosen by the Lawgiver to achieve His ends. The doctrine of unregulated benefits frees the jurist to add to those means, provided that the new

471. *Taqrīr*, 3:151–53. Cf. *Fawātiḥ*, 2:266.

472. *Mankhūl*, p. 365, gives some specific examples.

473. Ibn al-Ḥājib, *Muntahā*, p. 156.

474. *Fawātiḥ*, 2:266.

475. *Irshād*, p. 242.

476. Qarāfī, p. 394.

477. Sulaymān ibn ʿAbd al-Qawī al-Ṭūfī, *Risāla fī riʿāyat al-maṣlaḥa*, in ʿAbd al-Wahhāb Khallāf, *Maṣādir al-tashrīʿ al-islāmī fī-mā lā naṣṣ fīhi*, p. 116.

478. Al-Ṭūfī, *Risāla*, pp. 128–29. The Muʿtazilī Abū ʿAlī ibn Khallād (Ibn al-Murtaḍā, *Ṭabaqāt al-muʿtazila*, p. 105) already regarded the taking of the Prophet as an example (*al-taʾassī*) as applicable to ritual law alone (al-ʿAllāma al-Ḥillī, *Mabādiʾ al-wuṣūl ilā ʿilm al-uṣūl*, p. 167, n. 3). It should also be noted that the textual basis for al-Ṭūfī's argument, the tradition *lā ḍarar wa-lā ḍirār*, was cited by al-Āmidī as evidence for the validity of the method of appropriateness (Āmidī, 3:263).

rules are consistent with the old. For al-Ṭūfī, it is only the ends of the law that retain their imperative force. The choice of means to serve those ends is given over to the jurist.

For al-Ṭūfī, the progression from appropriateness in analogy to his own doctrine is a natural one. All the schools "except... the Ẓāhirīs are agreed in explaining the law in terms of benefits and the averting of harm."[479] All, too, are agreed with Mālik in supporting the law with unregulated benefits.[480] For al-Ṭūfī, analogy and benefit are inseparable. The universal practice of analogy is clear and convincing evidence of the nature of the law as a means to serve human goals. Where there is no place for analogy, there is no rationality of means and end, and there is no place for change.

The full implementation of his program required that al-Ṭūfī break the link between analogy and consensus. Al-Ṭūfī's doctrine is above all a rejection of certainty within the law. According to al-Ṭūfī, only where analogy is excluded is certainty attainable in the form of consensus. Elsewhere the demand for change requires an adaptable law. "Know that our aim is not to impugn consensus and not to annul it totally. Rather we stand by it in ritual law and fixed measures. Our aim is merely to explain that the principle of benefit taken from the Prophet's saying 'No harm and no retribution' is of greater force than consensus."[481] The old tradition of explaining abrogation in terms of changing human interests is taken up in its most radical consequences.

The restraint had hitherto come from the certainty of the revealed texts. They marked the final stage of change in human affairs, of such change at least as would call for a new legal order. All further adjustments were possible within the boundaries of analogy. And analogy itself tended to coalesce into consensus where again certainty was attained. The Ḥanafīs' doctrine of effectiveness is the strongest possible evidence of their adherence to the means chosen by the Lawgiver. The aim of analogy is not to explain these means, but rather to bring them to a higher level of generality. Should a consensus form, they will be fixed at that new level. To step beyond this limit is to legislate. Within this context, the line dividing jurists can be drawn not between analogists and anti-analogists but between the proponents of unregulated benefits and the others, analogists and anti-analogists alike.[482] The Ḥanafī objection to the method of suggestiveness, that is, appropriateness, was precisely that it did not contain inherent restraints against the tendency of men to remake the law in their own image. Appropriateness rests upon claims for human reason that the Ḥanafīs reject, claims embodied in al-Ījī's description of an inherently appropriate cause: "The appropriateness of the appropriate cause would be attainable by reason even if there were no law, like the relation of the quality of inebriating and prohibition. For its doing away with the reason required by man and its being

479. Al-Ṭūfī, *Risāla*, p. 166.
480. Al-Ṭūfī, *Risāla*, p. 166.
481. Al-Ṭūfī, *Risāla*, pp. 128–29.
482. Ibn Taymiyya, *Iqtiḍā*ʾ, p. 279.

appropriate for prohibition are among the things that it needs no revelation to know."[483] All that we lack is the fact of prohibition itself. The ways of the Lawgiver were patent.

VII. *Istiḥsān*

Although the subject of this chapter is analogy, the important related topic of *istiḥsān* cannot be passed over in silence. The legal issues raised by this topic are so complex that anything like an adequate treatment is out of the question. The opportunity will be taken, however, of addressing some fundamental misunderstandings of *istiḥsān*.

Istiḥsān may be defined broadly as the adoption of a rule of law recognized as a departure from analogy.[484] Corresponding to every such rule, also called *istiḥsān*, there is a rule based on analogy, a *qiyās*. It would seem that *istiḥsān* belongs under the same rubric as the doctrine of unregulated benefits. This is the point of view of the opponents of *istiḥsān*. Thus al-Ghazālī rejects the implementation of unregulated benefits to safeguard merely secondary interests of the law as "legislating on the basis of opinion and *istiḥsān*."[485] This condemnation recalls the famous statement of al-Shāfiʿī: "The practitioner of *istiḥsān* legislates" (*man istaḥsana fa-qad sharaʿa*)."[486] In fact, because every "preference" (as we may translate the term *istiḥsān*) involves a departure from analogy, it could even be said that we are dealing with a mitigated version of al-Ṭūfī's teaching (or that of Yaḥyā ibn Yaḥyā). This view of preference as the expression of expediency is that which dominates Western scholarship on Islamic law. Thus for Brunschvig, "*istiḥsān* consists in adopting without an underlying text or formal reasoning a solution judged good."[487]

The Ḥanafī explanation of preference, however, has been strangely ignored, and this despite the obvious canon of scholarship already enunciated by Abū 'l-Ḥusayn al-Baṣrī: "The partisans of a doctrine know best what their predecessors intended."[488] The Ḥanafīs' claim is that preference is reducible to procedures that are, if not universally accepted, at least within the range of debate. Their answer, in short, is that preference is merely a convenient technical term and is not to be taken in the sense of "I happen to prefer." [489]

483. Al-Ījī, *Sharḥ* 2:245.

484. Bukhārī, 3:311. Cf. Abū Yaʿlā ibn al-Farrāʾ's broader conception of the doctrine (*Musawwada*, p. 452).

485. *Shifāʾ*, p. 208; *Mustaṣfā*, p. 253.

486. *Mankhūl*, p. 374 and note; *Jamʿ*, 2:354. The mystic Muḥyī al-Dīn Ibn ʿArabī claimed that al-Shāfiʿī's followers misunderstood this statement, which was meant as praise (*Fawātiḥ*, 2:231).

487. Robert Brunschvig, "De l'aquisition du legs dans le droit musulman orthodoxe," *Mémoires de l'Académie Internationale de Droit Comparé* 3, pt. 4 (1955): 109.

488. *Muʿtamad*, 2:838.

489. Sarakhsī, 2:200; Bukhārī, 4:13. The commentator at *Jamʿ*, 2:344, who says that al-Shāfiʿī's use of the term should be taken in the ordinary sense is confused. What he means to say is that it should not be taken in the objectionable Ḥanafī sense. It may be observed that a consciously technical usage already

Of course, this reduction did not of itself save preference, for any or all of the procedures grouped under the term could be rejected. We will be concerned primarily with one element of preference, the specialization of the cause. This doctrine was rejected by some Central Asian Ḥanafīs who retained preference. And there were some Ḥanafīs who rejected preference entirely. [490]

Preference was not a problem for the Ḥanafīs alone. The Mālikīs,[491] Ḥanbalīs,[492] and even the Shāfiʿīs[493] inherited the problem of preference from their respective founders. All were confronted with deviations from analogy labelled "preference." Mālik is even supposed to have said that "Nine-tenths of knowledge is preference."[494] The task incumbent upon the later jurists was to show that preference was not a personal attitude elevated to a source of law, as its critics claimed.[495] This was accomplished by reducing preference to its elements. The Mālikīs, as might be expected, tended to see the answer to their problem of preference in the doctrine of unregulated benefits.[496] It was the Ḥanafis, however, who reasonably enough took the lead in this matter. Already Abū 'l-Walīd al-Bājī (d. 474/1081) reports that the Ḥanafīs of his day had ceased to use preference in public disputation.[497] This must be understood to mean that they no longer spoke of preference, not that they gave up their established rules. The Ḥanbalī al-Ṭūfī, moreover, compliments the Ḥanafīs on their masterful treatment of the topic.[498] But the truest indication of their success can be gathered from the words of the great Shāfiʿī al-Subkī (d. 771/1369). Alluding to al-Shāfiʿī's famous condemnation, he could say no more than "If there is a disputed doctrine of preference, then its practitioners do legislate."[499]

---

appears in al-Shaybānī's use of the noun *istiḥsān* and not merely the verb. This is opposed to *qiyās*, both referring to products not processes and impersonal results at that. See *Shorter Encyclopaedia of Islam*, s.v. "*fiqh*."

490. For example, Abū Jaʿfar al-Ṭaḥāwī (Ibn Ḥazm, *Mulakhkhaṣ*, p. 51; *Iḥkām*. 6:16). What this means concretely would make an attractive research topic. Bishr al-Marīsī, of course, rejected *istiḥsān*, the results of analogy being certain for him (*Jawāmiʿ*, f. 82b).

491. Qarāfī, p. 452; *Musawwada*, p. 458; Ibn Ḥazm, *Mulakhkhaṣ*, p. 9; *Iḥkām*, 6:16; *Baḥr*, f. 288b.

492. *Musawwada*, p. 400; *Madkhal*, p. 136.

493. Māwardī, 1:658; ʿAbd Allāh ibn Aḥmad ibn Qudāma, *al-Mughnī*, ed. Ṭāhā Muḥammad al-Zaynī et al. 10 vols. (Cairo: Maktabat al-Qāhira, 1388-89/1968-69), 6:281.

494. *Baḥr*, ff. 334b–335a; al-Shāṭibī, *al-Iʿtiṣām*, 2:138. *Istiḥsān* is explained as *ijtihād* by Ḥasan ibn ʿUmar al-Sīnawānī, *Kitāb al-Aṣl al-jāmiʿ li-īḍāḥ al-durar al-manẓūma fī silk Jamʿ al-jawāmiʿ* (Tunis: Maṭbaʿat al-Nahḍa, 1928), 2:109.

495. Taqī al-Dīn al-Subkī quoted in *Mankhūl*, p. 374, n. 1.

496. Al-Shāṭibī, *al-Iʿtiṣām*, 2:138–39; Ibn al-Anbārī quoted *Irshād*, p. 241.

497. Sulaymān ibn Khalaf al-Bājī, *al-Ḥudūd fī al-uṣūl*, p. 68.

498. Quoted in Ṣafī al-Dīn al-Baghdādī, *Qawāʿid al-uṣūl*, p.119, n. 1.

499. *Jamʿ*, 2:313. See also Ibn al-Ḥājib's discussion (*Muntahā*, pp. 155–56) and his conclusion that there is no disputed doctrine of preference (*Mankhūl*, p. 374, n. 1).

For the Ḥanafīs, there is no source of law named preference. Rather, there are many analogies that are not without competition of one sort or another. Preference is the label put on a solution seen in opposition to some analogy. To say even this much is to risk misunderstanding. Our definition of preference as a departure from analogy is a loose manner of speaking. It is a possible departure. For there are instances in which the Ḥanafīs favor analogy against preference.[500] Sometimes it is an outsider whom they regard as supporting preference against their analogy.[501] One can even find cases where analogy and preference do not clash.[502] A common misapprehension concerning preference is that it identifies a relaxation of the strict rule of analogy. The opposite, in fact, is not infrequently true. In ritual law (*ʿibādāt*) the principle of "precaution" (*iḥtiyāṭ*) is often the basis for preference.[503] In such cases, a more rigorous rule is sustained against analogy. This phenomenon is not confined to the ritual law. In the area of contracts, too, we find more restrictive rules identified as preference.[504] The point of these remarks is to stress that the distinction between analogy and preference is a technical one and is not simply to be identified with a tendency toward leniency.

Once preference is resolved into acceptable components, the question, as Abū Isḥāq al-Shīrāzī correctly says, is one of specific legal issues.[505] The labels analogy and preference, however, are indispensable to the study of a large body of legal doctrine and legal history. As yet modern scholarship has not been willing to follow the trail left for them by the classical jurists.[506] The distinction between analogy and preference goes to the heart of Islamic law understood as a system. Each preference signals a departure from what is perceived to be the direction marked out by systematic reasoning. In such cases, we must always ask what is the system that is being rejected. These were the questions that the Islamic jurists put to themselves, and on some points there were protracted debates over the proper classification of a rule, or more significantly an institution, as analogy or preference. It is incumbent on modern scholarship to determine what these debates were

500. Bukhārī, 4:10; Sarakhsī, 2:204; *Manār*, p. 815.

501. Jaṣṣāṣ, f. 296b; Nasafī, 1:166; *Manār*, p. 815.

502. Muḥammad ibn Aḥmad al-Samarqandī, *Tuḥfat al-fuqahā'*, ed. Muḥammad Zakī ʿAbd al-Barr (Damascus: Maṭbaʿat Jāmiʿat Dimashq, 1377–79/1958–59), 3:532.

503. *Al-akhdh bi'l-iḥtiyāṭ ʿamal bi-aqwā al-dalā'il* (*Manār*, p. 30). For specific examples, see Abū Bakr ibn Masʿūd al-Kāsānī, *Badā'iʿ al-ṣanā'iʿ fī tartīb al-sharā'iʿ* (Cairo: Zakariyyā' ʿAlī Yūsuf, n.d.), 1:147; *Madkhal*, p. 136. See also al-Ghunaymī, *al-Lubāb fī sharḥ al-Kitāb*, 1:79: *al-iḥtiyāṭ fī al-ʿibādāt amr ḥasan*, and more generally, Ibn Taymiyya, *Rafʿ al-malām ʿan al-a'imma al-aʿlām*, p. 47.

504. *Jawāmiʿ*, f. 83b (on the requirement of the immediate payment of the price in the *salam* contract); *Madkhal*, p. 136 (on the *ʿīna* contract).

505. *Lumaʿ*, p. 71.

506. Particularly cavalier in this regard is Chafik Chehata, "Études de philosophie musulmane du droit: II. L'"Équité' en tant que source du droit hanafite," *Studia Islamica* 25 (1966): 134. Contrast his attitude with that of Guido Cimino, the translator of Abdur Rahim, *I principî della giurisprudenza musulmana secondo le scuole hanafita, sciafeita, e hanbalita* (Rome: Casa editrice italiana, 1922), p. 383, n. 1.

about and what hinged upon their resolution. Particularly in the case of the Ḥanafīs, one must also not lose sight of another question: What does their consistent application of this distinction tell us about the development of their school?[507]

VIII. Specialization of the Cause

Closely related to *istiḥsān* is the obscure doctrine of the specialization of the cause (*takhṣīṣ al-ʿilla*). Simply put, the question is whether a putative cause is invalidated if a case can be found in which the cause appears without the proper legal qualification (*ḥukm*). This case forms an exception to the operation of the cause, and the cause, like a general term, is thus "specialized." Every case of *istiḥsān* would appear to be one of the specialization of the cause.[508] This is because opposed to every *istiḥsān* there is an analogy that is rejected in favor of some text, consensus, or a stronger analogy. The cause upon which the rejected analogy depends is present in each such case, but without the expected legal consequences.[509] Enough has been said to indicate that the specialization of the cause is the Islamic counterpart of the modern problem of statistical explanation.[510] Not only is the cause of only probable validity, but its operation in a given case is also only probable according to the proponents of specialization. Because no given case can invalidate a statistical generalization, establishing the truth or falsehood of such a generalization presents a particular difficulty.[511] Similarly, a major objection to the doctrine of the specialization of the cause was that it led to the infallibility of *ijtihād*. The specialization of the cause is thus a bridge between our discussion of analogy and that of *ijtihād*, the concluding subject of this study. At the same time, it extends our treatment of the models of the legal cause.

Later writers on *uṣūl al-fiqh* offer a highly compressed and unsympathetic account of what had come to be regarded as a dispute without substance.[512] The controversy surrounding the specialization of the cause is labelled as merely verbal (*lafẓī*).[513] Already,

507. Ibn Taymiyya, *Naqḍ al-manṭiq*, p. 40, is suggestive in this regard (extreme analogists such as Zufar created the background against which others practiced *istiḥsān*).

508. George Makdisi, "Ibn Taimīya's Autograph Manuscript on *Istiḥsān*: Materials for the Study of Islamic Legal Thought," in *Arabic and Islamic Studies in Honor of Hamilton A. R. Gibb*, ed. G. Makdisi (Cambridge: Harvard University Press, 1965), p. 460.

509. Sarakhsī, 2:213.

510. This is precisely one formulation of the doctrine: *ghalabat wujūd al-ḥukm ʿindahā* (sc. *al-ʿilla*) (Bukhārī, 4:33).

511. See Jennifer Trusted, *The Logic of Scientific Inference: An Introduction* (London: Macmillan, 1979), pp. 132–33.

512. Nasafī, 2:172; *Talwīḥ*, 3:13.

513. *Fawātiḥ*, 2:279; *Irshād*, p. 225.

however, al-Jaṣṣāṣ urged that the verbal solution that is readily available not be used to explain away the doctrine of specialization, which he attributes to the earlier Ḥanafī masters. Every case in which they applied *istiḥsān* could be reformulated in terms of causes not subject to the reproach of specialization, but this is simply not authentic Ḥanafī teaching.[514] The reformulation that al-Jaṣṣāṣ was referring to is quite simple. It consisted of adding further determinations to what was the putative cause; the absence of those features that characterize the exceptional case is taken as part of the cause or as a condition for its operation.[515] The question, then, is which is the correct analysis. Is the expected legal effect absent because the operation of the cause is blocked by an "impediment" (*mānic*), or is there no effect because there is no complete cause? The alternative analyses are always available.[516]

Within Ḥanafism, the dispute over the specialization of the cause constitutes the inner dimension of *istiḥsān*. The Ḥanafīs agree in recognizing preference. They differ as to whether preference is to be identified with the specialization of the cause. According to al-Jaṣṣāṣ the attribution of specialization to the early Ḥanafīs was almost universal among the Ḥanafīs of Baghdad.[517] Such was the view of al-Karkhī, al-Jaṣṣāṣ's teacher.[518] The Qāḍī al-Khalīl ibn Aḥmad al-Sijzī, who died in Samarqand (d. 378/989), is mentioned as another scholar who supported this attribution to Abū Ḥanīfa.[519] Among the Central Asian Ḥanafīs, support for the doctrine reached its peak with Abū Zayd al-Dabūsī, of whom al-Ghazālī speaks as "the most extreme proponent of specialization" (*ashadd al-nās ghuluwwan fī takhṣīṣ al-ᶜilal*).[520] Abū 'l-Muᶜīn al-Nasafī, the Bazdawī brothers, al-Sarakhsī, and al-Samarqandī are, however, all opposed to the doctrine.[521] Such, too, was the teaching of al-Māturīdī.[522] Along with the Ḥanafīs, and perhaps even more staunchly, the Mālikīs are adherents of the doctrine of specialization, and this is not surprising in view of their acceptance of *istiḥsān*.[523] Both the Ḥanbalīs and Shāfiᶜīs are split on the issue, with the latter the more solidly opposed to the doctrine.[524] Insofar as specialization could be identified

514. Jaṣṣāṣ, ff. 149a,b.

515. *Fa-najᶜal ᶜadam al-māniᶜ juzᵓ al-ᶜilla aw sharṭan lahu* (*Talwīḥ*, 3:13).

516. *Fa-'lladhī juᶜila ᶜindahu dalīl al-khuṣūṣ jaᶜalnāhu dalīl al-ᶜadam* (Nasafī, 2:178).

517. Jaṣṣāṣ, f. 299a. For *Jawāmiᶜ*, f. 79a, specialization is the doctrine of some of the later Ḥanafīs.

518. *Jawāmiᶜ*, f. 79a; *Fawātiḥ*, 2:278.

519. *Fawātiḥ*, 2:278.

520. *Shifāᵓ*, p. 465.

521. *Tabṣira*, f. 314a; Bazdawī, 4:36; *Ḥujaj*, f. 45b; Sarakhsī, 2:108; *Mīzān*, f. 166a.

522. *Mīzān*, f. 165b. The anti-specialization position is attributed to Abū Ḥanīfa in the Shiᶜi work, al-Ḥusaynī, *Munyat al-labīb*, p. 320.

523. Al-Shāṭibī, *al-Iᶜtiṣām*, 2:138; Ibn ᶜAqīl, p. 187.

524. Ḥanbalīs: *Rawḍa*, p. 172; *ᶜUdda*, f. 213b. Shāfiᶜīs: *Rawḍa*, p. 172; *Mīzān*, f. 165b; Māwardī, 1:542; Asnawī, 3:79. And on al-Shāfiᶜī, see *Mīzān*, f. 163a.

with *istiḥsān*, we are not surprised to find al-Jaṣṣāṣ claiming that even those jurists who reject specialization in name often practice it.[525]

Much of the obscurity surrounding the issue of specialization stems from the fact that, throughout the history of Islamic legal theory, specialization of the cause was merely a label for very different theoretical considerations. That a particular jurist is for or against specialization is not in itself especially informative. We will touch upon the main elements as they emerge from a survey of the literature in enough detail to suggest the complexity of the problem. Particular attention will be given to the teaching of several individual jurists: Abū ʿAbd Allāh al-Baṣrī, Abū Yaʿlā ibn al-Farrāʾ, and al-Samarqandī.

A fairly solid starting point for understanding the early doctrine of specialization is provided by al-Jaṣṣāṣ. As we have seen, al-Jaṣṣāṣ recognized that it would be a simple matter to reformulate Ḥanafī doctrine so as to avoid specialization. But this would have been dishonest. The early Ḥanafīs were not troubled by the fact that their causes did not operate without exception. Legal causes are signs, and as such they function almost like the signs of language, which, it is agreed, are subject to specialization.[526] Outside of language, the paradigm of such signs that are only probabilistic is the rain cloud. Heavy clouds function as a sign of rain even if they are not invariably followed by rain.[527] The identification of legal causes as signs is supported by the fact that the Islamic legal order followed a period in which causes were present without their legal consequences.[528]

Specialization as a direct consequence of the adoption of the sign model of the cause is well substantiated throughout the literature of *uṣūl*.[529] The standard version of the sign

525. Jaṣṣāṣ, f. 302a. On specialization as particularly characteristic of the jurist uncorrupted by an alien discipline, see *Shifāʾ*, p. 486, and Ibn Taymiyya, *Iqāmat al-dalīl*, 3:162.

526. Jaṣṣāṣ, f. 299b. Cf. *Mīzān*, f. 166b, and *Talwīḥ*, 3:14, which point out the specifically linguistic character of *iḍmār* and *taqyīd*. This assimilation of causes to words is the root of the rather unhelpful formulation of specialization in terms of the generality of concepts (*ʿumūm al-maʿānī*) as in Nasafī, 1:111.

527. *Muʿtamad*, 2:834; Bukhārī, 4:33.

528. *Jawāmiʿ*, f. 79a.

529. *Mughnī*, 17:86 (Abū ʿAbd Allāh al-Baṣrī's earlier position); *Musawwada*, p. 413 (Abū 'l-Khaṭṭāb al-Kalwadhānī); *Jawāmiʿ*, f. 79a; *Fuṣūl*, 1:48 (the Muʿtazilī interlocutor of al-Mufīd). The blurred image of the doctrine of specialization that emerges from the texts is in large measure due to the superimposition of another scheme on that of the sign model. Already Abū ʿAbd Allāh al-Baṣrī was able to combine specialization with his idiosyncratic version of the motive model. In later legal theory, which is dominated by the motive model, we find that the cause as motive is what is subject to specialization. Ibn Qudāma presents the sign and motive arguments for specialization side by side (*Rawḍa*, p. 172). Al-Qarāfī treats the justification of specialization along the lines of appropriateness as the standard understanding of the doctrine (Qarāfī, p. 400). So also al-Āmidī and al-Asnawī treat specialization as a technical question within the framework of appropriateness. The question for them is whether a benefit remains such even when it is equal to or outweighed by the detriment in a particular case (Āmidī, 3:50; Asnawī, 3:40). Ibn Taymiyya goes furthest in this direction. For him, specialization is especially reasonable (*qawī*) for one who accepts the motive model of the cause, as opposed to the sign model (*Iqāmat al-dalīl*, 3:162–63). See also *Baḥr*, f. 289a (Ibn al-Labbān [d. 749/1348]).

model not only allows for specialization, it requires it. This is because for the sign model, the function of the cause is to extend the legal qualification from the original case (*aṣl*). In the original case itself, the cause has no function, for the legal qualification is based on the text (*naṣṣ*), not on the cause. It is for this reason that the sign model will not allow for intransitive causes. The original case, according to this analysis, is always an instance of specialization.[530]

Opposed to the view of legal causes as mere signs that are subject to exception is that which assimilates them to rational causes (*al-ʿilal al-ʿaqliyya*).[531] These are the efficient causes (*al-ʿilal al-mūjiba*) with which theology, *kalām*, deals; and the role of theology as the paradigm of rationality is particularly clear in this topic of specialization. Many who rejected specialization distinguished between explicit and elicited causes. Elicited causes were invalidated by specialization, but explicit causes were known to be effective and remained valid even when subject to specialization. A more uncompromising opposition to specialization refused to accept the specialization of explicit causes. Specialization indicated that these causes were subject to unexpressed conditions. This was the position of al-Samarqandī, for example. Among Shāfiʿīs, it is associated with Abū Isḥāq al-Isfarāyīnī, and according to al-Ghazālī, this extreme view was a direct consequence of the impress of theology on al-Isfarāyīnī's thinking (*ghalaba ʿalayhi ṭabʿ al-kalām*).[532]

On the other hand, Abū ʿAbd Allāh al-Baṣrī, who always admitted some form of specialization despite changes in his teaching, is singled out by ʿAbd al-Jabbār for his insistence on the necessity of distinguishing between legal and rational causes.[533] The possibility of regarding legal causes in the light of rational ones depended on their acquiring such a validity within the Islamic legal order as to mark a break with their former ineffectiveness.[534] The assimilation of legal causes to rational ones was carried furthest by early theologian jurists, such as al-Aṣamm, his student Ibn ʿUlayya, and Bishr al-Marīsī. We are not surprised to find Bishr among those who rejected specialization.[535]

The views of the Muʿtazilī Abū ʿAbd Allāh al-Baṣrī and of the Ḥanbalī Abū Yaʿlā ibn al-Farrāʾ are examples of individual adaptations of the prevailing causal models. As noted above in connection with the intransitive cause, Abū ʿAbd Allāh al-Baṣrī abandoned the sign model for the view that legal causes represent "motives" (*dawāʿī*). This change was marked by a corresponding adjustment in his position on specialization. As a proponent of the sign model, Abū ʿAbd Allāh had allowed specialization under all circumstances

530. Al-Samarqandī defends anti-specialization at considerable length (*Mīzān*, ff. 149a, 167a–168b). Bukhārī, 3:317, strains to argue that the anti-*qāṣira* position is not related to specialization.

531. *Lumaʿ*, p. 67; Māwardī, 1:542.

532. *Shifāʾ*, p. 482; *Mustaṣfā*, p. 469. This was also the position of al-Isfarāyīnī's student ʿAbd al-Qāhir al-Baghdādī (Bukhārī, 4:32).

533. *Mughnī*, 17:335.

534. Ibn ʿAqīl, p. 187.

535. Jaṣṣāṣ, f. 299a.

(*ʿalā kull wajh*). His new position was that specialization was acceptable in the case of positive injunctions but not prohibitions.[536] This view followed from his understanding of the operation of motives.

Abū Yaʿlā, it may be recalled from our discussion of the ontology of the cause, distinguished between two sets of causes. The causes elicited by the jurist from the revealed texts were signs whereby the rule of law might be extended to new cases (*ʿillat al-ḥukm*). The jurist was not entitled to identify these causes with the policy behind the divine legislation. When a cause was explicitly specified in a text, however, it was to be taken to indicate the interest served by the law (*ʿillat al-maṣlaḥa*).[537] Revelation, in fact, was the only means of knowing these causes. But this ontological difference (itself resting on an issue of epistemology) did not lead Abū Yaʿlā to make a corresponding distinction in his doctrine of specialization. For him, the concept of a cause, even if that cause was a mere sign, required that it be uniformly accompanied by its qualification (*ḥukm*).[538] When an explicit cause turned out to be subject to specialization, this meant that what appeared to be the motive cause of the law was only part of the cause.[539] An elicited cause subject to specialization was no cause at all.

Such is Abū Yaʿlā's teaching in *al-ʿUdda*. According to Ibn Taymiyya, however, toward the end of his life, Abū Yaʿlā came to adopt a more favorable view of specialization.[540] Abū Yaʿlā now regarded specialization as sound Ḥanbalī doctrine, consonant with Aḥmad ibn Ḥanbal's legal rulings.[541] Clearly, this change required a corresponding change in Abū Yaʿlā's general conception of the cause. But we are not told if there was an accompanying change in his ontology. Did he continue to distinguish so sharply between explicit and elicited causes? Whatever the answer to this question, it is apparent enough how many features of the theory of analogy converged in the issue of specialization. The complexity of the problem of specialization is only symptomatic of the unusual instability of the doctrine of the ontology of the cause.

Somewhat surprisingly, the problem of the specialization of the cause did not remain merely a technical detail within the larger scheme of the causal models. The vehemence with which the topic came to be debated is suggested by the statement attributed to al-Bāqillānī that "if it were confirmed to me that al-Shāfiʿī held the specialization of the cause, I would not count him among the *uṣūlis*."[542] The theological implications of

536. *Mughnī*, 17:337–38. Al-Bāqillānī regarded this doctrine as a departure from consensus (*Baḥr*, ff. 288b–89a).

537. *ʿUdda*, f. 212b.

538. *ʿUdda*, f. 214a.

539. *ʿUdda*, f. 215a.

540. Ibn Taymiyya, *Iqāmat al-dalīl*, 3:161.

541. *Musawwada*, pp. 414–15.

542. *Baḥr*, f. 289a. Almost precisely the same language is attributed to al-Bāqillānī with reference to al-Shāfiʿī's position on the issue of *taṣwīb* (*Baḥr*, f. 357a; *Mankhūl*, p. 453).

specialization began to be drawn out, and the doctrine, seen in the light of these implications, became the focus of considerable animosity.

Within the Central Asian Ḥanafī tradition, a number of objectionable doctrines are derived from the acceptance of specialization. In the tenth century, it was the theological problem of ability preceding action (*al-istiṭāʿa qabl al-fiʿl*) that seems to have been uppermost in the minds of the opponents of specialization. If causes could be present without their effects, this supported the Muʿtazilī doctrine that humans had an ability to act that preceded their action. Thus Abū Bakr Muḥammad ibn al-Faḍl al-Kamarī (d. 371/981), in urging that rational and legal causes had to be distinguished as far as specialization was concerned, explicitly confirmed his adherence to the orthodox doctrine that ability could not precede action.[543]

Other Muʿtazilī dogmas that are cited in connection with specialization are the doctrine of the intermediate state of the sinner (*al-manzila bayna al-manzilatayn*), the eternal punishment of the unrepentant sinner, and the failure of the divine will to make the unbeliever believe.[544] But the weight of emphasis was placed on more obviously legal consequences of the doctrine of specialization. The predominant association here is that between specialization and the infallibility of *ijtihād* (*taṣwīb*).

Al-Māturīdī and in his footsteps al-Samarqandī see in specialization the attribution of inconsistency to the law (*nisbat al-tanāquḍ li'l-sharʿ*): the legal order supports the contention that a particular character is and is not at one and the same time a legal cause.[545] This line of argument focuses on the operation of the cause and is within the theological atmosphere that led to the association of specialization and the debate over ability. Al-Samarqandī in this context does not explicitly draw the connection between inconsistency and infallibilism, although he does so elsewhere.[546]

Another line of attack focused on the relation of specialization to the counterbalance of arguments (*takāfuʾ al-adilla*).[547] For when some putative cause is present in two original cases with conflicting legal effects, the two cases can be extended without regard to the fact that each one specializes the other. A position that recognizes the counterbalance of arguments opens the way to an arbitrary choice of one over the other, which in turn amounts to infallibilism.[548] Here, too, the reader is left to work out the chain of thought for himself.

543. Bukhārī, 4:188; *Ḥujaj*, f. 45b; *Tabṣira*, f. 314a; *Shifāʾ*, p. 459. That the issue of *istiṭāʿa* was largely a tenth-century one is suggested by the fact that neither al-Bazdawī nor al-Sarakhsī mentions it in his *uṣūl* work. It receives only brief treatment in *Tabṣira*.

544. Bukhārī, 4:39; Sarakhsī, 2:212.

545. *Ḥujaj*, f. 45b; *Mīzān*, ff. 166a, 170a.

546. *Mīzān*, f. 204a.

547. Bukhārī, 4:38; *Burhān*, f. 282; Ibn ʿAqīl, p. 187.

548. Bukhārī, 4:39.

Generally, however, the classical Ḥanafī texts made explicit the link between specialization and infallibilism. They do so by setting specialization within the context of public disputation. There it becomes clear that no counterexample can be invoked against a putative cause since the disputant can always fall back on specialization. Without a publicly recognized mode of invalidating causes, infallibilism will ensue.[549] A second step connects the infallibility of *ijtihād* with the Muʿtazilī doctrine of optimism (*al-aṣlaḥ*), that is, that God is obliged to do what is best for man.[550]

The doctrine of specialization went from a technical detail of the causal models to a topic of heated debate to an obscure point of legal theory. The last phase of its history resulted from growing uncertainty as to its theological significance. In the law, it was not clear whether specialization led to infallibilism or whether it was infallibilism that implied specialization.[551] If the latter was the case, then the real object of concern should be infallibilism, the root evil. But even apart from this, the two links in the chain leading from specialization to infallibilism to optimism were both severed. Infallibilism could rest as well on the orthodox doctrine of God's forbearance from imposing an impossible task (*taklīf mā la yuṭāq*) as on Muʿtazilī optimism.[552] Alternatively, infallibilism supported only the fact of God's having done what was best, not His obligation to do so.[553] As to specialization implying infallibilism, this depended on a disputant's insistence on the validity of his original cause in the face of specialization. He could, however, save his position merely by treating the counterexample as an exception and incorporating it into the original cause.[554] Once the theological significance of specialization became unclear, the issue was without substance. Its original setting within the causal models was now obscured. All that remained was a mere token. "Since the doctrine of specialization," wrote one scholar, "has become a watchword of the Muʿtazila in our region it should be avoided, just as one refrains from wearing a signet ring on the right hand because the Rāfiḍīs do so and from dressing like an unbeliever."[555]

Up until now we have been tracing the external history of the doctrine of specialization, that is, its treatment as a distinct issue capable of acceptance or rejection. In what follows, our concern will be with specialization in its relation to the work of the jurist. We have already mentioned that Abū Zayd al-Dabūsī was an extreme proponent of specialization. In part, al-Dabūsī's vehemence in defense of the doctrine undoubtedly grew out of his sensitivity to the theological attack that had been launched against it and that

549. Nasafī, 2:175; Bukhārī, 4:38.

550. Bukhārī, 4:38.

551. The latter was the view of ʿAlī ibn Muḥammad al-Ḍarīrī (d. 666/1268) quoted by his student al-Bukhārī (Bukhārī, 4:38). So also Nasafī, 2:176.

552. Bukhārī, 4:38.

553. *Manār*, p. 829, margin.

554. Bukhārī, 4:38.

555. Bukhārī, 4:38.

questioned the orthodoxy of its proponents. Significantly, al-Dabūsī attributed specialization not only to Abū Ḥanīfa but to al-Shāfiʿī as well.[556] But the main impetus for al-Dabūsī's campaign on behalf of specialization was that he saw it as part and parcel of the doctrine of effectiveness, which he had taken it upon himself to set down definitively.[557]

For Abū Zayd, the solution to the problem of a public test for the validity of a cause was found in effectiveness. Once a cause met the standard of effectiveness, its validity was not called into question by a simple counterexample. Legal causes are identified in the light of the revealed sources, and these same sources are the basis for our knowledge of the nature of these causes. For Abū Zayd, legal causes are signs in the sense that they do not constrain in themselves, but only insofar as the law makes them constrain.[558] For al-Dabūsī, this constraint simply does not entail that legal effect follow legal cause with absolute uniformity. Both the Ḥanafīs and the Shāfiʿīs, he notes, recognized rules that deviated from analogy.[559] The gist of al-Dabūsī's position is that law constitutes an integral domain. Those who have not come to understand the ways of the divine law are led to the superficial view that opposes specialization. For him, the alternative analysis that incorporates exceptional cases into the formulation of the cause is verbal (*lafẓī*) as opposed to legal (*fiqhī*). Human instinct inclines man to what is tangible rather than to what is intangible and inward.[560] The tone of Abū Zayd's treatment of specialization is entirely in consonance with his attack on the doctrine of consistency, which would, of course, oppose itself absolutely to specialization.[561]

While al-Dabūsī's doctrine of specialization is developed under the domination of his commitment to effectiveness, al-Samarqandī's work exhibits a thoroughgoing commitment to anti-specialization. And for him, this involved the careful reformulation of some issues that his predecessors had neglected to bring into line with their rejection of specialization. At the same time, however, al-Samarqandī is equally committed to the doctrine of effectiveness. We shall see how anti-specialization and effectiveness represent somewhat incompatible tendencies within legal methodology and how al-Samarqandī was called upon to work out an accommodation between the two.

556. *Baḥr*, f. 289a. Cf. *Mīzān*, f. 163a, which seeks to correct this attribution.

557. *Irshād*, p. 225 (quoting al-Samʿānī).

558. Dabūsī, ff. 133b–134a.

559. Dabūsī, f. 137b.

560. Dabūsī, ff. 137b–138a.

561. Bukhārī, 3:373: *ahl al-ṭard lā yarawna* (read thus) *takhṣīṣ al-ʿilla*. Bukhārī, 4:42: the *ṭardiyya* are *ashaddu inkāran li'l-takhṣīṣ min ahl al-taʾthīr*. This is the sense of the saying that the proponent of specialization is a pure jurist, but its opponent one of the crowd of the *ḥashwiyya* (*Shifāʾ*, pp. 459, 486). Al-Dabūsī, it will be recalled, labelled the *ṭardiyya* the *ḥashwiyya* of the analogists. Cf. Bazdawī, 4:41; *Manār*, p. 828, which connect specialization with the causes of the *ṭardiyya*. *Mīzān*, f. 166a, assumes the compatibility of *iṭṭirād* and *takhṣīṣ*. See also the quotation from al-Kiyā al-Ṭabarī in Bukhārī, 3:373. For a proposed solution, see *Fawātiḥ*, 2:342.

A crucial piece of evidence cited by al-Dabūsī in favor of specialization was the widespread recognition by the jurists that there were rules of law that represented departures from analogy.[562] It was, in fact, required of a correct analogy that it not be based on such a rule.[563] Al-Samarqandī, however, rejects the notion of a rule that is a departure from analogy, as consistent only with specialization. The recognition of a rule as a departure from analogy depends on the prior perception of an underlying analogy supporting an expected legal qualification that revelation disconfirms. But this analysis is precisely that involved in every case of specialization.[564] Rather than such a case being a departure from analogy, for al-Samarqandī it represents an outright arationality. It is not to be extended by analogy because it is unintelligible (*ghayr maᶜqūl al-maᶜnā*).[565] Imām al-Ḥaramayn, also a confirmed opponent of specialization, had similarly argued that an exceptional case could not be intelligible.[566] As a practical matter, it might appear that this is a distinction without a difference, since no extension proceeds from such an exceptional case, whether it is termed a departure from analogy or an arationality. But the difference between the two positions is not to be dismissed so lightly.

Exactly what is at stake becomes clearer if we look at another area of analogist doctrine that al-Samarqandī had to bring into line. Perhaps the fundamental notion at the heart of specialization is that of the specializing "impediment" (*al-mâniᶜ*),[567] and Abū Zayd had elaborated a complex scheme of causes and impediments to explain a variety of legal phenomena.[568] This scheme was already criticized by al-Samarqandī's immediate predecessors, al-Bazdawī and al-Sarakhsī.[569] It could obviously find no place within al-Samarqandī's even more consistent attack on specialization. Quite simply, al-Samarqandī has no place for the notion of an impediment. A cause that fails to operate is simply no cause at all.[570] In jettisoning the impediment, al-Samarqandī adopts a scheme that is ontologically simpler than that of al-Dabūsī. In place of the additional entity, the impediment, al-Samarqandī has a more complex cause, but the complexity is epistemological, not ontological. Every case of apparent specialization requires a further determination of what we supposed to be the complete cause. Abū Zayd's analysis preserves the cause as complete but introduces an impediment.

562. Such a rule being called by the Shāfiᶜīs *makhṣūṣ ᶜan al-qiyās* and by the Ḥanafīs *maᶜdūl bihi ᶜan al-qiyās* (Dabūsī, f. 137b; Bukharī, 4:33).

563. For example, Bazdawī, 3:302.

564. *Mīzān*, f. 170a; Bukhārī, 3:303.

565. *Mīzān*, f. 170a.

566. Asnawī, 3:80.

567. Sarakhsī, 2:212–13: "it is what they call a specializing impediment"; Bukhārī, 3:373, 4:39; Nasafī, 3:177.

568. Dabūsī, ff. 146a–47a.

569. Bazdawī, 4:40–42; Sarakhsī, 2:213–15. See also Nasafī, 2:178; *Manār*, p. 833.

570. *Mīzān*, ff. 160a–61b.

The crucial difference between the two analyses is that al-Samarqandī is constrained to allow more room for what is not open to explanation. In adopting the scheme that does without the impediment, al-Samarqandī sacrifices the apparatus required to explain the exceptional case, which must remain unintelligible. For Abū Zayd, however, the exceptional case can be further analyzed into the cause and its impediment. The impediment has to be appropriate to the specializing case (*māni*ᶜ *ṣāliḥ*).[571] This means that the impediment now shares in the explanatory force of the cause.[572] Once this possibility of explanation exists, the question of extending the exceptional case is put in a different light. This does not in itself mean that the longstanding Ḥanafī reservations against extending the exceptional case (*al-qiyās* ᶜ*alā mawḍi*ᶜ *al-istiḥsān*) immediately vanished.[573] The source of these reservations lies in epistemological issues of a different order from those that concern us at this point. What is true, however, is that there is now no inherent barrier to the extension of these cases as there is for al-Samarqandī.

The relation of specialization to effectiveness represents a particular concern for al-Samarqandī. Committed as he was to both effectiveness and anti-specialization, al-Samarqandī could not accept al-Dabūsī's position that specialization was of no consequence once effectiveness was established. But neither was al-Samarqandī content with the simple assertion that an effective cause was proof against specialization.[574] Insight into al-Samarqandī's nuanced accommodation of the two doctrines is provided by Ibn Taymiyya's illuminating exposition of legal styles. We quote this important passage at length:

> The dominant convention among the Iraqis in the fourth century, both before it and after it until close to the fifth century, was to require the propodent (*al-mustadill*) to present a consistent cause in his debates and writings. The Khurasanians, however, did not require this but required him to show the effectiveness of his cause. They allow a counterexample if he can offer a distinction (*yujīzūna al-naqḍ bi'l-farq*). This style gained dominance over the Iraqis after the fifth century. You will find the books written by us Ḥanabalīs and others on legal controversy (*al-khilāf*) according to the style of their time and place. Since the Iraqis at the time of Qāḍī Abū Yaᶜlā and Qāḍī ᶜAbd al-Wahhāb in Egypt and Abū Isḥāq al-Shīrāzī, etc., required consistency (*al-iṭṭirād*), their analogies were dominated by precision of expression (*taḥrīr al-*ᶜ*ibārāt*) and the achievement of consistent analogies. These are a source of universal principles (*al-qawā*ᶜ*id al-kulliyyāt*). But the distraction of the mind from the core of the question forces

571. Nasafī, 2:176.

572. Thus *al-ta*ᶜ*līl bi'l-māni*ᶜ (Asnawī, 3:116).

573. Bājī, p. 157; *Luma*ᶜ, p. 60; *Musawwada*, p. 399; *Mīzān*, f. 166b. Where *istiḥsān* is based on a stronger analogy, there is no bar to its extension. The two analyses agree. But the other cases of *istiḥsān* are the significant ones (Sarakhsī, 2:213).

574. As in Nasafī, 2:176, 178.

> the disputant or listener to occupy himself with what is not really relevant to the question, at the expense of what is. For this reason, they took the trouble to come up with a consistent analogy without observing that the causal character departed from the genus of legal causes and without establishing that the character was the cause of the legal qualification. Some even went into sheer *ṭardiyyāt*. But since the later Iraqis and some early Khurasanians did not require this, they opened the door for themselves to demand the effectiveness of the character. This method is a source of discussions of appropriateness and effectiveness according to their knowledge of traditions and legal reasoning. This method is more difficult for the proponent inasmuch as he is required to establish the effectiveness of his cause. The first is more difficult inasmuch as he is required to avoid a counterexample (*al-iḥtirāz ʿan al-naqḍ*).[575]

This passage points to the difficulty that faced al-Samarqandī. An uncompromising commitment to consistency would so encumber the system of effectiveness as to rob it of its role in validating legal causes. A single counterexample would mean that what appeared to be an explicit cause was not really such. As incomplete, the cause could not then be used as a paradigm for the identification of elicited causes. Al-Samarqandī's solution is an accommodation in the direction of specialization. The doctrine of effectiveness is preserved by positing a core or inchoate cause (*rukn al-ʿilla*), which is identified by effectiveness and which enters into the genetic relationships required by the system of effectiveness. But this core cause is not an operative cause without particular conditions being met.[576] Once again, al-Samarqandī adopts an epistemologically more complex scheme to preserve the ontological simplicity of a doctrine that does without impediments. For al-Dabūsī, the causes identified by effectiveness are complete in themselves. In al-Samarqandī's scheme, they are only potential causes. Their operation depends on their fulfilling particular conditions. "These conditions do not have the force (*athar*) of the core, but another force and another utility (*maṣlaḥa*) is attached to them."[577]

The complexity of al-Samarqandī's solution only highlights the facility with which analogy operates within the framework of specialization. In simplest terms, specialization means that once a cause has been identified, the jurist is entitled to use it without regard to any impediments as long as the counterexamples do not destroy his probable opinion (*ẓann*) that the cause is valid.[578] This is the practical difference between specialization and all varieties of anti-specialization. Al-Samarqandī's accommodation of effectiveness to anti-specialization removes effectiveness from the practical plane altogether. Effectiveness does not concern causes at all, but only their core. These are not subject

575. Ibn Taymiyya, *Iqāmat al-dalīl*, 3:160–61.
576. *Mīzān*, f. 156a.
577. *Mīzān*, f. 156a.
578. *Jawāmiʿ*, f. 79a; Badakhshī, 3:78.

to specialization because specialization is restricted to what purport to be causes. There thus arises a dual structure, the inner structure of effectiveness, which is theoretical, and the external, practical structure of the core causes surrounded by their epicyclical conditions. Its very subtlety ensured that this accommodation would have no following.

Summary

The controversy over analogy among the Muslim jurists is only one, though the most significant, side of the controversy over the role of probability in the law. Part of the anti-analogists' critique was their claim that there existed no authentic method of analogizing. The Ḥanafīs' answer to this challenge was the method of effectiveness, which relied on "causes" established by the Lawgiver or consensus to corroborate those put forward by the individual jurist. The success of this method ultimately made it possible to grade analogies numerically. In competition with effectiveness was the method of appropriateness, which depended on the recognition of the cause of the law in the light of its purpose. The compatibility of this method with their ethical doctrine was a problem for the Ashʿarīs. Appropriateness, furthermore, was allied to the controversial practice of "unregulated benefits" and to the still more radical thesis of Najm al-Dīn al-Ṭūfī. *Istiḥsān*, at least according to its Ḥanafī adherents, is a technical term for a departure from analogy on any of a number of grounds and is not to be taken in the sense of an arbitrary personal preference for what is less demanding. *Istiḥsān* does, however, raise the question of the specialization of the cause, which was hotly debated among the Central Asian Ḥanafīs. Although they were united in their adherence to the method of effectiveness, the Ḥanafīs, as the controversy over specialization indicates, were unable to reach agreement on the proper understanding of the causes that they were seeking: Were they identical to the motives behind the law, or were they merely the necessary apparatus for analogy?

Addenda to Chapter Four

In this chapter and the following references to issues in the philosophy of science make their appearance. The relevance of these issues to *qiyās* and *ijtihād* is not hard to explain. The legal theorists had to address well-known challenges to the entire practice of extending the law beyond its textual bases, challenges strikingly reminiscent of Hume's attack on induction that has now occupied many generations of philosophers. Once a version of *qiyās* became popular that appealed to legal causes *(ʿilal)*, debates among jurists naturally turned in the first instance on such formal considerations as *ṭard* and *ʿaks* that admitted of relatively easy assessment. It was only subsequently that substantive criteria such as *munāsaba* and *taʾthīr* came to dominate their debates. The interest of the *uṣūlī*s in formal methods parallels the efforts of philosophers of science under Hume's influence to develop a reductionist regularity theory of causation expressed in the logic of conditions. The adoption of substantive tests for legal causes left open the question of whether they were to be construed along realist or instrumentalist lines, a debate that parallels that between realist and antirealist interpretations of scientific theories.

Legal disputation (*jadal*) played a critical role in the development of the theory of analogy as we find it in the classical *uṣūl al-fiqh* literature. Yet despite its obvious importance for both theology and law, the subject of *jadal* has been sadly neglected. A rare exception is the unpublished Princeton University doctoral dissertation of Larry B. Miller, "Islamic Disputation Theory: A Study of the Development of Dialectic in Islam from the Tenth through Fourteenth Centuries" (1984). For the later theory, see Mehmet Kadri Karabela, "The Development of Dialectic and Argumentation Theory in Post-Classical Islamic Intellectual History" (unpublished McGill University doctoral dissertation, 2010).

Pp. 170–71

The Shiʿi jurist mentioned here and on **p. 361** is Abū Jaʿfar Muḥammad ibn ʿAbd al-Raḥmān ibn Qiba al-Rāzī (d. early fourth/tenth century). The confusion with the earlier Muʿtazilī Ṣāliḥ Qubba is addressed and clarified in Hossein Modarressi, *Crisis and Consolidation in the Formative Period of Shīʿite Islam: Abū Jaʿfar ibn Qiba al-Rāzī and His Contribution to Imāmite Shīʿite Thought* (Princeton: Darwin Press, 1993), 119–20.

P. 172

Al-Maghribī (Abū Ṭālib al-Maʿarrī in al-Ḥusayn ibn Muḥammad al-Marwarrūdhī, *al-Taʿlīqa*, ed. ʿAlī Muḥammad Muʿawwaḍ and ʿĀdil Aḥmad ʿAbd al-Mawjūd [Mecca: Maktabat Nizār Muṣṭāfā al-Bāz], 1:111) was an early Ẓāhirī jurist, whose legal opinions are occasionally cited in *ikhtilāf* works (e.g. Ibn al-Murtaḍā, *Kitāb al-Baḥr al-Zakhkhār* [Ṣanʿāʾ: Dār al-Ḥikma al-Yamāniyya, 1409/1988], 2:149).

Pp. 181–84

It is worth noting that the use of the label noncognitivism for a divine command moral theory departs from that prevalent in contemporary philosophy, which reserves the term for emotive and similar metaethical theories that deny that moral judgments admit of truth or falsity. This philosophical usage would classify both of the competing moral theories discussed here as cognitivist.

P. 184 n. 154

Van Ess has subsequently defended a far earlier dating for the use of the term *ʿilla* in legal analogy. Van Ess' only substantial evidence for this is a passage attributed to ʿAmr ibn ʿUbayd (d. 144/761) in Abū Ḥayyān al-Tawḥīdī's *al-Baṣāʾir wa'l-dhakhāʾir*, ed. Wadād al-Qāḍī (Beirut: Dār ṣādir, 1408/1988) 9:409–10, and apparently first noted by him in his article "The Logical Structure of Islamic Theology," in *Logic in Classical Islamic Culture*, ed. G. E. von Grunebaum (Wiesbaden: Harrassowitz, 1970), 42, and discussed and translated in his *Theologie und Gesellschaft*, 2:302 and 5:171–72. In *The Flowering of Muslim Theology*, trans. Jane Marie Todd (Cambridge, MA: Harvard University Press, 2006), 203–4, n. 42, van Ess suggests that the absence of the term *ʿilla* in the writings of al-Shāfiʿī reflects a lack of contact between different intellectual circles. I prefer to reject the authenticity of the critical passage attributed to ʿAmr ibn ʿUbayd as inconsistent with the overall evidence for the dating of the adoption of the term *ʿilla*. It is worth noting that the use of the term among those who practiced analogy remained controversial throughout the fourth/tenth century and probably beyond (al-Zarkashī, *al-Baḥr al-muḥīṭ*, 5:111, 126; see also the important preface to Ḥamd ibn Muḥammad al-Khaṭṭābī's commentary on the *Sunan* of Abū Dāwūd, *Maʿālim al-sunan*, ed. Muḥammad Rāghib al-Ṭabbākh (Aleppo: al-Maṭbaʿa al-ʿilmiyya, 1351/1932), 1:5). Translations of *ʿilla* as *ratio legis* and the like, in avoiding the literal translation "cause," fail to capture the "scientific" pretentions that the term originally conveyed. Unfortunately we still have nothing like an adequate account of Islamic theories of causation in theology and elsewhere to assist in situating the legal developments. The study of Ulrich Rudolph and Dominik Perler, *Occasionalismus: Theorien der Kausalität im arabisch-islamischen und im Europäischen Denken*, in *Abhandlungen der Akademie der Wissenschaften in Göttingen, Philologisch-Historische Klasse*; 3. Folge, Nr. 236 (Göttingen: Vandenhoeck & Ruprecht, 2000) obviously deals primarily with the rejection of causation. The recent edition and study of Jan Thiele, *Kausalität in der Muʿtazilitischen Kosmologie, Das Kitāb al-Muʾaṯṯirāt wa-miftāḥ al-muškilāt des Zayditen al-Ḥasan ar-Raṣṣāṣ (st. 584/1188)* (Leiden: Brill, 2011) is a useful step in the right direction but is limited to later Basran Muʿtazilism.

Pp. 185–86

One should not overestimate the extent to which logic ever came to "penetrate' classical *uṣūl al-fiqh* substantively. Certainly it would be rash to take the sections on logic found in some *uṣūl* works as indicative of anything like a reshaping of the field. These sections were sometimes entirely omitted from copies of the works in question (see, e.g., Plate VIII, facing p. 90, of a 686/1286 copy of al-Ghazālī's *al-Mustaṣfā* in *Catalogue of the Arabic Manuscripts in the Biblioteca Ambrosiana*, ed. Oscar Löfgren and Renato Traini [Vicenza: N. Pozza, 1995]; for the case of Ibn Qudāma's *Rawḍat al-nāẓir*, see ʿAlī ibn Saʿd al-Ḍuwayḥī, *Sharḥ al-muqaddima al-manṭiqiyya fī al-Rawḍa al-maqdisiyya* [al-Dammām: Dār Ibn al-Jawzī, 1431], 5–7), and even when left intact might be skipped in reading or glossed over: see the testimony of two modern Yemeni Zaydīs, hardly likely to be untypical, Aḥmad ibn ʿAlī al-Wazīr, *al-Muṣaffā fī uṣūl al-fiqh* (Beirut: Dār al-Fikr al-Muʿāṣir, 1417/1996), 32–35, and ʿAbd al-Karīm Aḥmad Jadbān in the preface to his edition of Ibn Luqmān, *al-Kāshif li-dhawī al-ʿuqūl ʿan wujūh maʿānī al-Kāfil bi-nayl al-sūl* (Ṣaʿda: Maktabat al-Turāth al-Islāmī, 1421/2000), 18–19.

P. 198

Felicitas Opwis deals with *maṣlaḥa* in analogy and more broadly in her *Maṣlaḥa and the Purpose of the Law: Islamic Discourse on Legal Change from the 4th/10th to 8th/14th* Century (Leiden: Brill, 2010).

P. 201

Al-Qaffāl al-Shāshī's *Maḥāsin al-sharīʿa* has appeared in both Beirut and Cairo editions. It does not support the conjecture in the text as to the origin of the *kulliyyāt*. I have tried to situate this jurist theologically in the article "Qaffal, Muhammad ibn 'Alī ibn Isma'il al-Shashi," *Oxford International Encyclopaedia of Legal History*, ed. Stanley N. Katz (Oxford: Oxford University Press, 2009), 5:60.

Pp. 204–5

Calling Abū Zayd al-Dabūsī *raʾīs al-qawm wa-muḥaṣṣiluhum*, al-Suhrawardī commends him for requiring *taʾthīr* in all cases (*al-Tanqīḥāt fī uṣūl al-fiqh* , ed. ʿIyāḍ ibn Nāmī al-Sulamī [Riyadh: n.p., 1418], 266).

P. 217

I now incline to take *al-sabr wa'l-taqsīm* as one of the numerous instances in which distinct technical terms came to be combined, for example, *al-naẓar wa'l-istidlāl* (often treated as a grammatical singular reflecting its status as a single *maʿnā*). If this is the case, then most likely the earlier term in usage was *al-taqsīm*, now clarified by the more familiar *al-sabr*. A similar way of understanding this terminology as referring to a single procedure seems to be reflected in the comment of Muḥammad al-Amīn ibn Muḥammad al-Mukhtār al-Shinqīṭī in *Sharḥ Marāqī al-suʿūd*, ed. ʿAlī ibn Muḥammad al-ʿUmrān (Mecca: Dār ʿĀlam al-Fawāʾid, 1426), 2:462.

Pp. 226–28

Abū ʿAbd Allāh al-Baṣrī's uncertainty is perhaps best understood in light of the well-known distinction in contemporary philosophy between justifying and motivating reasons. In Basran Muʿtazilism the distinction figures prominently in the discussion of the ground of the obligation to engage in reasoning (*naẓar*) leading to knowledge of the existence of God. Is this ground the justifying reason that knowledge of God is a *luṭf* or is it rather the psychological motive of fear that one may come to harm in failing to resolve the critical question of whether or not God exists?

P. 226, n. 414

See further Wilferd Madelung, "Zu einigen Werken des Imams Abū Ṭālib al-Nāṭiq bi-l-ḥaqq," *Der Islam* 63 (1986): 5–10.

P. 227

Luṭf and *shukr* (graditude) as competing grounds of legal obligation are discussed in my "Two Theories of the Obligation to Obey God's Commands," in Peri Bearman, Wolfhart Heinrichs, and Bernard G. Weiss, eds., *The Law Applied: Contextualizing the Islamic Shariʿa: A Volume in Honor of Frank E. Vogel* (London: I. B. Tauris, 2008), 397–421.

Pp. 232–33, n. 447

The theory of *asbāb* is discussed in my article "Muʿtazilism and Māturīdism in Ḥanafī Legal Theory," in Bernard G. Weiss, ed., *Studies in Islamic Legal Theory*, 257–63.

5

IJTIHĀD

I. *Ijtihād* and Probability

It is reported that the great Ḥanafī jurist ʿAlāʾ al-Dīn al-Kāsānī (d. 578/1182), the son-in-law of al-Samarqandī, once conducted a disputation with another Ḥanafī jurist in Anatolia. The topic was Abū Ḥanīfa's doctrine of *ijtihād*. Al-Kāsānī's opponent persistently maintained that for Abū Ḥanīfa, every *mujtahid* was correct. Losing his patience, al-Kāsānī finally raised his whip to strike the other jurist. The Anatolian ruler who witnessed this surprising spectacle readily agreed to send off the fiery al-Kāsānī as an emissary to Aleppo.[1] Writing of this very doctrine, that every *mujtahid* is correct, al-Bāqillānī said that, "Had al-Shāfiʿī not espoused it, I would not number him among the *uṣūlīs*."[2] What is common to these very different positions on the question of the infallibility of *ijtihād* is the fervor with which they are espoused. With the doctrine of *ijtihād*, we touch a very sensitive nerve of Islamic culture. For upon this doctrine hinges in large measure the role of law among the religious disciplines. The assessment of *ijtihād* is at the same time an evaluation of the activity of the jurist, for *ijtihād* of one sort or another is what the jurist practices.

Ijtihād literally means exertion of effort, and even in its most technical usages the word never totally loses its fundamental sense. Indeed, as we shall see, one important aspect of the sophisticated doctrine of the infallibility of *ijtihād* is the enhanced significance it gives to the act of the jurist, to the process of *ijtihād* as opposed to its product. Apart from this primary sense, it is most difficult to frame a satisfactory definition of

1. Ibn Abī ʾl-Wafāʾ al-Qurashī, *al-Jawāhir al-muḍiyya fī tarājim al-ḥanafiyya* (Hyderabad: Maṭbaʿat Majlis Dāʾirat al-Maʿārif al-Niẓāmiyya, 1332/1914), 2:244–45, quoted in the editor's introduction to Abū Bakr Ibn Masʿūd al-Kāsānī, *Badāʾiʿ al-ṣanāʾiʿ*, 1:77–78.

2. *Mankhūl*, p. 453. The Muʿtazilī Ibn al-Ikshīd had reported that al-Shāfiʿī supported infallibilism (Abū ʿĀṣim Muḥammad ibn Aḥmad al-ʿAbbādī, *Kitāb Ṭabaqāt fuqahāʾ aš-Šāfiʿīya*, p. 36).

ijtihād in the juridical sense that will concern us. One usage of the word that will not interest us directly is the *ijtihād* involved in an individual application of a rule of law (*ijtihād fī ḥukm khāṣṣ*), such as the determination of the direction for prayer (*qibla*).[3] Significantly, however, the *ijtihād* of finding the *qibla* is throughout the literature the model for the *ijtihād* involved in establishing a rule of law.[4] For Abū 'l-Ḥasan al-Karkhī, this was even the dominant sense of *ijtihād*.[5] For our purposes, however, we do better to accept al-Shafiʿī's identification of *ijtihād* with *qiyās*.[6] Although the precise sense of al-Shāfiʿī's statement is doubtful,[7] it at least puts us in the proper area of concern. The problem of *ijtihād* is largely that of the evaluation of the results of juridical analogy. The sphere of *ijtihād* is that part of the law where differences are most obvious, the realm of probability rather than certainty. These differences are the sociological starting point for the doctrine of *ijtihād*, which has to assess their legitimacy. For the majority of jurists, these differences are legitimate. But on one view, this legitimacy is by default. The one correct teaching cannot be identified with certainty. Legitimacy is a consequence of the mere probability that is attainable. The opposing view bestows an absolute legitimacy on the rival teachings. There is no one correct doctrine. All are equally correct. For this doctrine of *ijtihād*, probability is not a stage on the journey to truth but the very goal of the journey.

We have spoken of probability throughout this study, but we haven not stopped to look more closely at the concept of probability entertained by the Muslim jurists. Although the explicit treatments of the subject are few and most sketchy, it is clear that the dominant conception of probability held by the legal theorists was that of relative frequency. The application of the relative frequency concept to traditions seems rather straightforward. The incidence of lying, etc. varies with the character and mental qualities of the narrator. Its application to analogy raises the problem familiar to modern philosophers of whether the probability of theories can be treated in terms of relative frequency. The doctrine of effectiveness is an affirmative response to this question. Abū Yaʿlā ibn al-Farrā' expounds this line of treatment in his reply to the attack on the possibility of attaining probability in analogy:

> The objection is raised that probability depends on experience (*ʿāda*) so that if one sees thick, clustered clouds he expects rain. This appears probable to him because of his previous experience. But with respect to these legal rules there is no previous course of experience between us and God. The answer is that the path of probability is the occurrence of something in the majority of its analogues. For this reason it appears probable that a wall will tumble when it is

3. Māwardī, 1:497.
4. *Risāla*, paras. 1336–1349. There is an extended comparison in *Muʿtamad*, 2:988–89.
5. *Jawāmiʿ*, f. 67a.
6. *Risāla*, paras. 1323–24, 1326.
7. *Lumaʿ*, p. 56; *Mustaṣfā*, p. 395; Māwardī, 1:489; al-Samʿānī quoted Bukhārī, 3:268.

> cracked horizontally and that rain will follow thick black clouds, because rain generally comes from clouds of this sort and only infrequently fails to come. The opinion of a rational man corresponds to what is frequent rather than to what is infrequent (*al-ghālib dūn al-nādir*). This being so, probability of this sort in the rules of law is common, since the analogues there are many and recurrent, and it appears probable to the one reasoning that the point of contention (*al-mujtahad fīhā*) is like a given case.[8]

The very same objection against analogy had been raised earlier by al-Shaykh al-Mufīd in a disputation with al-Bāqillānī. While insisting that the *mujtahid* relied on his assessment of probability, al-Bāqillānī claimed that there was no special method for identifying legal causes. "What appears probable to me I act upon and treat as a mark and a sign. But if something else appears probable to someone else and he acts upon it, he is correct and does not err. Every *mujtahid* is correct."[9]

Al-Bāqillānī's concept of probability was an entirely subjective one and was the foundation of his radical infallibilism (*al-muʿammima fī al-taṣwīb*).[10] Famous formulations of this view of probability are put forth. Probability depends on the character of the subject rather than the object.[11] Probability amounts to a "preponderance of belief" (*rujḥān al-iʿtiqād*) rather than "a belief of preponderance" (*iʿtiqād al-rujḥān*).[12] Given the fact that everything depended on the individual jurist, the relation between any evidence and the subjective probability of the jurist was purely fortuitous (*ittifāq, ʿalā al-wifāq*).[13] The discontinuity between probability and the evidence for it appears, as al-Zarkashī suggests, to be at the root of the distinction sometimes made between "evidence" (*dalīl*) and "a sign" (*amāra*).[14] Knowledge follows directly from the examination of evidence, whereas probability may ensue in conjunction with a sign.[15] The distinction arose among the Muʿtazilī infallibilists and was taken up by some Ashʿarīs such as al-Bāqillānī.[16] For them, the usage common among the jurists that referred to signs as evidence was metaphorical.[17] The

---

8. *ʿUdda*, f. 195a,b.
9. *Fuṣūl*, 1:50.
10. *Musawwada*, p. 371.
11. *Musawwada*, p. 371.
12. *Musawwada*, p. 506.
13. Ibn Taymiyya, *al-Furqān bayn al-ḥaqq wa'l-bāṭil, in Majmūʿat al-rasāʾil al-kubrā* (Cairo: Muḥammad ʿAlī Ṣubayḥ, 1385/1966), 1:88; *Jamʿ*, 2:283; *Baḥr*, f. 348a.
14. *Baḥr*, f. 5a.
15. Ṭūsī, p. 10; *Musawwada*, p. 506.
16. *Musawwada* p. 506; Ibn Taymiyya, *al-Radd*, p. 253.
17. *Musawwada*, p. 506; *Mustaṣfā*, p. 505.

majority of jurists, however, continued to speak of evidence without discrimination.[18] And the distinction itself was subject to unfavorable criticism.[19]

Because every instance of probable opinion was fortuitous, every probability was like another. No gradation (*taqdīm wa-taʾkhīr, tartīb*) of probabilities was possible.[20] No particular method was inherently more reliable than any other. This, in brief, is al-Bāqillānī's doctrine of infallibilism as reported by al-Juwaynī and attacked by him as an "enormous lapse" (*hafwa ʿaẓīma*).[21]

II. Infallibilism

The classical legal theorists encountered no little embarrassment in ascertaining the *ijtihād* doctrine of the early jurists. In large measure, this was due to the formulations of the doctrine that were transmitted to them. These formulations were in the form of ambiguous slogans, the most famous of which held that "every jurist is correct" (*kull mujtahid muṣīb*). A formulation of this sort was inadequate. Other sources had to be drawn upon to clarify what the masters had meant. In what follows, several issues possibly relevant to the infallibility doctrine will be reviewed with a view to alerting the reader to the multifariousness of the problem rather than to pursuing systematically the scholarly researches of the legal theorists. Of course, these secondary issues were also ambiguous, and the theorists tended to treat them in conformity with their own positions.

Let us start with what appears to be a very narrow technical doctrine. For the purposes of ritual ablution, the works of substantive law classify the water left in a vessel from which an animal has drunk (*asʾār*). For example, water left by a horse is pure (*ṭāhir*). Water left by a mule or donkey, however, is, according to the dominant Ḥanafī view, of doubtful status (*mashkūk fīhi*). When no other water is available, one performs ablution with this water and also, to be safe, performs the cleansing with sand (*tayammum*).[22] Lurk-

18. *Lumaʿ*, p. 3; Sulaymān ibn Khalaf al-Bājī, *Kitāb al-Ḥudūd fī al-uṣūl*, p. 38; Bājī, p. 11, n. 12; *ʿUdda*, f. 7b.

19. Ibn Taymiyya, *al-Radd*, p. 165; *Muʿtamad*, 2:690.

20. *Mankhūl*, p. 334; *Musawwada*, p. 388; *Burhān*, f. 253; *Baḥr*, f. 348a.

21. *Mankhūl*, p. 334. Al-Zarkashī questions the accuracy of al-Juwaynī's understanding of al-Bāqillānī, since it should follow that al-Bāqillānī applies no methods of preference (*tarjīḥ*) among putative causes, whereas he in fact does (*Baḥr*, f. 348a). But the answer is supplied by al-Juwaynī himself at the beginning of his small work, *Mughīth al-khalq fī tarjīḥ al-qawl al-ḥaqq* (Cairo: al-Maṭbaʿa al-Miṣriyya, 1352/1934), p. 8. Al-Bāqillānī recognized those methods of preference that were themselves certain.

22. For example, al-Mawṣilī, *al-Ikhtiyār li-taʿlīl al-Mukhtār*, 1:19. The existence of such doubtful points is not confined to the Ḥanafīs. In Mālikī *fiqh*, there is a position that regards as doubtful the status of a small amount of water with an impurity but not to the point of a change in its character (Muḥammad ibn Aḥmad ibn Juzayy, *Qawānīn al-aḥkām al-sharʿiyya wa-masāʾil al-furūʿ al-fiqhiyya*, ed. Ṭāhā Saʿd and Muṣṭafā al-Hawwārī [Cairo: ʿĀlam al-Fikr, n.d.], p. 33; Aḥmad ibn Idrīs al-Qarāfī, *al-Dhakhīra* [Cairo: al-Jāmiʿa al-Azhariyya Maṭbaʿat Kulliyyat al-Sharīʿa, 1381/1961], 1:164). In Ḥanbali law, the status of a woman who

ing behind this narrow issue is the larger problem of the conflict or balance of evidence (*taʿāruḍ, taʿādul, takāfuʾ al-adilla*). It is clear that if the evidence were equally balanced for two solutions, this would lead to doubt on the point of law.[23]

The conflict of evidence is part of the complex of *ijtihād* doctrine. Confronted with a complete balancing of the evidence for different rulings, a jurist can take any one of several approaches. One is to freely choose whichever rule he wishes (*takhyīr*). This is a weak version of infallibilism. It was generally adopted by the infallibilists in preference to the second possibility of hesitation (*tawaqquf*).[24] For the infallibilist, each of the balanced probabilities was valid in its own right. The individual jurist was the locus on a small scale of the same phenomenon of equally established probabilities that was at work in the Islamic legal community as a whole. Thus we find al-Bāqillānī adopting the solution of free choice,[25] in agreement with such other prominent representatives of infallibilism as the Jubbāʾīs and Abū 'l-Hudhayl al-ʿAllāf.[26] This was also the view of ʿUbayd Allāh ibn al-Ḥasan al-ʿAnbarī, a Basran theologian-jurist notorious for his extension of infallibilism from law to theology.[27] Abū 'l-Ḥasan al-Karkhī, on the other hand, held the view that the jurist was bound to review his *ijtihād* until one ruling prevailed.[28] And it was precisely the Ḥanafī doctrine on the doubtful status of the water left over by the donkey that the Ḥanafī al-Jurjānī pointed to against al-Karkhī's teaching.[29] There were, of course, other ways of explaining the legal point.[30] And one Ḥanafī, Abū Ṭāhir al-Dabbās, was particularly offended by the term "doubtful," which he proscribed on the ground that there "is no doubt as to the rules of the Divine Law."[31]

The problem of the balance of evidence was posed in a much more pointed form for the Shāfiʿīs. The teachings of al-Shāfiʿī are commonly in the form of a former (*qadīm*) and a later (*jadīd*) doctrine. One possible interpretation of the two views (*qawlān*) of the

---

resumes bleeding within forty days after childbirth is doubtful (ʿAbd al-Raḥmān ibn Ibrāhīm al-Maqdisī, *al-ʿUdda sharḥ al-ʿUmda*, p. 58).

23. *Muʿtamad*, 2:856.

24. *Mīzān*, f. 185a.

25. *Mustaṣfā*, p. 508.

26. *Jawāmiʿ*, f. 92b; *Muʿtamad*, 2:853.

27. *Mustaṣfā*, p. 488; Bukhārī, 4:17; Ibrāhīm ibn Mūsā al-Shāṭibī, *al-Iʿtiṣām*, 1:147–48; Ibn Taymiyya, *al-Furqān*, p. 94; Ibn Taymiyya, *Qāʿida fī tawaḥḥud al-milla wa-taʿādul al-sharāʾiʿ wa-tanawwuʿihā*, in *al-Rasāʾil al-munīriyya*, ed. Muḥammad Munīr (Cairo, 1346 H. Reprint. Beirut: Dār al-Jīl, 1970), 3:156–57.

28. *Muʿtamad*, 2:959.

29. *Musawwada*, p. 446; *ʿUdda*, f. 237b.

30. *Musawwada*, p. 446; al-Mawṣilī, *al-Ikhtiyār li-taʿlīl al-Mukhtār*, 1:19.

31. *Manār*, p. 675. Al-Dabbās shunned the study of theology (ʿAbd al-Jabbār, *Faḍl al-iʿtizāl*, p. 320).

master was that they presented a balance of evidence.[32] Ironically, al-Shāfiʿī's view on *ijtihād* was also in this double form according to some.[33]

The great Shāfiʿī Ibn Surayj (d. 306/918) already wrote an extensive attack against the proponents of the balance of evidence.[34] But it was only with the increasing dominance of Ashʿarism among the Shāfiʿīs that the doctrine of *ijtihād* within the school was fully debated. Al-Bāqillānī, as we have seen, numbered al-Shāfiʿī among the infallibilists. Leading the opposition to this view were the Khurasanian Shāfiʿīs headed by Abū Isḥaq al-Isfarāyīnī (d. 418/1027).[35] Ibn Fūrak (d. 406/1015) and al-Isfarāyīnī's student ʿAbd al-Qāhir al-Baghdādī (d. 429/1037) are mentioned in this group.[36] And it is not surprising to learn that the attribution of infallibilism to al-Ashʿarī was also contested by these Khurasanian Shāfiʿīs. On the issue of *ijtihād*, they were at one with the leading Iraqi jurist, Abū 'l-Ṭayyib al-Ṭabarī (d. 450/1058),[37] who insisted that fallibilism was the doctrine of Shāfiʿīs, ancient and modern.[38]

Whereas al-Shāfiʿī's doctrine of *ijtihād* was most hotly debated within the ranks of Ashʿarism, for the Ḥanafīs the break here, as elsewhere, was between Iraqi Muʿtazilism and Central Asian orthodoxy. Of Abū Ḥanīfa, like al-Shāfiʿī, it was related that he held that every *mujtahid* is correct.[39] The association of infallibilism and Muʿtazilism was not fortuitous for the Central Asians. They saw the root of the erroneous doctrine in the Muʿtazilī principle of optimism (*al-aṣlaḥ*). God is bound to do what is best for man. Clearly, it is best for the jurist to hit upon the truth and receive his reward, rather than for him to risk losing it through no fault of his own.[40] The Central Asians were correct in linking infallibilism and the characteristic Muʿtazilī doctrine of optimism,[41] but the optimism

32. *Muʿtamad*, 2:862; *Mustaṣfā*, p. 511. The generally accepted solution appears to be that the later doctrine abrogates the former, and that when *fatwā* is according to the former, this is the view of the scholars and not to be attributed to al-Shāfiʿī (ʿAbd al-Raḥmān ibn Muḥammad al-Bāʿalāwī, *Bughyat al-mustarshidīn fī talkhīṣ fatāwā baʿḍ al-aʾimma al-ʿulamāʾ al-mutaʾakhkhirīn* [Cairo: Muṣṭafā al-Bābī al-Ḥalabī, 1371/1952], p. 8). There were other solutions such as that of al-Isfarāyīnī, who identified the preferred doctrine as that in opposition to Abū Ḥanīfa, on the ground that al-Shāfiʿī would not have opposed Abū Ḥanīfa without good reason (*Manār*, p. 675; *Jamʿ*, 2:360; *Musawwada*, p. 538).

33. *Lumaʿ*, pp. 76–77.

34. ʿAbd al-Qāhir al-Baghdādī, *Uṣūl al-dīn*, p. 309 (*Naqḍ kitāb al-jārūf*). See Josef van Ess, *Die Erkenntislehre des ʿAḍudaddīn al-Īcī*, p. 223.

35. *Mankhūl*, p. 334.

36. *Baḥr*, f. 356b.

37. *Fawātiḥ*, 2:380.

38. *Musawwada*, p. 497.

39. Bukhārī, 1:8, 46 (not a full version).

40. Bukhārī, 4:31; Nasafī, 2:174.

41. *Fawātiḥ*, 2:380, remarks that infallibilism cannot be the doctrine of all the Muʿtazila since they recognize objective value. But this is irrelevant to *ijtihād*, which operates precisely where there is no *ḥukm ʿaqlī*.

was not fundamentally one that concerned the reward of the jurist, but one that operated at a deeper level and satisfied a different imperative. In the rest of this chapter, we shall scrutinize a little more closely the theology of the *ijtihād* doctrines. Finally, we shall examine some of the implications of infallibilism that made it so objectionable to the Central Asians.

A useful distinction for a more nuanced discussion of the doctrine of *ijtihād* is that made between the act of the jurist, his process of *ijtihād* and the result of his act, the product. Fallibilism in its various versions holds that the result of *ijtihād* can be tested against an objective measure. The jurist can either "hit or miss" the target formed by the correct result. For infallibilism, there is no correct result, and the only measure of a jurist's work is the quality of his act of *ijtihād*.

The fallibilists, as their name (*al-mukhaṭṭiʾa*) indicates, are distinguished from the infallibilists by their recognition of the possibility of legal error within the sphere of probability. The significance of probability here is that it unites both infallibilists and fallibilists against those systems that allowed probability no place in the law (*lā majāl liʾl-ẓann fī al-aḥkām*). Apart from the Ẓāhirīs and Shiʿis, this second group includes such jurists as al-Aṣamm and al-Marīsī.[42] The Ẓāhirīs, the Shiʿis, and such Baghdādī theologians as Jaʿfar ibn Mubashshir and Jaʿfar ibn Harb rejected analogy. The others like al-Aṣamm and al-Marīsī accepted it. But all were united in eliminating *ijtihād* in its classical signification from their systems. Qāḍī ʿAbd al-Jabbār speaks explicitly of those who accept *qiyās* and reject *ijtihād*.[43] This distinction, however, is not maintained in the general body of literature, which speaks of al-Marīsī's doctrine of *ijtihād*, for example.[44] What al-Ghazālī refers to as al-Marīsī's raving (*hadhayān*) is the limit of the fallibilist position, as al-Ghazālī notes,[45] for al-Marīsī went so far as to expose to sanction the jurist who went wrong.[46]

Set against a system that would reward only the one jurist whose decision was correct, infallibilism, which rewards all jurists, can be identified with what is best (*aṣlaḥ*).[47] But al-Marīsī's was not the dominant doctrine. It was generally held that all jurists who made an honest effort were entitled to some reward, and al-Dabūsī accurately characterized

42. *Mustaṣfā*, pp. 490, 498 (*al-taʿlīmiyya*); *Fuwātiḥ*, 2:379.

43. *Mughnī*, 17:321–22, 369–70.

44. Bukhārī, 4:29.

45. *Mustaṣfā*, pp. 492, 497.

46. Although al-Marīsī, al-Aṣamm, and Ibn ʿUlayya are sometimes grouped together without distinction (*Baḥr*, f. 357a), some texts do differentiate among them. Punishment for the erring jurist is attributed to al-Marīsī (Ibn Taymiyya, *Rafʿ al-malām ʿan al-aʾimma al-aʿlām*, pp.32–33; Bukhārī, 4:18). Al-Aṣamm and Ibn ʿUlayya, on the other hand, are said merely to deny him a reward (Bukhārī, 4:18). Al-Aṣamm is associated with the doctrine invalidating the decision of a court that is based on error (Ṭūsī, p. 291: a minor error is forgiven). *Jawāmiʿ*, f. 94b, is less definite in associating Ibn ʿUlayya with these doctrines.

47. Bukhārī, 4:19.

the *ijtihād* doctrine that he defended as the moderate one (*al-qawl al-wasaṭ*), between the extreme of infallibilism, which puts all jurists on the same plane, and the narrow view that rewards only one. The optimism of infallibilism, then, is not to be sought in the reward that goes to the jurist. The appeal of the doctrine operated at another level, which may be termed theoretical. Infallibilism is an attempt to make theological sense of the legal reality of the Islamic world. The reality itself was quite simply described: the decision of every qualified *mujtahid* was as valid as that of any other. This is the reality that so discomfited Ibn al-Muqaffaᶜ (d. 140/757) in his famous *Risāla fī al-ṣaḥāba*. Optimism postulates the necessary identity of the actual and the ideal. The burden of infallibilism was to defend this postulate with respect to the working of *ijtihād*. Infallibilism and the other doctrines of *ijtihād* were seeking to grasp the elusive nature of the Islamic legal enterprise. Their attempts to capture the essential character of *ijtihād* generated a host of tortuous formulae, which al-Jaṣṣāṣ already decried.[48]

The starting point of Muᶜtazilī infallibilism is the legitimacy of disagreement on points of law. This indicates that all jurists are correct. If there were convincing evidence (*dalīl qāʾim*), in the form of a text or consensus, for one correct doctrine, then God would have made the discovery of that doctrine obligatory, and the jurist who failed in his search would be culpable.[49] Such is the situation in the rational sciences, that is, theology. There no disagreement is tolerated.[50] When it comes to extending the law, the only rule that is certain is the obligation of analogy. By applying this rule, the jurist can be certain that his result is valid. This is what we have termed the displacement of certainty. Certainty is no longer sought in the specific case, but the rule of the case derives its validity from the certainty of the master rule.[51] The rule governing analogy now functions like the rule requiring the worshipper to rely on probability when directing himself to the *qibla*. The effort involved in the application of such a lower-level rule to an individual case is also termed *ijtihād*. Infallibilism thus represents the reduction of analogy to the application of a rule of law that depends on the agent's assessment of probability. *Ijtihād* can, not misleadingly, be defined as the jurist's effort to achieve a probable opinion on a question of law.[52] Probability is the goal.

Essentially, infallibilism is a doctrine of solipsism. *Ijtihād* revolves about the *mujtahid*'s experience of probability. The same phenomenon is present in the other lower-level cases of *ijtihād*. The extent to which ᶜAbd al-Jabbār, for one, is ready to press the

48. Jaṣṣāṣ, f. 306a; Māwardī, 1:521.

49. Māwardī, 1:525: *li-anna jawāz ikhtilāf al-jamīᶜ dalīl ᶜalā ṣiḥḥat al-jamīᶜ*. See also Ibn Qayyim al-Jawziyya, *Mukhtaṣar al-ṣawāᶜiq*, p. 514, on al-Bāqillānī.

50. Jaṣṣāṣ, f. 246a; *Mustaṣfā*, p. 424.

51. Jaṣṣāṣ, f. 24a.

52. Muṣṭafā al-Iᶜtimādī, *Sharḥ Maᶜālim al-dīn fī al-uṣūl* (Qom: al-Maktaba al-Muṣṭafavī, 1377/1957), p. 358; *Mughnī*, 17:376.

point is striking. For him, the physical existence of the *kaʿba* is an incidental feature of the obligation of directing oneself toward the *qibla*. The *kaʿba* is necessary so that there be the required evidence (*amāra*) on which to base the assessment of probability. If this evidence could exist without an actual *kaʿba*, the requirement of directing oneself to a *qibla* would not suffer.[53] Evidence, however, is required for the assessment of probability to have legal or rational significance (*ḥukm*), as opposed to the experience of probability on the part of the melancholic person or the spontaneous intuition of probability on the part of someone normal.[54]

The difficulty that now faces ʿAbd al-Jabbār and Abū 'l-Ḥusayn al-Baṣrī, but not al-Bāqillānī, stems from the fact that, unlike him, they recognize an objective gradation of evidence. In most cases, one solution will be best supported by the evidence.[55] The question, then, is, Why this most cogent evidence does not take the place of a proof (*dalīl*) and the solution it supports is not imposed as the only correct one. The answer lies in the ethics of epistemology. The practice of the community indicates that a number of solutions are treated as of equal validity. This variety of solutions could only result if God failed to alert every *mujtahid* to the strongest evidence. This failure on God's part, however, is not objectionable (*qabīḥ*), as would be the case if God kept someone from knowledge where that was possible. This would amount to an objectionable "incitement to ignorance."[56] The relation of evidence to probability is, in modern terms, an analytic one, and provided that a jurist puts forth his best effort, he can never go wrong in what he regards as probable. "It is not objectionable to hold the *opinion* that Zayd is at home, when in fact Zayd is not at home."[57]

Even if it is accepted that the different answers of the *mujtahids* are equally valid, the question remains, why there cannot be another, qualitatively different, solution known to God.[58] That is, the question remains whether there can be one right answer known to God, which the *mujtahid* is, however, not obligated to discover. A positive answer to this question is given by the doctrine of verisimilitude (*al-ashbah*). The proponents of this doctrine hold that for God there is a solution that is most likely. The doctrine of verisimilitude is most closely associated with the Ḥanafīs.[59] It was the doctrine of Abū 'l-Ḥasan

53. *Mughnī*, 17:379; *Muʿtamad*, 2:985.

54. *Mughnī*, 17:359; ʿAbd al-Jabbār, *Sharḥ al-uṣūl al-khamsa*, p. 53. On *ḥukm*, see J. R. T. M. Peters, *God's Created Speech: A Study of the Speculative Theology of the Muʿtazilî Qâḍî l-Quḍât Abû l-Ḥasan ʿAbd al-Jabbār bn [sic] Aḥmad al-Hamaḏânî* (Leiden: Brill, 1976), pp.155–56.

55. *Muʿtamad*, 2:954–55; *Mughnī*, 17:359. The exception is where the evidence is balanced.

56. *Muʿtamad*, 2:963.

57. *Muʿtamad*, 2:963. See A. J. Ayer, "The Conception of Probability as a Logical Relation," in *The Structure of Scientific Thought: An Introduction to Philosophy of Science*, ed. Edward H. Madden (Boston: Houghton Mifflin, 1960), pp. 279–84.

58. Qarāfī, p. 441.

59. *Lumaʿ*, p. 76; *Musawwada*, p. 501; Ibn Taymiyya, *Iqāmat al-dalīl ʿalā ibṭāl al-taḥlīl*, in *Majmūʿat al-fatāwā*, 3:171.

al-Karkhī and al-Jaṣṣāṣ, who attributed it to Abū Ḥanīfa, al-Shaybānī, Abū Yūsuf, and Ibn Abān.[60] Verisimilitude was also attributed to al-Shāfiʿī, most notably by Abū Ḥāmid al-Isfarāyīnī (d. 406/1015).[61] Al-Isfarāyīnī may have been following Ibn Surayj, who was a noted adherent of the doctrine.[62]

Although verisimilitude is sometimes formulated in terms of one truth (*ḥaqq wāḥid*), this formulation is apt to be misleading.[63] Verisimilitude is rooted in the ethics of infallibilism. Where it differs from standard infallibilism is in its attempt to work out a more satisfactory epistemology, one that would have the advantage of the fallibilistic position. This it achieved by positing a uniquely correct result, which serves as a goal for juridical effort (*maṭlūb*).[64] The dominant image here is that of the *kaʿba*. Verisimilitude restores the *kaʿba* to the higher level *ijtihād*. In this sense, Abū ʿAbd Allāh ibn Zayd al-Wāsiṭī spoke of the doctrine as the "direction of *ijtihād*" (*taqwīm dhāt al-ijtihād*).[65] ʿĪsā ibn Abān suggested a helpful analogy with the various measures required by the sacred law (*al-maqādīr*). The precise actual measure is not required but only the measure based on one's best effort.[66]

For al-Jaṣṣāṣ, the right answer was that original case most like the one in controversy.[67] Others spoke of the right answer as the one God would send down if He were to do so.[68] This explanation has the virtue of emphasizing the peculiar function of the right answer for verisimilitude. Ibn Taymiyya notes that the proponents of verisimilitude would not label the right answer "a valid rule" (*ḥukm*).[69] For them, its validity, as the cited ex-

60. Jaṣṣāṣ, f. 306a. Sufyān ibn Saḥbān (or Sakhtān: see *Intiṣār*, p. 140, no. 112) attributed fallibilism to Abū Ḥanīfa (*Jawāmiʿ*, f. 94b; Ṭūsī, p. 391). *Muʿtamad*, 2:950, however, has Sufyān attributing verisimilitude to Abū Ḥanīfa. Note the omission of Abū Ḥanīfa in *Musawwada*, p. 502. On Abū Yūsuf's *taṣwīb*, see Walī Allāh al-Dihlawī, *ʿIqd al-jīd fī aḥkām al-ijtihād wa'l-taqlīd*, ed. Muḥibb al-Dīn al-Khaṭīb (Cairo: al-Maktaba al-Salafiyya, 1385), p. 5. Al-Karkhī's view is reported by his student, the Shāfiʿī ʿUbayd Allāh ibn ʿUmar in Ibn ʿAbd al-Barr, *Jāmiʿ bayān al-ʿilm wa-faḍlihi*, 2:73. The quotation, however, does not bring out that a version of infallibilism is being discussed. This may reflect an attempt on ʿUbayd Allāh ibn ʿUmar's part to bring verisimilitude over into fallibilism by isolating al-Muzanī, or, alternatively, carelessness on his part or on that of Ibn ʿAbd al-Barr, who quotes out of context.

61. *Mustaṣfā*, p. 504; *Mughnī*, 17:377 (Abū Ḥāmid).

62. *Mankhūl*, p. 458; al-Dihlawī, *ʿIqd al-jīd*, p. 5. For a passage from Ibn Surayj dealing with *ṭard* and infallibilism, see *Shifāʾ*, pp. 341–43. On Abū Ḥāmid al-Isfarāyīnī's following Ibn Surayj in *ẓawāhir al-fiqh*, see Tāj al-Dīn al-Subkī, *Ṭabaqāt*, 3:221.

63. *Musawwada*, p. 501.

64. Jaṣṣāṣ, f. 313a. This is the key element of the doctrine. Thus *Mughnī*, 17:379: *al-ʿayn al-qāʾima al-amr al-maṭlūb al-ashbah ʿinda Allāh*.

65. Jaṣṣāṣ, f. 306a; *Baḥr*, f. 358a.

66. Jaṣṣāṣ, f. 306b.

67. Jaṣṣāṣ, f. 307a.

68. *Musawwada*, p. 502; *Muʿtamad*, 2:982; *Mankhūl*, p. 458 (*Baḥr*, f. 358b, has the correct reading *la-ṭābaqahu*).

69. Ibn Taymiyya, *Iqāmat al-dalīl*, 3:171; *Jawāmiʿ*, f. 90b. Note also the formula attributed to Abū Yūsuf and some Iraqis in Māwardī, 1:527.

planation suggests, was only potential. The only valid rule for each *mujtahid* was the one that he deemed most probable. "This is the rule he is bound by and commanded to put into effect" (*tuʿubbida bihi wa-umira bi-infādhihi*).[70] The most likely rule has no force of its own. Insofar as it does achieve validity, its validity is precisely on a par with that of every other product of *iijtihād*.

The mainstream of Basran Muʿtazilism, despite some vacillation, remained unpersuaded that there was any need for a hypothetical most likely answer. There is no reason, Abū ʿAbd Allāh al-Baṣrī wrote, for the *mujtahid* to seek a result that he was not bound to arrive at.[71] Once it is agreed that every product of *ijtihād* is valid and the ethical underpinning of this system is worked out, there is no further ethical gain in postulating a most likely solution.[72] Infallibilism already had a goal that the *mujtahid* was bound to reach, and that goal was the rule based on his assessment of probability. It was this rule that was the source of benefit for him.[73] Abū ʿAlī al-Jubbāʾī (d. 303/915–16) apparently flirted with verisimilitude for a time before coming down against it.[74] ʿAbd al-Jabbār's teacher Abū Isḥāq ibn ʿAyyāsh entertained a weaker version of verisimilitude, which regarded the mere possibility of a uniquely correct solution as a sufficient goal.[75] But it was Abū Hāshim al-Jubbāʾī (d. 321/933) who set the pattern for the later Muʿtazila. For Abū Hāshim, the doctrine of verisimilitude was unintelligible.[76] This is also the position of ʿAbd al-Jabbār, who regards the doctrine as unintelligible as that of "nature."[77] This attitude was only reinforced by those proponents of verisimilitude who claimed that it was a notion incapable of verbal expression. They refused to go further than to speak of the most likely solution.[78]

Before turning to some of the broad consequences of infallibilism, we should look briefly at infallibilism within Ashʿarism. The fundamental theological difference between the Muʿtazilī and the Ashʿarī versions is that Muʿtazilī infallibilism is built around the doctrine of optimism, while for Ashʿarism infallibilism rests on the theological principle that God will not impose what is impossible.[79] The Muʿtazilī doctrine is mainly concerned

70. Jaṣṣāṣ, f. 307a.

71. *Muʿtamad*, 2:984.

72. *Muʿtamad*, 2:985.

73. *Muʿtamad*, 2:986. Al-Baṣrī treats *al-ashbah* as the *ḥukm*.

74. *Mughnī*, 17:377; *Muʿtamad*, 2:950; *Jawāmiʿ*, f. 90b.

75. *Mughnī*, 17:377.

76. *Mughnī*, 17:377.

77. *Mughnī*, 17:378.

78. *Lumaʿ*, p. 76; *Musawwada*, p. 502.

79. So Bukhārī, 4:31. This is not to say that *taklīf mā lā yuṭāq* is not part of the Muʿtazili version. See *Mughnī*, 17:367. But in the first instance, the principle is ethically, not textually, based in Muʿtazilism. Secondly, it is merely the epistemological starting point for the Muʿtazila, whereas for the Ashʿarīs it is the core issue.

with working out a positive account of the virtue of legal variety in terms of Muʿtazilī ethics. The Ashʿarī account, as elaborated by al-Bāqillānī, is analytical.[80]

The leading term in al-Bāqillānī's analysis is "communication" (*khiṭāb*). There is no general norm in the realm of probability because a valid norm requires an act of communication. The nature of probability for al-Bāqillānī is, as we have seen, such that there is no fixed relation between the evidence and the probability that ensues. In the absence of such a fixed relation, there is no definite act of communication involved in God's setting down this evidence. The message will depend entirely on the personal state of the individual addressee. Such is not the case with a proof (*dalīl*), which uniformly leads to the same knowledge. No one can be said to receive the particular information conveyed by what is merely evidence, because there is no particular information being conveyed, and "a communication without a communicatee is unintelligible."[81]

In place of a general norm for each case, there is the rule for analogy. This rule is certain, being based on consensus. Together with the rule laying down the principle of analogy, there were also the rules fixing its method. These rules guide the *mujtahid* in arriving at an acceptable probability. Outside of this clearly demarcated system, probability must not be the basis for action within the law.[82] Al-Bāqillānī's doctrine of analogy is thus marked by a particular rigidity. He was adamant in rejecting concomitance as a method of identifying the cause since it was not based on the practice of the Companions.[83] Similarly, he was set against the analogy of similitude.[84] The same character marks al-Bāqillānī's teaching on the unit-tradition: "Where there is conclusive evidence for the acceptance of any variety of unit-tradition, I accept it, but if there is no such evidence for it or against it, I am definite in rejecting it, since there is no evidence for accepting it." Here, too, consensus is the basis for his practice.[85] Al-Bāqillānī's infallibilism did not go unchallenged within Ashʿarism. We have already noted the opposition of Abū Isḥāq al-Isfarāyīnī. In al-Juwyanī, al-Isfarāyīnī found a successor. Al-Juwaynī rejected the displacement of certainty that was central to infallibilism. "What is probable in itself cannot possibly produce certain knowledge," he wrote.[86] He was firm in defending al-Isfarāyīnī's view that legal methodology was open-ended. The course of Islamic legal history showed that there were no fixed methods of analogy. Probability, not certainty, was the goal of the former jurists, and the paths to this probability were unlimited.[87] Al-Juwaynī's doc-

80. The same is true of the cardinal problem of the veracity of God. The Muʿtazili argument is ethical. That of the leading Ashʿarīs is metaphysical.

81. *Mustaṣfā*, p. 505.

82. Al-Juwaynī, *Mughīth al-khalq*, pp. 7–8; *Baḥr*, f. 340b.

83. *Mankhūl*, p. 349.

84. Qarāfī, p. 396.

85. *Mankhūl*, p. 259; *Musawwada*, p. 248.

86. *Burhān*, f. 169.

87. *Burhān*, f. 224; *Mankhūl*, p. 457.

trine was one of the autonomy of *ijtihād*. He could not, like al-Bāqillānī, definitely exclude the validity of a method that was not certainly acceptable. The decision had to remain with each *mujtahid*.[88] The Ashʿarī dispute over infallibilism did not come to an end with al-Juwaynī. Al-Juwaynī's student al-Ghazālī, after faithfully representing al-Juwaynī's position in *al-Mankhūl*,[89] ultimately came down for infallibilism in *al-Mustaṣfā*. "Our preference," he wrote, "and it is what we hold absolutely and opposition to which we brand as error, is that every *mujtahid* in the area of probability is correct."[90]

We have seen that infallibilism elevates the act of *ijtihād* to a value unto itself, subject to no external standard. The tension in the majority doctrine of fallibilism arises from the fact that it, too, recognizes an inherent value in *ijtihād*, but at the same time applies an independent standard by which to measure the success of the act. This tension is entirely absent from the *ijtihād* doctrine of al-Māturīdī and his follower al-Samarqandī. According to al-Māturīdī's formula, the *mujtahid* who does not reach the one correct result is wrong "beginning and end" (*ibtidāʾan wa-intihāʾan*).[91] That is, his act of *ijtihād* was wrong and so also was the result to which he was led thereby. There could be no reward for this incorrect act of *ijtihād* as the majority claimed. The blame ordinarily due for an improper act was, however, absent in questions of law because of their particular obscurity.[92] The jurist is, moreover, rewarded for his good intention since his failure alone does not call that into question. [93]

Al-Māturīdī's doctrine has its parallel elsewhere.[94] It represents the furthest possible approach to the position of those like al-Marīsī for whom *ijtihād* had no place in the legal system at all. It differs from their teaching in that it postulates results that are only probable. The jurist is thus not in a position to know that he has come upon the one right answer. This point was crucial for the Muʿtazilī infallibilists. Since the jurist could not know that his answer was correct, to charge him with coming upon the right answer would constitute the imposition of an impossible obligation. Therefore, one could not speak of a right answer. Al-Samarqandī, like the Muʿtazila, regarded the imposition of an impossible task as rationally excluded. But for him, the subjective certainty of the jurist is not necessary to avoid this objectionable result. All that is required is that there exist

88. *Musawwada*, p. 248.

89. *Mankhūl*, p. 455.

90. *Mustaṣfā*, p. 492.

91. *Mīzān*, f. 202a. For parallel formulations, see *Musawwada*, pp. 202–3; Māwardī, 1:532 (no reward or punishment), 532, 534 (intention rewarded). The Māturīdī formula is discussed in Bazdawī, 4:14, 18, and extensively in Nasafī, 3:171, margin. The doctrine that these sources accept is that which al-Samarqandī associates with Abū ʾl-Ḥasan ʿAlī ibn Saʿīd al-Rustughfanī, al-Māturīdī's student (*Mīzān*, f. 202a). See Manfred Götz, "Māturīdī und sein Kitāb Taʾwīlāt al-Qurʾān," *Der Islam* 41 (1965): 28–29.

92. *Mīzān*, f. 205b.

93. *Mīzān*, f. 205b.

94. Māwardī, 1:532, 534.

a real possibility of the jurist coming upon the right answer. This possibility is provided by the evidence in the revealed law, whatever its obscurity.[95] Although al-Samarqandī does not make the point,[96] this doctrine is of a piece with the characteristic Samarqandī dissociation of belief and action. The effective operation of the legal system does not require that the jurist know that he is doing the right thing. It is enough that he do what appears to him to be the right thing. What is important is that the level of belief reflect his uncertainty, that he not simply identify prudence with validity.

III. Consequences of Infallibilism

Al-Māturīdī's doctrine of *ijtihād* represents an uncompromising rejection of infallibilism in all its forms. In the rest of this section, we shall take up some of the objectionable consequences of infallibilism. These concern, on the one hand, the nature of the legal enterprise and, on the other, its value vis-à-vis the other religious disciplines. As to the first, infallibilism marks a rejection of the systematic quality of the legal process. As to the second, infallibilism involves a denigration of the importance of law in favor of theology.

The anti-systematic character of infallibilism appears most forcibly in its relativism. For infallibilism, the state of mind of the *mujtahid* is crucial, the attainment of probability being the act regulated by the master rule of analogy. Relativism is infallibilism's answer to the charge that it validates inconsistent rules. The act of *ijtihād* is treated not as issuing in a general rule of law but in a performative. "There is no contradiction in cohabitation with a particular woman being licit for one *mujtahid* and those who choose to follow him but prohibited to another *mujtahid* and those who choose to follow him, just as a woman is prohibited to the man who divorces her but licit for the man who marries her."[97] The full formulation of the rule issuing from an act of *ijtihād* must make reference to the *mujtahid* and those who choose to follow him,[98] since the Muʿtazilī version of infallibilism postulates distinct benefits for the *mujtahid* on the one hand, and for his followers, on the other.[99] While providing an answer to inconsistency in the law, this analysis in turn raises considerable difficulties.[100] Infallibilism is, for this reason, generally content to distinguish between the act of *ijtihād* and its cognitive content, only the former being of necessity individualized.

---

95. *Mīzān*, f. 205b.

96. Suggested, however, by *wājib al-ʿamal ẓāhiran* (*Mīzān*, f. 205a).

97. *Muʿtamad*, 2:957.

98. *Muʿtamad*, 2:957.

99. *Muʿtamad*, 2:968, 977, 982.

100. For example, no value to *munāẓara* and no possibility of *ijmāʿ*. And there is the problem of the fallibilist jurist who does not regard his solution as particular. Does his error affect the validity of his result? See Bukhārī, 4:24.

But even without the extreme of individualizing the content of a jurist's *responsum*, the act of *ijtihād* is still the crucial point. What is for the fallibilists a means to the result has an independent value for the infallibilist, inasmuch as the act of *ijtihād* is the *mujtahid*'s way of complying with the rule of analogy that obligates him. From this obligation, several important consequences follow, as reported by Ibn Ḥazm:

> There sprung up a group of Ashʿarīs who came up with a remarkably stupid doctrine of *taqlīd*. When a case arises the non-jurist is obligated to ask the most learned jurist in his vicinity. Once directed to him, he questions him and if given a response he is bound to adhere to it. The non-jurist is not allowed to adhere to the doctrine of a dead scholar, ancient or modern, Companion or Follower or their successors. Should the very same case befall the non-jurist a second time, he may not adhere to the response given to him by the jurist but has to question him a second time or question someone else. And he adheres to the second response whether it be the same as the first or different. They say that where there is no text each man's obligation is only the product of his *ijtihād*, and under these circumstances every *mujtahid* is correct.[101]

Ibn Ḥazm is here explaining the doctrine that calls for the renewal of *ijtihād* (*tajdīd*, *iʿāda*, *takrīr*) for every case. According to this doctrine, the jurist is bound to go through a full act of *ijtihād* even when he recalls his former line of reasoning.[102] This position was particularly consistent with al-Bāqillānī's epistemology, according to which the probable opinion of the jurist is unrelated to the evidence before him.

Infallibilism appears equally anti-systemic when looked at from the point of view of the layman (*muqallid*). This is true even apart from the reformulation of infallibilism in its most relativist terms. Suppose a stable body of doctrine elaborated by outstanding jurists. Each legal teaching of each *mujtahid* is correct. What keeps a layman from picking those solutions that most please him? With this question, we touch upon the threat posed by infallibilism to the dominant legal schools. This threat will be most clearly put if the position of the fallibilists is briefly outlined.

According to Abū Zayd al-Dabūsī, fallibilism "requires the layman to follow the one *imām* whom he regards, upon consideration, as the most learned and not to differ from him in anything according to whim."[103] This is so because if fallibilism is correct, the layman would seem to run some risk in not following the jurist most likely to be right.

---

101. *Iḥkām*, 6:119.

102. See *Muʿtamad*, 2:932–33. For al-Baṣrī, the jurist who recalls his earlier reasoning need not repeat it, but this is precisely "because he is like one doing *ijtihād* presently." There is thus something like an act of *ijtihād* credited to the jurist. It is not enough that the jurist recall his answer (*qawl*) alone. There is no possibility of developing a system of law in the face of this requirement that *ijtihād* be ever renewed. Only the termination of those capable of *ijtihād* could produce a stable body of doctrine.

103. Bukhārī, 4:24.

The virtue of affiliation with a recognized school is at the very least the certainty that it brings of not acting in violation of consensus.[104] But apart from this, choosing the school with the soundest method gives him the best chance of acting in accord with God's will in any given case. In choosing his *imām*, the layman takes him as his intermediary (*wasīla*) with God.[105] The selection of the most learned *imām* is, on this account, a sort (*ḍarb*) of *ijtihād*.[106]

As a result of this *ijtihād* of his, the layman believes that his school is correct, though possibly in error, while the opposing school is erroneous but possibly correct.[107] Under infallibilism, however, the layman is not warranted in any such belief. "The layman is not entitled to believe with certainty that what the scholar says is true and that what the opponent says is false. All that we allow him is to act in accordance with what the scholar says."[108] The real question for infallibilism is thus not how the layman chooses his *imām*, but why should he have to choose an *imām* at all? The proper formulation of a legal *responsum* must therefore indicate that the doctrine of the jurist is only binding if the questioner so chooses.[109] The upshot is that the nonjurist is granted a measure of freedom. At the very least, he may choose among the various solutions if they differ. In some cases, this will offer him a choice between a harsher and a more lenient view. There will even be cases where he will have the choice not to act. This will amount to the absence of obligation (*taklīf*).[110] Paradoxically, the layman is freer than the jurist, except in the sense that he is bound to consult some jurist or other with respect to his legal affairs.[111]

Some infallibilists could regard this situation with equanimity,[112] but others like al-Ghazālī were concerned to find a way to put some restraint on the potential freedom of the nonjurist. Al-Ghazālī requires the nonjurist to follow the scholar he regards as the most learned. But whereas for the fallibilist the basis for this requirement is the superiority of one system to another, for al-Ghazālī it is simply the decreased possibility that

---

104. *Mustaṣfā*, p. 479.

105. Taqī al-Dīn ibn ʿAbd al-Qādir al-Tamīmī, *al-Ṭabaqāt al-saniyya fī tarājim al-ḥanafiyya*, ed. ʿAbd al-Fattāḥ Muḥammad al-Ḥulw (Cairo: al-Majlis al-Aʿlā li'l-Shuʾūn al-Islāmiyya, 1390/1970), 1:4. The same notion of the leading jurists as *wasāʾil* is already found in the writing of Muḥammad ibn ʿAbd al-Malik al-Karajī (d. 532/1137), quoted in Ibn Taymiyya, *Naqḍ al-manṭiq*, p. 146.

106. Jaṣṣāṣ, f. 305a (quoting al-Karkhī); *Muʿtamad*, 2:939; ʿIyāḍ ibn Mūsā, *Tartīb al-madārik*, 1:78. It was for this reason that Abū Isḥāq al-Isfarāyīnī refused to speak of *taqlīd* (*Baḥr*, f. 361b).

107. Ibn ʿĀbidīn, *Radd al-muḥtār*, quoted in Aḥmad ibn Idrīs al-Qarāfī, *al-Iḥkām fī tamyīz al-fatāwā ʿan al-aḥkām wa-tasarrufāt al-qāḍī wa'l-imām*, ed. ʿAbd al-Fattāḥ Abū Ghudda (Aleppo: Maktab al-Maṭbūʿat al-Islāmiyya, 1387/1967), p. 245, n. 1.

108. ʿAbd al-Jabbār, *Sharḥ*, p. 63.

109. Jaṣṣāṣ, f. 266a.

110. *Muʿtamad*, 2:893.

111. *Muʿtamad*, 2:895.

112. *Muʿtamad*, 2:939–40.

the more learned jurist has bungled in a particular act of *ijtihād*.[113] Unlike his predecessor al-Bāqillānī, from whose doctrine he deviated on this point, al-Ghazālī was obviously troubled by the political consequences of loosening "the rein of obligation" (*lijām al-taklīf*). "As long as we are able to restrain people in some way this is better than giving them free choice and letting them loose like beasts or children."[114]

One of the central legal institutions threatened by infallibilism was the disputation (*munāẓara*). The opponents of infallibilism argued that there was no real point to disputations in which neither side was interested in convincing the other.[115] But this would have to be the case if infallibilism were correct. And it is clear that on the individualist version of infallibilism not only was there no point to disputation, but there could be no disputation. The *responsa* of the *mujtahid*s were never in conflict. The infallibilists sought to preserve the disputation by pointing to its other virtues, particularly its role in training for the rank of *mujtahid*.[116] Nonetheless, there is some truth in the fallibilist critique. It does not seem fortuitous that for al-Bāqillānī, the radical infallibilist, disputation consisted in a mere recitation of the *mujtahid*'s reasoning. For him, disputation was not a dialogue but a public performance of *ijtihād*.[117] A particularly pointed rejection of disputation is contained in a remark that the Sufi ʿAlī al-Khawāṣṣ liked to repeat: "Disputation in the law is a remnant of hypocrisy (*al-nifāq*).[118]

The irenic force of infallibilism was not limited to the wrangling of rival jurists. The unification of the Zaydīs under al-Mahdī Abū ʿAbd Allāh ibn al-Dāʿī (d. 359/970) was achieved by the introduction of the doctrine of infallibilism.[119] Infallibilism, on the other hand, could stand in the way of an energetic reformer, and we find Ibn Tūmart denouncing it as "a ladder to the destruction of the *sharīʿa*."[120]

If under infallibilism, law was a less significant subject of debate, it was equally less significant a subject of study. When Qāḍī ʿAbd al-Jabbār wished to study Ḥanafī *fiqh* with Abū ʿAbd Allāh al-Baṣrī, al-Baṣrī dissuaded him with these words: "This is a science in which every *mujtahid* is correct. I am a Ḥanafī. So you be a Shafiʿī."[121] The denigration of *fiqh* was accompanied by the elevation of those sciences where one truth was available.

113. *Mustaṣfā*, p. 521.

114. *Mustaṣfā*, p. 521.

115. Bukhārī, 4:20; *Muʿtamad*, 2:968; *Mustaṣfā*, p. 500.

116. *Mustaṣfā*, p. 501.

117. *Shifāʾ*, p. 295.

118. ʿAbd al-Wahhāb al-Shaʿrānī, *al-Mīzān al-kubrā* (Cairo: Muṣṭafā al-Bābī al-Ḥalabī, 1359/1940), 1:38.

119. Ibn al-Murtaḍā, *al-Baḥr al-zakhkhār*, 1:40; al-Ḥākim Muḥassin ibn Muḥammad al-Jishumī, *Sharḥ al-ʿUyūn*, in ʿAbd al-Jabbār, *Faḍl al-iʿtizāl*, pp. 374–7S. See R. Strothmann, "Das Problem der literarischen Persönlichkeit Zaid ibn ʿAlī," *Der Islam* 13 (1923): 37–38.

120. Ibn Tūmart, *Le Livre de Mohammad Ibn Toumert*, p. 25. This is another instance in which Ibn Tūmart differs from al-Ghazālī and takes the position of al-Isfarāyīnī and al-Baghdādī.

121. Ibn al-Murtaḍā, *Ṭabaqāt al-muʿtazila*, p. 119.

What were they? Theology, Sufism, and interestingly enough, *uṣūl al-fiqh*. It is no accident that the majority of theologians in the classical period held the doctrine of infallibillism.[122] At a later period, we find the famous Egyptian Sufi al-Shaʿrānī (d. 973/1565) following the lead of his illiterate master ʿAlī al-Khawāṣṣ (d. 939/1532), whose remark on disputation we have already quoted.[123] For al-Shaʿrānī, only the Sufi who had reached the end of his path could fully experience (*yashhad*) the truth of infallibilism.[124] Al-Shaʿrānī's famous work on legal differences, *al-Mīzān*, is devoted to displaying the harmony of the competing doctrines. Al-Suyūṭī (d. 911/1505) also accepted infallibilism, in its formulation at the hands of al-Ghazālī.[125]

While infallibilism precluded a direct attack on a legal school at the level of its rules of law, this was not true of methodology. *Uṣūl al-fiqh* was commonly regarded as subject to the same standard of certainty attainable in theology. This meant that only one doctrine was correct.[126] Al-Ghazālī, for example, regarded infallibilism itself as the exclusively correct doctrine.[127] The fallibilists were wrong. Consequently, doctrines in *uṣūl al-fiqh* could be used to eliminate rival systems from contention. If the errors at the level of methodology were significant enough, the rivals were not practicing *ijtihād* at all. Thus for al-Bāqillānī, Abū Ḥanīfa was definitely wrong in nine-tenths of his doctrine as a result of errors in *uṣūl*.[128] Al-Ghazālī agreed with this assessment of Abū Ḥanīfa,[129] and in *al-Mankhūl* he even stated flatly that Abū Ḥanīfa was no *mujtahid*.[130]

For fallibilism, there were no such differences between the various sciences. Law, as much as theology, was a matter of right and wrong. Basic to this perception of law is the view of analogy as declarative. Infallibilism introduces into the law a discontinuity between the revealed texts and the product of *ijtihād*. This dichotomy is foreign to fallibilism. Just as much as there can be no inconsistencies between the revealed texts, there can be none in the rules derived from those texts.[131] Infallibilism is thus a form of pragmatism as opposed to the realism of fallibilism. It is "essentially an extension of utilitarian ways of thinking (or speaking) from ethics to epistemology."[132]

---

122. *Musawwada*, p. 502.

123. On these two, see J. Spencer Trimingham, *The Sufi Orders in Islam* (Oxford: Oxford University Press, 1971), pp. 220–22.

124. ʿAbd al-Wahhāb al-Shaʿrānī, *al-Ṭabaqāt al-kubrā: Lawāqiḥ al-anwār fī ṭabaqāt al-akhyār* (Cairo: Muṣṭafā al-Bābī al-Ḥalabī, 1373/1954), 1:31.

125. Al-Suyūṭī, *Kitāb al-Taḥadduth*, p. 234.

126. Al-Suyūṭī, *Kitāb al-Taḥadduth*, pp. 208–9 (quoting Abū 'l-Ḥusayn al-Baṣrī, *Sharḥ al-muʿtamad*).

127. *Mustaṣfā*, p. 492. This is the answer to those who attack infallibilism as self-refuting (e.g., *Tabṣira*, f. 8b).

128. *Mankhūl*, p. 439. Recall also al-Bāqillānī's remarks about al-Shāfiʿī and infallibilism.

129. Māwardī, 1:442.

130. Māwardī, 1:471.

131. Bukhārī, 4:23; *Mīzān*, f. 204a.

132. Arthur Pap, *Elements of Analytic Philosophy* (New York: Macmillan, 1949), pp. 372–73.

Summary

The aspirations toward certainty evident in the doctrine of consensus found another and more immediate outlet in infallibilism, the theory that every qualified jurist could speak infallibly on points of law where probability was his only guide. Infallibilism worked to atomize the legal community and thus presented a grave threat to the institutionalized legal schools. Moreover, unlike the doctrine of consensus, which encouraged the communication of jurists through the medium of the disputation, infallibilism tended to remove law from the center of the intellectual stage in favor of other disciplines, above all theology, where there was a point to argument. Although infallibilism, particularly in the mitigated version of verisimilitude, had a wide following among the Ḥanafīs of Iraq, it never took hold in the solidly Ḥanafī region of Central Asia.

Addenda to Chapter Five

Despite the extensive writing on the subject of *ijtihād,* nothing like a comprehensive historical account of it is available. Unfortunately polemical positions are too often uncritically taken as historical reality. Since I intend to explore this subject fully elsewhere, I will content myself with noting a few recent contributions to the literature from the side of *taqlīd*. These include Sherman A. Jackson, "*Taqlīd*, Legal Scaffolding and the Scope of Legal Injunctions in Post-Formative theory: *Muṭlaq* and *ʿĀmm* in the Jurisprudence of Shihāb al-Dīn al-Qarāfī," *Islamic Law and Society* 3 (1996): 192–233; Mohammad Fadel, "The Social Logic of *Taqlīd* and the Rise of the *Mukhtaṣar*," *Islamic Law and Society* 3 (1996): 193–233 ; Wael B. Hallaq, *Authority, Continuity and Change in Islamic Law* (Cambridge: Cambridge University Press, 2001); Ahmed El Shamsy," Rethinking *Taqlīd* in the Early Shāfiʿī School," *Journal of the American Oriental Society* 128 (2008): 1–23. Bernard Haykel and I explore some problems for the theory of *ijtihād* raised by the traditional *madhhab* in our recent article "What Makes a *Madhhab* a *Madhhab*: Zaydī Debates on the Structure of Legal Authority," *Arabica* 59 (2012): 332–71.

P. 260

The dominant Basran Muʿtazilī as well as Ashʿarī interpretation of *ẓann* was subjectivist (personalist) and as such virtually tailor-made for the doctrine of the infallibility of the *mujtahid*s held by many of these theorists. For more extensive discussions of *ẓann* than appear in the *uṣūl al-fiqh* literature, one must turn to the few surviving works on the advanced part of theology (*laṭīf al-kalām*) such as Ibn Mattawayh's *al-Tadhkira fī aḥkām al-jawāhir wa'l-aʿrāḍ*, now available in the complete edition of Daniel Gimaret (Cairo: Institut français d'archéologie orientale, 2009), 2:648–60. These general treatments, however, leave many details to be filled in. The introduction of a logical interpretation of *ẓann* is commonly attributed to the Khwarezmian Muʿtazilī Ibn al-Malāḥimī (d. 532/1144) (e.g., by al-ʿAllāma al-Ḥillī, *Manāhij al-yaqīn fī uṣūl al-dīn,* ed. Yaʿqūb al-Jaʿfarī al-Marāghī [n.p.:

Markaz al-Dirāsāt wa'l-Taḥqīqāt al-Islāmiyya, 1415 (solar)] 185) and this attribution can now be confirmed from his *Kitab al-Fāʾiq fī uṣūl al-dīn*, ed. Wilferd Madelung and Martin McDermott (Tehran: Iranian Institute of Philosophy, 2007), 370–71. His position was anticipated by al-Sharīf al-Murtaḍā, *al-Dharīʿa ilā uṣūl al-sharīʿa*, ed. Abū 'l-Qāsim Gorjī (Tehran: Chāpkhane-yi Dāneshgāh-i Ṭihrān, 1967–68), 1:23–24. On the logical interpretation, reflection (*naẓar*) on given evidence (*amāra*) can under the right circumstances generate (*yuwallid*), that is determine, a single assessment of probability across individuals. On the subjectivist interpretation an assessment of probability is adopted by each individual in response to the evidence. The extent to which the implications of these interpretations of probability were consistently drawn is of course another matter.

P. 267

The exposition of the relation between evidence and probable opinion in the second paragraph needs to be refined to bring it into line with the subjectivist interpretation of probability held by these Muʿtazilīs. The relation cannot be analytic.

P. 276

The position that *uṣūl al-fiqh* is a *qaṭʿī* discipline like theology would appear to be particularly attractive to infallibilists in law, who, once admitting probability into *uṣūl al-fiqh*, would have been pressed to recognize infallibilism there as well. The question for fallibilists, on the other hand, would be to determine where to locate the certainty needed to ground appeals to probability, and this might not be in *uṣūl al-fiqh* as commonly understood. A brief critical discussion of the alleged certainty of *uṣūl al-fiqh* can be found in Muḥammad al-Ṭāhir ibn ʿĀshūr, *Maqāṣid al-sharīʿa al-islāmiyya*, ed. Muḥammad al-Ṭāhir al-Mīsāwī (Amman: Dār al-Nafāʾis, 1421/2001), 231–38. To the references cited there add Ibn ʿAqīl, *al-Wāḍiḥ fī uṣūl al-fiqh*, ed. George Makdisi (Beirut: Steiner, 1423/2002), iv/1, 217–18.

EPILOGUE

I. The Supposed Ẓāhirism of Ibn Tūmart and Ibn ʿArabī

In the preceding chapters of this study we have become acquainted with some typical systems of Islamic legal theory. For us, formalism in its most consistent version has been represented by Ḥanafism. For other slightly different varieties of formalism, we have looked to the teaching of the other leading Sunni schools. Given the historical dominance of these Sunni schools, we may properly speak of their legal theory as "normal." By way of contrast, Ẓāhirism has been presented as the type of the materialist legal system.

For the normal legal system, the bulk of the prophetic traditions, though not necessarily the most important ones, are of no more than probable authenticity. The interpretation of the Qurʾān and of the traditions brings to light further points of uncertainty. Finally, analogy introduces a growing body of legal rules that have no more than probable validity. This uncertainty is by no means entirely unwelcome, for it opens the door to *ijtihād*, to the personal effort of the expert jurist, which not only ensures him his otherworldly reward but also serves the interests of social stability. Nonetheless, the hope remains that the uncertainty within which *ijtihād* flourishes may ultimately be resolved by consensus, which stamps one of the competing solutions as correct. In some theological circles, a more immediate resolution to the problem of uncertainty was sought in the infallibilist version of *ijtihād*. A properly achieved probability bears its own stamp of certainty.

A materialist system does not allow for traditions that are not of certain authenticity. The interpretation of the legal texts is conducted according to principles that do not admit the uncertainty of the normal systems. Analogy and any other inferences that do not yield absolutely certain results are proscribed. Because these sources of uncertainty are eliminated, there is no need for consensus. Infallibilism can take no root here.

From our study it emerges that there are criteria by which one can determine the character of an Islamic legal system. One sure indication of a formalist system is the acceptance of unit-traditions coupled with the recognition that they are of only probable authenticity. Other likely criteria turn out to be unreliable. Such is the *argumentum a contrario*, the standard counterweight to analogy. It is true that the Ḥanafīs reject all forms of this inference so as to open the way for an untrammeled use of analogy. But others reject it out of scepticism toward all linguistic forms that are general in purport. Still others, anti-analogists, reject it as one more fallible inference.

Working with the criterion of the unit-tradition, let us look at some less well-known legal theories. We need not dwell long on the legal theory of the Almohad Mahdī Ibn Tūmart (d. 524/1130). Brunschvig has already shown that Goldziher was wrong in regarding Ibn Tūmart as aligned with the Ẓāhirism of Ibn Ḥazm. Brunschvig quite properly used the unit-tradition as the test for determining the character of Ibn Tūmart's system.[1] The possibility of Ẓāhirī affiliation is removed once Ibn Tūmart tells us that the unit-tradition is a source of law for him despite its uncertain authenticity.[2] Our classification of Ibn Tūmart as a formalist is confirmed when we find him using analogy.[3] Other features of his doctrine—his impatience with those who exhibit scepticism toward general linguistic forms, and his recognition of a body of traditions intermediate between concurrent and unit—indicate that al-Ghazālī was not, as has been suggested, a major source for Ibn Tūmart's legal theory.[4] Any Ashʿarī influence would have to go back to the line of Ibn Fūrak (d. 406/1015), Abū Isḥāq al-Isfarāyīnī (d. 418/1027), and ʿAbd al-Qāhir al-Baghdādī (d. 429/1037).[5]

Another Muslim of the West whom Goldziher sought to identify with Ẓāhirism was the Andalusian Sufi Muḥyī al-Dīn Ibn ʿArabī (d. 638/1240).[6] This identification is already found in the Arabic sources that Goldziher used and has persisted among contemporary students of the great mystic. Ibn ʿArabī, however, was no Ẓāhirī.[7] It is true that he rejects the use of analogy, but even on this point his doctrine is not to be identified with the straightforward rejection of the Ẓāhirīs.

Once again we are on firm ground when we observe that Ibn ʿArabī accepts unit-traditions but regards them as of only probable authenticity.[8] This already marks a decisive break with Ẓāhirism. Ẓāhirism does not recognize the discontinuity between action and knowledge involved in Ibn ʿArabī's doctrine. Those Ẓāhirīs like Dāwūd and Ibn Ḥazm who

1. Robert Brunschvig, "Sur la doctrine du Mahdī Ibn Tūmart," *Arabica* 2 (1955): 137–48 and further in his "Encore sur la doctrine du Mahdī Ibn Tūmart."

2. Ibn Tūmart, *Le Livre de Mohammed Ibn Toumert*, p. 4.

3. Ibn Tūmart, *Le Livre de Mohammed Ibn Toumert*, p. 157.

4. Brunschvig, "Sur la doctrine," pp. 147–48. On the legal issues, see Ibn Tūmart, *Le Livre de Mohammed Ibn Toumert*, pp. 38, 51.

5. See above, ch. 1, nn. 76–78, ch. 5, nn. 35–36, 120.

6. Ignaz Goldziher, *Ẓāhirīs*, pp. 169–71.

7. For example, Henri Corbin, *Histoire de la philosophie islamique* (Paris: Gallimard, 1964), p. 317.

8. Muḥyī al-Dīn Muḥammad Ibn ʿArabī, *Risāla fī uṣūl al-fiqh*, in *Majmūʿ rasāʾil fī uṣūl al-fiqh*, pp. 20–21, 23. (This treatise is an edited version of part of chapter 88 of Ibn ʿArabī's *al-Futūḥāt al-makkiya* [Cairo, 1393/1876. Repr. Beirut: Dār Ṣādir, n.d.] and corresponds to 2:162–65 of the Cairo edition of *al-Futūḥāt*.)

accept unit-traditions claim certainty for them. Those Ẓāhiris like Ibn Dāwūd who reject this claim exclude unit-traditions from their systems.[9]

Ibn ʿArabī's doctrine of analogy confirms the error of identifying him with Ẓāhirism. Far from rejecting analogy on epistemological grounds, Ibn ʿArabī regards some instances of its use as better founded than the unit-traditions he accepts.[10] He does not consider the use of this sort of analogy as incorrect for those who have been led by their *ijtihād* to accept it.[11] "And this is a doctrine that we alone hold as far as we know."[12] That is, Ibn ʿArabī extends the scope of *ijtihād* to embrace such fundamental issues of *uṣūl al-fiqh* as the legitimacy of analogy. He personally refrains from analogy because it increases the extent of human behavior that is regulated by the law (*ziyāda fī al-ḥukm*). This imposes an additional burden on the believers that is incompatible with the Lawgiver's declared aim of lightening (*takhfīf*) their load.[13]

We thus find that Ibn ʿArabī has a very personal legal theory. The unit-tradition he accepts despite its uncertainty, but not analogy. Analogy is, however, fully legitimate for other *mujtahids*. Whatever uncertainty is thus introduced is not resolved in the usual manner, by consensus, since Ibn ʿArabī does adhere to the Ẓāhirī doctrine that restricts consensus to the Companions.[14] Neither do we find him espousing the fully developed infallibilism found among later Sufis. He defends the standard fallibilist *ijtihād* doctrine that rewards the *mujtahid* for his effort even when his result is wrong.[15] Here, too, he diverges from Ibn Ḥazm, for whom error brings no reward.[16] Only one legal solution is correct, but there is no way to identify it. The validity of analogy, it should be stressed, is one such disputed issue for Ibn ʿArabī.

The true resolution of the problem of *ijtihād* in Ibn ʿArabī's legal theory is not epistemological but metaphysical. We must not forget that Ibn ʿArabī's legal theory is only part of an all-encompassing mystical system. For Ibn ʿArabī, the *mujtahid* is authorized to draw upon revelation for his own legislation (*tashrīʿ*).[17] It is in this sense that he took al-Shāfiʿī's identification of *istiḥsān* with legislation as praise.[18] There is legislative activity on the part of the *mujtahids*, and the source of this legislation is divine:

9. See above, ch. 1, sec. III, pt. 2.

10. Ibn ʿArabī, *Uṣūl al-fiqh*, pp. 20–21.

11. Ibn ʿArabī, *Uṣūl al-fiqh*, p. 20.

12. Ibn ʿArabī, *Uṣūl al-fiqh*, p. 22.

13. Ibn ʿArabī, *Uṣūl al-fiqh*, p. 30.

14. Ibn ʿArabī, *Uṣūl al-fiqh*, p. 29.

15. ʿAbd al-Wahhāb al-Shaʿrānī, *al-Yawāqīt wa'l-jawāhir fī bayān ʿaqāʾid al-akābir* (Cairo: Muṣṭafā al-Bābī al-Ḥalabī, 1378/1959), 2:98.

16. Ibn ʿArabī, *Uṣūl al-fiqh*, pp. 33–34.

17. Al-Shaʿrānī, al-Yawāqīt, 2:97–98.

18. See above, ch. 4, n. 486.

> Know that all the *mujtahid*s are firmly fixed in the Station of Prophetic Inheritance, but they do not know that they are in this Station. For this reason they engage one another in debate. For the divine succor (*madad*) flows to them with knowledge from this Station, and each seeks to persuade his fellow to accept the arguments that convince him, be it for obligation or prohibition, for approval or disapproval. Just as they do not know that they are in this Station, so also they do not know whence they receive this illumination and vision. They know it only through the intermediary of the legal arguments. Every *mujtahid* is correct since they all draw from the Source of Law (*ʿayn al-sharīʿa*).[19]

II. Twelver Shiʿism

The role that the unit-tradition can play in evaluating the character of a legal system is particularly clear in the case of Twelver Shiʿism. A sketch of the history of Imāmī legal theory will allow us to review the leading themes of this study, for in this one legal tradition we find a recapitulation of the Sunni developments. It should be noted, however, that some features peculiar to this new setting such as dissimulation (*taqiyya*) will be ignored.

The Shiʿis inherited from their Imāms, particularly Jaʿfar al-Ṣādiq (d. 148/756), strong warnings against the use of analogy.[20] This did not prevent Muḥammad ibn Aḥmad ibn al-Junayd al-Iskāfī (d. 381/991–2) from making use of analogy in his twenty-volume *Tahdhīb al-shīʿa*.[21] But for this very reason, Ibn al-Junayd's work fell out of favor. Similarly, no trace is found of his *Kitāb al-Ifhām fī uṣūl al-aḥkām*.[22]

By the time of al-Shaykh al-Mufīd (d. 413/1023), we find growing dissatisfaction with the dominant trend among the Imāmīs that looked to traditions from the Imāms, even unit-traditions, as the basis for all doctrine, theology as well as law. The dominant group, represented by the *ḥadīth* scholar Muḥammad ibn ʿAlī ibn Bābūya (d. 381/991–2), became known as the Akhbārīs. Al-Mufīd and his followers were known as the Uṣūlīs. The latter were above all concerned with the development of a Shiʿi doctrine that met the standards set by the Muʿtazilīs of their day.[23] For al-Mufīd, this meant that unit-traditions,

19. Al-Shaʿrānī, *al-Yawāqīt*, 2:97–98. (This is a free summary of Ibn ʿArabī, *al-Futūḥāt al-makkiya*, 2:161.)

20. See, for example, Abū Jaʿfar Aḥmad ibn Muḥammad al-Barqī, *Kitāb al-Maḥāsin*, ed. Jalāl al-Dīn al-Ḥusaynī, 2 vols. (Tehran: Dār al-Kutub al-Islāmiyya, 1370/1951), 1:209–15.

21. See Āghā Bozorg al-Ṭihrānī, *al-Dharīʿa ilā taṣānīf al-shīʿa* (Tehran and Najaf, 1353–98/1934–78), 4: 504.

22. See Abū Jaʿfar al-Ṭūsī, *al-Fihrist*, ed. Muḥammad Ṣādiq Āl Baḥr al-ʿUlūm (Najaf: al-Maṭbaʿa al-Ḥaydariyya, 1380/1961) p. 160. It is said that Ibn al-Junayd eventually gave up analogy (Muḥammad Amīn al-Astarābādī, *al-Fawāʾid al-madaniyya fī al-radd ʿalā man qāla biʾl-ijtihād waʾl-taqlīd ay ittibāʿ al-ẓann fī nafs al-aḥkām al-ilāhiyya* [n.p., 1321/1904], p. 135; Muṣṭafā al-Iʿtimādī, *Sharḥ Maʿalīm al-dīn*, p. 283, margin).

23. See *Encyclopaedia of Islam*, 2nd ed., s.v. "*Akhbāriyya*"; Wilferd Madelung, "Imāmism and Muʿtazilite

now regarded as fallible, had to be excluded as sources of law, not to speak of theology.[24] Al-Mufīd had been preceded in this course by Ṣāliḥ Qubba, a student of al-Naẓẓām's, who had offered rational arguments against the acceptability of unit-traditions.[25]

For al-Mufīd, the expulsion of uncertainty from the law meant that not only unit-traditions but also analogy and all forms of *ijtihād* were excluded.[26] The same doctrine was defended by al-Shaykh al-Mufīd's student al-Sharīf al-Murtaḍā (d. 436/1044) and by a series of prominent Imāmī jurists: al-Qāḍī ʿAbd al-ʿAzīz Ibn al-Barrāj (d. 481/1088), Ḥamza ibn ʿAlī Ibn Zuhra (d. 585/1189), Abū ʿAlī al-Faḍl al-Ṭabarsī (d. 548–552/1153–1158), and Muḥammad ibn Idrīs al-ʿIjlī al-Ḥillī (d. 598/1202). All rejected the unit-tradition in the name of certainty.[27]

We thus find a situation resembling that of early Ẓāhirism. The Akhbārīs, like Dāwūd al-Ẓāhirī, accept unit-traditions because they regard them as certain. Like Ibn Dāwūd, under the influence of Muʿtazilism, the Uṣūlīs exclude the unit-tradition, which they see as falling short of certainty. Because certainty is the standard, both groups are united in rejecting analogy. The gist of the Uṣūlī position is presented in the following characteristically Muʿtazilī language by al-Sharīf al-Murtaḍā:

> Know that for the rules of law one must have a source that leads to knowledge, for as long as we do not have knowledge of the rule and are not absolutely certain that it is beneficial (*maṣlaḥa*), we must allow for its being harmful (*mafasada*). And it is wrong (*yaqbuḥu*) for us to proceed to do what we are not sure is not harmful or wrong, for to proceed to do what we are not sure is not harmful or wrong is like proceeding to do what we know is bad. For the foregoing reason, we reject analogy, which our opponents accept, as a source of legal rules inasmuch as analogy provides probability not certainty.... And for this reason we reject action in accordance with unit-reports in the Law, since they support neither knowledge nor action, we holding it necessary that action correspond to knowledge.[28]

Theology," in *Le shiʿisme imâmite: Colloque de Strasbourg (6–9 mai 1969)* (Paris: Presses Universitaires de France, 1970), pp. 20–21. Fakhr al-Dīn al-Rāzī, *Maḥṣūl*, f. 179b, indicates that the Akhbārīs were originally dominant. See also *Intiṣār*, p. 99.

24. Al-Shaykh al-Mufīd, *Awāʾil al-maqālāt*, p. 100; al-Shaykh al-Mufīd, "*Uṣūl al-fiqh*," in Muḥammad ibn ʿAlī al-Karājakī, *Kanz al-Fawāʾid* (N.p., 1322 H), p. 193. See also the quotation from al-Mufīd's *Refutation* of Ibn Bābūya in Muḥammad Bāqir al-Bihbihānī, *al-Ijtihād wa'l-akhbār*, pp. 76–77.

25. Al-Murtaḍā al-Anṣārī, *Farāʾid al-uṣūl*, p. 23. His attack on *ẓann* is attributed to his *Kitāb al-Radd ʿalā al-Zaydiyya* in Muḥammad Karīm-Khān al-Kirmānī, *Risālat al-Ḥujja al-qāṭʿia*, with *Kitāb al-Fawāʾid* (Kirman: Maṭbaʿat al-Saʿāda, 1388 H), p. 295. On Ṣāliḥ Qubba (Ibn Qubba in the Shiʿi sources), see Josef van Ess, *Die Erkenntnislehre des ʿAḍudaddīn al-Īcī*, p. 168.

26. Al-Shaykh al-Mufīd, *Awāʾil al-maqālāt*, p. 115.

27. Al-Murtaḍā al-Anṣārī, *Farāʾid al-uṣūl* (Tehran: Dār al-Ṭibāʿa al-Muṣṭafawiyya, 1315/1897), p. 61.

28. Al-Sharīf al-Murtaḍā, *Jawāb al-masāʾil al-mawṣiliyya al-thāniya*, quoted in Muḥammad ibn Idrīs al-

A major break in the line of Uṣūlī thought came with al-Sharīf al-Murtaḍā's student Abū Jaʿfar al-Ṭūsī (d. 466/1068). In his work on *uṣūl al-fiqh*, *al-ʿUdda*, al-Ṭūsī claimed that the universal practice of the Imāmīs was to accept unit-traditions. This was despite the fact that they were of uncertain authenticity. The extent of disagreement on legal questions that already existed among the Imāmīs and that al-Ṭūsī had recorded in his works *al-Tahdhīb* and *al-Istibṣār* was clear evidence of the use of unit-traditions. So also was the Imāmī literature that concerned itself with the transmitters of traditions. The alternative of rejecting unit-traditions and appealing to some rational prelegal rule such as permission (*iṭlāq*) as al-Shaykh al-Mufīd had done, al-Ṭūsī rejected.[29] The rejection of the unit-tradition would mean that most rules of law would not come from revelation, and "this far scholars will not want to go." The long Shiʿi tradition against analogy al-Ṭūsī endorsed. Here there was no opposing practice that one could point to. That the Imāmīs accepted probability in the form of unit-traditions did not bind them to recognize the legitimacy of analogy, against which their Imāms had so firmly warned them.[30]

Al-Ṭūsī's writings did not bring the opposition to the unit-tradition among the Uṣūlīs to an immediate end. We have already noted that a line of prominent jurists maintained the rejection of the unit-tradition for at least a hundred years after al-Ṭūsī's death. But the practice of the community, to which al-Ṭūsī had pointed, strained the ability of the theorists to offer acceptable explanations. There was growing tension between the theory that Shiʿi law was based on the absolutely certain transmitted teachings of the infal-

---

ʿIjlī, *Kitāb al-Sarāʾir* (N.p., 1270/1853), pp. 2–3 (dropping *lā* before *naqṭaʿ* in the third line from the bottom of p. 2 and adding *al-ʿamal* after *al-sharīʿa* in the first line of p. 3).

29. Al-Shaykh al-Mufīd, *Sharḥ ʿaqāʾid al-ṣadūq aw Taṣḥīḥ al-iʿtiqād*, ed. Hibat al-Dīn al-Shahrastānī, p. 69.

30. Ṭūsī, p. 51. It seems to be unquestioned that al-Sharīf al-Murtaḍā's *al-Dharīʿa* was written before al-Ṭūsī's *al-ʿUdda* (for example, *Dharīʿa*, editor's introduction, p. 26 [the first complete work of Imāmī *uṣūl al-fiqh*]). But there are reasons to think otherwise. In the first place, al-Ṭūsī in justifying his work specifically notes that al-Murtaḍā had not produced a comprehensive treatment of the subject (Ṭūsī, p. 2). It is recognized that *al-ʿUdda* was written in al-Murtaḍā's lifetime (Āghā Bozorg al-Ṭihrānī's introduction to Abū Jaʿfar al-Ṭūsī, *al-Nihāya fī mujarrad al-fiqh wa'l-fatāwā* [Beirut: Dār al-Kitāb al-ʿArabī, 1390/1970], p. 19). This is indicated by formulas that refer to al-Murtaḍā as alive (e.g., *adāma Allāh ʿuluwwahu*, Ṭūsī, p. 2), although this usage is not consistent (e.g., Ṭūsī, p. 199). A similar fluctuation is found throughout al-Sharīf al-Murtaḍā, *Amālī al-Murtaḍā: Ghurar al-fawāʾid wa-durar al-qalāʾid*, ed. Muḥammad Abū 'l-Faḍl Ibrāhīm, 2 vols. (Cairo: 1373/1954; Repr. Beirut: Dār al-Kitāb al-ʿArabī, 1387/1967). *Al-Dharīʿa* was written in 430/1038–1039, that is, only six years before al-Murtaḍā's death (al-Ṭihrānī, *al-Dharīʿa*, 10:26; editor's introduction to *Dharīʿa*, p. 38). What appear to be citations in *al-ʿUdda* from *al-Dharīʿa* (e.g., that noted by the editor of *Dharīʿa*, p. 28) may go back to earlier writings of al-Murtaḍā. Al-Murtaḍā had already treated *qiyās* extensively nearly fifty years before *al-Dharīʿa* in *Jawāb al-masāʾil al-mawṣiliyya al-ūlā* (of 382/992–993 according to *Dharīʿa*, editor's introduction, p. 2, n. 5; three hundred eighty something [*nayyif*] as far as al-Murtaḍā could recall, quoted al-ʿIjlī, *Kitāb al-Sarāʾir*, p. 3). Of the works to which al-Ṭūsī refers in his *al-ʿUdda*, *al-Tahdhīb* was completed well before 430/1038–1039, the date of *al-Dharīʿa* (see al-Ṭihrānī's introduction to al-Ṭūsī, *al-Nihāya*, p. 18). Once the priority of *al-ʿUdda* is considered, it is not difficult to find a critical reference to al-Ṭūsī's work in *Dharīʿa*, 1:2–3.

lible Imāms and the actual practice of the jurists. In theory, the Imāmīs needed no *uṣūl al-fiqh*. In theory, they should not bother themselves with the transmission of unit-traditions, since these were not sources of knowledge. In theory, the Imāmī layman should not be consulting the scholar for his *fatwā*, since action had to be based on knowledge, and the *fatwā* of a single scholar could not provide this. But the practice was otherwise. Ibn Zuhra felt himself called upon to address these apparent contradictions. According to him, the cultivation of *uṣūl al-fiqh* was aimed particularly at the refutation of the views of the opponent.[31] Unit-traditions were transmitted so that concurrence might ensue.[32] The layman consulted the scholar not so as to act on a single *fatwā*, but to collect *fatwās* that might disclose the existence of a consensus.[33]

The contradictions between theory and practice proved insurmountable within the tradition of al-Sharīf al-Murtaḍā, which Ibn Zuhra so faithfully represents. By the time of Ḥasan ibn Yūsuf ibn al-Muṭahhar al-ʿAllāma al-Ḥillī (d. 726/1325), Uṣūlism had become Ijtihādism. Not only was the unit-tradition accepted as probable along the lines set down by Abū Jaʿfar al-Ṭūsī, but *ijtihād*, in the sense of effort directed at legal questions admitting only of probability, was now acknowledged.[34] In short, Imāmīsm was evolving into a "normal" legal system. The rejection of analogy was maintained, but ample space was afforded the exercise of *ijtihād*, for not only the unit-traditions but large parts of hermeneutics and subsidiary procedures like *istiṣḥāb*, the presumption of continuity, came to be regarded as within the realm of probability.[35]

By the beginning of the seventeenth century, a reaction had set in with the appearance of the renewer (*mujaddid*) of Akhbārism, Muḥammad Amīn al-Astarābādī (d. 1033/1624).[36] It was al-Astarābādī's master in the study of traditions, Mīrzā Muḥammad ibn ʿAlī al-Astarābādī (d. 1028/1619), who had bidden him "revive the way (*ṭarīqa*) of the Akhbārīs."[37] This al-Astarābādī did with his book *al-Fawāʾid al-madaniyya*, which he

31. Ḥamza ibn ʿAlī ibn Zuhra, *Ghunyat al-nuzūʿ ilā ʿilmay al-uṣūl waʾl-furūʿ*. In *al-Jawāmiʿ al-fiqhiyya* (Tehran, 1276/1859), p. 1 (pagination supplied).

32. Ibn Zuhra, *Ghunya*, p. 17.

33. Ibn Zuhra, *Ghunya*, p. 26.

34. Ibn al-Muṭahhar al-Ḥillī, *Mabādiʾ al-wuṣūl ilā ʿilm al uṣūl*, pp. 203, 240. See also A. K. S. Lambton, "A Reconsideration of the Position of the *Marjaʿ al-Taqlīd* and the Religious Institutions," *Studia Islamica* 20 (1964): 126.

35. See note 70, below. According to al-Iʿtimādī, *Sharḥ Maʿālīm al-dīn*, p. 352, al-ʿAllāma al-Ḥillī regarded the *argumentum a fortiori* as *qiyās jalī* in his *al-Tahdhīb*. This is not, however, the doctrine of al-Ḥillī's *Mabādiʾ al-wuṣūl*, p. 217. For al-Bihbihānī, the prohibition of analogy was beyond question but distinguishing it from legitimate procedures for extending the law was difficult (*Risālat al-Ijtihād waʾl-akhbār*, p. 8). On the possibility that *qiyās* is part of Imāmī doctrine, see Muḥammad Bāqir al-Yazdī, *Wasīlat al-wasāʾil fī sharḥ al-Rasāʾil fī ʿilm al-uṣūl* (Dār al-Ṭibāʿa Mullā ʿAbbās ʿAlī al-Tabrīzī, 1291/1874), p. 6.

36. Yūsuf al-Baḥrānī, *al-Ḥadāʾiq al-nāḍira fī aḥkām al-ʿitra al-ṭāhira*, ed. Muḥammad Taqī al-Ayrawānī (Najaf: Dār al-Kutub al-Islāmiyya, 1958), 1:169.

37. Muḥammad Bāqir al-Khvānsārī, *Rawḍāt al-jannāt fī aḥwāl al-ʿulamāʾ waʾl-sādāt*. Vol. 1. Ed. Muḥammad

sent to Najaf and the other holy shrines, where a following was quickly gained.[38] The ensuing debate generated a remarkable output of works on *uṣūl al-fiqh* that has lasted to our own day.[39] Muḥammad Bāqir al-Bihbihanī (d. 1205/1790) is supposed to have dealt a fatal blow to Akhbārism in his *al-Ijtihād wa'l-akhbār*.[40] But the familiar title, *Ḥujjiyat al-ẓann*, of al-Murtaḍā al-Anṣārī's (d. 1281/1864) *Farāʾid al-uṣūl* indicates that the current of ideas set in motion by Akhbārism did not die. In any case, Akhbārism, with modifications, was adopted by the Shaykhī sect, which is still active in Kirman.[41] Both Uṣūlism and Akhbārism exhibit considerable doctrinal variety, and we will confine ourselves to the salient features of the two schools.

Muḥammad Amīn al-Astarābādī was keenly aware of his role in history, and it is worth considering his account of the development of Imāmī legal theory, which differs substantially from our own. According to al-Astarābādī, a fundamental break with the Imāmī tradition occurred at the beginning of the Greater Occultation (*al-ghayba al-kubrā*, from 329/941) when Ibn al-Junayd and Ibn ʿAqīl fell under the influence of Muʿtazilī theology and legal theory. Al-Shaykh al-Mufīd kept this trend alive among his famous students al-Sharīf al-Murtaḍā and Abū Jaʿfar al-Ṭūsī. Rationalistic theology and legal theory became popular among the Imāmīs. Finally, al-ʿAllāma al-Ḥillī and the other scholars who followed him fell under the influence of Sunni writers. They accepted principles, distinctions, and terminology foreign to Imāmism and of which Imāmīsm had no need. They did this unwittingly, for their aim was to catch up, as it were, with the Sunnis in these sciences.[42] Al-Ḥillī, for example, was the first to introduce the four-fold classification of Shiʿi traditions.[43] The common theme running through this development was the attachment to probable inferences (*istinbāṭāt ẓanniyya*). Those Imāmīs who adopted these

ʿAlī Rawḍātī (Tehran: Dār al-Kutub al-Islāmiyya, 1382/1962), 1:311 (from al-Astarābādī's *Dāneshnāme-ye shāhī*).

38. Al-Khvānsārī, *Rawḍāt al-jannāt*, 1:332.

39. Note the complaint of Muḥsin Amīn, a product of this tradition, that it is hyperdeveloped (*Aʿyān al-shīʿa* [Beirut: Matbaʿat al-Inṣāf, 1960], 10:274). For modern Shiʿi legal theory, see Harald Löschner, *Die dogmatischen Grundlagen des šīʿitischen Rechts: Eine Untersuchung zur modernen imamitischen Rechtsquellenlehre*, Erlanger juristische Studien, 9 (Cologne: Heymann, 1971).

40. Abdoljavad Falaturi, "Die Zwölfer-Schia aus der Sicht eines Schiiten: Probleme ihrer Untersuchung," in *Festschrift Werner Caskel*, ed. Erwin Gräf (Leiden: Brill, 1968), pp. 81–82, n. 4.

41. Gianroberto Scarcia, "Intorno alle controversie tra Aḫbārī e *Uṣūlī* presso gli Imāmiti di Persia," *Rivista degli studi orientali* 33 (1958): p. 218. This and Scarcia's "A proposito del problema della sovranità presso gli Imāmiti" (*Annali dell'Istituto Orientale di Napoli*, n. s. 7 [1958]: 95–126) are the most significant discussions of the Akhbārī/Uṣūlī controversy in a Western language and among the best pieces on *uṣūl al-fiqh*. On Shaykhism, see Henri Corbin, *En Islam iranien*, 4 vols. (Paris: Gallimard, 1971–72), 4:205–300.

42. Al-Astarābādī, *al-Fawāʾid*, p. 56.

43. Al-Astarābādī, *al-Fawāʾid*, pp. 87–88. Cf. al-Baḥrānī, *al-Ḥadāʾiq*, 1:14 (either al-Ḥillī or his teacher Jamāl al-Dīn ibn Ṭāwūs); al-Khvānsārī, *Rawḍāt al-jannāt*, 1:150 (Ibn Ṭāwūs was the first).

inferences did not realize that the revealed law had an answer to every question that would arise until the Day of Judgment.[44]

The plenitude of revelation is the keystone of al-Astarābādī's Akhbārism. It explains, in the first instance, why al-Astarābādī distinguishes between al-Shaykh al-Mufīd, on the one hand, and al-Sharīf al-Murtaḍā and Abū Jaʿfar al-Ṭūsī on the other. For of this group, only al-Mufīd is mentioned in the line of those who accepted fallible inferences,[45] and elsewhere al-Astarābādī identifies al-Murtaḍā and al-Ṭūsī, along with Muḥaqqiq al-Ḥillī (d. 676/1277), as the best of the Imāmī jurists.[46] Al-Ṭūsī's *al-ʿUdda* is the best Shiʿi work on *uṣūl al-fiqh*.[47] In fact, al-Ṭūsī was an Akhbārī, contrary to what al-ʿAllama al-Ḥillī had maintained.[48] The integration of al-Murtaḍā and al-Ṭūsī into the ranks of the Akhbārīs was possible because their writings were sufficiently ambiguous for the Akhbārīs to effect a reconciliation of what appeared to be sharply opposed doctrines. Al-Sharīf al-Murtaḍā did reject unit-traditions, but for him this did not include most of the Imāmī traditions. These were certain by virtue either of concurrence or of some extrinsic corroboration. When Abū Jaʿfar al-Ṭūsī accepted unit-traditions, he meant the Shiʿi traditions, which were certain.[49] When al-Shaykh al-Mufīd, on the other hand, rejected unit-traditions, he had recourse to the fallible inference of *istiṣḥāb*.[50] It is clear that the status of the unit-tradition is still at the heart of Imāmī legal theory.[51] For the Uṣūlīs, the unit-tradition, which remained "the foundation (*ʿumda*) of most of the law," was of only probable authenticity. For the Akhbārīs, it was absolutely certain.[52]

44. Al-Astarābādī, *al-Fawāʾid*, pp. 158–59.

45. See n. 44, above.

46. Al-Astarābādī, *al-Fawāʾid*, p. 140.

47. Al-Astarābādī, *al-Fawāʾid*, p. 41. The second best is that of al-Muḥaqqiq al-Ḥillī, which is a reworking of al-Ṭūsī's (*al-Fawāʾid*, p. 83). The best Sunni work is al-Ījī's commentary to Ibn al-Ḥājib's *Mukhtaṣar* (*al-Fawāʾid*, p. 133). See on this last point, Scarcia, "Al proposito del problema della sovranita," p. 114.

48. Al-Astarābādī, *al-Fawāʾid*, p. 135.

49. Al-Astarābādī, *al-Fawāʾid*, pp. 49, 67. This understanding of al-Sharīf al-Murtaḍā's teaching is based on a quotation from his *Jawāb al-masāʾil al-tabbāniyāt* by way of al-Ḥasan ibn Zayn al-Dīn al-Shahīd's introduction to his *Kitāb Muntaqā al-jumān fī al-aḥādīth al-ṣiḥāḥ wa'l-ḥisān*. See also al-Baḥrānī, *al-Ḥadāʾiq*, 1:67 for the same reconciliation.

50. Al-Astarābādī, *al-Fawāʾid*, p. 159.

51. This is above all true for al-Astarābādī, for whom the Qurʾān and the traditions from the Prophet were legal sources only indirectly through the traditions from the Imāms, for these alone possessed the accompanying evidence (*qarāʾin*) necessary for certainty (*al-Fawāʾid*, pp. 40, 90). While this doctrine is of theological interest, it is not basic to Akhbārism as a legal theory, as has been suggested (Scarcia, "Intorno alle controversie," p. 230). In fact, some Akhbārīs did not hesitate to offer their own interpretations of the most obscure Qurʾānic passages (al-Baḥranī, *al-Ḥadāʾiq*, 1:27). But even with the Qurʾān as a direct source, the role of the traditions would be dominant.

52. Al-Bihbihānī, *Risālat al-Ijtihād*, pp. 12, 48.

From this fundamental disagreement, there follow the most significant differences between the two schools. Because the Akhbārīs work only with sources that are certain, they have no need for *uṣūl al-fiqh*.[53] The goal of this science is the *ijtihād* they reject. Such principles for dealing with conflicting sources as they require are part of the teaching of the Imāms. Among these the most noteworthy is the principle of "circumspection" (*iḥtiyāṭ*).[54] This is in distinction to the illegitimate resort to the principle of "original licitness" (*barāʾa aṣliyya*) practiced by the Uṣūlīs.[55] Since the law covers all possible questions, "there is nothing left in its original state of permission."[56] Because the traditions in the standard Shiʿi collections are of absolutely certain authenticity, there is no need to pursue the critical study of the biographies of the transmitters.[57]

The Akhbārīs, furthermore, have no need for consensus.[58] This point calls for further elaboration in view of the special character of the Shiʿi doctrine of consensus. Because for the Shiʿis consensus is of significance only insofar as it discloses the teaching of the hidden Imām,[59] it might appear that the Akhbārīs could have no objection to the doctrine. Scarcia has therefore surmised that the Akhbārī hostility to the doctrine must have its origin in some Uṣūlī abuse.[60] But this is an inadequate account of what is a much deeper issue. In the first place, we can identify a polemical rejection of consensus. The Uṣūlī system depends on a claimed consensus as to the legitimacy of the use of probability in the law in the face of the clear prohibitions in the revealed texts. This claim is countered with an attack on the validity of consensus in the first place.[61] At another level, consensus is simply redundant, as it always is, in a system that claims certainty for all its elements, and Akhbārism is precisely such a system. Once this is grasped, important questions arise. How did the Akhbārīs perceive the legislative role of the hidden Imām? Why do we find frequent claims of consensus in the writings of al-Murtaḍā and other

53. Al-Yazdī, *Wasīlat al-wasāʾil*, p. 60.

54. Al-Astarābādī, *al-Fawāʾid*, pp. 125, 155–56.

55. Al-Khvānsārī, *Rawḍāt al-jannāt*, 1:322 (point 17). Some Akhbārīs did accept the principle of original licitness where the nonexistent rule was one for which there would be general need (*ʿumūm al-balwā*) (Muḥammad Karīm-Khān al-Kirmānī, *Risālat Sawāniḥ safar Khurāsān*, with *Kitāb al-Qawāʿid* [Kirman: Maṭbaʿat al-Saʿāda, 1387 H.], p. 278).

56. Al-Astarābādī, *al-Fawāʾid*, p. 106.

57. Al-Bihbihānī, *Risālat al-Ijtihād*, p. 47.

58. Al-Astarābādī, *al-Fawāʾid*, p. 90 (*min mukhtaraʿāt al-ʿāmma*); al-Baḥrānī, *al-Ḥadāʾiq*, 1:39; Muḥammad Bāqir al-Bihbihānī, *al-Fawāʾid al-jadīda*, p. 2 (pagination supplied); al-Khvānsārī, *Rawḍāt al-jannāt*, 1:323 (point 26).

59. Al-Muḥaqqiq al-Ḥillī, *Kitāb al-Muʿtabar fī sharḥ al-Mukhtaṣar* (N.p., 1318 [/1901]), p. 6 is typical: "Consensus is a source of law (*ḥujja*) for us in virtue of the inclusion of the infallible Imām; so should a hundred of our jurists (agree) without his opinion being among them, that would not be a source of law."

60. Scarcia, "Intorno alle controversie," p. 234.

61. Al-Astarābādī, *al-Fawāʾid*, p. 90.

Shi'i jurists who, like him, rejected the fallible unit-tradition and insisted on certainty in the law?

The second question troubled the Akhbārīs themselves. One suggestion was that "consensus" in the writings of such "pillars of consensus"(*asāṭīn al-ijmā'*) as al-Murtaḍā and Abū Ja'far al-Ṭūsī was meant to identify what they took to be the traditions to be followed where there was conflict. This selection was required because it was precisely with these figures that Shi'i law passed from the mere collection of traditions to the production of systematically ordered works of law.[62] From our point of view, we can distinguish between al-Murtaḍā and al-Ṭūsī. For al-Murtaḍā, consensus must, at least in part, have served to fill the gap left by the removal of the unit-tradition.[63] With al-Ṭūsī and the introduction of probability, the role of consensus would have to grow. But only further research will give us an accurate picture of the changes.

For the Akhbārīs, the plenitude of legal sources means that the Imām has no legislative activity during the Greater Occulation. The corpus of traditions that he has left his followers is sufficient for their needs. Al-Astarābādī refuses to conceive of a consensus that does not go back to some tradition from the Imāms.[64] The Akhbārīs reject the intuitive (*ḥadsī*) recognition of the presence of the Imām that the Uṣūlīs were claiming. The direct intervention of the Imām they either deny or trace back to a tradition.[65]

The peculiar role of the hidden Imām for the Akhbārīs is brought out by another point of contention between the two groups. The Uṣūlīs claim that an absolute (*muṭlaq*) *mujtahid* can exist, one who can actually or potentially provide an answer to every legal question. The Akhbārīs deny this and assert that only the infallible Imām has a complete set of answers.[66] The legal system consisting of the available corpus of traditions is complete in itself but not in the sense that it provides the actual (*fī al-wāqi'*) rule of God to every legal question.[67] There are instances in which precaution is the only reasonable course to take in the face of uncertainty. There is thus an essential difference between those inside the legal system and the Imām, who stands outside. The consensus of the Uṣūlīs would brush over this distinction by drawing the Imām into the legal sphere of his followers. Similarly, the elevation of one or more followers to the rank of absolute *mujtahid* would make them rivals of the Imām. The role of those within the system is to

---

62. Al-Baḥrānī, *al-Hadā'iq*, 1:35–37. See also al-Astarābādī, *al-Fawā'id*, pp. 134–35. Cf. al-Kirmānī, *Risālat al-Sawāniḥ*, p. 297.

63. For the attribution of this doctrine to him, see al-I'timādī, *Sharḥ Ma'ālim al-dīn*, p. 311.

64. Al-Astarābādī, *al-Fawā'id*, p. 136.

65. Al-Yazdī, *Wasīlat al-wasā'il*, p. 7. On the methods of discovering the opinion of the hidden Imām, see Abdulaziz Abdulhussein Sachedina, *Islamic Messianism: The Idea of the Mahdi in Twelver Shi'ism* (Albany: State University of New York Press, 1981), pp. 139–48.

66. Al-Astarābādī, *al-Fawā'id*, p. 132; al-Khvānsārī, *Rawḍāt al-jannāt*, 1:321 (point 9); Abū Ṭālib ibn Abī 'l-Qāsim al-Mūsawī, *al-Tanqīd li-aḥkām al-taqlīd* (Tehran, 1315/1897), p. 69.

67. Al-Astarābādī, *al-Fawā'id*, p. 155.

concern themselves with the certainty of the traditions they rely upon, and this goal they can attain. Their role is not to seek out God's actual rules, for this course leads only to the use of illegitimate fallible inferences.[68]

Uṣūlism presents the sharpest possible contrast to the certainty of Akhbārism. As propounded by its leading defender al-Bihbihānī, Uṣūlism consists essentially in the overwhelming consciousness of the manifold sources of uncertainty that confront the jurist. This consciousness of uncertainty was, in fact, a requirement for the legitimacy of Uṣūlism. For it was a condition for acting according to probability or giving *fatwās* that there be knowledge that knowledge was no longer attainable, that the "gate of knowledge was shut" (*insidād bāb al-ʿilm*).[69] The majority of the sources of law, it was now recognized, provided no more than probability: the principles of original licitness and hesitancy, the presumption of continuity, consensus transmitted by a unit-tradition, the interpretation of the Qurʾān and traditions.[70] Despite the great attention given to the canonical collections of Shiʿi traditions, "there is hardly to be found a copy in which there are not serious errors and falsifying corruptions." It was no longer possible to claim, as had al-Sharīf al-Murtaḍā, that the traditions of the Shiʿis were accompanied by evidence that elevated them above mere probability.[71] The extrinsic evidence that the early jurists had relied upon was now dissipated.[72] The period in which knowledge was accessible (*infitāḥ bāb al-ʿilm*) was long past. Under these circumstances, the science of *uṣūl al-fiqh* was indispensable.[73] For *uṣūl al-fiqh* prepared the jurist to travel in the realm of probability.

The Akhbārīs denied that there was ever such a closing of the gate of knowledge as the Uṣūlīs claimed. They recognized that what was at stake was nothing less than the character of Shiʿism itself. According to the Shaykhī Muḥammad Karīm-Khan al-Kirmānī (d. 1288/1870):

> One who knows the history of the Shiʿis in ancient and modern times knows that the Family of Muḥammad has taught that acting according to probability is as much prohibited as wine, pork, and gambling (*maysir*), nay, seventy times more so, and that this is the difference between the Shiʿis and the Sunnis.[74]

---

68. Al-Astarābādī, *al-Fawāʾid*, p. 176.
69. Al-Bihbihānī, *Risālat al-Ijtihād*, p. 16: *sharṭ jawāz al-ʿamal bi'l-ẓann wa'l-iftāʾ bihi al-ʿilm bi-sadd bāb al-ʿilm*.
70. Al-Bihbihānī, *Risālat al-Ijtihād*, pp. 11–12.
71. Al-Bihbihānī, *Risālat al-Ijtihād*, p. 71.
72. Al-Iʿtimādī, *Sharḥ Maʿālim al-dīn*, p. 311: *wa'l-akhbār zālat qarāʾinuhā*.
73. Al-Bihbihānī, *Risālat al-Ijtihād*, p. 40.
74. Al-Kirmānī, *Risālat al-Ḥujja al-qāṭiʿa*, p. 295.

III. Conclusion

The development of Uṣūlism and the reaction of Akhbārism suggest some general considerations that apply to the confrontation of materialist and formalist systems in Islam. The discontinuity in the history of Shiʿi legal theory marked by the admission of probability brings out the close relation between materialism and the prophetic paradigm of Islamic law. "The mainstay of the argumentation of the Imāmīs," wrote Ibn Ḥazm, "is their saying that there must be an infallible Imām who possesses the totality of the knowledge of the Sharīʿa and whom the people consult on questions of religious law so as to be certain with respect to their obligations."[75] The Imām has total knowledge of the law because he has received this knowledge from the Prophet. He is the stand-in (*nāʾib*) for the Prophet.[76] For al-Shaykh al-Mufīd, only the religious law, not reason, prevents one from referring to the Imāms as prophets.[77] Although Ibn Ḥazm does not accept the doctrine of an infallible Imām, he, too, measures the limits of the legal system by the activity of the Prophet: "Since the Prophet did not respond except on the basis of revelation (*waḥy*), not otherwise, it is the greatest affrontery for those who do so to respond to religious questions on the basis of *raʾy*, or *qiyās*, or *istiḥsān*, or *iḥtiyāṭ*, or *taqlīd*, anything except revelation alone."[78]

The prophetic paradigm sees law as a static body of norms, the only dynamic element being the transmission of these norms from generation to generation. For the Shiʿis, this transmission, in its fullest form, is limited to the line of Imāms. Figures as far apart in time as the Ismāʿīlī Qāḍī al-Nuʿmān (d. 363/974) and the nineteenth and twentieth century Shaykhīs of Iran share this vision of the law. The proper role of man is not the elaboration of the law but its scrupulous preservation. The Imām is not a legislator but the trustee of the totality of the law, as was the Prophet. For the Sunni materialists like Ibn Ḥazm, the Muslim community as a whole has been entrusted with the revealed law. Every Muslim can and must share in its transmission.

When the Uṣūlīs abandoned the traditional Shiʿi understanding of the law, they did so because they recognized that it set standards that could no longer be met. The gate of knowledge was now shut, and there was no alternative but to rely on probability. But while the rank of the Imāmī jurist may have dropped in relation to that of the Imām, it rose in relation to that of the laity. For with the introduction of *ijtihād*, the role of *taqlīd*, the layman's adherence to the teachings of a legal scholar, was vastly enhanced, and along with it, that of the scholars, the *mujtahids*.[79]

75. Ibn Ḥazm, *al-Fiṣal*, 5:95.

76. *Mustaṣfā*, p. 405.

77. Al-Shaykh al-Mufīd, *Awāʾil al-maqālāt*, p. 12.

78. *Iḥkām*, 8:35.

79. Under the impress of Basran Muʿtazilism, al-Sharīf al-Murtaḍā allowed the *taqlīd* of the scholars

The triumph of Uṣūlism within Shiʿism is representative of the different fates of materialism and formalism in Islam at large. In both cases the same forces worked in favor of formalism. The passage of time and the attendant changes in culture and language would necessarily weaken the plausibility of the materialists' claim to possess the answer to every legal question in its original prophetic form. Furthermore, the authority of the jurists found a more satisfactory justification in formalism than in materialism. For those who rejected *taqlīd* the role of the scholar was merely to prompt (*yunabbihu*) the layman to attain his own knowledge of the relevant legal rule by setting him on the right course.[80] No system of legal reasoning designed to assess the relative weight of probabilities set the jurist apart from the layman. Nothing remained over and above the discrete legal rules, which both scholars and layman could come to know. What was missing was precisely the "understanding" (*fiqh, faqāha*) that was the central element in the self-definition of the formalist jurists, both Sunni and Shiʿi.

The peculiarity of Shiʿi formalism is that it marks an undisguised break in what had been a materialist tradition. The legitimacy of Uṣūlism is tainted to the extent that it originated as a measure of desperation like the eating of carrion flesh.[81] In contrast, Sunni formalism sees itself as rooted in the original prophetic legal order. At the very least, the Prophet instructed his followers in the use of analogy.[82] Some went further and held that the Prophet had himself exercised *ijtihād* on legal questions.[83] And one reason given for this is precisely that he might not be denied the reward that its exercise merited.[84] In its own way formalism, too, regarded itself as adhering to the prophetic paradigm.

Given their different perceptions of the standards for an Islamic legal system, it is not surprising to find materialism and formalism assuming characteristic postures in their historic confrontation. For materialism, the descent from certainty to probability is a betrayal of the prophetic legacy. This is the source of the tragic account of Islamic legal history that we already find with al-Naẓẓām.[85] Because the prophetic paradigm excludes individual contributions, those with the greatest ambition found it too confining. The introduction of probability enabled them to assume positions of leadership. For probability brought with it *taqlīd* and *ijmāʿ*, devices for the self aggrandizement of the so-called scholars.[86]

---

on the basis of consensus (*Dharīʿa*, 2:796–804). He continued to reject *ijtihād*, however (*Dharīʿa*, 1:236–37). Ibn Zuhra and the scholars of Aleppo persisted in rejecting *taqlīd* (al-Yazdī, *Wasīlat al-wasāʾil*, p. 6).

80. Ṭūsī, p. 293.

81. Muḥammad Karīm Khān al-Kirmānī, *Risālat al-Bayyina*, with *Kitāb al-Fawāʾid* (Kirman: Maṭbaʿat al-Saʿāda, 1388 H), p. 159.

82. Sarakhsī, 2:130.

83. *Muʿtamad* , 2.:261·, *Lumaʿ*, p. 78; *Musawwada*, p. 506 .

84. *Mustaṣfā*, p. 485.

85. *Mustaṣfā*, p. 405.

86. Al-Astarābādī, *al-Fawāʾid*, p. 45.

For their part, the formalists trace materialism to such unfortunate human characteristics as stupidity, self-deception, and eccentricity. Because it is impossible to base a legal system entirely on certainty, those who claim to do so must be either too ignorant to understand what they are doing, or under the domination of unworthy motives like the desire to attain notoriety. Because so many had already forsaken the prophetic standard, materialism had of necessity to assume the form of a call to renounce the past. Viewed from the vantage point of the formalists, the materialist program could only appear as the dissolution of the legal enterprise and their call a kind of false prophecy.

Addenda to the Epilogue

Pp. 280–82

Ibn ʿArabī's jurisprudence, including his alleged Ẓāhirism, is examined in Michel Chodkiewicz, *An Ocean without Shore: Ibn Arabi, the Book, and the Law* (Albany: State University of New York Press, 1993).

Pp. 282–91

The Akhbārī/Uṣūlī split is covered in two books by Robert Gleave. The legal theories of the Akhbārī Yūsuf al-Baḥrānī and the Uṣūlī Muḥammad Bāqir al-Bihbihānī are compared in his *Inevitable Doubt: Two Theories of Shīʿī Jurisprudence* (Leiden: Brill, 2000). The history of Akhbārism is treated in *Scripturalist Islam: The History and Doctrines of the Akhbārī Shīʿī School* (Leiden: Brill, 2007). An edition and translation of an Akhbārī text on the differences between the two groups, ʿAbd Allāh al-Samāhijī's (d. 1135/1722), *Munyat al-mumārisīn*, appears in Andrew Newman's "The Nature of the Akhbārī/*Uṣūlī* Dispute in Late Ṣafawid Iran. Part 1," *Bulletin of the School of Oriental and African Studies* 55 (1992) 22–51. Ahmad Kazemi Moussavi, *Religious Authority in Shiʿite Islam: From the Office of Mufti to the Institution of the Marjaʿ* (Kuala Lumpur: International Institute of Islamic Thought and Civilization, 1996) looks at the social implications of the Shiʿite adoption of *ijtihād.* My own effort at a brief intellectual history of this development can be found in the *Encyclopaedia Iranica* article "*Ejtehād* in Shīʿism."

BIBLIOGRAPHY

al-ʿAbbādī, Abū ʿĀṣim Muḥammad ibn Aḥmad. *Kitāb Ṭabaqāt al-fuqahāʾ aš-šāfiʿīya*. Ed. Gösta Vitestam. Leiden: Brill, 1964.

ʿAbd al-Jabbār ibn Aḥmad al-Hamadhānī. *Faḍl al-iʿtizāl wa-ṭabaqāt al-muʿtazila*. Ed. Fuʾād Sayyid. Tunis: al-Dār al-Tūnisiyya li'l-Nashr, 1393/1974.

——. *al-Mughnī fī abwāb al-tawḥīd wa'l-ʿadl*. Ed. Ṭāḥā Ḥusayn. Cairo: al-Muʾassasa al-Miṣriyya al-ʿĀmma li'l-Taʾlīf wa'l-Tarjama wa'l-Nashr, 1380–89/1960–69. Pt. 17. *al-Sharʿiyyāt*. Ed. Amīn al-Khūlī, 1962.

——. *Sharḥ al-uṣūl al-khamsa* [attrib.]. Ed. ʿAbd al-Karīm ʿUthmān. Cairo: Maktabat Wahba, 1384/1965.

Abdel-Rahman, Hassan. "L'argument *a maiori* et l'argument par analogie dans la logique juridique musulmane." *Rivista internazionale di filosofia del diritto* 48 (1971): 127–48.

Abū Dāwūd al-Sijistānī, Sulaymān ibn Ashʿath. *Risālat Abī Dāwūd ilā ahl Makka fī waṣf sunanihi*. Ed. Muḥammad al-Ṣabbāgh. Beirut: al-Maktab al-Islāmī, 1401 H.

Abū Shāma, Abū 'l-Qāsim ʿAbd al-Raḥmān ibn Ismāʿīl. *Mukhtaṣar Kitāb al-Muʾammal li'l-radd ilā al-amr al-awwal*. In *Majmūʿat al-rasāʾil*. Cairo: Maṭbaʿat Kurdistān al-ʿIlmiyya, 1328 H. Pp. 2–44.

Abū Yaʿlā, Muḥammad ibn al-Ḥusayn al-Farrāʾ. *al-ʿUdda*. Cairo: Dār al-Kutub. Uṣūl al-fiqh MS 76 (= Arab League Uṣūl al-fiqh Film 67).

Affifi, A. E. *The Mystical Philosophy of Muhyid Din-Ibnul Arabi*. 1939. Reprint ed. Lahore: Sh. Muhammad Ashraf, 1964.

Alchourron, Carlos E. and Eugenio Bulgin. *Normative Systems*. Vienna: Springer, 1971.

Allard, Michel. *Le Problème des attributs divins dans la doctrine d'al-Ašʿarī et de ses premiers grands disciples*. Beirut: Imprimerie Catholique, 1965.

al-Āmidī, Sayf al-Dīn Abū 'l-Ḥasan ʿAlī ibn Abī 'l-Ḥasan. *al-Iḥkām fī uṣūl al-aḥkām*. 4 vols. Cairo: Muʾassasat al-Ḥalabī, 1387/1967.

Amīr Bādshāh, Muḥammad Amīn. *Taysīr al-taḥrīr*. 4 vols. Cairo: Muṣṭafā al-Bābī al-Ḥalabī, 1350–51 H.

Amīn, Muḥsin. *Aʿyān al-shīʿa*. Beirut: Matbaʿat al-Inṣāf, 1960–.

Anderson, N. D. and N. J. Coulson, "Islamic Law in Contemporary Cultural Change." *Saeculum* 18 (1967): 13–92.

al-Anṣārī, ʿAbd al-ʿAlī Muḥammad ibn Niẓām al-Dīn. *Fawātiḥ al-raḥamūt sharḥ Musallam al-thubūt fī uṣūl al-fiqh*. With al-Ghazālī, Abū Ḥāmid Muḥammad ibn Muḥammad. *al-Mustaṣfā min ʿilm al-uṣūl*. 2 vols. Cairo, 1322 H. Reprint. Baghdad: Maktabat al-Muthannā, n.d.

al-Anṣārī, Murtaḍā. *Farāʾid al-uṣūl*. Tehran: Dār al-Ṭibāʿa al-Muṣṭafawiyya, 1315/1897.

Arnaldez, Roger. *Grammaire et théologie chez Ibn Ḥazm de Cordoue*. Paris: J. Vrin, 1956.

al-Asnawī, Jamāl al-Dīn ʿAbd al-Raḥīm ibn al-Ḥasan. *Nihāyat al-sūl fī sharḥ Minhāj al-wuṣūl*. 3 vols. Cairo: Muḥammad ʿAlī Ṣubayḥ, n.d.

——. *Ṭabaqāt al-shāfiʿiyya*. Ed. ʿAbd Allāh al-Jubūrī. 2 vols. Baghdad: Riʾāsat Dīwān al-Awqāf, 1390–91/1970–71.

al-Astarābādī, Muḥammad Amīn ibn Muḥammad. *al-Fawāʾid al-madaniyya fī al-radd ʿalā man qāla bi'l-ijtihād wa'l-taqlīd ay ittibāʿ al-ẓann fī nafs al-aḥkām al-ilāhiyya*. N.p., 1321/1904.

Ayer, A. J. "The Conception of Probability as a Logical Relation." In *The Structure of Scientific Thought: An Introduction to Philosophy of Science*. Ed. Edward H. Madden. Boston: Houghton Mifflin, 1960. Pp. 279–84.

al-Bāʿalāwī, ʿAbd al-Raḥmān ibn Muḥammad. *Bughyat al-mustarshidīn fī talkhīṣ fatāwā baʿḍ al-aʾimma al-ʿulamāʾ al-mutaʾakhkhirīn*. Cairo: Muṣṭafā al-Bābī al-Ḥalabī, 1371/1952.

al-Badakhshī, Muḥammad ibn al-Ḥasan. *Manāhij al-ʿuqūl fī sharḥ Minhāj al-uṣūl*. With al-Asnawī, *Nihāyat al-sūl*.

al-Baghdādī, ʿAbd al-Qāhir ibn Ṭāhir. *al-Farq bayn al-firaq*. Ed. Muḥammad Muḥyī al-Dīn ʿAbd al-Ḥamīd. Cairo: Muḥammad ʿAlī Ṣubayḥ, n.d.

——. *Kitāb Uṣūl al-Dīn*. Istanbul, 1346/1928. Reprint. N.p., n.d.

al-Baghdādī, Abū Bakr Aḥmad ibn ʿAlī al-Khaṭīb. *Kitāb al-Faqīh wa'l-mutafaqqih*. Ed. Ismāʿīl al-Anṣārī. 2 vols. Beirut: Dār al-Kutub al-ʿIlmiyya, 1395/1975.

——. *Kitāb al-Kifāya*. Hyderabad: Dāʾirat al-Maʿārif al-ʿUthmāniyya, 1357 H.

al-Baghdādī, Ṣafī al-Dīn ʿAbd al-Muʾmin ibn ʿAbd al-Ḥaqq. *Qawāʿid al-uṣūl wa-maʿāqid al-fuṣūl*. In *Majmūʿ mutūn uṣūliyya*. Ed. Jamāl al-Dīn al-Qāsimī. Damascus: al-Maktaba al-Hāshimiyya, n.d. Pp. 80–145.

al-Baḥrānī, Yūsuf. *al-Ḥadāʾiq al-nāḍira fī aḥkām al-ʿitra al-ṭāhira*. Ed. Muḥammad Taqī al-Ayrawānī. Najaf: Dār al-Kutub al-Islāmiyya, 1958.

al-Bājī, Abū 'l-Walīd Sulaymān ibn Khalaf. *Kitāb al-Ḥudūd fī al-uṣūl*. Ed. Nazīh Ḥammād. Beirut: Muʾassasat al-Zuʿbī, 1392/1973.

——. *al-Minhāǧ fī tartīb al-ḥiǧāǧ: L'art de la polémique*. Ed. Abdel Magid Turki. Paris: Paul Geuthner, 1976.

al-Bājūrī, Ibrāhīm ibn Muḥammad. *Tuḥfat al-murīd ʿalā jawharat al-tawḥīd*. Cairo: Dār al-Kutub al-Ḥadītha, n.d.

al-Bāqillānī, Abū Bakr Muḥammad ibn al-Ṭayyib. *Nukat al-Intiṣār li-naql al-Qurʾān*. Ed. Muḥammad Zaghlūl Sallām. Alexandria: Munshaʾat al-Maʿārif, 1971.

al-Barqī, Abū Jaʿfar Aḥmad ibn Muḥammad. *Kitāb al-Maḥāsin*. 2 vols. Ed. Jalāl al-Dīn al-Ḥusaynī. Tehran: Dār al-Kutub al-Islāmiyya, 1370/1951.

al-Baṣrī, Abū 'l-Ḥusayn Muḥammad ibn ʿAlī. *Kitāb al-Muʿtamad fī uṣūl al-fiqh*. 2 vols. Ed. Muhammad Hamidullah with the collaboration of Muhammad Bekri and Hasan Hanafi. Damascus: Institut Français de Damas, 1384–85/1964–65.

al-Bazdawī, Abū 'l-Yusr Muḥammad ibn Muḥammad. *Kitāb Maʿrifat al-ḥujaj al-sharʿiyya*. Cairo: Dār al-Kutub. Uṣūl al-fiqh MS 232 (= Arab League Uṣūl al-fiqh Film 109).

——. *Kitāb Uṣūl al-Dīn*. Ed. Hans Peter Linss. Cairo: ʿĪsā al-Bābī al-Ḥalabī, 1383/1966.

al-Bazdawī, Fakhr al-Islām ʿAlī ibn Muḥammad. *Uṣūl al-fiqh*. On the Margin of al-Bukhārī, *Kashf al-asrār*.

Bekir, Ahmed. *Histoire de l'école malikite en orient jusqu'à la fin du moyen age*. Tunis, 1962.

de Bellefonds, Y. Linant. "Ibn Hazm et le zahirisme juridique." *Revue algérienne, tunisienne et marocaine de législation et de jurisprudence* 76 (1960): 1–43.

——. *Traité de droit musulman comparé.* Vol. 1. Pp. 54–55. Translated in Herbert J. Liebesny, *The Law of the Near and Middle East: Readings, Cases & Materials.* Albany: State University of New York Press, 1975. Pp. 20–22.

Ben Choaib, Aboubekr Abdesselam. "L'argumentation juridique en droit musulman." *Revue du monde musulman* 7 (1909): 69–86.

van den Bergh, Simon. *Averroes' Tahafut al-Tahafut.* 2 vols. London: Luzac, 1969.

al-Bihbihānī, Muḥammad Bāqir ibn Muḥammad Akmal. *al-Fawāʾid al-jadīda.* With al-Rāzī, Muḥammad Ḥusayn ibn ʿAbd al-Raḥīm. *al-Fuṣūl al-gharawiyya fī al-uṣūl al-fiqhiyya.* N.p., 1261/1845.

——. *Risālat al-Ijtihād wa'l-akhbār.* With al-Ṭūsī, *Kitāb ʿUddat al-uṣūl.*

Bochenski, J. M. *The Methods of Contemporary Thought.* Trans. Peter Caws. New York: Harper & Row, 1968.

Brunschvig, Robert. "Averroès juriste." In *Études d'orientalisme dediées à la mémoire de Lévi-Provençal.* 2 vols. Paris: G.-P.Maisonneuve et Larose, 1962. Vol. 1, pp. 35–68. Reprinted in Brunschvig, *Études*, 2:167–200.

——. "Le culte et le temps dans l'Islam classique." *Revue de l'histoire des religions* 177 (1970): 185–93. Reprinted in Brunschvig, *Études*, 1:167–77.

——. "De l'acquisition du legs dans le droit musulman orthodoxe." *Mémoires de l'Académie Internationale de Droit Comparé* 3, pt. 4 (1955): 95–110.

——. "Encore sur la doctrine du Mahdī Ibn Tūmart." *Folia orientalia* 12 (1970): 33–40. Reprinted in Brunschvig, *Études*, 1:295–302.

——. *Études d'islamologie.* Ed. Abdel Magid Turki. 2 vols. Paris: G.-P. Maisonneuve et Larose, 1976.

——. "Ǧāmiʿ māniʿ." *Arabica* 9 (1962): 74–76. Reprinted in Brunschvig, *Études*, 1:355–57.

——. "Le Livre de l'ordre et de la défense d'al-Muzanī. *Bulletin d'études orientales* 11 (1945): 145–96.

——. "Polémiques médiévales autour du rite de Mālik." *al-Andalus* 15 (1950): 377–435.

——. "Pour ou contre la logique grecque chez les théologiens-juristes de l'Islam: Ibn Ḥazm, al-Ghazālī, Ibn Taymiyya." Convegno internazionale, 9–15 Aprile, 1969. Tema: Oriente e occidente nel medioevo: Filosofia e scienze, Roma. Accademia nazionale dei Lincei, Fondazione Allesandro Volta. *Atti dei convegni* 13 (1971): 185–209. Reprinted in Brunschvig, *Études*, 1:303–327.

——. "Rationalité et tradition dans l'analogie jurido-religieuse chez le muʿtazilite ʿAbd al-Ǧabbār." *Arabica* 19 (1972): 213–22. Reprinted in Brunschvig, *Études*, 2:395–403.

——. "Sur la doctrine du Mahdī Ibn Tūmart." *Arabica* 2 (1955): 137–48. Reprinted in Brunschvig, *Études*, 1:281–293.

al-Bukhārī, ʿAbd al-ʿAzīz ibn Aḥmad. *Kashf al-asrār ʿan Uṣūl Fakhr al-Islām al-Bazdawī.* 4 vols. Istanbul, 1308. Reprint: Beirut: Dār al-Kitāb al-ʿArabī, 1394/1974.

Chehata, Chafik T. *Essai d'une théorie générale de l'obligation en droit musulman.* Vol. 1. Cairo: F. E. Noury, 1936.

——. "Études de philosophie musulmane du droit: II. L'Équité' en tant que source du droit hanafite." *Studia Islamica* 25 (1966): 123–38.

Corbin, Henri. *En Islam iranien.* 4 vols. Paris: Gallimard, 1971–2.

——. *Histoire de la philosophie islamique.* Paris: Gallimard, 1964.

al-Dabūsī, Abū Zayd ʿAbd Allāh ibn ʿUmar. *Taqwīm al-adilla fī uṣūl al-fiqh*. Dublin: Chester Beatty. MS 3343.
al-Dawwānī, Jalāl al-Dīn Muḥammad ibn Asʿad. *Sharḥ al-ʿAqāʾid al-ʿaḍudiyya*. Istanbul: Dār al-Saʿādat, 1316 H.
al-Dihlawī, Walī Allāh Aḥmad ibn ʿAbd al-Raḥīm. *al-Inṣāf fī bayān sabab al-ikhtilāf fī al-aḥkām al-fiqhiyya*. Ed. Muḥibb al-Dīn al-Khaṭīb. Cairo: al-Maktaba al-Salafiyya, 1385 H.
——. *ʿIqd al-jīd fī aḥkām al-ijtihād wa'l-taqlīd*. Ed. Muḥibb al-Dīn al-Khaṭīb. Cairo: al-Maktaba al-Salafiyya, 1385 H.
al-Dimashqī, Abū ʿAbd Allāh Muḥammad ibn ʿAbd al-Raḥmān. *Raḥmat al-umma fī ikhtilāf al-aʾimma*. On the margin of al-Shaʿrānī, ʿAbd al-Wahhāb. *al-Mīzān al-kubrā*. 2 vols. Cairo: Muṣṭafā al-Bābī al-Ḥalabī, 1359/1940.
van Ess, Josef. *Die Erkenntislehre des ʿAḍudaddīn al-Īcī: Übersetzung und Kommentar des ersten Buches seiner Mawāqif*. Akademie der Wissenschaften und der Literatur, Veröffentlichungen der orientalischen Kommission, vol. 26. Wiesbaden: Steiner, 1966.
——. *Das Kitāb an-Nakṯ des Naẓẓām und seine Rezeption im Kitāb al-Futyā des Ǧāḥiẓ: Eine Sammlung der Fragmente mit Übersetzung und Kommentar*. Abhandlunden der Akademie der Wissenschaften in Göttingen, Philologisch-historische Klasse. Ser. 3, no. 79. Göttingen: Vandenhoeck & Ruprecht, 1972.
——. "Ein unbekanntes Fragment des Naẓẓām." In *Der Orient in der Forschung: Feschrift für Otto Spies zur 5. April 1966*. Ed. Wilhelm Hoernerbach. Wiesbaden: Harrassowitz, 1967. Pp. 170–201.
Falaturi, Abdoljavad. "Die Zwölfer-Schia aus der Sicht eines Schiiten: Probleme ihrer Untersuchung." In *Festschrift Werner Caskel*. Ed. Erwin Gräf. Leiden: Brill, 1968. Pp. 62–95.
Faruki, Kemal A. *Ijma and the Gate of Ijtihad*. Karachi: Gateway, 1373/1954.
al-Fayyūmī, Aḥmad ibn Muḥammad. *Kitāb al-Miṣbāḥ al-munīr fī gharīb al-sharḥ al-kābir li'l-Rāfiʿī*. Cairo: al-Maṭbaʿa al-Amīriyya, 1922.
Fyzee, Asaf A. A. *Outlines of Muhammadan Law*. Delhi: Oxford University Press, 1974.
al-Ghazālī, Abū Ḥāmid Muḥammad ibn Muḥammad. *al-Iqtiṣād fī al-iʿtiqād*. Ed. Muḥammad Muṣṭafā Abū 'l-ʿIlāʾ. Cairo: Maktabat al-Jundī, 1972.
——. *al-Mankhūl min taʿlīqāt al-uṣūl*. Ed. Muḥammad Ḥasan Hītū. N.p., n.d.
——. *Kitāb Miḥakk al-naẓar fī al-manṭiq*. Cairo: al-Maṭbaʿa al-Adabiyya, n.d.
——. *Miʿyār al-ʿilm fī fann al-manṭiq*. Ed. Muḥammad Muṣṭafā Abū 'l-ʿIlāʾ. Cairo: Maktabat al-Jundī, n.d.
——. *al-Mustaṣfā min ʿilm al-uṣūl*. Ed. Muḥammad Muṣṭafā Abū 'l-ʿIlāʾ. Cairo: Maktabat al-Jundī, 1391/1971.
——. *Shifāʾ al-ghalīl fī bayān al-shabah wa'l-mukhīl wa-masāʾil al-taʿlīl*. Ed. Ḥamad al-Kubaysī. Baghdad: Riʾāsat Dīwān al-Awqāf, 1390/1971.
al-Ghunaymī, ʿAbd al-Ghanī. *al-Lubāb fī sharḥ al-Kitāb*. 4 vols. Ed. Muḥammad Muḥyī al-Dīn ʿAbd al-Ḥamīd. Cairo: Muḥammad ʿAlī Ṣubayḥ, 1381–83/1961–63.
Gibb, H. A. R. *Mohammedanism*, 2nd ed. New York: Oxford University Press, 1962.
Gibb, H. A. R. and J. H. Kramers, eds. *Shorter Encyclopaedia of Islam*. Leiden: Brill, 1953.
Gibb, H. A. R., et al., eds., *Encyclopaedia of Islam*. New Edition. 12 vols. Leiden: Brill, 1960–2004.
Goldziher, Ignaz. *Introduction to Islamic Theology and Law*. Trans. Andras and Ruth Hamori. Princeton: Princeton University Press, 1981.
——. "The Principles of Law in Islam." In *The Historians' History of the World*. 25 vols. Ed. H. S. Williams. New York, 1908. Vol. 8, pp. 294–304.

——. "Über iǵmāʿ." *Nachrichten von der Königlichen Gesellschaft der Wissenschaften zu Göttingen*. Philologisch-historische Klasse, 1916. Pp. 81–85.

——. *The Ẓāhirīs: Their History and Their Doctrine*. Ed. and trans. Wolfgang Behn. Leiden: Brill, 1971.

Götz, Manfred. "Māturīdī und sein Kitāb Taʾwīlāt al-Qurʾān." *Der Islam* 41 (1965): 27–70.

Gräf, Erwin. "Zur Klassifizierung der menschlichen Handlungen nach Ṭūsī dem Šaiḫ Al-Ṭāʾifa (gest. 460) und seinen Lehrern." *Zeitschrift der Deutschen Morgenländischen Gesellschaft*. Supp. 3, pt. 1 (1977). Pp. 388–422.

Guidi, Ignazio. "*Sunnah e nadb presso i giuristi malechiti*." In *Festschrift Eduard Sachau zu siebzigsten Geburtstage gewidmet*. Ed. Gotthold Weil. Berlin: Riemer, 1915. Pp. 333–37.

al-Harawī, Abū 'l-Fayḍ Muḥammad ibn Muḥammad al-Faṣīḥ. *Jawāhir al-uṣūl fī ʿilm ḥadīth al-rasūl*. Ed. Abū 'l-Maʿālī Athar al-Mubārakfūrī. Medina: al-Maktaba al-ʿIlmiyya, n.d.

al-Ḥāzimī, Abū Bakr Muḥammad ibn Mūsā. *Kitāb al-Iʿtibār fī bayān al-nāsikh wa'l-mansūkh min al-āthār*. Ḥimṣ: Maṭbaʿat al-Andalus, 1386/1966.

——. *Shurūṭ al-aʾimma al-khamsa*. With al-Maqdisī, Abū 'l-Faḍl. *Shurūṭ al-aʾimma al-sitta*.

Heffening, W. "Zum Aufbau der islamischen Rechtswerke." In *Studien zur Geschichte und Kultur des nahen und fernen Ostens*. Ed. W. Heffening and W. Kirfel. Leiden: Brill, 1935. Pp. 101–118.

al-Ḥillī, al-ʿAllāma al-Ḥasan ibn Yūsuf ibn al-Muṭahhar. *Mabādiʾ al-wuṣūl ilā ʿilm al-uṣūl*. Ed. ʿAbd al-Ḥusayn Muḥammad ʿAlī ibn Yūsuf al-Baqqāl. Najaf: Maṭbaʿat al-Ādāb, 1390/1970.

al-Ḥillī, al-Muḥaqqiq Jaʿfar ibn al-Ḥasan. *Maʿārij al-uṣūl*. Ed. Ḥabīb Allāh al-Jīlānī al-Ashkfūrī. Tehran, 1310/1893.

——. *Kitāb al-Muʿtabar fī Sharḥ al-Mukhtaṣar*. N.p., 1318 [/1901].

Hītū, Muḥammad Ḥasan. *al-Ḥadīth al-mursal: ḥujjiyyatuhu wa-atharuhu fī al-fiqh al-islāmī*. Beirut: Dar al-Fikr, n.d.

Horovitz, Joseph. *Law and Logic: A Critical Account of Legal Argument*. Vienna: Springer, 1972.

Horovitz, Saul. *Über den Einfluss der griechischen Philosophie auf die Entwicklung des Kalam*. Breslau: T. Schatszky, 1909.

Hourani, G. F. "The Basis of Authority of Consensus in Sunnite Islam." *Studia Islamica* 21 (1964): 13–60.

——. *Ethical Value*. London: Allen and Unwin, 1956.

——. "Reason and Revelation in Ibn Ḥazm's Ethical Thought." In *Islamic Philosophical Theology*. Ed. Parwiz Morewedge. Albany: State University of New York Press, 1979. Pp. 142–64.

——. "Two Theories of Value in Medieval Islam." *Muslim World* 50 (1960): 269–78.

Hurgronje, C. Snouck. *Selected Works*. Ed. G.-H. Bousquet and J. Schacht. Leiden: Brill, 1957.

al-Ḥusaynī, Abū 'l-Fawāris ʿAbd Allāh ibn Majd al-Dīn. *Munyat al-labīb*. Ed. Farmān ʿAlī Jaʿfar. Lucknow, 1315 H.

Ibn ʿAbd al-Barr, Yūsuf ibn ʿAbd Allāh. *Jāmiʿ bayān al-ʿilm wa-faḍlihi wa-ma yanbaghi fī riwāyatihi wa-ḥamlihi*. 2 vols. Cairo: Idarāt al-Ṭibāʿa al-Munīriyya, n.d.

——. *al-Tamhīd li-mā fī al-Muwaṭṭaʾ min al-maʿānī wa'l-asānīd*. Ed. Muḥammad al-ʿAlāwī and Muḥammad al-Bakrī. Rabat: al-Maṭbaʿa al-Malakiyya, 1387–1412/1967–1992.

Ibn ʿĀbidīn, Muḥammad Amīn ibn ʿUmar. *Sharḥ al-manẓūma al-musammā bi-ʿUqūd rasm al-muftī*. In his *Majmūʿat rasāʾil*. Damascus: Maṭbaʿat Maʿārif Sūriya, 1301/1883.

Ibn Abī 'l-Wafāʾ al-Qurashī, ʿAbd al-Qādīr ibn Muḥammad. *al-Jawāhir al-muḍiyya fī ṭabaqāt al-ḥanafiyya*. 2 vols. Hyderabad: Maṭbaʿat Majlis Dāʾirat al-Maʿārif al-Niẓāmiyya, 1332/1914.

Ibn Amīr al-Ḥājj, Muḥammad ibn Muḥammad. *al-Taqrīr wa'l-taḥbīr*. 3 vols. Cairo: al-Maṭbaʿa al-Kubrā al-Amīriyya, 1316–17 H.

Ibn al-Anbārī, Abū 'l-Barakāt ʿAbd al-Raḥmān ibn Muḥammad. *Lumaʿ al-adilla fī uṣūl al-naḥw*. Ed. A. Amer. Stockholm: Almqvist & Wiksell, 1963.

Ibn ʿAqīl, Abū 'l-Wafāʾ ʿAlī. "Le Livre de la dialectique d'Ibn ʿAqīl." Ed. George Makdisi. *Bulletin d'études orientales* 20 (1967): 119–206.

Ibn al-ʿArabī, Abū Bakr Muḥammad ibn ʿAbd Allāh. *Aḥkām al-Qurʾān*. 4 vols. Ed. ʿAlī Muḥammad al-Bijāwī. Cairo: ʿĪsā al-Bābī al-Ḥalabī, 1376–78/1957–59.

Ibn ʿArabī, Muḥyī al-Dīn Muḥammad ibn ʿAlī. *al-Futuḥāt al-makkiyya*. 4 vols. Cairo, 1393/1876. Reprint. Beirut: Dār Ṣādir, n.d.

——. *Risāla fī uṣūl al-fiqh*. In *Majmūʿ rasāʾil fī uṣūl al-fiqh*. Ed. Jamāl al-Dīn al-Qāsimī. Beirut: al-Maṭbaʿa al-Ahliyya, 1324 H. Pp. 18–35.

Ibn al-Athīr, Majd al-Dīn al-Mubārak ibn Muḥammad. *Jāmiʿ al-uṣūl fī aḥādīth al-rasūl*. Ed. ʿAbd al-Qāḍīr al-Arnāʾūt. 11 vols. Damascus: Maktabat al-Ḥalwānī, 1969–73.

Ibn Badrān, ʿAbd al-Qāḍīr ibn Aḥmad. *al-Madkhal ilā madhhab al-Imām Aḥmad Ibn Ḥanbal*. Cairo: Idārat al-Ṭibāʿa al-Munīriyya, n.d.

Ibn Daqīq al-ʿĪd, Muḥammad ibn ʿAlī. *Iḥkām al-Aḥkām*. 4 vols. Ed. Alī ibn Muḥammad al-Hindī. Cairo: al-Maktaba al-Salafiyya, 1379 H.

Ibn al-Faraḍī, ʿAbd Allāh ibn Muḥammad. *Taʾrīkh ʿulamaʾ al-Andalus*. Cairo: al-Dār al-Miṣriyya li'l-Taʾlīf wa'l-Tarjama, 1966.

Ibn Farḥūn, *Kitāb al-Dībāj al-mudhhab fī maʿrifat aʿyān ʿulamāʾ al-madhhab*. Cairo, 1351 H.

Ibn Fūrak, Abū Bakr Muḥammad ibn al-Ḥusayn. *Muqaddima fī nukat fī uṣūl al-fiqh*. In *Majmūʿ rasāʾil fī uṣūl al-fiqh*. Ed. Jamāl al-Dīn al-Qāsimī. Beirut: al-Maṭbaʿa al-Ahliyya, 1324 H. Pp. 4–14.

Ibn Ḥajar al-ʿAsqalānī, Abū 'l-Faḍl Aḥmad ibn ʿAlī. *Lisān al-mīzān*. 6 vols. Hyderabad: Maṭbaʿat Majlis Dāʾirat al-Maʿārif al-Niẓāmiyya, 1329–31 H.

——. *Nuzhat al-naẓar sharḥ Nukhbat al-fikar fī muṣṭalaḥ ahl al-athar*. Medina: al-Maktaba al-ʿIlmiyya, n.d.

Ibn al-Ḥājib, Jamāl al-Dīn ʿUthmān ibn ʿUmar. *Kitāb Muntahā al-wuṣūl wa'l-amal fī ʿilmay al-uṣūl wa'l-jadal*. Ed. Muḥammad Badr al-Dīn al-Naʿsānī al-Ḥalabī. Cairo: Maṭbaʿat al-Saʿāda, 1326 H.

Ibn Ḥazm, Abū Muḥammad ʿAlī. *al-Fiṣal fī al-milal wa'l-ahwāʾ wa'l-niḥal*. 5 vols. Cairo, 1317–21 H. Reprint. Baghdad: Maktabat al-Muthannā, n.d.

——. *al-Iḥkām fī uṣūl al-aḥkām*. 8 vols. Ed. Aḥmad Muḥammad Shākir. Cairo: Maktabat al-Khānjī (vols. 1–3), Idārat al-Ṭibāʿa al-Munīriyya, 1345–47 H.

——. *Marātib al-ijmāʿ fī al-ʿibādāt wa'l-muʿāmalāt wa'l-iʿtiqādat*. Cairo: Maktabat al-Qudsī, 1357 H.

——. *Mulakhkhaṣ ibṭāl al-qiyās wa'l-raʾy wa'l-istiḥsān wa'l-taqlīd wa'l-taʿlīl*. Ed. Saʿīd al-Afghānī. Damascus: Maṭbaʿat Jāmiʿat Dimashq, 1379/1960.

——. *Risālatān lahu ajāba fīhimā ʿan risālatayn suʾila fīhimā suʾāl al-taʿnīf*. In his *al-Radd ʿalā Ibn al-Naghrīla al-yahūdī wa-rasāʾil ukhrā*. Ed. Iḥsān ʿAbbās. Cairo: Maktabat Dār al-ʿUrūba, 1380/1960. Pp. 85–135.

——. *al-Taqrīb li-ḥadd al-manṭiq wa'l-madkhal ilayhi bi'l-alfāẓ al-ʿāmmiyya wa'l-amthila al-fiqhiyya*. Ed. Iḥsān ʿAbbās. Beirut: Dar Maktabat al-Ḥayāt, n.d.

Ibn Ḥibbān al-Bustī, Abū Ḥātim Muḥammad ibn Aḥmad. *Ṣaḥīḥ Ibn Ḥibbān bi-tartīb al-Amīr ʿAlāʾ al-Dīn al-Fārisī*. Vol. 1. Ed. Aḥmad Muḥammad Shākir. Cairo: Dār al-Maʿārif, 1372/1952.

Ibn Juzayy, Muḥammad ibn Aḥmad. *Qawānīn al-aḥkām al-sharʿiyya wa-masāʾil al-furūʿ al-fiqhiyya*. Ed. Ṭāhā Saʿd and Muṣṭafā al-Hawwārī. Cairo: ʿĀlam al-Fikr, n.d.

——. *Kitāb al-Tashīl li-ʿulūm al-tanzīl*. 4 vols. Ed. Muḥammad Muḥammad ʿAbd al-Munʿim al-Yūnusī and Ibrāhīm ʿAṭwa ʿAwaḍ. Cairo: Dār al-Kutub al-Ḥadītha, n.d.

Ibn Khaldūn, ᶜAbd al-Rahmān. *Muqaddimat al-ᶜallāma Ibn Khaldūn*. Cairo, n.d.; reprint ed., Beirut: Dār Iḥyāʾ al-Turāth al-ᶜArabī, n.d.

Ibn al-Murtaḍā, Aḥmad ibn Yaḥyā. *Kitāb al-Baḥr al-zakhkhār al-jāmiᶜ li-madhāhib ᶜulamāʾ al-amṣār*. 6 vols. Beirut: Muʾassasat al-Risāla, 1975.

——.*Kitāb Ṭabaqāt al-muᶜtazila*. Ed. Suzanna Diwald-Wilzer. Bibliotheca Islamica, vol. 21. Wiesbaden: Steiner, 1961.

Ibn al-Nadīm, Muḥammad ibn Isḥāq. *Kitāb al-Fihrist*. 2 vols. Ed. Gustav Flügel. Leipzig: F. C. W. Vogel, 1871–72. Reprint. Beirut: Maktabat Khayyāṭ, 1964.

Ibn Qayyim al-Jawziyya, Muḥammad ibn Abī Bakr. *Iᶜlām al-muwaqqiᶜīn ᶜan rabb al-ᶜālamīn*. Ed. Ṭāhā ᶜAbd al-Raʾūf. 4 vols. Cairo: Maktabat al-Kulliyyāt al-Azhariyya, 1388/1968.

——. *Madārij al-sālikīn*. 3 vols. Ed. Muḥammad Rashīd Riḍā. Cairo: Maṭbaᶜat al-Manār, 1331–34 H.

——. *Miftāḥ dār al-saᶜāda wa-manshūr wilāyat al-ᶜilm wa'l-irāda*. 2 vols. in 1. Beirut: Dār al-Kutub al-ᶜIlmiyya, n.d.

——. *Mukhtaṣar al-ṣawāᶜiq al-mursala ᶜalā al-jahmiyya wa'l-muᶜaṭṭila*. Abridged by Muḥammad ibn al-Mawṣilī. Ed. Zakariyyāʾ ᶜAlī Yūsuf. Cairo: Maṭbaᶜat al-Imām, n.d.

Ibn Qudāma, Muwaffaq al-Dīn ᶜAbd Allāh ibn Aḥmad. *al-Mughnī*. 10 vols. Ed. Ṭāhā Muḥammad al-Zaynī et al. Cairo: Maktabat al-Qāhira, 1388–89/1968–69.

——. *Rawḍat al-nāẓir wa-junnat al-munāẓir*. Cairo: al-Maktaba al-Salafiyya, 1391 H.

Ibn Rushd, Abū 'l-Walīd Muḥammad ibn Aḥmad. *Bidāyat al-mujtahid wa-nihāyat al-muqtaṣid*. 2 vols. Cairo: al-Maktaba al-Tijāriyya al-Kubrā, n.d.

Ibn Rushd, Muḥammad ibn Aḥmad. *al-Muqaddamāt al-mumahhadāt li-bayān mā iqtaḍāhu rusūm al-mudawwana min al-aḥkām al-sharᶜiyya*. 2 vols. Cairo: Maṭbaᶜat al-Saᶜāda, 1325 H.

Ibn al-Ṣalāḥ, Abū ᶜAmr ᶜUthmān ibn ᶜAbd al-Raḥmān. *Fatāwā Ibn al-Ṣalāḥ*. Cairo, 1348 H. Reprint. Diyarbakr: al-Maktaba al-Islāmiyya, n.d.

Ibn Sīnā, Abū ᶜAlī al-Ḥusayn ibn ᶜAbd Allāh. *al-Ishārāt wa'l-tanbīhāt*. 4 vols. Ed. Sulaymān Dunyā. Cairo: Dār al-Maᶜārif, 1968–71.

——. *al-Shifāʾ, al-Manṭiq*: 4, *al-Qiyās*. Ed. Saᶜīd Zāyid. Cairo: Wizārat al-Thaqāfa, 1383/1964.

Ibn Taymiyya, Taqī al-Dīn Aḥmad ibn ᶜAbd al-Ḥalīm. *Bayān muwāfaqat ṣarīḥ al-maᶜqūl li-ṣaḥīḥ al-manqūl*. On the margin of his *Kitāb Minhāj al-sunna*.

——. *Bughyat al-murtād al-manᶜūt bi'l-sabᶜīniyya fī al-radd ᶜalā al-mutafalsifa wa'l-qarāmiṭa wa'l-bāṭiniyya*, in Supplement to Vol. 4 of *Majmūᶜat fatāwā Shaykh al-Islām Ibn Taymiyya*. Cairo: Maṭbaᶜat Kurdistān al-ᶜIlmiyya, 1329 H.

——. *al-Furqān bayn al-ḥaqq wa'l-bāṭil*. In his *Majmūᶜat al-rasāʾil al-kubrā*, 1:5–172. Cairo: Muḥammad ᶜAlī Ṣubayḥ, 1385/1966.

. *al Īmān*. Ed. Muḥammad Khālid Harrās. Cairo: Dār al-Ṭibāᶜa al-Muḥammadiyya, 1972.

——. *Iqtiḍāʾ al-ṣirāṭ al-mustaqīm mukhālafat aṣḥāb al-jaḥīm*. Ed. Muḥammad Ḥamīd al-Fiqī. Cairo: Maṭbaᶜat al-Sunna al-Muḥammadiyya, 1369/1950.

——. *al-Irāda wa'l-amr*. In his *Majmūᶜat al-rasāʾil al-kubrā*. 1:225–385. Cairo: Muḥammad ᶜAlī Ṣubayḥ, 1385/1966.

——. *Kitāb Iqāmat al-dalīl ᶜalā ibṭāl al-taḥlīl*. In vol. 3 of *Majmūᶜat fatāwā Shaykh al-Islām Ibn Taymiyya*. Cairo: Maṭbaᶜat Kurdistan al-ᶜIlmiyyah, 1329 H.

——. *Kitāb al-Radd ᶜalā al-manṭiqiyyīn*. Ed. ᶜAbduṣ-Ṣamad Sharafud-Din al-Kutubī. Bombay: Qayyimah Press, 1368/1949.

——. *Maᶜārij al-wuṣūl*. In his *Majmūᶜat al-rasāʾil al-kubrā*, 1:175–211. Cairo: Muḥammad ᶜAlī Ṣubayḥ, 1385/1966.

——. *Minhāj al-sunna al-nabawiyya fī naqḍ kalām al-shīʿa wa'l-qadariyya*. 4 vols. Cairo: al-Maṭbaʿa al-Amīriyya, 1322 H. Reprint. N.p., n.d.

——. *al-Musawwada fī uṣūl al-fiqh*. Ed. Muḥammad Muḥyī al-Dīn ʿAbd al-Ḥāmid. Cairo: Maṭbaʿat al-Madanī, 1384/1964.

——. *Naqḍ al-manṭiq*. Ed. Muḥammad ibn ʿAbd al-Razzāq Ḥamza, Sulayman ibn ʿAbd al-Raḥmān al-Ṣāniʿ, and Muḥammad Ḥāmid al-Fiqī. Cairo: Maṭbaʿat al-Sunna al-Muḥammadiyya, 1370/1951.

——. *Qāʿida fī al-muʿjizāt wa'l-karāmāt*. In his *Majmūʿat al-rasāʾil wa'l-masāʾil*, ed. Muḥammad Rashīd Riḍā, 5:2–36. Cairo, 1349 H. Reprint. Lajnat al-Turāth al-ʿArabī, n.d.

——. *Qāʿida fī tawaḥḥud al-milla wa-taʿaddud al-sharāʾiʿ wa-tanawwuʿihā*. In *Majmūʿat al-rasāʾil al-munīriyya*, ed. Muḥammad Munīr, 3:128–165. Cairo, 1346 H. Reprint. Beirut: Dār al-Jīl, 1970.

——. *Rafʿ al-malām ʿan al-aʾimma al-aʿlām*. Damascus: al-Maktab al-Islāmī, 1383/1964.

Ibn Tūmart. *Le Livre de Mohammed Ibn Toumert, Mahdi des Almohades*. Ed. J. D. Luciani. Algiers: Pierre Fontana, 1903.

Ibn al-Wazīr, Muḥammad ibn Ibrāhīm. *Īthār al-ḥaqq ʿalā al-khalq fī radd al-khilāfāt ilā al-madhhab al-ḥaqq fī uṣūl al-tawḥīd*. Cairo: Sharikat Ṭabʿ al-Kutub al-ʿArabiyya, 1318/1900.

Ibn Zuhra, Abū 'l-Makārim Ḥamza ibn ʿAlī. *Ghunyat al-nuzūʿ ilā ʿilmay al-uṣūl wa'l-furūʿ*. In *al-Jawāmiʿ al-fiqhiyya*. Tehran, 1276/1859.

al-Ījī, ʿAḍud al-Dīn ʿAbd al-Raḥmān ibn Aḥmad. *Sharḥ mukhtaṣar al-muntahā al-uṣūlī*. 2 vols. Ed. Shaʿbān Muḥammad Ismāʿīl. Cairo: Maktabat al-Kulliyyāt al-Azhariyya, 1394/1974.

al-ʿIjlī, Muḥammad ibn Idrīs. *Kitāb al-Sarāʾir*. N.p., 1270/1853.

al-ʿIrāqī, Zayn al-Dīn ʿAbd al-Raḥmān ibn al-Ḥusayn. *Sharḥ alfiyyat al-ʿIrāqī al-musammā bi'l-Tadhkira wa'l-tabṣira*. 3 vols. Ed. Muḥammad ibn al-Ḥusayn al-Irāqī al-Ḥusaynī. Fez: al-Maṭbaʿa al-Jadīda, 1354 H.

——. *al-Taqyīd wa'l-īḍāḥ sharḥ Muqaddimat Ibn al-Ṣalāḥ*. Ed. ʿAbd al-Raḥmān ʿUthmān. Medina: al-Maktaba al-Salafiyya, 1389/1969.

al-Iʿtimādī, Muṣṭafā. *Sharḥ maʿālim al-dīn fī al-uṣūl*. Qom: al-Maktaba al-Muṣṭafavī, 1377/1957.

ʿIyāḍ ibn Mūsā. *Tartīb al-madārik wa-taqrīb al-masālik li-maʿrifat aʿlām madhhab Mālik*. 5 vols. Ed. Aḥmad Bakīr Maḥmūd. Beirut: Dār Maktabat al-Ḥayāt, 1387 H.

Jadaane, Fehmi. *L'Influence du stoicisme sur la pensée musulmane*. Beirut: Dar El-Mashreq, 1968.

al-Jazāʾirī, Ṭāhir. *Tawjīh al-naẓar ilā uṣūl al-athar*. Medina: al-Maktaba al-ʿIlmiyya, n.d.

al-Jaṣṣāṣ, Abū Bakr Aḥmad ibn ʿAlī al-Rāzī. *al-Fuṣūl fī al-uṣūl*. Cairo: Dār al-Kutub. *Uṣūl al-fiqh* MS 229 (= Arab League Uṣūl al-fiqh Film 6).

al-Jishumī, al-Ḥākim Muḥassin ibn Muḥammad. *Sharḥ al-ʿuyūn*. In ʿAbd al-Jabbār, *Faḍl al-iʿtizāl wa-ṭabaqāt al-muʿtazila*.

al-Juwaynī, Abū 'l-Maʿālī ʿAbd al-Malik ibn ʿAbd Allāh. *al-Burhān fī uṣūl al-fiqh*. Cairo: Dār al-Kutub. Uṣūl al-fiqh MS 714 (= Arab League Uṣūl al-fiqh Film 18).

——. *Mughīth al-khalq fī tarjīḥ al-qawl al-ḥaqq*. Cairo: al-Maṭbaʿa al-Miṣriyya, 1352/1934.

al-Kaʿbī, Abū 'l-Qāsim ʿAbd Allāh ibn Aḥmad. *Dhikr al-muʿtazila*. With ʿAbd al-Jabbār, *Faḍl al-Iʿtizāl*.

——. *Kitāb Qabūl al-akhbār wa-maʿrifat al-rijāl*. Cairo: Dār al-Kutub. Muṣṭalaḥ al-ḥadīth MS 14.

Kaḥḥāla, ʿUmar Riḍā. *Muʿjam al-muʾallifīn: tarājim muṣannifī al-kutub al-ʿarabiyya*. 15 vols. Damascus: Matbaʿat al-Taraqqī, 1957–61.

Kaplan, Abraham. *The Conduct of Inquiry: Methodology for Behavioral Science*. Scranton: Chandler, 1964.

al-Kāsānī, ʿAlāʾ al-Dīn Abū Bakr ibn Masʿūd. *Badāʾiʿ al-ṣanāʾiʿ fī tartīb al-sharāʾiʿ*. 10 vols. Cairo: Zakariyyāʾ ʿAlī Yūsuf, n.d.

al-Khayyāṭ, Abū 'l-Ḥusayn ʿAbd al-Raḥīm ibn Muḥammad. *Kitāb al-Intiṣār*. Ed. H. S. Nyberg. Cairo, 1925. Reprinted with a translation by A. N. Nader. Beirut: Imprimerie Catholique, 1957.

Kholeif, Fathalla. Introduction to *Kitāb al-Tawḥīd* by al-Māturīdī. Beirut: Dar el-Mashreq, 1970.

al-Khvānsārī, Muḥammad Bāqir. *Rawḍāt al-jannāt fī aḥwāl al-ʿulamāʾ wa'l-sādāt*. Vol. 1. Ed. Muḥammad ʿAlī Rawḍātī. Tehran: Dār al-Kutub al-Islāmiyya, 1382/1962.

al-Khwārizmī, Abū ʿAbd Allāh Muḥammad ibn Aḥmad. *Mafātīḥ al-ʿulūm*. Cairo: Maṭbaʿat al-Sharq, 1342 H. Reprint. Cairo: Maṭbaʿat al-Sharq, n.d.

al-Khwārizmī, Jalāl al-Dīn ibn Shams al-Dīn. *al-Hidāya maʿa sharḥihā al-Kifāya fī al-masāʾil al-fiqhiyya wa'l-dalāʾil al-naqliyya wa'l-ʿaqliyya*. 4 vols. Ed. Hukeem Mouluvee Abdool Mujeed. Calcutta: al-Maṭba al-Ṭibbī, 1831–34.

Király, Tibor. *Criminal Procedure, Truth, and Probability*. Trans. Kornél Balázs, rev. Árpád Erdei and Imre Gombos. Budapest: Akadémiai Kiadó, 1979.

al-Kirmānī, Muḥammad Karīm-Khān. *Risālat al-Bayyina*. With *Kitāb al-Fawāʾid*. Kirman: Maṭbaʿat al-Saʿāda, 1388 H. Pp. 134–88.

——. *Risālat al-Ḥujja al-qāṭiʿa*. With *Kitāb al-Fawāʾid*. Kirman: Maṭbaʿat al-Saʿāda, 1389 H. Pp. 230–377.

——. *Risālat Sawāniḥ safar Khurāsān*. With *Kitāb al-Qawāʿid*. Kirman: Maṭbaʿat al-Saʿāda, 1387 H. Pp. 236–320.

al-Laknawī, ʿAbd al-Ḥayy Muḥammad. *al-Rafʿ wa'l-takmīl fī al-jarḥ wa'l-taʿdīl*. Ed. ʿAbd al-Fattāḥ Abū Ghudda. Aleppo: Maktab al-Maṭbūʿāt al-Islāmiyya, n.d.

Lambton, A. K. S. "A Reconsideration of the Position of the *Marjaʿ al-Taqlīd* and the Religious Institutions." *Studia Islamica* 20 (1964): 115–135.

Laoust, Henri. *Contribution à une étude de la méthodologie canonique de Taki-d-din Aḥmad Ibn Taimiya*. Cairo: L'Institut Français d'Archéologie Orientale, 1939.

——. *Les schismes dans l'Islam*. Paris: Payot, 1965.

López Ortiz, José. *Derecho musulmán*. Barcelona: Labor, 1932.

Löschner, Harald. *Die dogmatischen Grundlagen des šiʿitischen Rechts: Eine Untersuchung zur modernen imamītischen Rechtsquellenlehre*. Erlanger juristische Studien, 9. Cologne: Heymann, 1971.

Madelung, Wilferd. "Imamism and Muʿtazilite Theology." In *Le shiʿisme imâmite: Colloque de Strasbourg (6-9 mai 1969)*. Paris: Presses Universitaires de France, 1970. Pp. 13–29.

——. *Der Imam al-Qāsim Ibn Ibrāhīm und die Glaubenslehre der Zaiditen*. Studien zur Sprache, Geschichte und Kultur des islamischen Orients, ed. Berthold Spuler, n.s., vol. 1. Berlin: Walter de Gruyter, 1965.

Makdisi, George. "Ibn Taimīya's Autograph Manuscript on *Istiḥsān*: Materials for the Study of Islamic Legal Thought." In *Arabic and Islamic Studies in Honor of Hamilton A. R. Gibb*. Ed. G. Makdisi. Cambridge: Harvard University Press, 1965. Pp. 446–79.

Makhlūf, Muḥammad ibn Muḥammad. *Shajarat al-nūr al-zakiyya fī ṭabaqāt al-mālikiyya*. 2 vols. Cairo: al-Maṭbaʿa al-salafiyya, 1349–50 H. Reprint. Beirut: Dār al-Kitāb al-ʿArabī, n.d.

al-Maqdisī, Abū 'l-Faḍl Muḥammad ibn Ṭāhir. *Shurūṭ al-aʾimma al-sitta*. Ed. Muḥammad Zāhid al-Kawtharī. Cairo: Maktabat al-Qudsī, 1357 H.

al-Maqdisī, Bahāʾ al-Dīn ʿAbd al-Raḥmān ibn Ibrāhīm. *al-ʿUdda sharḥ al-ʿUmda*. Cairo: al-Maktaba al-Salafiyya, n.d.

Marçais, William. "Le *Taqrīb* de en-Nawawi, traduit et annoté." *Journal asiatique*, n.s., 16 (1900): 315–46; 478–531; 17 (1901): 101–49, 193–232, 524–40; 18 (1901): 61–146.

Martin, R. L. "The Identification of Two Muʿtazilite MSS." *Journal of the American Oriental Society* 98 (1978): 389–93.

Massignon, Louis. *La Passion de Husayn Ibn Mansour Hallaj*. 4 vols. Paris: Gallimard, 1975.
al-Māwardī, Abū 'l-Ḥusayn ʿAlī ibn Muḥammad. *Adab al-qāḍī*. 2 vols. Ed. Muḥyī Hilāl al-Sarḥān. Baghdad: Riʾāsat Dīwān al-Awqāf, 1971–72.
al-Mawṣilī, ʿAbd Allāh ibn Maḥmūd. *al-Ikhtiyār li-taʿlīl al-Mukhtār*. Ed. Maḥmud Abū Daqīqa. Cairo, 1951. Reprint. Beirut: Dār al-Maʿrifa li'l-Ṭibāʿa wa'l-Nashr, 1395/1975.
Meron, Yaʿakov. "The Development of Legal Thought in Ḥanafi Texts." *Studia Islamica* 30 (1969): 94–101.
al-Miklātī, Abū 'l-Ḥajjāj Yūsuf ibn Muḥammad. *Kitāb Lubāb al-ʿuqūl fī al-radd ʿalā al-falāsifa fī ʿilm al-uṣūl*. Ed. Fawqiyya Ḥusayn Maḥmūd. Cairo: Dār al-Anṣār, 1977.
al-Mufīd, Muḥammad ibn al-Nuʿmān al-Shaykh. *Awāʾil al-maqālāt fī al-madhāhib al-mukhtārāt*. Ed. Faḍl Allāh al-Zānjānī. Tabriz: Maṭbaʿat Riḍāʾī, 1371 H.
——. *al-Fuṣūl al-mukhtāra min al-ʿuyūn wa'l-maḥāsin*. 2 vols. Najaf: al-Maṭbaʿa al-Ḥaydariyya, n.d.
——. *Sharḥ ʿaqāʾid al-ṣadūq aw Taṣḥīḥ al-iʿtiqād*. Ed. Hibat al-Dīn al-Shahrastānī. With al-Mufīd, *Awāʾil al-maqālāt*.
——. *Uṣūl al-fiqh*. In al-Karājakī, Abū 'l-Fatḥ Muḥammad ibn ʿAlī, *Kanz al-fawāʾid*. N.p., 1322 H. Pp. 186–94.
Mullā Ḥusayn ibn Iskandar. *Kitāb al-Jawhara al-munīfa fī sharḥ Waṣiyyat al-Imām al-Aʿẓam Abī Ḥanīfa*. Hyderabad: Maṭbaʿat Dāʾirat al-Maʿārif al-Niẓāmiyya, 1321 H.
Mūsā, Jalāl Muḥammad. *Manhaj al-baḥth al-ʿilmī ʿinda 'l-ʿarab*. Beirut: Dār al-Kitāb al-Lubnānī, 1972.
al-Mūsawī, Abū Ṭālib Muḥammad ibn al-Qāsim. *al-Tanqīd li-aḥkām al-taqlīd*. Tehran, 1315/1897.
Nallino, Carlo. "Classificazione del '*ḥadīth*' dal punto di vista dei tradizionisti." In *Raccolta di scritti editi e inediti*. 6 vols. Ed. Maria Nallino. Rome: Istituto per l'Oriente, 1939–48. Vol. 2, pp. 142–45.
al-Nasafī, Abū 'l-Barakāt ʿAbd Allāh ibn Aḥmad. *Kashf al-asrār fī sharḥ al-Manār*. 2 vols. Cairo: al-Maṭbaʿa al-Kubrā al-Amīriyya, 1316 H.
——. *Sharḥ al-Manār wa-ḥawāshīhi min ʿilm al-uṣūl*. Istanbul: al-Maṭbaʿa al-ʿUthmāniyya, 1315 H.
——. *ʿUmdat ʿaqīdat ahl al-sunna wa'l-jamāʿa*. Ed. William Cureton. London: Society for the Publication of Oriental Texts, 1843.
al-Nasafī, Abū 'l-Muʿīn Maymūn ibn Muḥammad. *Kitāb Tabṣirat al-adilla*. Istanbul. Carullah. Veliyeddin MS 1128.
al-Nashshār, ʿAlī Sāmī. *Manāhij al-baḥth ʿinda mufakkirī al-Islām*. Cairo : Dār al-Maʿārif, 1967.
al-Nāṭiq bi'l-Ḥaqq, Abū Ṭālib Yaḥyā ibn al-Ḥusayn. *Kitāb Jawāmiʿ al-adilla fī uṣūl al-fiqh*. Milan. Ambrosiana. MS Arabic B49.
al-Nawawī, Abū Zakariyyāʾ Muḥyī al-Dīn ibn Sharaf. *Tahdhīb al-asmāʾ wa-'l-lughāt*. 4 vols. Cairo, n.p. Reprint. Tehran: Maktabat al-Asadī, n.d.
al-Nīsābūrī, al-Ḥākim Muḥammad ibn ʿAlī. *Kitāb Maʿrifat ʿulūm al-ḥadīth*. Ed. Muʿaẓẓam Ḥusayn. Cairo: Matbaʿat Dār al-Kutub al-Miṣriyya, 1356/1937.
al-Nuʿmān ibn Muḥammad, Qāḍī. *Kitāb Ikhtilāf uṣūl al-madhāhib*. Ed. S. T. Lokhandwalla. Simla: Indian Institute of Advanced Study, 1972.
Oertmann, Paul "Interests and Concepts in Legal Science." In *The Jurisprudence of Interests*. Ed. and trans. M. Magdalena Schoch. Cambridge, MA: Harvard University Press, 1948.
Pap, Arthur. *Elements of Analytic Philosophy*. New York: Macmillan, 1949.
Paton, George Whitecross. *A Text-book of Jurisprudence*, 4th ed. Ed. G. W. Paton and David P. Derham. Oxford: Oxford University Press, 1972.
Patton, Walter M. *Aḥmed Ibn Ḥanbal and the Miḥna*. Leiden: Brill, 1897.

Peters, J. R. T. M. *God's Created Speech: A Study of the Speculative Theology of the Muᶜtazilî Qâḍî l-Quḍât Abû l-Ḥasan ᶜAbd al-Jabbār bn [sic] Aḥmad al-Hamaḏânî.* Leiden: Brill, 1976.

al-Qafṣī, Muḥammad ibn ᶜAbd Allāh. *Kitāb Lubāb al-lubāb.* Tunis: al-Maṭbaᶜa al-Tūnisiyya, 1346 H.

al-Qarāfī, Shihāb al-Dīn Aḥmad ibn Idrīs. *al-Dhakhīra.* Vol. 1. Cairo: al-Jāmiᶜa al-Azhariyya Maṭbaᶜat Kulliyyat al-Sharīᶜa, 1381/1961.

——. *al-Iḥkām fī tamyīz al-fatāwā ᶜan al-aḥkām wa-taṣarrufāt al-qāḍī wa'l-imām.* Ed. ᶜAbd al-Fattāḥ Abū Ghudda. Aleppo: Maktab al-Maṭbūᶜat al-Islāmiyya, 1387/1967.

——. *Sharḥ tanqīḥ al-fuṣūl fī ikhtiṣār al-maḥṣūl fī al-uṣūl.* Ed. Ṭāhā ᶜAbd al-Raʾūf. Cairo: Maktabat al-Kulliyyat al-Azhariyya and Dār al-Fikr, 1393/1973.

Qāsimī, Jamāl al-Dīn. *Qawāᶜid al-taḥdīth min funūn muṣṭalaḥ al-ḥadīth.* Ed. Muḥammad Bahjat al-Bayṭār. Cairo: ᶜĪsā al-Bābī al-Ḥalabī, 1380/1961.

al-Qasṭallānī, Aḥmad ibn Muḥammad *Irshād al-sārī ilā sharḥ Ṣaḥīḥ al-Bukhārī.* 10 vols. Cairo: al-Maṭbaᶜa al-Kubrā al-Amīriyya, 1304–5 H.

Rahim, Abdur. *I principî della giurisprudenza musulmana secondo le scuole hanafita, sciafeita, e hanbalita,* Trans. Guido Cimino. Rome: Casa editrice italiana, 1922.

al-Rāzī, Fakhr al-Dīn Muḥammad ibn ᶜUmar. *Kitāb al-ᶜArbaᶜīn fī uṣūl al dīn.* Hyderabad: Maṭbaᶜat Majlis Dāʾirat al-Maᶜārif al-ᶜUthmāniyya, 1353 H.

——. *Kitāb Muḥaṣṣal afkār al-mutaqaddimīn wa'l-mutaʾakhkhirīn min al-ᶜulamāʾ wa'l-ḥukamāʾ wa'l-mutakallimīn.* Cairo: al-Maṭbaᶜa al-Ḥusayniyya, 1323 H.

——. *al-Maḥṣūl fī uṣūl al-fiqh.* London. India Office. MS 1445.

——. *al-Masāʾil al-khamsūn fī uṣūl al-kalām.* In *Majmūᶜat al-rasāʾil.* Cairo: Maṭbaᶜat Kurdistān al-ᶜIlmiyya, 1328. Pp. 330–87.

——. *Munāẓarāt Fakhr al-Dīn al-Rāzī fī bilād mā warāʾ al-nahr.* Ed. and trans. Fathalla Kholeif in *A Study on Fakhr al-Dīn al-Rāzī and His Controversies in Central Asia.* Beirut: Dar El-Machreq, 1966.

——. *al-Tafsīr al-kabīr.* 32 vols. Cairo: al-Maṭbaᶜa al-Bahiyya al-Miṣriyya, n.d.

Sachedina, Abdulaziz Abdulhussein. *Islamic Messianism: The Idea of the Mahdi in Twelver Shiᶜism.* Albany: State University of New York Press, 1981.

al-Sakhāwī, Shams al-Dīn Muḥammad ibn ᶜAbd al-Raḥmān. *Fatḥ al-mughīth sharḥ Alfiyyat al-ḥadīth li'l-ᶜIrāqī.* 3 vols. Ed. ᶜAbd al-Raḥmān Muḥammad ᶜUthmān. Medina: al-Maktaba al-Salafiyya, 1388/1968.

al-Samᶜānī, Abū 'l-Muẓaffar Manṣūr ibn Muḥammad. *Qawāṭiᶜ al-adilla.* Istanbul. Feyzullah Efendi. MS 627 (= Arab League Uṣūl al-fiqh Film 73).

al-Samarqandī, ᶜAlāʾ al-Dīn Abū Bakr Muḥammad ibn Aḥmad. *Mīzān al-uṣūl fī natāʾij al-ᶜuqūl.* Princeton. Garrett. MS 1626.

. *Tuḥfat al-fuqahāʾ.* Ed. Muḥammad Zakī ᶜAbd al-Barr. 3 vols. Damascus: Maṭbaᶜat Jāmiᶜat Dimashq, 1377–79/1958–59.

al-Ṣanᶜānī, Muḥammad ibn Ismāᶜīl al-Amīr. *Irshād al-nuqqād ilā taysīr al-ijtihād.* In *Majmūᶜat al-rasāʾil al-munīriyya.* Ed. Muḥammad Munīr. Cairo: Idārat al-Ṭibāᶜa al-Munīriyya, 1343 H. Vol. 1, pp. 1–47. Reprint. Beirut: Dār al-Jīl, 1970.

——. *Subul al-salām.* 4 vols. Cairo: Muṣṭafā al-Bābī al-Ḥalabī, 1379/1965.

——. *Tawḍīḥ al-afkār li-maᶜānī Tanqīḥ al-anẓār.* 2 vols. Ed. Muḥammad Muḥyī al-Dīn ᶜAbd al-Ḥamīd. Cairo: Maktabat al-Khānjī, 1366 H.

Santillana, David. *Istituzioni di diritto musulmano malichita con riguardo anche al sistema sciafiita.* 2 vols. Rome: Istituto per l'Oriente, 1926–38.

al-Sanūsī, Abū ʿAbd Allāh Muḥammad ibn Yūsuf. *ʿUmdat ahl al-tawfīq wa'l-tasdīd sharḥ ʿAqīdat ahl al-tawḥīd al-kubrā*. Cairo: Muṣṭafā al-Bābī al-Ḥalabī, 1353/1936.

al-Sarakhsī, Abū Bakr Muḥammad ibn Aḥmad. *Uṣūl al-Sarakhsī*. 2 vols. Ed. Abū 'l-Wafā al-Afghānī. Hyderabad: Lajnat Iḥyāʾ al-Maʿārif al-Nuʿmāniyya, 1372–3/1953–4.

Scarcia, Gianroberto. "A proposito del problema della sovranità presso gli Imāmiti." *Annali dell'Istituto Orientale di Napoli*, n. s. 7 (1958): 95–126.

——. "Intorno alla controversie tra Aḫbārī e Uṣūlī presso gli Imāmiti de Persia." *Rivista degli studi orientali* 33 (1958): 211–50.

Schacht, Joseph. *The Origins of Muhammadan Jurisprudence*. Oxford: Oxford University Press, 1967.

Schreiner, Martin. *Studien über Jeshuʿa ben Jehuda, Achtzehnter Bericht über die Lehranstalt für die Wissenschaft des Judenthums in Berlin*. Berlin: H. Itzkowski, 1900.

al-Shāfiʿī, Muḥammad ibn Idrīs. *al-Risāla*. Ed. Aḥmad Muḥammad Shākir. Cairo: Muṣṭafā al-Bābī al-Ḥalabī, 1358/1940.

al-Shahrastānī, Muḥammad ibn ʿAbd al-Karīm. *Kitāb al-Milal wa'l-niḥal*. Ed. ʿAbd al-ʿAzīz Muḥammad al-Wakīl. Cairo: Muʾassasat al-Ḥalabī, 1387/1967.

——. *Kitāb Nihāyat al-iqdām fī ʿilm al-kalām*. Ed. Alfred Guillaume. Oxford: Oxford University Press, 1934.

al-Shaʿrānī, ʿAbd al-Wahhāb ibn Aḥmad. *al-Mīzān al-kubrā*. 2 vols. Cairo: Muṣṭafā al-Bābī al-Ḥalabī, 1359/1940.

——. *al-Ṭabaqāt al-kubrā: Lawāqiḥ al-anwār fī ṭabaqāt al-akhyār*. 2 vols. Cairo: Muṣṭafā al-Bābī al-Ḥalabī, 1373/1954.

——. *al-Yawāqīt wa'l-jawāhir fī bayān ʿaqāʾid al-akābir*. 2 vols. Cairo: Muṣṭafā al-Bābī al-Ḥalabī, 1378/1959.

al-Sharīf al-Murtaḍā, ʿAlī ibn al-Ḥusayn. *Amālī al-Murtaḍā: Ghurar al-fawāʾid wa-durar al-qalāʾid*. 2 vols. Ed. Muḥammad Abū 'l-Faḍl Ibrāhīm. Cairo: 1373/1954. Reprint. Beirut: Dār al-Kitāb al-ʿArabī, 1387/1967.

——. *al-Dharīʿa ilā uṣūl al-sharīʿa*. 2 vols. Ed. Abū 'l-Qāsim Gorjī. Tehran: Chāpkhāne-yi Dāneshgāh-i Ṭihrān, 1967–68.

al-Shāshī, Abū ʿAlī Aḥmad ibn Muḥammad. *Uṣūl al-Shāshī*. Hyderabad, 1306.

al-Shāṭibī, Abū Isḥāq Ibrāhīm ibn Mūsā. *al-Iʿtiṣām*. Ed. Muḥammad Rashīd Riḍā. Cairo: al-Maktaba al-Tijāriyya al-Kubrā, n.d.

——. *al-Muwāfaqāt fī uṣūl al-aḥkām*. Ed. Muḥammad Muḥyī al-Dīn ʿAbd al-Ḥamīd. 4 vols. Cairo: Muḥammad ʿAlī Ṣubayḥ, n.d.

al-Shawkānī, Muḥammad ibn ʿAlī. *Irshād al-fuḥūl ilā taḥqīq al-ḥaqq min ʿilm al-uṣūl*. Cairo: Muṣṭafā al-Bābī al-Ḥalabī, 1356/1937.

——. *Irshād al-sāʾil ilā dalāʾil al-masāʾil*. In *Majmūʿat al-rasāʾil al-munīriyya*. Ed. Muḥammad Munīr. Cairo: Idārat al-Ṭibāʿa al-Munīriyya, 1346 H. Vol. 3, pp. 84–97. Reprint. Beirut: Dār al-Jīl, 1970.

Shehaby, Nabil. "The Influence of Stoic Logic on al-Jaṣṣāṣ's Legal Theory." In *The Cultural Context of Medieval Learning: Proceedings of the First International Colloquium on Philosophy, Science, and Theology in the Middle Ages, September 1970*. Ed. John E. Murdoch and Edith D. Sylla. Boston Studies in the Philosophy of Science, 26. Boston: D. Reidel, 1975. Pp. 61–85.

al-Shīrāzī, Abū Isḥāq Ibrāhīm ibn ʿAlī. *al-Lumaʿ fī uṣūl al-fiqh*. Cairo: Muḥammad ʿAlī Ṣubayḥ, n.d.

——. *Ṭabaqāt al-fuqahāʾ*. Ed. Iḥsān ʿAbbās. Beirut: Dār al-Rāʾid al-ʿArabī, 1970.

Ṣiddīq Ḥasan Khān, Muḥammad. *Ḥuṣūl al-maʾmūl min ʿilm al-uṣūl*. Istanbul: Maktabat al-Jawāʾib, 1296.

al-Sīnawānī, Ḥasan ibn ʿUmar. *Kitāb al-Aṣl al-jāmiʿ li-īḍāḥ al-durar al-manẓūma fī silk Jamʿ al-jawāmiʿ*. 2 vols. Tunis: Maṭbaʿat al-Nahḍa, 1928.

Spies, O. and E. Pritsch. "Klassiches Islamisches Recht." In *Orientalisches Recht*, Handbuch der Orientalistik, pt. 1, supp. 3. Leiden: Brill, 1964.

Strothmann, R. "Das Problem der literarischen Persönlichkeit Zaid ibn ʿAlī." *Der Islam* 13 (1923): 1–52.

al-Subkī, Tāj al-Dīn ʿAbd al-Wahhāb ibn ʿAlī. *Jamʿ al-jawāmiʿ*. 2 vols. Cairo: Īsā al-Bābī al-Ḥalabī, n.d.

———. *Ṭabaqāt al-shāfiʿiyya al-kubrā*. 10 vols. Ed. ʿAbd al-Faṭṭāḥ Muḥammad al-Ḥulw and Maḥmūd Muḥammad al-Ṭanāḥī. Cairo: ʿĪsā al-Bābī al-Ḥalabī, 1964–76.

al-Subkī, Taqī al-Dīn ʿAlī ibn ʿAbd al-Kāfī. *Maʿnā qawl al-imām al-muṭṭalibī idha ṣaḥḥa al-ḥadīth fa-huwa madhhabī*. In *Majmūʿat al-rasāʾil al-munīriyya*. Ed. Muḥammad Munīr. Cairo: Idārat al-Ṭibāʿa al-Munīriyya, 1346 H. Vol. 3, pp. 98–114. Reprint. Beirut: Dār al-Jīl, 1970.

Summers, Robert Samuel. *Instrumentalism and American Legal Theory*. Ithaca: Cornell University Press, 1983.

al-Suyūṭī, Jalāl al-Dīn ʿAbd al-Raḥmān ibn Abī Bakr. *Kitāb al-Iqtirāḥ fī ʿilm uṣūl al-naḥw*. Ed. Aḥmad Muḥammad Qāsim. Cairo: Maṭbaʿat al-Saʿādah, 1396/1976.

———. *Kitāb al-Taḥadduth bi-niʿmat Allāh*. Ed. E. M. Sartain as vol. 2 of *Jalāl al-Dīn al-Suyūṭī: Biography and Background*. 2 vols. Cambridge: Cambridge University Press, 1975.

———. *Taqrīb al-rāwī fī sharḥ Taqrīb al-Nawāwī*. Ed. ʿAbd al-Wahhāb ʿAbd al-Laṭīf. Medina: al-Maktaba al-ʿIlmiyya, 1379/1959.

———. *Taʾrīkh al-khulafāʾ*. Beirut: Dār al-Thaqāfa, n.d.

al-Taftāzānī, Saʿd al-Dīn Masʿūd ibn ʿUmar. *Sharḥ al-ʿaqāʾid al-nasafiyya*. Istanbul, 1326 H. Reprint. Baghdad: Maktabat al-Muthannā, n.d.

———. *al-Talwīḥ*. 3 vols. Cairo: al-Maṭbaʿa al-Khayriyya, 1322–24/1904–6.

al-Tamīmī, Taqī al-Dīn ibn ʿAbd al-Qādir. *al-Ṭabaqāt al-saniyya fī tarājim al-ḥanafiyya*. Vol. 1. Ed. ʿAbd al-Fattāḥ Muḥammad al-Ḥulw. Cairo: al-Majlis al-Aʿlā li'l-Shuʾūn al-Islāmiyya, 1390/1970.

Tashköprüzāde, Aḥmad ibn Muṣṭafā. *Miftāḥ al-saʿāda wa-miṣbāḥ al-siyāda fī mawḍūʿāt al-ʿulūm*. 3 vols. Ed. Kāmil Kāmil Bakrī and ʿAbd al-Wahhāb Abū 'l-Nūr. Cairo: Dār al-Kutub al-Ḥadītha, 1968.

al-Ṭihrānī, Āghā Bozorg. *al-Dharīʿa ilā taṣānīf al-Shīʿa*. 26 vols. Tehran and Najaf, 1353–98/1934–78.

Trimingham, J. Spencer. *The Sufi Orders in Islam*. Oxford: Oxford University Press, 1971.

Tritton, A. S. "Some Muʿtazilī Ideas about Religion: in Particular about Knowledge Based on General Report." *Bulletin of the School of Oriental and African Studies* 14 (1952): 612–22.

Trusted, Jennifer. *The Logic of Scientific Inference: An Introduction*. London: Macmillan, 1979.

al-Ṭūfī, Sulaymān ibn ʿAbd al-Qawī. *Risālat al-Ṭūfī fī riʿāyat al-maṣāliḥ al-mursala*. In Khallāf, ʿAbd al-Wahhāb, *Maṣādir al-tashrīʿ al-islāmī fīmā la naṣṣ fīhi*. Kuwait: Dār al-Qalam, 1390/1970. Pp. 106–44.

Turki, Abdel Magid. "Argument d'autorité, preuve rationelle et absence de preuves dans la méthodologie juridique musulmane." *Studia Islamica* 42 (1975): 59–91.

al-Ṭūsī, Abū Jaʿfar Muḥammad ibn al-Ḥasan. *al-Fihrist*. Ed. Muḥammad Ṣādiq Āl Baḥr al-ʿUlūm. Najaf: al-Maṭbaʿa al-Ḥaydariyya, 1380/1961.

———. *Kitāb ʿUddat al-uṣūl*. Tehran: Maṭbaʿat Mīrzā Ḥabīb Allāh, 1317/1899.

Tyan, Émile. "Méthodologie et sources de droit en Islam." *Studia Islamica* 10 (1959): 82.

Versteegh, C. H. M. *Greek Elements in Arabic Linguistic Thinking*. Leiden: Brill, 1977.

Wensinck, A. J. *The Muslim Creed: Its Genesis and Historical Development*. 1932. Reprint. London: Frank Cass, 1965.

von Wright, Georg Henrik. *The Logical Problem of Induction*, 2nd ed. New York: Macmillan, 1957.

——. *A Treatise on Induction and Probability*. London: Routledge and Kegan Paul, 1951.

al-Yazdī, Muḥammad Bāqir al-Ḥasanī. *Wasīlat al-wasāʾil fī sharḥ al-Rasāʾil fī ʿilm al-uṣūl*. Dār al-Ṭibāʿa Mullā ʿAbbās ʿAlī al-Tabrīzī, 1291/1874.

al-Zajjājī, Abū 'l-Qāsim ʿAbd al-Raḥmān ibn Isḥāq. *al-Īḍāḥ fī ʿilal al-naḥw*. Ed. Māzin Mubārak. Cairo: Dār al-ʿUrūba, 1378/1959.

al-Zanjānī, Shihab al-Dīn Maḥmūd ibn Aḥmad. *Takhrīj al-furūʿ ʿalā al-uṣūl*. Ed. Muḥammad Adīb Ṣāliḥ. Damascus: Maṭbaʿat Jāmiʿat Dimashq, 1382/1962.

al-Zarkashī, Badr al-Dīn Muḥammad ibn Bahādur. *al-Baḥr al-muḥīṭ*. Paris. Bibliothèque Nationale. MS Arabic 811.

Zarrūq, Abū 'l-ʿAbbās Aḥmad ibn Aḥmad. *Qawāʿid al-taṣawwuf*. Ed. Muḥammad Zahrī al-Najjār. Cairo: Maktabat al-Kulliyyāt al-Azhariyya, 1388/1968.

WORKS CITED IN THE ADDENDA AND PREFACE

ʿAbd al-Barr, Muḥammad Zakī. *Taqnīn uṣūl al-fiqh*. Cairo: Maktabat Dār al-Turāth, 1409/1989.

Abdul Hussain, Arif, trans. *Principles of Islamic Jurisprudence: Shiʿi Law* [partial translation of Muḥammad Bāqir al-Ṣadr's *al-Durūs*]. London: ICAS, 2003.

Ahmad, Ahmad Atif. *The Fatigue of the Shariʿa*. New York: Palgrave Macmillan, 2012.

——. *Structural Interrelations of Theory and Practice in Islamic Law: A Study of Six Works of Medieval Islamic Jurisprudence*. Leiden: Brill, 2006.

Ali, Mohamed M. Yunis. *Medieval Islamic Pragmatics: Sunni Legal Theorists' Models of Textual Communication*. Richmond, Surrey: Curzon Press, 2000.

al-ʿAwnī, al-Sharīf Ḥātim ibn ʿĀrif. *al-Yaqīnī wa'l-ẓannī min al-akhbār: sijāl bayna al-imām Abī 'l-Ḥasan al-Ashʿarī wa'l-muḥaddithīn*. Beirut: al-Shabaka al-ʿArabiyya li'l-Abḥāth wa'l-Nashr, 1432/2011.

Bedir, Murteza. "An Early Response to Shāfiʿī: ʿĪsā b. Abān on the Prophetic Report (*khabar*)." *Islamic Law and Society* 9 (2002): 285–311.

Bercher, Léon. *Les fondements du fiqh: Kitab al-Warakat fi uçoul al-fiqh: le livre des feuilles sur les fondements du droit musulman*. Paris: Iqra, 1995.

Brown, Jonathan A. C. "Did the Prophet Say It or Not? The Literal, Historical, and Effective Truth of *Ḥadīths* in Early Sunnism." *Journal of the American Oriental Society* 129 (2009): 259–85.

——. *The Canonization of al-Bukhārī and Muslim: The Formation and Function of the Sunnī Ḥadīth Canon*. Leiden: Brill, 2007.

Chaumont, Éric, trans. *Traité de théorie légale musulmane* [translation of al-Shīrāzī's *Kitāb al-Lumaʿ fī uṣūl al-fiqh*]. Berkeley: Robbins Collection, 1999.

Chodkiewicz, Michel. *An Ocean without Shore: Ibn Arabi, the Book, and the Law*. Albany: State University of New York Press, 1993.

Coady, C. A. J. *Testimony: A Philosophical Study*. Oxford: Clarendon, 1992.

al-Ḍuwayḥī, ʿAlī ibn Saʿd. *Sharḥ al-muqaddima al-manṭiqiyya fi'l-Rawḍa al-maqdisiyya*. Dammam: Dār ibn al-Jawzī, 1431.

El-Omari, Racha. "Accommodation and Resistance: Classical Muʿtazilites on Ḥadīth." *Journal of Near Eastern Studies* 71 (2012): 231–56.

El Shamsy, Ahmed. "Rethinking *Taqlīd* in the Early Shāfiʿī School." *Journal of the American Oriental Society* 128 (2008): 1–23.

van Ess, Josef. *The Flowering of Muslim Theology*. Trans. Jane Marie Todd. Cambridge, MA: Harvard University Press, 2006.

——. "The Logical Structure of Islamic Theology." In *Logic in Classical Islamic Culture*. Ed. G. E. von Grunebaum. Wiesbaden: Harrassowitz, 1970. Pp. 21–50.

——. *Theologie und Gesellschaft im 2. und 3. Jahrhundert Hidschra*. 6 vols. Berlin: de Gruyter, 1991–1997.

Fadel, Mohammad. "The Social Logic of *Taqlīd* and the Rise of the *Mukhtaṣar*." *Islamic Law and Society* 3 (1996): 193–233.

Gleave, Robert. *Islam and Literalism: Literal Meaning and Interpretation in Islamic Legal Theory*. Edinburgh: Edinburgh University Press, 2012.

——. *Scripturalist Islam: The History and Doctrines of the Akhbārī Shīʿī School*. Leiden: Brill, 2007.

——. *Inevitable Doubt: Two Theories of Shīʿī Jurisprudence*. Leiden: Brill, 2000.

Hallaq, Wael B. *Authority, Continuity and Change in Islamic Law*. Cambridge: Cambridge University Press, 2001.

——. *A History of Islamic Legal Theories: An Introduction to Sunnī uṣūl al-fiqh*. Cambridge: Cambridge University Press, 1997.

Hansu, Hüseyin. "Notes on the Term *Mutawātir* and Its Reception in *Ḥadīth* Criticism." *Islamic Law and Society* 16 (2009): 383–408.

——. *Mutazile ve hadis*. Kızılay, Ankara: Kitâbiyât, 2004.

Haykel, Bernard and Aron Zysow. "What Makes a *Madhab* a *Madhab*: Zaydī Debates on the Structure of Legal Authority." *Arabica* 59 (2012): 332–71.

al-Ḥillī, al-ʿAllāma al-Ḥasan ibn Yūsuf ibn al-Muṭahhar. *Manāhij al-yaqīn fī uṣūl al-dīn*. Ed. Yaʿqūb al-Jaʿfarī al-Marāghī. N.p.: Markaz al-Dirāsāt wa'l-Taḥqīqāt al-Islāmiyya, 1415 (solar).

al-Ḥusayn ibn al-Qāsim. *Kitāb Hidāyat al-ʿuqūl ilā ghāyat al-sūl fī al-uṣūl*. 2 vols. Sana'a: al-Maktaba al-Islāmiyya, 1401/1981.

Ibn ʿAqīl, Abū 'l-Wafāʾ ʿAlī. *al-Wāḍiḥ fī uṣūl al-fiqh*. 4 vols. in 5. Ed. George Makdisi. Beirut: Franz Steiner, 1423/2002.

Ibn ʿĀshūr, Muḥammad al-Ṭāhir. *Maqāṣid al-sharīʿa al-islāmiyya*. Ed. Muḥammad al-Ṭāhir al-Mīsāwī. Amman: Dar al-Nafāʾis, 1421/2001.

Ibn al-Fakhkhār. *al-Intiṣār li-ahl al-madīna*. Ed. Muḥammad al-Idrīsī. Rabat: Markaz al-Dirāsāt, 2009.

Ibn Fūrak, Abū Bakr Muḥammad ibn al-Ḥusayn. *Mujarrad maqālāt al-shaykh Abī 'l-Ḥasan al-Ashʿarī*. Ed. Daniel Gimaret. Beirut: Dar al-Machreq, 1987.

Ibn Ḥazm, Abū Muḥammad ʿAlī. *al-Iʿrāb ʿan al-ḥayra wa'l-iltibās al-mawjūdayn fī madhāhib al-raʾy wa'l-qiyās*. 3 vols. Ed. Muḥammad ibn Zayn al-ʿĀbidīn Rustam. Riyadh: Aḍwāʾ al-Salaf, 1425/2005.

Ibn Luqmān. *al-Kāshif li-dhawī al-ʿuqūl ʿan wujūh maʿānī al-Kāfil bi-nayl al-sūl*. Ed. ʿAbd al-Karīm Aḥmad Jadbān. Ṣaʿda: Maktabat al-Turāth al-Islāmī, 1421/2000.

Ibn al-Malāḥimī. *al-Tajrīd fī uṣūl al-fiqh* (facsimile ed.). Ed. Sabine Schmidtke and Hasan Ansari. Tehran: Markaz-i Dāʾirat al-Maʿārif-i Buzurg-i Islāmī, 2011.

——. *Kitab al-Fāʾiq fī uṣūl al-dīn*. Ed. Wilferd Madelung and Martin McDermott. Tehran: Iranian Institute of Philosophy, 2007.

Ibn Mattawayh, Ḥasan ibn Aḥmad. *al-Tadhkira fī aḥkām al-jawāhir wa'l-aʿrāḍ*. Ed. S. N. Lutf and F. B. ʿAwn. Cairo: Dār al-Thaqāfa, 1975. 2 vols. Ed. Daniel Gimaret. Cairo: Institut Français d'Archéologie Orientale, 2009.

Ibn al-Murtaḍā, Aḥmad ibn Yaḥyā. *Kitāb al-Baḥr al-zakhkhār al-jāmiʿ li-madhāhib ʿulamāʾ al-amṣār*. 6 vols. Sana'a: Dār al-Ḥikma al-Yamāniyya, 1409/1988.

Ibn al-Qaṣṣār. *al-Muqaddima fī al-uṣūl*. Ed. Muḥammad al-Sulaymānī. Beirut: Dār al-Gharb al-Islāmī, 1996.

Jackson, Sherman A. *Islamic Law and the State: The Constitutional Jurisprudence of Shihāb al-Dīn al-Qarāfī*. Leiden: Brill, 1996.

——. "*Taqlīd*, Legal Scaffolding and the Scope of Legal Injunctions in Post-Formative Theory: *Muṭlaq* and *ʿĀmm* in the Jurisprudence of Shihāb al-Dīn al-Qarāfī." *Islamic Law and Society* 3 (1996): 192–233.

Kamali, Mohammad Hashim. *Principles of Islamic Jurisprudence*, 3rd ed. Cambridge: Islamic Texts Society, 2003.

Karabela, Mehmet Kadri. "The Development of Dialectic and Argumentation Theory in Post-Classical Islamic Intellectual History." Unpublished Ph.D. dissertation, McGill University, 2010.

Kemper, Michael. *Sufis und Gelehrte in Tatarien und Baschkirien, 1789–1889: Der islamische Diskurs unter russischer Herrschaft*. Berlin: Klaus Schwarz, 1998.

al-Khaṭṭābī, Ḥamd ibn Muḥammad. *Maʿālim al-sunan*. 4 vols. in 3. Ed. Muḥammad Rāghib al-Ṭabbākh. Aleppo: al-Maṭbaʿa al-ʿIlmiyya, 1351/1932.

Krawietz, Birgit. *Hierarchie der Rechtsquellen im tradierten sunnitischen Islam*. Berlin: Duncker & Humblot, 2002.

Löfgren, Oscar and Renato Traini, eds. *Catalogue of the Arabic Manuscripts in the Biblioteca Ambrosiana*. Vicenza: N. Pozza, 1995.

Lowry, Joseph E., ed. and trans. *The Epistle on Legal Theory* [translation of the *Risāla* of al-Shāfiʿī]. New York: New York University Press, 2013.

——. *Early Islamic Legal Theory: The* Risāla *of Muḥammad ibn Idrīs al-Shāfiʿī*. Leiden: Brill, 2007.

——. "The Legal Hermeneutics of al-Shāfiʿī and Ibn Qutayba: A Reconsideration." *Islamic Law and Society* 11 (2004): 1–41.

Lucas, Scott. "The Legal Principles of Muḥammad b. Ismāʿīl al-Bukhāri and Their Relationship to Classical Salafī Islam." *Islamic Law and Society* 13 (2006): 289–324.

Madelung, Wilferd. "Zu einigen Werken des Imams Abū Ṭālib al-Nāṭiq bi-l-ḥaqq." *Der Islam* 63 (1986): 5–10.

Mānkdīm Shāshdīw. *Sharḥ al-uṣūl al-khamsa* [attrib. ʿAbd al-Jabbār ibn Aḥmad al-Hamadhānī]. Ed. ʿAbd al-Karīm ʿUthmān. Cairo: Maktabat Wahba, 1384/1965.

al-Marjānī, Shihāb al-Dīn. *Nāẓūrat al-ḥaqq fī farḍiyyat al-ʿishāʾ wa-in lam yaghib al-shafaq*, ed. Ūrkhān ibn Idrīs Anjaqār and ʿAbd al-Qādir ibn Saljūq Yılmaz. Istanbul: Dār al-Ḥikma; Amman: Dār al-Fatḥ li'l-Dirāsāt wa'l-Nashr, 1433/2012.

al-Marwarrūdhī, al-Ḥusayn ibn Muḥammad. *al-Taʿlīqa*. 2 vols. Ed. ʿAlī Muḥammad Muʿawwaḍ and ʿĀdil Aḥmad ʿAbd al-Mawjūd. Mecca: Maktabat Nizār Musṭafā al-Bāz, 1998.

Matilal, Bimal Krishna and Arindan Chakrabarti, eds. *Knowing from Words: Western and Indian Philosophical Analysis of Understanding and Testimony*. Dordrecht: Kluwer Academic, 1994.

al-Māzarī, Muḥammad ibn ʿAlī. *Īḍāḥ al-maḥṣūl min Burhān al-uṣūl*. Ed. ʿAmmār al-Ṭālibī. Beirut: Dār al-Gharb al-Islāmī, 2001.

Melchert, Christopher. *The Formation of the Sunni Schools of Law, 9th–10th Centuries C.E.* Leiden: Brill, 1997.

Miller, Larry B. "Islamic Disputation Theory: A Study of the Development of Dialectic in Islam from the Tenth through Fourteenth Centuries." Unpublished Ph.D. dissertation. Princeton University, 1984.

Modarressi, Hossein. *Crisis and Consolidation in the Formative Period of Shīʿite Islam: Abū Jaʿfar ibn Qiba al-Rāzī and His Contribution to Imāmite Shīʿite Thought*. Princeton: Darwin Press, 1993.

Moussavi, Ahmad Kazemi. *Religious Authority in Shiʿite Islam: From the Office of Mufti to the Institution of the Marjaʿ*. Kuala Lumpur: International Institute of Islamic Thought and Civilization, 1996.

Mottahedeh, Roy Parviz, trans. *Lessons in Islamic Jurisprudence* [partial translation of Muḥammad Bāqir al-Ṣadr's *al-Durūs*]. Oxford: Oneworld, 2003.

Nasser, Shady Hekmat. *The Transmission of the Variant Readings of the Qurʾān: The Problem of Tawātur and the Emergence of Shawādhdh*. Leiden: Brill, 2012.

Newman, Andrew. "The Nature of the Akhbārī/Uṣūlī Dispute in Late Ṣafawid Iran. Part 1." *Bulletin of the School of Oriental and African Studies* 55 (1992): 22–51.

Opwis, Felicitas. Maṣlaḥa *and the Purpose of the Law: Islamic Discourse on Legal Change from the 4th/10th to 8th/14th* Century. Leiden: Brill, 2010.

Özen, Şükrü. "Ebû Mansûr el-Mâtürîdî'nin fıkıh usûlünün yeniden inşası." Unpublished Ph.D. dissertation. Marmara University, 2001.

Ramić, Šukrija (Husejn). *Language and the Interpretation of Islamic Law*. Cambridge: Islamic Texts Society, 2003.

Reinhart, A. Kevin. "'Like the Difference between Heaven and Earth:' Ḥanafī and Shāfiʿī Discussions of *Wājib* and *Farḍ*." In *Studies in Islamic Legal Theory*. Ed. Bernard G. Weiss. Leiden: Brill, 2002. Pp. 205–34.

———. *Before Revelation: The Boundaries of Muslim Moral Thought*. Albany: State University of New York Press, 1995.

Rudolph, Ulrich and Dominik Perler. *Occasionalismus: Theorien der Kausalität im arabisch-islamischen und im Europäischen Denken*. In *Abhandlungen der Akademie der Wissenschaften in Göttingen, Philologisch-Historische Klasse*; 3. Folge, Nr. 236. Göttingen: Vandenhoeck & Ruprecht, 2000.

al-Samāhijī, ʿAbd Allāh. *Munyat al-mumārisīn*. In Newman, "The Nature of the Akhbārī/*Uṣūlī Dispute*."

al-Samarqandī, ʿAlāʾ al-Dīn Abū Bakr Muḥammad ibn Aḥmad. *Mīzan al-uṣūl*. Ed. Muḥammad Zakī ʿAbd al-Barr. Doha: Maṭābiʿ al-Dawḥa al-Ḥadītha, 1404/1984. Ed. ʿAbd al-Malik ʿAbd al-Raḥmān al-Saʿdī. Mecca: Wizārat al-Awqāf, 1407/1987.

Schöck, Cornelia. *Koranexegese, Grammatik und Logik: Zum Verhältnis von arabischer und aristotelischer Urteils-, Konsequenz- und Schlusslehre*. Leiden: Brill, 2006.

Schwarb, Gregor. "*Uṣūl al-fiqh* im jüdischen *kalām* des 10. und 11. Jahrhunderts: Ein Überblick." In *Orient als Grenzbereich?: Rabbinisches und außerrabbinisches Judentum*. Ed. Annelies Kuyt and Gerold Necker. Abhandlungen für die Kunde des Morgenlandes 60. Wiesbaden: Harrassowitz, 2008. Pp. 77–104.

———. "Capturing the Meaning of God's Speech: The Relevance of *Uṣūl al-Fiqh* to an Understanding of *Uṣūl al-Tafsīr* in Jewish and Muslim *Kalām*." In *A Word Fitly Spoken: Studies in Medieval Exegesis of the Hebrew Bible and the Qurʾān Presented to Haggai Ben-Shammai*. Ed. Meir M. Bar-Asher, Simon Hopkins, Sarah Stroumsa, and Bruno Chiesa. Jerusalem: Ben-Zvi Intitute, 2007. Pp. 111–56.

al-Sharīf al-Murtaḍā, ʿAlī ibn al-Ḥusayn. *al-Dharīʿa ilā uṣūl al-sharīʿa*. 2 vols. Ed. Abū 'l-Qāsim Gorjī. Tehran: Chāpkhāne-yi Dāneshgāh-i Ṭihrān, 1967–68.

al-Shāshī, Abū Bakr Muḥammad ibn ʿAlī al-Qaffāl. *Maḥāsin al-sharīʿa*. Ed. Abū ʿAbd Allāh Muḥammad ʿAlī Samak. Beirut: Dār al-Kutub al-ʿIlmiyya, 2007. Ed. ʿAlī Ibrāhīm Muṣṭafā. Cairo: al-Fārūq al-Ḥadītha li'l-Ṭibāʿa wa'l-Nashr, 2008.

al-Shinqīṭī, Muḥammad al-Amīn ibn Muḥammad al-Mukhtār. *Sharḥ Marāqī al-suʿūd al-musammā Nathr al-wurūd*. 2 vols. Ed. ʿAlī ibn Muḥammad al-ʿUmrān. Mecca: Dār ʿĀlam al-Fawā'id, 1426 H.

al-Shīrāzī, Abū Isḥāq Ibrāhīm ibn ʿAlī. *al-Lumaʿ fī uṣūl al-fiqh*. Ed. Éric Chaumont. *Mélanges de l'Université Saint-Joseph* 53 (1993–1994 [1997]).

Sklare, David E. *Samuel b. Ḥofnī Gaon and His Cultural World: Texts and Studies*. Leiden, Brill, 1996.

Stewart, Devin. "Muḥammad b. Dāwūd al-Ẓāhirī's Manual of Jurisprudence: *Al-Wuṣūl ilā maʿrifat al-uṣūl*. In *Studies in Islamic Legal Theory*. Ed. Bernard G. Weiss. Leiden: Brill, 2002. Pp. 99–158.

——. *Islamic Legal Orthodoxy: Twelver Shiite Responses to the Sunni Legal System*. Salt Lake City: University of Utah Press, 1998.

al-Suhrawardī, Shihāb al-Dīn Yaḥyā ibn Ḥabash. *al-Tanqīḥāt fī uṣūl al-fiqh*. Ed. ʿIyāḍ ibn Nāmī al-Sulamī. Riyadh: n.p., 1418 H.

al-Tawḥīdī, Abū Ḥayyān. *al-Baṣāʾir wa'l-dhakhāʾir*. 9 vols. Ed. Wadād al-Qāḍī. Beirut: Dār Ṣādir, 1408/1988.

Thiele, Jan. *Kausalität in der Muʿtazilitischen Kosmologie: Das Kitāb al-Muʾaṯṯirāt wa-miftāḥ al-muškilāt des Zayditen al-Ḥasan ar-Raṣṣāṣ (st. 584/1188)*. Leiden: Brill, 2011.

Tillschneider, Hans-Thomas. *Die Entstehung der juristischen Hermeneutik (uṣūl al-fiqh) im frühen Islam*. Würzberg: Ergon Verlag, 2006.

al-Usmandī, Muḥammad ibn ʿAbd al-Ḥamīd. *Badhl al-naẓar fī al-uṣūl* [attrib. to al-Samarqandī as *al-Mīzān*]. Ed. Muḥammad Zakī ʿAbd al-Barr. Cairo: Maktabat Dār al-Turāth, 1417/1997.

Vishanoff, David R. *The Formation of Islamic Hermeneutics: How Sunni Legal Theorists Imagined a Revealed Law*. New Haven, CT: American Oriental Society, 2011.

——, trans. *al-Waraqāt* of Imam al-Haramayn al-Juwayni. Online: http://faculty-staff.ou.edu/V/David.R.Vishanoff-1/Translations/Waraqat.htm (accessed 13 March 2013).

al-Wazīr, Aḥmad ibn ʿAlī. *al-Muṣaffā fī uṣūl al-fiqh*. Beirut: Dār al-Fikr al-Muʿāṣir, 1417/1996.

Weiss, Bernard G. *The Search for God's Law: Islamic Jurisprudence in the Writings of Sayf al-Dīn al-Āmidī*, rev. ed. Salt Lake City: University of Utah Press, 2010.

——, ed. *Studies in Islamic Legal Theory*. Leiden: Brill, 2002.

——. *The Spirit of Islamic Law*. Athens, GA: University of Georgia Press, 1998.

al-Zarkashī, Badr al-Dīn Muḥammad ibn Bahādur. *al-Baḥr al-muḥīṭ fī uṣūl al-fiqh*. 6 vols. Ed. ʿAbd al-Qādir ʿAbd Allāh al-ʿĀnī. Kuwait: Wizārat al-Awqāf, 1413/1992.

Zysow, Aron. "Muʿtazilism and Māturīdism in Ḥanafī Legal Theory." In *Studies in Islamic Legal Theory*. Ed. Bernard G. Weiss. Leiden: Brill, 2002. Pp. 235–65.

——. "*Ejtehād* in Shīʿism." *Encyclopaedia Iranica* 8 (1998): 281–86.

——. "Two Theories of the Obligation to Obey God's Commands." In *The Law Applied: Contextualizing the Islamic Shariʿa: A Volume in Honor of Frank E. Vogel*. Ed. Peri Bearman, Wolfhart Heinrichs, and Bernard G. Weiss. London: I.B. Tauris, 2008. Pp. 397–421.

——. "Qaffal, Muhammad ibn 'Ali ibn Isma'il al-Shashi." In *The Oxford International Encyclopaedia of Legal History*. Ed. Stanley N. Katz. Oxford: Oxford University Press, 2009. Vol. 5, p. 60.

TABLE OF PAGE CORRESPONDENCES

INDEX OF QUR᾽ĀN CITATIONS

INDEX OF ARABIC TERMS AND PROPER NOUNS

RESOURCES IN ARABIC AND ISLAMIC STUDIES

Number 2
The Economy of Certainty: An Introduction to the Typology of Islamic Legal Theory
by Aron Zysow
(2013)

Number 1
A Reader of Classical Arabic Literature
by Seeger Bonebakker and Michael Fishbein
(2012)

CPSIA information can be obtained
at www.ICGtesting.com
Printed in the USA
BVOW03s1650030617
485724BV00015B/10/P

9 781937 040093